D0772852

A HOMELAND IN THE WEST

A Homeland in the West

UTAH JEWS REMEMBER

EILEEN HALLET STONE

The University of Utah Press Salt Lake City

© 2001 by the University of Utah Press
All rights reserved

Printed on acid-free paper

07 06 05 04 03 02 01
5 4 3 2 1

Library of Congress Cataloging-in-Publication Data
A homeland in the West : Utah Jews remember /
[edited and compiled by] Eileen Hallet Stone.
p. cm.
Includes bibliographical references (p.) and index.
ISBN 0-87480-702-6 (hardcover : alk. paper)
1. Jews—Utah—Social life and customs. 2. Jews—
Utah—Identity. 3. Jews—Utah—Interviews.
4. Utah—Ethnic relations. I. Stone, Eileen Hallett, 1943–
F835.J5 H66 2001
978.2′004924—dc21 2001003862

TO DANIEL

PREFACE

When a Jew Is a "Gentile"—What does it mean to be an American Jew during the last century and a half, especially in an isolated western state so engrossed in its own religious struggle for identity that as a Jew you are not only a minority, but also a Gentile? (In the Mormon culture, a non-Mormon is a Gentile.)

A Homeland in the West: Utah Jews Remember explores the myriad reasons motivating Jewish individuals to go west and examines the modification of cultural practices that such a move may have required. Through oral history interviews primarily, distinct voices abound with stories of the struggle to maintain independence and cultural identity, while adapting Judaism to the demands of western life.

Historical Conversations—This book is not a history of Utah Jews, which would be impossible to compile in one volume. It is a book about historical conversations steeped in the unique experience of Utah; it is about lifestyles, attitudes, issues, events, traditions, legacies, and the personal searches for Jewish authenticity. Compiled of a cross section of Jewish experiences throughout the state of Utah, these stories weave the threads of an otherwise uncaptured ethnic experience into the fabric of Utah history. They are here to represent Jewish immigrants, from the early pioneer era up to the modern day, and to portray their influence and commitment to the settlement of the West. These earnest accounts will define in personal terms the economic, educational, and social challenges Jewish families experienced, the adversity they endured, the discrimination they faced, the failures they overcame, and the successes they achieved. Their

A scribe adds the last letter to the Torah. (Photo by Eileen Hallet Stone)

Waiting tallits. (Photo by Eileen Hallet Stone)

stories, accounts, memoirs, interviews, explicit conversations, excerpted articles, and even tales are presented to become visible to a population that continues to have little or no awareness of the Jewish existence. They are here to help others develop the ability to challenge the many forms of discrimination that face all ethnic minority groups in contemporary American culture.

Authentic Voices—Although these stories gain color through the medium of colloquial history, they expose intimacies and a depth of character that are recognizable and therefore accessible in their humanity. Their very existence adds to the matter of history. Authentic voices, rather than constructed texts, bring alive myriad aspects of life and viewpoints that a reader can dispute, deny, agree with, or relate to, which in itself makes the experience tangible and real—something to be reckoned with.

A Process in Sensitivity—Collecting more than ninety archived and current Jewish oral history interviews, I tried to select a wide representation of diversity in life histories, and used approximately sixty-five interviews for this book. When I had the opportunity to reinforce one interviewee's story with the observations of another, I abstracted the material to complement the work.

Many of the interviews were from ten to one hundred typed pages. Of those included in this book, a rare few were complete by themselves; others were usable in large sections of transcript form. To bring most of the interviewees' stories into focus, I had to delete content, shift paragraphs, and add transitions. Since most interviews ebb and flow with thought, sections of content were carefully subtitled to allow smooth transitions and a way of indexing, and at times to act as a visual respite. I strove for sensitivity to the nuances of pauses, the mulling over of facts, the facial expressions and body stances, so that we all would hear rather than surmise what was being said. In this way, the eighty-year-old voice could find solace among the pages while relating the effects of an *inferred* tone of voice when an elder asks what he, a Jewish boy of twelve, is doing among a group of young Mormon Boy Scouts. Similarly, a reader will sense the panic that lifts off the pages in disbelief as a six-year-old child is accused in a small Utah mining-town ward house of killing Christ. Or see the blinding color of racism that emerges from pages of muddied yellow imprinted with the word *Jude.*

Revisiting—I was fortunate to be able to visit with several interviewees to clarify information found in interviews conducted more than ten to twenty years ago, at that time asking them to delve into experiences thirty, forty, or fifty years earlier. I was fortunate to hear relatives recount stories, sometimes offering such different interpretations of a sibling's tale that both had to be included.

Carrying the Torah, Scott Cramer. (Photo by Eileen Hallet Stone)

Language and Memory—To reduce the risk of misinformation on factual data, I searched technical data for corroboration or enlightenment. To reduce the risk of rumors, I listened for the undercurrent akin to hearsay, the sigh of contradiction, a desire to please, and the play of memory. Throughout the editing choices, I willingly delved into the challenge of retaining the language styles and oral presentation of the interviewees.

Out of the Blue—To my unexpected delight, copies of original manuscripts emerged from seemingly nowhere but goodwill, including an original and rare copy of Solomon Nunes Carvalho's travels into the West, as well as the journals of Eveline Brooks Auerbach and her husband, Samuel Auerbach. Kibbitzing produced a memoir on Senator Sol Selvin by his ninety-year-old-daughter, Min Selvin Crutcher. Professor Robert Goldberg's enthusiasm for the back-to-the-land movement in Utah added to the treasure chest.

While searching for photographs from family albums and homes, the Special Collections at the University of Utah's Marriott Library, and the Utah State Historical Society, original postcard portraits of Clarion colonists literally fell into my hands. A 1902 advertisement for a Jewish firm was discovered on the back of a matte board used to frame an unrelated although quite interesting portrait being cleaned in the basement of the old Rock Church in Parowan, Utah, by Marriott Library's preservation librarian, Randy Silverman. A neighborly comment from Phil Notorianni to Pete Mirabile led to the discovery of a hitherto-unknown plate-glass image of former Salt Lake City mayor Louis Marcus—who would have guessed! As a result of these

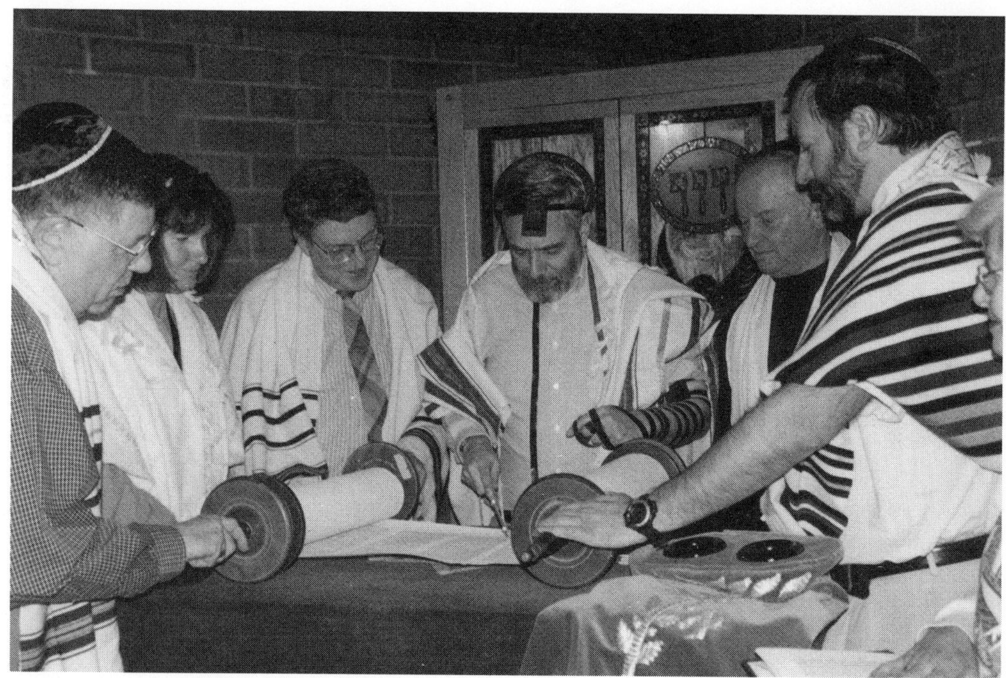

Monday-morning minyan *(l–r)*: Ira Tannenbaum, Terry Treseder, Rabbi Frederick Wenger, Cantor Laury Loeb, Herman Spiegal, and Scott Cramer. (Photo by Eileen Hallet Stone)

outpourings of interest and generosity, roughly 150 representations of Utah Jewish life are now out in the open to be seen.

Pictures of Life—Historical photographs have the ability to create a backdrop of experiences and traditions that convey visual concepts with immediacy, directness, possibly familiarity, and, one hopes, scrutiny. Included in this book is a series of stunning photographs depicting Utah Jewish life. This growing photograph collection was a "find." Loaned with both reservation and commitment to make more clear the human experience, the photographs also position the interviewees in their rightful place in the new West.

A Reality Rich in Drama—The book may be read on many levels: as a historical overview, a social commentary, a personal and psychological journey, a revelation of a past, or a look into the future. Yet, until we understand stories of ethnicity, such as the Jewish story, our own Utah story is not complete, and its history is not complete with the richness and drama of its people. It is with the help of these stories, memorabilia of the past, and accounts of the present that Utah's true history will become visible, recognized, and, perhaps, understood.

ACKNOWLEDGMENTS

Born and raised in Boston and Maine, where one does not readily ask for directions, and transplanted to Utah, which by its very girth demands independence, I am grateful therefore for the intuition, encouragement, and support of friends who helped guide me on roads familiar and new throughout the writing of this book. I am grateful to my friends Gail Bernstein Ciacci, for her generous outpouring of information and access from conception to completion; Don Gartman and Sue Herbst, for their attentiveness to the importance of minute details; and Donna Barnow Balandrin, for the power of proverbs and order.

I thank Dr. Gregory Thompson, assistant director of the Marriott Library, Special Collections, for his encouragement to take on this project to help establish at the University of Utah a rich archival byway. I am indebted to Marriott Library's Paul Mogren, Walter Jones, Stan Larson, Lorraine Crouse, Elizabeth Rogers, Mary Ann Curtis, Lezann Keshmiri, Karen Carver, and Judy Jarrow, all of whom extended help in numerous ways. I thank Max Evans of the Utah Historical Society for proffering an extensive collection of early Utah photographs; Sue Richards for locating glass-plate negatives of early Jewish-owned stores; Joan Sturhan for her insightful comments on Solomon Nunes Carvalho; and Dr. Philip Notarianni for guiding the scope of this project. Thanks to Marriott Library Digital Technologies librarians, Kenning Arlitsch, Kelly Taylor, and Clifton Brooks, for their diligence in creating our digital library of Jewish photographs. I also thank Jonathan Taylor and Michelle Ortega at the Ritz Camera (Inkley's) Store for their expertise in photographic reproductions. I am grateful to the board members of Common

Ground Productions who directed me to travel unimpeded in search of the most genuine stories to bring strength and beauty to this book; and to the Utah Humanities Council.

To help complete this phase on ethnic diversity, I thank the United Jewish Federation of Utah, the Ruth Eleanor and John Ernest Bamberger Memorial Foundation, Price Development Co., the Rosenblatt Foundation, Michael Wolfe, Robert D. Wolff, Herbert Wolfe, the McGillis Foundation, the Reagan family, F. Lee Auberbach, Daniel and Carol Kotler, David and Anne Dolowitz, Fred and Irene Tannenbaum, Congregation Kol Ami, and other friends and members of Utah's Jewish community.

I thank my son, Daniel Ian Gittins Stone, and Randy Silverman, *mein geliebte,* for putting up with my work-driven goals and giving me the right signals to go full speed ahead. I thank Jeff Grathwohl, Dawn Marano, Rodger Reynolds, and Marcelyn Ritchie, at The University of Utah Press, copyeditor Annette Wenda, and book designer Kristina Kachele for bringing this project to its tasteful and stunning fruition. I apologize for whatever mistakes or omissions may have occurred.

A HOMELAND IN THE WEST

INTRODUCTION

A Brief History of Utah Jews in the West

EARLY JEWS OF THE WEST

Strangers in a Strange Land—In the early 1800s, a Jewish emigrant arrives in the territory of Utah, pauses overnight, a few days perhaps, and then continues on his way to seek adventure and fortune in the West. Jewish trapper, trader, explorer, wandering entrepreneur, peddler, one wonders whether he carries with him the trappings of religious unity. Traveling alone, or with non-Jewish companions, who shares with him Talmudic studies and Jewish commentaries? Does a mezuzah consecrate his tent? In the wilderness, does he don tefillin, wear a tallith, and daven? How did he face the religious dilemmas of kashrut, shehitah, Passover seders, Jewish burials,[1] and minyans, which require a gathering of ten men over the age of thirteen? And what about his Jewish bride, his mishpoche and *mechutanim*? Strangers in a strange land, most of them were recent émigrés to the United States, barely able to speak English and unversed in American customs. Far away from established eastern Jewish communities, what was the life of the Jewish pioneer in the West?

Emmanuel Lazarus, one of a sixteen-man trapping and exploring party headed by Jedediah Smith, set out from the Great Salt Lake in 1826 to find trade routes to California and the Northwest.

In 1844, seventeen-year-old Moses Schalienberger, a member of a trading party, camped for a time at the Great Salt Lake as well, before departing for adventures in the new frontier. Within four years, mineral discoveries—not just gold but also copper and silver—encouraged "large numbers of young, restless Jewish men who were both pushed from Europe by the political reaction following the revolutions of 1848 and pulled by the news of the discovery of gold in California."[2] Mormon leader Lorenzo Brown noted in his journal, dated March 1, 1851, that he "called to see some Hungarian Jews living in the ward . . . emigrants bound for the [California] mines . . . forced to leave their native land because of the revolution."[3]

Joseph Smith and the Mormon Church—The Church of Jesus Christ, later renamed the Church of Jesus Christ of Latter-day Saints, was founded by Joseph Smith and his associates in Fayette, New York, on April 6, 1830. The son of a New England farmer, living near Palmyra, New York, Joseph Smith reported several times seeing heavenly beings, considered by him to be God the Father and Jesus Christ. Later, Smith told of an angel named Moroni who spoke about the existence of gold plates on which, engraved in ancient writing, was the history of the early people of the Western Hemisphere. According to Joseph Smith, he discovered these plates on Cumorah, a hill near his home, and published the translations in what is called *The Book of Mormon,* believed by members (often referred to as Mormons, LDS, or Saints) to be divinely inspired.

Facing Discrimination—A fast-growing church, the Church of Jesus Christ of Latter-day Saints had a thousand members by the end of its first year, yet its members constantly faced discrimination by suspicious and hostile non-Mormon neighbors and were driven from their communities in Ohio, Missouri, and Illinois. When Joseph Smith was shot to death in Nauvoo, Illinois, Brigham Young undertook Smith's plan to move his people from the East to the Great Basin in the Rocky Mountains where they believed they would be safe from persecution.

This Is the Place—In 1847, Young, later elected church president, led an advance party of 148 Mormons into the Great Salt Lake Valley. Saying "This is the place," Young then helped with the migration of thousands of other Mormon pioneers traveling overland along the Mormon Trail. In 1849, the Mormons established the "State of Deseret" and set up a temporary government with Brigham Young as governor. By the time the first transcontinental railroad line was completed at Promontory, Utah, in May 1869, more than 60,000 Mormons had come to the territory by covered wagons and handcarts. After decades of political conflicts and cultural misunderstandings, Utah became America's forty-fifth state on January 4, 1896.

Freedom—While the Mormon flight to the West was one of religious liberty, the prospect of opening up new lands and seizing new opportunities had its effect on the early Jewish pioneers. Western Jewish migration was spurred by a sense of adventure, romance, economics, risk, and personal and religious freedom away from the stigma of anti-Semitism encountered in Europe. Even though isolated from their families and the religious traditions that shaped their lives, the West offered Jewish emigrants the opportunity to make their own decisions: in occupations, later in politics, and in religious practices; for some, it required adjusting to the spirit of the times.

On the Pioneer Trail—From 1846 through 1869, thousands of Mormon pioneers traveled along the Mormon Trail. They had the advantages of safety in companionship and unity in their cause, and were under the command of able leaders. "The early Jews who made the trip, on the contrary, traveled alone or at best with one or two companions of their own faith among the group."[4]

Different Routes—Some Jewish pioneers traveled overland from Independence, Missouri, known as the "jumping-off" point for travelers going across the Plains. Others embarked on an all-water route down the Atlantic Coast, around Cape Horn, to the Pacific Ocean and north to San Francisco. From there, they joined a wagon train and headed toward Utah. Still others chose a faster but more difficult route, sailing to the Isthmus of Panama, traveling through the jungle on mule back, and then booking passage to San Francisco.[5]

An Expedition with the Pathfinder—One of the most adventurous Jewish newcomers to Utah was the thirty-eight-year-old artist, daguerreotypist, and writer Solomon Nunes Carvalho, whose work attracted the attention of Colonel John Charles Frémont. Looking at the thirty-eighth parallel across the Rocky Mountains as a viable route for this country's first transcontinental railroad, Frémont wanted Carvalho to join his expedition to record and photograph his military mapmaking excursion into the West. Although Frémont never published his report or the daguerreotypes, Carvalho's journal, *Incidents of Travel and Adventures in the Far West; with Col. Fremont's Last Expedition across the Rocky Mountains: Including Three Months' Residence in Utah, and a Perilous Trip across the Great American Desert to the Pacific,* captures and preserves Frémont's near fatal expedition. Fraught with peril, the party nearly perished in the high altitudes of the Wasatch Mountains. They grappled with disorientation, lost routes, blinding snowstorms, swollen rivers, freezing temperatures, sleep deprivation, dwindling supplies, and a constant lack of food. After varied scenes of vicissitudes remote from civilization, the expedition journeyed into the Mormon settlement of Parowan where, weighing one hundred pounds and suffering from dysentery, Carvalho was nursed back to health.

Observations—This early Jewish observer's journal, essays, and drawings give an unparalleled snapshot of the Mormon community in its infancy to those who have never been west of the Missouri River. Making his way to Salt Lake City, Carvalho engaged in long conversations with territorial governor Brigham Young, conducted geographical surveys, gathered reports on Mormon philosophy, and opened a cotillion with one of Young's wives. Carvalho was granted independence to make observations for later publication if he would "only publish facts." Openly moved by the devotion of the Mormon pioneers, and believing them to be "the most earnest religionists I have ever been among," Carvalho questioned whether the early Mormon practice of polygamy "harmonizes with the requisite of peace and justice, and the good order essential to the happiness of all," and noted that "polygamy is practiced to a great extent among the high-priests and officers of the church. There are thousands of Mormons, however, who reprobate, and disapprove of it."[6]

Early downtown Main Street, circa 1880s. (Courtesy of Utah State Historical Society)

Before rejoining Frémont's westward-bound expedition, Carvalho painted several portraits of Brigham Young, Lieutenant General Wells, General Ferguson, Bishop Smoot, Mrs. Wheelock, and several other Salt Lake City notables. His portraits of Native Americans offer anthropologists a rare look at the headdress and clothing of the Great Basin tribes.

Work Opportunities—The development of the West opened up floodgates of work opportunities and adventures. Responding to the promise emanating from this newest frontier, early Jewish pioneers were resourceful, intrepid, entrepreneurial, and individualistic. If one place did not work out, they moved on to the next. If one plan failed, they devised another. If one enterprise proved successful, they expanded. Such is the case with the first documented Jewish couple to reside in Utah. Julius and Fannie Brooks, formerly from Central Europe, left civilization behind in 1854 and traveled overland in a prairie schooner to Salt Lake City. (Prior to immigration, the family's name was "Bruck.") After traveling throughout the western territory, opening stores in rough mining camps, like Timbuctoo in the Sierra Nevada, and mercantile shops in San Francisco and Malad, Idaho, they returned to Salt Lake City to settle, raise a family, set up shop, and undertake a series of business ventures, both large and small, that required them to continue traveling in and out of the state. Listed in the *Mormon Millennial Star* among the new city's twenty-two business establishments is Mrs. Brooks's Millinery and Bakery Shop.[7] Not listed was her restaurant establishment, consisting of a crudely hewed wooden-plank table and two benches, serving breakfasts to long lines of emigrants on their way to one gold mine or another. In 1891, on a narrow lot of land on the west side of Main Street, north of Third South, Julius Brooks had built what became known as the Brooks Arcade, a Richardsonian-Romanesque building of elaborately carved gray stone that still stands more than a hundred years later.

A Military Base—The appearance of United States Army troops, under the command of Colonel Albert Sidney Johnston, in the fall of 1857 drew pioneer merchants Nicholas Siegfried Ransohoff and his brother, Elias, who brought a load of freight from the West Coast to supply the troops. In response to reports listing charges against the Mormons of unfair treatment and murder of non-Momons, President James Buchanan intended to replace Governor Young with a new governor and sent Colonel Johnston's federal troops to establish a military base, Camp Floyd, and quell the near warfare among the Mormons and heavy-handed "runaway [federal] judges" and territorial governors.[8]

Risky Business—Inclement weather, Indian attacks, reports of entire parties being butchered, and losses of wagon trains that "left cattle dying" resulted in human and financial ruin for those in the highly speculative business of hauling freight goods across the Plains from the East. These risky ventures justified the sound profits given to freighters such as the Ransohoff brothers whose supplies were very much in demand in the territory. Nicholas Ransohoff established a freight company in Salt Lake City and had one of the best stone-built stores in the city. He was on such good terms with Governor Brigham Young that he loaned the president of the Mormon Church thirty thousand dollars to purchase pork left over when Colonel Johnston's departing army was called back to the States at the outbreak of the Civil War in 1861.

One of the founders of Congregation B'nai Israel, which was incorporated in 1881 and dedicated in 1891, Ransohoff was also a leader in the only Gentile (non-Mormon) political party. (Ironically, regardless of whether it was proposed by LDS Church leaders, all non-Mormon people, including Jews, are more often than not considered "Gentiles" by members of the LDS Church.) At the height of Ransohoff's success, he established branches in Ogden and at the "Gentile" city of Corinne, Utah.

Early Pioneers—Freighter Samuel Kahn, whose partner had been murdered in 1859 while crossing the Plains, arrived in Utah with a load of merchandise in 1860 and became a partner in the firm of N. S. Ransohoff & Co. Three years later, Samuel joined George Bodenberg and became one of the leading distributors of groceries in Utah, Idaho, and Montana. Rather than haul freight across the Plains, in his experience an oftentimes dangerous endeavor, his firm advertised shipping goods from the East by boat, sailing around Cape Horn to California, and then traveling by wagon train to Salt Lake City. Later, Samuel joined his brother Emanual, opened the firm of Kahn Brothers, and became a leading wholesale grocer in Utah. Active in politics and civic affairs, in 1864 Samuel was one of the financial backers of the *Peep o'Day,* "a Salt Lake Magazine of science, literature, and art," reputed to be the first magazine published west of the Missouri.[9] Both brothers were on the board of directors of Congregation B'nai Israel; in 1882, Samuel was the congregation's president.

Portraits of early Utah entrepreneurs *(l–r):* Gilchrist, Horace, and partner Samuel Kahn. (Courtesy of Special Collections, Marriott Library, University of Utah)

Until the late 1860s, the gold-rush frenzy opened the gates to opportunity. Jewish entrepreneurs chased chance in and out of towns, from territory to territory, setting up tent stores by railroad lines; proffering a gathering place for prominent miners and freighters; safekeeping gold dust, nuggets, and bullion; and supplying itinerant miners with picks, shovels, clothes, food, and prospecting pans.

Booms and Busts—The Auerbach brothers, Frederick, Samuel (who later married Julius and Fannie Brooks's daughter, Eveline), and Theodore, took the path set forth by many young immigrants of the time: going where business could be had. Setting out for California by way of the Isthmus of Panama, the Auerbachs experienced the quixotic ups and downs of operating tent and wood-shack stores during the booms and busts of mining towns across the western territories.

In 1864, Fred Auerbach arrived in Salt Lake City, called upon Brigham Young, who offered assistance in locating a store on Main Street, and began a friendship with the president of the Mormon Church that endured for many years, even during the bitter struggle between Mormons and Gentiles and the ensuing trade wars that threatened the very future of every Gentile business. In 1864, Frederick and his brothers, Samuel and Theodore, opened the Peoples Store, F. Auerbach & Bros., in Salt Lake City. They opened branch outlets in Ogden and Corinne and sent traveling salesmen throughout Utah and Idaho in light horse-drawn "buckboards," and by 1883 reached a half-million dollars a year in sales and real estate. In business for more than 120 years, until 1979 when they closed the doors on the oldest department store in the West, the Auerbach Brothers were most likely Utah's most successful Jewish merchants.

Concern for Safety—In the 1860s, increasing numbers of Gentiles in the Utah Territory posed a threat to Mormon autonomy. Retaliating against a perceived invasive population they believed was cheating them, and to preserve temporal unity of the Mormon people, LDS Church

Kahn Brothers on Main Street, one-half block of First South, circa 1880s. (Courtesy of Utah State Historical Society)

leaders adopted a resolution pledging its members to be self-sustaining. By 1866, the bitterness between Gentiles and Mormons reached such heights that the Gentiles feared not only for their future as Salt Lake City merchants but also for their safety. Their concern was exacerbated by two murders, the April 2 murder of S. Newton Brassfield, a Gentile from Nevada who married a plural wife of a Mormon and was in Salt Lake City on business, and the October 22 shooting of Dr. J. King Robinson, a physician at Fort Douglas and superintendent of the town's only non-LDS Sunday school, accused of anti-Mormon activities. Utah historian Orson F. Whitney describes the acrimony and distrust between the two factions:

> Much bitterness of feeling was now manifested between the two classes of the community. Many Gentiles persisted in the belief, which they did not hesitate to express, that it was the purpose of the Mormons to compel them to leave the Territory, and that the Brassfield and Robinson murders were events indicating a settled policy in that direction. This, the Mormons indignantly denied, asserting still their innocence as a people of those crimes, and

denouncing as a slander the charge that they were bent upon compelling a Gentile exodus. That there was a class of men in the Territory whom the Saints regarded as enemies, and did not care how soon they departed, was admitted, but that the feeling against them was due to the fact they were Gentiles, or that it arose from any reason that would not have been deemed good and sufficient and have called forth similar sentiments in any State or Territory in the Union, was disclaimed. It is true, however, that so far as that particular class was concerned, the Saints, or their leaders, had hit upon a plan which they hoped would have the effect of weakening if not dissolving what they deemed an organized opposition to the peace and welfare of the community. It was to boycott such of the Gentile merchants and traders as it was believed were conspiring against the best interest of the people.[10]

A Request from Gentile Merchants—Dr. Robinson's death, which took place outside his home, drew a crowd of passersby leaving a theater. It also awakened Mr. and Mrs. Julius Brooks who ran outside to help. Mrs. Brooks told her daughter, Eveline, that she recognized one of the perpetrators. Fear became so instilled in the Gentile merchants of Salt Lake City that they wrote to President Young with a compelling request:

To the Leaders of the Mormon Church,
Gentlemen: As you are instructing the people of Utah, through your Bishops and missionaries, not to trade or do any business with the Gentile merchants, thereby intimidating and coercing the community to purchase only of such merchants as belong to your faith and persuasion, in anticipation of such a crisis being successfully brought about by your teachings, the undersigned Gentile merchants of Great Salt Lake City respectfully desire to make you the following proposition, believing it to be your earnest desire for all to leave the country that do not belong to your faith and creed, namely: On the fulfillment of the conditions herein named. First—The payment of our outstanding accounts owing us by members of your church; Secondly—All of our goods, merchandise, chattels, houses, improvements, etc., to be taken at cash valuation, and we to make a deduction of twenty-five percent from the total amount. To the fulfillment of the above we hold ourselves ready at any time to enter into negotiations, and once final arrangements being made and terms of sale complied with we shall freely leave the Territory.

Respectfully Yours,

Walker Bros.,
Bodenburg & Kahn,
C. Prag of firm of Ransohoff & Co.
J. Meeks,
Gilbert & Sons,
Wm. Sloan,
Ellis & Bros., by J. M. Ellis,
McGrorty & Henry,

Seigel Bros.,
L. Cohn & Co.,
Klopstock & Co.,
Gluksman & Cohn,
Morse, Walcott Co.,
J. Baum & Co.,
Morris Elgutter,
Thos. D. Brown & Sons.
F. Auerbach & Bros.,
Oliver Durant,
S. Leeser & Bros.,
John H. McGrath,
Wilkinson & Fenn,
I. Watters,
M. B. Callahan,

Great Salt Lake City, Dec. 20, 1866[11]

President Young's Reply—Had President Young acquiesced to the Gentile merchants' request and the Salt Lake City merchants had left, it is likely the remaining Gentile population would have departed as well. Several Salt Lake City Gentile merchants had already established stores in the nearby tent city and railroad town of Corinne, hoping to wait out the dilemma. Most likely, the merchants' petition was also sent to draw the attention to their plight from the federal authorities in Washington.

The following day, they received President Young's reply, which explained the position of the Mormon Church in light of the existing situation in Utah:

Gentlemen:

Your communication of December 20th, addressed to "The Leaders of the Mormon Church" was received by me last evening. In reply, I have to say that we will not obligate ourselves to collect your outstanding accounts, nor buy your goods, merchandise, and other articles that you express your willingness to sell. If you could make such sales as you propose, you would make more money than any merchants have ever done in this country and we, as merchants, would like to find purchasers upon the same basis.

Your withdrawal from the Territory is not a matter about which we feel any anxiety; so far as we are concerned, you are at liberty to stay or go, as you please. We have used no intimidation or coercion toward the community to have them cease trading with any person or class, neither do we contemplate using any such means, even could we do so, to accomplish such an end. What we are doing and intending to do, we are willing that you and all the world should know.

In the first place, we wish you to distinctly understand that we have not sought to ostracize any man or body of men because of their not being of our faith. The wealth that has been accumulated in this Territory from the earliest years of our settlement by men who were not connected with us religiously, and the success which has attended their business operations prove this: In business we have not been exclusive in our dealings, or confined our patronage to those of our own faith. But every man who has dealt fairly and honestly, and confined his attention to his legitimate business, whatever his creed, has found friendship in us. To be adverse to Gentiles because they are Gentiles, or Jews because they are Jews, is in direct opposition to the genius of our religion. It matters not what a man's creed is, whether he be Catholic, or Episcopalian, Presbyterian, Methodist, Baptist, Quaker or Jew, he will receive kindness and friendship from us, and we have not the least objection to doing business with him; if, in his dealings he act in accordance with the principles of right and deport himself as a good law abiding citizen should.

There is a class, however, who are doing business in the Territory, who for many years have been avowed enemies of this community. The disrupture and overthrow of the community have been the objects which they have pertinaciously sought to accomplish. They have, therefore, used every energy and all the means at their command to put into circulation the foulest slanders about the old citizens. Missionaries of evil, they have no arts too base, no stratagems too vile for them to use to bring about their nefarious ends. While soliciting the patronage of the people and deriving their support from them, they have in the most shameless and abandoned manner used the means thus obtained to destroy the very people whose favor they found it to their interest to court. With the regularity of the seasons have their plots and schemes been formed; and we are warranted by facts in saying that, could the heart's blood of the people here be drawn, and could be coined into the means necessary to bring their machinations to a successful issue, they would not scruple to use it. They have done all in their power to encourage violations of law, to retard the administration of justice, to foster vice and vicious institutions, to oppose the unanimously expressed will of the people, to increase disorder, and change our city from a condition of peace and quietude to lawlessness and anarchy. They have donated liberally to sustain a corrupt and venal press, which has given publicity to the most atrocious libels respecting the old citizens. And have they not had their emissaries in Washington to misrepresent and vilify the people of this Territory? Have they not kept liquor, and surreptitiously sold it in violation of law and endeavored to bias the minds of the Judiciary to give decisions favorable to their own practices?

Have they not entered into the secret combinations to resist the laws and to thwart their healthy operations, to refuse to pay their taxes and to give the support of schools required by law? What claims can such persons have upon the patronage of this community, and what community on earth would be so besotted as to uphold and foster men whose aim is to destroy them? Have we not the right to trade at whatever store we please, or does the Constitution of the United States bind us to enter the stores of our deadliest enemies and purchase of them? If so, we would like that provision pointed out to us. It is to these men whom I have described, and to these alone, that I am opposed, and I am determined to use my influence to have the citizens here stop dealing with them and deal with honorable men. There are honorable men enough in the world with whom we can do business, without being reduced to dealing with the class referred to. I have much more to say upon this subject.

Brigham Young.

Great Salt Lake City, Dec. 21st, 1866.[12]

Orson F. Whitney concludes that "Brigham Young, even had he desired all non-Mormons to leave Utah, was too shrewd to have given his enemies such a terrible advantage over him. A Gentile exodus was the very thing that he and his people did not desire, as everything goes to prove."[13]

Waiting It Out—Although President Young personally told Fred Auerbach that he should wait things out, by 1868 the Mormon-run Zion's Cooperative Mercantile Institution (ZCMI) opened its doors to discourage Mormon patronage of Gentile merchants. Gentile stores were indeed boycotted. Eveline Brooks reports that her mother, who rented homes to Mormon tenants, was suddenly left with empty houses, while the Auerbachs survived in Salt Lake by replacing their signature bags with plain brown-paper wrappings stuffed inside empty flour sacks called "Mormon suitcases." Few merchants dared to walk outside at night. When they did, they took to the middle of the road and carried guns. More Gentile merchants relocated to Corinne, but many others were forced out of business, as the LDS Church promoted cooperative business among its members and lowered prices to destroy competition.

Harmony Restored—Fortunately, by 1869, development spurred by the transcontinental railroad and mining enterprises precluded all possibilities of Mormon seclusion, and the LDS Church ceased to urge its members to boycott Gentile establishments. Harmony was restored.

Acquisitions—Earlier, in 1865, Simon Bamberger headed west as a young man to collect an overdue debt at a tough, primitive railroad tie camp and never looked back. "Being alone and far away from home, I engaged in buying up 'pay checks' for workers and, by this means, accumulated quite a little money by re-discounting them," he said in an interview with Utah Jewish historian Leon Watters.[14] Going from one venture to the next, roaming the Utah and Nevada mining districts, Bamberger acquired valuable experience and properties in Big Cottonwood, Park City, and the Oquirrhs. Although he could have retired a wealthy man, his desire to play a further role in the development of the state impelled him to build railroads, public transportation, and an amusement park called Lagoon, which still delights crowds of people. A founder of Congregation B'nai Israel, Bamberger later entered the political arena.

A Stream of Jewish Pioneers—In the wake of these early Jewish pioneers came a slow but steady stream of other emigrants, including the first Jewish rancher in Utah, Charles Popper; pioneer merchant Joseph Farmer, who drowned while swimming at Black Rock; Henry Cohn, who traded in furs and pelts; the grocer Gumpert Goldberg; the jeweler Ichel Watters, whose business was touted as manufacturing the first gold chain ever made in Utah; the realtor and

Eureka mine owner Anna Rich Marks; the Kuhn Brothers, who prospered in wholesale dry goods and clothing in Ogden; the Simon brothers, who, after venturing in businesses throughout rural Utah, established the Paris store, in downtown Salt Lake; and Professor H. S. Krouse, who organized and conducted the choir at Congregation B'nai Israel. As early as 1865, these Jewish names and others were prominent in Masonic lodge rosters; by 1866, they were among the early founders of the Odd Fellows—both organizations being non-Mormon fraternities. One of many Jews active in public life, in 1874 Louis Cohn was elected as a member of the city council and served again in 1888. The 1887 records of the Salt Lake City Chamber of Commerce list as members J. E. Bamberger, M. H. Lipman, and Fred H. Auerbach.

By the end of the 1890s, more than two hundred Jews lived in the Utah Territory. During this period, Salt Lake City enjoyed a sizable generation of peddlers, traders, cattle dealers, butcher shops, slaughterhouses, merchants, manufacturers, industrial workers, wholesalers, and miners.

Back to the Soil—In 1911, Utah's Jewish population saw geographic changes as they witnessed the remnants of the last major attempt of Jewish colonization on land in the United States. Taking part in a "back-to-the-soil movement," the establishment of an agricultural experiment was created to revive the agrarian life for Jews. Between 1880 and 1920, 2 million Jews left Eastern Europe for the urban centers of New York and the eastern seaboard. This mass immigration created overcrowded conditions. Looking toward the West, emigrant Jews enamored with becoming self-sufficient and independent farmers pooled their funds to help establish an agricultural colony called Clarion, near Gunnison, Utah. Underwritten by Jewish families and friends of the movement, encouraged by the governor of Utah and the Mormon Church, Clarion heralded the transformation of a dream into reality and the promise of a future in farming. However, lack of water, inclement weather, and inexperience sealed the colony's fate; it died as an organizational entity in 1916. Its leader, Ben Brown, became active in the Utah Poultry Association, and colonist Maurice Warshaw's produce marketing efforts led to the Grand Central Markets. Although the Clarion project failed, the courage, determination, and demise of this farming community have become a critical part of the Jewish western experience and, as Robert Goldberg explains, "a crucial part of the larger mosaic of Jewish history."[15]

Jews in Utah Politics—In 1903, Simon Bamberger was elected to the state senate and served until 1907. In 1916, he was nominated for governor. Elected for a four-year term by the controlling non-Mormon vote, Bamberger was the first Democrat, only Jew, and first non-Mormon to become governor of Utah. In 1932, Louis Marcus was elected mayor of Salt Lake City, and Sol Selvin of Tooele was first elected to the Utah State Legislature in 1934 and in 1942 served as mayor of Tooele.

A. Wally Sandack was elected Salt Lake County Democratic chairman in 1952. Fifteen years later, he ran for the office of the chairman of the State Democratic Committee and made national headlines as "Utah Democrats Select Jewish Chief." After retiring from his medical practice as an ear, nose, and throat specialist, a full-time professor and head of the Department of Otorhinolaryngology at the University of Utah, in 1980 Dr. David A. Dolowitz headed two hours south of Cedar City and became the small town of Toquerville's beloved mayor. Fourth-generation native-born Patrice Arent entered Utah politics in 1996 as a member of the Utah House of Representatives. In her third term, in 2001, Arent became the House Democratic whip and the highest-ranking woman in the Utah legislature. In 2000, David Litvack also threw his hat into the political ring and was elected member of the Utah House of Representatives, District 27, Central City, Utah.

"Jewish Row"—Between the world wars, Salt Lake City was abuzz with Jewish-owned shops on State and Main Streets, South Temple, and Third and Fourth East Streets. By the 1930s, nearly one hundred businesses lined the downtown streets and neighboring areas: clothing and department stores, jewelers, furniture stores, luggage shops, ladies and men's apparel, and a millinery; florists, candy companies, manufacturers, sporting goods, factories, meat packers, and industrial warehouses; bakeries, restaurants, taverns, and pawn brokers; insurance, specialty floors, janitorial supplies, food markets, and insurance agencies. Apropos to a western town, among them were a Jewish cowboy, a kosher butcher, a *shochet* (who is authorized to slaughter animals), and a rancher who drove cattle down from surrounding areas such as Park City.

War Years—During World War II, approximately two hundred Utah Jewish soldiers were counted in the armed forces rolls. Different Jewish women's organizations—such as the National Council of Jewish Women, Hadassah, the Jewish Relief Society, and the synagogues' Sisterhoods—set up hospitality dances and socials at the Covenant House on South Temple, rolled bandages, brought soldiers into their homes for seders and get-togethers, and participated in the Red Cross and in the sales of savings bonds.

After the Korean War, the James L. White Jewish Community Center was constructed on property at Seventeenth South and Foothill Drive. Named in honor of a prominent Jewish leader and financier, the land was deeded by James E. Hogle jointly to the Jewish community and to the All Saints' Episcopal Church.[16]

Innovations—By the 1960s and 1970s, Utah's Jewish population swelled again with westward-moving pioneers eager to teach and research, invent and heal, influence business and entertain. Radio entrepreneur Sid Fox established a television station, while Sid Cohen tinkered with something mysteriously called "cable."

Survivors and New Homes—Stories of Holocaust survivors living in Utah raise one's consciousness about a significant chapter of world history, its impact, and the continual need to recognize, expose, and challenge discrimination in its many forms. Operation Exodus, a nationwide program relying on funds to help bring Russian refugees to America, has broadened the history of the West with a continuous migration of Soviet Jewry to Utah.

Unofficial Counts—In 1993, Utah's estimated Mormon population was 1,425,000 people who

DAL SIEGEL

If we want to come up to date a little bit, the Covenant house had been sold in 1948, irrespective that a report came out that said 1949. And we were without a community center and very definitely felt the loss of it during the next ten years. Several people were appointed as committee chairman to try to advance the building or the procurement of a new community center. And yet until I held that position, a new community center did not appear on the scene. I was finally given the chairmanship for a new community center in about 1956. I told them at the time, I am persistent in my nature; and before I finish my job, you will have a community center. We proceeded from that point on with studies and meetings, people getting interested, fund drives being held, and actually progressing to the point where we hired an architect and signed a contract to have a center named the James L. White Jewish Community Center built on Foothill Drive and Seventeenth South. As you ask what was my contribution to the community, I would say it was the work I did from 1956 through 1962 to see that this center got built. My personal goals, though, were to bring Jewish people together, to improve the image of the Jew in a non-Jewish community (because the better you knew a person, the better you liked them, which helps eliminate prejudice), and perform community service to both the Jewish and non-Jewish community.[17]

worshiped in 405 stakes (state-level facilities), 3,045 ward houses (county level), 104 branches (town level), 3 missions (world division), and 10 temples (holiest of cathedrals). Mormon converts from all other nations continue to swell these numbers. Yet, Utah also attracts newcomers of all faiths, and a strong, vibrant, and diverse Jewish community thrives. Today, Utah's Jewish population unofficially numbers more than 6,000 people with 5 different Jewish movements providing places for worship.

Religious Community—It is probable that as early as 1860, religious services were held in the homes of Jewish merchants. The *Salt Lake Telegraph,* on October 11, 1864, wrote:

> The respectable portion of our Israelite citizens commenced the celebration of the Atonement at sundown on Sunday and held over till the going down of the same orb. Being without a synagogue, the faithful met in the house of one of our East Temple Street merchants and commemorated the High Priest entering the holy of holies to make atonement for the sins of the people. The conveniences for observance being rather meager, there was little conformity to the Law of Sacrifice. We have respect for the religious sentiments of all men, whatever we may think of interpretations. We should be nothing sorry to learn that some of the Israelites were drawing nearer to Moses. We mean it.

In 1865, Charles Popper, who later became Congregation B'nai Israel's first treasurer, closed his butcher shop on Rosh Hashanah and Yom Kippur. Respected by Mormon butchers,

Temple B'nai Israel. (Courtesy of Utah Historical Society)

they too closed up shop; this gesture was reciprocated by Popper during the Mormon "Pioneer Day" celebrations.

One Synagogue—On March 21, 1881, twenty-three Utah Jews met to incorporate B'nai Israel of Salt Lake City. Their objectives were to give the Jewish people a religious and educational opportunity "not for pecuniary profit." Tanner's Lot, at First West Temple and Third South, was purchased for the sum of twenty-six hundred dollars; seven hundred dollars was borrowed from M. C. Phillips to build a schoolhouse first and then add a synagogue. That year, the first religious services of the incorporated congregation were held at the Odd Fellows hall. The sum of ten dollars was paid for the use of the hall.[18]

Congregation dues were set at twelve dollars a year; masquerade balls were held at the Salt Lake Theater to raise money for the congregation, and the Ladies Hebrew Benevolent Society both contributed and loaned money for the building construction. In 1889, dues were raised to twenty-five dollars a year for married men and lowered to ten dollars for single people, the old synagogue was sold, and land was purchased on Fourth East to build a new temple.

Congregation Montefiore. (Courtesy of Utah State Historical Society)

In 1891, the city's Jewish house of worship, B'nai Israel, was dedicated. Designed by Phillip Meyer, a nephew of Frederick H. Auerbach brought to Salt Lake from Germany, the rock-faced native kyune-stone building was constructed with a magnificent dome that rises to a height of eighty-eight feet, with stained-glass windows and a seating capacity of five hundred people. (Returning home, Phillip Meyer died in a German concentration camp on October 15, 1943.)

A Second Synagogue—Prior to 1875, most of Salt Lake City's Jews were German-speaking immigrants from the newly unified Germany. In the subsequent decades, a more massive immigration of Russian Jews occurred; these immigrants spoke Russian and Yiddish. Whereas Congregation B'nai Israel began its services steeped in traditional Orthodox customs, many of its earlier (German) congregants leaned toward Reform Judaism, a newly introduced movement that was spreading across the country. Upon arriving in Salt Lake City, the new emigrants from Eastern Europe and the traditional "irreconcilables" from B'nai Israel were disenchanted with the new ideology that "bared" heads, integrated seating arrangements for men and women, and combined Hebrew and English services. A schism among the Jews developed along social, language, and religious preferences. Passionately defending their Orthodoxy, this more Conservative group began looking for a new house of worship. In 1889 with thirty members, Congregation Montefiore took form in the home of Nathan Rosenblatt at Eighth South and State Streets. Eventually, with contributions led by Isadore Morris of $150 in gold dust, the twin-domed, Moorish-looking Congregation Montefiore was dedicated in 1904.

A Short-Lived Synagogue—Declaring Congregation Montefiore less Orthodox than desired, several congregants moved over to a lesser-known third synagogue, Shaarey Tzedek, on Second East. Lack of money forced its closing in the 1930s; facing similar problems, the other two synagogues struggled with deteriorating building conditions, the need for improvements, and the requirements of running both a synagogue and a religious school.

Considering a Merger—University of Utah professor Louis Zucker wrote that the golden age for both B'nai Israel and Congregation Montefiore took place in the 1920s, 1930s, and 1940s. These were different synagogues with different rituals: each had something wonderful to offer and traditions to uphold. Yet, among the diversity of Jewish thought and Jewish ideology, a common bond between the two synagogues also created another desire—one that motivated their unification. Just as the original three synagogues were unable to move ahead because of finances, neither could the two remaining synagogues continue to have separate rabbis, separate cantors, or separate religious schools. Besides, some of their traditions were beginning to merge, even to the point of intercongregational dating; hence, Montefiore member Surki Lehrer crossed "boundaries" and "traditions" when she married B'nai Israel member Ira Tannenbaum on July 10, 1960.[19]

The Merger—The idea of a partnership between the two synagogues began with talks in 1947 and accelerated into more debates and meetings by 1956, and as congregation members Ben Roe and Wally Sandack maintain, "unification was only a matter of time, once everyone in the community [got] used to the idea." In 1969, the two congregations merged their educational programs to form the United Jewish Religious School. Still, questions needed to be answered. In a combined congregation, should yarmulkes be worn, was there a place for the choir and organ, should bar mitzvahs read from the Torah, how would the kosher kitchens fit in, how would they remain kosher, who would be qualified to read from the bema, and would women be counted in a minyan? In the summer of 1972, 77 percent of the Jewish community voted for the merger, and Congregation Kol Ami was created. Louis Zucker reflected, "As Jews, we are free to the utmost, in this Mormon Zion, to shape our ends and means as a community and a congregation as we ourselves desire."[20]

Finale—In 1976, Abe Bernstein, Sam Bernstein, Bruce Cohne, Max Cowan, Geraldine Dupler, Lionel Frankel, Richard McGillis, Ben and Morris Pepper with Phil Perlman, Henry Pullman, Milton Rosen, Harold Rosenberg, A. Wally Sandack, Joel Shapiro, Sam Shapiro, Dal Siegel, Jack Spritzer, Fred Tannenbaum, Ralph Tannenbaum, and Elliott Wolfe collectively signed a

A blended community: Congregation Kol Ami. (Photo by Eileen Hallet Stone)

promissory note with the former Walker Bank to buy land and build a new synagogue. By the year's end, dedication ceremonies took place and Congregation Kol Ami (which means "All My People") became a blend of two traditions merged into one.

"When the Jewish people first came here, life was not only physically hard, it was psychologically very difficult, and that produced a kind of toughness and independent-mindedness that is part and parcel of the strength of this community," said Rabbi Frederick Wenger of Congregation Kol Ami. Just as Utah is unique, our Jewish identity in Utah is unique. "These Jewish 'pioneers' who came to Utah specifically wanted to live in a community where they would have an opportunity to advance themselves," continued Rabbi Wenger. "They were not afraid to move out of the major centers of Jewish life and come here to live among a dominant religious majority. Of course, I think it's fair to say there's been no time in the Jewish community, even in the best of times, when they did not feel they were endangered. The challenges for Jewish survival were many."[21]

Ogden Jewry—In the 1800s, the railroad made the northern Utah city of Ogden a clearinghouse for Jewish immigrants coming west. Those early pioneers, primarily peddlers and cloth-

A welcoming walk to the I. J. and Jeanné Wagner Jewish Community Center and the Early Childhood Education Program. Salt Lake City. (Photo by Eileen Hallet Stone)

ing merchants, who remained in Ogden to raise families formed Congregation Ohab Sholem in 1890; services were held in the local Odd Fellows hall. Congregation Brith Sholem (which means "To Complete the Covenant") was formed in 1916. Partially destroyed when vandals set fire to the synagogue in 1989, it was rebuilt and remains on the National Register of Historic Places as the oldest continuously operating synagogue in Utah.

Places of Worship—Since 1990, Rabbi Benny Zippel, his family, and other members of the Orthodox Chabad Lubavitch movement arrived in Utah. The Chabad synagogue, Bais Menachem, in Salt Lake City, is named after Rabbi Menachem Schneerson, the seventh and last rabbi in the Dynasty of the Chabad rabbis. Rabbi Benny Zippel explained that the Chabad is one of the world's largest Jewish outreach organizations designed to educate Jews. "Our main purpose," said Rabbi Zippel, "is to make Jewish people more aware of their Judaism, to immerse themselves in a more traditional style, to increase their knowledge, and to make Judaism more accessible to them." Members of the Lubavitch movement believe they must adapt their lives to the Torah. "If you are a Jew, you can be a Jew twenty-four hours a day, seven days a week," said Rabbi Zippel.[22]

Relatively new to Utah is the Chavurah B'Yachad, a Reconstructionist movement based on a modern-day American-Jewish philosophy. "The Chavurah takes into account the political and cultural situation in which Jews presently live," explained Chavurah member and teacher Elizabeth Paige. "It sees all of humanity as being chosen, perhaps for different things, but nonetheless chosen." Living in Utah has impacted Paige's Reconstructionist experience. "Being away from a larger Jewish community has given me time to think carefully about how to create a Jewish home and to make this a sacred place for me and my family. It has taught me how to celebrate lighting Friday night candles in my home, celebrating Simchat Torah with my friends, and sharing Shabbat services in the canyons."[23]

Utah's most recent emigrant, Reform Temple Har Shalom in Park City, founded in March 1995, thrives in mountain Jewry. As visiting rabbi Jerry Weider of Brooklyn, New York, said during 1992 High Holy Day services in Park City, "At a time when despair rules the thinking of those who evaluate the future of American Jewry, I felt an excitement and a confidence that Jewish life was not dissolving, but evolving into a beautiful new form. Sensitive to Israel, mindful of the Holocaust, and searching for G-d in their lives, and in the lives of their children the Park City Jewish Community is pioneering a new chapter in American Jewish history."

In the site of a former polygamous home in Salt Lake City, Beit Midrash offers one an agreeable place to study traditional Jewish text, make a minyan, and read Torah.

A Place to Be—Dedicated to meeting the needs of families at all stages of life, nestled high in the foothills of Salt Lake and offering a stunning, panoramic view of the entire valley, the I. J. and Jeanné Wagner Jewish Community Center is creating history with remarkable achievements. A vital reality for now and a legacy for the future, Utah Jews from all walks of life and viewpoints have joined together to preserve Jewish heritage and traditions.

The Undiscovered American West—Different motivations continue to impel Jewish individuals to move to new frontiers. The "undiscovered" American West was the breeding ground for adventure, diversity, independence, and precarious living. Today, for small ethnic groups, the same definition may be its calling card. Although still a minority people, Utah Jews struggle with the paradox of living among a predominantly homogenous culture with practices and theologies quite dissimilar from their own that both embraces the Jew and subtly rejects him as a Gentile. Consequently, to make a place for themselves in the West, Utah Jews have had to adapt to the circumstances of another culture first, and then, within this uniquely different environment, maintain their religious identity, culture, and traditions.

The following oral history interviews, diaries, newspaper accounts, articles, journals, and photographs explore how Utah Jewish individuals, representing all walks of life, experiences, and attitudes, not only became at home in the American West but settled into the new chapter of western history as well.

ONE

A Wandering Jew on the Thirty-eighth Parallel

Solomon Nunes Carvalho

While encamped on this spot we met a party of gold explorers from Los Angeles. They had been down on the Colorado, looking for gold, but had been unsuccessful. They were under the command of a man with one leg, known as "Peg-leg Smith," a celebrated mountaineer.

He told me he had been several times across the continent, and had been in this part of the world for some years. He says he crossed the Rocky Mountains in 1824—thirty years ago. He is a weather-beaten old chap, and tells some improbable tales.[1]

Into the Far West—Seven years after the Mormons arrived in Utah, Sephardic Jew Solomon Nunes Carvalho, a deeply religious man who believed that Jewish culture could coexist with American life, traveled with Colonel John C. Frémont's ill-fated expedition across the Rockies, nearly died from exposure, and found himself on the mend in Utah in 1854, a Gentile among Mormons.

A Commitment to Judaism—Coming from a long line of Spanish-Portuguese Sephardic Jews who fled the Spanish Inquisition and migrated to the Canaries, Holland, London, the British West Indies, South America, and the United States, Solomon Nunes Carvalho was born in Charleston, South Carolina, on April 27, 1815. At the time, John Charles Frémont was two years

Solomon Nunes Carvalho, half-plate daguerreotype. (Courtesy of the Library of Congress)

old. That the two would later meet in 1853 to undertake "the Pathfinder's" last and near fatal expedition into the Far West, and that Carvalho would be the first Jewish person to spend any length of time in Utah, was far from serendipitous.

Solomon Nunes Carvalho was born into a "family which prized culture, piety, and refinement."[2] In 1798, Solomon's uncle Emanuel Nunes Carvalho trained as an artisan in England,

and became the *hazzan* of the Portuguese congregation in Barbados. As a cantor, he eventually held pulpits in Barbados, Charleston, New York, and Philadelphia. The first of many Jewish leaders in America, Emanuel wrote a Hebrew-English prayer book so that the vibrant language and compelling Judaic content would ensure continuing participation among Jews in the New World.[3] In New York, the uncle also taught Hebrew and Jewish literature in the school of Shearith Israel. For four years, he was the hazzan of Beth Elohim Congregation in Charleston before departing for Philadelphia.[4] Most likely, it was during Emanuel's residency in Charleston that he brought his younger brother David to the United States.

Solomon's mother, Sarah D'Azevedo, is reputed to have been a descendant of Moses Cohen D'Azevedo, the chief *chachem* (rabbi) of a Spanish-Portuguese community in London. His father, David Nunes Carvalho, made his living as a merchant in the marble-paper manufacturing business. Believing that "Judaism was not fixed and unchangeable," he was drawn toward adapting Jewish traditions to contemporary existence and sensibilities while living a Jewish life devoted to social justice and ethics. Like his brother Emanuel, he also emphasized the important role of secular and religious literature.

> In Charleston, during the War of 1812, David saw service with the volunteers who defended the city against the British. . . . David made his living as a merchant, but engaged in a multitude of cultural and religious activities. He had a penchant for writing and composed several works which were never published, including a metrical translation into English of the Book of Psalms, and a five-act drama, "Queen Esther." . . . David was also the founder of the controversial Reformed Society of Israelites of Charleston, the first Reform congregation in the United States; he served as a member of its Committee on Correspondence, and acted, without remuneration, as minister at its divine services. In 1827, shortly before his removal to the north, he was honored with election as lecturer of the congregation.[5]

Solomon revered his father's commitment to Reform Judaism, although his own views were more traditional. As a child, he devoted many hours to Torah study and reading abstracts written by medieval Jewish writers. When his love of learning extended to the arts, a portfolio of religious drawings emerged. Later, the adult Solomon became an active leader devoted to developing Jewish institutions and sounding the clarion on Jewish issues. In Baltimore, he joined the Hebrew Young Men's Literary Society, and reiterated his belief that traditional Orthodox Judaism was to be upheld, though he also recognized the significance of modification. In a letter to his friend and mentor the Reverend Isaac Leeser, the hazzan of Philadelphia's Mikve Israel synagogue, Carvalho stressed the challenges facing contemporary American Jewish life.[6]

> Look at the numberless young men who have deserted the ship by escaping over the side (intermarriage) preferring to swim to some shore rather than remain on board. When

> there is so much strife and contention about things of no consequence [ritual details], is it not imperiously demanded that we should let our children know that there is a true course to be steered and that our religion is not one of contention but of peace and good will?[7]

Solomon revered Judaism and maintained his interest in Hebrew Scriptures throughout his entire life; in 1884, he wrote a treatise titled *The Two Creations: A Scientific, Hermeneutic, and Etymologic Treatise on the Mosaic Cosmogony from the Original Hebrew Tongue.* In this lengthy work, he attempted to prove that no conflict existed between the scientific theories on the creation of the world and the biblical version presented in Genesis. This book was not published, but in a letter he alluded to the source of its inspiration:

> While traveling in the Grand Canyon of the Colorado, I made geological examinations and saw for myself the gigantic fossiliferous remains of ancient creations all arranged in stratifications like the shelves in a library. I there realized the immeasurable duration of time which must have elapsed since they were created. I promised myself if I ever lived to return, I would examine the original text of Genesis, etymologically and dialectically, to see what Moses really saw.[8]

From Portrait Painter to Daguerreotypist—By the time Carvalho was in his twenties, he had achieved a considerable reputation as a portrait painter. In 1849, he opened an art studio in Baltimore, then in Charleston, and later in New York, and was soon experimenting with photography. Credited with having been the first Jewish photographer in history, Carvalho made artistic improvements to the fashionable daguerreotype process by offering exclusive "Crayon Daguerreotypes," portrait miniatures that he claimed were superior to most competitors' offerings.[9] The daguerreotype process involves treating a thin sheet of silver-plated copper with the fumes from heated iodine crystals to sensitize the silver plating to light. The sheet, mounted on a wooden plate holder, is then placed inside a camera. When the lens cap is removed, the plate is exposed to light through the camera lens. After stopping the exposure by replacing the cap, the sheet is removed from the camera, placed in a special developing chamber, and developed by vapors from mercury that have been heated. At the points where the mercury combined with the silver have been affected by light, a detailed image will emerge. The plate is removed and bathed in several solutions so the image will become fixed, insensitive to light and portraying a more brilliant finish. To complement the portrait, a fine brush of color is applied. Because a daguerreotype plate is susceptible to deterioration, to protect the image it is placed between a brass mat and a piece of glass with the edges sealed with paper tape. Popular in the 1840s and 1850s, daguerreotype experimentation resulted in improved exposure times of less than a minute, making it an ideal system for traveling.[10]

A Vivid Account of the West—By 1853, most likely, it was Carvalho's reputation as a daguerreotypist that attracted the attention of Colonel John C. Frémont. Frémont was looking for a photographer and artist to accompany him on his fifth, and last, expedition into the Far West, a journey intended to prove the viability of the thirty-eighth parallel through the Rocky Mountains as a feasible route for the country's first transcontinental railroad.

Frémont wanted to publish a survey report replete with illustrations, maps, and photographic images. He also wanted to include Carvalho's journal as a companion piece to his 1856 promotional campaign as the country's first Republican candidate for president of the United States. Frémont lost to James Buchanan, the survey report was never published, and, in fact, many of the daguerreotypes were lost over time. Solomon's book, *Incidents of Travel and Adventure in the Far West,* reprinted four times before 1860, remains the only contemporary account of Frémont's near fatal expedition.[11] Eloquent in language, rich in detail, *Incidents of Travel* is a narrative and visual epic that preserves an important milestone in the West. It gives voice to the contemplation of an American artist, intellectual, and Jew who, away from the comforts of civilization, experiences the unconquered wilderness of desert, plains, and mountains that embodies America's destiny. It captures this country's panoramic vistas, its fauna and flora, and it meticulously details the geological and archaeological diversity intrinsic to the West. It exposes the severity of challenges, reenacts the disasters, regales with humor, portrays the loneliness of travel and the absence of comfort, and imbues the inquisitive reader with western lore. In Utah for almost four months, Solomon's fascinating account sheds light on the Mormon principles of faith, the geographic surveys of early settlements, and Solomon's indisputable quest for scientific and intellectual observation.

The following excerpts are taken from the 1857 book, an extraordinary treasure archived within miles of Parowan at Utah State University's Rare Book Collection in Cedar City, *Incidents of Travel and Adventures in the Far West; with Col. Fremont's Last Expedition across the Rocky Mountains: Including Three Months' Residence in Utah, and a Perilous Trip across the Great American Desert, to the Pacific.*

On the 22d August, 1853, after a short interview with Col. J. C. Fremont, I accepted his invitation to accompany him as artist of an Exploring Expedition across the Rocky Mountains. A half hour previously, if anybody had suggested to me, the probability of my undertaking an overland journey to California, even over the emigrant route, I should have replied there were no inducements sufficiently powerful to have tempted me. Yet, in this instance, I impulsively, without even a consultation with my family, passed my word to join an exploring party, under command of Col. Fremont, over a hitherto untrodden country, in an elevated region, with the full expectation of being exposed to all the inclemencies of an arctic winter. I know of no other man to whom I would have trusted my life, under similar circumstances.[12]

Solomon Nunes Carvalho and Col. John C. Frémont taking observations. (From the first edition of *Incidents of Travel and Adventure in the Far West*)

Travels and Members of the Expedition—Entertaining these feelings, the dangers and perils of the journey, which Col. Fremont pointed out to me, were entirely obscured by the pleasure I anticipated in accompanying him, and adding my limited skill to facilitate him in the realization of one of the objects of the expedition—which was to obtain an exact description of the face of the country which we were to travel.

The party consisted of twenty-two persons; among them were ten Delaware chiefs; and two Mexicans. The officers were: Mr. Egloffstein, topographical engineer; Mr. Strobel, assistant; Mr. Oliver Fuller, assistant engineer; Mr. S. N. Carvalho, artist and daguerreotypist; Mr. W. H. Palmer, passenger. The expedition was fitted out, I think at the individual expense of Col. Fremont. [18–19]

Daguerreotypes in the Mountains—To make daguerreotypes in the open air, in a temperature varying from freezing point to thirty degrees below zero, requires manipulation from the processes by which pictures are made in a warm room. My professional friends were all of the opinion that the elements would be against my success. Buffing and coating plates, and mercurializing them, on the summit of the Rocky Mountains, standing at time up to one's middle in snow, with no covering above save the arched vault of heaven, seemed to our city friends one of the impossibilities—knowing as they did that iodine will not give out its fumes except at a temperature of 70 *degrees* to 80 *degrees* Fahrenheit. [20]

Arrival at Kansas—When we landed, we met Mr. Palmer and several of the men who were to accompany the Expedition as muleteers, etc. The equipage of the camp that had been previously shipped from St. Louis, had arrived safely. As soon as our baggage had landed, it, together with the rest of the material, was transported by wagons to camp near Westport, a few miles in the interior. [23]

On the night of the 20th, all hands slept in camp, a heavy rain-storm drenched us completely, giving to the party an introduction to a life on the prairies. The necessity of India-rubber blankets became evident, and I was dispatched to Westport to procure them. There were none to be had. I sent a man to Independence to purchase two dozen; he travelled thirty miles that night and by ten next morning I had them in the camp. They were the most useful articles we had with us; we placed the India-rubber side on the snow, our buffalo robes on top of that for a bed, and covered with our blankets, with an India-rubber blanket over the whole—India-rubber side up, to turn the rain. [24–25]

Engagement of Delawares—The distribution of arms and ammunition to the men occupied a portion of the next day. Each person had a rifle and Colt's revolver. Some of the Delawares had horsemen's pistols, also. The messenger Col. Fremont sent to the Delaware camp returned, with a number of braves, some of whom had accompanied Col. Fremont on a former expedition—he selected ten, among whom was a chief named Solomon, who had been with him before, and for whom Col. Fremont felt a great friendship. They were entertained with dinner, and after a smoke, each had a small quantity of the brandy we brought for medicinal purposes. They left us, to make preparations for the expedition, and to join us near the Kansas River, about one hundred miles westward. [25]

Catching a Mule—I had never saddled a horse myself. My sedentary employment in a city, never having required me to do such offices; and now I was to become my own ostler, and ride him to water twice a day, besides running after him on the prairie for an hour sometimes before I could catch him. But, dear reader, follow me to a camp on the mountains of snow, where I exchanged my horse for a mule, at daylight, with the thermometer 20 degrees below zero. . . . My mule sees me, and know[s] that my errand is to prepare him for his day's journey, without first giving him provender to perform it. . . . I have reached it, and at the moment I think I have him securely, he dashes away at a full gallop, pulling me after him through the snow. . . . I lie breathless on the icy carpet. I am now a mile from camp. . . . I renew my exertions, and gently approach him; this time he stands quiet, and I gather the rope in my hand and pat him for a few minutes, and then mount him bare backed. The life and activity he possessed a few moments before, is entirely gone; he stands like a mule in the snow, determined not to budge a step. I coax. I kick him. . . . I, worn out, and almost frozen, remain chewing the cud of bitter reflection, until one of my comrades comes to seek and assist me; he goes behind the mule, and gives him a slight touch *a posteriori,* when, awakening from his trance, he starts at a hard trot into camp. . . . "Stubborn as a mule." [26–27]

Shawnee Mission—We remained at the Methodist Mission until the next day, when we proceeded to the Shawnee Mission, a few miles further, and camped for the night. It was at this spot that Mr. Max Strobel made his appearance. . . . He requested Col. Fremont to allow him to accompany his expedition as a volunteer. . . . Col. Fremont hesitated as his company was complete, but finally yielded to his continued entreaties. Col. Fremont, who had been slightly indisposed during the day, finding himself worse, decided to return to Westport, requesting us to continue on our journey until we meet the Delawares, and then encamp and await his return. [29]

Reflections on the Prairie—My heart beat with fervent anxiety, and whilst I felt happy, and free from the usual care and trouble, I still could not master the nervous debility which seized me while surveying the grand and majestic works of nature. Was it fear? No; it was the conviction of my own insignificance, in the mist of the stupendous creation; the undulating grass seemed to carry thoughts on its rolling surface, into an impenetrable future;—glorious in inconceivable beauty, extended over me, the ethereal tent of heaven, my eye losing its power to distant vision, seemed to reach down only to the verdant sea before me. [30]

The Twenty-seventh—To-day we met our Delawares, who were awaiting our arrival. A more noble set of Indians, I never saw, the most of them six feet high, all mounted and armed *cap-i-pie,* under command of Captain Wolff, "Big Indian," as he called himself. Most of them spoke English, and all understood it. Washington, Welluchas [*sic*], Solomon, Moses, were the names of some of the principal chiefs. They became very much attached to Col. Fremont, and every one of them would have ventured his life for him. [31]

Camp Life—Dear [Sarah]: The duties of camp life are becoming more onerous as the weather gets colder. It is expected that each man in camp will bring in a certain quantity of fire-wood! My turn came to day, and I am afraid I shall make a poor hand in using the axe; first, I have not the physical strength, and secondly, I do not know how. I managed by hunting through the woods to find several decayed limbs, which I brought in on my shoulder. I made three trips, and I have at all events supplied the camp with kindling wood for the night.

I certainly, being a "Republican," do not expect to warm myself at the expense of another; therefore, arduous as it is, I must, to carry out the principle of equality, do as the rest do, although it is not a very congenial occupation. [37][13]

Kansas Territory—Kansas lies between the thirty-seventh and fortieth degrees of north latitude. The Indian Territory bounds it on the south, Utah and New Mexico on the west, Nebraska on the north, and Missouri on the east. . . . Grasses of a hundred different kinds, some of them rank and high, but the most of them possessing highly nutritive qualities, grow spontaneously on the prairies, and afford nourishment to immense quantities of game.

The water of the Kansas partakes in color of the character of the soil over which it passes. It is, I am inclined to believe, always turbid. I found it quite unfit for daguerreotype purposes, and had to preserve many of my plates until we approached the crystal streams from the Rocky Mountains to finish them. During our long camp on Salt Creek, our topographical engineer and myself explored the country for miles. Coal in abundance is to be obtained with but little exertion; in many instances it crops out on the surface of the ground. The general character of the formation of this country is the same as Missouri—a secondary limestone. [41]

Dear [Sarah]: Yesterday two beaver trappers came into the Delaware camp, and traded for sugar and coffee with the Delawares. I have my suspicions that our mules conveyed them away, as they are no longer on the creek where they set their traps yesterday.

I must leave off my journal, as it is my usual hour for rifle practice; I have become quite an expert; at one hundred paces, I have hit the "bull's eye" twice in five times, which is not bad shooting, considering I have had no practice since I was a member of a rifle volunteer company in Charleston, some twenty years ago. [45]

Illness of Captain Wolff—The ceremony was conducted in secret, but I found out afterward the place, and from the mode which was explained to me, I understood the rite perfectly. A small lodge, composed of the branches of trees, high enough for a man to sit upright in, was built; in this the patient was placed in a state of perfect nudity. "The Medicine Man," who is outside, takes a "pipe," filled with "*kinnikinick* and tobacco," and hands it in to the patient. While the Medicine Man recites the all powerful words, the patient puffs away until the lodge is filled with smoke; . . . he is taken out, wrapped in his blankets, and conveyed to his own lodge.

Feeling anxious about him, I went in to see him about an hour afterwards; I found him in a high state of febrile excitement, which had, no doubt, been increased by his extraordinary treatment; he complained of a dreadful headache and pain in his back. . . . I told him if he would submit to my advice, I thought I could cure him—he consented, and I administered ten grains of calomel, and [then] Epsom salts. He is now considerably relieved. . . . Indigestion was the cause of his suffering.

Colonel Fremont has not yet arrived. . . . I am afraid Col. Fremont is seriously ill. [46–47]

A Pleasant Time—Last night our camp was visited with a heavy storm of rain and sleet; it was bitter cold. It rained considerably yesterday, but the temperature was not lower than 65 degrees. The wind increased during the night, and one sudden gust blew our cotton tent completely over, exposing us to the peltings of the merciless storm of sleet. Several of us essayed to raise the tent, but the ground had become saturated with moisture, and afforded no hold for our tent-pins, and we consequently lay down, wrapped ourselves in our India-rubber blankets, and bewailed our fate. [49]

Discovery of a Herd—After about three hours' gentle trotting, one of the party startled a *"cayote,"* and we chased him until he disappeared in the brush. When we reached the brow of a hill, Weluchas ejaculated, in deep, low tones, "Buffaloes," "big herd"—I turned my eyes and, for the first time, beheld a large herd of buffaloes occupying an extensive valley, well wooded and watered, and luxuriant with the peculiar short curled grass, called "Buffalo grass" *(Lysteria Dyclotoides),* on which this animal principally feeds. I gazed with delight and astonishment at the novel sight which presented itself. There must have been at least 6,000 buffaloes, including cows and calves. It was a sight well worth travelling a thousand miles to see. Some were grazing, others playfully gambolling, while the largest number were quietly reclining or sleeping on their verdant carpet, little dreaming of the danger which surrounded them, or of the murderous visitors who were about to disturb their sweet repose. [51]

Mode of Attack by the Delawares—A Delaware Indian, in hunting buffaloes, when near enough to shoot, rests his rifle on his saddle, balances himself in his stirrup on one leg; the other is thrown over the rifle to steady it. He then leans on one side, until his eye is on a level with the object, takes a quick sight, and fires while riding at full speed, rarely missing his mark, and seldom chasing one animal further than a mile. [53]

Solitary and Alone—After recovering from my fright, and the intense excitement incidental to the chase, other sensations of a different character, although not less disagreeable, immediately filled my mind. I discovered that I was entirely alone, in an uninhabited, wild country, with not a human being in sight. I had chased my bull at least five miles. . . . My mind was fully alive to the perils of my situation. I had left my pocket compass in camp, and I did not know in what direction to look for it. I mounted my horse and walked to the top of a hill to see if I could find any traces of the party. I discovered looming in the distance, Smoky Hills some twenty miles off. My mind was in a slight degree relieved, although I was almost as ignorant of my geographical position as I was before. I did not despair, but unsaddling my horse, I gave him an hour's rest; the grass was fresh, and he appeared totally unconcerned at my situation. [53–54]

Pony Killed for Meat—Poor fellow! Little did I think that day, as he carried me, so full of life and high spirit, that in a few weeks he would be reduced to a mere skeleton, and that I should be obliged, in order to save my own life on the mountains of snow, to partake of his flesh. I shed tears when they shot him down, and I never think of his generous, willing qualities, but I lament the stern necessity that left his bones bleaching on the mountains. [54]

Prairie on Fire—During the day, the sun was completely obscured by low, dark clouds; a most disagreeable and suffocating smoke filled the atmosphere. . . . We were on the prairie, between Kansas River on one side, Solomon's Fork on another, Salt Creek on the third, and a large belt of woods about four miles from camp on the fourth. We were thus completely hemmed in, and comparatively secure from danger. . . . About this time the prairie was on fire just beyond the belt of woods through which Col. Fremont had to pass. . . . The fire had reached the belt of woods. . . . The fire on the north side had burned up to the water's edge, and had there stopped. The whole horizon now seemed bounded by fire. Our Delawares by this time had picketed all the animals near the creek we were encamped on, and had safely carried the baggage of the camp down the banks near the water. When day dawned, the magnificent woods which had sheltered our animals, appeared a forest of black scathed trunks.

The fire gradually increased, yet we dared not change our ground; first, because we saw no point where there was not more danger, and, secondly, if we moved away, Solomon, the Indian chief, who after conducting us to the camp ground we now occupied, had returned to guide Col. Fremont, would not know exactly where to find us.

We thus continued gazing appalled at the devouring element which threatened to overwhelm us.

After breakfast, one of our Delawares gave a loud whoop, and pointing to the open space beyond, in the direction of Solomon's Fork, where to our great joy, we saw Col. Fremont on horseback followed by "an immense man," on an "immense mule," (who afterwards proved to be our good and kind-hearted Doctor Ober); Col. Fremont's "Cook" and the Indian Solomon galloping through the blazing element in the direction of our camp. . . . The keen sense of the Indian directed him under all difficulties directly to the spot where he had left us. . . . We passed through the fiery ordeal unscathed; made that day over fifteen miles, and camped for the night on the dry bed of a creek, beyond the reach of the devouring element. [56–61]

Reflections—Near by our camp, a rugged mountain, barren of trees, and thickly covered with snow reared its lofty head high in the blue vault above us. The approach to it was inaccessible by even our surefooted mules. From its summit, the surrounding country could be seen for hundreds of miles. Col. Fremont regretted that such important views as might be made up from that point, should be lost, and gave up the idea as impracticable from its dangerous character. I told him that if he would allow two men to assist me in carrying my apparatus up the mountains, I would attempt the ascent on foot, and make the pictures; he pointed out the difficulties, I insisted. He then told me if I was determined to go he would accompany me; this was an unusual thing for him and it proved to me, that he considered the ascent difficult and dangerous, and that his superior judgment might be required to pick the way, for a misstep would have precipitated us on to the rugged rocks at its base; and it also proved that he would not allow his men or officers to encounter perils or dangers in which he did not participate.

After three hours' hard toil we reached the summit and held a panorama of unspeakable sublimity spread out before us; continuous chains of mountains reared their snowy peaks far away in the distance, while the Grand River, plunging along in awful sublimity through its rock bed, was seen for the first time. Above us the cerulean heaven, without a single cloud to mar its beauty, was sublime in its calmness.

Standing as it were in this vestibule of God's holy Temple, I forgot I was of this mundane sphere; the divine part of man elevated itself, undisturbed by the influences of the world. I looked from nature, up to nature's God, more chastened and purified than I ever felt before.

Plunged up to my middle in snow, I made a panorama of the continuous ranges of mountains around us. Col. Fremont made barometrical and thermometrical observations, and occupied a part of his time in geological examinations. We descended safely, and with a keen appetite, discussed the merits of our dried buffalo and deer meat. [82–83]

Intense Cold—Eating, sleeping, and travelling, continually in the open air, with the thermometer descending, as we gradually ascended the immense slopes of country between the frontiers of Missouri and the Rocky Mountains, until I have found myself in temperature of 30 degrees below zero, prepared my system for the intense cold, which we endured during our journey through that elevated country. Twice only did our party find it too cold to travel longer than half an hour, without stopping, and making a large fire to keep ourselves from freezing. We were all mounted at the time, but we find it necessary to walk a greater part of the way, to keep up a circulation of blood. [84]

My First Journey on Foot—It was a very cold day in December; the snow covered the immense mountain, over which we had to travel, and right merrily we all followed each other's footsteps in the deep snow.

When we arrived at the foot of the rugged mountain, it was found necessary to dismount, and lead our animals along the intricate and tortuous path. . . . I plunged frequently up to my neck in chasms of snow. . . . My efforts to extricate myself cost me some time, and when I regained my footing, I discovered my pony about fifty yards ahead, trying to regain the party. . . . I sank down exhausted on a rock, with the dreadful reality that I was alone, and on foot on the mountains of eternal snow, with a long day's journey before me.

Gathering fresh strength and courage from the serious position I found myself in, I scrambled up that mountain with a heart palpitating so loudly, that I could count its pulsations. In this manner, alternately resting, I reached the top. On looking on the other side, the only indication of the party, was their deep trail in the frozen snow.

I commenced descending, and at considerable distance below me, I fancied I saw a moving object under a tree. . . . Captain Wolff saw my pony riderless, and suspecting that he had escaped from me, caught and tied him up in the place where he was sure to be found; thus repaying me a hundred fold for my medical advice and attendance on Salt Creek. [85–86]

Fifty Animals Rolling Headlong—Several days after we came down from the Cochotope Pass, it became necessary to ascend a very high and excessively steep mountain of snow. When we were half way up, one of the foremost baggage mules lost his balance, from his hind feet sinking deep in the snow. Down he tumbled, heels-over-head, carrying with him nearly the whole cavalcade, fifty odd in number, several hundred feet to the bottom.

It was a serious, yet a most ludicrous spectacle, to witness fifty animals rolling headlong down a snow mountain, gaining fresh impetus as they descended, unable to stop themselves. The bales of buffalo robes, half buried in the snow, lodged against an old pine tree, the blankets scattered everywhere; my boxes of daguerreotype materials uninjured, although buried in the snow. . . .

. . . [W]e found one mule and one horse were killed. This scene made a deep impression upon me. Night came upon us before we were ready to leave the spot. We camped on the same place of the night before. . . .

That night the thermometer sank very low, and the men stood to their waist in snow, guarding the animals to prevent their running away in search of grass, or something to eat.

We descended the mountain the next day. Our tent poles, belonging to the large lodge, were broken by their contact with the trees in the winding path. The lodge, afterwards, became useless, and the men, myself among them, had to sleep out upon the open snow, with no covering but our blankets, etc. . . . We at this time were on rations of meat-biscuit, and had killed our first horse for food. [87–89][14]

Wild Horse Killed by Indians—We travelled that day nearly twenty miles, and encamped outside of a Utah Indian village, containing a large number of lodges and probably several hundred persons. . . . We made several purchases, and traded for several small lots of fat venison.

About nine o'clock, after placing double guard around our animals, . . . we heard loud noises approaching the camp; voices of women were heard in bitter bewailment. . . . [T]he horse our

A Utah Indian village, daguerreotype by Solomon Nunes Carvalho. (Courtesy of the Library of Congress)

Delawares had killed the evening before, some twenty miles away, belonged to one of the squaws then present, who valued it very highly, and demanded payment. [91]

Colonel Frémont's Justice—On informing Col. Fremont, who denied himself to the Indians, he remarked that "we had no right to kill their horse without remunerating them for it."

The Indians having seen our assortment, wanted a part of everything we had, including a keg of gunpowder. To this demand Col. Fremont gave an absolute refusal. . . . The Indians then threatened to attack us. Col. Fremont defied them. After considerable parleying, we succeeded in pacifying them.

As it was the intention of Col. Fremont to leave camp at an early hour, I unpacked my daguerreotype apparatus, at daylight, and made several views. While engaged in this way, one of the Utah Indians brought into camp a beautiful three-year-old colt, and offered to trade him with me. . . . My poor Pungo had, three days before, been shot down for food, and in consequence I was literally on foot, although I was using one of the baggage animals for the time.

With permission of Col. Fremont, I traded for him; I gave him in exchange one pair of blankets, an old dress coat, a spoiled daguerreotype plate, a knife, half an ounce of vermilion and an old exhausted pony. [91–92]

The Six-Shooters—When we left the Utah village, we travelled a long day's journey, and camped on the Grand River, thirty miles from the last camp; my pony behaved admirably well on the road, and I would not have parted with him on any account.

While at supper, about fifty or sixty mounted Utah Indians, all armed with rifles and bows and arrows, displaying their powder horns and *cartouche* boxes most conspicuously, their horses full of mettle, came galloping and tearing into camp.

They had also come to be compensated for the horse we had paid for the night before; they insisted that the horse did not belong to the woman, but to one of the men then present, and threatened, if we did not pay them a great deal of red cloth, blankets, vermilion, knives, and gunpowder, they would fall upon us and massacre the whole party. . . .

Very much alarmed, I entered Col. Fremont's lodge, and told him their errand and their threats. . . . He tore a leaf from his journal, and handing it to me, said,: here take this, and place it against a tree, and at a distance near enough to hit it every time, discharge your Colt's Navy six shooters, fire at intervals of from ten to fifteen seconds—and call the attention of the Indians to the fact, that it is not necessary for white men to load their arms.

I did so; after the first shot, they pointed to their own rifles, as much as to say they could do the same (if they had happened to have the powder), I, without lowering my arm, fired a second shot, this startled them.

I discharged it a third time—their curiosity and amazement were increased; the fourth time, I placed the pistol in the hands of the chief and told him to discharge it, which he did, hitting the paper and making another impression of the bullet. . . .

We effected a trade for three or four apparently sound strong animals; Moses, one of the Delaware chiefs, also traded for one, but in a few days they all proved lame and utterly useless as roadsters, and we had to kill them for food. [96–98]

Crossing the Grand River—The crossing of the Grand River, the eastern fork of the Colorado, was attended with much difficulty and more danger. The weather was excessively cold, the ice on the margin of either side of the river was over eighteen inches thick; the force of the stream always kept the passage in the centre open; the distance between the ice, was at our crossing, about two hundred yards. I supposed the current in the river to run at the rate of six miles an hour. The animals could scarcely keep their footing on the ice, although the men had been engaged for half an hour in strewing it with sand. The river was about six feet deep, making it necessary to swim our animals across; the greatest difficulty was in persuading them to make the abrupt leap from the ice to the roaring gulph [*sic*], and there was much danger from drowning in attempting to get on the sharp ice on the other side, the water being beyond the depth of the animals, nothing but their heads were above water, consequently the greater portion of their riders' bodies were also immersed in the freezing current.

To arrive at a given point, affording the most facilities for getting upon the ice, it was necessary to swim your horse in a different direction to allow for the powerful current. I think I must have been in the water, at least a quarter of an hour. The awful plunge from the ice into the water, I never shall have the ambition to try again; the weight of my body on the horse, naturally made him go under head and all; I held on as fast as a cabin boy to a main-stay in a gale of wind. If I had lost my balance it is most probably I should have been drowned. I was nearly drowned as it was, and my clothes froze stiff upon me when I came out of it. Some of the Delawares crossed first and built a large fire on the other side, at which we all dried our clothes standing in them. [100]

Solemn Scene—At last we are drawn to the necessity of killing our brave horses for food. The sacrifice of my own pony that had carried me so bravely in my first buffalo hunt, was made; he had been running loose for a week unable to bear even a bundle of blankets. It was a solemn event with me, and rendered more so by the impressive scene which followed.

Col. Fremont came out to us, and after referring to the dreadful necessities to which we were reduced, said "a detachment of men who he had sent for succor on a former expedition, had been guilty of eating one of their own number." He expressed his abhorrence of the act, and proposed that we should not under any circumstances whatever, kill our companions to prey upon them. "If we are to die, let us die together like men." He then threatened to shoot the first man that made or hinted at such a proposition.

It was a solemn and impressive sight to see a body of white men, Indians, and Mexicans, on a snowy mountain, at night, some with bare head and clasped hands entering into this solemn compact. I never until that moment realized the awful situation in which I, one of the actors in this scene, was placed. . . .

It was a clear, cold night, on the Eagle Tail River, after a long fast, and a dreary walk, our men had returned supperless to sleep on their snowy bed, and with no prospect of anything to eat in the morning, to refresh them for another day's tramp. . . .

We had been twenty-four hours without a meal. Mr. Fuller was on guard and it was a few days before he gave out, . . . hungry as the rest of us; while patrolling up and down the river on the banks of which we were encamped, his keen eye discovered a beaver swimming across the stream; he watched it with rifle to his shoulder, and as it landed, he fired and killed it. Our beaver was dressed for breakfast. [100–103]

Grass Seed for Food—The descent into the valley of the Green River was over the most dangerous projections of different strata of rock, thrown into its present state by the convulsion of nature. . . . We crossed the river, and were conducted by the Indians to a fertile spot on the western bank of it, where their village was. We found that they lived on nothing else but grass-seed, which they collected in the fall. Their women parch it, and grind it between stones. In this manner, it is very palatable, and tastes very much like roasted peanuts.

This, their only article of food, was very scarce, and we could procure only a small supply. I parted with everything out of my daguerreotype boxes that I did not require, and several articles of necessary clothing, for about a quart of it. The quantity I had lasted me for three days. [104–5]

Dinner on Porcupine—A large porcupine was killed and brought into camp today by our Delawares, who placed it on a large fire, burning off its quills, leaving a thick hard skin, very like that of a hog. The meat was white, but very fat; it looked very much like pork. My stomach revolted at it, and I sat hungry around our mess, looking at my comrades enjoying it. The animal weighed about thirty pounds.[15] [107]

Horse—When it became necessary to slaughter our animals for food, I refrained from eating it in the vain hope of killing game, until exhausted nature demanded recuperation. I then partook of the strange and forbidden food with much hesitation, and only in small quantities. The taste of young fat horse meat is sweet and nutty, and could scarcely be distinguished from young beef, while that of the animal, after it is almost starved to death, is without any flavor. You know you are eating flesh, but it contains no juices—it serves to sustain life, it contains but little nutritive matter, and one grows poor and emaciated, while living on it alone. Mule meat can hardly be distinguished from horse meat, I never could tell the difference. [113]

Terrible Rainstorm—I had been on foot all day, travelling over a rugged country of volcanic formation, with an apology for moccasins on my lacerated and painful feet. I slept soundly until twelve o'clock, when I felt the cold water insinuating itself between my clothes and body. I uncovered my head, over which I had my robe and blankets, to find it raining fast and steadily. In an hour, I found myself lying in water nearly a foot deep. I could not escape my present situation. Wrapping my India rubber closely around me, I remained perfectly passive, submitting to the violence of the heaviest and most drenching rainstorm I experienced on the whole journey. Darkness reigned supreme. Our campfires were extinguished. [114–15]

Oliver Fuller Gives Out—Mr. Egloffstien [*sic*], Mr. Fuller, and myself were generally at the end of the train, our scientific duties requiring us to stop frequently on the road. Mr. Fuller had been on foot several days before any of the rest of the party, his horse having been the first to give out. . . . [O]f the three, I was considered the worst off. One of my feet became sore, from walking on the flinty mountains with thin moccasins, and I was very lame in consequence. Mr. Fuller's feet were nearly wholly exposed. The last pair of moccasins I had, I gave him a week before; now his toes were out, and he walked with great difficulty in the snow. He never complained when we started in the morning, and I was surprised when he told me he had "given out." Mr. Fuller was the strongest and largest man in the camp when we left Westport, and appeared much better able to bear the hardships of the journey than any [other] man in it. . . .

When we realized his conditions, we determined to remain with him; to this he decidedly objected. "Go on to camp," said he, "and if possible send me assistance. You can do me no good by remaining, for if you do not reach camp before night, we shall all freeze to death." [118]

Colonel Frémont Sends for Fuller—It commenced to snow. We travelled in this manner ten long hours, until we came to camp. Mr. Egloffstien [*sic*] and self both informed Col. Fremont of the circumstance, and we were told that it was impossible to send for Mr. Fuller.

While we were speaking at our scanty fire of the unfortunate fate of our comrade, Col. Fremont came out of his lodge, and gave orders that the two best animals in camps be prepared, together with some cooked horse-meat [provisions]. He sent them with Frank Dixon, a Mexican, back on the trail, to find Mr. Fuller. There was not a dry eye in camp that whole night. We sat up anxiously awaiting the appearance of Mr. Fuller. Day dawned, and cold and cheerless was the prospect. There being no signs of our friend, Col. Fremont remarked that it was just what he expected. Col. Fremont had allowed his humanity to overcome his better judgment.

Solomon Nunes Carvalho's children.
(Courtesy of the Library of Congress)

Towards night, the two Delawares supporting Mr. Fuller were seen approaching; he was found by the Delawares awake, but almost senseless from cold and starvation; he was hailed with joy by our whole camp. Col. Fremont, as well as the rest of us, rendered him all the assistance in our power; I poured out the last drop of my alcohol, which I mixed with a little water, and administered it to him. His feet were frozen black to his ankles; if he had lived to reach the settlements, it is probable he would have had to suffer amputation of both feet. [119–20]

Another Nearly Gives Out—After we crossed the Green River, the whole party was on foot. The continued absence of nutritious food made us weaker every day. One of my feet was badly frozen, and I walked with much pain and great difficulty; on this occasion, my lameness increased to such a degree, that I was the last man on the trail, and my energy and firmness almost deserted me. Alone, disabled, with no possibility of assistance from mortal man, I felt that my last hour had come; I was at the top of a mountain of snow, with not a tree to be seen for miles. Night approached, and I looked in vain in the direction our party had proceeded, for smoke or some indication that our camp was near. Naught but a desert waste of eternal snow met my anxious gaze—faint and almost exhausted, I sat down on the snow bank, my foot resting in the footsteps of those who had gone before me.

I removed from my pocket the miniatures of my wife and children, to take a last look at them. Their dear smiling faces awakened fresh energy, I had still something to live for, my death would bring heavy sorrow and grief to those who looked to me alone for support. I determined to try and get to camp. I dared not rest my fatigued body, for to rest was to sleep, and sleep was that eternal repose which wakes only in another world. Offering up a silent prayer, I prepared to proceed. I examined my gun and pistols, so as to be prepared if attacked by wolves or Indians, and resumed my lonely and desolate journey. As the night came on, the cold increased, and a fearful snowstorm blew directly in my face, almost blinding me. Bracing myself as firmly as I could against the blast, I followed the deep trail in the snow, and came into camp about ten o'clock at night. [122–23]

Fifty Days on Horse Meat—The rule adopted was, that one animal should serve for six meals for the whole party. . . . We lived on horsemeat fifty days. [126–27]

Little Salt Lake Valley—Four days before we entered the Little Salt Lake Valley, we were surrounded by very deep snows; but as it was necessary to proceed, the whole party started to penetrate through what appeared to be a pass on the Wasatch Mountains. The opening of this depression was favorable, and we continued our journey, until the mountains seemed to close around us, the snow in the canyon got deeper, and further progress on our present course was impossible. . . .

The mountains, which intercepted our path, were covered with snow four feet deep. The ascent bore an angle of forty-five degrees, and was at least one thousand feet from base to summit. Over this, Captain Wolff said it was also impossible to go. "That is not the point," replied Co. Fremont, "we must cross. The question is, which is most practicable, and how we can do it?" [128–29]

After the council, Col. Fremont told me there would be an occultation that night. . . . [He] remained several hours making observations, first with one start, then with another. . . . The next morning, Col. Fremont told me that Parowan, a small settlement of Mormons, forty rods square, in the Little Salt Lake Valley, was distant so many miles in a certain direction, immediately over this great mountain of snow; that in three days he hoped to be in the settlement, and he intended to go over the mountain, at all hazards.

We commenced the ascent of this tremendous mountain, covered as it were, with an icy pall of death, Col. Fremont leading and breaking a path. The ascent was so steep and difficult, that it was impossible to keep on our animals; consequently, we had to lead them and travel on foot—each man placed his foot in the tracks of the one that preceded him. The snow was up to the bellies of the animals. . . .

We none of us had shoes, boots it was impossible to wear. Some of the men had raw hide strapped round their feet, while others were half covered with worn out stockings and moccasins. Col. Fremont's moccasins were worn out, and he was no better off than any of us. . . . [He] commenced the descent. I could see no mode of extrication, but silently followed the party, winding round the base of one hill, over the side of another, through defiles and, to all appearance, impassable "cañons," until the mountains, which were perfectly bare of vegetation, gradually became interspersed with trees. Every half hour, a new snow-scape presented itself, and as we overcame each separate mountain, the trees increased in number. . . .

Deer tracks were visible over the snow, which gave fresh life to the men. The Delawares sallied out to find some. They were out several hours, and Welluchas was seen approaching, with a fine buck across his saddle. . . .

We had now triumphantly overcome the immense mountain, which I do not believe human foot ever attempted; . . . and on the very day and hour previously indicated by Col. Fremont, in Little Salt Lake Valley, which could not be distinguished two miles off, thus proving himself a most correct astronomer and geometrician. Here was no chance work—no guessing—for a deviation of one mile, either way, from the true course, would have plunged the whole party into certain destruction. [129–31]

It is worthy of remark, and goes to show the difference between a person "to the manor born," and one who has "acquired it by purchase." That in all the varied scenes of vicissitude, of suffering and excitement, from various causes, during a voyage when the natural character of a man is sure to be developed, Col. Fremont never forgot he was a gentleman; not an oath, no boisterous ebullitions of temper; when, heaven knows, he had enough to excite, from the continued blunders of the men. . . . He never wished his officers or men to undertake duties which he did not readily share. [132–33]

Mr. Fuller's Death—The death of Mr. Fuller filled our camp with deep gloom; almost at the very hour he passed away, succor was at hand. Our party was met by some Utah Indians, under the chieftainship of Ammon, a brother of the celebrated Wakara, who conducted us into the camp on Red Creek Cañon. [134]

Mr. Heap and His Three Wives—I was riding side by side with Egloffstien [*sic*] after Mr. Fuller's death, sad and dejected. Turning my eyes on the waste of snow before me, I remarked to my companion that I thought we had struck a travelled road. . . . I stopped my mule, and with very great difficulty alighted, and thrust my hand into the snow, when to my great delight, I distinctly felt the ruts caused by wagon wheels. I was then perfectly satisfied that we were "saved!" . . .

When I was actually in the town, and surrounded with white men, women, and children, paroxysms of tears followed each other, and I fell down on the snow perfectly overcome.

I was conducted by a Mr. Heap to his dwelling, where I was treated hospitably. I was mistaken for an Indian by the people of Parowan. My hair was long, and had not known a comb for a month, my face was unwashed, and ground in with the collected dirt of a similar period. Emaciated to a degree, my eyes sunken and clothes all torn into tatters from hunting our animals through the bush. My hands were in a dreadful state; my fingers were frost-bitten, and split at every joint; and suffering at the same time from diarrhea, and symptoms of scurvy, which broke out on me at Salt Lake City afterwards. I was in a situation truly to be pitied, and I do not wonder that the sympathies of the Mormons were excited in our favor. For my personal appearance being but a reflection of the whole party, we were indeed legitimate subjects for the exercise of the inner feelings of nature. When I entered Mr. Heap's house, I saw three beautiful children. I covered my eyes and wept for joy to think I might yet be restored to embrace my own. . . .

Mr. Heap was the first Mormon I ever spoke to, and although I had heard and read of them, I never contemplated realizing the fact that I would have occasion to be indebted to Mormons for much kindness and attention, and to be thrown entirely among them for months.

It was hinted to me that Mr. Heap had two wives; I saw two matrons in his house, both performing to interesting infants the duties of maternity; but I could hardly realize the fact that two wives could be reconciled to live together in one house. I asked Mr. Heap if both these ladies were his wives, he told me they were; [and that] they had been three sisters, but one mother was deceased. . . . [135–37]

I remained from the 8th to the 21st of February at Parowan. I was very ill during the whole time; . . . my physician advised me not to accompany the expedition; the exertion of riding on horseback would have completely prostrated me, my digestive organs were so much weakened, and impaired, by the irregular living on horsemeat, without salt or vegetables, that I was fearful that I should never recover. . . . I left for Salt Lake City, in a wagon belonging to one of a large company of Mormons, who were on their way to "Conference." I was so weak, that I had to be lifted in and out like a child. [139]

Salt Lake City—We arrived at Great Salt Lake City on the night of the 1st of March, 1854, and took lodging at Blair's hotel. . . . After I was comfortably settled, I called on Governor Young, and was received by him with marked attention. He tendered me the use of all his philosophical instruments and access to a large and valuable library. . . .

[In Salt Lake City,] the principal business streets run due north and south, a delicious stream of water flows through the centre of the city, this is subdivided into murmuring rivulets on either side of all the streets. The water, coming directly from the mountains, is always pure and fresh, affording this most useful element in any quantity. . . . Cotton-wood trees grow in the main stream, and saplings had just been planted while I was there, on the sides of the streets. Most of the dwelling houses are built a little distance from the sidewalk, and to each dwelling is appropriated an acre and a quarter of ground for gardening. . . .

The governor's residence, a large wooden building of sufficient capacity to contain his extensive family—nineteen wives and thirty-two children, was nearly finished. I made a daguerreotype view of it, and also a drawing. [140–42]

Morality of the Mormons—Under the operation of this law, nobody but Mormons can hold property in Great Salt Lake City. There are numbers of citizens who are not Mormons, who rent properties; but there is no property for sale—a most politic course on the part of the Mormons—for in case of a railroad being established between the two oceans, Great Salt Lake City must be the half way stopping place, and the city will be kept purified from taverns and grog shops at every corner of the street. Another city will have to be built some distance from them, for they have determined to keep themselves distinct from the vices of civilization. During a residence of ten weeks in Great Salt Lake City, and my observations in all their various settlements, amongst a homogeneous population, . . . it is worthy of record, that I never heard any obscene or improper language; never saw a man drunk; never had my attention called to the exhibitions of vice of any sort. [143]

Gov. Brigham Young—I received a good deal of marked attention from his Excellency, Governor Young. He often called for me to take a drive in his carriage, and invited me to come and live with him, during the time I sojourned there. This invitation I refused, as I wished to be entirely independent to make observations. I told Brigham Young that I was making notes, with a view to publish them. He replied, "Only publish 'facts,' and you may publish as you please." [146]

Author's Views on Polygamy—Polygamy is practised [*sic*] to a very great extent among the high-priests and officers of the church. There were thousands of the Mormons, however, who reprobate, and disapprove of it.

The following questions seem to suggest themselves as bearing upon the polygamy practised by the Mormons. What is their rational plea from revelation as true believers? Is such a system in conformity thereto—with right reason, and with the requirements of civilized society? Will it improve the physical powers of man; impart additional mental energy, and increase the period of human existence? Is it calculated as a wise providence indeed, to perpetuate his species? Does it harmonize with the *requisites* of peace and justice, and the *good order* essential to the happiness of all? In my limited reading of the Scriptures, I find nothing to sanction such a course. [150–51]

Ball at Salt Lake City—Towards the end of April, 1854, about ten days previous to the departure of Brigham Young, on his annual visit to the southern settlement of Utah, tickets of invitation to a grand ball, were issued in his name. I had the honor to receive one of them.

If the etiquette of dress, which is a necessary preliminary to the *entre* of her Majesty's drawing-room, had been insisted on in the vestibule of Gov. Young's ballroom, the relation of the following incidents would never have emanated from my pen.

When I arrived at the great city of the Mormons, I was clad in the tattered garments that I had worn for six months, on the journey across the Rocky Mountains. In vain, I applied to every store in Salt Lake City for suitable clothes; a pair of black pants or a broadcloth coat was not to be purchased. I, however, succeeded in having a pair of stout cassimere pants made for my intended journey to California, and a gentleman by the name of Addoms, a merchant from Cedar Street, N.Y., contributed a new coat from his wardrobe. I was indebted to him also for a great deal of kindness and attention during my illness. [155–56]

At the invitation of Gov. Young, I opened the ball with one of his wives. The Governor, with a beautiful partner, stood *vis-à-vis*. An old fashioned cotillion was danced with much grace by the ladies, and the Governor acquitted himself very well on the "light fantastic toe."

I singled out from among the galaxy of beauty with which I was surrounded, a Mrs. Wheelock, a lady of great worth, and polished manners; she had volunteered her services as a tragedienne, at different times during my visit to Salt Lake, at the theatre, where she appeared in several difficult impersonations. . . . I had the pleasure of painting Mrs. Wheelock's portrait in the character of "Pauline" in "Claude Melnotte." She was the first wife of her husband, whom she married in England, about eight years before; her parents, who are estimable people, came over after they had embraced Mormonism. When this lady married, the spiritual wife system had not yet been revealed.

Mr. Wheelock is a president of the seventies; and . . . had at this time three wives, the last one visited the ball as a bride; I was introduced by Mrs. Wheelock senior, to all of them; they looked like the three graces as they stood in the room, with their arms enfolding each other like sisters. . . .

I returned to my quarters at twelve o'clock, most favorably impressed with the exhibition of public society among the Mormons. [157–59]

Sketch of a dead child. (Courtesy of the Daughters of Utah Pioneers (DUP), Parowan, Utah)

Departure from Great Salt Lake City—Having determined to go to California by the Southern route from Great Salt Lake City, through the settlements, and over the trail of Col. Fremont of 1843, which I wanted to illustrate with views, etc., I took advantage of the opportunity which [was] offered on the 6th May, 1854. [180]

A Return Trip to Parowan—We entered Parowan about five o'clock. I was affectionately greeted by those persons who administered to my sufferings some few weeks before. I had changed so much, and grown so fat, that not one of them knew me. [208]

I renewed my acquaintance with Henry Lunt, [and] remained at his house during my stay. . . . The morning after my arrival, I arose very early, and taking my sketch-book along, I sauntered around the city. In the course of peregrinations, I saw a man walking up and down before an adobe shanty, apparently much distressed; I approached him, and inquired the cause of his dejection; he told me that his only daughter, aged six years, had died suddenly in the night; he pointed to the door, and I entered the dwelling.

Laid out upon a straw mattress, scrupulously clean, was one of the most angelic children I ever saw. On its face was a placid smile, and it looked more like the gentle repose of healthful sleep than the everlasting slumber of death.

Beautiful curls clustered around a brow of snowy whiteness. It was easy to perceive that it was a child lately from England, from its peculiar conformation. I entered very softly, and did not disturb the afflicted mother, who reclined on the bed, her face buried in the pillow, sobbing as if her heart would break.

Without a second's reflection I commenced making a sketch of the inanimate being before me, and in the course of half-an-hour I had produced an excellent likeness.

A slight movement in the room caused the mother to look around her. She perceived me, and I apologized for my intrusion; and telling her that I was one of the Governor's party who arrived last night. I tore the leaf out of my book and presented it to her, and it is impossible to describe the delight and joy she expressed at its possession. She said I was an angel sent for heaven to comfort her.

She had no likeness of her child.

I bid her place her trust in Him "who giveth and taketh away," and left her indulging in the excitement of joy and sorrow. I went out unperceived by the bereaved father, who was still walking up and down, buried in grief. I continued my walk, contemplating the strange combination of events, which gave this poor woman a single ray of peace for her sorrowing heart.

When I was about starting the next day, I discovered in the wagon a basket filled with eggs, butter, and several loaves of bread, and a note to my address containing these words—"From a grateful heart." [211–12]

TWO

European Jewry

AN OVERVIEW

PETER BLACK

Reason and Restrictions—East of the Rhine and north of the Alps, prior to the nineteenth century, Jews were not living as equals to the non-Jewish population, but they were also not living as serfs or on the lowest end of the economic ladder.[1] The Jews occupied an odd position that made them rather vulnerable in times of trouble, in their relationships both with the ruling classes, who were primarily aristocratic and bureaucratic, and with the lower classes, particularly the peasantry.

In Central and Eastern Europe, Jews had been invited by kings in the late medieval and early modern periods to settle in specifically designated areas and were given specific rights, privileges, and restrictions. The rights and privileges had to do primarily with licensing to produce products and, in particular, to move products. Jews were encouraged to settle for employment in managing various affairs of the royal bureaucracy and, in some states, for individual landlords, particularly in the Republic of Poland, in what became the Romanian principalities, and in western Russia after the partitions of Poland. This occupation involved management of anything from tax collection for which the state was responsible, as in Prussia, for instance.

In Poland, the landlord was usually responsible for collecting what passed for taxes. The same was true in Romania. Often, Jews were engaged to run a landlord-owned tavern or a trading post where peasants would come to drink, get food they could not grow themselves, or buy seed and equipment, if they could afford it. If they did not have any money, which was often the case, credit could be extended. If the crop failed, for whatever reason, peasants quickly fell into debt. Whereas, in fact, they would be in debt to the landlord, it was the Jewish manager of the landlord's affairs with whom they would have to deal. Thus, the Jew was often the personification of those issues that made for landlord-peasant tension in Eastern Europe.

The Jew also became the point of tension between the centralized state and royal bureaucracy and the more regionally oriented nobility. In other words, it was rather a no-win position. If anything went wrong, whether it was indebtedness, poor production, or failure to pay debts, the Jew as a personification was already around to blame.

Having said this, I should add that the Jews had come to Central and Eastern Europe with significant restrictions. It is true that certain professions were open to them in which they were influential and even dominated. In addition to commerce, finance, and supply, they were also engaged in free professions, such as journalism, which was beginning to develop by the seventeenth and eighteenth centuries; theater; arts; medicine; and, to a certain degree, law, particularly in Prussia, although not in Eastern Europe. By law, I do not mean a position as state prosecutor or state investigator, but more as legal consultant to a royal bureaucrat, a king, or a landlord.

But Jews were forbidden to own land. They were restricted to residing in designated areas in certain cities and the countryside. They were forbidden to join the civil service, including the army; if they were conscripted, they were certainly blocked both socially and legally from rising to the rank of officer. Not until the early nineteenth century could Jews serve in Germany and Austria, and not until later that century were they conscripted into the czarist army. In France, during the French Revolution, Jews did serve and could rise to officer status, and, in fact, had equal citizen rights. But France is a different story. Since teaching was part of civil service, Jews were excluded from that profession; however, Jewish instructors did teach at Jewish private schools and religious schools.

The average Jewish inhabitant in the Russian Pale was generally poor, and probably spoke some Ukrainian or Russian, because he lived among the Ukrainians and Russians. How comfortable Jews were speaking those languages is open to question. Most Jewish inhabitants of the Pale, who were educated beyond elementary school, learned Hebrew and spoke Yiddish in the home. There was nevertheless a small, educated elite who knew the local languages as well as the "cultured languages," such as French and German, and, when they had to, were able to function in Christian society.

One should not get the image of the average Jewish resident of Central and Eastern Europe—particularly in Prussia or at least half of Prussia and, of course, all of what is today Poland,

Romania, and Russia—as being part of the middle class. When one says Jews dominated in commerce, statistically, that could mean a Jewish merchant bought timber from one peasant in one village and, if he were well off enough to own a wheelbarrow, wheeled it to the next village to sell at whatever profit he could make. Contrasted with a relatively small minority, he was doing quite well, but in prominent positions in commerce, banking, trade, and supply as Central Europe prospered, most Jews were poor and getting poorer in the early modern era, by the late eighteenth and early nineteenth centuries.

In addition to the traditional religious prejudice of the Protestants in Prussia, the Catholics in Poland, and the Orthodox in Romania and Russia, a prejudice developed against the Jews as a favorite group of the elite, since Jews were dependent for their privileges upon whomever was in charge. Thus, if there was dissatisfaction with the ruling power, there was dissatisfaction with the Jews. By the same token, since Jews relied on the ruling class, they tended to support them not only for their privileges, such as they were, but also for their very safety and livelihood. And so Jews came to be associated with a wealthy and manipulative financial, commercial, and, by the nineteenth century, increasingly industrial entrepreneurial class that was perceived as threatening to landlords, who were unable to keep up with the inroads that modern capitalism was making in Eastern Europe. Their relationship was also strained by the peasantry, whose own traditional rights and privileges were being undermined. Transformed from peasants into agricultural wage laborers, or from serfs, briefly, to independent peasants in 1861, they saw their status sink again to peasants.

In Eastern Europe, the Jews were seen as a people apart not only by religion but also by economic status, class, and language, since most Jews east of the Elbe and north of the Alps still spoke Yiddish, their mother tongue. This perception as prejudice was further aggravated when emancipation laws were passed, particularly in the middle of the nineteenth century, in Central and Eastern Europe. The laws that granted Jews equal rights ended their privileges and the restrictions applied to their residence and business activities. In Central Europe, many moved into professions that had been dominated by Christians, including the civil service, the army, and landownership to a certain degree. It also stirred the pot for a newer type of prejudice. Sons of peasants were trying to rise, and sons of landlords who were in danger of losing their lands were moving into the middle class. They were getting an education and seeking entrée into professions in which Jews had traditionally predominated.

Through all of this, three layers of anti-Semitism were developing toward a fever pitch by the end of the nineteenth century throughout Central and Eastern Europe: traditional religious prejudice, economic-status prejudice, and job-competition prejudice, which developed from the dropping of restrictions on Jewish participation in political and economic life.

Into the Russian Pale of Settlement—A plurality of European Jews by the twentieth century, about 5 million of the 11 million Jews counted at the end of the nineteenth century and up to the beginning of World War II, was invited to settle in what had formerly been Poland. Poland in the fourteenth and fifteenth centuries, in union with Lithuania, stretched from western Latvia at the Baltic Sea all the way south to the Black Sea by Bessarabia, and, at times, extended as far east as Kiev and Smolensk. It was during this period that Polish kings permitted Jews, and other non-Polish urban dwellers, to settle and essentially manage local commerce and, where it existed, finance. The newcomers also provided personal services to Polish aristocrats.

Poland was a relatively hospitable place for Jews escaping the extreme intolerance in France and Spain during the late fifteenth and early sixteenth centuries. Spain was enduring the Inquisition in the late fifteenth century. The earliest auto-da-fé of the Spanish Inquisition took place in Seville in 1481, in which Jews and other "heretics" were turned over to the "secular authorities" and burned at the stake. Andalusian Jews were expelled, and those caught secretly adhering to Jewish practices were tortured. France was engrossed in a series of religious civil wars that lasted more than thirty years in which the Jews came to be associated with the Huguenots (that is, Protestants). When the Huguenots were killed or exiled during the Massacre of Saint Bartholomew's Day, the Jews were expelled along with them. Immigrating to Poland resulted in a significant Jewish population living in areas that later became the Pale of Settlement. The Pale was virtually all of Poland in the sixteenth century, but after the final partition of Poland at the end of the eighteenth century, it fell to either the Russian Empire or the Hapsburg monarchy of Austria-Hungary.

By the end of the nineteenth century, roughly 4.9 million (formerly Polish) Jews lived in the Russian Pale of Settlement. When compared to the 11 million Jews living in Europe, this was a significant plurality. A number of Polish Jews were dispersed in Prussia, Austria, Galicia, and the eastern regions of Hungary. The remainder of the Polish Jews were in the principality of Moldavia, which is still a province of Romania, and Bessarabia, which became part of Russia in 1812, was taken back by Romania in 1918, and is now the Republic of Moldova. So, essentially, the origins of the Pale of Settlement are the Russian Empire.

Russia had traditionally barred Jews from settling in their country under the Romanov dynasty, beginning in 1613, when Michael Romanov was crowned czar of Russia, and lasting until 1917. They offered Jews a choice to convert, leave, or die. They also intended to expel the Jews to the borders. Between 1772 and 1812, Russia had annexed large tracts of Polish land. Before the partitions in Poland, 150,000 Jews were living in the entire Russian Empire. Afterward, 430,000 Jews were immediately added to the Russian population, creating a Jewish problem for the Russians because of traditional Russian antipathy to Jews and in terms of geography. The Russians decided to restrict the area of Jewish settlement to a pale, which roughly covered what is now central Poland, Moldavia, most of the western and central Ukraine (including the Crimea), Lithuania, and White Russia, which we now call Belarus.

The Pale was officially created according to a series of statutes that were passed during the first two decades of the nineteenth century. Within the Pale was a significant amount of rural countryside, but most of the Jews living there were engaged in pursuits that were primarily urban: management, commerce, supply, and handicrafts. Because of their isolation, the restrictions on their movements, and the constraints placed upon them by Jewish leaders who were deeply religious, the Jews in the Russian Pale of Settlement tended to be Conservative and adverse to changes of any kind.

Jewish Poverty—The laws themselves were fairly unstable, and, of course, there were seemingly indiscriminate additions. But the arbitrariness came more or less from the laws' enforcement, which was by no means stable or consistent—sometimes deliberately so. Sometimes the authorities wanted to promote more prosperity and would relax some of the restrictions. Sometimes the relaxation was just a matter of bureaucratic incompetence. Again, the community was generally poor, and getting poorer during the course of the nineteenth century. There was also somewhat of a difference in terms of Jewish property as opposed to the property of the non-Jews. The literary critic Ba'al Makhshoves explains:

> The endemic poverty of the Jews of Eastern Europe is that it is not a poverty of the great European cities nor is it the poverty of the Russian peasant. Jewish poverty has no idea what a factory looks like for it exists in the *shtetl* where it has its origins in fathers and grandfathers who had been wretchedly poor since time immemorial. The Russian peasant, as poor as he may be, is the proprietor of a small piece of land and his condition is not hopeless. One feels that sooner or later it will improve. But Jewish poverty is utterly without a cure. The Jew has no available means for improving his condition, which will remain abject as long as he lives among alien people. In villages, where life should have brought him closer to the earth, he lives as though he were in the city.[2]

Many of the larger cities in the Pale of Settlement had, and maintained, majority Jewish populations until the German invasion of the Soviet Union in 1941. For instance, a city such as Pinsk, which is in White Russia, was 62 percent Jewish; many smaller towns had even higher percentages of Jewish inhabitants.

Along with a series of restrictions, taxes, and decrees that placed a heavy hand on Jewish rights and religious traditions, Russia did offer several opportunities to the Jewish populace. Jews could convert; they could enroll in Russian schools. This allowed for a certain degree of movement for those Jews who wished to assimilate and for those who maintained their customs but were driven to become educated and increase their skills.

While Jews still could not be employed by the state, which was a significant factor, they had fewer restrictions on employment in the private sector, and virtually all professions were open to them as long as they remained in the Pale of Settlement. Finally, the Russians were interested in encouraging loyalty among the settlers, that is, loyalty to the czar. They were even prepared to offer Jews land if they would move to the southern part of the Pale, toward the southwestern

Ukraine and Bessarabia, border areas that the Russians had just taken from Bessarabia, Turkey, and Poland in order to secure Russia's western border.

It was a double-edged sword. Jews were permitted to own land only in troubled border regions, which accentuated their somewhat delicate position in the dynamic between landlord and the land-hungry peasantry. The peasantry in Russia tended to be exploited and oppressed anyway, and when the peasants could articulate at all, they voiced their frustration against established authority or, more often, against that which appeared to be the local face of established authority. When they could not rise against gendarmes and soldiers, they tended to rise against Jews who appeared to be the favorites of the distant regime.

Crimes against Jews—Pogroms always existed in terms of disturbances against the Jews. If one looks at Europe in the early Middle Ages, one finds riots from time to time, encouraged by or tolerated by authorities. What made the pogroms of 1881–1884 different was that they occurred on such a widespread scale. In 1881, when Czar Alexander II was assassinated, a wave of pogroms raged throughout more than one hundred Russian communities. Twenty thousand Jews were left without homes. Thousands more were beaten, raped, or murdered. These pogroms appeared to have been spontaneous in origin, but were aggravated by official incompetence and slow reaction. This may well have been the result of an increasingly feeble autocracy that lacked the flexibility to respond well to social disturbances. After all, the czar had just been assassinated by the revolutionaries, which had bluntly exposed the sheer weakness of the security system. In a dictatorship, particularly in an aristocratic autocracy, any kind of social disturbance is a potential threat to authority. And when peasants and poor people in the cities riot and destroy or loot property, it is very hard to blame one minority.

When the pogroms began that year, particularly in the southern Ukraine, the official reaction was extremely slow and inconsistent, which further exacerbated the disturbances. They were also aggravated by the fact that local officials tended to be hostile to the Jews. This, of course, fed on the reluctance to intervene locally because local gendarmes did not want to appear as protectors of the Jews, and they did not want to shoot their own fellow Christians, even as the situation started to get out of hand. The pogroms were intensified further when soldiers and policemen, who did finally get involved and were under explicit orders from their superiors to stop the disturbances, participated in the destruction and plunder of Jewish property and in the killing of Jewish individuals.

There are numerous theories that suggest the pogroms were officially inspired, and there are some documented cases of local officials trying to use the pogroms, and even encouraging them. Most scholars now discount a broader conspiracy on the part of the central government to promote these disturbances as a distraction from the economic and political problems of the day.

Similar riots took place in Prussian Pomerania and Bohemia-Moravia, but they did not have the same effect as the Russian pogroms. Riots in Russia were not new; Russians had been subject to these events before, and although there was a certain intensity that was foreign in the early 1880s, it was not beyond the range of their experience. The pogroms did happen, however, at a time in which Russia was beginning to modernize, albeit slowly. Modern ideas about economy, politics, commerce, and industry were beginning to seep into the Russian fabric. It was also a period of slow but expanding secularization, with an increasing withdrawal of religion as the most important part of an individual's life. And so the Jewish response to the pogroms in the early 1880s was a little different from past responses. More individual Jews began to think in terms of whether it was really worth staying and enduring such events and whether they had any other options. A large part of that response represented not only a disillusionment of the Jews with the economic or political prospects in Russia, but also a sense that as individuals they needed to make the decision to pick up and leave, and break the bonds with the old society.

Out of Europe—In the forty years before 1880, only 200,000 European Jews emigrated overseas. In the next thirty-four years, from 1881 through 1914, between 2.4 and 2.7 million European Jews emigrated, mostly to North and South America, South Africa, and Palestine. Most of this emigration came from Eastern Europe where the majority of Jews lived. In fact, 83 percent of European Jews lived in Russia, Austria, Hungary, and Romania.

Between 1889 and 1910, 750,000 Jews came from Russia to the United States. Virtually all of the exoduses resulted from individual decisions rather than forced emigration. Another 180,000 came from eastern Hungary. In it interesting to note that, due to medical advances, the population birthrate and survival rate were such that even this mass emigration did not significantly dent the European population totals.

These emigrants were, like most other emigrants, less skilled, less educated, and less established. They were also less integrated and less assimilated. They came from manufacturing classes and from employment in domestic and personal services. Poorly paid in Eastern Europe, these Jews were mostly from backward rural areas. The big difference between the Jewish emigration from these regions is that unlike other Europeans, the Jews had no intention of returning home.

These Jews tended to come as families, and 75 percent of all emigrants were female, an astounding statistic in comparison to non-Jewish emigration. Jewish women came over with their husbands or followed shortly afterward; the plan was to get the entire family out and to stay out. Poverty and potential for economic improvement played significant roles in their emigrating to a new country, but after 1881, these reasons were reinforced by the heightened fear of personal security and pogroms. A different perception of the future of Russia and the future role of the Jewish communities also played a part, as well as a desire to detach from the extra- and intracommunity bonds. America with its religious freedom and separation of church and state and its equal status for Jews and non-Jews offered a myriad of spiritual, economic, social, and political opportunities that Russia simply could not offer.

German Jews—Prior to the nineteenth century, Germany was made up of several dozen individual states, virtually all ruled by a king or a prince or a series of aristocratic electors. These rulers often employed Jews to manage their legal and financial affairs. Jewish families prominent in those areas were permitted to live in certain areas of cities. In each of the German states in the seventeenth and eighteenth centuries, there were periods in which the Jews were expelled from the cities and had to resettle in the countryside, but then those restrictions were relaxed and the Jews moved back into the cities. The majority of Jews in Austria and Bohemia and in eastern Germany lived in the countryside, often in positions of management for aristocrats and in a somewhat better economic position than Jews farther to the east in Poland and after the partitions in Russia.

Assimilation—In Germany, Austria, and Hungary, Jews were granted civil rights in 1867 and 1871. This opened all kinds of economic and even political and social opportunities for the Jews. They actively sought to assimilate. Some went so far in their assimilation as to convert. Even if they did not convert, there was a general tendency with the middle classes throughout Europe, particularly in Central and Western Europe, to move away from religion and, in a sense, go with the movement of the times in which religion was becoming less important as a factor of self-identification. For many Jews who sought assimilation, loyalty to the nation and to the nation's culture was becoming a more important consideration in developing their personal and collective identities.

Most German Jews, particularly in the middle and upper classes, but not excluding the lower working classes, identified with the German Reich as it grew in prosperity and then developed into a European power after unification in 1871. Many were strong German patriots, particularly in the western and central regions. To the east, Jews were a little less assimilated and a little less well-to-do, and those who emigrated to Germany were often poorer, less educated, and less skilled than their German counterparts. But even more so than the Jews coming from Russia, they had better educations and more skills.

Galicia, in Austria, was a province of the Hapsburg monarchy and was under Austrian rather than Hungarian control. A place of heavy settlement of the Jews at the time of the First World War, approximately half a million Jews lived there. It was also the first stop, so to speak, for Russian Jews and political refugees trying to escape Russia. A number of Russian Jews migrated from Russia to Galicia, and from there went to Germany in search of economic opportunity and better personal security.

Some of these Galician emigrants to Germany who found it difficult to get German citizenship wound up going to the United States, as well as South Africa and South America. It was less likely that well-to-do, middle-class German Jewish citizens would leave unless there was some political or personal reason that was exceptional.

The Lessons of Hate—Economically, German Jews' influence was negligible, as they represented less than 1 percent of the population. However, looking for ways to be good Germans, Jews who assimilated played a fairly significant role in the development of an all-German culture, including some of the nationalist and unpleasant aspects of it that we have all come to know and disparage. There were even some right-wing Jewish organizations, including veterans' organizations, that petitioned Hitler in 1933 to participate in the New Nationalist Order that he was promising to create in Germany!

It also bears mention that the Nazis understood when they came to power in 1933 that the German people, as such, were not what the Nazis called "racially conscious." They had to be prepared not only for a war that the Nazis intended to fight for what they perceived as racial survival, but also to stop, to isolate, and to ultimately expel the German Jews. This was not easy since the experience of most Germans who had dealt with Jews in the urban areas could not always "distinguish" them from other German citizens.

So while there was certainly anti-Semitism in Germany, particularly of the intellectual variety, and there were harsh stereotypes of Jews, in general the population was not prepared to exclude, let alone expel or kill, their Jewish neighbors without some "prompting" and "re-education." It took the Nazis roughly four or five years to accomplish that end.

THREE

Early Jewish Utah Pioneers

"FANNIE, LET US TAKE OUR FEW DOLLARS AND GO WEST"

Julius and Fannie Brooks

Business in Breslau—My father, Julius Gerson Brooks, was born in the year 1825, at Frankenstein, a small village near Breslau [southwest Poland, formerly in Germany].[1] Father was a fine looking man, dark, five feet eight inches tall and very slight; always wore a small moustache. He came from a large family of 24 children, fourteen girls, and ten boys. Father related that in 1845, 22 of his siblings were still living.

Father spoke very little about his father, who died when he was quite young, but he said he was a very tall, heavy, and smooth shaven man. His hair was combed over his forehead, he wore a black broadcloth suit, a stiff bosom shirt front, standing linen collar with a small bow tie, and looked somewhat like Beethoven. While he kept a small dry goods and notion store, he was usually absent from home, going twice a year to the fur market at Leipzig to buy furs, which was quite a business in those days. When away at business, Grandmother took charge of the store and was the business as well as the finance man. She was a tall stately woman with piercing black eyes, pointed nose, and always wore a lace cap with three ruffles. She was well educated, speaking German and Hebrew, and had a wonderful faculty for giving advice. She was called the *Rabbinavich* of the village. Anyone desiring advice went to her and what she told them was usually considered good judgment.

Father was never a great student and at an early age was apprenticed to a trade, as weaver of cloth. He received no money and had to pay some for his apprenticeship. He said the hours were long and tedious and his goods poor; many times he went to bed hungry. When his two years were up, he quit and went to work for a tanner. There he met a peddler who spoke of the adventures of traveling and Father decided to run away.

He did not write his mother for he knew that if he had, she would make him go back to work. So he took his few belongings, tied them up in a square green cloth and, with a stick through it, put it over his back, and went straight to Breslau. There, he bought such notions as pins, hairpins, threads, needles, shoelaces, pearl buttons, and he started peddling. At first he was very timid. When he rang a bell or knocker at the door, the lady of the house would answer. If she looked cross, he would ask for some Mr. *So-and-So,* knowing he never existed. If she looked pleasant, he would tell her a hard luck story. He was very successful, being full of humor and always giving full value for the money, and soon had more orders than he could fill.

Opening a Continent—After nine months, he decided to visit his mother, but in 1847, wanted to travel again. This time, he would go to the New World. His mother was very set against his going. With the little money he had saved up, about $35.00, Father bought his ticket on a sailing vessel. He took the few clothes he had, and put them in a carpetbag. In a box, he packed some crackers, sausage, cheese, and black bread as he had heard that mostly bacon and ham was served on the boat.[2] He took his straw bed and blankets, and, as a going away present from his uncle, a handsome rifle. Father was five weeks out at sea, during which time part of his food supply got moldy and had to be thrown overboard. The vessel's rocking put him more in his berth than on deck. Landing in New York, he took a room near the Battery in a sailor's home, and paid $1.50 a week. His money did not last long, so he was forced to sell his rifle. It was a handsome rifle, and he got $100.00 in gold. With this money, he opened a small shop in New England.

Homesick—When the gold rush fever struck, thousands of people were ready to go West, but father stayed in the East for five more years and then decided to go home and visit his family. At his mother's house, he told wonderful stories about "gold" found on the streets. People believed him because they had read about such wonderful discoveries. Among his listeners was a young girl just home from college who was the most interested of all. She was handsome, educated, full of life, and not quite sixteen. She exclaimed, "Uncle Julius, when you return to America, take me with you." Father said, "Yes, if you will marry me. Otherwise, not." She said, "If my parents are willing, I will."

On the 18th of August 1853, my parents were married and, during that same year, they set sail for America. Mother spoke beautiful German and French and had some knowledge of English. Father, of course, was a dreadful sailor; mother was not sick for a moment and spent her time entertaining the evening crowd with folk songs and jokes. She played the piano and guitar, and sang very beautifully.

Respite before Heading West—When they arrived in New York, they took a room at a boarding house on East 14th Street for $2.50 a week. Mother said everything was very cheap and the food was excellent. Their stay in New York was not long, as just at that time, the excitement of gold mines was in the air again and Father say, "Fannie, let us take our few dollars and go West." Mother, being only 16 years old, thought it would be great. In 1854, they departed for Galena, Illinois, where they heard that a company was leaving the following June for California. Galena was an important commercial center; large supplies for the westbound emigrant trains were obtained there. Since they arrived in the late spring, too late to head West, they had to wait until the following June to begin their trek. They stayed at a large farmhouse called an "Inn" where among the several other boarders was a Captain Ulysses Grant of the United States Army. His father had a leather goods store in Galena, and the Captain spoke about how he and the Hudson Bay Company had been in Utah trying to open up trade between the two.

Wagon Train—Mother and Dad bought a little team with two mules, and although Mother had never driven a horse in her life, she learned within a couple of days how to harness and unharness them quicker than any man. The animals became attached to her and after a week, no one could come near them but Mother! Ten people were the numbers allotted to a wagon and one tent. One hundred pounds of luggage, including beds and clothing for all persons over eight years of age; fifty pounds to those between eight years and four years; all under four years of age had no luggage privileges.

The wagons were ordered in Cincinnati and St. Louis and were brought by steamer to the camping ground. The wagon bed was twelve feet long, three feet and four inches wide and eighteen inches deep. Boxes were made to fit inside the wagons to put utensils and clothing in. Cattle purchased from cattle dealers in Western settlements were driven to the camping grounds. Wagon covers were made of very superior twill cotton brought from England. For the emigration of 1854, the material was supplied long before their departure and they made the tents and covers for the voyage, thus saving great expenses. The material was twenty-seven inches wide and forty-four yards were used for the tent, twenty-six yards for the wagon cover. The cost was forty dollars.

Each wagon that year cost $65.00. They were supplied with one hundred pounds of flour, fifty pounds of sugar, fifty pounds of bacon, fifty pounds of rice, thirty pounds of beans, twenty pounds of dried apples, twenty pounds of dried peaches, five pounds of tea, one gallon vinegar, ten bars of soap, twenty-five pounds of salt. It was hoped that these articles, the milk from their cows, the game caught on the plains, and the fresh water streams would furnish them better food and would sustain them through the journey.

The entire cost to cross the plains with a wagon train was about $65.00 per person. As soon as a sufficient number of wagons could be gotten together, in some cases, a hundred or more, they moved off under the leadership of a captain. To each emigrant as he traveled, his wagon served as a bedroom, parlor, kitchen, and sometimes as a boat crossing over fordable streams, and being carried on rafts over deep waters near the Missouri. Constructed for carrying man, beast, and wagons, ropes were attached to rafts and pulled back and forth until the entire train had crossed the river. Mother said where the rivers ran deep, the bottoms of the wagons would fill with water, and clothes and provisions would get wet. Sometimes, they would even lose kettles or buckets that were not properly tied to the wagon's exterior. She said after one wet crossing, they had to hang their clothes on the lines strung from the wheel of one wagon to the wheel of another wagon, and balance their shoes on the sagebrush to dry before they could move on. After rainstorms, the roads became like muddy streams and the poor animals could barely pull their load.

The Slow Trek—At the beginning of their journey, the heat was intense, the dust suffocating, and their day's journey slow. An average day's journey did not exceed thirteen miles. Traveling by the overland route required three months and more. On July 5, they had reached Florence, Nebraska, six miles from Omaha, where they stayed a week making preparations to cross the plains. Some were opposed to going to Utah so late in the season, suggesting they spend the winter in Nebraska. A meeting was called. Eager to reach Salt Lake, the greater part decided to continue with their journey.

They worried about depleting the flour, and decided that each wagon would take an extra 90 pounds. Some people grumbled. They thought their load was already heavy enough. During the trip, wagons broke and often the whole train was delayed for days until repairs had been made. One night, their cattle stampeded. The men went in pursuit and rounded up their herd. The following morning, they discovered they were quite a few heads short, but they went forward without them. The further west they pushed, the colder it got. Their bedding and clothing were insufficient to keep them warm. Cold weather, scarcity of food, and fatigue soon produced bad results; many were taken ill and several died. My mother lost her first baby. She was to lose two more children in infancy before I was born.

Mother said they had a few Indian scares, but they turned out to be peaceful Indians who were hungry and left after they had been given food. One day, they suddenly saw a black cloud. Frightened by this sight, fearing Indians again, it turned out to be a herd of buffaloes. Their fear was not groundless. An earlier wagon train had been attacked upon by Indians, and the whole train had been practically wiped out.

As they neared Indian country, women and children went to sleep at night while the men kept watch with loaded rifles. In the day, the women drove the teams so the men could sleep. Before they arrived at Fort Laramie, everyone was dusty and dirty. There was no wood or sagebrush. Children gathered buffalo chips so that fires could be started.

At night in the valley of the Platte, the wagons were drawn up in a semi-circle on the banks of a river, forming a defense on one side. The tongues of the wagons were placed outside, the fore wheel of each was placed against the hind wheel of the wagon before it. All the horses and cattle were brought inside the closure. Their corral was oblong with an opening at either end, where there was a guard.

The wagon train had traveled to Independent Creek, Big Blue River to Walnut Creek, Oxen Creek, Little Blue River, Platte River, and Fort Kearney. They followed the south bend of the Platte River and then went northerly to where Ash Creek empties into the North Fork of the Platte River, passing Court House Rock, Chimney Rock, Scott's Bluffs. Now, they were entering Fort Laramie where they paid $15.00 to take the ferry across the Platte River. They moved on to Deer Creek, and Independence Rock.

Hardship at the Pass—Arriving at Rocky Ridge near the summit of the South Pass, the wind freshened into a gale and then a hurricane, howling incessantly for thirty-six hours. Snow drifted in every direction. The company camped on a branch of Sweetwater for two nights to wait for the storm to pass. Tents and wagon tops were blown away; the wagons buried almost to the tops of their wheels in snow banks. No fire could be lighted, little food could be had, no aid was in sight, although they were within a few days march of the valley. After two days, the storm abated and they made their way to Willow Copse. The men found nearly half their cattle lying dead amid the snow banks, but not a human life was lost in that storm.

At South Pass, they met pioneers of the Handcart Expedition.[3] Somewhat primitive in construction, the shafts were about five feet long and made of hickory or oak with cross pieces, one of them serving for a handle, the other for the bed of the cart, and under the center of which was a wooden axle tree. The wheels were made of wood with a light iron band; the entire weight of the vehicle was sixty pounds. To each one hundred persons were furnished twenty handcarts, five tents, three or four milk cows, and a wagon with three yoke of oxen to convey the provisions and camp supplies. The quantity of clothing and bedding was limited to seventeen pounds per person, and the freight of each cart including cooking utensils was about one hundred pounds. When the handcarts reached Salt Lake City on the 9th of November, sixty-seven handcart pioneers out of the total of 420 died. Three weeks later, a mother company of 600 emigrants crossed the plains, and a smaller percentage died.

My parents' wagon train crossed Little Sandy, Big Sandy, and the Green River. They arrived at Fort Bridger, and went to Echo Canyon. After Weber Canyon, they chose the Hasting Cutoff, which was so impassable, they had to cross toward the lake. Then came the desert, forty miles wide and dreary. The company chose the northern route and reached Black Rock and the Great Salt Lake, twenty-two miles from Salt Lake City. Unable to drink the salty water, they pushed on and camped on the banks of the Jordan.

A Campsite for Emigrants—Early in the morning, the wagon train left for Salt Lake City and arrived at Haymarket Square, which occupied a square block on West Temple and First South. Used as a campsite for emigrants, it was also a general market place, where hay was sold, animals bought and sold, and vegetables and fruit exchanged for clothing, sugar, tea, and coffee.

My parents had just finished feeding their horses and built their campfire to make supper when a curious crowd of Mormons, who seemed to be the only inhabitants of Salt Lake at that time, gathered before them. Among them was a small thin man with a round, ruddy face, sharp eyes, and a briar pipe in his mouth. He walked up to Father and said in German, "Who are you? Where do you come from?" My father answered, "My name is Brook [Bruck]. I came from Breslau with my bride and we are making a wedding trip through to California." This man, Alexander Neibaur, said, "I, too, come from Breslau. Your aunt married an uncle of mine."

A Mormon Convert—Mr. Neibaur was born in 1808. He studied to be a rabbi, was well versed in the Talmud, and spoke beautiful German, French, Hebrew, and English without an accent. He was a dentist by profession. When he saw my mother, he said she was the first Jewish woman that had come overland to Utah. As they believed him to be a Jew, mother and father were surprised to hear he had joined the Mormon Church.[4]

Until they left for California in the spring, Mr. Neibaur invited my parents to board with his family. His home, on 2nd West between 2nd and 3rd South, was a one-story adobe house with six rooms, two rooms deep with a door for his three wives, and an added shed for a kitchen. The house stood back in the yard some twelve feet, and was a full lot in which he raised vegetables and had a cow. I remember it well. I was eight years old when his first wife died. His second wife was still living, but they were not very happy, and later he took a third wife. Her name was Elizabeth. I remember Father, who had very little religion, say to him, "You, Neibaur, as a Jew, don't believe those [gold] plates were real." And Neibaur reply, "Brooks that is none of your business." Years later, when Neibaur died, he had no tombstone. My parents set one for him.

Wherever Business Could Be Had—In May, my parents left with a heavy heart, but promised to return some day, little dreaming they would return soon. I was born in Timbuctoo, in the Yuba District, California, on November 16, 1859, in a shack that consisted of three rooms, two were used as a kitchen and bedroom, and the third as a store for general merchandise. My father acquired some mining claims and had a gold camp on the Yuba River near Marysville. By 1860, my father tired of the business and we went to San Francisco. In May, they then decided to continue on to New York to visit Mother's family who had come from Germany six years earlier. My brother George was two years old at the time and I was three months. Just before leaving, I was taken very sick and not expected to live. A large boil appeared on my cheek, which had to be lanced. From that moment, I improved.

It took two weeks to go from San Francisco to Panama. When walking out of doors, Mother wore a heavy veil because of the heat, moisture, and insects. She said we had to wait ten days for a boat and arrived in New York by the end of June. Grandparents, uncles and aunts were down at the pier to meet us. I had not yet been named, but was called "baby." My mother's youngest sister, Aunt Mary, was reading a book, in which the heroine's name was Eveline. So I was called Eveline.

Fannie and Julius Brooks with children. Eveline is standing between her parents. (Courtesy of the Bancroft Library, University of California)

My father returned to Timbuctoo, alone. It was a terrible, God forsaken place, and we stayed with Mother's family for a while. Later, we joined Father in San Francisco, and then left with a company of eight wagons heading for Oregon, where my father and a partner John McGowan opened a store on Front Street. Business was not as good in Portland as in those days, the country was overrun with get-rich-quick people, and Father had problems with his partner. We lived in Portland for two and a half years, and my brother Eddie was born there. He was web-footed.

Hearing about a large gold strike in Idaho, my father sold most of his merchandise, and took the rest with him, including one hundred sacks of flour. He opened another little store and since flour was scarce, he made money. But the flour had to be sifted first, owing to the dampness in Portland. Mother's neuralgia continued to trouble her and in late fall of 1864, my folks sold out, bought a wagon and returned to Utah where the climate is bracing, healthy and dry, and before the first fall of snow.

Returning to Salt Lake City—Of course, my parents' first visit was to see Mr. Neibaur. They found him hale and hearty and overjoyed to see them. He now had two wives and twelve children, so, of course could offer us no accommodation. But he took us to a rooming house on Main Street where Mother rented two rooms and did her own work. Around the corner from us on 2nd South were the McCalls stables where the Pony Express and the stagecoaches used to come. George and I always knew a little while ahead when the coach was coming, as the drivers would whip up their horses causing a cloud of dust that could be seen for blocks away. In the back of our house was a gambling saloon, very common in the West, which was raided by the Mormon police who took all the money they could find, then threw bottles, glasses, and furniture out the window. Next morning, George and I picked up some vases and whiskey glasses.

The only hotel that I can remember at the time was the Salt Lake House, run by Mr. Townsend, a Mormon convert from Maine. We rented only for a short time. On November 18, 1865, the house on the corner of Main Street and 3rd South was sold to Fannie Brooks for $2300.00. Mother kept boarders.

Federal Intervention—Colonel Patrick E. Connor was a friend of my parents. I knew him well. He was sent out to Utah in 1863 on account of the Mormons trying to keep out all non-Mormons. He came here from California with 1,000 volunteers and declared an area of the foothill, Camp Douglas, as a military reservation. At first, only one square mile was taken up for the camp. Jake Ornstein and Charles Popper had taken up all the land on the east bench, but the Government claimed they had only right for a certain amount, and took 2,500 acres from them, adding it to the Fort.[5] Popper built a few houses near his slaughterhouse and called it Popperton. Later, it was called Darlington, as a man by that name bought it, and put up several rows of houses. It is now known as Federal Heights.

A Practical Joke That Lands Them in Jail—Jake Ornstein and Charles Popper had immense cattle interest; they had a slaughterhouse and in connection with their butcher business, they manufactured soap. We had a little pony and often Mrs. Ornstein would send me out to the slaughterhouse to get Jake. I thought nothing of jumping on the pony bareback and riding out to Popperton, which was three miles from the 8th Ward. Ornstein was a short, thin man. He was cross-eyed, had blond curly hair and a little mustache. They first lived on 3rd South and later moved on Cathedral Hill, where they built a home. One Sunday evening, they were giving a housewarming as was customary and invited all their friends. They were to have a dance, forbidden on Sundays, and Mr. Popper thought he would play a joke on the crowd and informed the police. Just as the dancing was at its height, in walked five policemen who arrested all the men. They took them to jail and refused them bail. Mr. Popper later found the joke was on him when everybody was so angry, they wouldn't speak to him for months.

General Garfield—We used to walk up to the Fort with our lunch and spend the day. There was always a fine military band, a dress parade on Sunday. The fort was kept in wonderful condition. There were four cannons pointing towards Brigham Young's house, in case of emergency,

COLONEL PATRICK E. CONNOR

Born March 17, 1820, in Ireland, Patrick Edward Connor immigrated with his parents to New York City. In 1839, he enlisted in the United States Army; five years later, he went into the mercantile business in New York; in 1846, he moved to Texas to join the Texas Volunteers. Severely wounded during the war between the United States and Mexico (1846–1848), Connor returned briefly to the mercantile business in California and then enlisted in the Third California Infantry.

On October 24, 1861, with eastern and western work crews converging in Salt Lake City, the first transcontinental message was sent by Chief Justice Stephen J. Field of California to President Abraham Lincoln, declaring the state's loyalty to the Union. Handed the command to guard the overland mail and telegraph line, Colonel Connor and his California Volunteers were ordered to Salt Lake City in 1862, the year the Morrill Anti-Bigamy Act was passed, to establish Fort Douglas. The very presence of these soldiers enlivened the Gentile merchant trade and offered non-Mormon business owners a sense of security during the city's trade war between Mormons and non-Mormons.

In 1863, Connor received the brigadier general's star for his ruthless slaying of 250 Shoshone men, women, and children at Bear River. He burned 70 lodges, captured 175 ponies, and seized "a large quantity of grain, implements, and other property believed to have been stolen from emigrants. . . . On his side, Colonel Conner lost fourteen men and forty-nine were wounded."[6]

Colonel Connor was one of the founders of the Liberal Party, a non-Mormon political party, and also became involved in finding Utah's valuable minerals. Recognizing the richness of Utah mines with their untapped resources in gold, silver, copper, zinc, lead, iron, and coal, Colonel Connor sent his troops into Utah's canyons and mountains in search of precious metals.[7] Named the "Father of Utah Mining," he located the first silver mine in Little Cottonwood Canyon. He hoped mining would bring in non-Mormon miners and others to Utah to help diffuse the Mormon's political and economic clout.

Two Jewish soldiers arrived with Colonel Connor's California Volunteers in 1862. One, Solomon Cahen, did not stay long in Salt Lake City, although his son later married a daughter of Salt Lake residents Mr. and Mrs. Fred Simon. As soon as the other soldier, Isidore Morris, a pious Jew, completed his tour of duty in 1864, he worked in the mercantile business in Salt Lake, opened a store in the mining town of Bingham, Utah, and later married a Mormon woman who converted to Judaism. Their daughter married a Cincinnati engineer who laid out the Bamberger Railroad. According to Leon Watters, in his book *The Pioneer Jews of Utah,* Morris "won the gratitude of the Mormon people when he intervened in their behalf in 1886 at the time when forty-nine Mormon 'Elders' were incarcerated in the Utah Penitentiary charged with violation of the Federal law against polygamy."[8]

Riding on the *General Garfield* on the Great Salt Lake to Corinne. (Courtesy of Utah State Historical Society)

but, of, course they were never used. In 1868, Colonel Connor built and launched a small steamer called Katie Conner, used for carrying Union Pacific railroad ties and telegraph poles from the North to the South shore. I remember the first excursion boat was built in 1870. It was called the "City of Corinne." Mother, Dad, and I took a short trip on her; also later on the "General Garfield."

Houses for Emigrants—In 1867, gold was being discovered in both Utah and Nevada. Father told Mother that there was a great crowd of emigrants expected in Salt Lake City next fall and that they were fencing off the 8th Ward Square (where now stands the City and County Building) with an eight foot solid board fence for a public camping ground. Father had brought a couple of thousand dollars with him from Portland and Idaho. He said he could buy the southeast corner opposite the square for $300.00 and build some cheap frame houses, which he was sure could be rented over the winter, as emigrants had to stay in Salt Lake until the Spring. Mother thought it would be a good idea to buy.

That evening, Father went over to an old man named Acey, who with his twelve sons lived in an adobe building on the corner of Main and 3rd South. They were all builders. Father talked things over with Acey and it was agreed that he would build seven lath and plaster houses. Consisting of four rooms, a kitchen and sitting room downstairs, two bedrooms upstairs, a long porch would run across the front of the house. Each house was to be twenty feet front and thirty feet deep, with an artesian well on the one side and the outhouse on the other side. The whole lot of houses was to cost $2500.00.

Acey began to build in the spring and when he was half through, his nails gave out. There were none to be had in town, so he had to wait until the freight came in from Omaha, which took a couple of months. Auerbach's were the first to receive a shipment and they charged father $1.00 a pound for ten penny nails. There were fourteen to a pound. Of course, when Acey got through, it cost $1000.00 more than they had planned. In the meantime, on the back of our little adobe house, father had built two rooms, a bedroom and a kitchen, which we occupied in

AN ASIDE

by Samuel Auerbach

In 1867, Mr. Julius G. Brooks bought a corner facing on the Eighth Ward Square and began to build several frame and plaster houses. It was his intention to live in one of these and to rent the others. The nails cost him $1.00 per pound and putty $1.00 per pound. He bought these nails from F. Auerbachs & Bros. In later years, after I married his daughter Eveline, he often twitted me about our high priced nails.

About this time, J. G. Brooks opened the Pioneer Corral located on 3rd South, between 2nd and 3rd East. He was the proprietor of the Pioneer Corral for several years.

Mr. Brooks told this story on one of his tenants by the name of Acey. Acey had eleven sons, and of a cold winter's evening, when sitting before the log fire, he would say, "John, bring in some wood." John would ask Jim to go, Jim would say, "Dick, you go." Dick would tell Robert to go, and so on down the line until at last Dad went for the wood.

A fire occurred at Camp Douglas in 1867 and a great many goods were burned. General Connor, who knew J. G. Brooks, as well as Fred and myself, very well, spoke to us about this sale. Mr. Brooks and we bought some of these damaged goods and then resold them. Much of the fat J. G. Brooks secured was used in the making of soaps, of which there was then a great scarcity in Salt Lake.

He arranged with a man named Snell who hired out as an expert soap-maker to direct the soap-making operations and they turned out vast quantities of soap. The cakes were stacked up in great heaps all over the place, and J. G. Brooks almost pictured himself as a soap king. Snell, however, had put too much lye and not enough fat. As a consequence, when the soap dried, the large bars of soap shrank to almost nothing. They had also made a great lot of candles. Although these sputtered profusely, they refused to burn.

For a long time, soap and candle manufacture was a subject of great merriment among the Brooks family and their friends. With Mr. Brooks, however, it was a very sore subject, and provoked his ire to such a degree that we no longer thought it wise to mention it in his presence.

order to rent the adobe house. When the tenants moved on to California, and the coming winter was very severe, we moved back into the front of our house.

Fifth South was then the end of town. The pastures began there and cattle were turned out to graze. George and I used to go fishing in the deep creek from Parley's Canyon that ran through 5th South and emptied into the Jordan River. In the winters, we skated; in the summers, we'd go to Warm Springs Lake. We attended the 8th Ward schoolhouse, as there were no Gentile Schools at the time.

Assassination of Dr. Robinson—On October 22, 1866, while we still lived on Main Street, Dr. King Robinson was murdered. A native of Maine, he practiced his profession in Salt Lake, was appointed surgeon to Camp Douglas, and was the superintendent of the Gentile Sunday School which George and I attended. The year prior, he married the daughter of Dr. Kay, who was an apostate of the Mormon Church.

While at Camp Douglas, Dr. Robinson heard that certain ground in the neighborhood of Warm Springs was unoccupied and supposing it to be a portion of the public domain, he took possession of it and erected a building. The City Council claimed that the land belong to the city and ordered him to move. The doctor brought the matter before the court, but the chief justice decided the matter against him. His property was razed, along with other property belonging to him. Dr. Robinson said he would hold the city responsible. Some time later, at midnight, he was called up to attend to a man who was supposed to have been injured. Just as he left the house, he was hit on the head by a blunt instrument and then shot. We heard the terrible cries. Mother and Father jumped out of bed, as did we children. We were ordered back to bed and to keep absolutely quiet. Mother said she was sure of one of the criminals, but dared not tell.

After the assassination of Dr. Robinson, fears of violence seized the whole non-Mormon community. Many a man who before this incident went unarmed now carried pistols or revolvers. Respected citizens in Salt Lake forsook the sidewalks after dark and walked in the middle of the streets, carrying a bull's eye lantern. The excitement following this murder reached such a pitch that all non-Mormon merchants joined in a letter to Brigham Young offering the church their merchandise and estate at 25 percent less than actual value, saying they would leave the territory. Brigham Young replied, "I did not ask you to come in the Territory and I do not ask you to leave it."

Trade Wars in the City—Brigham Young had forbidden all the Mormons to buy, sell, or trade with Gentile merchants. When the country saints claimed they did not know the difference between a Mormon or Gentile store, it was determined that the words "Holiness to the Lord" was written under a bull's eye (meaning an all-seeing eye) and out on every sign above the door of a Mormon shop owner. But even this did not suffice, and in the following year the idea of uniting all Mormon stores into one grand cooperation, Zion's Cooperative Mercantile Institution (ZCMI) took form.

The above cut represents the Mormon "Co-operative Sign"—called by the Gentiles the "Bulls Eye." At the Mormon conference, in the fall of 1868, all good Mormon merchants, manufacturers and dealers who desired the patronage of the Mormon people, were directed to place this sign upon their buildings in a conspicuous place, that it might indicate to the people that they were sound in the faith.

The Mormon people were also directed and *warned* not to purchase goods or in any manner deal with those who refused or did not have the sign,—the object seemed to be only to deal with their own people, to the exclusion of all others.

The result of these measures on the part of the church was to force many who were Gentiles or Apostate Mormons to sacrifice their goods, and leave the Territory for want of patronage. Some few, however, remained. Among whom was J. K. Trumbo, an auction and commission merchant, who procured the painting of what was known as the

"GENTILE SIGN."

This sign was placed in position on the front of his store, on the morning of the 26th of February, 1869, in a similar position to those of the Mormons. All day wondering crowds of people of all classes, little and big, hovered about the premises, and many opinions were expressed as to the propriety of the sign, and whether it would be allowed to remain by the Mormons; but at about 7 o'clock in the evening the problem was solved, by a charge made by several young Mormons, who, with ladders climbed upon the building and secured ropes upon the sign, while the crowd below tore it down, and dragged it through the streets, dashing it to pieces. This should be a warning to all "Gentiles" in future, not to expend their money in signs to be placed on their stores in Utah—*unless they have permission.*

"Holiness to the Lord," the Zion's Cooperative Mercantile Institution. (Courtesy of Special Collections, Marriott Library, University of Utah)

Mormon Tenants Vacate—Except when there was emigration, our livelihood depended on the trade of Mormons. Upon the issuance of this anti-Gentile edict, our houses, rented to Mormons, were vacated at once. Mother and Father decided they would move back to California because they had seen such hard times while in Salt Lake and now they lived in fear of their lives. Mother asked Mr. Neibaur to go with her to see Brigham Young. She wanted to ask him if he would buy her property, so they could go to California. Mr. Neibaur took mother to see Brigham Young at his office in the Council House.

She told him since "you have forbidden the Mormons to trade with the Gentiles, our houses are empty. President Young, all our money is tied up in property. If we can't rent them, we will starve." Brigham Young told her how some of the Gentiles came to Salt Lake and wanted to run the town, but that they [the Brooks family] have always paid their tithing and have never hurt the Mormons in any way. "We would hate to have you leave," he said, and told her to go home; have patience and everything would turn out right. The next Sunday the Bishop preached to his people to be nice to Brother and Sister Brook and rent from them. Soon, all the houses were rented.

But shortly before this took place, some Chinese of note came from Frisco to go to New York. They were great on bathing and every day they were in the tub, as we had no bathrooms. And at night, they would walk around the house burning punk. Dad asked them why they did that and they said to keep the devil away. We never knew whether it was they or Brigham Young that brought us luck. But from then on, things began to improve.

On with Business—One of our tenants was Mrs. Anderson, a Swedish woman. She said if my father would get her some buckskin, she would make up some gloves very cheaply. The Indians brought quite a few skins to town, which were tanned in Salt Lake at William Pickard's place. Mrs. Anderson cut some of them out, and put cuffs on the gloves, making gauntlets out of them. Other gloves were embroidered with sprays of rose or forget-me-nots in silk. Some were trimmed with beaver tops. Father sold some of the gloves to Auerbach's and ZCMI.

In 1869, gold fever hit again and a great many Easterners were coming through on their way to the mines. The following spring, one hundred and fifty wagons arrived and Mother decided to offer breakfasts, serving forty people at a time at an ordinary wooden table with plain board benches. Mother did the cooking, along with Billie the cook and a fine woman, the second wife of a man who was treating her badly, who hired on as a waitress. A line of people formed standing half way down the block, waiting to get in to breakfast. Sometimes they would feed one hundred fifty people in a day, all emigrants, camping on the 8th Ward Square. Father put in a few groceries to sell and did quite a nice business. As soon as the fall began, though, the emigrant trains stopped and Dad owed so much at the Bank and to the Auerbachs, we had to save and scrape to pay interest.

A Death in the Family—That same year, mother was making pies and George, who was twelve years old, came into the house and asked if he and his friend could ride a pony to Warm

East Temple Street showing stores with ZCMI sign, "Holiness to the Lord," and Zion's Cooperative Mercantile Institution. (Courtesy of Utah State Historical Society)

Springs. Mother didn't want him to go, but relented after they promised not to be gone too long. The two started off on a small pony, one sitting behind the other. Poor fellows, they did not stay long. Inside of an hour, George was brought home dead. The horse had stumbled and thrown both boys. While his friend was not hurt, poor George struck his temple and was instantly killed. We thought mother would lose her mind. He was a darling boy, the second person to be buried at the Jewish cemetery in Salt Lake City. That same year, our four-year-old brother, Milton, died. We blamed the doctor because he did not know what his sickness was. Later, both he and Milton were moved into the Brooks vault, built when Father's remains were brought to Salt Lake City.

I remember, earlier, having a little dog that was run over by a large dray while playing with George and me in the yard. We were beside ourselves with grief. George, who was two years older than I, made a coffin out of cigar boxes and we buried him under our beloved cherry tree. I remember, after George died, we sold the pony although it was as gentle as a lamb.

After my brothers died, my parents decided to go to California on a visit.

Business—By 1870, Fred Auerbach loaned father money to buy condemned goods, most in good condition, at Fort Douglas: tea, coffee, sugar, rice, beans, shoulders of hams and sides of

Eveline Brooks, sixteen years old. (Courtesy of the Bancroft Library, University of California)

Eveline Auerbach. (Courtesy of the Bancroft Library, University of California)

The eight children of Sam and Eveline Auerbach (*l–r*): Jennie (born 1889), George (born 1885), Madeline (born 1895), Herbert (born 1882), Josephine (born 1884), Selma (born 1887), Bessie (born 1886?), and Frederick (born 1889?). (Courtesy of Stan Sanders)

bacon, old saddles, bridles, and leather goods of all sorts. Father bought the entire lot for $250.00. He realized from the leather goods alone $800.00. The ham and bacon were trimmed and sold to restaurants; the undesirable parts used to make soap. Later we went to Elko, Nevada and then to California. It was in the year 1870 after a big earthquake when any property could have been bought for a song. In the spring we returned. Father bought and sold cloth. Mother continued to take in boarders, and that year the first circus came to town.

Future Works—In 1872, Father opened Brooks Furniture Store, but sold it and went to California on business for a short time. In 1873, my parents decided to go to New York to live. In the meantime, Father returned to Salt Lake City and bought some property. Four years later, my family returned again. Mother opened the first millinery shop in Utah on 3rd West and 1st South Streets. Sometimes she was paid in eggs and butter, fish or fruit. Father could not order the goods fast enough. (My father was always looking for bargains, and I remember a time when he bought a carload of damaged buttons, which Mother and I sewed on fresh cards and Father made quite some money.)

Some of the girls during that time were beginning to go in society. There were Fannie Levy Wolff, Rose Moritz Kahn, Leah Phillips, Phoebe Symon Siegel, Rosanna Kahn, and a couple others. The young men that came to see us were Mr. Lipman, Abe Cohn, Louis Bamberger, Mr. Moritz, Emil Friedman, Simon Friedman, Joe Simon, Mr. Kahn, and once in a while a few travelling salesmen from California. I think we girls all liked Louis Bamberger best; perhaps it was because he was blond, full of fun, and had no idea of marrying anyone.

Josephine and Herbert Auerbach, circa 1887. (Courtesy of Stan Sanders)

In 1878 Sam Auerbach and I were engaged only a few days when Leon Watters was born and I was chosen as Godmother. That same year my mother and father celebrated their silver wedding. In 1879, I married Sam Auerbach. Five years later, my father got the idea of building The Brook's Arcade.[9]

We lived forty years in Salt Lake City. As a child, growing up among families where a man had one wife or half a dozen, and where they called each other "Sister" or "Brother" even though they were not related meant nothing to me. We were so accustomed to that way of living.

GENTILE PIONEER MERCHANTS

Samuel H. Auerbach

King of Prussia—My father, Hillel Tobias Auerbach, was a horse and cattle dealer; in leather, grain and flour; and a teacher at the college in Fordon.[1] He spoke five languages fluently and was regarded as one of the leading Talmudists in Germany. I had four sisters: Rose, Joanna, Augusta and Rebecca; and two brothers, Frederick, born in 1836, and Theodore. I, Samuel Hillel Auerbach was born in Fordon on the Weichel on June 15th 1847.

I remember incidents happening when I was four years old. I used to go to the ferry to see my poor father depart on his trips to the country and occasionally wait for his returning. In July 1851, I was blind for about four weeks. One night I awoke and called out that I could see. That night my poor father passed away. It was the nineteenth day in the month of Ab.[2] My father was coming home from the country on a loaded wagon. He fell off and sustained such injuries from which he did not recover.

We lived in a small apartment in a large and high building, like a tenement building, that at one time, was used by the government to collect duties from passing sailing vessels, called Berliner Kahn Boat, and other duties. My mother, Biele (or Bertha), would tell me to go downstairs and sit on the step. Sometimes I was tempted to go down to the river to see what boats are passing or what rafts were floating by.

In the winter, which started early in the middle of December, blocks of ice would come floating down the river, and as the frosty night began, the shallow water would freeze and stop the blocks of ice from floating. The river would freeze solid and the ferryboats could not be operated. The town officers appointed men to test the ice if it was strong enough for traffic. They would cut holes in the ice and put limbs of pine trees in and make a roadway for teams and passengers to go over. I have seen, say, twenty wagons loaded with twenty sacks of wheat, each sack weighing one hundred pounds, and some heavier, and four horses crossing the ice. Owners of estates, some with titles, some plain citizens, would send their farm produce, wheat, rye, oats, barley, alcohol, and other products to the city of Bromberg, returning, carrying machinery and

Samuel Auerbach, 1904. (Courtesy of Stan Sanders)

below
Frederick Auerbach. (Courtesy of Stan Sanders)

other supplies across the ice, saving the expense of having them ferried when the river is open for navigation.

I do not remember much of that time until I was to go to a private school. I refused to go. My sister Rebecca offered to go with me and remain until I was accustomed to being there. When I was seven years old, I attended the public school for several years. As I grew older, I would arise at five o'clock in the morning to go to college where I attended lectures and discussions on religion, law, and literature.

My oldest brother, Fred, while but a young boy, went to work as an apprentice in a grocery store. No fire was kept in the store, his hands were frequently swollen from frostbite; and his master gave him barely enough to eat. Fred finally quit the place to become an apprentice in a leather and fur business. He was always extremely ambitious, unusually bright, and well liked. He had read and heard a great deal of America, and its wonderful attractions, especially of the great opportunities in California, so he determined that's where he would go. Our uncle, Louis Auerbach, who lived in Berlin and was a manufacturer of silks, promised to help my brother reach America.

At Sea—When I was thirteen years old, I went to learn the trade of a furrier, and was apprenticed to a man to learn the tanning and preparation of leather and furs. I was no success at all. I lodged and boarded at home and gave up my apprenticeship. I had an Aunt Sarah Levy in Culmese whose sons were merchant tailors. She wrote to my mother, who was her sister, to send me to them, and I could learn the tailor trade. I started to work there, and it was like home, but that trade did not just suit. My brothers wrote to me to come to America.

Before leaving, I went to take leave of my sister Rebecca. She told me if your heart does not carry you, do not go, you will make a living here also. My pride made me go. On June 16, 1862, I sailed on the Hamburg-Amerika Liner *Borussia.* The steerage quarters were congested, dark and dingy, dimly lighted by faint-flamed lanterns, poorly ventilated and ill smelling. While at sea, we encountered two big storms, saw several large icebergs, had to sail amid heavy fogs in the vicinity of Newfoundland. I was seasick for several days, homesick, too. The drinking water was very poor and smelled stagnant. It required seventeen days to reach New York. Shortly before we docked, we were ordered to throw our mattresses and pillows overboard. It seemed a shame to destroy these things, miserable though they were.

New York Sights—The Civil War [1861–1865] was then in progress and New York was a martial city. The City Hall Square and Union Square were dotted with tents, and soldiers were constantly marching up and down the streets and to and from the ferries to the sounds of fife and drums and military music. The excitement was intense.

Fred sent money to New York to cover my steamer ticket, pocket money, and traveling expenses to the diggings at Rabbit Creek, California. Within several weeks time, I endeavored to see as much of New York and its sights as possible. From the spire of Trinity Church, I got a bird's eye glimpse of the city. I walked up and down Broadway until I was tired out from looking at the fine buildings and the shop windows along this busy thoroughfare. I recall the Stewart Marble Palace, at Broadway and Chambers Streets, the biggest dry goods emporium in New York; Lord and Taylor's Marble Store; and Tiffany and Company. Barnum's Museum on Broadway consisted of a wild animal menagerie, some birds, various wax figures, mechanical figures, and numerous curios. A minstrel show, which I visited, amused me exceedingly. I noted with interest that in hotels and lounging rooms, it was customary for many of the people to tilt their chairs against the wall and recline with their feet stuck up on railings or other chairs. I had never seen anything like that before.

Travels to Rabbit Creek—On July 12, 1862, I left New York on a side-wheeler, which carried nearly 650 passengers on board. During the sea voyage, the Captain was anxiously on the lookout for Confederate boats. I was seasick again. The trip through the West Indies, past Cuba and Haiti, and the Caribbean Sea was beautiful, but as we neared the Isthmus of Panama, the heat became stifling. The railroad from Aspenwall on the Atlantic Coast to Panama on the Pacific Coast was about 48 miles long. Fever was prevalent upon the Isthmus and the water was undrinkable; but the oranges and bananas were particularly fine, and here I tasted my first sugar cane.

In the evening of July 31, we left Panama on the Steamer *Orizaba,* another side-wheeler that was so overloaded, she was unable to take on a full load of coal at Panama and ran slower than her usual speed. At night we sailed without lights, for this Captain too had been warned that the Confederate steamers *Alabama* and *Ariel* were cruising the Pacific on the lookout for northern boats.

Early Sunday morning, August 17, we entered Golden Gate Bay and the famed city of San Francisco. The business district extended from Montgomery Street to the Bay, and between Washington and California Streets. The jobbing houses were on Front and Battery and California Streets. Most of the retail dry goods stores held forth on Sacramento Street. Montgomery was the most important and busiest street, with beautiful stores and shops, and tremendous throngs of people by day and night. There were many hotels, theatres, and amusements; and near Sacramento Street, the curb brokers held their exchange on the sidewalk, trading in mining and other stocks amid the perfect bedlam.

I went on to Sacramento and Marysville before getting on the stage to go to Rabbit Creek, sixty miles away. I was overjoyed to find my brother Fred waiting as the stage drove up to the Union Hotel. We had supper, walked up the street to his main store, and spent an extremely happy evening answering questions about mother, sister, relatives and friends. The next day, to my great delight, Theodore came from Port Wine to meet me. I recall vividly that he gave me a bright silver dollar to buy peaches.

Rabbit Creek lay hidden in a very beautiful valley amid the elevated peaks of the Sierras. It was the trading headquarters for thousands of miners scattered through the surrounding camps and mountains. Pack-mules constantly carried supplies to the workers in the mountains. It was a real boom mining camp, engaged in bed-rock or placer mining, with all the absorbingly interesting life and activity. Some of the principal camps in the vicinity of Rabbit Creek rejoiced in the euphonious names of Port Wine, Wahoo, Poverty Hill, Whiskey Diggings, Spanish Flat, Eureka City, Poorman's Creek, American House and Poker Flat.

Weighing Gold—Minted money was rather scarce and a large part of the business was transacted by means of credit, trade, or barter. Paper money was frequently used, but was not worth face value. One saw an occasional "Gold Slug." Gold dust was current and every merchant had a pair of gold dust scales on the counter. A piece of Brussels carpet was usually placed under the scale. From time to time, the carpet was burned and its gold contents saved. A "pinch" of gold dust consisted of as much dust as could be held between the thumb and index finger, and was figured at approximately "two bits" [a quarter]. Some barkeepers could pinch very liberal pinches. Good barkeepers were measured more by their ability to take extravagant pinches than

A BREAK-IN AT THE STORE

Auerbach's in Rabbit Creek was located where the women were considered rare and referred to as "cute little hens." Auerbach's main store in Rabbit Creek was a gathering place and headquarters for many of the prominent miners and freighters of the district whom Fred often advised in their important deals and transactions. Many of them left their gold dust, nuggets, and bullion with the Auerbachs for safekeeping. At times, the brothers had very large amounts of treasures in their safe. The night that Fred went to San Francisco, the safe was full to capacity.

Sam, asleep in the back of the store, was awakened by a noise and discovered two men near the safe; and one of them pointing a pistol at him. It was by far the biggest pistol he had ever seen. It looked like a cannon. Sam looked straight down the inside of the barrel, and it was blacker and deeper than he ever imagined a cannon could be. The men themselves were eight feet tall!

"Open that safe and open it damn quick!" Sam knew that to do so meant ruination. He told them he didn't have the combination; didn't know it. They threatened to shoot him, but he maintained that his brother would never trust him with the combination. The witless outlaws cursed Sam profusely. They tied his feet and hands, fastened a bandanna-handkerchief across his mouth, and then began drilling into the safe door. After what seemed like hours—although it may have been a matter of minutes—a group of latecomers had stopped to talk near the store entrance where the Auerbachs always had a light burning. Fearful of detection, the safecrackers dropped what they were doing and made a hasty escape through a back window. After hours of wiggling and squirming until his bonds loosened up enough for him to break free, Sam hurried over to a friend whom he routed out of bed, and together they awakened the sheriff. The bunglers were long gone, the gold was secure in the safe. Sometimes knowing "nothing" turns out to be quite an asset in itself.[3]

by their drink-mixing ability. Gold dust was usually carried in buckskin or leather sacks, but often, too, in bottles, fruit jars and cans.

Business Enterprises—Our main store on Main Street—we had a branch in Rabbit Creek and Port Wine, carried a general line of dry goods, ladies' and men's clothing, furs, hats, boots, shoes, groceries, mining supplies, blankets, mattresses, hardware, notions, carpets, wall paper and drugs. We specialized in men's and ladies' Indian tanned buckskin gloves, with cuffs, embroidered with silk in fancy floral designs. We also sold considerable merchandise to both commission merchants and merchants in Virginia City, Nevada; Helena, Montana; Virginia City, Montana; Fort Benton, Montana; Great Salt Lake City, Utah, and Fort Bridger, Utah. Returns for these goods were received mostly in gold coin and gold dust, and this gold would be sent to San Francisco and Sacramento in order to pay the merchants there from whom these goods had been purchased. Merchandise was exchanged for oats, butter, eggs, cheese, dried fruits, and other products, and sent to Virginia City, Nevada, where they could be disposed of for gold coin.

Fred and I slept in the rear of the store. That was the custom among merchants in order to protect the store and its merchandise. Theodore spent much time at our store in Port Wine, known as "Lavenberg & Company." We were the "company." Theodore also worked as a messenger for a banking house; and, for a short, hectic time, Fred and I operated a train of pack mules out of Rabbit Creek.

Fred Took Sick—Business at Rabbit Creek quieted down during the spring and summer of 1863, and in the fall times, became very dull. That year, Fred went to Austin, Nevada, to try out a new mining camp. He took sick and lay on the dirt floor of a small shed in the back of the store for several days and then for many weeks on a rough bed made from packing cases. As he belonged to the IOOF [Independent Order of Odd Fellows], he eventually received valuable nursing and attention from the Lodge.[4] Reduced in weight from 140 pounds to ninety, he pulled through.

Meeting Brigham Young—In March 1864, Fred drove a mule team to Great Salt Lake City, taking with him all the remaining merchandise, which barely filled a mountain schooner. Just at dusk, he became acquainted with Henry Heath and spent his first night at his home. Henry, an adopted son of Bishop Hunter, had come to Great Salt Lake with the Edwards Hunter Company in 1847 at the age of 18. Shortly after arriving, he became an officer on the local police force, and was, for many years, a bodyguard of Brigham Young. Heath was reputed to know more than he cared to tell regarding the shooting incident of Dr. Robinson.

Fred looked about the town and was favorably impressed with it. He told Heath he contemplated relocating to Great Salt Lake City. Heath took him to the Church office on South Temple Street and introduced him to "President Brigham." The two of them chatted for some time. President Young told Fred to come back the following morning when he would see if he could find a suitable location for him to open a store. The following day, Fred inquired about a small adobe cabin on the westside of Main Street, just below 1st South Street, which was then occupied temporarily by a carpenter shop.

Setting Up Shop—President Young visited the carpenter, and said, "Brother Stephens, build yourself a shop in the back of the yard. Fred Auerbach is going to open a store in this cabin." From this time dated Fred's friendship with Brigham Young. Fred employed the carpenter to build a counter and some shelving from the wooden packing cases, which contained his stock

Auerbachs in the mid-1870s. (Courtesy of Utah State Historical Society)

of merchandise. In a few days, he secured a crudely made sign above the door, which read, "The People's Store. F. Auerbach & Bros," and opened the Salt Lake store. Shortly afterwards, in the spring of 1865, my brother Theodore and I joined him at Great Salt Lake City to live.

Samuel's Acquaintances—After my arrival, I became acquainted with Mr. and Mrs. Brooks, and frequently visited them with my brother Fred. I lived in a one-story adobe house on Main Street between 1st and 2nd South Street, and later moved to a boarding house on the eastside of West Temple Street, between 1st and 2nd South Street. In those days, we used coal-oil for lighting which cost $10.00 per gallon. Each morning, before breakfast, I would sweep out the store, and clean and fill and trim the wick of the single hanging lamp. I would then place merchandise displays, including sacks of grain, flour, groceries, shovels, brushes, brooms, etc., upon the sidewalk in front of the store.

Advertising Opportunities—One morning, hearing quite a commotion, I hurried outside to discover a team of oxen had strayed upon the sidewalk and each one was munching a broom

Auerbach float, 1897, fiftieth anniversary of the Mormon settlement. (Courtesy of Stan Sanders)

with every evidence of keen relish. A large crowd had gathered to watch. The oxen ate as far as the broom handles, but these they rejected. The news soon spread along the street and all that day amused and curious crowds came to view the scene of the broom comedy. Business was unusually good. Thus, by accident, I learned that unusual happenings often have great advertising value.

In our store, we carried a mixed stock of goods, such as groceries, hardware, mining supplies, boots, shoes, drugs, notions, dry goods and clothing. We bought considerable merchandise at San Francisco; but most of our goods came overland from St. Louis and points farther East. When we had produce for sale, we'd hang a sign out in front of the store and teamsters who wanted "Loading" for towns in Montana, Idaho, Wyoming, or Nevada would drop in to see what we had to offer. We also traded in and bought furs and hides; handled maybe thousands of beaver, mink, marten, fox, wolf, cougar, lynx, bear, buffalo robes and otter skins, and deer and elk buckskins. Some of these were brought in by white trappers; many others were brought by

Indians, like Chief *Washakik* and his Indians who often traded with us. He was a real chief, a sincere friend of the white people, and of a very peaceful nature. He was exceptionally interesting, and I was always very glad to see him.

Mormon Script—Shortly after we started in business, the Bishop of one of the wards came to the store and told us that many of the people in his ward were sick and needed medicine. He asked if we could contribute a few bottles. As we all had suffered from sickness—Fred in Nevada, I on the boat—we sympathized and, though in poor financial circumstances, gave him our entire stock of remedies. Some time later, Brigham Young learned of this contribution and was so pleased he came into the store and thanked us. He said he had given orders that we would be permitted to redeem L.D.S. Church tithing script at face value. As far as I know, we were the only non-Mormon firm to whom this unusual privilege was ever granted.

Window display at Auerbachs, 1909.
(Courtesy of Utah State Historical Society)

Candling, Salt, Customers—There was a time we did a large butter and egg business and had a room in the cellar of our store for candling. With aid of a lit candle and a piece of cardboard with a hole cut in it, we candled eggs. We purchased salt in large quantities and then put them up in five and ten pound bags having our signature "F. Auerbach & Bros., Salt Lake City, Utah" stamped on them. We were very careful to pack only the best grade of salt that it was possible to obtain, and we built up a very good reputation. We sold many hoop skirts. It was quite a trick to fold up a hoop skirt prior to wrapping it.

When customers or friends came in from out of town, it was customary to permit them to sleep in the aisles or on the counters. Blankets would be taken out of the stock and they would roll themselves in these blankets and sleep. The next morning, after they had arisen, the blankets would be placed back in stock. Most of the people slept in their boots, and some of them did not remove any part of their outer clothing.

Street Scenes—In the 1860s there were no paved streets or sidewalks. The sidewalks at times became so muddy, merchants laid a plank or two along the walk in front of their shop and I have often seen it so muddy, if one stepped off this planking, they would sink into mud over

A modernization sale at Auerbachs, 1934. (Courtesy of Utah State Historical Society)

their shoe tops. In those days, deep ditches were at the sidewalk's edge on either side of Main Street and were filled with water from City Creek.

At night, the streets and sidewalks of Salt Lake City were inky black (no lights of any kind) and any attempt to take a walk after dark frequently resulted in a collision with some woodpile stored upon the sidewalk, or with boxes and wagons left upon the walk by thoughtless residents.

Cows, horses and pigs roamed at random along the streets and sidewalks, often damaging fences and gardens. Main Street was a favorite playground for horses, cows, pigs, and dogs, while chickens came from coops located blocks away that they might disport themselves and make merry in the deep dust of Main Street. I recall one man, who resided in an adobe house on the west side of Main Street, between 2nd and 3rd South. He had a vegetable garden and corn patch in his front yard, and the horses and cows broke through his fence times innumerable; on each occasion provoking a string of profanity that was simply incomparable.

During the summer the dust was very deep. When herds of cattle were driven along Main Street, we were forced to close windows and doors to prevent merchandise from being ruined by the dust.

During the rainy season, the mud was almost bottomless, and of a consistency and stickiness to put glue to shame. At times, it was nearly impossible to cross a street. Main Street was frequently a river of mud. It was no unusual sight to see arriving stages and freighting teams stuck in the mud; and many times I have seen oxen mired so deep in the mud on Main Street. In stormy weather, mud was king, and when we placed wooden planks on the walks in front of our stores, we had started the first round in a battle to free ourselves from the tyranny of mud.

In those days, men wore boots and drank and swore and chewed tobacco. I made frequent trips to the outlying villages and settlements, where I took orders for merchandise and bought farm products to be delivered in Salt Lake.

A Pioneer Lodge—In May 1865, Fred with his friends Captain Willard Kitteredge of Fort Douglas, Mr. Wohlgemuth, R. Westbrook, J. Ellis, Joseph Merril, Charlie Popper, and L. Whitney started the first Odd Fellows Lodge in Utah. They had their lodge room upstairs in the rear of a two-story building on Main Street, and members used empty coffee and canned goods boxes as substitutes for chairs. Fred was the first Grand Master of the Grand Lodge in Utah. Afterwards, he was appointed by the Grand Lodge in Baltimore as Deputy Grand Sire, and when more lodges were installed in Utah, he received, every six months, the password, whereupon he would visit these lodges and transmit the password to them.

Mount Moriah Masonic Lodge No. 1. was one of the first lodges in Salt Lake. It was organized by a number of men including my brother Theodore in 1869.

General Connor and Unease in the City—Fred and I became acquainted with General Connor shortly after we came to Salt Lake and a warm friendship had sprung up between us. General Connor often came in to discuss new strikes at the mines and to show us assays, which ran unusually high. We were interested with him in several of his mining properties. In 1864, General Connor founded Stockton, the first Gentile town in Utah. The following year, he took over the Great Basin Mine in Stockton District. Later renamed the Honorine, it proved to be a very rich property, its production in excess of three million dollars. General Connor also controlled the Quandry, the Silver King and the General Connor Tunnel and Mining Co.

Knowing General Connor, as a natural consequence, we were also acquainted with many of the officers and soldiers at Camp Douglas who did considerable trading at our store. The non-Mormon element regarded the military as their friends and protectors, and the military fraternized with the non-Mormons. Needless to say, the Mormons viewed the military with feelings ranging from dislike to deep hatred, and always as an enemy.

The Murder of Dr. Robinson—Mr. McLeod was an ex-army chaplain. He was in charge of the Congregational Church services held at Independence Hall on West 3rd South Street. Dr. Rob-

THE MAKING OF A DEPARTMENT STORE

In 1864, store keeping began as early as six-thirty and ended long after midnight. F. Auerbach & Bros., in Salt Lake City, was a busy place. They carried all kinds of groceries, sacks of flour and grains, coffee, tea, sugar, and spices. Common drugs and medicines were offered, among which was asafetida, worn in little bags around the necks of children and grown-ups alike to ward off epidemics. In corners and on floor displays, on shelves, in cases, and on countertops were boots and shoes, stoves, farming tools and miners' equipment, crockery and glassware, eating utensils, pots and pans, hardware, coal oil, wallpaper, towels, soaps, ropes and twine, wood, saws, shovels, buckets and brooms, jewelry and notions, tapes, ribbons, buttons, needles and threads, men's ready-wear clothes and furnishings, cloth, ticking for mattresses and pillows, unbleached muslin for sheets and underwear, and hoops and bustles.

In front of the shop, prospectors would tie up their pack mules to hitching posts, and bring in gold dust to exchange for provisions, blankets, clothes, blasting powder, and tools. Miners purchased their supplies, and trappers dropped off stacks of fur pelts and buckskins to exchange.

The newest and most appealing merchandise was put outside on the street to stop passersby. In 1869, long tin bathtubs, shaped to fit the body, were introduced. There was no plumbing attached to the tub, no running water, and no outlet for used water, but the tub represented such an advance over the washtub placed in front of the kitchen stove that the item created quite a sensation.

inson was superintendent of the Sunday school. In his sermons, Mr. McLeod had made many bitter attacks on polygamy. Possibly by association—that and being married to an apostate's daughter, a fine looking girl, Nellie Kay, the daughter of Dr. Kay—Dr. Robinson had incurred the animosity of certain Mormons.

In October, 1866, at about 11:00 P.M., a man rapped at the door of the home of Dr. John King Robinson, situated on 3rd South, west of Independence Hall, and requested him to set a fractured limb for a man who had just met with an accident. Mrs. Robinson begged the good doctor not to go, but Robinson was a brave man and declared that it was his duty to answer any and all such calls. Halfway across the street, he was attacked by his caller and four other men with guns. As they shot him, he shouted, "Murder!" and died. Mrs. Robinson ran out of the house and witnessed the assault. There were many other people on the street, for the theatre had just let out, and they too saw what happened. Mr. and Mrs. J. G. Brooks, who lived just above the corner of Main Street and 3rd South heard the outcry and the sound of gunshots. They ran to the sidewalk in time to see men hurrying away.

Following this wanton murder, there was intense feeling, great unrest and uneasiness in Salt Lake, and many Gentiles procured and carried firearms. The officers and men at Camp Douglas, and particularly, General Connor, were greatly wrought up over the assassination of their comrade. No real action was ever taken by the authorities to apprehend or to punish the murderers, although, I believe, rewards were posted to make it appear as if their arrest was desired. It was claimed that the murderers were all members of the Salt Lake police force.

Unfair Competition—These actions took place during the time Mormons were ordered not to buy at Gentile stores. The Salt Lake City police, whose wages we as tax-paying citizens helped pay, patrolled our store at Conference time and warned the Saints away from entering. We had many good friends among the Mormons, as well as among the non-Mormons, and had established a reputation for fair dealing and for selling at lower prices than many other merchants.

It became necessary for our Mormon customers to come at night by way of the back entrance in order to make their purchases secretly, for they dared not be seen by the spies of the church. In shipping their goods, we disguised the cases and were extremely careful to obliterate the name "Auerbach & Bros.," or any other marking that would enable someone to trace the origin of the cases. If Mormon customers purchased smaller items, some of them used what was called "Mormon Suitcases." Actually, these were sugar sacks or flour sacks, which they carried in their pockets, filled with their purchases, and slung over their back before starting for home.

Gentile Merchants React to Trade War—On December 20, 1866, the Gentile merchants prepared a petition to Brigham Young in which they offered to sell their stocks at a sacrifice and agreed to leave Utah. Two years later, at the Fall Conference, Brigham Young held a meeting with the Mormon merchants at the City Hall and directed that a sign be made reading "Holiness to the Lord," below which was drawn a picture of the All-Seeing Eye. This sign was placed over the front doors of all Mormon stores, so that the Mormon brethren could not mistake a Gentile store for a Mormon store. As a result of this action, many of the smaller Gentile merchants were forced to the wall, losing everything they possessed. Conditions were getting desperate even for the larger merchants, who had means and credit.

Fred decided to take up matters with President Brigham Young. President Young would frequently come to our store and often sit upon the counter for hours, discussing theology and the bible with Fred, who was an unusual scholar and a deep student of the Talmud and of the Bible. Fred met with President Young and spoke to him of existing conditions. He said they were becoming unbearable and that if they were to continue in this manner, we must soon get out of Salt Lake. Brigham Young told Fred that Auerbachs had always been good friends of the Mor-

The Wild West liberal town of Corinne. (Courtesy of Special Collections, Marriott Library, University of Utah)

mons, and that he did not want us to leave Salt Lake. He said, he had told the Mormons not to trade with their enemies, but added, the Auerbach Brothers were not the enemies. President Young complained that many of the Gentiles were slandering and injuring the Mormons and working against them, and he flatly stated that he intended to drive that type of Gentile from the territory. He counseled us to be patient and said everything would come out all right.

On October 16, 1869, Z.C.M.I. opened in Salt Lake City. Within a short time, branch co-ops were founded in many of the smaller towns. These co-ops each had the same particular sign over their door, which added to the persecution of the Gentile merchants. For us, this was the "last straw," and Fred and I discussed very seriously the matter of moving back to California. However, following Brigham Young's avowal of friendship, we decided to await developments for a reasonable time. As a last hope, we all pinned our great faiths to the mines, believing that with the development of Utah's wonderful ore deposits, the Gentiles would again have a chance in Utah.

Times were dull. The boycott was strongly enforced. It looked as though the Gentile concerns would surely be out of business, and out of Salt Lake City. We started a branch store at Ogden, and one in a large tent at Promontory, which we later moved to Corinne. From 1869 to 1870, I was away from Salt Lake a considerable part of the time, being often in Ogden, Promontory, and occasionally at our branch stores in Bryan, which was a notoriously tough railroad camp in Wyoming, and in Malad, Idaho. I also made trips to Virginia City, Montana, and Cheyenne, Wyoming, and spent a good portion of time in Corinne.

Nearing the end of March, 1869, about six miles north of Great Salt Lake, Corinne was built by Gentiles fleeing Salt Lake City and the Union Pacific Railroad. It was named after the daughter of General Williamson, the Commissioner of Land of the Union Pacific Railroad. With a direct spur to the town, the railroad encouraged merchants and business people to move there.

An All-Gentile Town—At that time, Corinne was the only Gentile city in the territory of Utah. A canvas city, it was a very lively town, with a population that ran as high as 5,000. Some of the stores consisted of a wooden frame, covered with canvas, but most of the places were plain canvas tents. Many people were convinced that, being on the railroad, it would soon be a larger city than Salt Lake City. It was the starting point for stage lines and freighting outfits to Idaho and Montana, and became an important forwarding point. Large quantities of ore and lumber, as well as supplies of every kind, were handled by these freighters.

Our store consisted of a wooden frame with canvas stretched over it, and carried a sign: "California Store. F. Auerbach & Bros." It was located on the south side of Main Street, or Montana Street, at the corner of 4th Street. The Metropolis Hotel, operated by Malsh and Greenwald, was on the north side of Main Street. The Uintah Hotel was the main hostelry of Corinne and consisted of a wooden frame covered with canvas. A hall extended down the center with "rooms" on either side. These rooms were mere stalls divided off by canvas sheets, and each contained a small crudely built bed. The floor was a dirt floor, but beside each bed lay a splintery board to serve as a rug for tender feet. Fred Kiesel started his business in Corinne. Mr. Farmer had a good-sized store there. A. Kuhn and Brother also had a good-sized store, as well as George A. Lowe, another early merchant, and Gumpert Goldberg.[5]

Corinne became the supply station for Brigham City, about six miles east. Brigham City farmers brought fruit, vegetables and produce to Corinne, and disposed of it for cash. However, as Brigham City was a Mormon community and Corinne was a Gentile town, the farmers would not spend a cent at Corinne, and when Corinne citizens went to Brigham City, they were anything but welcome there.

Corinne was a wide-open town with a large proportion of sporting population coming from as far away as Elko, Nevada. At that time, there were twenty-one bars and all the grocery stores carried stocks of liquor. Corinne was also quite a region for stock raising, and was the gateway to Montana. All freight outfits bound to and coming out of Montana were outfitted at Corinne. [Of course, when railroad baron Jay Gould built his narrow-gauge railroad from Corinne to Montana, the freighting by teams ceased, and Corinne began to decline.][6]

The Golden Spike and the Transcontinental Railroad—I was doing business at Corinne on May 10, 1869, and drove to Promontory Summit to attend the laying of the last tie and the driving of the last spike connecting the Union Pacific and the Central Pacific Railways, and uniting the Atlantic Coast with the Pacific Coast.[7] All along the Great Salt Lake was a long stretch where the Union Pacific and the Central Pacific grades paralleled, each company having graded as far as possible in order to obtain the greatest mileage from the United States government.

Construction trains and workmen were early on the scene, followed by excursion trains and settlers in conveyances of every sort and description, as well as on horse back and mules. Mr. and Mrs. J. G. Brooks with part of their family, including Eveline Brooks, were there, having driven up from Salt Lake City with Mr. Pat Quinn and his family.

At about 11 o'clock, a Union Pacific train carrying officials, excursionists, several companies, and the band of the 21st Infantry from Camp Douglas arrived. Soon after, a train from California pulled in, then another train from the East, carrying Easterners, more excursionists, and the 10th ward band from Salt Lake.

Beside the Central Pacific and the Union Pacific official parties and the newspapermen, there were representatives from Ogden and Salt Lake. There were very few women. I met Mr. C. R. Savage, who took several photographs of the celebration. Among the track gangs were many Chinamen and Mexicans.

It was a strange place for such a celebration. A dreary, desolate area of sagebrush and dwarf cedar, high above the blue waters of the Great Salt Lake, which stretched away to the south, while grey sand and grey sagebrush lay on every side of us. A little before noon, the officials and their parties gathered around the gap in the track, and soon after the last tie, which was a polished California laurel tie inscribed with a silver plate, was placed, several of the railroad officials each tossed a shovel full of earth upon it. Representing the Central Pacific Railroad, a gang of Chinamen carried the last Central Pacific rail to its place. Then a gang of Irishmen carried the last Union Pacific rail to its place. The bands played and everybody cheered wildly.

The two silver spikes from Nevada and Arizona were then driven in, and President L. Stanford of the Central Pacific grasped the silver-headed sledge and struck at the California Golden Spike. He missed it at its first blow, to the delight of the crowd. He then struck it on the second blow. Dr. T. C. Durant, vice president of the Union Pacific, also struck at it. He too missed the first blow, which greatly amused the crowd, especially the construction crews. General Dodge, too, had a swing at the spike. Then the telegraph operator signaled each blow—*click, click, click*—to the waiting world. The bands played. The crowd cheered themselves hoarse and the engines whistled and tooted. The long dreamed of transcontinental railroad had become a reality.

Ventures in Real Estate—On January 13, 1872, Fred Auerbach & Bros. and J. S. Barnes bought from Edwin B. Trowbridge, and others, 25 feet by 165 feet on Main Street for $15,000.00. Fred asked Mr. Barnes what profit he would take to sell him his half interest, and he replied, "$500.00." This was our first venture in city real estate.

A Loan for President Young—One morning early in 1872, Brigham Young came into the store. Fred and I were in the office. President Young said he had come to see us on a matter of finance, and asked if we could loan him $20,000 for fourteen days. We immediately replied we would be glad to do so, and after fourteen days, President Young repaid the loan. He offered to pay interest, but we refused to accept any interest. We did think it rather strange that President Young should borrow money from us, because he was reputed to be very wealthy and to have at all times great sums of cash on hand.

In 1875, we purchased one-half of the Trowbridge Building from David Day. In the spring of 1878, I made a trip to the Exposition at Paris and while there, stopped in London for several days. While there, I met Mr. Simon Bamberger, who was at the time financing some mining properties and a railroad in Sanpete. That same year, we opened a store at the mining camp of Silver Reef, Utah.

A Wedding—On Wednesday, December 16, 1879, I married Eveline Brooks. Mr. and Mrs. Brooks, Edgar Brooks and Fred Auerbach were present; also forty of the men employees of the Auerbach store. We were married in a little cottage, which stood in back of the Colonial Theatre. The house was beautifully decorated with flowers, which Fred ordered from San Francisco. We were married by Judge Emerson of Ogden.

Eveline wore a white satin dress having a plain waist with square neck, trimmed with duchess lace. The gown had long tight sleeves, fitted tight at the elbows and closed with four white buttons. The skirt was quite full, with four deep flounces and a long train, probably two yards in length. She had a veil of tulle, and a wreath of orange blossoms. The wedding dress, made by Mrs. Swenson, who was considered the best dressmaker in town, cost $30.00 for the making.

Outside of the family and employees, the following persons were present at the wedding: Joe Simons, M. Friedman, S. Friedman, H. Cohn, Alex Cohn, Charles Berry, Charles Ensign, Mr. Smith, Mr. Franke, Mr. Goblin, Mr. Gabriel, C. Madsen, Hyrum Pursons, C. Dunbar, Mr. Atkins, H. Barnett, S. J. Friedman, and E. Friedman. We had a lovely wedding supper and spent the first night at the Townsend House, at the corner of 1st West and 2nd South, that being the only first class hotel in Salt Lake.

More Real Estate—James Townsend in the 1850s was the owner of a piece of property on the east side of Temple Street, about 82-1/2 feet frontage by 15 rods depth. The property was known as "Townsend Row." Its north boundary was the center line of the block between 1st and 2nd South and it extended south from this line 82-1/2 feet. It was here that the well-known Townsend Hotel, or "Salt Lake House," was located.

On March 1, 1864, Townsend quit-claimed to Brigham Young Senior and Feramorz Little the north quarter of lot 4 and the west half of the north quarter of lot 3, block 70, plat A, being 5 rods by 15 rods, or 82-1/2 feet by 247-1/2 feet.

On June 13, 1883 the District Court of the Third Judicial District, Salt Lake County, gave a decree of partition to Feramorz Little for 43-3/4 feet on Main Street by 269-1/4 feet deep, which was the south portion of the Townsend property.

On April 25, 1887, Feramorz Little and his wife Rebecca E. Little conveyed this property by Warranty Deed to F. S. Auerbach and Samuel H. Auerbach, the property having a frontage of 43-3/4 feet and a depth of 269-1/4 feet, the consideration being $26,250.00.

COHNS' DRY GOODS CO.

Louis and Alexander Cohn, natives of Dobrzyn, Russian Poland, organized the firm of L & A Cohn in Salt Lake City in 1867. When Joseph D. Farmer drowned at Black Rock, the two brothers moved their business into Farmer's then vacant "One Price Store" at 55 East Temple Street. They renamed it the Cohn Dry Goods Company.[8]

Salt Lake Herald, Friday, Jan. 16, 1885

GREAT ANNUAL SALE!

At Cost!

AT

COHN BROTHERS.

THE LADIES' OPPORTUNITY TO BUY

Silks, Velvets, Plushes, Cloaks, Shawls, Hosiery, Dress Goods, Embroideries, Trimmings,

AT ENORMOUS REDUCTIONS!

Our stock is still very large, and according to our principles we never carry Goods from year to year, and the reduction made throughout our Entire Stock is **SIMPLY ENORMOUS.** Space will not permit us to enumerate everything, and we will only quote a few of the leading articles.

SILKS AND VELVETS

Everything in this Stock at Cost, without Reserve. Colored Velvets at $2, former price $2.75, and our Cheaper Quality at $1.50, reduced from $1.85. Plushes at $1.75 and $2.30, former prices, $2.25 and $4. The Reduction in Prices in our Line of Black Velvets is still greater. Brocade Velvets and Silks at **LESS THAN COST.**

Foreign Dress Goods, at Cost.

Ladies' Cloths and Tricots, at Cost.

Heavy Cloakings, at 50 c on the Dollar.

CLOAKS AND WRAPS

Everything in this Department will be Sold at a **GREAT SACRIFICE, REGARDLESS OF COST.**

FLANNELS AND BLANKETS AT COST!

Tremendous Bargains in our Attractive

WHITE GOODS STOCK,

Table Linens, Napkins and Towels. **EVERYTHING AT COST**

OUR LARGE ASSORTMENT OF

MERINO and **MUSLIN UNDERWEAR AT COST.**

HOSIERY, HOSIERY, HOSIERY, and WOOLEN GLOVES,

AT COST

Corsets, Corsets, Corsets, at Cost.

On this property we built the six-story Progress block. On December 14, 1905 Samuel H. Auerbach and his wife deeded one half interest in the above property to the Salt Lake Tribune Publishing Company, the consideration being given as $66,250.00.

By Association—I noticed that many people were eyeing us with great interest, and I later learned that a travelling man on the train had been pointing us out to the passengers as a Mormon with his third wife, en route to Chicago.

Bashful Eveline—While in Chicago, I bought some merchandise and shipped it to Salt Lake City. We stopped at the Palmer House, then a new hotel, and a very popular one. It was the first big hotel Eveline had ever seen, and she said it looked like a palace. She was particularly impressed by the immense dining room with its walls and high ceiling beautifully frescoed and decorated, and the large, ornate crystal chandeliers with their many gas lights.

Eveline was exceedingly bashful. We took our places at the table, and a colored waiter was placed back of each of our chairs. Eveline was dressed in a navy blue travelling dress, with a hat to match, a sealskin coat and diamond ear-drops which were quite the rage in throughout the west. Of course, the waiters could see that we were newly-weds, and they outdid themselves to give us every attention and service. Eveline was so bashful that she could not eat, and kept ordering one thing after another as a subterfuge to get rid of the waiter at her chair; but he simply passed the order to another waiter, who went to the kitchen for it, so that the waiter she wanted to get rid of, scarcely left her chair. After dinner, Eveline said she was hungry; so we went to a coffee place to get something to eat.

FROM TIE CAMP TO POLITICAL TIES

Simon Bamberger

Young Man in the West—I was born in Eberstadt, Hesse-Darmstadt on February 27, 1846.[1] My father was Emanuel Bamberger and my mother Helen Fleisch. The family had lived there for several generations. There were two daughters by his first wife and five more children by his second, my mother. The eldest was Herman; then came myself, Jacob, Setta, who became the wife of Louis Rothenberg, and the youngest, Louis.

I left home at the age of fourteen in the company of a cousin who had been earlier in America. Landing at Castle Garden and after a few days in New York, I set out for Cincinnati, Ohio, where I had two half-sisters. There were no through trains in those days and one had to know where to get off to change. I failed to change trains at Columbus, having fallen asleep, and so was carried on to Indianapolis instead. Fortunately, I had a cousin at the former city so stopped off there and worked in his store for a few months and then joined my brother, Herman, in his store at Wilmington, Ohio. I tended store while my brother Herman was a soldier in the Civil War, his duty being to guard bridges.

After the war, Herman and I went to St. Louis where we manufactured clothing. We sold considerable goods to a trader who was a contractor, following the Union Pacific Railroad as it was being built westward. This man was in our debt and, as money was scarce, I started West to collect it. I crossed the Missouri River on a ferry, as Council Bluffs, not Omaha, was the starting point of the new Union Pacific. That was in the year 1865. I followed the road as far as Piedmont, then in Utah but now somewhat inside Wyoming.

Looking for Opportunities—It was then a "tie camp" for the railroad and was typical of many such camps built as the railroad pushed westward. Both the life and the men were tough and primitive, but I managed to make my way till I heard, after several months, that the business in St. Louis had failed. Being alone and far away from home, I engaged in buying up "pay checks" of the workers and, by this means, accumulated quite a little money by re-discounting them. There was considerable gold-mining excitement in the vicinity and I saw an opportunity in

Lagoon fun house, 1923. (Courtesy of Utah State Historical Society)

erecting tents and "shacks," which readily rented. So I invested quite a little of my small fortune in these.[2]

Shortly, a great deal of Indian excitement developed and ultimately the Indians cleared out the whole settlement. It happened that Bolivar Roberts, who was later well known in Salt Lake, was also heavily interested in Piedmont and his description of Utah caused me to decide to go on west, as I had no other objective in view.

I went through Bryan, Wyoming to Ogden, a distance of 110 miles and stopped at the "Lester House," owned by a Mormon Bishop. It was run by Mr. and Mrs. Briner Cohen, who later moved to Salt Lake. I think this must have been about 1869, as Corinne was already established, the railroad being far west of the town and the town very small.

And Finding Them—Charles W. Penrose was very influential in Ogden and was very friendly to me. I bought a half interest in the hotel, but soon thereafter an epidemic of small pox broke out and Union Pacific passengers were not permitted to come up to the town, so I gave up. I

Fourth of July picnickers at Lagoon, 1931. (Courtesy of Utah State Historical Society)

took the Utah Central to Salt Lake and there bought the "Delmonico Hotel," which was on the southwest corner of Main Street and Second South streets, and renamed it the "White House," in partnership with B. Cohen of Ogden. West of the hotel was the home of Charles Popper, and further west was "Little's Row," built by Feramorz Little, once the mayor of Salt Lake.[3] At that time, the old "Salt Lake House," on Main Street between First and Second South, east side, was run by Captain Barratt; there were also the "Valleyhouse" and the "Townsend House."

Mining Interests—About 1872, I became interested in mining, first in the "Silver Mountain" mine, then in "Sailor Jack" mines in Tintic. My brothers, Jacob and then Herman and Louis came on, and I set them up in business. I became interested in the "Centennial Eureka" mine, along with Woodman, Chisholm, McCornick, and others.[4] This venture proved successful and made fortunes for all of us.

Building a Railroad—I then looked into some coal mines in Sanpete County and found that, to operate the mines, a railroad to Nephi, about forty miles away, was essential. In 1874, at the

Simon Bamberger, first Democrat and only Jewish governor of Utah. (Courtesy of Special Collections, Marriott Library, University of Utah)

suggestion of Mr. Maxwell, engineer of the "Flagstaff" mine, I went to England, raised a million dollars and built the railroad to Nephi; but the coal turned out to be of inferior quality, and the venture was a failure.

I then turned my attention to a project for building a railroad running north from Salt Lake and, about 1891, I obtained a franchise for a road from that point to Ogden. Work was started

EXCERPT FROM SIMON BAMBERGER'S INAUGURAL ADDRESS, JANUARY 1, 1917

It is indeed with great pride and satisfaction that I have taken the oath of office as Governor in the State where for so many years I have made my home, and to which I have become so attached, that it seems as though it is the only home I have ever had.

Although it is true that when I first set foot in Utah, I had already relinquished my former national ties and had taken the oath of allegiance to this glorious United States, yet it was here in the free and open, whole-hearted, broad-minded, generous West, and surrounded by the hospitable, home-loving people of this mountain empire that I learned the real message of America and became a true American citizen.

For forty-eight years I have lived and toiled here. I have traveled the State over from Cache Valley to St. George; from the Western deserts of Deep Creek to the Eastern limits of the Uintah Reservation. I have always met with the most cordial greetings and friendly welcomes, so typical of our Utah people with their intolerance of rank and caste, their distaste for sham and show, their desire for free thought, free speech, and religious toleration.

The West is coming into its own, and the eyes of the World are being turned upon it for guidance and inspiration. We should therefore take special care to so conduct our Government that we may win the admiration and confidence of all other States.

Twenty years ago the first Governor of this State was inaugurated. In that brief time what a remarkable development has occurred. What beautiful cities have been built; what industries have been completed; what resources have been developed; what magnificent structures erected.

. . . This valley lying before us, such a short while ago but a bare plain with here and there a little stream of water, along which a few willows and rushes, and here and there a clump of sage brush, has indeed been made "to blossom like the rose" and we can truly say, "This is the Place."

. . . I shall ever strive to be a Governor of the State of Utah, not Governor of any religious, social, racial or industrial faction, but Governor of a united people, desirous of obtaining a good, clean, honest, progressive, business-like administration.

Economy will be our Watchword, yet we will NOT allow our desires for economy to interfere with efficiency, but will always strive for the further improvement of the heritage of our great State, the broadening of her influence, the conserving of her energies, the development of her resources, and the enhancing of your glory.

. . . Fellow citizens, I thank you.[5]

SUPREME COUR

Governor Bamberger hearing concerns of farmers. (Courtesy of Special Collections, Marriott Library, University of Utah)

opposite

Simon Bamberger's inauguration day. (Courtesy of Special Collections, Marriott Library, University of Utah)

on Third West Street, opposite the Union Pacific depot, and the road was completed to Beck's Hot Springs. Shortly thereafter I built the "Lagoon."[6] The road was first run with steam locomotives when it was completed to Ogden, in 1908, but in 1910, it was electrified.

Political Life—I was on the School Board, first by appointment and then by election. I was elected to the State Senate while John C. Cutler was Governor. I, myself, was elected Governor of the State in 1916.[7]

GOVERNOR GIVEN MEED OF PRAISE

Jewish Society Gives Banquet at which Executive Divulges Political Views

Governor and Mrs. Bamberger were the guests of honor at the twenty-fifth anniversary of the founding of the B. F. Peixotto lodge of the Independent Order of B'nai Brith at the Hotel Utah last night.[8] The celebration of the founding of the lodge, together with the festivities in connection with the supper dance, brought together not only those of the later days of the organization, but a number of the charter members of the organization.

Governor Bamberger was given the toast, "The Jew in America," and after commenting upon the pride, which should come to the Jew who lives in the United States, he made an appeal to patriotic Americans. He reviewed the hardships through which he went before he made the goal to which he aspired and asserts that every man of his own creation should thank God that the United States was created.

Louis Marcus was the toastmaster of the evening and first introduced W. L. Jacobs, who spoke on the affairs of the organization.[9] E. K. Baer spoke on benevolence, Daniel Alexander addressed the diners on brother love, Simon Shapiro spoke on "Harmony," and Rabbi William Rice on "The Jew in Utah." Max Aaron addressed the diners on the work of the lodge and Moss Woolf gave a short address in which he dwelt on the most part on his acquaintance with Governor Bamberger, which has extended over forty years. He asserted that the state in choosing a governor could not have done better than to choose Governor Bamberger, who, he said, knew the needs of the poor.[10]

"ANNA GOT HER GUN"

Anna Rich Marks

She Was Not a Weak Woman—Born in Russian Poland on March 15, 1847, Anna Rich Marks was a woman of indomitable spirit and chutzpah. Running away from the constant threat of pogroms and breaking the bonds of poverty, Anna fled her native country when she was barely into her teens, promising never to be poor or powerless again. In 1862, she married Wolff Marks in London. The two of them emigrated to New York and journeyed to the Utah Territory around 1870. Bound to this new frontier and unrestrained by protocol, Anna found opportunities unheard of for women in the East. She was not a weak woman. She set her own goals, made her own decisions, and stood behind her words, albeit uttered with such blasphemies they were capable of shaking the recipients asunder.

A Folk Hero of Sorts—Anna and her husband engaged in business in Salt Lake City for several years and in 1880 moved to Eureka City in the Tintic mining district of Utah, sixty miles south of Salt Lake City. Whereas her husband was a quiet gentleman who ran the family store, Anna was active in pursuit of riches, hoping to make her fortune in land and mining ventures. One wonders if she made up her name. Anna was a very determined woman as the town folk of Eureka would soon learn. On October 25, 1963, Sam F. Elton wrote in the *Eureka Reporter:*

> In the early days of Tintic, two men, John O. Feckleston and Hyrum Gardner, claimed the land in the west end of Pinion Canyon. They opened the first road through Pinion Canyon. They placed a toll gate in the narrow part of the canyon charging a fee for all who entered.
>
> Jewish lady, Anna Marks and her husband, Wolff, hearing of the opportunities in Tintic, headed towards Pinion Canyon with their outfit. She was in the lead in a buggy followed by many wagons loaded with everything necessary to open a store. When she came to the gate, she refused to pay the toll. A verbal war was on, the air turning blue with Anna's cuss words. She summoned her bodyguard and with guns drawn they tore down the toll gate and went on to Eureka.

Anna Rich Marks (*left*) in Eureka, Utah. (Courtesy of the Tintic Mining Museum, Eureka)

Not stopping there, Anna took possession of a piece of land on the south side of the main road and opened her doors for business. Some of the townspeople believed her occupancy was a matter of taking and not legally procured. Elton reported:

> Her right to the ground was hotly contested by a man named Pat Shea. Many verbal arguments followed. Finally, she pulled her guns on Pat. He went flying and so did the bullets. He made it to a pile of posts. He wasn't hit, but she sure made the bark fly.
>
> From then on, no one crossed Anna Marks. Her husband was a pleasant, law-abiding man, and when any of the kids visited the store, they were always treated to a stick of horehound candy.

Riches—Anna owned controlling interests in two mines, the Anna Rich and the White Cloud. She invested money in diamonds, made a fortune in real estate in Eureka and Salt Lake City, and was known as a stubborn businesswoman with a penchant for foul language. In a dispute over boundary lines, she once held up at gunpoint the Denver and Rio Grand Railroad Building until they agreed to pay her price to cross her land.

In 1912, Anna died of a heart attack. Reporting on her death, the *Eureka Reporter* wrote, on April 26, 1912, that in "the early days of Eureka, Mrs. Marks became involved in much litigation, most of which resulted from disputes over the boundary lines of town lots and these suits, which were aired in the courts, are still fresh in the minds of many of the older residents of the camp." Interned, not to be forgotten, at the B'nai Israel Cemetery in Salt Lake City, Anna and her husband's headstone shows two hands touching.

A NEWHOUSE MONOGRAM

Samuel Newhouse

Son of Immigrants—Born in New York City in 1854, a son of Russian-Jewish immigrants, Samuel Newhouse began his career in law, but after an unsuccessful law practice in Pennsylvania, he headed west in search of opportunities and adventure. Landing in Leadville, Colorado, Newhouse established a freighting business and fell in love with a comely sixteen year old, Ida Stingley, who waited on tables at her mother's boardinghouse. After a brief courtship, Ida and Samuel married in 1883 and opened a hotel business.

On to Riches—One day, an English guest fell ill and was nursed back to health by Ida. Grateful for the care, this man became a friend and financial backer, providing for the first of Newhouse's entrepreneurial mining ventures. Samuel Newhouse, a flamboyant personality in the early mining days of the West, became one of the world's wealthiest men—exactly what the unrefined Mrs. Stingley had been seeking for her daughter.

Owning numerous mines in Colorado, Newhouse later sold them for millions of dollars. He set his sights on Denver where he became a speculator and a promoter, recognized in U.S. and British financial circles. He secured a tutor to teach his wife to speak properly and behave in the manner of European high society. She was an apt student, an Irishwoman fashioned with clothes and jewels that bespoke nobility. After Newhouse paid a notable Englishman to introduce her to the right people, Ida traveled frequently to Europe. She was presented at the Victorian court and, upon Queen Victoria's death in 1901, at the court of Edward VII. Easily picking up the nuances of royal society, Ida became an emissary for Newhouse and his interests.

His Own Town—When Newhouse turned his attention to Utah, he purchased the Highland Boy Property at Bingham Canyon. He then bought and developed the Cactus silver mine and mill on the western slope of the San Francisco Range. He built the nearby town of Newhouse in Beaver County to house miners and their families. Originally called Tent City, workers lived in tents and in covered wagons. Newhouse spent more than $2 million with investments from foreign stockholders and resurrected the town of Newhouse. Constructed of stone, brick, concrete, and tended fields, the company town housed forty-two two- and three-room cottages,

Newhouse Mill, Newhouse, Utah, 1908. (Courtesy of Utah State Historical Society)

thirty two-room houses, and two boardinghouses. Newhouse then built a school, park, restaurant, hospital, livery stable, several stores, and a company-owned and -operated hotel, dance hall, and the "Cactus Club" for entertainment. Free dancing was held every weekend, but the town of Newhouse outlawed a "red-light" district.[1]

The silver boom period lasted only five years before the Cactus mine gave out. The area then became the focus for cattlemen and sheep men, who built large sheepshearing pens. The town of Newhouse did make it into the motion pictures, and was the site for the film *Covered Wagon.* Nonetheless, it just as quickly became a ghost town.

Opulence—Newhouse's fortune continued to grow. He hobnobbed with the British royal court, and conceived and built the Flatiron Building in New York. He gained the first mineral rights in China, although he lost them during the Boxer Rebellion when foreigners were driven from the country in 1900. Newhouse had estates in Salt Lake City, London, and Long Island and a chateau in France. He and his wife led a spectacular social life. Their home on Brigham Street in Salt Lake City was an elegant colonial mansion. Entering a palatial foyer with Italian marble

Samuel Newhouse party at inauguration of first steam turbines in Utah. Front row *(l–r)*: Louis N. Kramer, Mary Moore, Samuel Newhouse, Ida Moore, George Moore, Charles Parsons, Lafeyette Hanchett. Behind Newhouse is A. J. Bettles. At extreme left is Roger Knox. (Courtesy of Utah State Historical Society)

floors, one was greeted by opulent Persian carpets, deep-piled stair carpets, and a winding staircase with copper railings. Salons were appointed with velvet upholsteries, red draperies, green silk tapestry, gold-framed paintings, stained-glass windows, and a bronze statuary. In the dining room, while sitting on high-backed chairs, guests dined at a large mahogany table. On the nearby mahogany credenza was a silver service and candelabra. Highly polished mahogany walls were separated by silk wall coverings illuminating the splendid green-onyx detailed fireplace. Two built-in cabinets displayed glass and stemware bearing the Newhouse monogram. The Newhouses hosted extravagant parties, and it was not uncommon for guests to eat the finest cuisine from solid gold plates.

Female guests would gather in the Palm Room where sheer green draperies, white-background wall coverings sprinkled with a green leaf design, and white wicker furniture upholstered in yellow and green material set a convivial atmosphere. This same room also concealed an electric button that released a trap door and exposed a stair ladder. Aided by rod and ropes, one would descend into an enormous and elaborate room containing a mahogany table, sitting chairs, and

The Newhouse Building (*at right*), on Main Street, Salt Lake City, 1917. (Courtesy of Utah State Historical Society)

opposite
Samuel Newhouse (*third from left*) at the University Club Roof Garden, Salt Lake City. (Courtesy of Utah State Historical Society)

a glassware cabinet. It also held at least thirteen hundred bottles of wine, an extensive collection of steins brought from Germany, and, in an adjacent room, innumerable bottles of imported liquors.[2]

Skyscrapers in Utah—In 1907, Newhouse financed the construction of the city's first skyscrapers. Initiating a city building project on Main Street, he built the Newhouse and Boston Buildings. Several years later, he built the Newhouse Hotel with a banquet room that replicated the Louis XV room at Versailles.[3] East of the skyscrapers, Newhouse donated land for the Salt Lake Stock Exchange and Commercial Club Buildings. Here on a short street named Exchange Place, Utah's stockholders, bankers, and mining kings held business, traded, and negotiated in the largest mining exchange in the United States. At the nearby Commercial Club, these same men would retire to negotiate, exchange news of the day, dine, and enjoy the athletic facilities. At night, the city's socialites would hold lavish parties in private quarters of the club.

Ebb and Wane—Newhouse developed thirty other structures throughout the city. Among his acquisitions, he purchased a slaughterhouse in the east section of Salt Lake City called Popper-

ton, previously owned by cattle baron Charles Popper and Jake Ornstein. But in the days prior to World War I, Samuel Newhouse could no longer obtain the loans he needed. He could secure neither enough financial help nor assurances from his friends. His financial fortunes began to unravel.

As a result, the Newhouses' opulent home on South Temple, worth millions, was sacrificed for seventy-five thousand dollars. The entire contents, including jewelry whose worth exceeded $1 million, was put on the auction block and bought by a New York firm. By 1914, Ida had spent so much time in Europe and away from Samuel that their marriage ended. Ida moved to California and lived in the Beverly Hills Hotel until she ran out of money. In 1937, she lived on the charity of friends and died in poverty.

Samuel Newhouse joined his sister at Marnes le Coquette, the French chateau he had bought for her. While he continued in the world of finance, Newhouse never could recoup his staggering losses. He no longer had the Midas touch. Newhouse died in France on September 22, 1930.

A PIONEER IN UNDERGROUND MINING MACHINERY

Joseph Rosenblatt

A Russian Past—I was born January 13, 1903, in Salt Lake City. My older brother, Simon, was fourteen years older than I.[1] My other brother Morris was twelve years older. No sisters. That my brothers were grown and out of the house while I was still a child, I, therefore, was an only child around my parents, which was a substantial advantage in many ways. It set habits and standards that molded my years all the time. I was not dependent upon outside activities. My mother, Tillie [Sheinbaum] used to love to turn on the phonograph and my father, Nathan, read extensively. As I've thought about it, he always sat in a very firm straight, upright chair and would sit for hours, reading.

They were self-educated, yes. My father's education was limited to that which was available to a youngster in a big industrial city in Russia called Brest-Litvosk. The only schooling that was open came through the Hebrew school. He was well versed in biblical stuff, if you please, but that was it. My mother was from the same city. She was bitter about it all her life, that education was denied to women, not only because that was part of Orthodox Judaism, but it was the way of life throughout that part of Europe. [She taught herself], but it was a struggle, a bitter struggle. While her father was educated and a successful businessman, there was no recognized or accepted responsibility to educate a girl child.

Let me divert a bit. All general business activities were forbidden to Jews except two: local transportation and lumbering or wood supply.[2] My mother came from a family that was a little bit above the average. Her father had a franchise for hauling and moving in the city. My father's family had a small mill and stocked and sold sized lumber.

Primitive Conditions—There was a condition, which affected the lives of many of the families in those years. There were no doctors, just neighborhood midwives. There was no medicine even remotely close to what we think of today. There was no sanitation. There was nothing which represented the equivalent of hospitals, so children were born in homes under almost primitive conditions. Not that that area was worse than any others, but it was a way of life in the 19th century and, of course, in previous years. Mothers frequently lost their lives giving birth to children. This happened both in my mother's family and in my father's family. [Both fathers remarried], but the trauma of being a stepchild of that kind of environment one had no concept of recreation or fun. So when my mother came to America, it was a matter of her father saying, "This is the situation." She was the first child, a girl. After that she had one sister, and then the mother died and a new family came in. The inevitable controversies drove her away. But just the very fact of living was so difficult it was all consuming.

For One's Own Good—My father came to America on his own. He would tell about when his father came to him one night and said, "Pack your things!" He pushed him out the door and said, "I don't know what's going to happen to you [by leaving]. I do know what will happen if you stay here. So maybe this is a chance." Dad was fourteen when he came.

My father would [later] say, "I can't tell you what it meant to come to this town as a kid. I didn't know any [English] language and I had to fight for everything and my total assets was one thin dime." I can't conceive that it was possible, but then you bring yourself to understand that there was a good deal of that, particularly in Utah. It was shortly after the Mormons had come with pushcarts, unbelievable disadvantages, so the struggle to live did something to the people. The need for work in order to live created an ethic of work that was highly respected in my own family and generally in the community.

A Ticket Out West—The ticket his father gave him was to Denver. He didn't even stop in New York. His father had given him a letter written to a man he had earlier helped to leave Russia and go to America. The family's name was Radinsky. The letter said, "This is my boy. If you can help him, I'll appreciate it."

In the beginning of the year 1880, the Radinsky family had nothing. Dad said, "It was a question of begging for food and it was obvious [having] another mouth to feed was just overwhelming. They couldn't know how to deal with it." So, through the remaining days of the early winter months, my father somehow got word that he might have a chance in a place called Salt Lake.

Meeting the Auerbachs—When he got to Salt Lake, it was May 1, 1880. He went to see Mr. Auerbach. Somebody had told him, "Go see Auerbach." There were three Auerbach brothers, one of them was a bachelor. Either out of pity or out of other motives, Auerbach—they then had the beginnings of their dry goods store, which later grew into a very large place—says, "I'll give you a pushcart and load it with stuff. You just go around town and sell it. I'll give you a piece of paper telling what to do, how much to ask, and so forth."

Overcoming Barriers—The Auerbachs were Germans, who hardly knew Yiddish, but for Dad, if language was a handicap, it was simply something he had to get over. He would say, "I don't like to talk about those years. There was no fun." He didn't live with the Auerbachs, no; just wherever there was a place to wrap a blanket around him. I don't know if he had outgrown the pushcart, but he made a success of the pushcart.

Remembering Russia—I remember his talking through the years of his hatred of Russia. There's no doubt in my mind. Anything about Russia that came known in the news or people would talk about, he would just not permit conversations concerning Russia in his presence. My parents spoke their own patched up English. Dad would remember Yiddish expressions, in which he was quite fluent. I never heard them speak Russian. Dad would have been opposed to that. And we never learned Yiddish. He was a very charitable man and a kind man. He always sent sums to his father and to relatives who later came along as members of the family that he had never known. He was a patriotic American. I never knew him to hear the "Star Spangled Banner" but what he cried. But he had no love for Russia.

Matchmaking—My mother came to the United States, really as a child. She used to tell me the horror of crossing the ocean in steerage. She would sit there with tears running down her face describing it: the constant nightmare left her with an intuitive fear of water.

My father didn't have any more ideas as to what this girl, that was being sent to be his wife, looked like or anything. He knew who her family was and remembered seeing her running around the neighborhood. Since her ticket was also for Denver, he met her there for the first time and they were married. Nine months after they met, my brother Simon was born. In Denver, things didn't go well; it was still a struggle. Shortly after Simon's birth, Dad said, "Let's go back to Salt Lake." That was in about 1884.

On to a New Life—Mother repeated often that when she got to Salt Lake, my father expected the maintenance of a kosher household. She says they would bring meat and poultry in from Denver, where that was the only source of people who knew how to treat food with the traditional certainty of kosher requirements. [Sometimes] it would arrive spoiled and she just declared, "No more! We will have a household like everybody else has and we will make our own requirements of cleanliness and sanitation."

Cleanliness was so ingrained in her thinking that she became a slave to it. An absolute slave. This big house that we lived in later years had to be dusted twice a day. The floors had to be polished every week. That was part of the requirement that I was subjected to. When you came home, you had these duties to take care of. You gave nothing else consideration until that was done. I don't remember it any other way.

The first house we lived in, on 8th South and State Street, was in front and the scrap yard was in the back. Mother, of course, was always telling us that she pitched in, but that kind of an arrangement was one that she was going to put an end to as soon as she could. In about 1907 or 1908, they moved to a new terrace that had been built upon 6th South and State Street by Mr. Thomas Kearns.[3] This house was only two blocks away from their scrap yard. After they moved, she purchased a pony and a little buggy. I remember when I first went to school, she took me by pony and wagon. In 1910 or 1911, we moved to a new, three-story house on 6th East and 3rd South. Mother hated it because it was so much to keep clean. Olga, dear Olga, always lived with us and helped her. Mother says, "Too much for her." But it was a beautiful house, a fun place to live. It's still there, cut up into three apartments, I think.

For years, Mother's allowance was twenty-five dollars a week, which was to supply the household with food and other necessities. When they got into the difficulties on the steel mill after the first war, she was the only one who had saved enough to help them out of the crisis. "Enough of this moaning and feeling sorry for yourselves," she said. "I've got this savings. Here it is."

Viewpoints—My mother was a strong character. In many ways, a rebel. My father built the first synagogue in Utah and she gave notice. She said to him, "When that synagogue is built, the traditional Orthodoxy of putting the women upstairs will not be observed in this building." And sure enough, when she gathered the few women, I think about eight of them, downstairs they came. They moved right in the back row of where my father sat and throughout the years, your Orthodox rabbis would come and they would say, "we can't stay here. You must change this." Mother made it very clear, she had enough clout in those years, "if you can't live with this kind of clear understanding of what religion means, you better pack your things, and get out."

When my father decided to build the synagogue, there was a shortage of money in those days, and he felt that they [members of the Jewish community] should go to the Mormon Church and ask for a contribution. In later years, I asked him, "Why did you send Mr. Shapiro to see the church presidency?" "Well," he says, "Shapiro has more chutzpah than I have. He likes that kind of thing and I hate it. And he got the contribution."[4]

Solo Flight—Circumstances were considerably better when I grew up. Even though Dad had a car, a Buick, I think, he did not drive a car and neither did Mother. They had the buggy and a sled. What great fun that was! In wintertime, snows were heavy in those years, and the three of us would get in the sled and go riding. I started driving the car when I was twelve years old. After school, I would always go home and do whatever driving he wanted me to do for him.

Home Life—My mother was a wonderful cook. My own wife, who has no skills in the kitchen, of which she is the first to admit, I'm sure tires all the time of my saying, "Ah, my mother's lemon pie!" [Laughs.] Or her roasted chicken! Those relatively simple activities constituted the foundation of a family: Sunday dinner, or the family getting together, or the assignment of tasks within the family's own organization.

My task was always to get up early, in the years when I was able to do that, and light the fire for the morning. I always had to take the tub from beneath the icebox and empty the water. The only method of heat for home furnaces was soft coal. And in the wintertime, Salt Lake was a fearful place because the whole air was filled with smoke. I remember when the wagon would come around with the coal supply to go into the basement, Mother would cover everything up with white sheets because the dust coming up would annoy her; it upset her. So, on the days when they would deliver coal, I would dread it because that meant that my mother was going to be demanding all kinds of extra cleaning.

Quarantine—We had a furnace in the basement. This reminds me of the kind of little event that stays with us when we have occasion to reminisce. As a little child of maybe four or five, six years, I caught measles. In those years, if you had measles or scarlet fever, they would plaster a sign on the outside of our house, which, in effect, meant you were quarantined. The remedy for measles was to put the child in a darkened room from which the sunlight was completely restricted, as sunlight was dangerous for eyes. I remember being put downstairs in the little den in the basement. The blinds were drawn and I stayed there alone for a couple of weeks.

My Father's Career—Around 1893, my father had, from his description, a large wagon with a team loaded with various and sundry things—machinery, some clothing, gloves—to sell to the mining work that was going on in Northern Idaho—Kellogg, Wallace, that whole lead and zinc belt up there. The trip from Salt Lake to Spokane, Washington [near the Idaho border] took him about four months. He'd make a couple of miles a day. Well, he succeeded in disposing of everything and was ready to come home. Then, the Pullman Panic came along.[5] As I recall it was a very, very difficult time in which the banks were closed. The towns were issuing scrip instead of money. So, my father was stuck up there and didn't get home until about a year later. I always remembered that from my mother's descriptions because it was very hard for her at home with the two boys. She said that she greeted him [not too kindly], when he came back, because on his way he had stopped at a place called Cache Valley, Logan, and scribbled in a note, "This is so beautiful, I just have to stop a day and enjoy it." She used to throw it at him for years later.

Family Business: Midvale Smelter and Rolling Mill, a Bitter Experience—Throughout Utah, wagons or even carloads would come in with scrap. Yards on 9th South and 4th West were huge piles of scrap. Somewhere around 1910, 1911, my Dad and two brothers bought a smelter in Midvale. It was part of what had been known as the Utah South Mines. The first year they had it, it was a big steel building with traveling cranes, they rented it to the contractor who was to supply stone for the capitol building. Then in 1913, Morris had the idea of building an iron and steel rolling mill as the best way to profitably use Dad's accumulation of scrap iron and steel.

Bundling the scrap, getting it hot, melting it, and then putting it through the rolls, [this process] produced iron (angled iron forms and mine rails, principally) and was a reasonably successful operation. When World War I came along in 1914, the demand for rolled steel products was immense. Morris got the idea that we would build what is known as the open-hearth furnace, a fifty-ton furnace, and they were really pouring stuff out of there, three thousand tons a month. But when the war was over in 1918, there was no provision on the part of the government for what later we knew as reconstruction finance, etc. All the orders were cancelled, and that created a great crisis in the family. The open-hearth furnace was built on borrowed money, and Dad had accumulated excess quantities of scrap.

The closing of the Midvale operations was a bitter experience for my father and my brothers. They ended up with debts that were company debts he couldn't pay. Simon's company, the

American Foundry and Machine Company, was a separate entity, yes, but everything else went down the drain.

I remember part of it so well. I was fourteen or fifteen years old at the time. I did the driving for my father. Then, on weekends, I would go down and work in the plant, in the office and in the mills. The value to me was that as a companion to my father, I was the listening post for all of his worries and doubts and plans. So my thinking was entirely controlled in those years by a participation in the activities that the family was going through, much beyond what normally would be available to a youngster growing up.

I remember my father making a declaration to himself and to Mother that it would not be possible for him to live with his head up until all of those debts had been paid. It took him, I think, close to ten years, but the great joy was that he would say, "I'm going to buy a new suit and a hat because today I can walk down the street. I don't owe anybody anything."

Bird of Paradise—Every two years, my father would go to the tailor and buy himself three suits of clothing. My mother was very fussy about her appearance. I used to take her shopping when I'd get home from school or on Saturdays. Her clothes were ready-made. I remember taking her to a millinery store, which in those years was important, the Paris Millinery store. She fell in love with a hat that had a bird-of-paradise on it. She paid seventy-five dollars for that hat. She was horrified; my father was horrified.

High School Days, College, and Some Trauma—During the later years of World War I, the ROTC [Reserve Officers' Training Corps] had just started in high school.[6] I was the captain of the adjutant of the ROTC, if you please. Our drill days were Monday, Wednesday, and Friday. Mother thoroughly enjoyed it. She took me to a tailor and he made me a magnificent whipcord officer's uniform. I got a beautiful nickel-plated sword, so that on drill days I was really all dressed up. As for buying the sword at a time when money was an issue, mother would have nothing to interfere with that kind of success.

I went to East High School. It was a beautiful new building, opened in the year 1916, and I went to Stanford University in 1921. I remember very well the train ride; first time I had been on a train by myself. As I recall I was very excited with the ferry ride from Oakland to San Francisco and getting on the train in San Francisco to go to Palo Alto, and being over-awed with the drive up the University Avenue to Stanford, and seeing old Encina, where the freshmen stayed.

I got sick right away, had difficulty breathing. I remember being frightened at the idea, being in a strange place, nobody knew me, and going to see a doctor somewhere around the school. He took a quick look at me and said, "You've got asthma. You better get out of here." So I went home. I wasn't sure really but that there wasn't more joy about the fact that I had come home, than there was disappointment.

I recovered when I got home. But Dad said, "I think you ought to give it another try. Seems you're in perfect shape to me." So after Christmas, off I went again and the same thing happened. I returned home and went to the University of Utah and law school.

At the Shop—In the summers, I worked mostly at the machine shop because the business had turned itself around. I knew by my second and third year of law that I was not going to practice, but I enjoyed it, but when that was done, in 1926, that was it. I packed it all up and gave the books away.

Eastern Iron and Metal Company (EIMCO)—My father said, "Look, here it is. Here's this little thing called Eastern Iron and Metal. It's yours, go ahead and see what you can do with it." Dad had bought it maybe ten years earlier but it was just more or less neglected. This was machinery, second-hand machinery, exclusively mining items. We bought it and repaired it to its totally operable condition, advertised it, and sold it. There were things like pneumatic drills and ore cars for the underground, but the principle items were metallurgical, the equipment for recovering metals: crushers, ball mills, concentrating tables, pumps and a variety of other items in those categories.

The state of the minerals industry was recovering very well. In the days from about 1910 and beyond through the end of the war, too, mineral industries in Utah were at their prime production. The copper and the lead and the zinc in Bingham and Lark. Of course, the silver in Park City. Some mining operations in Southern Utah, well, the whole state, and both southern and the panhandle of Idaho.

Salt Lake, with its concentration in those areas, attracted geologists and metallurgists and people who are the backbone of the mining industry. Many of the essential items of machinery that made the metallurgical recoveries possible were invented in Salt Lake and because of the position of American Foundry and Machine, they built the pilot models of most of the machinery that was created. That became a source of general information and knowledge that encouraged the diversification at EIMCO in later years. But the first big effort was the one that was undertaken at Ray, Arizona at the end of 1927 and the beginning of 1928, when we bought the Arizona Hercules [owned by Kennecott], which was then a property adjoining the big Ray Mines operation.

A Risky Venture—We paid eighty-five thousand dollars. It was a substantial investment. My father felt it was a little risky, but he thought it was worth the gamble. It was enormously difficult for me, because the family said, "Okay. Out you go. You're going down to Ray, Arizona, and take this job on." Eighty miles south and east, as I remember, from Phoenix, the last twenty-five miles were tough going over the mountains and over the roads that had been dug out for single wagons, originally. It was really the first venture for me away from home, so that I found immediately that I was required to do things for myself that had always never been thought about. Simple things. Having a clean place in which to live. Bed linens and towels and clothing to be kept in shape.

The arrangement with the Kennecott people was that we would have a couple of rooms available in their boarding houses. Or else, they had a cottage, which they turned over to me, which was the most lonesome. I had never encountered temperatures like I walked into at Ray, Arizona. It was in the summer, and the advice that I got from people around was that the only way to get to sleep was to take a sheet, put it into the cold water, get it wet, throw it over you and if you could fall asleep before that sheet dried, you were in pretty good shape. [Laughs.]

Snakes in the Grass—The other thing that bothered me was the abundance of snakes around the place. Rattlesnakes and sidewinders. One of the fellows over at the Kennecott office said, "Digging around all that old stuff over at Arizona Hercules, the big thing that you need is a terrier dog. Get yourself a terrier dog and that will take care of the snakes." I did. When you'd see this little terrier grab a snake by the back of its neck and shake the life out of it, you wouldn't dare move. You wouldn't go into a shack, either, without being extremely careful to have the dog with you.

Along That Time, an "Interesting Happening"—The mill, which had run for a long enough period, had accumulated a lot of concentrates in various places around the mill, under the stairs, and around some of the filters. Word got to Mr. Smith, who was the general manager for Kennecott, that we were looking to see if there was going to be any cleanup. He said, "Young man, I just want to tell you not to waste your time, because we have swept that place thoroughly. There's nothing there. Don't waste your time or money."

That was passed off and nothing more was said. But as we started working there, it became apparent to me that that was not such a good cleanup job. We started taking machines out and very carefully cleaning up all of the concentrate that we found. I went over to see Smith after a few months. I said, "By the way, we're finding a few pounds of concentrates that we regard as valuable cleanup." He sat up on the edge of his chair and the first thing he did was offer me a cigar. [Laughs.] I took it.

I was a little worried about [our discovery] because Smith might feel he had a claim on it. When I had enough so that it could be shipped, instead of shipping it six miles away to the smelter at Hayden, where the Ray concentrates were shipped, I got a railroad car and shipped it to Superior, which belonged to Magma. The long and short of it is, it went through the smelter and it yielded $14,000, which in the 1920s was a big chunk of money. It was a windfall. Of course, Smith was concerned it might reflect on his responsibilities and reputation. But that was the end of it. I sent the check home. Everyone was delighted and it was fun.

Sale to Lead Zinc Company of Metalline Falls, Washington—The most interesting sale was to the people who made the decision to build the Metalline Falls plant. They called themselves Lead Zinc. We had the opportunity of selling them buildings from the Ray Mine that could be used to house their mill in northern Washington where they had an abundance of snow and everything. To come home and get the drawings made for some of the layouts that we were committed to build was a big job, a tremendous job. When the people of Metalline didn't see how they were going to go through the job of moving it to northern Washington, that's when we said, "We'll do it."

Taking apart a huge, old operation that consisted of all the things necessary for a mining and milling operation was a serious challenge. Today, you'd get a mobile crane and you'd get in there and it would be rather simple. Things of that type were not available. In many cases, they had just not been designed or built. So the task of going into a mill and picking up a great ball mill that had a total weight of maybe fifteen or twenty tons and moving it—you didn't do it quickly but you did it safely. We even had to rig up a way to pull the power lines out of the shaft because they were heavily covered copper wire.

Well, I spent most of my time for about two years, but we built the mill. In terms of the kind of dollars that we think about now, it was nothing. But it covered the total cost and a reasonable profit, not only for the machines themselves, but also for the work of construction that was done.

Diversification—That job became the basis of the decision to diversify and move from second-hand equipment only into the building of new equipment. For example, in 1935, we started to design and build our own filters. We had American Foundry and Machine that was my brother Simon's. Morris was over the fabricating shop, where you take rolled steel products that you buy from steel mills around the country and make buildings and bridges. That was Structural Steel and Forge Company. The company of EIMCO did not become EIMCO until the early '30s. I've forgotten the exact date but we were sitting around one day at lunch and I said, "This Eastern Iron and Metal business is no good, it's not descriptive of anything that I'm doing now." One of the fellows said, "Why not just call it EIMCO?" I said, "All right, let's settle for that." So the whole operation became EIMCO after the acquisition of the mucking machine patents from Finlay and Royle.

The Finlay-Royle Loader, a.k.a. the Mucking Machine—The mucking machine was the beginning of a total change in our method of operation. The construction of mine plants was pretty well finished. I think the last plant I built, a gold mill, was over at a little town, near Lead [South Dakota]. The mucking machine was developed at Eureka, at the North Lily mines, an area where they felt they could expect to get some gold production. To save money, the pressure was on Mr. Finlay, who was in charge of the job. Mr. Royle was the hoistman who got the idea of the rocker shovel, the rocker arm. The principle was that you could crowd your bucket into the muckpile while you were lifting it up, so that it was like the human movement of pushing with your shovel point with your leg and your arms lifting it up. The mucking machine would pick up a load in the bucket, and then deposit it overhead in very limited headroom. This meant, instead of driving a drift or a tunnel eight feet by eight feet, the size needed for a human being to dig into a hard muck pile and to deposit it, the area cut down in size. This enabled them to get more total footage within a limited space and budget.

After seeing it, we started the process of convincing Finlay and Royle and Anaconda that we were the logical place for them to call home. We built hundreds of those. The original, the smallest, was known as Model 11, determined by the horsepower of the motor. They were Ingersoll-Rand motors until about 1944. That's when I decided we'd make our own motors. We built a plant and designed the motors. From then on, we were the best builders in the country of that air motor. After working out the patent and completing the contracts with Anaconda and with Finlay and Royle, we lived happily together for seventeen years under the patent.

Broadening Horizons—Our first machines were sold to the gold mines in Canada and then all over the world. The Philippines was a tremendous market for us not only for the loaders but for all the things we were then making. When we got to South Africa, the attraction was that we were able to take these young men out of the bush who were as primitive as it is possible to imagine, no education, no language, and we were able to take those young men and teach them how to run that EIMCO-Finlay Loader. After World War II, we started to manufacture in the coal mines of Leeds.

In those early years, in effect, I put the loader on my back and went around to the gold mines. As business moved out, we developed the idea of working through the mails and working through telephones and telegrams and telexes. We had our own advertising department. We built up our own print shops. We had, at one time, one of the biggest and the best print shops in town with all kinds of color presses, and we printed our own bulletins, parts lists, and instruction books.

We did this in many languages, with translations. German, Italian, and Japanese, which was very difficult, but we did it. We had all that under our own control. Yes, we became one of Utah's largest employers. We didn't exceed people like Kennecott, but in terms of manufacturing we were the largest employer for many years right here in the city. Then, of course, over the years, we moved into broader lines, and into other countries like Israel, South America, Mexico. We continued to grow.

A 1934 Experience—At that moment, I didn't need to expand my operations, but I felt that was the time to make my connections so that as I went along and the needs became more pressing, [I could] expect a line of credit. When I went to New York in 1934 I explained the situation to Fred Searls, my best friend in those years.

He put on his little cap and says, "Well, let's start with the best." Crossing the street, we went to J. P. Morgan, on the corner of Broad and Wall. It's a magnificent building. It had a huge vaulted ceiling with beautiful décor, and all the partners' desks were lined up in a row.

As you walked in the entry, three tall, husky men stood there waiting to see who you were and what in heaven's name were you doing there. Mr. Searls said we had an appointment that he made with Mr. Anderson. So in we went. That was a very crucial experience for me because I had never encountered that kind of a necessity to be sophisticated in dealing with that sort of an environment. And mind you, in my mind what I had was an immense amount of money, seventy-five thousand dollars of extra cash. My statement was a good, sound endorsement of the company. I didn't owe anybody anything.

They were quite understanding. I made it plain I intended to keep the plant in Salt Lake City. That was my home. That's where we lived. That's where we worked. That's where the mining industry was in those years. Utah was the center of mining in the United States in the 1920s, and that I needed references. At times when we were soliciting business in other areas of the country, I needed to say, "Our bank is J. P. Morgan." You couldn't do better than that.

Well, we talked at some length and Mr. Anderson said, "We'll let you know." We left, and I never heard a word from them for about three or four months. Then came a letter, which said, "We have completed our investigation and we are pleased to tell you that we will take your account." It came as a very exciting event not for the economics that were involved, but what it did for my confidence.

Speaking of this, some years later in France, we were going to expand our plant and needed some financing. There, too, I wanted the French people and our people to have associations that could always be helpful. My mother always drummed in, "Be careful of the people you associate with. If you associate with bad people, you're going to get into trouble. So always make sure that you're with good people." In France, it was known as *Morgan et Cie.* Their banking quarters were in a palace or villa that belonged to one of Louis XIV's brothers. A magnificent place.

Well, we walked in and I was overwhelmed with the beauty of it. My appointment was with Mr. Pierre Jay, the manager of Morgan's in France. In his room, a magnificent room, he could see I was a little nervous and edgy, uncomfortable. He reached over, pushed himself forward in his chair, looked at me, and said, "Rosenblatt, relax. I come from Kansas." We got along very nicely.

Revisiting Tillie—As I said my mother was a tyrant in her demand for cleanliness. I can remember when the first vacuum cleaner was a manual one. You created the vacuum by pumping up and down, and Mother said, "This ought to do for getting dirt out of these carpets that I can't do with a sweeper."

When we moved out of the house, which she hated because it was so hard to keep clean, we moved into an apartment on 13th East. We lived on the second floor. Someone moved into the first floor. After they had been there for a couple of months, Mother thought she saw a cockroach and she was furious. She pulls herself up and goes downstairs and she just lays into that lady. It was a scandal. That was the end; the place was cleaned up.

As for keeping kosher, she said, "It was good a couple of thousand years ago. It doesn't mean that it makes any sense now. I will have one compromise with you. On the Passover holiday, I will turn this into as kosher a house as you will want to see." That was done as long as she lived. The Passover week was celebrated with all the family in attendance.

She insisted the family be there for all meals or, if they were going to eat at home, they had to take the unleavened bread, the matzos, home with them. Otherwise, everybody was eating in her house. As the family grew, it became a wonderful means of gathering. Dad would recite some of the prayers and her food was just wonderful. She was a great cook, a great baker, a master of her kitchen and her pastries, and very demanding if anybody else was there. You had to do it her way or else.

My mother was a snob. Her grandchildren, like Esther [Landa] and Barbara [Burnett], called her a tyrant and a snob. That was a reasonable description. She was both. She was also very much concerned about the families and the connections in which my brothers had married, and the women-wives coming without training, without knowing what to do in the kitchen. They lived close by and she would undertake to go over in the morning and teach them [housekeeping]. So you can imagine the kind of conflicts, but before a very long time went by, her goal was achieved.

My mother struggled to teach herself, but she had no feeling whatever for Orthodoxy or anything that was a part of a religion that was dependent upon traditions and history. She would say to Dad, "Ten Commandments is enough for any intelligent person."

He would say, "Well, when the Messiah comes, the yoke will be off man's back. There will be answers, and cruelty and persecution will stop." She would say, "You men are crazy. There is no Messiah. You say that the Messiah is yet to come and your Christian friends say that he's been here. The truth is you're both wrong. There is nobody like that. You just created a figure."

My Father—He was a wonderfully kind man, my father. He stayed away from any kind of publicity. He was shocked by publicity, and he was afraid of it. When you realize in Russia, any record in writing that was kept became a self-destroying document. When the army came around looking for boys to take into the army, or during the pogroms, when they looked around for people or businesses to destroy, *no* record was much safer than *any* record. So Dad didn't like to keep family records or anything. He kept away from it.

But my father would take the occasion of holidays, like the Passover or the Day of Atonement. We would gather together after the services and he would read a passage about Isaiah. He would say, "What Isaiah tells you is that prayer and fasting and observance won't get you atonement. What you have to do if you want to have atonement is to know that you have to help the poor; you have to cure the sick. In this day and age, it has a broader meaning. It means using your head to relieve the kind of conditions that breed sorrow and disproportionate treatment. You have to know that a thing like freedom has to be protected. You have to be willing and concerned not about your privileges all the time, but to worry about meeting your obligations." That was the way he thought. That's the way he worked. And that's what he wanted his family to do, to live by. He always said, "You know, I never turn anybody down who asks for help. I would rather make a mistake in giving than turn someone who needs it down." And that's what he did.

Changes—The holidays of Yom Kippur, the Day of Atonement, my father felt he should do what his father used to do. They would walk on that day to the synagogue. They wouldn't dare ride. They wouldn't use the telephone. He would take Mother and they would go down to the hotel and rent a room for the night so they wouldn't have to walk far.

When we moved out of the big house and into the apartment, Mother said, "It has nothing to do with religion. It's a different day and age." So she said, "We're going to ride." We had a car

Lou Burnett Jr., Joe Rosenblatt, and Simon Rosenblatt (*l–r*). (Courtesy of Esther Landa)

then, a good car. "You'll take us," she said. "You can let us off a half a block before the synagogue so we're not going to be embarrassed by anybody seeing you falling away from [tradition]."

The first time we did that, lo and behold, on the way home after services, we got a flat tire. What a crisis! Mother in her practical way said, "Don't be silly. Get out there and change the tire and let's go." Dad was fretting and stewing, but they didn't take a hotel room after that. They stayed at home and used the car.

FOUR

Turn-of-the-Century Arrivals

FOR LOVE OF YIDDISH

Abe B. Cline

A Hebrew Education—My father, Hyman [or "Hotchka" in Yiddish], was born in the large city of Nishtat in the country of Lithuania.[1] He was a child when he left there. My grandfather, who was an intensely religious man, would go to Germany, I guess, every winter and tutor children in a wealthy family. Later, he moved his family to England. From what I learned from my father and others who knew him, my grandfather was a highly respected man because of his learning and his intense religiousness. The making of a living, though, is something that was a by-product for him. My Dad was telling me that one time my grandfather sold books. I asked him how did he do? Not very well, because the only books he would sell were religious books and nobody wanted to buy any. Practicing his religion was the main object. One of his boyhood chums said he was so highly respected they always mentioned his name in a whisper. He and my grandmother are both buried in the Holy Land.

Only one of my grandfather's sons followed in his footsteps. Dad was probably the most non-religious one, but he was intensely Jewish! He loved to talk Yiddish. He was educated in Hebrew and, having come over from England, spoke English with an English accent. My father never went to school for any length of time, but I would say he was a mechanical genius, a builder.

Knife Edges and Bone Carvings—Dad was the first one of five brothers that came over to America. First to New York; everybody came in through Ellis Island, then to Philadelphia where he peddled. While he knew the language all right, he got some notion that they [immigrant Jews] peddled in those days, so he went out into the country, walking and calling on farm houses, selling pins and needles and thread and stuff. Of course, he was never any good in business, and calling on people and urging them to buy stuff was not to his liking. So he went to a barber school, graduated, and from there found work at the best hotel barbershop in Philadelphia, which was unusual, but if you knew him, you know how well he could do things.

When he was twelve years old in Lithuania, Dad apprenticed in a home where they had a business of bone carving. They carved bones to make handles for knives. He hadn't been there but a short time before they discovered he could sharpen their knives like nobody else. In Philadelphia, they went around making bets, saying there's a kid out of barber college that can hold a razor better than any experienced barber! He just had a genius for putting an edge on something; he was so good you could shave with one of his kitchen knives.

Footloose and Fancy—I'm not sure why my father came to Salt Lake City, except that he was free and footloose and the West appealed to him. The first time he came, he opened up a barbershop but, for some reason, he moved to Butte, Montana, which was a mining camp town, and then back to the Chicago area, where he married and opened another barbershop. It was then that he started having trouble with his feet, getting sores on his toes and an almost gangrene-like condition setting in. He healed, but as a barber, he couldn't stand on his feet long enough, so he had to look at another occupation. He learned to become a cigar maker; and if you knew my father, in a very short time, he became a very special cigar maker.

Stripping Tobacco—Dad returned to Utah and I was born in 1895. When I was a year old, he went back to Chicago. I don't know why he went back and forth except he was always in search of some way to make a better living. No matter how painful things were physically for him, there was no such thing as a lazy bone in my father. He wanted to work as long as he could. When I was four or five years old, he came back to Salt Lake City, worked for a fellow in a west-side factory-home making cigars. When I was about eleven, we moved again. This time to Blackfoot, Idaho where Dad started his own cigar factory. His equipment consisted of a few tools for making cigars. To prepare tobacco for cigars, you have to strip the big stem out of the leaves. This is a job usually done by women and children because it requires a small hand to do it properly. I used to strip the leaves. I was hired to strip tobacco for fifty cents a day. It doesn't sound like very much, but in those days, you could hire a man to work in the field for fifty cents a day. I was probably the only person in southern Idaho who knew how to strip tobacco. I would work six, eight, ten hours a day, sitting there and stripping tobacco while my Dad was making cigars.

At one point, my Dad, because he was not a good businessman, sold the business to another gentleman, Abe Mishkind, and worked for him. Later, the two of them opened up a haberdashery store in Boise. They both worked at it but the business didn't work. The two of them would sit in the shop and play chess. A customer would come in and he'd have to wait until one or the other made a move. Then they would take care of their customers! They sold the business in 1910.

When we lived in Boise, Idaho, I remember they had a very small Reform Temple. Come High Holidays, the junk peddlers—all Eastern European Jews—wanted to hold services. Since my Dad had a tremendously retentive memory, he became the Rabbi! When I turned thirteen, my brother and I had to stay there in order to make the minyan. Without us, they didn't have a minyan. Of course, we were still kids, so they watched us with an eagle eye because we wanted to go out and play ball.

Haggadah by Memory—Now to give you an idea of what a memory my father had. Ben Roe and I are very good friends, and our families used to have seders together.[2] One year, I decided we were going to have a real Orthodox seder; everything in the *Haggadah* would be read in Hebrew. Of course the only ones who could read Hebrew were my Dad and Ben Roe. My Dad's eyesight was so bad, he couldn't see to read, so he said he would recite from memory. Since this seder took place on a Friday night, my Dad had to read a passage said only on that day. Ben said, "You better let me read this because you won't be able to remember this after so many years." And Dad replied, "Who can't say it?" and rattled it off letter perfect.

I told you my father loved to talk Yiddish and he loved to tell stories, especially Yiddish stories. When we moved back to Salt Lake, my Dad opened one store on 1st South between 5th and 6th East. That didn't work out and so he opened up another one on 2nd South between 6th and 7th East. It was a little store, he ran it by himself, and we were able to get by. People would come in, even young fellows, to listen to his tales. A lot of Jewish families lived in that neighborhood then. You might call it a little ghetto, except these are not ghetto homes. These were Jewish homes and every one of them was immaculate and inside each one was a woman proud of her house.

Jewish Cooks—My mother had three kids and she was one of those meticulous housekeepers who had to have everything just exactly right. She had a reputation, even among Jewish women, for being a wonderful housekeeper and an excellent cook. She used to do with very little money and she turned out gourmet meals. Her cooking was Jewish, of course. She never read a cookbook in her life. She couldn't give my wife a recipe because she would say, "You put in a little of this, a little of that in there." "How much?" my wife would ask. "Oh, just the right amount."

My mother didn't just get one fish to make gefilte fish, she had to get two or three different kinds of fish to blend together to taste just right. There was a time when we had a kosher butcher and she would make stews. Her veal stew was just out of this world.

My mother was from a small village in Lithuania. Her parents died when she was young and so she was raised by an older sister. This is at a time when Jewish girls never went to school, yet, my mother could read and write Yiddish and Slavic when most women couldn't. She learned to read English. When my mother was trying to be more religious, my father went along without believing it at all.

The Healing Process—When the doctors amputated my father's legs—they got so bad gangrene-like symptoms began—he walked on two artificial legs and used two canes. He could never rid himself of the pain but he still kept his sense of humor, could always tell a story, and never complained. Neither did my mother. She was bitter about a lot of things; it's true, there was no money, no security, no financial security. But she believed his amputations were God's verdict. "*Bashert.*" Do you know what that means? It's fate, she would say.

A Change in Course—In those days, there was no such thing as welfare. And if there had been, my father would never have accepted it. I stopped going to school and started working when I was fourteen years old. Oh, I registered for high school. I wanted a classical course. I was interested in reading. I would read anything I could get ahold of. I was interested in knowledge. I was not interested in becoming a bookkeeper. But my uncle said if I took a classical course, I would have some knowledge but no knowledge that I could sell, unless I went to college. And the idea of going to college in those days was unheard of. They decided I should take a commercial course. I said I wouldn't and I didn't. So I didn't go to school. Of course, looking at it right now, it was the entirely wrong thing to do.

So I went to work. Sometimes I'd work seven days a week and on Saturdays 'til ten or eleven o'clock at night. There was no such thing as time and a half, but we never felt abused. We contributed to the household; if I made six dollars, I'd give my mother five. Not because they demanded it of me, but because I was going to be independent. I worked in other stores in merchandising. What can a fourteen-year-old kid do? Mop up the floor, wash the windows. And sell. The trick in those days was when somebody came in to buy a handkerchief, you're supposed to sell him a suit. Well, I couldn't do that. I could sell him a handkerchief, and I would try to sell him the best kind of handkerchief, but a pair of shoes or a suit from a handkerchief? I wasn't any good at that!

The Orthodox Way of Selling—There were gangs in those days, sure, but they were groups of boys who gathered together for fun. If there was a fight—and I myself got into very few fights—there was a feeling you had to fight fair. Now, I remember the West Colfax boys, like Charlie McGillis and his brother.[3] Tough. Real tough. They came from Denver and they were in business where you were either tough or you didn't stay in business very long. Charlie was a distributor for the newspaper, the *Salt Lake Telegram.* There was tremendous rivalry between newspapers here in Salt Lake for street sales and advertising and the newspaper brought him in because he was tough, a scrapper. He wouldn't let anybody take his kids' corners.

I was one of them. There were quite a few kids out on the street then. We never read the paper, but they would tell us what we should yell. Not the headlines, generally. They were smart

The newsboys' Thanksgiving Parade. (Courtesy of Cal McGillis)

enough to know people were really interested in the local stuff. So whatever they wanted us to yell, we would yell. We were a noisy bunch. And we would move around. If you stood in one corner, in one spot and yelled, it didn't do you any good. Anytime you saw a man walking by, you had to go over to him, yell and wave the paper at him. That was the orthodox way of selling papers.

Youthful Spirit—When we were kids, in the winter, we went tobogganing. I never owned a sled, but somebody else did. We would go on up to the top of South East Temple, we called it Brigham Street then, and we'd coast clear down as far as we could, which was generally about 5th East, walk back up there, dragging the slides and coast down again.

I was always very physically active. I did a lot of walking. I had a lot of jobs in little stores and I used to work at a Jewish store. Can't think of the name of it, something like Eastern Patterns. My cousin and best friend, Abe Cline, was going to the University but he worked on Saturdays, too, so afterwards, he'd meet me at the shop. We didn't have any automobiles in those days. We'd change to hiking clothes in the store, take the streetcar to Holladay and then hike up into the canyon all night. In the morning, the sun would get so it's warm enough and we'd lie down generally in the shade of the trees and sleep for a couple of hours. Of course, we had something to eat with us there. Then we'd hike back. One time we hiked all night and day. We went 32 miles, from 4200 feet in altitude to 9600 feet in height. It took us 12 hours and 40 minutes. It was an adventure to hike all night.

In those days there was no such thing as fear of anybody bothering you either in town or out of town. That was unheard of. I walked all over Salt Lake City. And if you had a date with a girl who lived way out in the country there and it was after midnight, why, you'd have to walk her home. That's what we did. So going on an all-night hike was okay. We were already conditioned for it.

Enlisting Together—In 1916, Abe, we called him "Doc" even when we were kids because we knew he was going to become a doctor, and I joined the National Guard. I wasn't twenty-one years old then, so I had to get my mother's signature, which was easy because she didn't know what she was signing. When she did understand, she threatened to go to the Governor, Simon Bamberger, and get me kicked out. I said if she did that she would probably never see me again. She knew I was stubborn, so she let me go. We went down together, down to Arizona. We were going to catch Pancho Villa who was shooting up some American towns. The following June we were mustered back into service and before World War I ended, we were in France.

Now, I'll tell you. Abe and I were both Abe Clines in one company and our records would get all balled up, so I decided to take the initial B to avoid confusion. Why did I pick B? What does it stand for? Nothing. Just "B." Abe B. Cline. (Of course, if you could find my birth certificate, which you can't, my last name would be Klein. But my father, who was as stubborn as I was, decided that Cline was the correct American spelling.)

We were always together, Abe and I. In 1918, he was commissioned a Second Lieutenant and as an officer could ride first class. As an enlisted man, I had to ride second class. But you couldn't separate us even then. Once I got in the first class car with him and an MP came along and looked at our orders with all our names on there: First Lieutenant A. Cline and Sgt. A. B. Cline. He asked, "Are you brothers?" We said, "Yes." "Well," he says, "I'm sorry, you can't ride first class." As an enlisted man, I had to ride second class. So he kicked me off at this end [of the car] and I went around the other end and got back on because by this time he was out of the train. This was the way we operated then. All the time.

Business and Fly-Fishing—Coming back from the army, I was unsettled. I didn't want to go back into the kind of job I had. Eventually, I got my own company selling pumps, water softeners and air conditioners. It was a good life. When I retired, I opened up a small fishing tackle shop. Abe and I—we'd get together and go fishing up in Idaho. I happen to be a fly fisherman. It's not just a hobby for me. It's a way of life!

"NEXT TO WATER SOFTENERS!"

by Roseanne Cline Gordon

My father was a dry-fly fisherman who loved to fish.[4] He'd go to Wyoming or Idaho to fish. He was not a Utah fisherman. He didn't ever say anything negative about it but he always went to Wyoming. And in his last years, he went to the North Fork of the Snake River where he had a guide with a raft. They adopted one another, it was like father and son, and the fellow got a special seat so that Dad could sit comfortably in the raft.

Why did he love fishing? Why does anyone like fishing so much? He loved it because it was outdoors, in the mountains, and quiet. He loved the quiet. He hated noise. In his later years, he had a hearing problem and he could not stand to go out in the crowd because he couldn't understand anybody. All he heard was noise.

Like I said, my father was a dry-fly fisherman. Dry flies float on top of the water, whereas the wet flies float underneath. And to the true fisherman, that's a fine distinction, because dry fly fishermen are purists.

A man by the name of Keith Cook taught my father how to tie flies. And, like my grandfather, he learned well. My Dad was considered an expert fly tier. He would never sell his flies. Gave them to people, but he never sold any. After he retired from the Cline Equipment Company, my Dad decided that it would be great fun to open a fishing tackle store. He opened a little store called The Royal Coachman, which is the name of a fly. The store was on 4th South and West Temple. It was a wonderful place, a lot of friends coming by, but he found out that you can't run a retail store and be there just when you want to be and it got so my mother would go down so that he could go to lunch with his friends.

top Abe B. Cline with his wife and little Roseanne. (Courtesy of Roseanne Gordon)

bottom Abe B. Cline in the outdoors. (Courtesy of Roseanne Gordon)

He followed fishing right to the end of his life. Yes, that was his passion. He lived to be just barely 88 years old and he probably went on his last fishing trip when he was 85 years old. He had kidney failure, and was on dialysis for the last years of his life. The dialysis group arranged a fishing trip to Lake Powell. They did dialysis right there on the houseboat. And though it almost did him in, and it turned out to be his last fishing trip, he loved every moment of it. He was ahead of his time, my Dad. He was ahead of his time because now fly fishing is a big rage!

Abe B. Cline and Elliott Wolfe in the great outdoors. (Courtesy of Roseanne Gordon)

NATHAN ROSENBLATT, ACCORDING TO MY DAD

told by Abe B. Cline

My Dad told me there were quite a few Jewish junk peddlers in Salt Lake City at the time. And these were East European Jews who immigrated. They had no skills and they generally didn't have enough money to start into business. So, the one thing they could do was peddle junk. And some of them were highly educated in Hebrew and most of them were quite intelligent. But very few of them had any experience in business.

Now Nathan Rosenblatt was one of the men who was very well educated in Hebrew, but also had good business sense, and was highly intelligent. And some of these poor junk peddlers, when they would pick up a wagonload of junk and take it to the dealer to sell, they were robbed blind because they didn't know! They knew that they were not getting the value, but they didn't know what to do to take care of their interest. So they used to get Nathan Rosenblatt to go with them to sell their junk. Well, the dealers couldn't slip anything over on Mr. Rosenblatt because he was too smart.

In short time, I imagine, he opened up a junk store and bought junk from these peddlers. And of course, when he did that, they all looked to him because they knew they would get a square deal, which they got.

But in the meantime, he became quite well to do and eventually quit. When the boys grew up and were all college graduates and they had a technical education, they started into the manufacturing business as well as the junk business and became successful.

My dad told me this story. I don't know how accurate. But it's true as far as he knew. I'm sure.

COLLATERAL: CHARACTER, FAITH, AND WHATNOT

Simon Frank

Early Beginnings—I was born in Murray, Utah but moved to Salt Lake soon after.[1] For a very short time, we lived on 3rd South and 2nd East and then on 9th East and South Temple. I went to Wasatch Public School, and one of my first mistakes was going from first through eighth grade in five years. The result of this is I don't retain anything. [Laughs.] Well, things were actually pretty normal, but I'll tell you briefly. When I was twelve years old, World War One was a world event that changed the times for many of us in school. I started high school in 1918, when I was twelve years old, almost thirteen years old, and the boys coming back from the army were now going back into school as seventeen-, eighteen-, even twenty-year-old students! So I went with a much older group, and probably picked up some experiences trying to keep up with them. I loved high school! It was easy. I didn't want to give it up—even said that at graduation, but I did. I went through four years at the University of Utah, and then went to work with my Dad. That's the only job I ever had.

My father and mother, Arthur and Bertha Frank, were from Russia. Dad had been a successful businessman, relatively speaking for people of Jewish faith in the old country. He was a railroad contractor. That's what I always would have liked to do. There's a much greater feeling of accomplishment building railroads. Being a merchant, the only consolation is you may or may not do a better job than your competitors. But I guess an uncle must have sung the praises of America because Dad came over in 1901 and worked for him in the mercantile business. A year later, he offered to buy my uncle's store. My uncle said, "With what?" He said, "I'll go to the bank and borrow it." My uncle said, "Well, that's pretty good. I've been here for several years and I can't borrow any money from the bank. How do you think you're going to?" Dave Macmillan, the president of the bank, took a liking to my Dad and loaned him the money to buy the store. In those days, you didn't always have to have collateral. They did that on your character, faith, and what not. He was a great benefactor to our family and to my dad.

The jitney. (Courtesy of Steve Goldsmith)

The Jitney—Around 1911 or 1912, my dad acquired diabetes, and sold everything out and we went away to California for a year. When we came back, he had an idea of buying a fleet of Fords that were called jitneys. They looked like Model-T-Fords. I can see ten or twenty of them on various streets. There were streetcars, of course, in the center of the street. But the drivers of the jitney had an advantage. They could drive right up to any curb to pick up or drop off a passenger for a nickel fare. It didn't last long though; something about licensing, and Pop went back into the retail business.

Laughter and Tears—I called my dad, Pop, and my mother, Mother. They had a great verve for living and a great sense of humor. We had lots of laughter, lots of tears, and marvelous moments of understanding. Particularly with my Dad because we were associated in business all the time. For years, I used to play pinochle with him. We played a dollar a game, and the money, we'd have to put the money out on the table, in cash. Invariably, I'd beat him. After the first game, it wasn't so bad. The second game, he started getting mad. By the third one, he got worse. I'd take one look at Mother and she'd look at me; we'd start to laugh so hard—heartily. You talk about rolling on the floor. Of course, the more we laughed, the angrier he got. But we finally got over it through exhaustion. My father was very meticulous. He would write everything down, and kept records even on the pinochle games, every single game we played, who won, who lost, the amount and the total.

We used to have Passover seders at my parents' home. We were always very close to the Rabbi—Rabbi Gordon and then Rabbi Luchs—and I'm sure whoever was conducting the seder would like to have killed us, but we used to have so much darn fun with the degree of speed getting through it all. Especially on Yom Kippur: the Day of Atonement and fasting. Mother, I think, used to fast. But Pop never did. We'd go to B'nai Israel for services, but my dad and I never went to the daytime services. Instead, we'd go to the Hotel Utah for lunch. Oh, so many funny things!

Before the Talkies—I remember in 1918, we used to see movies with Fatty Arbuckle, Harold Lloyd, and Gloria Swanson. Fatty Arbuckle was a very good comedian, and I remember this one movie where they arrived in a Ford automobile and there must have been a hundred people getting out of the car. It was such a new thing to witness. How in the hell do they do that? You know, the tricks of photography, of course, but things like that are very impressive when you're young. There was another time in one of the films when they arrived at a little old shack and just down below it, on the cliff side, was a magnificent mansion. I thought that was wonderful.

I also remember the first national broadcast of radio very well. We didn't have a radio. We went over to a friend's house and listened to it in the back yard. When was that? It had to be before talking movies, around 1927 or 1928. I know when we were growing up we listened to the Victrola and played all kinds of records on it. In those days, people called every phonograph a Victrola, which was a commercial name for the product. But I always sang along with Caruso. My mother could never tell the difference, whether it was Caruso singing or I. But radio, some time after that, became my favorite. Jack Benny was a favorite.

In the summertime, as a family, we went on loads of picnics to various canyons around here and to Saratoga Springs. We'd visit relatives who lived in small towns like Tooele and Nephi. And we'd go out for dinners. What impressed me most was the Hotel Utah in Salt Lake, which I thought was real elegant; the Ship Café at Saltair, which was also very elegant. And I remember restaurants out in small towns that were famous in their days, like Beefstead Harrison in Springville.

Business Deals—In those early days, there were loads of traveling salesmen and my dad would do his buying on a Sunday in the hotel with these salesmen. Very often, I'd go with him. That was my training; more through osmosis than actual training. After six months, I took over much of the buying. We had a store called the Union Clothing. Like many stores, our name was on the sidewalk. Of course, a lot of them have been torn up. But it was right there. My dad then picked up four or five other stores right in Salt Lake. One was called The Wonder. One was The Regent. Another on the same side of the street was The Day and Night Clothes Shop. We didn't

BUSINESS PORTRAIT OF ARTHUR FRANK, A MAIN STREET PIONEER

At the age of 80, Salt Lake City businessman Arthur Frank walks with a spring stride, his big frame erect, his whole look that of a man accustomed to the rugged outdoor life of an engineer or construction worker.[2]

Which is what the head of the mens-wear shop that bears his name was nearly half a century ago. "I was a railroad contractor and foreman in Europe before deciding the future lay in America. . . . I laid the roadbed and track from Grodno to Lodz and Warsaw, and walked every tie as we built the line."

Born in Grodno, April 2, 1873, in what was then the Lithuanian province of Russia, Mr. Frank made a 16-day crossing of the Atlantic from Bremen to Hoboken in the belief life could prove a bit more stable in the USA. . . . Coming to Utah to hunt up Harry Baron, a brother-in-law, Mr. Frank found himself working in the retail business, rather than in the railroad building, and "hasn't much regretted it."

The band plays in front of Arthur Frank's store. (Courtesy of Utah State Historical Society)

Those were the days when opportunities beckoned, he asserts. "I arrived in Murray in 1903 to work at the Baron store. By 1907, I had opened a chain of twelve leading clothing shops called 'The Leader' stores in such Utah cities as Midvale, Spanish Fork, Brigham, and Bingham." But the men's specialty shop he opened in 1907 . . . in Salt Lake City soon became his principal interest.

It was "one of the first of its kind in the state," Mr. Frank says with pride. "Main Street was quite a place, utility poles in the middle of the street, trolley tracks, and unpaved below 4th South. . . . We sold suits for $5, those narrow waisted models. A derby hat sold for $1.98. Walkover shoes, a brand selling for about $25 now [in 1953], were $1.98 to $3.50 a pair. Shirts were 95 cents, socks a dime. Vests were just as loud, then as now."

Moving his "Union Store" to the present-day "Arthur Frank" location in 1910, the retailer . . . was particularly proud of the new Romney Building's electric lights, the hitching posts outside, and the size of the haberdashery stock. A "Main Street booster," he initiated a jitney bus line to bring more people downtown in 1913, but quickly "left the transit game to others."

. . . "The boys run things pretty much now," he says referring to sons, Harry, Boris and Simon, who have been "raised in the business." But Mr. Frank still takes pride in work, and is "'specially proud of long-range matters, such as the fact we've been handling one brand, Hart Schaffner & Marx for more than a quarter-century."

[Retired, Mr. Frank still plays] "five or six holes of golf, whenever I get the chance . . . but I find myself looking forward to going to the store. I could no more retire than I could forget what this country—and Utah—have done for me."

run them. We bought them out, closed them out, and brought the merchandise into our Union Clothing store.

Facing the Depression with Aplomb—We had a store and with it, we had a family. One of the interesting things about our business is that in our day we rarely lost an employee except through death. When they came with us, they came for life. During the depression, they worked for almost nothing. We gave them what we could afford, which was very little, and they stayed with us. We encouraged them, knowing that we'd work it out some day. We were quite well-to-do before the depression. We lost almost everything and then we had a mighty comeback. But

I believe you should be young to go through a depression, not old. It was "youth" that helped.

I remember my father would come down and say he was going to close out the store and save what he could and the rest of us could go out and do what we could for ourselves. I said, "No, Pop, we don't do that. We'll fight this thing through and some day it's going to change and we'll make it." The very next day, he comes down and says, "Well, we'll put in dollar shirts and ten dollar suits."

The inactivity was so bad, it just drove him crazy. Being in the store all day long, and I told you, our employees working for practically nothing. But we held out, and lo and behold, we made it! My dad was then fifty-seven years old. Having worked all of his life and being successful, to lose everything is not much fun. So it was gratifying to know that we did the right thing in holding out. It was hard times.

And Humor—But speaking of humor, at that time during the depression, we were down on 210 South Main. We had two entrances that were side by side with enough space to accommodate setting up a table from the hat department in between the two doors. My father and I used to sit there and talk. Incidentally, Rabbi Gordon used to come in almost every day and talk. Most of what I learned, my father was a student of the Talmud and very learned, came from these conversations. Well, one day at work, my father was reading a magazine [article] in which somebody was dunning a merchant for a bill he owed. The merchant wrote back, "Dear Sir. Let me tell you how I pay my bills. I put all my bills in a hat and I pull out as many as I can pay. If you get too touchy with me, I won't even put your name in a hat!" Well, that was the tragic truth almost all that time. And my father and I started to laugh, and that sort of broke the strain. Thank goodness for a sense of humor, you can get through. It was about the bottom, those depression days, it was almost the tragic truth. But, by 1933, it was already the beginning of prosperity.

We had some wonderful stores. It's kind of sad to see them gone. Auerbachs was an old, old store. Fine people. The Paris is gone now. That was the Simon brothers in those days. We had L&A, an old, old family. Billy Rice, who is in the advertising business; his father was the rabbi who confirmed me. His mother was a Cohen who had a rather large junior department store. Can't forget Makoffs, one of the best stores in town. And our store, Arthur Frank. We were second to none in reputation, integrity, and honor in the business community of Salt Lake. I'm very proud of it. But you know, I'm really jealous of the guy who can design and build railroads.

Naches IN NEPHI

Eva Siegel

Bundled Washings—I have lived during the transition from the horse and buggy days to the automobiles.[1] There were telephones, yes, but very expensive and with very few customers. Coal stoves. We didn't have central heating and Utah winters were severe. We had a cook stove in the kitchen and a little heating stove in the dining room. We'd get up in the morning, grab our clothes, and run to the dining room where Dad would have a fire made. He'd warm our long underwear on the stove and then we'd get dressed. Long underwear and long stockings, we needed them. We lived in the country and we'd walk to school. Outdoor plumbing? No. Wherever we lived, my father insisted on indoor toilets. The outdoor ones were sometimes too far away from the house. I remember when we first moved to Nephi, the outhouse was so far away, my little brother froze going out there. So we always found a closet or a porch or something like that where my father would have a toilet put in. For washing clothes, we would take a bundle of washing to the washwoman twice a week. She would wash it, iron it, fold it and we would get it back. Later, when we moved to Salt Lake, we had a wash room on the back porch of our house. It wasn't an electric washer, and so all the clothes were washed in cold water. The Troy laundry, just north of Murray, used to come in and pick up the sheets and shirts.

The Spirit of Adventure—My parents were Louis and Bertha Frank. My father had a brother here who came because of his brother-in-law. You know how they did

Bertha Frank and her daughter, Eva, 1906. (Courtesy of Eva Siegel)

this, one family member following the other to America. My mother came, though, simply out of the spirit for adventure that had swept Europe at the time. A new world. A wonderful place to go. She was eighteen years old. Her brother had a passport to Switzerland to learn watch making. It was a passport for two, and that's how she convinced her parents that she should go, on her brother's passport. She went as far as Berlin with him, then she was able to secure passage on the ship the Bismark. I don't think she knew anyone. Her parents gave her money to come with and to come back with, but she never returned. She liked it here.

From Yiddish to English—My father was already living in Utah, while my mother was in New York. But they must have had a correspondence with each other because, finally, she married him in his brother's home in 1905. I was born a year later, in 1906, and practically grew up in Nephi. I did all my grammar school there. It was a very lovely community to live in. Had a good school system. We were accepted by most of the people. They were English, Mormon converts from England, and they were very nice, refined people. They were crazy about my folks and wonderful to them. After all, my parents hardly knew English, but my father was sociable and my mother was really pretty. Everybody liked her. It's remarkable how they learned English, but they did learn, and very quickly. My mother's handwriting was also very beautiful. She didn't go to American schools, but she never misspelled a word. She went into the store right away to work. She met people and she assimilated. When I was young, my parents spoke Yiddish. But after that, it was all in English. They were so anxious to learn the language, and to be Americanized.

South of Salt Lake City—For a short time, my parents lived in Murray and then for a short time in Midvale. When they heard of the silver boom further south in Mammoth and Silver City, they set up a general merchandise store. My father had no money, but he was able to get credit. The store was so busy, my father brought in my mother's brother, Ben. They worked together until the silver mines suddenly closed and the price of silver dropped. They set up a store in Eureka, too, but it was the same thing: the silver mines shut down. So they went further south to Nephi in about 1911 and opened up a general merchandise store. They sold shoes and clothing for children, women and men. We lived in Nephi for ten years. It was a farming community.

We liked our small town living. Not the big city pressures that we get now. And we did see our relatives often, so we felt very close growing up. Every summer, we used to get together in Provo Canyon, which was a half way meeting point for many of us. Sometimes we'd go to Saratoga Hot Springs, out in Lehi. We'd take family picnics. We'd go to Salt Lake to Uncle Arthur and Aunt Bertha's home and spend some time there; they came out to visit us. Of course, in those days, it was quite a distance to get to Salt Lake, but when we got the car in 1916, it was nice. Driving on a one-lane road, after a hundred miles and five punctures along the way, because the tires were never any good, we could get to Salt Lake in three hours. On Sundays, sometimes my parents would just relax and read the paper. Other times, my father would rent a horse and buggy and take us on little rides around the countryside.

Eva Frank Siegel, handmade lace, hat, and spats, 1912. (Courtesy of Eva Siegel)

In Salt Lake, my uncle and aunt belonged to both synagogues. We joined Temple B'nai Israel. But even after we moved to Salt Lake, my dad attended services because the family did, but he didn't really care about it. Mother was a little more involved. Living in Nephi, we were rather isolated from the day-to-day activities of Jewish life. Nephi was a typical Mormon town. There were no paved streets, but there was always a Main Street, which had a few shops like ours.

There were a couple of schools, Mormon ward houses, usually two, one at each end of the town. The houses were set off from the street and they lined maybe three blocks on either side of the street. The town was about five blocks long, and that was it. Most of the people were involved in farming because the mining industry was closed.

We had a store in Gunnison and Richfield, too, although we didn't spend much time in Richfield. At the time, there were a number of Jewish-owned stores in rural Utah towns. My Uncle Sol Selvin, who was married to my father's sister Fanny, had a general merchandise store in Tooele. My mother's brother Ben Douglas had a clothing store in Delta. (Their Polish name is Dlugatch.) Mother's other brother Albert had a clothing store in Lehi. They stayed only a few years and went back to New York. Everybody worked very hard in those days.

The Selvins of Tooele—I remember my Aunt Fanny (Fannia Frank, who was my father's sister). She worked in the store, too, but she spent a lot of her time reading. She was an intellectual. The Selvins had four children, and when we were children, we used to go to Tooele to visit. It was pleasant to go there. They lived in a house on about an acre of ground with fruit trees. We could all be around, playing indoors and out, and my aunt would be into a book and never hear us. My uncle was a Senator for many years and then became the mayor of Tooele where he served many terms. I believe he introduced a series of civil rights laws into Utah. Every year, they were voted down, but he kept reintroducing bills until finally some of them were passed. The Selvin children were all very bright people. Herman finished school by the age of 12 and went to Berkeley and graduated by the age of eighteen. He was the youngest law student in that school. Min, the second child, went to Berkeley when I did. We all went to Berkeley. Min became a writer for the movie industry. The other son David has been a newspaper man for as long as I remember, and the youngest daughter, Florence, who moved to Canada, became well versed in Italian Art.

Visiting Clarion—During the time we lived in Nephi, when my father bought the little store in Gunnison, my parents worked both stores, and we would stay maybe a week or two down there. My mother's sister Rae Riegert worked there too. Gunnison is about 40 miles south of Nephi. It's next to Clarion, the Jewish agricultural settlement. I was young, about seven years old, but I remember being out there one time to see that it was a very desolate desert. I remember the Jewish colonists got their water from a wagon. My parents were close to the Basow family. They came from Philadelphia, had been in Clarion, and moved to Gunnison. They had three daughters and one son, all young like we were. Many years later two of the girls came back and visited my mother. We knew the Browns; Ben Brown was very involved in the Clarion project.[2] He had a daughter Lillian who was about my age, and two sons, Eugene and Isadore. We knew them when they lived in Gunnison. When Mr. Brown left Clarion, he just moved down the road and developed the Utah Poultry Association. I think after he died, the family moved on to California.

Brother to Brother—My father was the youngest Frank brother, but between him and Uncle Arthur, they took care of their four sisters. Uncle Arthur was an autocrat, the head of the family, whereas my father was very lenient. Never heard or said a harsh word in my family at all. In fact, if my father thought that anyone said, "shut up," it was the most terrible thing they could say. He wasn't a high-powered person, but people liked him. For example, during the depression, the family struggled with their ladies shop here on 37 East Broadway. My father lost the business and was contemplating closing the one in Nephi when a storeowner across the street on 3rd South, who knew what was happening to Dad, intervened. He was friendly. But not too much. He came over and said, "Louis, if you need money, I'll give you what you need." And he did. He was a Mormon and he liked my father and he voluntarily came over and set him up in business again.

A Maimonides Club outing. *From the top:* Claire Steres Bernstein, Eva Frank Siegel, Burt Pepper Barlow, Jackie Zlotnick Bernstein, Ida Wax, Bessie Rosie, and Rose Epstein Pepper. (Courtesy of Gail Bernstein Ciacci)

My dad had a good reputation and a good sense of humor. He played pinochle with a group of Jewish men in Salt Lake who are no longer here: Jack Tannenbaum, Joe Dupler, Manny Crocker. It was a fun game. They used to laugh, tell jokes, and kibitz. Abe Cline used to go just to watch them because it was so much fun.

A Sense of Jewish Community—We moved back to Salt Lake because my parents wanted me to go to a larger high school and probably get more involved in the Jewish community. I grew up in the temple. Rabbi Gordon was the rabbi then. I dated the Jewish boys. After I came back from college, I went to all the Maimonides Club events.[3] I did that until I married Max.

I had little Jewish background when I was a child. No Jewish education. And I don't know, it's still very strange, but I have a strong feeling of identity. My husband was very involved. He owned the Salt Lake Loan Office, a family business. His father died when he was 16 years old and he was left with his mother and two brothers to support. He worked long hours, always has, but was an ardent worker for Jewish objectives.

During the war, I remember we did a great deal of work—war work—at the old Covenant House on South Temple. There was a group of women who met twice a week to roll bandage and knit sweaters for the war effort. Then we had functions for USO. I cooked in the kitchen. There were several big army camps around here: Kearns, Hill Field, Camp Williams, Fort Douglas. Clearfield was a big center of distribution. Often, the Jewish soldiers would gather at the Covenant House.

I remember, after the war, Max wanted to raise money for Israel and did a lot of personal solicitations. Had meetings. Had dinners. Max would go to Ogden and have a dinner and a drive there. He went to Boise a few times. He never felt frustrated by his attempts. He was a very easy-going person who just took things as they were. I remember we entertained people from national organizations and had big dinners. Once, we had a big dinner at the Hotel Utah with probably a couple of hundred people to hear Jack Benny. He came to help raise funds.

It was in 1955, I think, that we sold our old Covenant House to have a Jewish Community Center. James White was a strong leader in this community, a brilliant speaker with a forceful personality, who worked to make the transition a reality.

He and Max worked together. Max was very involved in United Jewish Appeal. He was the president of the council here for almost twenty years. Very instrumental, very strong. When it came to supporting the [synagogues'] merger, Max supported the idea, felt strongly that there shouldn't be this division of two congregations. We had several meetings in our home with representatives from each congregation. All men. There was antagonism. Some believed Reform Jews were *goyish.* But everybody was losing money. And losing their rabbis. Finally, they set up a committee to merge the two religious schools. Joel Shapiro was the chairman and did a magnificent job. For two or three years, the two Sunday Schools met together. The kids liked it. The parents saw that it was working. So they decided to have a fund drive. First, we sold B'nai Israel and then we sold Montefiore. We got a building committee, bought property, and hired an architect. I thought it made sense. I still think so.

WITH THE ENCOURAGEMENT OF STRANGERS

Sol J. Selvin

Sol and Fannia Selvin with children Herman and Min, before coming to America. (Courtesy of Nancy Selvin)

For the Children's Future—I was born in a small town in Lithuania, then under the rule of Czarist Russia.[1] Education in Russia at that time was neither compulsory nor universal. Schools were very few and sparse. Children of poor parentage or of minority groups were unable to receive even an elementary education. As I came from a minority and of poor parentage, I was unable to get the desired education. I educated myself. By the time I was 18 years old, I passed the examination of an elementary teacher. At 20, I was drafted into the Czarist Army and served four years there. After I was released from the army, I married a teacher and both of us opened a private school and taught there for awhile. Two children were born to us. Then our minds were settled on the future of the children. There was no future for them in that country. My wife and I decided to emigrate to the United States where we thought a better future could be had for them.

Working in America—Early in 1909, we arrived in the United States and settled in Murray, Utah. I had a younger brother there and he put me to work in a clothing store. Not knowing a word of the English language and not being acquainted with the customs and ways of this country, life certainly was not a bowl of cherries.

The reception of the American people given us in the respective communities on our landing was cordial and helpful. The neighbors and our newly made friends were kind in many ways and were very helpful to us in adopting the new ways and customs of our newly adopted country. They were very encouraging and praiseful in our learning the English language; their friendly attitudes towards "strangers" helped us to get acclimated to the habits and way of living in this land of ours.

The attitude of our competitors in business was not as friendly as those of our neighbors at

The Selvins at home in Tooele. (Courtesy of Nancy Selvin)

first. They changed in time and became more neighborly and tolerant when they learned more of our intentions, character and attitude.

The store where I worked started me out with $50.00 a month. It was a little amount certainly at that time, but we made a go and lived within our means. At the end of 1909, I moved to Tooele. A smelter was being built there and I was offered $75.00 per month. I worked in that store until the end of 1911. The store quit business and I lost my $75.00 a month job. A friend of mine, who was in the mining business in Tooele, offered me two thousand dollars as a loan to enable me to go into business for myself. I accepted the generous offer of my friend and opened in the same location of my former business. My wife was by my side as much as possible. We worked diligently in the business and at the same time kept our dreams about the children alive. It was not money we were after. We wanted to fulfill our promise to give our children a better home and a better future than they would have had if we had not emigrated to this country. Above everything else, our desire was to become one of the community and we took an interest in communal affairs as much as our business would allow us.

Struggling through Debts—Our business grew steadily and when the First World War broke out in 1914, and a small depression set in our community, we lived through the crisis. There were many bills to pay and not much income. We struggled and watched every penny and by the middle of 1915, we succeeded in going over the top. Every creditor received 100 percent on the dollar we owed.

MY FATHER'S BIOGRAPHY

by Min Selvin Crutcher

My Father's Past—The country of Lithuania that my father refers to is a troubled strip of land lying between Germany and Russia, torn by greed and strife between emperors and kings, kaisers and czars.[2] Since the days of Genghis Khan. It is a corridor that has been, in turn, Germany, Poland, Russia, Lithuania, Russia again and Poland. The Jews in this dismembered land suffered even more galling afflictions than [did] their Christian countrymen. Discrimination and persecution made up the everyday fabric of Jewish life, and for special occasions there were the dreaded pogroms, "the organized massacres of helpless people," an irregular certainty of life for the Jews. The Selvins were Jews in the ghetto-like village of Kuznetsa in the province of Grodno in the country that was then Lithuania.

My father's parents were as harsh and uncompromising as the barren piece of land they farmed for a meager existence. Grandfather Zelwiansky was an ardently religious disciplinarian. In the Jewish tradition, whatever time and energy he could spare from cultivating his farm was spent in the Synagogue in the nearby village.

Display of affection was as scarce as money in my father's home, although my father often said he knew his mother loved him even though she never said so, or showed it by any overt act. Despite this apathy, my father knew the anguish of homesickness when, at the age of 13, he was sent to live with a rabbi in Kuznetsa to become a yeshiva bocha, apprentice to the rabbi. Yearning for home, he broke the rule which forbade him to leave the premises of the synagogue and trudged the nine miles to the isolated farm. He arrived at the wooden shack that was his home late at night, cold, hungry, and tired. His father met him at the door. "You have run away," he said. "You have broken the rule." My father was left outside the door, his only alternative was to return to the synagogue. "My mother stood behind my father that night," Dad said. "She didn't say a word. But it was the only time in my life I saw her cry."

Mishpoche—Somehow, with his limitless energy for molding his life to realize his dreams, in spite of the difficulties of being a poor Jew in that country at that time, my father educated himself. In the course of his self-education he met Fagile (Fannia) Fraktovnik, who later became his wife. The Fraktovnik and Zelwiansky families were distantly related. Grandfather Fraktovnik was a house builder in Grodno, the capital city of the province. His wife had died when my mother was nine years old; thus, she became child-mother to her two brothers and three sisters. By comparison to the Zelwiansky family, the Fraktovniks were very well to do city dwellers, and when my father went to Grodno in pursuit of learning, it was natural for him to stay with his *mishpoche*. It was then that he fell in love with and married the well-educated, intellectual, and serious oldest

Fraktovnik daughter who volunteered to teach him Russian. When my parents finally received their teaching credentials, they rented a house in Kuznetsa and opened a school, restricted by law and custom to Jewish students.

In 1904, their first child Herman was born. My father was in the Russian army and, by virtue of his proficient Russian and legible penmanship, he became a company clerk, a rare distinction for a Jew. He was a fast walker, the result of four years in the Czar's army. He stood and walked like a soldier—ramrod straight, he walked with long, quick strides his entire life. I never learned to keep up with him.

The Czar's Army—My dad wrote letters for illiterate Russian officers who refused to pay him but gave him permission to attend a nearby Polish university so he could listen to lectures; occasionally he acquired enough money to pay for private tutoring. In this way, he was educated.

I was born in 1907, while my father was still in the Czar's army. He was given a brief leave for this event, but an unseasonable storm delayed the train. After walking all night through the blinding snow, he arrived in Kuznetsa with hardly enough time left to greet his family before he had to plow his way through hip-high snowdrifts to return to camp. After his final discharge from the army, my father rejoined my mother in teaching, but they recognized the futility of trying to support themselves and two children on the limited income from their school. They decided to emigrate where they "thought a better future could be had for them and their children."

Certainly Lithuania offered no future for Jews. Lithuanian Christians, sorely oppressed by the Russians, in turn oppressed the Jews, even excluding them from joining the patriots in their struggle against the tyranny of the Czar. Jews were thus forced to ally themselves with Russian revolutionary groups if they were to fight the ruthless despotism of their rulers. Mom and Pop were in sympathy with the aims and ideals of those who sought to overthrow the Czar, but they never engaged in revolutionary activities. Two of my mother's family, her younger brother Louis and sister Ray, however, were deeply involved. Uncle Louis had to sneak over the German border to escape arrest, and my brother Herman remembers going to jail to visit Aunt Ray when she was imprisoned for making a speech against the Russian tyrants.

Passage to America—The migration pattern had already been established in the family. Earlier, in 1906, the combined resources of the Fraktovnik and Zelwiansky families had been pooled to finance the trip to the United States of Mom's oldest brother, Arthur Frank. Pop's youngest brother, Isadore, had saved enough money while working in Germany to pay his own passage, and Uncle Arthur provided transportation for Uncle Louis when he had escaped to Germany. These three members, now in Utah, sent Dad enough money to join them. He sailed for the "Promised Land" in November 1908. Two years later, we followed. Later, David and Florence would complete our family.

When asked why my father went to Tooele, he always said, "You didn't go where you wanted to, you went where you could afford it." Among the few fortunate people who could afford to escape economic entrapment in the big eastern cities was my mother's oldest brother, Arthur Frank. On his arrival in New York, in 1906, he was advised by landsleit who had preceded him to invest the pooled resources of the Fraktovnik and Zelwiansky families in a men's clothing store in Salt Lake City, Utah.

Within three years, Uncle Arthur opened two additional stores. One was in Salt Lake in which he installed his younger brother Louis as manager; the other in the farming community of Murray and managed by my father's brother Isadore. At that time, if you established credit, as Uncle Arthur had, opening another store meant renting a location, installing a few wooden tables, and piling them with merchandise bought on credit. If the profits didn't accumulate fast enough, the merchandise was repossessed. Fortunately, both new stores were successful and it was not long before Uncle Arthur was reimbursed for his original investment and my uncles became independent store-owners. On his arrival in the United States, distant relatives in New York tried to dissuade Father from going West. But Dad felt a family, as well as a financial, obligation to go directly to Utah where he immediately went to work for $50.00 a month in the Murray store.

Jewish Heritage—Although our life was more similar to the "Gentile" pattern than the Mormon, my mother and father were ardently anti-ritualistic. We never observed any of the religious holidays or services in our home, nor did we ever attend the Synagogue in Salt Lake. We were, however, instilled with a deep sense of pride in our Jewish heritage, and we learned about Jewish history and folklore in family discussions, but only in a secular sense. We were, except for a brief few years, the only Jews in town; and the social taboos of our European background, added to our Jewish traditions, widened the gap between the accepted social values in Tooele and our family.

Pickled Herring—I realize, especially in trying to reconstruct the early years in Tooele, that childhood memories evoke images that betray reality. I remember Pop's buying trips to Salt Lake long before we had an automobile or bus transportation was available. He would leave early in the morning and return late at night, long after Herman and I were asleep. But we were always allowed to get up and have a cup of cocoa with the rich, crusty pastries he always brought for us. We disdained the "foreign" delicacies—the dark, rough pumpernickel bread, the fat, salty pickled herring, the cream cheese, smoked salmon and bagels—which Mom and Pop ate with such relish.

And, sitting at the kitchen table, we would listen to a report of his day's activities. We heard news about our aunts and uncles and cousins in Salt Lake; and tidbits of gossip about other people we knew that he picked up from the owners of the Jewish market that he stopped by on the way to the depot in Salt Lake. He also gave us a recital of the business he had transacted, what he bought, how much and from whom, often interspersed with an "Oh, that reminds me," and he would open one of the large bundles he brought and pull out a surprise present. Sometimes it would be a new dress or coat, or a box of candy sent by one of the "drummers," salesmen, or a trinket bought with money the salesmen would give him for expenses.

The Real McCoy—But for the real story of Father's buying trips in Salt Lake. He used to take the 7:30 "shift train" from the Smelter to the depot. Then Earl Tate, the stationmaster, would flag a train going into Salt Lake. There, Dad would walk from the depot in Salt Lake to the business section and, around midnight, back again to catch the westbound train for Tooele. In the course of the day, he would have walked at least ten miles. He would walk to the Zion's Cooperative Mercantile Institution (ZCMI), the Mormon Church–owned store and then walk on Main Street to visit with Uncle Arthur. He would then walk over to the small wholesale district on West Temple Street to buy overalls and work shirts from Levi-Strauss. He'd move on to the Salt Lake Knitting Mills, which was the only authorized manufacturer of LDS garments, the button-less long-sleeved, long-legged underwear that the "Word of Wisdom" required good Mormons to wear. Loaded with bundles, he would make his final stop at the Jewish delicatessen on his way back to the depot in Salt Lake and home.

"I used to be so tired," he told us, "I'd stand at the Tooele depot and be afraid to start out because I didn't think I could make it home. In the winter, they wouldn't clean the streets with snow plows that far out of town, and I'd have to push my way through the snow. Lots of times, I'd stumble and fall, and sometimes the packages would break open and I'd sit on the ground and tie them up. But I lived through it. It just goes to show that work never killed anybody."

A Matter of Citizenship—One of my father's continuing contributions to his adopted country was to help countless immigrants acquire citizenship. He was never too busy to help them accumulate the required data, coach them for their examination, and appear as a witness for them. I am sure the records of the courts will reveal that during his lifetime, my father witnessed more citizenship papers than any other individual in the County. He contributed time and money to every welfare activity, and for more than twenty years was the chairman of the Tooele County Public Welfare Board.

A Debt to Pay—The most endearing quality of my father was humility: an absence of arrogance or pride in his achievement. He never considered himself a self-made man. Rather, he believed he was a man fortunate enough to have friends help him take advantage of the opportunities afforded in this wonderful land. When all his children were college-educated, Dad had discharged his major obligation, but he believed he owed another debt that he must somehow repay. This was a debt to the people and to the country, which had been good to him. Inspired by President Roosevelt's political leadership, Dad became active in a partisan sense for the first time in his life. He became an outstanding Democratic leader in Tooele County, campaigning for Democratic candidates in state and national elections. When he was considered the choice for the Democratic candidate for the state legislature in 1934, he accepted with gratitude and humility. He was also considered a most unusual politician.

Stubborn as a Mule—He never took a position on a legislative matter until he studied it thoroughly. He read everything he was given by proponents and opponents; he talked to everyone who sought an audience with him. He made independent surveys, conferred with specialists, researched subjects at the library, sought information from other states, and when he reached a conclusion, nothing could sway him. He served in the legislature as a representative from Tooele and Juab Counties until 1941. During the legislative sessions, he and Mom lived in Salt Lake, and kept tabs on the store by daily correspondence and weekend visits. In between sessions, he partitioned off a section at the back of the store, installed a desk and some chairs, and held forth daily.

Lunch on the State—Stories about Pop's quaint figures of speech are legion. When occasion and time allowed, he would illustrate a point he wanted to make with an earthly homily. Once when he was leading a fight for increased appropriations for a state institution, he invited a member of his loyal opposition to have lunch with him, and took him into the main dining of the elegant Hotel Utah. "Sir, you are my guest," he announced, "and I want you to eat a good lunch. Please order whatever you like as long as it doesn't cost more than 12-1/2 cents. That," he explained, "is what the state allows per meal at the State Institution, and I assume you feel that anyone can get along on that."

In 1938, my father was re-elected by the biggest popular vote ever received by any other candidate running for any office in Tooele. He loved it.

The year 1918 was the hardest we experienced. The slump in business arrived. The mines and smelters shut down. Men were idle and desperate. Accounts receivable could not be collected. Sales were at zero. We owed considerable money and no money in sight to pay it with. The little stock we had on hand was sold at a sacrifice in order to raise some money with which to satisfy some of our debtors. By the end of 1919, our assets, accumulated since 1911, were gone. On top of that, we owed several thousands of dollars to various distributors and manufacturers.

Children, Business, and Politics—Our oldest son Herman just graduated from high school and made up his mind to enter the University of California at Berkeley. The problem was before us: how to bring about our long dream of giving the children a better chance in this world than we had. In the middle of 1920, the mines and smelters resumed work on a limited basis. We started over again, worked hard, and were able to pay off our indebtedness of 1919 and most of 1920. Our daughter Min enrolled at Westminster College. And we sailed along cautiously. Business resumed its steady growth. From 1911 to 1954, I was the sole proprietor of The Economy Store.

In 1934, I entered in active political work, being elected to the Utah State Legislature, the House of Representatives. I served there continually to 1941. In 1940, my beloved wife, who was always by my side, died. In 1942 and 1943, I served as Mayor of Tooele.

FROM THE *Salt Lake Tribune*, NOVEMBER 29, 1944

Mr. Selvin, a Democrat, reports he favors greater equalization of educational opportunities and costs and maintenance of the state's educational system on a high plane. He is open minded on the question of a nonpartisan judiciary. "I have," he said, "no axes to grind and pet bills to introduce."

FROM THE *Transcript Bulletin*, AUGUST 19, 1958

It was under [Sol Selvin's] orders that polio vaccine was made available to all children of the Tooele county, from local polio funds and there has not been a single polio case in the county since this order was given.

He has been the chairman of Tooele County Welfare Board for fifteen years, and was the chairman of NRA of Tooele County in 1933. He was the first chairman of Defense Council and rationing board of Tooele County during WWII.

FROM THE *Utah Labor News*, FEBRUARY 9, 1945

The Senator of Tooele is taller sitting in his rocker than standing beside it. He steps down to get up and gets up to sit down. But the Senator of Tooele is one of the mighty men of the Senate. He is almost always in the right, and when in a battle on the floor of the Senate, he will go a mile to win a point but wouldn't give an inch to sacrifice a principle.

KEEPING KOSHER IN VERNAL

Claire Steres Bernstein

My father had gone to Vernal originally with the backing of Jewish people from Salt Lake City to buy hides and furs on the reservation.[1] And I believe when he decided to make Utah his home, he settled in Vernal because that was the center of where he was working. He brought my mother there. And after a few years, he started selling the Watkins household products on the reservation so that together with the hide and fur business he had another income.

My father immigrated to Canada first from Ukraine. I don't know how long he was there, but he then went to Utah in about 1905. He got out of Russia at the beginning of the Sino-Russian War. It was always a kind of miracle to him and to his friends, because his class was called up within two months *after* they let him out of the country. He was lucky.

A Rescue—My mother came from Russia in 1906. She always talked about having survived the Cossack raids in Nicolaia, "Raising the Red Cock." One time, on the day of the Czar's birthday, which happened to be the same day as my mother's birthday, the first of May, the Cossacks made a sweep of the Jewish section. A Gentile man, who owned a lumberyard, grabbed my mother and her three small children and hid them in his lumberyard. He saved them from that pogrom.

My father's parents, we never met. I remember from hearsay that he was the most religious Jew in the small town of Nicolaia and probably one of the backbone of the synagogue. Being his eldest son, my father was given the responsibility of greeting those religious men who came to the community. And all I know is that he rebelled against the strict religious life he led in Russia when he came to the United States. What I know about my mother's family is her father was a musician; and both her parents came to the United States.

I think my mother had a difficult time getting to the United States. Her husband went first, so it was just a matter of finances. The first time she left, she took her three children and went to a relative in London, expecting her husband to send her money to bring her to the United States. The money never came to her. After a difficult time, I imagine at least six months, she

ARTICLES IN THE *Vernal Express*

The Jew Store is no more. (March 29, 1902)

Mrs. Rosetta Jensen has sold two acres of land on Uintah Avenue in the eastern part of town, upon which the old blacksmith shop stands, to Max Weiss and Morris Glassman, two Jews, for the sum of $1,300. The purchasers intend to start a store on the property. (August 11, 1906)

Of our unusually long list of serious accidents lately, the most serious one is the accident which occurred Thursday night. Max Weiss, of the Vernal Trading Company, is the victim. About two weeks ago while out at Price, he was kicked by a horse, the part injured being his thigh just below the hip. He managed, however, to continue work, though very lame. Thursday evening, while unloading beef hides, the bone of the injured leg snapped in two and he fell helpless. He called for help and finally Frank Young came to his assistance and helped the family remove him to the house. Dr. Brownfield set the bone and pronounced this the worst fracture he has seen for some time. (November 24, 1906)

The Jewish Easter holiday began last Wednesday and will continue until next Wednesday. (April 17, 1908)

Mr. and Mrs. Glassman attended the Jewish New Year services in Salt Lake City on the 11th and 16th. They don't get to their services very often and appreciated the privilege. (September 24, 1909)

In Ogden, Wm. Glassman was elected Mayor, with the entire Republican ticket. (October 9, 1909)

Watkins Remedies, Extracts and Spices

Cash Paid for Hides, Pelts and Furs, 1/2 mile east of Co-op

I. Steres. Phone 41a. (advertisement, April 17, 1911)

New Citizens. Wednesday morning, Judge John E. Booth of the 4th Judicial District Court issued to Isaac Steres naturalization papers making him a citizen of the United States of America. (September 8, 1911)

Wind Plays Pranks. The hurricane that struck Vernal about 2 A.M. Tuesday morning played pranks on the premises of Isaac Steres in the east part of town. Among other things, it took off the top of two buggy sheds, carried away two horse blankets, one of which was found entangled in the telephone wires at the top of a tall telephone pole, the other has not been found yet. Across the street from Steres, it shattered a plate glass window in the residence of Mr. Smith. When the gust struck the Steres residence, the door was open. A young man attempted to close it and was thrown backward into the room by the force of the wind. Everything about the place that was moveable was shifted about promiscuously. (October 13, 1911) got to the point where her children didn't have enough food to eat, and the family there was not able to help enough. She returned to Russia and had to wait until he got funds to her.

Deep Snows and Warm Bread—I was born in Vernal in 1907. We lived there at least until 1914. I remember the deep snow in the winter, and going to the Congregationalist school because I could read before I was of kindergarten age. I walked through that deep snow not wearing overshoes but galoshes; that's how deep the snow was. My mother took care of the garden, raised vegetables, and helped support us by baking bread.

Fashion statement, Claire Steres and Burt Pepper. (Courtesy of Gail Bernstein Ciacci)

Two other Jewish families were living in Vernal at the time: The White family and the Glassmans. Mrs. White was like an aunt to us. We seemed to have this landsman feeling of living in the same area, a feeling I've always had about them. When my mother came to Vernal, she had never seen a cook stove. In Yiddish, the two of them, Mrs. White and my mother, would complain. They didn't know how it worked. Fortunately, one of her neighbors explained how to open and close a damper, then my mother started to bake. She would get up in the middle of the night and set the bread, and then bake bread two or three times a day. My father was probably just eking out a living, barely. He traveled and my mother would bake this gorgeous, really, good bread—the best we ever ate. She baked bread until she was 85 years old.

It was a wonderful, warm community. And you know even with the prevailing culture and the feeling that everyone must be given the opportunity to join the [LDS] church, there were never any [overt] pressures. I did go to Sunday School when I was young. When they taught us that the Jews killed Christ, I came home crying, and my father wouldn't let me go any more.

The Shochet—We kept a very, very Orthodox home. Of course, my mother had never eaten nonkosher food. When she traveled across to Utah, on a train for four or five days, she said she carried her own food. In fact, she ate no meat at all until my father, like a *shochet,* learned how to ritually kill a chicken. I don't know when she started eating meats besides chicken. I do remember my father had a ritual knife and killed a calf in our backyard. The reason I remember this so vividly is because there was a family who came out from New York: a shoemaker, his wife, and two young children. They were very observant, traditional Orthodox Jews. The wife wouldn't eat anything except vegetables. When they told her my father was a *shochet,* then she started eating chickens. My father felt that at least he kept this woman eating.

When my mother prepared the house for Passover, we very carefully ate no leavening after we went to school. We had a strong cultural background in Judaism even though by that time we were the only Jews living in Vernal.

Claire and her father at the market in Salt Lake City. (Courtesy of Gail Bernstein Ciacci)

Isaac and Rose Steres at home on 9th South and 3rd East. (Courtesy of Gail Bernstein Ciacci)

A Jewish Life in Salt Lake City—When we did move to Salt Lake City, my father kept traveling. He'd go back to the reservation, and be gone for days buying hides and furs. The first house we owned in Salt Lake was on 8th South and Blair Street, between 3rd and 4th East. Then my father built a big house with a grocery store on the corner of 3rd East and 9th South. My mother would work there because he hardly stopped traveling. I think they kept the store for fifteen years, and later when my father died, my mother sold it.

The incident at Sunday school might have had something to do with our moving to Salt Lake. But probably, a more important reason was that my mother's two oldest children were getting to be pre-teenagers, and she was anxious for them to get closer to a Jewish community. We were sent to religious school immediately. My brother, the third child, was almost ready for his bar mitzvah, so he went to Hebrew school. We attended Congregation Montefiore. At about that time, there was a split in the synagogue. The Orthodox group left and formed its own congregation, Shaarey Tzedek. My father called them Bolsheviks; my husband's family went there. Well, in the end, all the "Bolsheviks" came back to Montefiore.

A Ku Klux Klan Scare—I want to tell you an incident that happened when we were teenagers in high school that affected me because of what it represented. We had a close relationship with the Ogden Jewish community and on weekends, on Saturday night, a whole bunch of us would get together and climb the mountains. We'd sleep over, come down on Sunday, and picnic. We'd go in kind of family groups, brothers and sisters. And in that way, we didn't really need chaperones. We always had a good time.

On one of those weekends, there was a crime. A Ku Klux Klan rally was taking place and they were burning a cross on the mountain. We had enough sense to keep away from them; and we knew better than to barge in. They were protesting against Catholicism, Blacks, and they were naming Jews, too. Of course, they didn't know many of us, but I think this is what fascinated us: that we could be there, unseen, and hear these terrifying things. The Ku Klux Klan also held rallies on State Street below 9th South. There was a big truck garden and kind of a campground set up, too. We were just kids and I don't think we understood how dangerous it could have been for us to be around them, had they taken notice of us hiding. It was only afterwards, years later I realized just how frightening it really was and could have been for us.

I was working in an office in 1924. The office manager, who was considerably older than I, was telling us how proud she was that members of the Ku Klux Klan had bought a new organ for her church. She said they were going to attend services on Sunday and have a big dedication. She said they would even come in wearing their masks. I'm positive this is true because she was so excited about it. I knew it was something I would never be excited about or proud of or wanted to be a part of, ever.

The Steres family in the Great Salt Lake (Claire, floating, *right side*). (Courtesy of Gail Bernstein Ciacci)

BORN OF IMMIGRANT PARENTS

Abe Bernstein

Always a Peddler—As I understand it, my father spent a good part of his time in the Austrian army, and when his folks were asked his age, they added two or three years onto it, thinking that would get him out of Austria sooner.[1] He could neither read nor write. I believe he left his wife and came alone to New York City around 1904. He worked in New York for a while and realized that he did not come to the United States to work in the sweatshops. So in 1905, he picked up jobs along the way to the St. Louis' World's Fair and worked there as a waiter in a beer garden until he got enough money to come to Salt Lake City where he had an aunt who owned a boarding house.

This aunt's husband was traveling around with horses and a covered wagon. He made two or three trips between Salt Lake City and Chicago so he kind of left her to get by as best she could. Since she had boarders, she took her nephew in. Her name was Bernstein, as it so happens, but it was just a coincidence because the old man was no relative of my family.

My father was a young man, so these boarders put together a few dollars and bought him a horse and wagon. They told him to go out and buy whatever he could buy for as little as he could buy it and sell it for as much as he could sell it for. I guess he went door to door to start peddling around. In those days, you didn't have to go very far from where my aunt lived on 8th South between Main and West Temple before you were in the country. He earned enough money to bring his wife. The year after she arrived in Salt Lake City, I was born on January 17, 1907.

When I was six months old, they tell me the old man, the uncle, talked my father into going to Arizona with him. Painted a big picture about buying junk there and making a fortune. So they loaded up a covered wagon with water, flour, meat, and whatever else they could get in and left Salt Lake City to go to Tucson. When he got there, my father missed his family, but he had a relative in Los Angeles, so he sold his half of the wagon and horses to his uncle, got on a train, and went to California. At the time, it was nothing but a big swamp, I guess, because he didn't like it. He left there and came back to Salt Lake.

My father was always a peddler. He bought a Model T truck after the horses, and he used to drive up into the mountains of Kamas, Coalville, and Rockport in the summer to take up a load of fruit to sell. He would buy fruit at the market around 5:00 o'clock in the morning and head out. It wasn't an easy life, but he had a lot of friends who trusted him. He still didn't know how to read or write in English, but he could hand a man a checkbook. The customer would make out the check and he would sign it. Over time, we had taught my dad how to sign a check.

Between West Temple and 1st West and 6th and 5th South, all the farmers would bring their crops and my father would go in and buy this one farmer's entire load of cherries or that farmer's entire load of peaches or pears or apples. He'd buy vegetables too, and take them to these various areas, summer after summer until, oh, I believe into the middle 1920's.

In the winters, he would look for fur hides and pelts to sell. He was constantly on the road. Leave on Tuesday morning and wouldn't come back until Friday. But he always came in on Friday so he wouldn't have to work Saturday. Sometimes in the summer, when we were kids, we would go with him. We would get in the horse and wagon here and it would take us all day to get to the summit; and from there, we would go to Wanship and then he would either go to Coalville one time or Kamas the next time. Farmers all knew him and all waited for him.

I remember there was a young man in a town by the name of Abe Bloom, who was pretty friendly with my father. They formed a partnership where they were going to take fruit into Wyoming. They bought enough to have three truckloads. I was thirteen or fourteen years old at the time, and who was going to drive the third truck? I was. So here are the three trucks going together. We drove to a town just east of Evanston, the first day. Then one of them took off for Piney, one of them went east and I went south. We were all to come back and meet at the same place that evening. When we all three met up, the trucks were empty! We sold everything.

Years later, after we were married, Claire and I would go up into those areas where my father did business and visit with the good friends he made. We'd stay with them over night, go on picnics with them. They were real nice people.

Yiddish Only—In 1912, there was quite a group of Jewish families living around Eighth and Nine South and State Street and Main. We lived at 844 South 3rd East. Until I started school, I never knew a word of English. I spoke Yiddish to my mother and father. That's all they knew. Mother could write pidgin German, I guess you would call it. I started school when I was somewhere between five and six. There were maybe eight or nine or ten of us living around that area and we would all meet together and go to school together because if we didn't, the non-Jewish boys, if they caught one or two of us alone, we'd be in one heck of a fight. It wasn't easy. I guess we were living in the wrong end of town. But maybe we also got in so much trouble because we thought *we* were a tough bunch. If anyone wanted to fight, we fought with sticks and stones. In fact, we even had a football team and, oh, boy, I am telling you, this Ben Garelick was big and he had a cousin that was twice as big as he was! Those football teams with the Gentile kids were real bad games.

The Shochet and the Mohel—At home, we lived under very strict Orthodox laws. There were a couple of kosher Jewish butcher shops. One of the main ones was run by a man by the name of Rubin Kaplan. He had a butcher shop down on 8th South between State and 2nd East. Everybody bought meats from Mr. Kaplan in those days. Most of us were kosher, so it was very easy to buy meat and keep a kosher home. He was a *shochet,* too. He used to kill chickens in the back yard. And he was a mohel, yeah. When he wasn't in the shop, he'd be performing at Congregation Shaarey Tzedek, davening, reading the torah, leading the prayers. He was kind of a short, about 5′6″ or 7″ heavy-set man with a white beard and a mild voice. I can remember his wife was very peaceful.

Batter up! *L–r:* Harry Wax, Abe Bernstein, and Sam Pepper. (Courtesy of Gail Bernstein Ciacci)

Shaarey Tzedek, the "Other" Synagogue—At first, I went to Hebrew School at Congregation Montefiore. My Hebrew teacher's name was Mr. Alder; his son David [was] in the insurance business. Then, my father and maybe twenty other families broke away from Montefiore because they felt the synagogue wasn't Orthodox enough for them. English started to get in their services and this is what the group objected to; they wanted services to be strictly Orthodox. But, Montefiore had translations. If you attended a Saturday service, there will be no English. But on Friday nights, services were in English. I remember that. In my estimation, it's not a real service unless it's done just at sundown and after sundown it is Saturday and whatever happens after that isn't part of the old Orthodox Jewish religion or the Conservative type of service. So it is a Reform type of service. And I think maybe it's because the German Jews wanted a more Reform service. So I guess they had a big argument.

Until Shaarey Tzedek was built, they had meetings in our home and the Garelicks' home. Let's see, there were Morris Garelick, Sam Garelick, Allan Mednick, Harry Mednick, Joe Bernstein, Joe Doctorman, Ben Doctorman, the Kaplans, though Kaplan kind of vacillated between the synagogues. Sometimes he was up in Montefiore and then back to Shaarey Tzedek. There was Mr. Bettman, and the Shaeffers, the Sussmans, Mr. Wagner from Wagner Bag Company. Abe Miller, he was a teacher and a good one. We met in the basement of Shaarey Tzedek after it was built and he had quite a class. I can remember the summer time when the older fellows would meet at nine in the morning, and the younger students come at ten. Then we'd all get together and he'd tell stories about the Jews. Monday, Tuesday, Wednesday and Thursdays, those are the days we met, and then most of us attended the Saturday morning services. We didn't go to Sunday school. I remember, too, there were the Goldsteins and there was old man Rosenthal who had the grocery store on State Street, Mr. Feldman, the women that had the feedstore, Mrs. Katlovich, Charlie Grossman, and the two Agoshen brothers.

There wasn't a hundred people, but Shaarey Tzedek wasn't a small membership either. There was a lot of immigration into this country and they all had relatives or friends that would come into Salt Lake City. And here was a group practicing their Orthodox religion the way they remembered it from Europe. The building was built with what we call a bimah in the center, and an altar at the east end. The men would sit downstairs and the women upstairs, which was the old Orthodox way of conducting a service, and all the prayers were in Hebrew. We never had a rabbi, but they appointed a real good cantor and teacher by the name of Strinkowsky. He, his wife and children lived right next door to the synagogue, on the south side.

I was about ten or eleven when Shaarey Tzedek was built and we lived right in back of where it was being built. In about 1920, I remember being a bar mitzvah at the Rabbi's, in the teacher's home. At the time, it was during the war and there was a big epidemic of influenza in the area. My mother was very sick and was not there at my bar mitzvah. I remember, too, they hired a teacher to teach Hebrew, but then the Mormon church hired him and took him down there. And then Shaarey Tzedek was built and my other two brothers were bar mitzvahed there.

I remember we had a Jewish governor at the time, Simon Bamberger. One Sunday, when they were raising some money by auctioning off cornerstones, he was very much interested and gave quite a donation, bought one cornerstone. And old man Ruthbard, he was a cattle buyer, didn't have a family, but I think he agreed to buy the other one for $500.00. I think the Mormon Church gave a thousand dollars. And this little handful of Jews built this building, and had their own cemetery. The Garelicks' parents were buried there and the family still takes care of the cemetery.

Holding One's Own—Shaarey Tzedek men knew what they wanted and nobody interfered with them. I don't think there were any fights although I can remember in somebody's home, Sam Hayden saying, "Hold me back, I'm going to fight!" That's the kind of fights they had: verbal ones. They were smart! That's right. I will tell you something interesting.

This was during Prohibition days. The congregation would go to the State and get permission to bring in wine for services, for *kiddush,* High Holy Days and Passover. You have a little glass of wine. So they would bring in four, fifty-gallon barrels of wine. That is 200 gallons of wine, see? So, say there was forty families at Shaarey Tzedek. There is just no way they could consume 200 gallons of wine during the year. So what did they do? They sold it to their members for $25 a gallon so they'd have enough money to run the synagogue. That kept the congregation going for a long time.

The Return to Montefiore—Congregation Montefiore has its own cemetery and so does the

Peddlers—They were peddlers.[2] Grandpa Isaac Steres, my mother's father, traded fur pelts with the Indians. My Aunt Dora Steres told me a story about Grandpa. At first, when Grandpa had no trade, he met up with two men who were going out in the country and buying hides and pelts. These men taught him the trade, but in the meantime, they were fleecing him. That meant he was doing all the work but hardly getting any of the money. Fortunately, Grandpa became friends with Hebe Bortal, a rancher who was one of those patriarchs with a great white, flowing beard. To protect Grandpa's money, Mr. Bortal told these men that my grandfather owed *him* money and that he was going to put a lien on some of these furs and pelts until he got it. But what he actually did was give the money to my grandfather, which saved him.

Then Grandpa stayed in Vernal and worked on his own, trying to get enough money to bring the family out from Russia. Once they arrived, they lived in a great big tent on the property of this Hebe Bortal, in Vernal, until Grandpa bought a two-room log cabin about a half mile from the center of town. It was called Hatch Town, because all the Hatch families lived there. Grandpa had another friend who lived in a different part of town. This man, also a rancher, was Mr. Williams.

After Grandpa was in Vernal for a while, it seems he still owed money on the log cabin and the banker took the cabin back. I believe the banker's name was Marse. He was ninety years old and still working at the bank, the last time my uncle Eiman came through in 1975. Well, Grandpa went to Ogden with the family and tried to find work. When he couldn't, his friend Mr. Williams came and got the whole family; brought them back to Vernal. They got their log cabin back, and they added on a third room. They didn't leave Vernal for Salt Lake City until 1914. That's where he opened a grocery store on 9th south above 3rd East.

Now, Grandpa Joseph Bernstein had been on his way to find gold when he, like so many others, stopped in Salt Lake City. As was the way of the times, Jewish people would seek out other Jewish people for a kosher meal and news. That's when these people told my grandfather that the Gold Rush days were long over. They gave him pencils, or shoe laces, and told him to learn English so he could sell his wares on the corner of 1st South and Main Streets.

That's what he did first. Over the years, though, he bought a horse and wagon and traveled all over the country selling vegetables and fruits. When my father was a young boy, he'd go along with them. If my father went too far, he'd stay with people over night, but he would always be back home in time for *Shabbes*. He always made it home on time.

The Stereses visiting Mr. Williams. (Courtesy of Gail Bernstein Ciacci)

Frum—My parents were first generation Americans. My mother always koshered the kitchen for Passover, but they were very poor in the beginning of their marriage and they had to decide how they were going to run their lives. Their parents all had accents, came from the old country, and came as Orthodox Jews. My grandmother, Gussie Bernstein, not only placed doilies on every piece of furniture in the house but she had a reputation for being an excellent cook. She kept a *frum* kitchen and took in Jewish boarders. She was the woman whose house was open for any religious Jew passing through Utah to go to—that's how kosher she was.

My grandmother Gussie was an educated Jew who wrote letters in Yiddish to family and friends throughout the United States. She was president of the Talmud Torah, a woman's club at Congregation Montefiore. She lived down on Custer Court, which was a little street between 3rd and 4th South on 3rd East. If you go halfway down that block, and turn east, you would have seen a little corridor of stuck-together houses. A lot of Jewish families used to live in that area. It was of course within walking distance of the synagogue and was like a courtyard with grass. It's not there now, but we used to go there on holidays. She was a strict no-nonsense type of woman with her hair pulled back into a tight bun. Whenever we went to her house, we had to behave.

Dropped Like a Hot Potato—I'd say it was different growing up in Utah as a Jew. Sometimes we felt isolated from other Jewish families because no other Jew lived nearby. I saw my friends at synagogue and when I took the bus after school to go downtown to *heder* at Congregation Montefiore. My mother didn't drive in those days but my father would pick me up after work. Anita Nord and I were the first girls who were bat mitzvahed with Rabbi Cardon.

I was fortunate in elementary school because I was usually accepted during school time. It was only afterwards that I was dropped like a hot potato. Why? Because I wouldn't go to primary with the Mormon kids and nobody gave me any respect for my religion. They just told me that I was going to go to hell because I didn't join the right church. And I can remember to this day, in the third grade, the teacher said, "All Christians stand up." And I knew I wasn't Christian, but I wasn't going to sit there either. So I stood up. I don't know what would have happened if I didn't stand up. In those days, you didn't make waves.

Life got easier in the higher grades. I went to East High where you could count the number of Jewish kids on your left hand. By this time, I had several non-Jewish friends and I was the first Jewish girl selected for Pep Club at East High. I felt good about it, like I was breaking new ground. Finding a Jewish date though was a problem because all the local boys we knew were like brothers to us. I finally went to college in Boulder, Colorado where the campus was heavily populated with Jews and I joined a Jewish sorority.

Third Generation—Knowing how isolated I felt in grade school, when my two children, who are six years apart in age, started at the same elementary school, I wanted them to feel comfortable with their Judaism and be in a school where they could hold their heads high and be proud of their heritage. So I got involved right away, explaining the different traditions and symbols, always bringing in Chanukah treats, and showing the kids how to play Jewish games like spinning the dreidel and singing songs. I didn't get into religious issues, there is no reason to, but wanted to share the customs and traditions that are part of my children's life so that other kids could understand and accept the differences. I feel that way about other ethnic minority groups with their fascinating traditions and customs. I think we're all in the same boat, and I hope today's parents are going into schools, explaining traditions and customs, showing the real diversity that exists in our state.

My kids are grown up now and on their own, *kayn aynhoreh*. But the teachers always called me back and so they were upset when twelve years later they had to go on without me!

Temple B'nai Israel, so we know who is going to be buried at the congregation and who is going to be buried at the Temple.[3]

I don't remember when Shaarey Tzedek disbanded. Maybe it was happening that when immigration was cut off and the next generation was growing up, and, why, we didn't want to live that way anymore. We liked what was going on at Congregation Montefiore. When I was a teenager, they got a young rabbi by the name of Burstein, who formed a Jewish club called Maimonides. It was a social club, so eventually it got us with a lot of other Jewish kids and drew us away from Shaarey Tzedek. I have to say there was a lot of us who met our future wives in this club.

Seeking Work—I went back to Congregation Montefiore because I quit high school in my sophomore year and went to business college to become a stenographer. Then I got myself a job after college to pay my way through school so my folks wouldn't find out that I wasn't still really going to high school. They never did find out until the truant officer came after me.

Improving One's Prospects—My father had aspirations to see all of us boys become professional men. In 1924, I went from business college and worked for a man by the name of Alex Sims in an automobile agency. He sold parts, accessories for automobiles, to dealers. In those days, cars never came equipped with bumpers or trunks. He had gone broke during the depression and lost himself over a million dollars, but gradually he got into the building material business. That's when I went to work for him, first starting as a stenographer to learn the business. By 1930, I went into business for myself representing Soule Steel Company. Later I opened my own company called Associated Specialties. I sold and installed building materials. We furnished a lot of materials to build the Huntsville monastery; we put in the steel joists that hold their Quonset hut together. We made the floors in the monastery in Ogden. We just got through with the aluminum finishing on the LDS Church Administration Building. I still go to the school of hard knocks and I've learned over the years that I can read plans and am a self-made engineer. My brother Sam became an attorney. Herm went to the university for one year and then he was drafted into the army. When he was discharged, he went into business with me. Father died in 1934.

Sacrifice—What my Dad did in those days always amazes me because it required an awful lot of sacrifice, as far as I am concerned, to stay out on the road all that time away from your family to take care of them. My father had tremendous dedication. He had a mother, brother and some sisters in Europe. He would get letters telling them how bad things were over there, you know. So my father, who didn't know how to read or write, not only tried to keep his own family together here, he tried to keep those people over there from starving to death by sending his hard-earned money. He tried to get them to America. After the First World War, he sent money for his youngest brother and a nephew of his oldest brother to come to the United States. They got to Hamburg and this youngest brother had spent the whole war as a prisoner in Siberia, so they had nothing.

They couldn't get a visa into the United States. They were told to get on the ships going to Mexico City. In Mexico, all you had to do is walk across the border into the United States.

So, Uncle Morris gets into Mexico City, and he's in a community that is European, strictly Orthodox, and living the life the way he wanted to live. So he married there and stayed, and we have been down to Mexico for the weddings of their children. They're all married and keep kosher homes so their mother and father could eat in their homes.

My father had he come here twenty years later than he did would have had a tough time making it. Things were changing. Everybody would be driving automobiles. This way, you can imagine going in with a couple of bare horses and a wagon loaded with fruit, driving up into the rural areas where it takes you a day to go to the summit and another day to get some place else. These people were living in areas where they couldn't raise their own fruit. They were looking forward to somebody who had enough fortitude to survive the hardships of travel. My father did that. And during the depression, he helped put my two brothers in school. They worked too; and I was working. That's what we did. This is the story of immigrants and the history of people my age born from immigrant parents.

RED-HOT COALS

Esther Klein

Early Downtown Scenes—I don't think the streets were paved.[1] They were dirt streets uptown and I can see the old trolley cars, and one old-fashioned store, dry goods store on Main Street between Second and Third South. I think it was called Cohn Bros. This is when they didn't have cash registers in every department; instead, they had those wire baskets that stretched overhead. They had a contraption on the balcony where tube-like pipes would extend out to the different departments and a salesman would twist open a little container, put the sales slip and the money in, and send the container back up the tube. If there was change due back, then someone would send the container back down with the right amount.

I remember the Walker Brothers building. I was still playing with dolls and they were having some kind of sales gimmick that little girls of a certain age could get dressed up, bring their dolls, and have hot chocolate in the display window. My sister Elizabeth fixed my hair in curls, and we did end up with a little cup and saucer that I kept for years. (You know my hair was long. I never did have a haircut until after I got up to high school and decided to have it cut like the rest of the girls. My mother was so disappointed. Elizabeth and I went into the bathroom and she proceeded to cut my hair and put it up on rollers. That was so funny. My mom said we were crazy, and I finally did get to go to a barber that did it right.)

Packing Ice Cream—Klein's Bazaar was located just a few stores below on Main Street from Third South on the eastside of the street. This man's name was Klein, like ours, but we weren't related.[2] He used to sell candy at the store, but the shop was more like a bazaar with dishes, household goods, and a whole bunch of stuff. Right next to that store was Freshman's Jewelry Store. This was around 1919, but I can remember even earlier times when we were growing up. In the summertime there was a railroad that would go by on 1st West. It used to deliver beer which, of course, would come packed in ice. My father, Joseph Klein, would say, "If so-and-so would take the wagon and pick up some ice, I'll help Mama fix some ice cream." If there were neighbor kids with us, we'd go east to a place called Putnam's. He had an ice cream parlor, but

Looking south on Main Street with Cohn's Ready-to-Wear Store on right, early 1900s. (Courtesy of Utah State Historical Society)

he'd sell us the cones without the ice cream if we wanted. My mother would make the ice cream and she and my father would treat the neighborhood.

My mother had an old ice cream freezer, a little wooden bucket that you had to take turns cranking. When my dad was younger, he used to really keep it going, but, gee, by the time it was our turn, we were young and didn't have too much stamina to keep it up. We were always there though to have a small taste when my dad and mother took out the middle part of the ice cream and then packed it with ice so it would freeze up a bit faster. And, of course, we always had salt that we could pack around the freezer and then cover it with an old gunny sack to keep the ice from melting too fast. Later in the day, my mother would serve the ice cream and I can remember this one scoop. It was round at the bottom and came up to a peak with little prongs on the inside that would loosen the ice cream into the ice cream cone.

In the summer time, the ice cream wagons, horse-drawn no less, would go by with their ding-a-ling. Why, when we heard it, we went running. The ice cream man would serve six scoops of

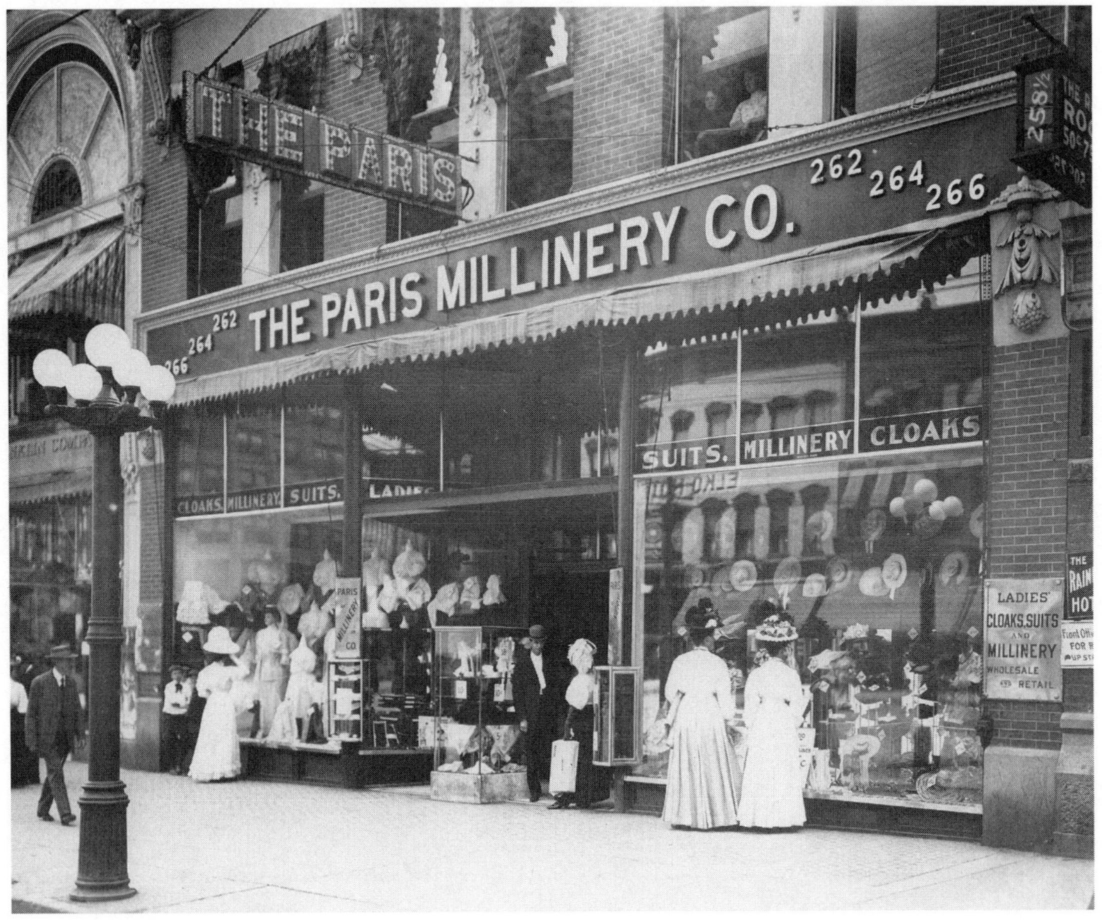

The Paris Millinery Company, on 262-266 South Main Street, 1908. (Courtesy of Utah State Historical Society)

ice cream for a quarter. We'd bring our bowl out with a quarter and have quite a treat. That's generally what would happen after we had our dinner. I remember that plain. From there, the ice cream wagons kind of changed to carts, you know, where the kids would push carts and sell ice cream.

Secondhand Baths—I was born in November 1906. I think by then we were living in a little adobe house on 2nd South and West Temple. That was before you had indoor bathrooms. When the weather was warm enough, my mother would fill a round tub of water and let the sun heat it as best it could in the back yard so we could all take a bath. I was the youngest and got the bath water at the tail end. Oh, shoot. I hated that. It was the same water and by the time I got into it, it would be just lukewarm—and probably not really clean. I must have been three or four years old then but I won't forget it. Later we moved to a place where we had electricity: an electric stove and an electric heater to heat the water. It was like seventh heaven to have all that hot water.

Blue Eyes—My dad didn't have much schooling, but his mind was real sharp and he always claimed that he taught himself to read the newspaper and talk in English. He was real fair-skinned and had kind of strawberry red hair, a thick head of hair, that looked like it was curly but only because of the way he combed it. He always had a moustache, would never let any one of us trim his moustache, had to do that himself. His eyes were really blue and he was a little on the tall and wiry side. He traveled quite a bit in his younger days. He came here from Hungary when he was around eighteen years old. One of his first jobs was with a railroad crew. When work was slow, he'd pick fruit in the orchards. I know he went down Miami way because he mentioned that one time he was sick and put into a Catholic Hospital; he said nuns were nice to him. He could remember going west, and even getting near Yellowstone Park, but he never actually went inside the park. I guess he was working on the railroad then and got as far as Denver. I know that's where my mother and father met. They were married in Pueblo, Colorado.

Ellis Island Names—My mother was from Warsaw, Poland. Her last name was like Rosencuss, but not that. As we go through the records that name has been misspelled so many times it is really a shame. My dad, too, always used to say in later years that he didn't think Klein was the right spelling of his name. But I guess they didn't have anyone to correctly translate his last name when he arrived at Ellis Island; so they translated what they heard. Klein.

Mother was dark skinned with black hair and brown eyes. She wasn't very tall. She came to America on board a ship and carried her bedding and stuff; I think I still have her little trunk. She came with her three sisters, but only her older sister Aunt Molly and she went west to settle in Pueblo. The other two sisters didn't get any further from New York City than when they arrived. Eventually they lost track of each other.

A Laborer—Even though my father did rough work, he never used rough language around us. He was a laborer and worked at the smelter. He didn't have a profession so it was just plain labor work, but it was really nice. Like I say, he never used coarse language and he always had a firm rule that he thought people of foreign heritage should talk American when they were out in public. In the homes, it was different. Besides speaking Yiddish, my parents spoke Czechoslovakian or Hungarian if they didn't want us to know what they were talking about. We caught on and understood Yiddish and German, but not Czech or Hungarian. And we never really picked up any language, other than English, enough to carry on a conversation.

Cramped Quarters—Golly, you just wonder about how our parents got along because for a long time we didn't have any modern conveniences. One lone light globe hung in our bedroom and in our kitchen. One bedroom for the parents, two beds in one room for the girls, and my brother slept on a couch in the living room of a particular home that I remember in Salt Lake. There are a lot of things I guess I won't forget. Somewhere along the line, I had just started going to Grant School when we moved to another house in a little court on 8th South between West Temple and 1st West. It was called Jefferson Place.

Chased by a Rooster—Now, I had an odd occurrence there. After I started school, they used to dress me in red—I'm not sure why—and I'd come home from school and there'd be a darn old rooster chasing me out in the street. He would never let me walk on the sidewalk. I'd run out in the street and cry. I guess I cried my head off. The minute my mother heard me crying, why, here she'd come, no matter what she was doing, with a broom in her hand to shoo the darn rooster away from me. That was the craziest thing. I just can't imagine that rooster didn't seem to bother anybody else. But I guess it just knew that I was afraid of it.

"Rehearsing for tonight's show."
(Courtesy of Utah State Historical Society)

The Circus Comes to Town—When we lived in that little court, a lot of vacant fields were around there and when the circus was coming, you'd see people put up billboards all around the fields. Railroad tracks led into these fields and at that time, why, the circus used to come in on the railroad and unload their equipment and animals. Of course, they'd come early in the morning and so we wanted to stay up all night long so we wouldn't miss them. Mom said we couldn't but Dad would always awaken us on time so we could watch the men that worked in the circus lead the animals out of the boxcars. It was really quite interesting because the young boys in the neighborhood would get jobs carrying water to the different animals and hosing them down. There'd be a lot of noise and confusion. We'd watch them put up the tents. The people were so different from what we were used to seeing. They had their shirts all pushed up over their elbows. But I don't remember if they talked rough other than shouting at the animals and ordering the kids around.

At other times, the medicine show would hit town. They would set up on the other side of the field from where we lived. The men would look like they do in the old western movies: some would have a wagon with pots and pans and medicine. They'd have singing and dancing girls, ladies that traveled along with them; and at certain times of the year, they'd have pie-eating contests. It was generally the boys that would join in that and their hands would be behind their backs since they weren't supposed to use their hands to eat the pie. Pie filling and crust would be all over their faces.

They had shows in the evening and we'd go as a family to hear them hawk patent medicine like "Lydia Pinkham" which had ingredients, they used to say in later years, with enough potency to produce a baby from every bottle. When you think about how medicine shows kept their medications, why, they always had a joke about how it was mostly alcohol, even though it was supposed to be good for anything that ailed you. People believed in that, you know, because there weren't too many doctors out West at that time. They had a lot of pharmacies and pharmacists who acted like doctors, but not doctors. I don't think my parents ever bought medicine from medicine shows although I know they used to patronize the pharmacies.

This was way before my time, in Pueblo, my sister Katie, the one who passed away in October [1982], told me how my mother used to fix a lunch and some lemonade, put the kids in an old wicker buggy and go to the circus. Katie said she saw Tom Thumb and that he was a really little person who could stand in the palm of your hand but was just as normal as normal.

Pearl White—We also used to go to the old Pantages for live entertainment. We'd go through the ads in the newspaper and cut out free passes to go to the theatre before show time. That's how a lot of times we got to go to the shows. Further down the street was another playhouse that showed movies. I think it was named Mahesy, and it was just above Broadway. They showed serials every week. You had to go to see if Pearl White was saved. Have you ever heard of her? She's the one on the railroad tracks; each chapter would always end where she was in a terrible predicament. We went there often on Saturdays. On certain nights, you'd deposit part of our ticket and if you were lucky enough to have the other part of our ticket called, why, sometimes, they'd give money prizes. Whenever my dad won, he'd always share his luck. Of course, it was never very much in those days, but we had a good life together.

The Working Trades—My older brother stopped going with us when he took a job delivering millinery for the store, Adrian and Emily's. He also got a job on the newspaper and had a paper route on West Temple below 9th South. In the winter, Dad said it wouldn't hurt us to help him deliver papers, so we stacked the papers on the sled and afterwards I always got to ride home on the sled. My brother had a bike, too. If a paperboy missed leaving a paper at one of the homes, they'd call my brother and he'd deliver it. Of course, he still had to attend Hebrew School at Congregation Montefiore. It was only for boys then. Girls didn't go to Hebrew School.

A Matter of Yiddish—I remember a time when my mother wanted me to be friends with a Jewish girl my age. I was over to her place visiting and this girl was talking in Yiddish to her mother about me. It was nothing bad about me, but it bothered me and I excused myself and went home. I told my mother, "Don't they realize that I can understand Yiddish, even though I don't speak it?" So my mother says, "What do you expect, being raised in a Jewish home and not speaking Yiddish?" I guess it was strange that we didn't speak Yiddish. In fact, on my first trip with my sister to a wedding in New York, they thought it was really strange that we didn't speak Yiddish.

A Matter of Difference—What was even more strange to me was when I was young—I don't remember how old—the kids I used to play with said I was going to have to go to Jerusalem to live. I said, "Why would I ever have to go to Jerusalem to live?" "Well," they said, "That's where Jews come from originally." And I said, "I don't think so. I was born and raised here. Why should I have to go there?" That was the first time I'd ever heard about having to leave this country because I was Jewish. I was just as much an American as they were. They were all LDS kids and as a rule we got along pretty good. But you know, if I was playing with one Mormon girl, that was fine, but the minute a couple of other Mormon girls came along, then, I was deserted. Alone, I'd go home.

A Difference in Religious Traditions—My father was not especially religious. The only thing he ever mentioned was that he had hoped to become a religious person. But when he was farmed out to his uncle in Hungary, why, his uncle expected my father to do all the farm work, and left no time for his prayers or to study. So my dad got his fill of farming, and somewhere along the line, why, he didn't get to carry on his religion like he wanted. I guess he lost his ambition. He did go to Synagogue on Friday nights and Saturday mornings and High Holy Days. We lived on 2nd East and 6th South near Congregation Shaarey Tzedek. He would go there because it was so close to the house, but he actually felt more at home there. They were store people and they were more religious, he believed, than the others.

Congregation B'nai Israel seemed to have a wealthier class of people: business people and people that had stores, like Arthur Frank. He always came in late and it took him forever to get settled in the pew. At Montefiore, they were store people, too, but they were more religious than at B'nai Israel, and maybe not as outgoing. We weren't outgoing either. Maybe if we had been, we would have made more friends. Well, we went to B'nai Israel and in between services, which were said in both Hebrew and in English, we'd wander over to Shaarey Tzedek and sit with Mother. At some point, Mama would tell my sister Katie to go home and start the farfel.

Soup—They call it a different name nowadays, but Mama made what they called egg barley. You don't need very much barley. You'd put it in hot water and then have it to go in the chicken soup. Mother used to make all of her noodles. She was a very good cook and was never at a loss for soup. If we ever called up and asked what was for dinner," she would say "Soup." We'd say, "Soup again?" And she said, "There'll come a time when you'll wish you had some of this soup."

Traditions—Dad used to sneak out of services during High Holy Days. It was a tradition. He'd go to a show downtown and always come back with a great big sack of grapes. My mother could always tell 'cause he did the same thing every year, sneak out of services, walk uptown, go to a show, and bring back a present. She believed if that was his pleasure, I guess, it was okay. Mother always held the fast. Afterwards, she would pour a little glass of wine to go with her sponge cake. When we were little, we'd dunk our sponge cake into the wine, and it would taste like a real grownup treat.

Years later, when I was in high school, I wanted to get a part-time job earning money, but my sister said I could be a lot more help to my mother than making the amount anyone would pay me. Still, when I saved a quarter, I'd buy a World War I saving stamp to put in a little book. One time my tonsils were a mess and I turned the books in to pay for my tonsillectomy. I wanted to save the tonsils so I could see what they looked like. I was really curious, but the doctor told me they were so abscessed and full of holes, they couldn't be saved for me to even look at.

I paid for the surgery with these savings stamps, because we all wanted to pay for whatever happened to us. Dad never did make an awful lot of money, but we never went hungry. He always used to check my mother's purse to see if she had enough money to go shopping, so she wouldn't be penniless. That's why we always wanted to pay for board and room. When it was my turn, I got a job after high school, and my mother said, "Buy yourself some decent clothes and a winter coat, maybe a pair of shoes." I said I'd do something else. For a dollar a week, I signed up at the Utah Power and Light for our first vacuum cleaner.

Careers—My first job was with the Metropolitan Life Insurance. I did clerical work. I started after high school, in 1926, and spent my whole life there. I think I retired in 1967. Like I say, we always got jobs as soon as we could to kind of help out with the family things. Sometimes when we lived on the other side of West Temple, on 8th South, my mother would pack a lunch and we'd walk all the way to Liberty Park, have a picnic and listen to the band concert. We'd always have enough money to buy a bottle of pop to drink with our lunch. We all went together to the park and we all walked home together. Oh, gee, that used to be the longest walk home.

Red Coals—Sometimes we'd catch a train to go to Saltair. Everybody used to try to ride in the pen cars, and there we'd be, all of our family and a big lunch box. My father and mother went with us all the time but I don't think my mother ever went into the water. The water was so deep that as the train would come into the depot and drop us off, we could just go bathing on the south side of the railroad tracks. When I got my first car in '29—the salesman had to teach me how to drive the car—we'd drive out to Black Rock where the Great Salt Lake would be just like the ocean, the tide coming in and going out. (In later years, the water receded and I don't think it ever came back to what it used to be.) They had a bathhouse, in '29 or '30, and it was quite a thing to go out there in an evening. As they dumped all the red coals from the smelter into the water on that black and full night, it was such a pleasure to be in that warm water. And it was like watching fireworks to see those red coals coming down the side and breaking into the water.

Father Has an Accident—My dad always worked, even after having several accidents at Kennecott, so around 1929 or so, he decided to go into peddling. He got a horse and wagon, went to different buildings to see if he could pick up any of their scrap iron or other things they wanted to get rid of. I know he went to the Newhouse and Boston buildings because he had friends there. I know that for sure. And I know that there were times when he would be gone overnight and go clear up to Bingham. Can you imagine? That used to be a long, steep drag to get up there. They had a one-way tunnel and you'd have to wait until that light turned green to let you know the tunnel was clear for you to pass through.

One day, my father was down on State Street and the horse went over a cement log and felled the wagon and my father. Dad must have landed on his head or face in the gravel. He was an awful mess and the doctor out there wouldn't take care of him until he could show that he had money to pay for treatment. My dad gave him a name of a person who would verify that he could pay—he gave a Jewish man by the name of Louis Block. I think this same Mr. Block came to take care of the horse. Well, the doctor stitched him up badly. He didn't even do a decent job cleaning his face and nose. Dad ended up having to go into the hospital where our family doctor could take care of him.

It took a long time for him to recuperate, but every once in awhile, he'd go visit all these old clients, and eventually he rented another horse and wagon to get rid of the trash that these buildings would accumulate. He must have been in his early seventies then, but he was always independent. After my mother died and my father's hearing got bad, he'd go to services with us at B'nai Israel.

THE TRAVELING SALESMAN

Simon Shapiro

Simon Shapiro was born in Russia and entered this country with his father and brother in 1890. Before he opened his trunk factory in Salt Lake City, Simon Shapiro traveled west at a time soon after the turn of the century when men still wore guns on their belts.

"My father was a city boy," says son and Salt Lake merchant Joel Shapiro. "He was a city boy when he was born; he was a city boy when he came west and got into the mercantile trades. At five-foot-eight, he was anything but the raw-boned tough cowboy. I rarely heard him swear. A mild man, he spoke structured English laced with an Old World perception. But he was the butt of many jokes. Many of these cowboys types would seize on him as this young, skinny, sallow Jewish boy traveling the little towns of the West. They'd play jokes on him, which he learned to "take"—which, Shapiro philosophizes, "many minority people, at that time, learned to take."

His father rode horses. "He wasn't great. He told us he just wanted to get along. Once in a western town, in a saloon, they set him up for a ride into the countryside. He and a 'set-up' companion got on their horses, nice little saddle horses, and ambled off. Half a mile down the road, the man turned and said, 'What's that in back of us?' My father's horse reared and turned, taking off like a streak of lightning, down the street, back into town, with my father hanging on to his neck in pure terror.

"Unbeknownst to him," says Shapiro, "the town had a custom of racing horses on command from the edge of town to the saloon. Like a bullet, his horse shot back to the saloon where everybody was waiting out front, laughing with great hilarity at this poor man, just barely hanging on, scared to death. They made a fool of him, but this is the kind of thing they did to a young, skinny Jewish kid. And my dad had to get along with them because he had come to that little town to see a merchant and to sell his wares."

At about this time, Simon Shapiro learned to play poker. "He didn't die until he was ninety-one," Shapiro says. "And he used to play poker two or three afternoons a week. Some of his

Shapiros in the 1920s: Prosperity before the crash. Note the Bakelite toiletries. (Courtesy of the Shapiro family)

poker 'maters' would accuse him of being too slow. As he told me, he had learned to play with both hands on the table since he was playing with guys with guns on their hips. I remember my mother would yell at him when they were playing bridge. 'You're too slow,' she'd say. 'You don't have to open and close the cards after every bid. You're holding up the game.'

"But he learned to look at a poker hand, bid, fold it, and keep both hands on the table." He learned in the West.[1]

AMERICAN BUSINESS

Comments by Joel Shapiro

Most of the stores I'm talking about are family held kind of stores, like ours [Shapiro's Luggage, Gifts, and Leather], where there's a great deal of passing on to the second and third generation.[2] There's also a great deal of closing up when there is no one to pass on to. There's quite a bit of buying out. That is, maybe a guy doesn't have the sons or daughters who want to take it over.

Even if they're good, some of them just close up and disappear in the night. That's the end of it. That's the story of American business. Go on for fifty years, and all of a sudden, it quits.

I've not pushed my boys to be interested in retailing. I've not given them any speeches about the glories of retailing. In fact, I've tended to talk the other way around. I think retailing has many rewards, many rewards: emotional, psychological, and so forth. It's also got to be the most difficult mistress in the world. It's a

Shapiros in the 1930s, catering to travel. (Courtesy of the Shapiro family)

driving thing, with retailing deals, essentially, six months from now, a year from now. You're constantly being asked to look around the corner in time.

Your judgements are on the line every day to predict tomorrow. It's a high-risk business. Any form of retailing; very high risk. You can lose your bundle of potatoes in six months. And anybody who wants to have fun and enjoy retailing has got to have a bit of daring. You've got to have a willingness to take chances and high risks without getting ulcers. New things? Constantly. You can never stick with anything. You no sooner get something nailed down, a procedure or method, a technique, a line or service, something happens and it's got to be uprooted and changed again.

It allows no resting, and for most people, it requires all the human energy and analytic thinking you can throw at it. It's not a forty-hour a week job. I've told my kids, I think with very fair accuracy, there's better ways to make a living, in the sense that one can have more time for himself. If you're a person who wants to work thirty-five to forty hours a week, and go boating, and enjoy the pleasures of raising a family, stay out of retailing. It won't allow you that much time, if you're the boss.

I just figured out how to do it a few years ago. The question of what it offers and why I do it, maybe are two different things. I was not trained to do anything else. I drifted into it and I just stayed here. I just kept at it 'til I learned how to do it right and I'm still learning. What does it offer me in mature life? A sense of self and self satisfaction, an ability to provide for my family with a decent living, and a decent way of making a living.

It's given me peer acknowledgement as a nice person. I've conducted my affairs on a high level. Good service. Integrity. A nice relationship with banks, suppliers, and salesmen. I'm looked upon as a decent chap, by most. Those are conventional and reasonable values. People see retailers as being narrow and dumb. I'm trying to suggest to you that most of them who survive are neither narrow nor dumb. Their sense of public service is broad. Their sense of public awareness is broad. And their intellectual grasp of what's happening in the world has got to be attentive and keen, and "with it" all the time.

FIVE

Minyan in a Railroad Town

AN OGDEN NATIVE

Ralph Benowitz

Wide-Open Spaces—Many Jews I think came to the West to look for a different life than they might have witnessed or their parents might have witnessed coming from Europe.[1] Most immigrants came to New York City; many to Baltimore, Maryland, but the conditions living in the eastside of New York, like my father and his family did, were very difficult. They lived in a small two-room apartment with six children in one of the crowded tenement buildings on the eastside. For Jews and Italians, primarily, it was very difficult living. In my father's case, when he came to the United States, he didn't feel that the opportunity was there for him.

Joseph Benowitz, my father, was brought over to America with his family in 1891 from Bialystok, Poland. At that time, Russia had control of that portion of Poland. My father's family left to get away from the long arm of the Russian czar in which Russian soldiers would come into a community and take away any eligible, young Jewish boy they thought would serve their purposes in the army. In many cases, the family never saw that child again. My father's parents thought the thing to do was leave if they could, which they did. They arrived in Ellis Island in 1891. Now, in New York, my father worked in one of the sweatshops to learn a cap trade. This was in the days when sweatshops were really sweatshops. There were very little or no facilities at all that were proper for the working conditions. He worked for several years; the first many weeks for nothing, and then finally they paid him a dollar a week. He brought home a dollar and gave half of it to his parents. I assume that his brothers did the same.

New Horizons—Sometime around 1901, my father and a friend, whom he had met coming over from Europe, decided to go to Waco, Texas. They wanted to go there because they heard about the possibilities of making a fortune. A hurricane struck Galveston that year and killed about 6,000 people, destroyed a lot of property, communities. Now they were rebuilding, making a 17-foot sea wall, and building up towns and communities. There was a lot of work done.

Each of the two men had about five hundred dollars. They packed their clothes and went to Waco, but the opportunities just weren't there and the result was they lost their money and they returned to New York broke. Then my father heard about St. Joseph, Missouri. St. Joseph had been a site in the United States where before the transcontinental railroad came into being, manufacturing had begun and the wagon trains would go through St. Joseph to get supplies on their way westward. My father traveled there and got a job in the cap factory known as the St. Joseph Hat and Cap Company. Incidentally, that cap factory is still in existence and is now the home of Stetson Hats.

On to Utah—My father became acquainted with a number of people in St. Joseph, several of whom talked about the possibilities in Utah. It was then he decided he would like his own business. He had saved some money, since he was still single, and he came on a train from St. Joseph to Utah. First, the train would go to Ogden and then to Salt Lake City, and my father's intent was to go to Salt Lake City.[2] He got off the train at the old Ogden Depot to stretch his legs, and saw the hustle and bustle and the tremendous activity that was taking place. A lot of people were there because the railroad was building a trestle over the Great Salt Lake that would shorten the route from Utah to the West Coast. The old route went around the north part of the Great Salt Lake; the new one would cut off a number of miles.

So there were lots of people still there: a lot of Chinese labor, a lot of Italian labor, and, particularly from the bottom of 25th Street going up to Washington Boulevard, a matter of three blocks, a lot of Jewish clothing stores. There were also a lot of saloons, hotels, and brothels. My dad told me, and he would laugh when he said it, there were 30 brothels, and 30 saloons and 30 clothing stores.

So, my father got off the train in 1907, saw the activity, the beautiful mountains—he came early in the fall—and said, "I'm going to stay here." He never got to Salt Lake to open a business, but he did open a small store and then his brother, my Uncle William and his family came. They operated their first store, under the trade name of Benowitz Brothers, on 25th Street. It was called the B.B. Clothes Store. That was the original name, but it evolved into a slightly different name over the years after I came in the business. My father's business, as well as the other Jewish storeowners, was to meet the needs of the many railroad workers who had been work-

Early religious school at Temple Brith Sholem. (Courtesy of Brith Sholem)

ing on the lake cut-off. He sold workingman's clothes. By the end of the year, the project had been completed, and it was not long before many other workers left. Soon thereafter, so did other Jewish families.

Early Jewish Pioneers—It is said that the first Jews arrived in Ogden about 1890, but exactly who they all were is not certain. If there was one family that may have been the earliest to arrive, it was the Kuhn Brothers, who moved to Ogden in 1880 and established a wholesale dry goods business. Apparently, they did not become founders of the religious Jewish community, although they were very successful business people in those days. As I understand it, in the later years, there was some intermarriage and when the Kuhn family had some deaths, the Orthodox Jews controlling the cemetery wouldn't allow them to have burial in the Jewish cemetery. There is a good-sized vault immediately on the north side of the Jewish cemetery with the Kuhn name on it.

A Synagogue in Ogden—The synagogue that now exists was built by a half a dozen or more businessmen of the community of that time, and my father was one of them. It was built in 1921. Before then, Jewish families living here held Orthodox religious services in the Independent

Order of Odd Fellows (IOOF) Hall on Grant Avenue between 24th and 25th Streets. They rented space there, but they wanted their own place of worship, their own structure. So these individuals, including my father, formed the nucleus of the community that officially organized Congregation Brith Sholem in 1921 and finished construction of the building at 2750 Grant Avenue.[3] At the time, the location was still a desirable community area and close to many stores on 25th Street. It was a thriving Jewish community with family names such as the Kreines Brothers, Rosenberg, Oppman, Benowitz Brothers, Lutzker, Rubin, Rubenstein, Smith, Gordon Brothers, Kertz Brothers, Medoway, Oliash, Hersovitz, Greenband, Lavin, Booth, Siner, and Sugar. In the 1920s and into the late 1930s, other Jewish families joined the community: Saperstein, Bruckner, Swartz, Seidner, Diamond and Morrison.

At home in Ogden (*l–r*): Grandpa Lieberman (Mollie Benowitz's father); Joseph Benowitz, brother of William and husband of Lillie; Marian Benowitz (Swartz) (seated, age eight), daughter of Mollie and William; Mollie Benowitz; Lillie Benowitz; Evelyn Benowitz (Rosenblatt), daughter of Mollie and William; and William Benowitz

I was born in 1918 only about two blocks from the Congregation Brith Sholem building. Just a short time later, when I was three years old, in 1921, my father and mother bought a home up the hill at 916 23rd Street. It was a good sized home.

Life's Lessons—When I was in grade school, life in school was rather pleasant and times were economically better. Then, in junior high school, it was different at different times. What I mean is that in junior high, it was depression time and things change. As a matter of fact, and this does not relate to school, but it had an uncomfortable influence on us during that time. The Ku Klux Klan had an organization in Ogden and in the foothills in Ogden, on occasion, when we kids were playing, we could see them burn a cross on the hillside. That's my only recollection, burning the cross. It had no real bearing on me, by that I mean we were only kids, but it probably had an effect on my father.

There were several Jewish families in Ogden with children who got together in a group. They were older than me. I remember, Rachelle Medoway, who lives in Salt Lake City, was one of the Jewish groups of friends. And there were three sisters from the Greenband family. My cousins, Marion and Evelyn Benowitz, who later married Joseph Rosenblatt, were part of that group. Evelyn is my first cousin. She is the daughter of William and Molly Benowitz. And William Benowitz is the brother of my father, who was in business with my Dad.

A Hint of Exclusion—In high school, there was only about three or four Jewish students. I was one of them, and it was impossible for a Jewish person to belong to clubs. That was impor-

Congregation Brith Sholem, Ogden. (Photo by Eileen Hallet Stone)

tant to a kid in high school in Ogden in those days. When I was in ROTC, we wore World War One regular uniforms with the wrapped leggings, but as a Jew you wouldn't be able to become a commissioned officer in the ROTC in high school, which was kind of a big thing in those days. We're talking 1933–1934 and I graduated in 1935. I was a good student, I had good grades, and I knew a lot of kids in school but I couldn't get it. I would never be given a commission. I was a sergeant, but that's all. That's as much as they could give you. I could never get into a club, neither did any of my Jewish friends, and socially, we were out more or less in left wing. The overall community of kids didn't want to take any of the Jewish people into their groups. I must say I had two good Mormon friends who went to school with me; one of them is a lifelong friend. Larry Evans, whose father was a bishop, lived right across the street

MRS. SINER DONATES SYNAGOGUE STONE

The cornerstone of the synagogue being erected by the Brith Sholem congregation in Ogden, was donated by Mrs. A. Siner in memory of her husband, who died about two years ago. The cornerstone was laid last Sunday in the presence of more than 1,000 people.

At the time of his death, Mr. Siner was president of the congregation, and was instrumental in securing the lot on which the synagogue is being built. Mrs. Siner is president of the Hebrew Ladies Benevolent Society.

A total of $761 in voluntary donations have been received by the building committee, it is announced by A. Rosenberg, president of the congregation.[4]

VANDALS BURN, RANSACK BRITH SHOLEM IN OGDEN; NO LEADS

When at 4 A.M., Saturday, Dec. 30, vandals broke into the Brith Sholem synagogue in Ogden, UT, they set seven fires in the 67-year-old building.

On the south side of its vestibule, prayer books and a tallis rack were destroyed. An American flag by a back door was burned. Areas that held printed matter were also burned. Areas behind the Ark were ransacked. The sanctuary itself received considerable smoke damage. However, an Israeli flag was found intact and fortunately, the Torahs, found lying on the synagogue floor, sustained no further damage.

According to Dr. Robert Brodstein, spokesperson for Brith Sholem, the Torahs were "not unrolled, marked, or slashed with knives."

At the time of desecration, the synagogue was empty, according to Detective David Lucas of the Ogden City Police. Although one set of footprints was discovered, all leads to the unknown perpetrator "are pretty well exhausted." Lucas described the incident as "possibly being one of a person who, looking to steal, broke in, and when not finding anything, got angry, took out his Bic lighter and started fires on his way out."

Because of drifting winds, the scent of fire was in the air, alerting firemen of its presence but not location. . . .

A community without a rabbi, the residents relied on the older Jewish men to lead Friday night services and teach the young children. Like many congregations common in small cities and towns, a handful of educated Jewish people strive to keep Jewish traditions and customs alive. . . .

"There is a strong Jewish spirit in the community of Ogden," said Rabbi Wenger of Congregation Kol Ami in Salt City. "They are fiercely loyal to their synagogue, to Judaism and to the Jewish people. They have a tremendous spirit of volunteerism, and maintain their congregation with their own services and enthusiasm."

. . . Shortly after news of the fire reached the ears of other residents, there were offers of help. "This tragedy has brought our own congregation closer to the general population and has provided heartwarming responses," said Brodstein. "Telephone calls have poured in with offers from other churches to use their buildings for services as well as contributions from a variety of individuals. The County of Morgan offered a cleanup crew. We've been holding *minyans* at Ogden's McKay Dee Hospital." Since the fire, more people have been attending services.[5]

from us and he was very friendly to the Benowitz family. Larry went to the University of Utah and was a student of a Jewish professor who was well known in those days, Dr. Louis Zucker, and he always talked about how great a man he was. Larry became a professor of Philosophy at Weber State University. A dear friend, he died a few years ago. He was my friend growing up from the time, well, even before we went to school, before kindergarten. I never talked with him about the relationship with Jews and clubs, no, no, we didn't talk about it. I went away to the University of California, Berkeley, in later years and we didn't see as much of each other. But we came together several years before he died and he was the same wonderful person I knew when we were very young.

Rabbis Come and Go—After they built Temple Brith Sholem, rabbis did come for awhile. Rabbi Finkelstein, who was a very fine person and a very fine rabbi, left after a few years, but there were one or two other rabbis.[6] I remember Rabbi Barris who was there teaching half a dozen of us young boys. He was a very strict Orthodox individual and knew how to use a ruler on your hand if you didn't pay attention. What else do you want from a bunch of nine-, ten- or eleven-year-old kids that came after school and who weren't totally interested but went to Hebrew School because their parents want them to? We were all boys who went to Hebrew School. In those days, girls did not go to Hebrew School in Ogden. Rabbi Barris left after just a few years. I don't think he got a 100 percent attention from us.

Changing Ways—Brith Sholem began as an Orthodox synagogue. When the older men, who were now in their 70s and then into their 80s became fewer in number, and several of them had died, their sons and a younger generation began to take over, including myself. We relied on those elders who were still there at that time, including my father, Mr. Kreines and Mr. Isadore Gordon, and for the most part followed the kind of services that were performed. That was what we did until some of us either moved away or another set of young people, mostly from out of state, moved in and became members of the synagogue. They have done a marvelous job in recreating the synagogue, especially after it was burned, and they are responsible for the wonderful activities that exist in Ogden today.

Of course, Brith Sholem has changed again. The present day Congregation is Reform with tendencies towards Conservative. Yes, because a number of the newcomers who are now leaders in the community and the synagogue are from areas where they had substantial Jewish education and not particularly from Reform homes. I am very proud and pleased to know what they've done to revitalize the synagogue in the community. My wife Regie and I still continue to be members of the Ogden Synagogue as well as we are here at Congregation Kol Ami.

Depression Struggles—My father and his brother had two stores at one time on 25th Street in Ogden. And they were successful up until the depression came, then there was a struggle for everyone. My family still did well and we lived comfortably; not extravagantly, but comfortably. My father and uncle had connections with certain manufacturers that they'd been doing business with and had a good reputation as far as their credit was concerned. So we were able to do that and get by.

SYNAGOGUE IN OGDEN

With the laying of the cornerstone of the Hebrew synagogue, on Grant Avenue between Twenty-seventh and Twenty-eighth streets, on Sunday, Ogden was assured a house of worship for the members of a religious body which has existed thirty centuries.

At the dedication one of the speakers gave the following quotation from an address by James Russell Lowell on the Jew:

"All share in the government of the world was denied for centuries to perhaps the ablest, certainly the most tenacious, race that had ever lived in it—the race to whom we owe our religion, and the purist spiritual stimulus and consolation to be found in our literature."

The Jews gave to the world the moral code and the worship of one God. They drove back idolatry and helped to lay the foundation on which was built modern civilization.

The erecting of the synagogue is a reminder that Ogden is growing and with that growth has come a demand for an ever increasing number of houses of worship in which all shades of religious belief may find expression.

The synagogue was first erected in Babylon, during the period of exile of the Jews. It was a piece of assembly for prayer and study. During their Babylonian captivity, the Jews grew stronger in their faith and finally gained their freedom.

From their earliest history, they have been a people subjected to persecutions, but the one country in which they have been free from discrimination has been America and here they have found their greatest development.

The Orthodox Jew is intensely devoted to his religion and now that a synagogue is assured them in Ogden, those of that belief who are residents will be given the consolation of having a house of worship in which they may commune with their God according to their dictates of conscience.

Every place dedicated to religion adds to a city's moral forces of uplift and makes for a better community.[7]

A Look to the Future—In the mid-1930s, when I was a young man who helped my father during the depression days, I suggested that we change the kind of merchandise that we were carrying. Instead of just workingmen's clothes, I decided why not carry more fashionable clothes of that date? I thought going on a different avenue would promote better opportunities to help revive a business that had been hurt tremendously during depression days, like all the other businesses. And so we did. By then there were very few stores on 25th Street, and we were the only store on 25th Street that had that kind of merchandise. Washington Boulevard was the main street and there were maybe two or three stores, particularly one, that were larger and had even higher-priced merchandise and catered to Mormons. The largest store, Fred M. Nye, was owned by Presbyterians, and they had their own customers. So we sold a dressy type of clothing for men. Not tuxedos, although to a certain extent, people bought them, but there was still the depression going on and there was little opportunity, to speak of, for the working class.

The Stopover in Ogden—The railroad was very strong in those days in Utah, and had their repair shops in Ogden, since it was a stopover place for the Union Pacific going from Chicago to the West Coast. There were a certain number of porters and waiters that would temporarily stop in Ogden and stay over at one or two of the hotels here. And, of course, there were a lot of people who worked on the engines, as well as conductors and brakemen who also had homes in Ogden because of its location to the railroad. So, I thought with so few stores left, yes, it would be the right time to offer a change to people, selling a nicer brand of clothing. That's the direction our business went and we did all right over the years until 1979, when we closed the shop and I left the clothing business. The following year, my wife and I moved to Salt Lake City.

Lone Politician—I've been a Democrat all my life. My father had that background, as many Jews did when they came to the United States. As a matter of fact, a lot of them became Socialists. Over the years, I supported the Democratic Party in Weber County and they came to me in 1972 and asked me to run for the Utah State Senate. After some thought, I decided to do it. We've always been interested in politics in our family, but the reason I decided to, I thought it would be nice to have Jewish representation in the Utah State Senate. I knew our Democratic Governor then and I had been on several committees, done various kinds of work in the community, sat on some boards. I knew of Sol Selvin, and that he was a State Senator, and retired in 1972. I had to run against a Mormon Bishop in a Republican District, and I had never run before. In politics, you know, often name recognition is very important. I was known in the community for various things, but not in politics. In any event, I got 45 percent of the vote, and didn't win but that was pretty good. Maybe it showed a little change.

A Slap in the Face—There is an incident that does stay in my mind from my youth. My friend Larry invited me to come to join the Boy Scout Troop in his Mormon ward, and because there was no Jewish Boy Scout troop in Ogden, I did. One summer, we went to camp up in South Fork Canyon above Ogden. The regional Boy Scouts had a camp there. I went along and I had a very disturbing experience because the regional director of the Boy Scouts of that area was a Mormon who many years later became one of the members of the Seventies Quorum in the LDS Church. He saw me, and he said to me, and I am like twelve years old, and he said to me, and he knew me, incidentally, because he lived only two blocks away from my house, and he knew the Benowitz family, although we were never close, but he said to me, "What are you doing here?" That was devastating to me and I was never comfortable in that camp. I stayed for the rest of it, and then I eventually dropped out of the Boy Scouts.

FARM LIFE AND THE *Jewish Daily Forward*

Doris Neiditch Guss

Escape from the Czar's Army—My parents, Pearl and William Neiditch, were born in Russia and went to America when they were about sixteen years old.[1] My father left to escape the army. My mother left because her mother had passed away and her father had remarried. They had a bakery and all the family, of course, lived there. But she felt it was time for her to move on. Consequently, she made the move along with my dad and they came to New York. As I recall from family stories, they met other Jewish couples and were taken in by a very gracious Jewish family already established in New York. The husband, a rabbi, married the young people and gave them each a place to live. My mother worked in a garment factory for awhile. I don't recall what my father did.

Log Houses for City Folk—My parents then moved to Chicago. My mother gave birth first to a girl and then to a boy. A diphtheria epidemic in the city took both of them. I was born in 1909; and several years later, I had a sister. My father learned the trade of painting buildings in Chicago, but one fine day, he, an uncle, and three friends read that the government was distributing 160 acres per family of dry farming in Dairy Creek, Idaho. He said that all one had to do was improve the property within five years and it could be yours. So, in 1916, five Jewish pioneers left Chicago for Idaho land. I was about seven years old at the time and stayed behind with mother until my father could get us settled. By the time we went to Idaho, it was winter. Two log homes had been built but the logs that my father had gathered earlier were deep in snow. We lived with my aunt and uncle during the winter and in the spring they started building our homestead.

No Minyans, No Matzo—Coming from a busy city like Chicago to a little area like Dairy Creek, Idaho was quite a change. My mother was a very religious person. When Passover arrived, my father told her not to worry about it. He told her we would get matzo and everything else needed for a Passover seder. Of course, we couldn't. My dad took a horse and wagon and went to Arimo, which was the closest little village that had a merchandise store, and bought flour. At home my parents made matzo, but they didn't have the right roller to roll and prick little air holes in the matzo. My father was a clever man. He took apart a clock and used the little balance wheel with the saw teeth on the edge to make holes in the rolled out dough. But I can tell you, and I remember this clearly, my mother's tears could have washed the entire state of Idaho. She was heartbroken to have come to this kind of situation.

A Child's Delight—From my point of view, I was happy on the farm. It was a different atmosphere. I enjoyed getting out in the wagon with my father, whether it was going for the water or errands. I enjoyed riding our horse in the field. For one reason or another, though, we ended up moving to Ogden, Utah, where my father got a job painting boxcars, freight cars, in enormous roundhouses, as they called them. Since World War I was coming to an end, my parents had trouble finding housing. We moved in with a family who let us have a bedroom and kitchen privileges.

Learning Experiences—I don't recall the name of the family, but he was what they call a *melamed*, a teacher. He felt sorry that I couldn't understand a word of Yiddish. Actually, I never wanted to speak Yiddish. I never wanted my mother to speak Yiddish in front of my friends. I was embarrassed by it. When I was a child, in Chicago, and we'd take the streetcar, whenever she took out the *Jewish Daily Forward* to read, I'd say, "Mama, please, put it down."[2]

She would tell me, "Doris, never be ashamed of who you are. Don't ever do that to yourself because you'll never be a happy person." So when we came to Ogden, this man recognized the fact that my mother wanted me to learn Yiddish and have it be part of my experience. He taught me how to speak and write Yiddish. I was really happy because I became part of the family that understood our roots. To this day, I am grateful for that lesson in life.

Ogden's Jewish Community—Ogden had a small Jewish community of maybe fifty Jewish families living there with their own synagogue, Brith Sholem. They didn't have a rabbi at the time, but a man by the name of Kraines knew the Torah inside out. He would daven and he would cover his head to pray. A young woman named Lillian Rubin taught Hebrew lessons.

Merchants—Ogden had Jewish merchants, too. Do you know where Washington Avenue is? Well, most of the merchants were from Washington Avenue West, from 25th Street where the depot is. I had an uncle who was a tailor in Ogden. Everybody knew Harry the Tailor. His shop was just a block away from the depot, and anybody that came from that direction would stop in and have a pair of pants shortened or lengthened or they could buy a jacket. There was a shoemaker, but most of the Jewish merchants were in clothing. Benowitz had a store near 25th Street and the Rubins had a store near 23rd Street. It was all within walking distance.

Friends—I knew the Benowitz girls. One of them, Evelyn, married Joe Rosenblatt. Several of them moved to San Diego. The Addelson family had a number of children, and their twin girls and I were friends. Her mother was quite a baker. She'd bake bagels, put a few in a shopping bag, go along and stop at one of her friend's shop, give a couple of bagels, sit and talk, and maybe knit or crochet while she was talking. I have nice memories of Rachelle Finkelstein. She was an

Ogden girl, younger than I am. Her parents were the Medoways, who both passed away. Sonia Pepper, Dr. Pepper's wife, was also an Ogden girl.

Parks—When we were kids, as a group, we used to go up the canyons in the summer and sometimes spend the night. With warm weather coming, women would take their young children, walk to the park in the evening and sit around on benches and talk while the children played. Sometimes, we'd stop and buy an ice cream cone. By this, I mean it was a very nice community.

A Crisis in the Home—When I was I around thirteen years old, my father passed away from dropsy; that's when fluid drowns the heart. He was just a young man, forty years old. My mother had to take care of me and my sisters Sylvia, Fannie, and Helen, the baby who was only three months old at the time. Four sisters, it was quite a struggle for her. I was in the 11th grade and went through school quite rapidly. Because of the situation at home, I needed to learn a profession so I could help support my mother.

A Solution—Fortunately, I had done well in school and the so-called Jewish Relief Society in Ogden offered me a scholarship to go to business college where I could learn shorthand and typing. I worked my way through school in the evenings. I worked for Ora Bundy. I took dictation once a week, transcribed it over at the business college, and took it back to him the next day. He paid me so much a page, so I was soon able to return the money to the Jewish Relief Society. After working for a couple of years, I met my beloved when I was seventeen, had the blessings of a beautiful family, and got married the following June.

Beloved—Sam had a truck and bought and sold cattle. Saturday was our day. We'd go out and often times buy a record and in the evening after dinner, we'd turn the record player on and dance and dance, just the two of us. We were always together. We didn't have to say very much to one another but our thoughts were much alike in every way.

Raising Two Families—When my mother passed away on her fiftieth birthday in 1933, we took in and raised Helen and Fannie, who were eleven and sixteen years old. Sylvia had a heart condition and died right after I was married. We also had four children of our own, so it wasn't always very easy raising six children. We lived on what he made from buying and selling a cow.

The Good Life—And we did it and our life was always good, and when it was bad, we comforted each other. We rarely ever argued. And when we did have cross words, never did an evening pass until it was all smoothed out. Never throughout almost fifty-seven years of marriage. I miss him. He was a fine person, for his family and for his fellowman. I find myself talking to him as if I expect an answer. But he was always there by my side and there was never, as God is my witness, a night that we went to bed that I didn't say to him, "May God give you to me all the rest of my life." And he would say, "I thank God for you."

Letting Go—Sam was sick with cancer. He didn't know it, and we didn't know that it was just a matter of how long or what. When he was in the hospital the last two weeks, he started failing. The rabbi visited him and said everyone was praying for his well being. Sam told the rabbi,

Doris and Sam Guss. (Courtesy of the Guss family)

"God owes me nothing. I have had a good life." I knew then that he knew he was dying. When the rabbi said he would return to visit, Sam told him, "I appreciate your coming, but I want you to know I am not afraid." When he was moved into Hospice, I put my body actually on him and put his arms around me. He looked at me with his blue eyes and didn't say anything. But the question was there. I told him, "Sam, don't worry about me. I'll be all right." I did not want him to worry about me or to suffer any longer. He said, "Are you sure?" I said, "Yes." Those were the last words I heard from him.

Kaddish—If mourning is what I'm doing, I haven't stopped. I'm from the old school and for the first thirty days, I did not go anywhere. I did not listen to music or turn the radio on. We said the Kaddish for the whole year. That's the way we are. His memory deserves our revering it, carrying on his memory with dignity, with honor, like his life was. It doesn't have to be mourning when you say a Kaddish. You pray that you can be a blessing to his memory, that none of us ever do anything to desecrate his name, or to shame him, or do anything that would be a discredit to him. That's what a memorial is. It isn't crying over it. My tears come because I just truly miss the partner of my life. They say it comes easier with time. Maybe it will. I sit here and he always sat right there.

SIX

Back to the Land

A BRIEF VIEW OF CLARION

ROBERT ALAN GOLDBERG

If you get on Interstate 15 to go towards Los Angeles, and you turned off the road some 135 miles from Salt Lake City, you will find a place called Clarion.[1] You know you are there when you can say, "This place looks like a lunar landscape." Rocks. Weeds. Sagebrush. Then your eye will pick up something very interesting in the southern Utah desert. You will see two gravestones in a very small cemetery. Inscribed in Hebrew, one of them is the grave of a man named Aaron Binder, a Jewish farmer killed in a logging accident. The other grave is of a baby dead before its first birthday.

If you go north a half a mile from the cemetery, you will find something else. Among the weeds and sagebrush foundations of some homes, and the concrete foundation of the schoolhouse. You'll also find the broken walls of a water storage system. What you will see, stretched out over six thousand acres, are pieces of a dream, a dream called Clarion—the remnants of a back-to-the-soil movement that began as recently as the 1880s but died in the early part of the twentieth century.

Only occasionally is the modern Jew reminded of his agrarian biblical roots. On Succoth, the Feast of Tabernacles, Jews still construct booths to commemorate the final gathering of the harvest in ancient Israel; and, of course, the Five Books of Moses, the words of the Prophets, and the Psalms abound with agricultural allegories and allusions. . . . Few Americans realize, however, that they need not look back thousands of miles to the Israeli *kibbutz* to come face to face with their Jewish agrarian heritage, for no group in modern America was more obsessed with the agrarian idea in their fashion than their forefathers who between 1881 and 1915 founded over forty agricultural colonies across the length and breadth of the American continent.[2]

Agricultural colonies were created in New Jersey, New York, the Dakotas, Louisiana, Colorado, and one in Utah. At the same time Jews were planning agricultural colonies in the United States, they were also creating Jewish agricultural colonies in Argentina, Canada, and Palestine. The colony of Clarion was the largest Jewish colony involving people and land area, and it existed longer than any other colony west of the Appalachian Mountains.

The back-to-the-soil movement saw settlement on the land as a way to remedy Jewish problems: to help Jewish immigrants leave the crowded cities, the tenements, the sweatshops, and the slums by offering agricultural solutions to end urban overcrowding and economic oppression. Farming would "productize" Jewish immigrants, create a beneficial environment for their children, and discourage anti-Semitism. When living in the *shtetls* of Europe, Jews were forbidden to own land, and very few of them were farmers. Here now was an attempt to change Jewish lives, to make Jews productive not just in the cities but also on the farms, and to bring about a Jewish spiritual and physical revival. The movement fostered self-help and work rather than charity and dependency for the Jewish poor, and it also helped change the image of the Jewish person. The Jew no longer had to be the factory worker, or the peddler, or the innkeeper. The Jew could be the farmer, proving to both Jews and Christians that Jews could live productive lives working the land.

The Clarion Colony arose first in the mind of Russian emigrant Benjamin Brown, who agitated for an organization of a nonreligious Jewish farming colony. Returning to the soil, Brown believed, would not only get Jews out of the ghettos, but also enable them to prosper. Clarion would be their trumpet call; their shofar, calling them out of the city and back to the land, like their forefathers and foremothers in Israel. Brown delivered impassioned speeches to small and large groups in Philadelphia and New York; he spoke of the values and ideals of agrarian living. His message reached a wide range of people, among which were socialists, anarchists, Zionists, communists, and religious Orthodox. "[Brown sought] 150 to 200 young married men with approximately three hundred dollars each whose savings would generate an operating capital of between forty-five thousand and sixty thousand dollars for the purchase of land, equipment, livestock, and building materials—a substantial outlay for at the time that would prove insufficient" (71).

Isaac Herbst surveying the land and marking the colony's main road. (Courtesy of Robert Goldberg)

One of the original Clarion pioneers, Abe Sendrow: determined to make a new start. (Courtesy of Eileen Hallet Stone)

After looking at properties in Colorado and New Mexico, Brown and Isaac Herbst, who was a civil engineer, traveled to Utah to look at land that would eventually be irrigated with water from a canal that was then under construction. Near the town of Gunnison, the State of Utah was offering prime property at a low price and promised the prospective clients that the canal would provide abundant water to take care of their crops. The colony was near a railroad, they hoped to sell their harvest in other parts of the West and ship it back east.

On September 10, 1911, Ben Brown arrived with the first eleven colonists. Only two of these Jewish pioneers had any farming experience, while the others had been chosen for their mechanical skills, experience with horses, and com-

Abe Sendrow: Harvesting with hope.
(Courtesy of Eileen Hallet Stone)

mitment to the project. The first stage was to create a communal farm in which everybody worked the land together and shared in the harvest. They set up four large tents to serve as communal living and winter shelters. The following day, they began to clear the land for cultivation. With their joint funds, they would buy a tractor to till the land. They intended to divide the land into tracts for later use for farmsteads.

Closer inspection of the soil showed a sandy, gravelly consistency underlain by a hardpan subsoil. The situation of the canal construction necessitated fixing the initial area of cultivation in what was the worst land of the tract. There were no wells on the land. Twice a week, water was hauled in in a large tank from nearby Gunnison. The governor of the state sent agricultural experts from Utah State College, in Logan, to teach them about what crops to plant and where to plant them. Mormon neighbors would also lend a helping hand with advice, food, and encouragement.

Jews were invited to Gunnison to participate in parties and dances. The Mormons made no attempt to proselytize them, no attempt to convert during the three or four years that the colony was there. The Mormons believed the Jews would help the local economy, buying tools and equipment. Mormons also saw Jews as their biblical brethren, cousins who had come to the land.

That fall, the men prepared fifteen hundred acres of land and dug irrigation channels from the canal to the fields. By winter, though, they were facing their first economic crisis. Their money, spent on tools, wages (for his work, each man received fifteen dollars a week), and livestock, was almost depleted. The colony owed the State of Utah its first installment for the land, and purchases bought on credit were now due. Ben Brown was sent back east to raise funds and recruit new members. His appeal was successful and by the spring of 1912 the farmers had planted their crops: wheat, oats, and alfalfa. By late spring, sprouts were beginning to appear. The colony was ecstatic, but their joy was short-lived. Dust storms, strong winds, and mosquitoes plagued the farmers, and their promised water from the state-built canal didn't appear.

Crucial to the existence of the colony, the canal was poorly constructed and its banks were breached, so the water disappeared before it could reach the Jewish colony. Throughout the summer there were weeks when there was no water at all. Once, despite the attempt to repair the canal by the colonists and the state, the colony was without water for thirty-three days. For only two days during that summer was the water flow sufficient to irrigate all the colony's fifteen hundred acres. The only crop to grow that year was dissension among the colonists. Benjamin Brown's judgment and qualifications came under attack, and he was accused of mismanagement and dictatorial practice.

The first year's harvest was a disaster. In the second year, the colonists divided the land up into homesteads. Each family was given a house on forty acres of land, and the farming cycle began again. They dug a well. They planted trees. They built a school and by the spring of 1913, there were 156 colonists living in Clarion, and twenty-four hundred acres had been planted.

The greatest conflict occurred with the school. While having a school symbolized permanence, compromises in curriculum had to be reached.

> What began in harmony and cooperation degenerated into bitter feuding when the program of Jewish education was considered. . . . [D]issension and debate can only be understood in the context of the ideological diversity that pervaded the Jewish immigrant world. Nationalists wanted to hire a teacher who would support Jewish identity through instruction in the Yiddish language, literature, and folklore. Radicals felt an emphasis on "Jewish" subjects would distract students from the international struggle for socialism. The religious minority sought instruction in the Hebrew liturgy. Finally, some were content to employ only the Mormon teacher selected by the school board. A compromise was eventually reached. It called for a teacher who would support the [nationalist view] and at the same time interpret Jewish history from an international socialist perspective. Hardly anyone was satisfied. Colonist Abe Wernick wrote, "Long after these meetings there was tension in the air and the opposing factions did not look at each other when they met" (77).

That spring, another disaster struck the colony. This time the problem wasn't a lack of water; this time the problem was too much water. Heavy rains filled the canal to overflowing. Once the canal banks were flooded, the water spilled over, flooded the farmlands, and destroyed the crops. Around the same time, colonist Aaron Binder died, and one baby who had been born in the colony died, and the Jewish farmers were beginning to question whether their venture was worth it.

By the winter of 1914, they were running out of money and were borrowing money from relatives back east. They were selling off whatever they had. They took odd jobs and some of the families remember eating cats in order to survive that winter. Once again, Ben Brown was sent to the East to sell Clarion's bonds and succeeded in raising six thousand dollars. The colonists decided to stay on the land, to rebuild, repair, and replant. They planted again—and again there was tragedy.

In the spring of 1914, the water appeared in the canal on schedule, but still the soil cracked under the sun and the crops withered. This time, the problem wasn't flooding or a break in the canal. Rather, the colonists experienced a water shortage. Their neighbors, farmers who lived upstream, took more water than was allotted to them. As a result, by the time the water reached the colony, there was not a sufficient amount to water their land. "After repeated appeals to state officials brought no redress, thirty frustrated and angry colonists led by Brown marched along the canal, seized control of the water gates, and closed off those belonging to the Mormon farmers. Order was eventually restored, but no one benefited" (79).

The harvest that came in was insufficient to boost the colony. Many of the colonists decided they could not survive on the land. By 1915, there were approximately fifty members left in Clarion. Ben Brown resigned as president. Members from the Salt Lake Jewish community, who had helped before by buying bonds, donating money for equipment, and depositing lumber to build homes—now raised money to buy railroad tickets to send the colonists back to Philadelphia or New York. Some colonists went on to become farmers in California, Michigan, Pennsylvania, and even New York.

A brother of one of the colonists, Maurice Warshaw, moved to Salt Lake and started what was to be called Grand Central, an important business concern in the city for many years. Ben Brown stayed in Sanpete County, near Clarion, and helped found the Utah Poultry Association, which later became the Intermountain Farmers Association. With a Mormon partner, he also pioneered a company, which later became Norbest Turkey.

Three other Jewish families stayed in Clarion until the 1920s. They were successful farmers and left the Clarion area only because they were worried that their children would intermarry with Mormons. They moved on to California where they became part of the Jewish community.

The Clarion farmers did not sound the Clarion call and lead scores of Jews out of the city, but what they did is most important. Their story is one of hope, determination, and courage. They failed and they succeeded. They took an incredible risk against all odds. And they took a risk not just for themselves; they had in mind the welfare and importance of the Jewish people. As models, they speak not only of their achievements, but of Jewish achievements as well.

THE AGRICULTURAL COLONY CLARION: A RETROSPECTIVE

SEVERAL CLARION COLONISTS

Benjamin Brown—When I was still a young man, about 23 years old, I felt the necessity for a wide colonization movement here in this country.[1] At the time, the thought to "productize" our people was widely spread. The seeds that the enlightenment period had shown [for Jews] brought forth such growth as the Bund, Zionism, and Territorialism. One special and unusual growth was in the leadership of Dr. Chaim Zhitlovsky.[2] His philosophy brought me to an aroma of fruitful earth, with Jewish *yosher* (justice) and a special folk direction, which led me to write in Dr. Zhitlovsky's journal, *Dos Naye Leben (The New Life),* an article under the title, *Varoom Bit Mir (Why Not We).* This article caused the creation of an organization which evolved into the colony "Clarion of Utah."

In 1909 and 1910, groups were formed in Philadelphia and New York for the purpose of settling in a colony that should serve as an example for other colonies. Everyone was accepted for membership who could invest $300.00 and declare his accord with the following principles. The organization of the colony was formed with the slogan that 1) culture, party, and religion are private things and that society as such should not mix in such private matters; 2) the principle of owning land shall be an equal amount for every family and that one should not have the right to buy out another's land; 3) the buying and selling of products should be cooperative; 4) a voluntary group of members will be involved in the cultivation of the land; and 5) the leadership for the colony should be through direct and equal vote.

Isaac Friedlander—While tramping about in the United States, Benjamin Brown wrote that he had seen in the West farming communities of Germans, Norwegians, and Danes as well as Americans which looked successful, peaceful and happy.[3] He wrote, why shouldn't we Jews, who are choking in the big Eastern cities, emulate them? Why can't we? Brown's articles were read by some very interested young men and stirred a lively response. The men formed a group in Philadelphia. Then, some other young Jewish men in New York [who] were sweatshop workers, petty shopkeepers, tailors, and carpenters, invited Brown to speak to them. He kindled great enthusiasm; that very evening, a New York branch was formed, which soon surpassed the Philadelphia group in numbers and activity. The little savings these men had, they turned over as their share in the agricultural association. This made them partners in the enterprise, a much better way to redeem themselves from wage-slavery and urban ugliness. Full of hope, they looked forward to the day when they would finally settle on their own land.

Abraham Bassin (on his father, Morris F. Bassin)—My father, Morris Bassin, was born and brought up in a small village where every Friday, regardless of the weather, all the Jewish residents thoroughly bathed themselves in the Drieper River, after soaping themselves on the bank, and then swimming or walking until they were neck deep in the water.[4] This regular custom was done in the nude. Part of the bank was for the men and further down was for the women. Dad explained that an important part of our heritage and Mosaic Law was cleanliness and Jewish descendants carried this tenet to the utmost degree. It was a rule among Jews everywhere to do this Friday evening at the mikvah so that on the Sabbath, you can rest and do your religious duties. He also explained that a farmer can always raise enough money to meet his needs for comfortable existence, which is why he attended agriculture school in the evenings and on days away from his bricklaying work.

Benjamin Brown—[Looking at different lands to establish our colony], we first voted in a Land Commission of three people and sent them to New Mexico to inspect the area. That trip was disappointing. In the meantime, we got a message that the Governor of the State of Utah invited our commission to come to Utah to investigate a tract of land, which the State Government was offering to sell. The lucky coincidence came as a result of that fact that one of the leader's sons had business dealings with a Samuel Newhouse, a Salt Lake Jew, who was very close to the Governor.

Isaac Friedlander—The leaders considered land in New Mexico, Arizona, and Utah. Why did they prefer the Far West to the East to build an agricultural colony? Land costs were less in the Far West, and had been used less. At a distance of 2,500 miles from New York, it wouldn't be so easy for colonists to quit and go back to the big city. Finally, because eastern Jewish farmers too often became hotelkeepers, depending for income on summer boarders. At the heart of this agricultural project was a sacred vision: Jewish farmers deriving their livelihood from their own labor in the field, with hoe and plough, tractor and threshing machine. "Boarder-farming" would be a desecration.

Why did they choose Utah? The State promised to bring an irrigation system to the whole area in which the colony would be situated. The colony would be not further than eight miles from the good-sized, thriving town of Gunnison, which had a railroad station for transportation. In the capital city of Salt Lake, resided a number of Jews of wealth and influence, who were agreeable to having the proposed colony in their state and who could be relied upon to look after it and support it. These outstanding Jews were Simon Bamberger, the Auerbach brothers,

Daniel Alexander, and Harry Joseph. Finally, Utah was chosen because the Mormons, who called themselves, "Children of Zion," would be friendly, and a constant example. Had they not themselves suffered persecution? Won't they remember the struggle it was to establish themselves on this land? And won't they sympathize with the Jews in their trials and errors as pioneers? The leaders purchased the land. The colony came into official existence. It was to be a shining example and inspiration to Jews all over America.

Samuel Chatzky—MONDAY, APRIL 17, 1911. I have been thinking about this all morning.[5] It is a warm but cloudy spring morning. Ten people have gathered at the Pennsylvania Railroad Station at Broad and Market to say goodbye to our two dear friends Isaac Herbst and Ben Brown who are leaving as an Expedition Committee to investigate land in the Far West.

We are happy and hopeful. Perhaps now the cornerstone will be laid for our great undertaking. Looking back at the past few months, I can't believe that we did so much work. Six or eight months ago, the idea of sending out an expedition was no more than a dream, a glorious dream. Here are Brown and Herbst with their valises, joking and laughing, their eyes glowing with optimism and faith in our goals and our members.

We shook hands with the travelers, extending best wishes. We waited until the train left, and with hearts full of hope, went out to the street. Someone suggested we have a drink to celebrate this very special day. We, brave and happy people, agreed unanimously. The saloon keeper on the Northwest corner of Broad and Filbert must have thought we were all crazy, coming in during breakfast time to drink glass and glass of beer or whiskey. To be honest, I had a glass of milk.

Benjamin Brown—According to the arrangements with the State of Utah, we received a tract of land amounting to 6,000 acres, irrigated, the sum to be paid out within ten years. At the time, we did not have all the 150 members needed, and since we decided to buy ten acres for each settler, we purchased 80 acres on some names, temporarily. A 6,000-acre tract is not the same throughout. Naturally, on such a tract there are hills and flat land, ravines for water flow, rocky places, etc. It was therefore understood also that the organization would have to survey the land in portions of equal value for every member.

On August 11, I traveled to Utah to conclude the contract and to make necessary preparations for the first settlers, the "pioneers," as we called them. The tract of land was about 13 miles long, at the foot of a mountain chain, a virgin land never before worked at. Westward, it stretched out near the narrow Sevier River; across, eastward, is the Gunnison Valley, which is encircled in a theatre of high clouds and cut by the Wasatch Mountain ring. Spread out in this broad valley are several Mormon settlements far away from each other, in the manner of European villages. On the very lowest part of this long valley, there is a snake-like railroad that unites the few forlorn areas with the wide world which, as Mormons declare, begins with Salt Lake City, about 150 miles towards the North. As is known, there is very little rain in this area, especially in the flat valley where the air is dry. The summers are very hot, and even during the winter there is sunshine. It is pleasant to work outside. The nights are, therefore, cold, almost like in the State

With hope for a good harvest.
(Courtesy of Robert Goldberg)

of New York. The soil is forever covered with a growth that is called sagebrush, little dry, low trees that give out a strong smell of turpentine.

Isaac Friedlander—Two men who like to work together tell at the supper table that "today" they dug out in the field huge rocks and carried them to the border of our land in order to build a dam. Now the torrents of spring rain run off at random across the land wastefully. One man tells that for the first time he ploughed a large area with the help of an eight-horse team. This required skill equal to that of the long-experienced Gentile farmers.

Joseph Furman, or Yuskeh, the "Fifteener," called because he wears a size 15 shoe, is a tall, bony, strong young man, a carpenter by trade, who sees here a beginning that will fulfill his Zionist-Territorialistic dream. He often declares, "Let us make a good go of it here, and you'll see the whole Jewish people returning to the land."

Benjamin Brown—We were very democratic. No work was considered better or worse and everyone received an equal amount, $15.00 a week. For instance, our engineer Herbst participated in cleaning the horse stables together with the others; each one had to work in the kitchen to help the [main] man cook, whom we exchanged every week. And if ever anyone complained about the meals, he was punished at once to become the cook for two whole weeks.

Samuel Chatzky—DECEMBER 27, 1911. In a letter which Brown wrote to us on December 19, he says, "Today, Sunday, heavy snow covered the land and mountains. A strong wind battered our tents. I remained like a '*shaygets* without a whistle,' i.e. I had not work to assign and nobody to do it. We stayed in our tents reading, writing, or discussing. In tent number two, the cold weather stimulated hot debate. Eli Sendrow, a free thinker, is very angry at God, and can prove that He doesn't exist. Sam Levitsky, on the other hand, claims there positively is a God, saying, 'Since I was in the army, I am convinced there must be a leader everywhere.'[6] Sendrow shouts, 'If there was a God, He would see to it that nobody had to serve in the army!' Aaron Binder, in his serene bass voice argues that there 'must be a God because even the *Goyim* believe in Him.'"

Benjamin Brown—Forest and natural grass grow only on the mountains. You find there various animals like bears, lions, deer. They come to the valleys, except a small kind of wolf, which is a combination of a wolf and fox.[7] They make frequent visits, but aside from the fact that they cause unpleasant music with their howling and they steal chickens, small pigs, and similar household animals, they don't cause very much damage.

It is here on such a tract of land, in this area, did I, Hurvitz and a few other members put up four tents: three for sleeping and one for a kitchen and dining room. In these tents, on 11 September 1911, we welcomed our pioneers. Twelve men, they numbered. Hurvitz and I met them in this forsaken station in Gunnison, far, far, in the valley, about nines miles from our tents. The day, as usual, was sunny. The pioneers took their places in the wagon, but didn't forget to take along their umbrellas, which they opened up, and traveling so they stretched out and sang a Ukrainian song, *(Ach, Doba, Dona).* When we passed by a Mormon village, children and grown-ups, *kind un kait,* young and old, came out to admire the pioneers with umbrellas, dressed in city clothes, singing elegantly but so strangely. The Mormon farmers shouted, "Pioneers with umbrellas!"

At first the days were really interesting. The umbrella pioneers have brought this virgin, wild area into cultivation. We used to greet each sunrise with song and labor, and every sunset used to bring us restfulness and spiritual happiness. During the fall and winter, we cleaned about 1500 acres of wild growth. At the time, the tractors for land cultivation just appeared. We were enthralled with the newness of this machine. Of course, I must record my mistake: not recognizing the high cost of such equipment, not having mechanics to work such a machine, and at the time not realizing that these tractors were not quite ready for practical usage. Nevertheless,

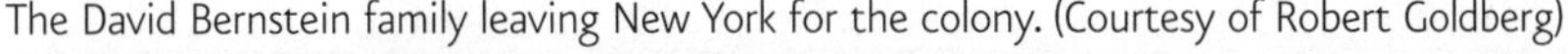
The David Bernstein family leaving New York for the colony. (Courtesy of Robert Goldberg)

The Bernstein family in Clarion. (Courtesy of Robert Goldberg)

we did seed about 1500 acres of wheat, oats, and alfalfa. This brought out the admiration of our non-Jewish neighbors, and some came with friendly visits, like equals to equals. Later, when the fields were already seeded did we build a few small houses and our pioneers brought their families.

Harry Bernstein (on his father, David)—My father's formal education, all in Russia, ended at the mid–high school level, or its equivalent.[8] He was an intelligent, well-read, versatile and idealistic man, and to a large extent, self-educated. He could speak and read in four languages. Although well versed in matters pertaining to the Jewish religion, could read and speak Hebrew, he professed to be an agnostic. Nevertheless, he attended services on High Holy Days, perhaps as an example for his children, and insisted on (and enforced) our obedience to the views of my mother, who was religious, kosher, and followed most of the rituals, often difficult to do in our primitive farm environment. From the earliest days of her marriage, my mother had to skimp and save. When my father died in Clarion, my mother was 32 years old. Left with seven young children, she lived on the farm. Her life was full of hardship.

The earliest group of pioneers, including my father, arrived in Utah in Spring 1912, to prepare for the arrival of their families as few months later. By the time we left for Utah, our family had grown to six children, the oldest was nine years old. The trip, which took three days, was a memorable one. Leaving our drab home and surroundings and boarding one of the luxurious trains of those days, watching the fascinating scenery exceeded anything we could have imagined. But the contrast between what we anticipated and what we found when we arrived, was something of a let down.

Since the house we were to live in was not yet completed, we all crowded together, two adults and six children, in our temporary shelter, a crudely built shack of two small rooms. Our furniture had not yet arrived, so we slept on the floor with a few blankets and pillows my father had purchased. Cooking was done from a stove, the only one, for this small group, in a centrally located shack, and there were yet no outhouses. Water came out of barrels and had to be brought in from Centerfield or Gunnison, seven miles away.

Moshe Melamed—JUNE 8, 1912. All the men were so sunburned that it was hard to recognize them.[9] One of them approaches me. I see glowing, dark eyes beneath a forehead covered

Reviewing the books: Benjamin Brown (*second from right*) and Isaac Herbst (*right*). (Courtesy of Robert Goldberg)

with long, uncut hair. We wave at each other warmly, and still I don't know whose hand I am pressing.

"Don't you recognize me?" he laughs, and tells me his name. I am stunned. We embrace. Young women stand in the doorways of the frame houses, holding the hands of their children, who are all dressed up, coming to greet their "green" guests.

Clarion now has nine frame dwellings for the first settlers, and a few tents for recent arrivals, whose families have not yet joined them. In the center, where an American flag flies, stands the business office. We have a few barns for our horses and wagons, and everything is managed and under the control of our energetic and tireless Ben Brown. He doesn't rest for one minute. Several times a day, he makes the rounds of the colony—from one end to the other, on his beloved pony Nicky.

In this short time, there were only twelve settlers here, and only eight of them worked on the land. Of the remaining four, one was the cook, one the secretary, one the manager (Brown), and one went every day to town to buy food. Until now, we have planted 1400 acres; about 1,000 have been irrigated by artificial canals that transport the water from the huge reservoir 60 miles away. The fields are green and promise a good crop.

Right now is the critical time. The sun beats down pitilessly, the fields cry for water, and all our "hands" are occupied with irrigating the thirsty fields. We work late, irregular hours. No

Russian attire in American fields. (Courtesy of Eileen Hallet Stone)

one looks at the clock. By six in the morning, we were in the fields. We come home long after sundown. Even on Sunday, we work half a day, sometimes more, and nobody complains. City people don't have the slightest idea what it is like to endure such physical and spiritual hardship; to be far from friends, without the accustomed comforts of city life.

The challenge we are facing is many times greater than what we endured until now. There are still 4500 acres to be cultivated, and a [school] curriculum for the children must be decided upon.

Isaac Friedlander—AUTUMN. The leaves are falling; the mornings are cold, frosty. Work is being done less in the field and more in the camp. Wagons are repaired, a harness is mended, and machinery lubricated to prevent rusting during the winter. Roads are straightened, holes in the roads are filled in, bridges are strengthened. Men make trips into town to shop for the winter.

On a fair, sunny Sunday morning, the entire group, taking sacks, axes, and rope, ride out in open wagons into the interior of the mountains. The two-fold purpose is to gather firewood and to acquaint ourselves with the reality of the interior of those neighboring mountains, huge, often misted over, mysterious, evoking in us a religious exaltation.

The mountain walls are hued rose and yellow. We see forms like sphinxes, artistically sculptured by nature. Riding in open wagons, we keep gazing, with heads thrown back, towards the colorful heights. As we approach the canyon, we see on its horizon a glistening lake. As we draw nearer, it forever recedes. A mirage! We ride through this canyon in silence, amazed by the concurrence here of summer and winter. Below, Indian Summer prevails, while the wooded ridges and high crevasses are mantled with snow. Somewhere in the depths of the mountains, a sudden clap of thunder is heard and then fades away.

WINTER. It's getting colder. We lack warm clothing and proper, waterproof shelter. The roads are not good. Innocently beguiled by Brown's praises of his newly discovered land and by the promotional literature of the merchants and the Chamber of Commerce of Gunnison, we believed this area enjoyed perpetual summer, so we left our warm clothing back East. Reality is the opposite. We find the summers are short and terribly hot, the winters long and severe. This is our first disillusionment and a painful one.

During the first winter, all our connection with the town was not seldom completely cut off by the snowfalls and storms. More than once, we were left without bread or drinking water, and there was no delivery of letters from our families. Neighbors tell us, this is an unusual winter, they could not remember ever having such a hard winter before. We reconciled ourselves and resolutely hoped for better times.

The ground was hardened by winter. We managed to plough a good part of the land, both with the tractor and the horse and plough. The tractor is not always in good working order; many a time, we have to seek outside help both to repair it and to operate it. Although the winter strikes early, we got planted a winter wheat, which, if the harvest turns out, would be ready in late spring.

Harry Bernstein—There was little rain or snow during the three years we lived in the colony and irrigation was absolutely necessary for proper crop growth. There was a general down slope on both sides to the Sevier River, more uniform on our (West) side of the Wasatch Valley, as this whole area is known. The contour of the land thus made it ideal for flow and distribution of water. The source of our water was from a canal on the upside, about a half a mile to the West, and properly placed supply ditches that led to the canal. A small stream of water for household use, such as washing clothes, dishes, or bathing, flowed steadily; but when needed for irrigation, the flow was increased by opening the shut-off valves at the canal and allowing the water to flow into the furrows in the seeded areas. This was done at intervals by pre-arrangement with others in the colony to avoid overuse or the complete loss of available water at the lower end of the canal. While the supply was available, there was no lack of cooperation by the colonists in the use of water, but it was indispensable to the colony's survival that this water be available when needed. Perhaps due to our location, the water level in the canal was frequently low or it was completely dry, at that point.

Benjamin Brown—Through the summer of 1912, the 1500 acres were plowed up and the seeded tract of land bloomed attractively in the Spring. The irrigation canal was brought closer to our fields and we began to irrigate the large tract of land with singing. But the canal, being new, could not hold the large quantity of water that the seeded land required, especially for the first year. In addition to that, the inexperience with irrigation resulted in our not making the best use of the water. Most of the land went to waste, and the income from the land which did receive enough water wasn't enough to pay for the seeds.

Isaac Friedlander—That first spring and all summer, the basin was enlivened with hard work and happy song—in Yiddish, of course. Binder, in particular, was happy. He never complained. He would dig out the most ponderous rocks, however deep they were imbedded. When the honeymoon was fading away into realism, it was Binder who kept up the spirits of the doubters and the disappointed. The harvest of winter planting was not satisfactory.

Harry Bernstein—My father had a rare versatility and could find ingenious solutions to the many problems faced by the early colonists, especially, and informed himself in matters that were important so he could instruct others. His mechanical skills were often needed in repairing farm machinery, and he took part in the building of houses, stables, chicken coops, the derricks used for stacking hay and straw, and many other projects.

Before the local school was built, the Colony children were sent for about a year to the school in Centerfield, five miles away. Father selected and rebuilt the vehicle used to take them to school. It was a surrey-type wagon with a roof. He rearranged the seats so he could install a small stove for heat in the winter during the one-hour trip to school.

For over a year, water had to be brought in by barrel from the nearest town of Gunnison. The Colony could afford only one well, and the project was assigned to my father. He did the planning, chose the centrally located site, assisted the man drilling, and helped assemble the tower and water storage tank. The pump frequently needed repair, and he was the only one there who could do this. Irrigation problems arose as well, due to improper channeling of the water. This became another area in which he helped. As time went on, he became a key figure and an important voice in the counsels and meetings of the colonists, until his death in September 1914.

Sam Chatzky—I want to record the fact that the 24th of July is a State Holiday, when all of Utah commemorates the first pioneers who came here in the first half of the last century. One of the neighboring towns sent us, "The Jewish Colony," or "The Pioneers of 1911," an invitation to celebrate "Pioneer Day" with them. We accepted and prepared a float, decorated with Clarion's products: oats and corn; wheat and fresh-cut alfalfa; and added big and small American flags. The nationalist group asked, "What about a Jewish flag?" At a special meeting, it was clearly stated that we, as a Jewish colony, should also have our own flag. For the first time, Clarion was adorned with the blue and white flag, fluttering in the wind for all to see.

Isaac Friedlander—The original group was getting worried over the insufficiency of money to ensure the progress of this project. Ben Brown went East to raise a needed $10,000. In New York, he was welcomed by members with enthusiasm. He dwelt on the more favorable aspects. We will establish a flourishing Jewish settlement, a farm colony that will be a model for the entire Yiddish-cultural world. As far as the financial strengthening needed to tidy the colony over these early hard times, the *Yehudim* (American Jews of German extraction) of Salt Lake City were also ready to help.

We needed clothes, shoes, food, implements, etc., and most of all this we bought from the merchants of Gunnison. The banker of Gunnison, a down-to-earth man, had some doubts about us as pioneers. He regarded us as extravagant and decided, therefore, that the Jews had money. Therefore, we were trustworthy for bank loans. The merchants followed suit. The Jews, for their part, were confident they could meet all their financial obligations.

Benjamin Brown—In short, a difficult period began. I sent an SOS message to Dr. Krauskopf. He sent us Rabbi Landsman, and I was able, with his help, to interest people of means in Salt Lake City, who incorporated, in June 1912, a help-organization under the name of "Utah Colonization Fund." A young lawyer, by the name of Daniel Alexander, prepared for us all the papers for issuing bonds. With a whole pack of letters from the business people, as from the Governor of the State, and from the head of the Mormon Church, I left to peddle with this pack of bonds.

A colony home in Clarion. (Courtesy of Robert Goldberg)

We still did not have enough money and so it was decided that the land should be divided among the members. Since there were no houses for everyone, the Salt Lake Jews bought bonds for $5,000 and the Jewish Governor, Mr. Simon Bamberger, sent in some building materials valued at $2,000. We were encouraged and I continued with the peddling of bonds, traveling as far as St. Louis where I got all of $6,300. What was important was not so much the amount as the renewed confidence that it had called out among our members.

Isaac Friedlander—Our brothers the Yehudim could not remain indifferent, whether they wished to participate or not. They were impelled to serve as "big brothers," these philanthropists. They approached the Jews of Clarion with caution, as was their way in dealing with East-Europeans, and involved themselves more and more. They kept a watchful eye on the colony to make sure nothing was being done that would reflect disgrace upon them.

Harry Bernstein—In general, the winters were not severe and we were accustomed to inconvenience when we finally moved into our house during the Spring of 1913, our furniture having arrived about that time. Among the early arrivals with my father was a close, long-time friend, named Joseph Furman, a carpenter by trade. Furman and my father worked together to build our house and three others nearby, including Furman's. The houses had a concrete foundation and were built of lumber, with a shingled gable roof, and unplastered. For insulation, tar paper, or other heavy paper was nailed to the inside walls. A brick chimney to drain the smoke out of the stove used for heating and cooking was installed from the kitchen through the roof.

With seven children, our home was one of the larger ones, divided into four rooms, with a small pantry with shelves, near the kitchen. My mother was scrupulously clean, and she was very religious, which increased her work in many ways. With three sets of dishes, for milk foods, meat foods, and for Passover, she took on the task of keeping track of, storing, and cleaning separately each set, as required by the rituals. Wood brought in from the mountains was the fuel used; kerosene lamps the source of light. In the summer, there were some problems with food storage. There was no refrigeration, of course, so we made complete use of the daily supply from our own cow. Excess milk was allowed to turn sour and then consumed as such. Meat, from locally slaughtered chickens or lambs, was all cooked and used within a day or two, and when purchased from town, was kept from spoiling with ice wrapped in burlap and given by the butcher. Garden vegetables and potatoes were homegrown, picked as needed, with the excess canned or pickled. Fruits were brought in from outside as the colony had no fruit trees. Water was brought in and used from barrels. In the winter, the water froze in the barrels and had to be melted by pouring heated water from the supply kept in the house.

Farm animals, usually two or three horses and a cow, a few sheep or a goat, and a dozen or two chickens, were individually owned. A wagon, buggy, buckets, barrels, shovels, rakes were among our prized possessions, and every farmer had a rifle used to ward off predators of chickens or lambs. Coyotes and hawks were frequent visitors to the coops or corrals. Shared ownership of some small equipment existed, although the larger ones, such as the reaper and thresher, were community owned and rotated for use by different colonists at harvest time.

Isaac Friedlander—In the canal, there was scarcely enough water for the planted fields that summer. Nor was this water fit for human drinking. A filtering system was required. When the families came out, the shortage of culinary water was a great hardship. The topography of our locality was unfavorable to well digging. We were close to the foothills, and to the hard, stony soil. We used a "water witch" to search over the length and breadth of our land. When the branch responded to a spot in the northern part of the area, the joy was great. But the digging yielded no water. A second spot showed signs; digging was done. Much trouble yielded just a little bit of water, and then this source dried up altogether.

Isaac Herbst, one of the original twelve, and an engineer, was charged with the responsibility of building a reservoir. Working with a committee, they fashioned a structure 30′ by 40′ across with 8′ high walls. Wooden forms were made for the walls, and into these forms concrete was poured. Faucets and a filtering system were elements built in. Across the walls, a cover was laid, to keep out insects. The concrete was allowed ample time to dry out before the water was let in slowly over the course of three days.

On the fourth day at midnight, a frightful crash resounded. We heard the roaring of waters from the direction of the reservoir. The reservoir had broken apart. The stored up water went to waste. As we learned later, the material used was not of standard quality. The construction was not professional. The wooden forms should have been reinforced with iron rods and wire, so that the concrete would have the strength to withstand the pressure of thousands of gallons of water. Disappointed, ashamed, and disgraced, Herbst left the colony. Water remained scarce.

Benjamin Brown—During the summer of 1913, the situation in the colony became almost unbearable. Rather than a bountiful crop, we suffered a harvest of failure. Former comrades were divided into various fighting groups. Then during the summer, something else happened that shocked all of us. Brother Binder went to the mountains to gather wood for his barn and turned the wagon full of wood on himself.

Samuel Chatzky—AUGUST 1913. Aaron Binder died on the way home from the hills, where he and others had gone to get wood to build a barn for the horses and cows. The steep road is a dangerous one. His wagon turned over, rolled down the hill, and he was buried under the timber. He died instantly. Can anyone imagine what a shock it is for young people who are building a home for themselves when one of their most capable and devoted farmers is suddenly torn from here? Aaron Binder, who was less than 30 years old, worked tirelessly. He was a simple man, a child of the people, with a pure and honest soul.

Isaac Friedlander—Aaron Binder was the personification of *folksteemlichkait* [a common man]. He was not interested in our ideological motivation in returning to the land; he was simply called by the land, and he helped to transform Clarion into a human habitation. He even helped in the building of cabins. I see him now by the narrow stream, not far from our tents, and there he is working on a goodly stretch of ploughed land free from weeds and ready for planting. His farming and expertise and devotion to the land were, as I said, unapproachable by any of us. When he learned something from the Mormon farmers, he lost no time trying it out, and he made it work. Old-time farmers admired him as an expert and hard worker, and he became known throughout the valley as "the big Jew."

Binder was buried on the boundary of his farm. His solitary grave was the first to be cut out in that remote, wild valley, and bears this epitaph:

HERE LIES
Baurch ben Abraham
A son of our people, a humble, hardworking Jew,
With a great Jewish soul.
He died a martyr, in the cause of raising our level
And not permitting shame on the Jewish name.

Samuel Chatzky—It was a terrible blow for us. Binder left a wife and four children. Our Gentile neighbors came to offer their sympathy. We were one big family who had lost one of its children. One can never find such togetherness and devotion in the city with its lodges and fraternities, such concern for one another. It took us a long time to come to ourselves; at his grave, we swore to continue our work.

Harry Bernstein—My father's death, about a year later, had a similar effect on the colonists. His work required being outdoors in the most severe weather, sometimes all day. The toes of one of his feet were badly frozen; sometime later, gangrene set in. Delay and neglect, and difficulties in getting to a doctor resulted in the spread of infection. My father went to Salt Lake City, and later, to Chicago for treatment. He died in 1914. That year, two other deaths occurred. One was an infant who died soon after being born. He was buried in Clarion. The other was an elderly woman who came and lived with a married son.

Life was quite difficult for the adults. My mother would recall years later, any reference to the farm with a shudder. All who were then children, though, have some pleasant memories. We had our share of work, as do all farm children, mainly picking stones from the fields, weeding, chopping wood, and watering the animals. But during our free time, there were many interesting places to see. The "salt mine" was one. An excavation where highly saline water from an abandoned enterprise had accumulated, it was very deep and clear but because of its salinity, we could swim and float with safety. Within a mile or two from our home, climbing the nearby hills or going to the Sevier River were frequent adventures. Day or night, it was safe to play outdoors.

Yetta Bassin Farber (on her father, Morris F. Bassin)—The stories I remember hearing from my family were of great difficulties.[10] My father, Uncle Zeital, Cousin Louis Levine, and my brother Abe Bassin invested in a total of 160 acres in Clarion. My father and other members of the family worked constantly to build homes for many members of the colony. They built their own cabin and my mother told of sleeping with large sticks near the hand as coyotes would come and howl under the floor.

I remember hearing about strong disagreements when they talked of a school for the children. Some colonists were Socialists, others were anarchists, and some had no political leanings. There were squabbles for weeks on end.

Isaac Friedlander—Through all the trials, the desire for the Yiddish culture did not die. The people of Clarion were practically all drawn from the Yiddish-language intelligentsia, and wanted the colony to become an enclave of the higher Yiddish culture. In this little, remote nook in the Far West, then, we started our Yiddish day school, but opinion was still divided as to what precisely should be taught. The national-minded majority demanded a Yiddish-national education. The international socialists demanded the opposite. After some passionate debate, we compromised to allow a choice between Yiddish language and literature, Jewish history, Jewish customs and traditions and history from the international-socialist view, and folk song. There was general satisfaction with this compromise; the parties were tolerant of the differences.

Harry Bernstein—The Clarion School was completed about late 1913. Like the colonists' homes, but somewhat larger, it was a lumber structure on a concrete foundation with unplastered walls, and had a stove for heating. It was adequately equipped with school desks, about 12 in each room, had blackboards and textbooks. For about six months, our only teacher was Mr. Charles Emily Jr., who was the principal at the school in Centerfield; and only one of the classrooms was used. Early in 1914, when we got a second teacher—Abe Schwartz, a younger graduate from Philadelphia, who was a relative of one of the colonists—the second classroom was put to use. We virtually idolized our new teacher, who [living] on our side of the colony, walked to school with us and gave lectures on cleanliness by properly using our meager water supply. A young woman later came to the colony; he left with her to get married and they returned to Philadelphia in the Spring of 1915. It was for all of us a great tragedy.

In addition to classes, the school building was used as a meeting place for colony members to discuss problems or plan for various enterprises. Because of its central location and size, it served as a synagogue during holidays and for celebrations. After the colony broke up, we learned that the school building was used as a church by residents of the area.

Isaac Friedlander—In the heat of the mid-summer, we had high hopes for an excellent, profitable harvest. The day began fair and clear; then towards evening, suddenly, here and there, a small cloud appeared on the horizon. A few worried that it might rain. When night fell, the skies were heavily clouded over; no stars were visible. Around midnight, a tremendous storm was let loose from the mountains, waking everyone. This was a heroic storm. The wailing cry and ripping of the wind, the roaring of the mountain winds, the whining of the coyotes, and the torrents racing from the hills, carrying rocks—all these, intermingling with the unceasing thunder and lightening, terrified us. We were aware that a great misfortune was befalling us.

It was too dangerous to step outdoors. Fragments of metal and wood and broken-off tree branches flew through the air. The frail houses of wood and roofs rocked. The women and children cried. Others prayed. By morning, the rain had stopped. A thick fog moved in; anyone seen outdoors looked like apparitions. The havoc the colonists found was worse than they ever imagined. The damage was terrible; the despair, even greater. The area looked as if it had hailed rocks all night. Whole patches of field, once full grown with stocks of grain, were partially buried under rocks, broken branches, and weeds. The water and the wind had flattened the stocks to the ground. All the hard work of spring planting of the summer cultivation and watering was, in the half of one night, annihilated.

Broken was the resistance, the stubbornness of even the strongest and most patient. Anxious speculation returned. There was no money. Personal possessions were badly damaged by the storm and flood. The dissatisfaction with the land-ownership became all too apparent. This was only one of the faults of which the people, in their depression or despair, became acutely conscious. The other faults were the climate, the water scarcity, the land itself, and overall, the inexpert management. Before sixty families had arrived and settled on the land, some were leaving, and for those who stayed and the new pioneers who arrived, they lived between doubt and hope.

It continued to be difficult to make a living in Clarion, and to pay the debts and taxes. But the hope for better times was persistent. We were raising chickens, turkeys and pigs. We were told it was profitable. The women at first recoiled, but were persuaded that pig-tending was worth the trouble. The Yehudim Jews, wanting to help, sent us a load of lumber to build chicken coops, fences, etc. We tried all sorts of things, not to abandon hope. We were still dreaming of that ideal way of life.

Later, we did not have the water needed to water our fields and we lost another year's crop, which nearly ruined us. Then on the third year, we were told the colony was required to pay the State Land Board's loan of no less than $60,000, payable no later than January 1, 1915. The town banker was owed about $3,000. The merchants in town were owed for groceries. The colonists did not lose their heads. People who came with documentary evidence of debts demanding payment were referred to the Utah Colonization Fund, the proprietor of all the colonial property. Inventory . . . liquidation . . . creditors. But everyone realized this was the beginning of the end. Ben Brown resigned the presidency and left Clarion. And the others? Backbone lost, all was lost.

Yetta Bassin Farber—Father and Mother thought very well of Ben Brown, the Auerbachs, Julius Rosenwald, and the Garelicks, with whom Dad traded in Salt Lake, for their ability, foresight and charity. My father believed that U.S. government bureaucrats, the pressures and stress prior to World War I, and anti-Semitism played important parts in Clarion's failure. My parents were not bitter about their experiences, but did feel poorly about Clarion's failure, although Dad mentioned they were lessons for the future.

Harry Bernstein—Only in the last year when problems developed which threatened their very survival did they realize the futility of continuing this venture. The events and difficulties which led to their discouragement were cumulative: unrelieved financial problems, the death of two colonists, problems in getting enough water, and the departure of other colonists. Yes, we were greatly saddened by the failure of the Colony and in seeing all their hard work come to nothing. Many wept as we boarded wagons to leave, among them my mother, despite the hardship she endured.

Benjamin Brown—It seems that the five principles upon which the colony was organized were quite ordinary principles, with the exception perhaps of the clause that the ownership of land should be equal for every member. This clause was the beginning of the decline of the colony. The second reason was the mish-mash—conglomeration—of the membership. For instance, we had among us anarchists of all sorts, left and right socialists, nationalists of all varieties, and atheists and religious Orthodox, and the question of language also caused a division. Finally, the working of the land cooperatively by voluntary groups caused enmity between old friends in a very short time.

Isaac Friedlander—A number of the "older" pioneers were loath to leave this area; they felt they had invested too much toil, energy, money in Clarion, to a sacrificial degree, to drop it.

CLARION REVISITED—JUNE 2000

Armed with a set of plats and a lot of drinking water, my husband Randy and I entered the western hills of Gunnison to find Clarion Cemetery. "You mean the Jew graves," one young farmer said, as we ventured onto a side road. "We went there a lot when we were kids. It's over there."

After a fair number of dead ends, Randy spotted a loop of twisted wire wrapped around a gated fence beyond which the hot sky draped low across a series of flat hills. As far as one could see, sagebrush, cracked soil, ant dwellings, thorny piles, dry washes, and drought dominated the landscape. This was not prime farmland. We walked in one direction, varied onto another, and then in the heat of day came upon two graves surrounded by a white railing and decorated with pink plastic flowers.

What in the Sam Hill?—A man, wearing a cowboy hat, white shirt, denim jacket, and jeans, riding what could have been a horse but was a motorcycle, came out of nowhere and pulled up short in front of us. Bruce Sorensen, a local farmer, wanted to know what we were doing. He has a connection with the Clarion colonists and an affinity for the territory. "You can only imagine what it must have been like for these people living in this desert," he said. For the next several hours we combed the colony land together.

Long after the Jewish farmers moved away, the town pitched fences in the small cemetery to protect the graves from being knocked over by wandering cattle. Sorensen takes time off from his chores to tend the site. He is a gentle caretaker, and on Memorial Day he places flowers for remembrance. For most visitors, he has become the resident historian.

"People with roots in Clarion come here from all over the country, and I want them to know these pioneer farmers are not forgotten," he said. "I show them around the cemetery, and what's left of the school, the foundations and the cisterns. I tell them how the Mormons held meetings in the schoolhouse after the farmers left. You can still see the foundation. I tell them how people like my grandparents moved into the empty houses to live, and later how these houses were moved to nearby towns and farms. Nothing goes to waste here. I answer whatever questions I can. It is something I want to do. Why? Right over there is where I live, where I farm. But I'm out here all the time, and just like the Jewish farmers, this land is a part of me, and my history. We share the same problems even today. Even today we still have to fight for water."

Also, they had burned their bridges to the city; they dreaded going back to the city, whose evils [the sweatshops and crowded tenements] they had fled. Despite all the calamities and disappointments they had suffered, they felt they had integrated themselves into the land. They loved it, from the song of the mountain birds and the smell of the mountain woods to the dreamy white nights and blue-rose dawns. These natural delights of the healthy, close to the earth way of life, they could not anymore live without. They sought, on their individual responsibility, to obtain government-owned land nearby. To rigorous labor, these pioneers were already accustomed. They rode wild, almost unbroken horses bravely, as if their fathers had been doing this all their lives.

Yetta Bassin Farber—When the colony failed we moved to Salt Lake City. My father worked trading with farmers, buying hides, furs, scrap metal and such. Much later, in 1945, Dad bought a farm in Lakewood, New Jersey; he raised chickens and peddled eggs until his death in 1947.

Isaac Friedlander—Thus tragically, Clarion came to an end. A chapter of the Back to the Land movement among Jews in America. A movement, an idea, an ideal which, during the years 1910–1915, caught up many Yiddish-progressive young men and women who dreamed of, and strove for, a lovely, free workers-life in the lap of Mother Nature.

Clarion did not perish because the colonists were Jews. This was never the explanation. Jewish Clarion perished because of the climate; the soil; the lack of water, transportation and market distance. Against this combination of hindrances, the Jews contended in vain.

SEVEN

Networking

BEFORE THE TALKIES

Howard Marcus

Louis Marcus—My father Louis Marcus was born in Brooklyn, New York; his parents were born in Philadelphia.[1] Their ancestors, I believe, were from Holland, and possibly some from Germany. I'm under the impression that the Jews from Holland were Sephardic Jews from Spain. My mother was from Chicago. Her parents came from Germany, northeast of Berlin, in Stetein. When my grandparents left Germany, it had been a part of Poland as well. My grandfather had been in the wholesale liquor business. I believe he had tuberculosis and was advised to move to Pueblo, Colorado. That's where my mother spent most of her life until she married. She had come to Salt Lake City to visit a cousin and met my father here. They were married in 1912. I was born April 22, 1919 and am an only child. My maternal grandfather died before I was born but my grandmother lived with us in Salt Lake City for a number of years.

In 1907, when Dad was twenty-seven years old, he left Philadelphia. His brother, Eugene, had come to Utah some time prior and persuaded my father to join him. Eventually his other brother came here as well and they all got into the distribution of motion picture films. My father is the only one of the three that was successful at the business. I don't know what his

The Capitol Theatre, June 1937. (Courtesy of Utah State Historical Society)

experience was before that, but I was told before he came to Utah, my dad and one of his two brothers used to act in minstrel shows in the East. They were very popular around the turn of the century. I think he did it more as a hobby than for a living.

Before the Talkies—As far as I know, my dad got a job with a rather well-known character by the name of Max Florence, a pioneer in exhibiting motion pictures in Salt Lake City. For a few years he worked for Max as a projectionist and an amateur electrician who knew how to wire things up and fix projectors. I believe the theatre where he worked was called the Isis, which is on Broadway between State and Main and is now the Broadway Theatre. After a few years, he got into film distribution for the Famous Players Laskey Corporation; it later became Paramount Pictures. By the early 1910s, Dad sold silent movies to theatres all over the Intermountain West.

Theatre Owner—He began as a local manager, became a regional manager, and then opened theatres of his own. I think he finally got up to about fourteen theatres in Salt Lake City, Ogden, Provo, Idaho, and possibly Montana. His first one, no longer in existence, was called the Paramount Empress, renamed the Paramount, and changed later to the Uptown. It was torn down at the time the ZCMI Center was built. Then there was the Victory Theatre on Third South across the street from the Isis. Among other theaters that have come and gone, Dad and his business partner, an attorney, bought the Capitol Theatre, which had been in my family for forty-nine years until it was condemned and extensively remodeled into the Center for the Performing Arts.

Old Friends—When my dad first came to Salt Lake City, he rented a room from an old, old German Jewish family here called Mrs. and Mrs. Schiller. They had a son somewhat younger than Dad by the name of Herbert. He went to Harvard Law School and my father was instrumental in getting him appointed as a city judge in Salt Lake. The family owned Continental Cleaners on 2nd Avenue. The room my dad rented was in their basement. Later, the Schillers lived in the Knickerbocker Apartments on South Temple and 13th East. The friends my father had when he first came here and the friends he made after he was married, well, most of them have disappeared, either they moved away or died. There are a couple of exceptions. There's the Sweet family, the Lovingers, the Kahn Brothers, the Oppenheimers, and the Simon family. Max and Charles Simon owned the real estate where the Paris Company was. Oh, and there was the Strauss family and the Bambergers. Simon Bamberger became Utah's first Democrat and only Jewish governor.

Home Movies—The first house I can remember living in is the duplex on 2nd South and 5th East where the Radio station KWHO is located. It had a nice garden out in the back. I have some old movies showing it. I guess my father was the first person in Salt Lake City to have home movies because he was in the business and he hired professional movie photographers to come and take pictures. Originally taken on 35mm film, he later had them reduced to 16mm, and then I put them on videotape.

At first, my father made an adequate living. As the years went by, he did extremely well in the business. He made a lot of trips to the corporate offices in New York and then with his attorney partner built some offices for all the film distributing company under one building complex on 1st South and 2nd East. Undoubtedly, in the early days, the 1920s and 1930s, he was the number one showman in Salt Lake. There were other operators, but they were smaller. They told me that my dad could have run them out of business, if he wanted to. But he never did. He believed in letting the little man survive. He was fair.

The Marcus family in Italy, 1931. (Courtesy of Pete and Carolyn Mirabile)

My father was always interested in business in general. It could have been the coal business, the oil business, theatre business, real estate, securities, it didn't matter what it was, just as long as it was business. When he went to Europe in 1931, Dad had to fill out some documents and state his occupation. He was at that time retired from business, he had sold out, but he put his occupation as "capitalist." That was before it became a dirty word. That's what he was, though, and successful at it. He did a lot of negotiating. His judgment, as far as investments go, was generally very good. And he got along with people.

Reform Services—My family was active at Congregation B'nai Israel. My father insisted that my mother and I go to temple every Friday night, so we did. I used to enjoy going, because most of the service was done in English and at least I had an idea of what it was all about. But I would never wear a hat or a prayer shawl. My father had great admiration for Rabbi Gordon. He was a good friend and his services were extremely Reform. Dad was one of the organizers and founders of the first Jewish community center on South Temple, in what is now the LDS Business College. He was very interested in Jewish affairs and at the same time was a leader in community affairs. I suppose that's how he got to be elected mayor of Salt Lake City in the fall of that year, 1931.

Good Showing—Initially, my dad didn't want to run for mayor. The year before, he retired from business, and sold out his theatres to Paramount Pictures. He was asked to put on a celebration for the Pioneer Day on the 24th of July. Pioneer Day celebrates the coming of Brigham Young and the pioneers to Utah. As the general chairman, my dad organized quite a parade and an elaborate show at the University of Utah stadium. It was very successful and he got quite a bit of publicity. I don't think, though, that he had in mind it would be used to propel him into political office, but that was the result of it. The government had not been operating particularly well at the time. The city was in dire financial straits. And a number of businessmen got together and decided my father would be a logical choice to be mayor of Salt Lake. They persuaded him to run for office.

Into Politics—Dad was a life-long Republican. Of course, it's pretty apparent that had the Mormon community or the Mormon leaders not wanted him to be mayor, I don't think he could have been mayor. He could not have been elected nor would he even have accepted the opportunity to run. But he did run and he was elected. According to some of his successors, mayors and members of city government, they said he did an outstanding job and was the finest mayor Salt Lake City had.

He went into office during the depth of the depression, and the very first thing he did was to cut his salary, his own personal salary. Then he asked all the other city employees to do the same. He also refused the use of a city car. The government always bought a new car for the mayor, but he decided to use his own. Until prohibition was repealed, while he was still mayor, my father went along with anything that was the law and disposed of every bottle of liquor and wine that we had in our house. This is not to say he didn't enjoy a drink before dinner at someone else's home, but he would never have it around or serve it at his own home. The most important thing he did was deal with the water problem. We would not have had enough water today if it had not been for his foresight in 1931. He was instrumental in setting up the Metropolitan Water District, which resulted in the building of the Deer Creek Reservoir, our chief source of water.

Dad got along with the governor who happened to be a Democrat. He did very well with the Mormon Church, and was friendly with Herbert J. Grant, president of the LDS church at the time my father was mayor. He had a knack of getting along with people, a wonderful smile, and a lot of charm. To my knowledge, he never had a speech written up since he was a very good extemporaneous speaker. He went along with anything that was the law. I would go with my mother to a political meeting when he gave a talk, but most of the time the talks were held during the day when I was at school.

Busy Times—It was hard for me as child, though, especially when he was mayor. I think he was a better businessman, public servant, husband, and leader of the Jewish community than he was a father. He didn't have a great deal of time for me. My fondest memories are the numerous occasions when, in the last couple of years of his life, he took me fishing and duck hunting. Those experiences left an impression on me because they are activities I still enjoy.

Defeated by Friends—When my father was up for re-election, it was a cinch that he would win. He got sixty to seventy percent in the primary and he had only to run against one opponent. Everybody assumed he was going to win by a landslide. Bookmakers were giving five to one odds that he would be elected in the general election, and so his own friends and even his own employees, he had gone back into business, didn't bother to vote. My father was defeated by 1100 votes in one of the lightest turnouts in Salt Lake City's history. He was defeated by friends who failed to vote. A lot of friends at that time said it really broke his heart because he died six months later at age fifty-six.

Up until the time I went to college, I was raised and spent all my life in Salt Lake City. I had traveled quite a bit, but always lived here. I went to Stanford University. I had wanted to be a chemist. My father was against that and, in retrospect, I think he was very short sighted. He did not have a college degree, but he was a great reader and student of history. He wanted me to be in business. During the war, I was exempted for physical reasons but worked for the Office of War Information. Later, I went to Los Angeles and worked for my cousin in the plastic business. That's where I met my wife. I loved being in California and especially San Francisco. It is the most beautiful city in the United States. When I was at Stanford, they were building the Golden Gate Bridge and the Oakland Bay Bridge. I saw them go up, I saw them completed, and what a thrill it was to drive across them. I loved everything about San Francisco and thought I would like to spend the rest of my life there.

But as things worked out, business interests and my mother being a widow and I her only child, I came back to Salt Lake. All these things brought me back. I worked with an advertising agency for about five years and then got into investments. James White, after whom the Jewish Community Center is named, was an attorney and a good friend of the family who made a considerable amount of money investing in bankrupt railroad bonds.[2] He had two daughters, but no son. He came to me and said he'd like to teach me something about investing in what he called special situations. With capital from my mother, I got out of the advertising business, went into investments and for the last decade got into real estate. It's treated me well. But, like I told you before, the Capitol Theatre was in my family for forty-nine years. It turned out as an old movie theatre that outlived its usefulness as such, it is quite well adapted to its new use, and for that, I am very proud.

RADIO DAYS

Sid Fox

Young in the West—I was born in St. Louis, Missouri in 1889, left home when I was 17 years old, and went to Denver for my health.[1] I landed in Denver as a young inexperienced boy on a Sunday morning. The depot is at the end of 17th Street. I got off the train, took my grip, started to walk up 17th Street to look for a place of lodging. In 1906, rooms could be found for a dollar a day.

When you're 17 years old and out into the world, you have to make a living and support yourself right away. I was fortunate to meet a man named Al Hirschfield, who had a small print shop. He helped me find a room and a job selling business cards.

Denver was an old typical mining town with a number of music halls attached to saloons. Miners from various parts of Colorado went to Denver to relieve themselves of the work they had to put in, mostly underground. Hirschfield showed me around and he directed me to a district where there was at least 500 girls, "soiled doves," who represented themselves and needed business cards. Within two weeks, I was in business with 200 sales.

Talent—I didn't stay with Hirschfield for long. I really wanted to be an actor. I could tap well. I was a fair dancer. But I didn't have much of a voice. Nevertheless, I tried it out. I worked with a young fellow my age who was a good piano player. We formed a little vaudeville act, which I went out and sold to one or two saloons. Without a voice, though, I soon had to give up the act. Still, I wanted to work where I could at least "see" talent, so I got a job working as an usher in a vaudeville theatre.

A Million-Dollar Product—I loved show business. I worked as a salesman in the film business, then as a salesman on the road calling on theatres, always looking for business. I'll tell you a story. When I started radio, I occupied the ninth and tenth floors in the Walker Bank Building, the tallest building in downtown Salt Lake City. On the ground floor was a firm called Crazy Crystals. It was a laxative. Packaged in a rather ordinary looking box. Sold for about $1.00 or $1.50 a box. I found out they had a sort of franchise proposition in which they sold territories. The salesmen were reputed to be making two or three million dollars a year. The product was taken from the wells of Texas, and dried into a powder-like substance that resembled diamonds. The advertising was that the product would clear out the system.

A fellow named Bowers and another called Capson had it in mind that I form a company and produce a product similar to Crazy Crystals taken from the Great Salt Lake. They tried to interest me, and they did; but, how to market it? I was running a radio station and I knew a number of radio operators. I figured, if I could get them interested, I could sell it across the country.

Miracle Diamonds—I formed a company and decided to call Crazy Crystals, "Miracle Diamonds." They looked like diamonds. Sparkled like diamonds. And when you dried them out and put them into a box, they poured out like diamonds. Instead of ordinary packaging, I got drawings of a beautiful woman coming out of a diamond to put on the package. I decided if I learned about the distribution of the drug business, I could place Miracle Diamonds in drugstores. Then if I made a set of shows about famous diamonds, I could sell Miracle Diamonds to the public all across the country through the medium of radio. All Bowers and Capson had to do was furnish the product.

With a few shares given to the two of them, I owned all of the company. I hired eight or ten writers to come up with 26 stories about diamonds, and made a series of recordings in L.A. Now, they were good stories, otherwise I couldn't have sold them "after" I was put out of the Miracle Diamond business. Oh, we got started out all right. We had a good-looking package, better than our competitors. I sold Miracle Diamonds in Northern California, Southern California, and Colorado, and I was getting pretty good at it, when all of a sudden I got notice from the Postal Department. Our advertising copy had to be changed.

A Case of Misinformation—The advertising we used was how the system would respond when you took Miracle Diamonds to eliminate material from the body. "That it would eliminate faulty elimination of the waste material of the body that causes problems of various medical problems." We had to say it was a "laxative." And we hadn't used the word "laxative" once. The postal service said that had to change. I considered that change of words carefully, and decided that was the end of Miracle Diamonds. All I got from my investment were the recordings on famous diamonds. Fortunately, they were good enough to sell to 700 radio stations on my first effort, all the way from five dollars to fifty for a show. Finally, I got all my investment money back.

A Tough Business, Promoting—Pioneering in radio, selling radio promotions is the toughest racket to be in because you haven't got any background to work with. After the war, my wife had a cousin who told me about a convention coming up in Paris for ex-servicemen. Now, how to sell that on radio was a challenge. First I went to the American Legion. And I came up with a proposition that the American Legion is going to have the first convention after the war in Paris. Popular appeal! Patriotic appeal! Three men representing the army would be sent to Paris. Well, I proceeded to create a contest. All I had to do was get hold of the American Legion

KDYL at night. Note Dupler Furs on street level. (Courtesy of Special Collections, Marriott Library, University of Utah)

"On the scene with KDYL."
(Courtesy of Special Collections, Marriott Library, University of Utah)

In 1922, the pioneer radio station, KDYL, was the thirteenth commercial radio station in America.[2] In 1927, it was also a struggling radio station with a net asset value of $4,000.[3] Sid Fox established an Operating License Account for $11,000. In 1930, KDYL showed a profit of $14,000, and by December of that year, Fox and his wife, Miriam, owned the majority of outstanding stock. In 1938, Fox opened the KDYL Playhouse in the Masonic Temple on First South and Second East. The following year, NBC sold Fox a television demonstration unit consisting of a camera, control unit, six receivers, and a small closed-circuit transmitter, which were installed in a local department store for public demonstrations and then at the Utah State Fair.

According to Denver's *Rocky Mountain Magazine*, "when 45,000 persons jammed [the] three-day demonstration in a Salt Lake department store the summer of 1939, Fox waxed enthusiastic, 'Brother, television's the thing.'"[4] Shortly after, Fox applied to the Federal Communications Commission for an experimental license to operate a commercial television station. As Utah's only NBC station, in November 1946, KDYL became the first independent television station to broadcast test patterns in the United States.[5] After two years of experimental broadcasting, in 1948, KDYL began its daily broadcasting, running approximately twelve hours a week on a five-day schedule. Not too long after the advent of television, this country's most famous vaudeville stars, Milton Berle, Jack Benny, George Burns, and Gracie Allen, were beginning the trek from radio to TV screen. Ten days after KDYL-TV went on air, the American entertainer Jimmy Durante was at the fairgrounds to deliver a program for a fund-raising drive for the American Cancer Society. Mr. Durante was

A dapper Sid Fox and wife, Miriam. (Courtesy of Special Collections, Marriott Library, University of Utah)

The Fox family in repose. (Courtesy of Special Collections, Marriott Library, University of Utah)

escorted from the Hotel Utah by Salt Lake mayor Earl J. Glade and Utah's governor, Herbert B. Maw, in a party led by the "Ute Rangers," and followed by a brass band. A. Wally Sandack was the master of ceremonies; the music was supplied by Eugene Jelesnik and his twelve-piece orchestra.

Approximately seven hundred television sets were installed in Salt Lake homes and taverns, at a time when forty-four thousand homes were listening to radio. Within two years, Fox believed at least one thousand televisions would be illuminating his programs within the metropolitan area. Yet, by 1953, Fox, his wife, and other family members sold the business to TLF Broadcasting, a subsidiary of Time Incorporated. While Fox remained on board as a consultant, he was eventually lured to new adventures, managing the Royal Nevada Hotel in Las Vegas, Nevada, at first, dipping into a short-lived venture producing films for television, and rebounding with trampoline centers.

Salt Lake resident Ralph Tannenbaum remembers Sid Fox and his entourage of followers. "Wherever Fox went, dressed to the nines with clean collar and spats, his people were always behind him. You would see this as he walked down Main Street and went into one restaurant or another. There was his brother-in-law, Dr. Loeb; his stepsons, Myron Fox and Fred Provol, and different people who came along at different times. I don't think he was ever alone. No doubt, he was an exciting fellow, an innovative man with many ideas, and a philanthropist who did a lot for a lot for people. He was also a compulsive gambler."[6]

Sid Fox's Achilles heel, gambling, took over his entire life, although he tried many times to reform himself. By the early 1970s, Fox was broke. "A group of men in the Jewish community and the non-Jewish community took care of him," said Tannenbaum. "They put him up in the Belvedere Apartments in downtown Salt Lake City. They pooled their money every month to see Sid through. Up until the end of his life, he was always dapperly dressed, although sometimes his monogrammed cuffs were slightly frayed."[7] Sid Fox died March 3, 1980, in a Salt Lake nursing home. He was ninety-one years old.

and have them enroll a certain number of ex-servicemen who were interested in winning a contest to go to Paris. It'd cost about $6,000 to send them.

I established a voting headquarters, rented a room downtown, and put up ballot boxes on all sidewalks and back walls. And a big sign: "Free Trip to Paris Campaign for Servicemen." Before there were trading stamps, I sold votes like stamps to merchandisers. With the backing of the American Legion, I got 200 men who wanted to go to the Convention. Now, I had to have merchants buy these votes and give them out with each ten-cent purchase. Whoever got the most votes would go to Paris.

But to make it work, I needed more than that. Every merchant who wanted to participate had to buy radio time. They had to buy an announcement that ran every night on a program that lasted two hours. They also had to run full-page ads that were placed around a patriotic story that I ran in the newspaper. And I had the theatres make a film. The campaign ran for three months. It was a good idea. Of course, it took a million votes to come in on that deal. But, when the merchants heard their announcements and saw their selling copy, they were sold on the idea of radio as an advertising media. They saw that I was able to do it and I was able to do that because it was a patriotic idea, and it had that punch to sell the businessman. But, see, I had to promote that deal from scratch. It cost $6,000 to send the three men, and I made about $5,000 net on the deal. And one of the men, why, I remember, he wanted to take the cash and stay home.

Show Business Again—I have to laugh. I really have to laugh at some of the things that my life was involved in. Song and dance. Real Estate. Radio. Television. It all really started when I couldn't make it in show business. In 1927, Fred Provol, my stepson, worked for Hudson Bay Fur Company and was partner of an advertising man, ran a dancehall, and a ready-to-wear shop called "Just Sixteen." [At the time, Fred was also president and a major stockholder of Intermountain Broadcasting Corporation.] He come to me and says, "I can get hold of a radio station. The newspaper owns it and they want to get rid of it for $1500." So we bought KDYL, and we started from scratch. That's what you had to do if you were going to be one of the pioneers in the great and new media of radio and television. And that's what I was, a pioneer.

THE NEWSIES

RICHARD MCGILLIS

Charlie McGillis

Our Life in Salt Lake: Exploring Charlie's Background—Wherever there were newsboys in Salt Lake City and a need for a rhythmical hawker, there was always my dad, Charlie McGillis.[1] There was a time when the *Salt Lake Tribune,* a morning paper and the *Telegram,* an evening paper, fought for street corners with the *Deseret News.* Because it grew into such a competitive situation, Ian McKay, publisher of the *Salt Lake Tribune* and *Telegram* newspapers brought my father, Charlie McGillis, over from Denver. He knew my Dad was tough and could fight well. They wanted him to establish the territory, so he became street sales manager for Newspaper Agency Corp., which distributed the city's two major dailies. Dad was so tough, if one of "Charlie's newsboys" had a corner, nobody else would get it. He saw to that.

My Dad was born in 1889 in Cripple Creek, Colorado and then moved to Denver. When he was about eighteen years old, he became the Street Circulation Manager of the *Rocky Mountain News.* He fought professionally until he was twenty-one. But he came over here, to Salt Lake, specifically to fight for corners. Charlie was with the newspaper for sixty-three years until he retired at the age of 84. During this time, he developed a lasting friendship with the financier Russel L. Tracy, worked with the newsboys, and in 1910 owned a newspaper wagon that stood on the corner of the old National Bank of the Republic at 202–204 S. Main Street in Salt Lake City. That wagon was the most complete street wagon with an electric sign and room enough to display an array of newspapers. Quite a beauty, it's in the Smithsonian Institution now, where they have all the newspaper memorabilia.

A Rite of Passage—A lot of Jewish kids sold papers for my father in Denver and in Salt Lake. Michael Wolfe's grandfather, Hubert Wolfe, sold papers for my father. In Denver, David Zinik, of Zinik Sporting Goods, his father sold papers for my father. Joe Dupler sold papers for my

top Newsies: Outside the News Development Room, Salt Lake City, 1908. (Courtesy of Utah State Historical Society)

bottom The most complete news wagon, 1910. (Courtesy of Utah State Historical Society)

Charlie McGillis's sons, Sydney and Dick, early 1920s. (Courtesy of Cal McGillis)

father. Joe moved here. He had a fur and mink farm and he had a fur store. His father owned the Chi Chi Club, which later became the Manhattan Club. Until Izzy Wagner, of Wagner Bag Company, went into the army, he had the club, too, with his partner Hymie Guss. But it was called a different name then, yeah, maybe, *The Officers' Club.*

Losing a Brother—My mother Zelma, they called her Sally, was born in Colorado Springs. Her father was a retail merchant. She had a hard life. Her mother was deaf and never communicated with her. When Dad died, she lived with us for a while. She was a very gentle, sweet disposition woman who throughout her entire life was a kind person. My parents had their ups and downs, sure, their temperaments were different, but they loved each other and went through a lot together. I had a brother who was eight years older than I was but he died of a disease that today would be curable with penicillin; my other brother Cal lives here in Salt Lake City.

Another Ellis Island Name—My father never knew any other name but McGillis. It was probably changed when his parents came over from Europe. It might have been Margoles. That's what we guess it was. McGillis, as a name for us, is unusual. It sounds like an Irish name and my father, you might say, was a pugilist who looked like he could have been Irish. Like I said, he was a professional fighter. He used to have fistfights in later years. When people got out of line at pool halls, someone would call Dad to come down and my Dad would take the offender out in the alley.

Jack and Dad—When he wasn't doing most other things, Dad promoted boxing matches, marathons, and bicycle races. He was five feet six inches tall, weighed, when he was fighting, about 135–140 pounds. In later years, he was 170 pounds. He was friendly with a lot of people, like Jack Dempsey. Dempsey was originally from Denver, like Dad. But when Dempsey moved to Salt Lake, Dad took me to his house and I met him. Dad promoted the fight between Dempsey and Primo Carnera.[2] I was probably about five or six years old at the time, and he looked awfully big. Dempsey was the U.S. heavyweight champion from 1919 until 1926; that's when Gene Tunney defeated him.

Charlie McGillis (*right*) with Dick (*center*) leading the newsies' Thanksgiving Parade, 1926. (Courtesy of Cal McGillis)

Jewish Mayor at the Dinner—When I was five years old—I was born in 1920, so this had to be around 1926—I remember marching up Main Street with the newsboys, my Dad and Mr. Tracy. I remember going to the Hotel Utah for Thanksgiving dinner and sitting with my father. When Dad entered the lobby of the hotel, he would bellow something about the newsboys and the Russel Tracy dinner. He would shout loudly, in the same voice he used when teaching the newsboys how to sell papers on the street. I actually remember, too, when I was ten or eleven years old, seeing Lou Marcus, the Jewish mayor, sitting at the head table with Russel Tracy. Marcus was interested in what the newsboys were doing although his participation was only coming to dinner. Afterwards, Lou Marcus would take me to the football game. He was very well liked, a successful mayor. I heard he ran it like a business, which is why it worked, and he didn't make enemies.

Friendship with Tracy—When I was thirteen years old until the time I went in the army at twenty, I, too, worked at Tracy Loan and Trust Company. Russel L. Tracy was the owner of the bank and I was his protégé. When I was working at the vault as a messenger boy, Mr. Tracy would call me up to his house to play with him on his pitch-and-putt golf course, or his pool table. He'd have his chauffeur, Edward, drive us up to his Boy Scout camp, the Tracy Wigwam in Mill Creek Canyon, that he built in 1921. This is the same Russel L. Tracy who in 1938 donated the bird sanctuary, Tracy Aviary, at Liberty Park. He was a wonderful human being and good to me.

Now, if you want to go way back, why did Mr. Tracy hire me? He was close to my father due to the newsboys, he was kind to us, and subsequently he hired me. Of course, he couldn't hire me, per se, I wasn't old enough. You had to be sixteen years old before you could work. So Mr. Tracy paid me out of his own pocket rather than from the bank. I got nine dollars a month when I worked after school and fourteen dollars when I worked full time. Mr. Tracy and his wife attended my confirmation class and promised me a gift of a hundred dollars if I didn't smoke or drink until I was twenty-one years old. I abstained from those vices and received the hundred dollars; unfortunately, that night, I lost it in a card game.

Another Way to Make a Living—Mr. Tracy died while I was in the army. He left me three shares of stock in the bank and had decreed that I should come back and work my way up through the different offices. I chose not to go back. I wasn't making very much money when I went into the army and knew I wouldn't be making much when I came out. So I had to find another way to make a living. I will say, Mr. Tracy gave me a good start.

Charlie McGillis in Denver—Dad grew up in West Colfax, a Jewish area in Denver, and yes, it would be a tougher area. A very tough and poor neighborhood. He had to learn to protect himself, that's why he became quite a fighter. There were a lot of Jewish fighters in those days. It had to do with being poor. The Jewish fighters, because they were poor; then the Irish fighters because they were poor; and then it became the black fighters, because they were poor. It usually had to do with being an immigrant too, although Dad wasn't, but he was poor.

Taking a Stand—I grew up with some friends who were Jewish and some friends who were not Jewish. I did not actually run into any anti-Semitism. My father did a little bit at the Elks Club and got into a couple of fights. Joel Shapiro's father, Simon, would come running to Dad and say this one fellow said something about the Jews. Simon was a nice man, would never raise a hand to anyone. But he'd tell Dad and Dad would go punch the offender in the mouth. My Dad would not be considered religious. He was Jewish. It was his heritage, his culture, and frankly in my father's case, it was also a protective feeling. He would rise up! It had to be done. Harry Miller, who came to Utah later was a very tough guy himself, into boxing, too, but I think even he would admit Dad was the toughest.

An Unmatched Fight—I remember an incident with my Dad. There was a man here in the early days by the name of McCullough. He was a very difficult man, tough too, let's put it that way. He promoted wrestling matches and Dad promoted boxing matches. They were both about forty-five years old and there were rumors that wrestling was fake. So McCullough challenged my father's boxers in a mixed ballot. On top of that, he challenged my father. He would wrestle; my father would box. I was five years old at the time, and I went there. It was in McCullough's arena on 9th South and Main Street. Every one of the wrestlers won their matches. They won because the boxers wore gloves and the minute they entered the ring, they'd be wrestled to the ground and couldn't do anything about it. So Dad got in the ring with this guy, and just as they came into the center of the ring, Dad hit him, knocked him down, pounded on him. This guy went to the hospital the next day. I went to see him. Imagine as a five-year-old kid walking into a hospital. They were both tough guys. At some time or another, they worked together and promoted bicycle races. But the finale to this story is they eventually ended up in the same rest home. This fellow really lost it; and my father wasn't so much with it, himself. But Dad did come out of the rest home and took an apartment with my mother at the Charleston Apartments on 5th South and 13th East. They lived there until he died.

> **NEWSIES' GRATITUDE GLADDENS BANK HEAD**
>
> *Paper Sellers Enjoy Banquet Provided by Russel L. Tracy, Salt Lake Financier*
>
> Business success, world tours, and other triumphs faded into insignificant oblivion for Russel L. Tracy Thursday when a twelve-year-old newsboy opened a heart full of gratitude.
>
> The youngster, Alma Soronsen, "stole the show" with his 150-word presentation of a book of photographs of the newsboys, the highlight of Mr. Tracy's thirtieth Thanksgiving dinner for *Tribune-Telegram* newspaper salesmen. Here is what he said: . . .
>
> "We are proud to know at heart you are one of us. We all wish you many happy returns of this glorious day, and hope that we will be able to celebrate the fiftieth annual newsboys' dinner together."[3]

A Dare Devil—Dad would try anything. They used to have horse races out at the Fair Grounds and so he had to ride the horses. Not professionally, of course, but he rode them to see what it was like. One time, I even saw him out there riding a motorcycle. He was involved in the dog races. He had a concession there, I think, and one up in Evanston where they had a western deal. For awhile there was one out at Saltair. Dad owned one pool hall in Park City and two in Salt Lake. He was part owner of the Horseshoe, and he owned the Windsor Billiard Parlor that was in the back of the Windsor Hotel. That hotel was a very small, second rate place on Main Street between 2nd and 3rd South on the eastside of the street. My dad said he had a bus down at the railroad station to bring people to the hotel. He didn't make much money, but he always made a very good living because of his newspaper work and his other little enterprises of which he had many.

Home Life and Jewish Involvement—We lived on the Northeast corner of Virginia Street and South Temple, and lived quite well. Had a maid, but never had a surplus of money. My mother was a religious woman. We used to go to the Reform temple (Congregation B'nai Israel) for all holidays. I grew up and was confirmed from the community center when I went to Sunday school up on South Temple at the Wall Mansion that later became the LDS Business School.[4] It was a beautiful building, still is. On the third floor was a ballroom, and below that were classrooms. I didn't go to Hebrew School. We didn't have one at the Reform temple. But I went to the Covenant House, as it was called, every Sunday. I really think I got more involved in Judaism later in life because of my wife Joanne. She got involved with the Jewish community and all its programs and I went along with it. Although, actually, when we were first married, I was already doing things in some ways, giving to the various Jewish projects. I gave commensurate with my income at that time.

SANTA PLANS ANNUAL VISIT TO NEWSBOYS

A visit to the home of each of 100 newsboys to be sure that Santa Claus will make his annual Christmas appearance will be made next week by C. W. McGillis, street circulation manager of *The Tribune* and *Telegram*.

Mr. McGillis will see that each newsie is provided with new warm clothing on the day before Christmas. He also plans to study the needs of each newsie's family and insure against want. If the family requires food, fuel, or clothing, it will be cared for, Mr. McGillis said. . . . Gifts will include shoes, sweaters, underwear, gloves, stockings, shirts and caps. Baskets of food and sacks of coal also will be distributed.[5]

A Small Jewish Population—When we moved out of that lovely building and into the James L. White Community Center, I was one of the signers—there were twenty of us who guaranteed the mortgage on the Center on 17th South. Subsequently, when we talked about the merger of Congregation Montefiore and B'nai Israel into Congregation Kol Ami, I was also involved. There were several Reform Jews who were against the merger and some Conservatives who were almost like Orthodox Jews and very much against the merger. But it was a necessary move. We had a small Jewish population. We couldn't afford to have a Conservative Rabbi and a Reform Rabbi and keep up with two separate buildings that were in pretty bad shape. Well, the first time we tried to work out a merger they gave up on it. Some people believed that Conservative and Reform Jews wouldn't be able to get along what with their various ways of adhering to Jewish traditions. They said there would have to be a lot of compromises made. But it was necessary because anyway you look at it we couldn't afford both congregations. So, most of us agreed and by doing that, we ended up with a nice big building and synagogue, Congregation Kol Ami.

Blending of Traditions—My wife says it worked out because we had children who were being totally polarized from one another, as if having two distinctly different communities. During

A STORE ON WHEELS

In the early 1970s, a replica of McGillis's 1910 newspaper wagon, originally built by Phil Kipple, became part of the National Museum of History and Technology of the Smithsonian Institution in Washington, D.C. According to both Richard and Cal McGillis, every day the newspaper wagon was placed on Second South and Main Street in Salt Lake City, on the corner of the National Bank of the Republic. Periodically, because it obstructed his view, the bank president would order the police to remove it. The following day Thomas Kearns, co-owner of the paper, would order it back to its corner site.

A Complete Store—The cart and horses were both parked at night at the old McCoy Livery Stable near the Cullen Hotel. The wagon measured ten feet high by six feet wide, had a thirty-inch sign and twenty-four-inch spoke wheels. The *Salt Lake Tribune* on March 25, 1910, described the news wagon as "the most complete street newspaper ever built." Sleek with eye-catching newspaper logos, it had a red body, yellow wheels, and black trim. On top of the wagon, an electric sign brightened up the night with its call to "Read the Salt Lake Tribune." To protect the newspaper stock when not in use, the wagon's doors and shutters closed into a box. When preparing to greet the public with the daily news, the wagon was opened into a unique store with its own counters, benches, and display panels.

Nowhere to Be Found—At some point in time, the original news wagon disappeared from the city streets, perhaps hauled away for the last time by the police. In 1971, the *Salt Lake Tribune* offered an award of one thousand dollars to find it. Many calls were received and leads were offered, but it was to no avail; the original news wagon was nowhere to be found. To make a replica significantly close in detail, the Smithsonian had to rely upon photographs, descriptions, and the craftsmanship of a cabinetmaker in Harrisburg, Pennsylvania. With the exception of the electric sign, which would violate building codes, the news wagon was constructed and is part of a permanent exhibition devoted to the history of news reporting in America.

the final merger deliberations, the children were brought together and educated under one roof. It was no longer a "them" or "us," and it worked out.

A Jewish Way of Life—I'm a Jew because I was born a Jew. For me, this is not a religious end. It's just a way of life. When we were in Israel in 1980, the gift I gave to Israel I gave for what Israel had done for us. For improving the situation for American Jews, we owe Israel. Instead of being looked on as pawn brokers and moneylenders, and other such stereotypes, we were seen as

THE DENVER-UTAH CONNECTION

"The Publisher's Desk," by Max Goldberg

SALT LAKE CITY, UTAH. No one knows how many Jewish families there are in Salt Lake City. Best estimates, between 450–500. Of this number 250 are affiliated, the rest, unaffiliated.

This community can easily boast of one of the best per capita responses to the UJA [United Jewish Appeal] in the country. In their 1970 drive, the Salt Lakers raised $250,000, an average of $1,000 per family. True, this $1,000 figure consists of pledges from both husbands and wives. And, in many instances, the children, too. But nothing can detract from this impressive goal.

To me, Salt Lake City is like a second home. I have two brothers there—William and Morris, and two sisters-in-law, Sarah and Augusta, and a nephew Charles, and his wife, Selma.

I once worked on the old *Salt Lake Telegram* writing sports and remember being present when Salt Lake's first Jewish Mayor, Mayor [Louis] Marcus, was introduced to cheering thousands from the balcony of the *Salt Lake Tribune* building.

I also have fond memories of writing about Jack Dempsey when he came to Salt Lake to visit his mother on West Temple Street.

Salt Lake City is also the scene of my only hole-in-one, which I shot several years ago at the Bonneville Golf Course. I was playing with my brothers and nephew when the ball hit the side of a hole, rolled on the green and dropped into the cup. The first definite confirmation came from Dal Siegel, who was playing at the hole below and excitedly waved his club to signal to us that [indeed] something unusual had occurred.

There are so many ex-Denverites living in Salt Lake City, it is hard to keep track of them. With a number of children marrying Denver boys and girls, and vice versa, the Salt Lake–Denver link remains as strong as ever. At Sabbath services at the Montefiore Congregation and, at their annual picnic held at Lagoon the next day, I was showered with regards for scores of Denver relatives.

After services, I had a pleasant chat with Max Cowan who is in Denver quite often. Max is an exponent of Jewish history and *Yiddishkeit*. He was the *Bal Korah* at the Shabbes service. "This is the second time I have done this," he told me. His reading of the Torah was masterful and was handled with warmth and skill.

fighters, farmers, builders, Jewish pioneers, doing whatever was necessary for what we had to do. And I believe we were accepted much better in the United States by business people, by clubs, and other societies, because of their respect for Israel at that time. I believe this.

My Dad wasn't particularly religious, like I said, but he, too, was a participant in his time because being Jewish *is* a way of life. My Dad gave money for the Jewish Community Center

Abe Guss, married to a Denver girl, Sophie, as always, helped conduct the service with dispatch. Abe is one of the real *balebatim* of the city and a lifelong pillar of the Montefiore synagogue. . . . I met Norman Nathan who enjoys writing quotations and short commentaries on life. I also met Mr. and Mrs. Harry Glow. Their daughter is married to Bob Brody, a Denver financier.

At the Montefiore picnic, I saw the Manny Peppers and the Jerome Peppers, the Melvin Richtels, Harry Shers, Sam Saptiskys, Lou Kaufmans, Mrs. Sid Safran, Phil Mednicks, Ben Mednicks, and a host of others. I saw Steve Rosenblatt, whose brother, Norman, is the 1970 UJA chairman. Another engaging person, whom I always enjoy seeing, was Attorney Sam Bernstein and his wife, Jackie. Sam, throughout the years, had held just about every major office that the community has to offer.

A visit to Salt Lake is never complete without my calling on Charlie McGillis, a walking encyclopedia of early Denver newsboy history. He left Denver over 55 years ago. Charlie has been ill and had just returned from the hospital when my brother, Willie, and I paid him a short visit. The conversation turned to Jack Dempsey and to the time when McGillis was the ONLY boxer to defeat a wrestler. . . .[6]

Charlie McGillis, outside the newsboys' headquarters, Salt Lake City. (Courtesy of Richard McGillis)

that was on South Temple. During Jewish Welfare Drives back then, he worked at raising funds. He was a good guy. He was a very tough guy. A strong guy. Very active in the Elks Club, he promoted their boxing matches.

Charlie McGillis in His Time—For most of his life, at least sixty-seven years of it, my father was very involved with the "newsies" holding their own on street corners and barking out the local news; the newspaper wagon that sold papers from all parts of the country; and his spiel that has become part of his legend: "If you've got a home, I have your home paper."

RUSSEL LORD TRACY AND THE NEWSIES' THANKSGIVING CELEBRATIONS

Russel Lord Tracy Gives a Gift—Thanksgiving Dinners traditionally held after the holiday parade for the *Tribune-Telegram* newsboys came to life in 1902 when, on his way to work, Russel Lord Tracy, president and chairman of Tracy Loan and Trust Company, met a tow-headed newsboy hustling papers on a street corner. Only six years old, this young lad, Ralph Nielson, had lost his father, brother and one sister within a period of six months and was forced to become the sole supporter of an invalid mother and a surviving sister. They lived on meager funds in a small two-room home. A resourceful child, however, Ralph found the only occupation offered to boys of his age, selling newspapers, and took his stand as a downtown vendor of the daily *Tribune*. Touched by his story, Mr. Tracy became his regular customer.

"It's Swell"—The following Thanksgiving, Mr. Tracy asked Ralph if he liked turkey. The young boy replied he had never tasted it before, but that his sister had once and said, "it's swell." Understanding there would be little festivities in the Nielson family's home during the holidays, Mr. Tracy offered them a turkey with all the trimmings. The boy expressed profound appreciation for Mr. Tracy's generosity, and the financier and the young newsie's friendship deepened and became the "deciding factor" in Mr. Tracy's desire to help young newsboys improve their quality of life, and develop characters of "honesty, self-reliance and moral uplift." Thus began the custom of giving a Thanksgiving dinner to a growing number of boys who made their living selling newspapers on downtown Salt Lake City streets.

Payment for Good Grades—When Ralph was ten years old, he left the streets and worked after school and on Saturdays as a telephone operator in Mr. Tracy's office. At this time, a second tradition took hold. Mr. Tracy believed that if given the proper kind of encouragement children would have the incentive for "good living and achievement." Newsboys began to show their report cards to Mr. Tracy and depending upon their grades were rewarded monetarily for achievement in studies. Excellent reports in "Deportment, Application and Scholarship" received fifty cents and accolades; "very good" garnered twenty-five cents; "good" secured a dime.

Unruliness Lands Them in Trouble—Corralling high-spirited lads to a sit-down dinner ignited a new set of challenges. In 1903, more than seventy-five hungry newsboys took their seats for a Thanksgiving banquet at Bonds Restaurant. With dinner nearly over, several older boys attempted to steal slices of pies from the younger newsboys, who in turn threw cups and saucers at the rascals, sometimes completely missing the human target. When they broke a large glass mirror that hung in back of a counter, the police were called in, Mr. Tracy had to pay $15 to $20 in damages, and he had second thoughts.

Charlie McGillis Gets Involved—After two years of such experiences, the do-gooder was ready to relinquish all offers when Charlie McGillis, amateur fighter and street sales manager for the newspaper, stepped in and took control of the boys. Thus armed, Tracy and McGillis did much together. In fact, for twenty-eight years, during the winter season, the men provided each newsboy with warm stockings and good shoes. In 1911, Mr. Tracy rented the third floor of a building (which later housed the Utah State National Bank), and Charlie McGillis helped build the newsboys' gymnasium. Instrumental in keeping the youth off Salt Lake City's mean streets and away from street gangs, monthly boxing and wrestling contests were held. Before the Boy Scouts became an American organization in 1910, Mr. Tracy also helped establish a summer newsboys' camp in Big Cottonwood Canyon.

Mr. Tracy's friendship with Charlie McGillis lasted their lifetime and extended to their families. Mr. Tracy used to carry McGillis's young son in his arms; when Richard grew older, Mr. Tracy would lead him by the hand while walking the annual parade; and later offered Richard a job at the bank.

A Who's Who of Newsies—Over the years, prominent people, attorneys, physicians, bankers, legislators, and contractors graduated from the ranks of newsboys. Heavyweight champion boxer Jack Dempsey was a newsboy, as was Senator Gordon Weggeland. As far as the boy who initiated the food riot in 1903? That was Herbert B. Maw who, in 1941, was the Democratic Governor of Utah.[7]

HARRISON LOST GREAT BATTLE IN 1911

OGDEN FIGHT FANS CAME HERE BY CARLOAD

Boxer Suffers Pairs of Broken Ribs—Once upon a time, along about 1911, there was a mighty tough little hombre up in Ogden named Kid Harrison. The Kid was a lightweight and had been all over the Pacific coast in the fight game. He was going great guns and was a popular scrapper in Utah.

Roy Shumway was the Kid's manager, and Roy was always on the outlook for a big drawing card. So he heard about Chick McGillis, the fighting newsboy of Salt Lake, and a bout was arranged. Incidentally, folks, that was one of the greatest fights ever staged in the old Manhattan Club in Salt Lake. . . .

Fans by Carload—The big night arrived, and several special carloads of fans came down from Ogden to see the Kid in action. And Salt Lake fistdom was out in force to "holler" for the fighting newsboy.

Here was Harrison, a rugged fighter, with many a scrap under his belt, including fights with such men as Ad Wolgast and the best lightweights in the game.

And here was Chick, the gamest little fighting cock of the walk in Salt Lake.

Words fail us to describe that battle, but perhaps an old newspaper clipping of the scrap will help: "After the big crowd of fans had started to leave the hall, thinking Chick had been put down and out by Harrison, the local newsboy came back to score a knock-down himself in the third round and wind up by getting a draw. The boys made good.

"Against a cool hard-hitting and experienced boxer who likes the twenty-round route better, McGillis kept his windmill swings and by sheer gameness and 'abysmal brute,' as Jack London would term it, turned the tide of battle to even honors again.

"In the first round, McGillis went down for the count of nine from a left to the eye. He took the count twice in the second round and it was the second time that he was down that fans began to say goodnight. (Incidentally, Chick received two broken ribs in this round.)

Strong Cheer—"McGillis, however, was not down and as he came up strong the cheer that greeted him was worth hearing. In the third round McGillis landed one of his swings and Harrison was down. Chick had the better of this round. The fourth was even with McGillis making the Kid lose much of his precision in landing. Seemingly in better condition, Harrison's terse muscles would not allow him to keep fresh."

Salt Lake fans will long remember the setting of that fight card, remembering the hard-hitting Mexican who faltered, and the newsboy who came back to secure a draw.[8]

CHANGING TIMES

September 2, 1941
Mr. Charlie McGillis
Tribune-Telegram Publications
Salt Lake City, Utah

My dear Charlie:

I realize school will begin tomorrow and you should have a reply from me as to what I wish to do regarding school boys' reports and what plans we should make regarding the Thanksgiving day celebration.

During the past thirty-eight years I have greatly enjoyed my relations with you and the little newsboys, and I deeply regret the necessity of discontinuing any further activities with them. In years past, it was a real pleasure to ask them to bring their school reports to me every month when I would reward them with from ten to fifty cents according to the standing of their reports. I could also talk with them regarding their future and give a suit of clothes to the one with the best report for the year and actually promise a spanking to those who had any more red "U's" or "Unsatisfactory" marks. But, that was when we actually had newsboys who were seven, nine and ten years old.

Now, under the new laws, newspaper salesmen must be sixteen and most of them are eighteen or more and you can imagine how I would feel or they would feel to have me address them as above or how they would like you or myself visiting their homes and discussing their school reports with their mothers; or to establish camps in the canyons and instruct them how to cook, make their beds, etc.

It is not because I have lost interest in the little boys or lack of funds for such work, but simply because you have no longer any material, for there is now no such thing as a newsboy; therefore, you will have to excuse me from participating hereafter with their school reports or with the Thanksgiving Dinner, and we can both feel very happy because in the years past we have had an opportunity to be of real service to boys when they were just starting in life and only from six to ten years of age.

Sincerely, Russel L. Tracy[9]

JUDAISM, POLITICS, PR, AND WAR

A. Wally Sandack

Not a Green Horn—My mother was born in the United States.[1] My father claimed he was born in St. Louis. But I'm sure he was born in Russia, Poland, Lithuania, or in one of those places. He was an American citizen, of course, by the fact that his father was naturalized after coming to this country. But I think he felt there would be more opportunity in America if he were known as a natural-born citizen rather than as a "green horn." I assume he came here for the hope and future of America and to get away from the strict life of his past. I don't know if he was ever the product of any pogrom himself. I do know his father, Israel Isaac Sandack, showed me his trigger finger on his right hand. He told me that his mother bent it back and broke it so he couldn't be drafted into the czar's army.

A Shul Mensh—Well, they escaped the army and came to Chicago. My grandfather was a real *shul mensh.* He lived, ate, slept, and breathed the synagogue. In the years I knew him, he was an old man with many sons and daughters, all of whom supported him. His sole occupation in later days, which were in Los Angeles, California, was to attend shul meetings morning, noon and night. I would watch him put on his tefillin and say his morning prayers and his evening prayers. He'd wrap his arms with the tefillin straps. I went to shul with him out of curiosity more than dedication. Although I was bar mitzvahed in Los Angeles in 1926, I didn't really become a great scholar.

Living for Family and Shul—My grandmother's name was Annie and she was a wonderful lady. She'd have family over every Friday night for a beautiful Sabbath dinner. She cooked everything. I'd get out of school early in the afternoon and watch her make *luchen kugel.* She didn't have any of the pasta-cutting equipment. She had her fingernails and a very sharp knife. She'd engineer those noodles, cutting perfectly with her knife, using her fingernails as a guide, and getting just thin, beautifully-sized *luchen* noodles. She made beautiful chicken soup, too. A fine woman, she lived for her family. Her husband lived for the synagogue. They were not wealthy people, but between the two, they were happy old people with sons and daughters who loved and adored them.

The Only Child to Survive—On my mother's side of the family, grandfather Grossman and his wife, Goldie, came to the United States in about 1882. They lived in Pittsburgh for a while, and settled in Chicago. Grandfather Grossman was an old Jewish transient watch dealer who worked the gold pawnshops between St. Louis and Chicago. He met my Dad who was then working in a St. Louis jewelry store. Said he had a beautiful girl for him. They were introduced and my father and mother married in about 1907. I was born in Chicago in 1913. My own mother passed away in childbirth when I was about three years old. I am the only child to survive. After her death, my father remarried twice to very fine women.

Tent Stores—When my Dad first came to this country, he worked with his father, grandfather Israel, on the building of the Tex-Arkansas Railroad, out of St. Louis. They didn't work on the railroad. They set up a tent store and as the railroad ties moved down the line, they moved their tent down the line. Laborers could buy boots and socks and gloves and clothing. It was a six-o'clock-in-the-morning job to a twelve-o'clock-midnight job. They were opened any hour of the night to serve the needs of the railroad laborers. My father didn't do manual labor. He just tore down the tent and moved it down the road a half a mile and put it back up again and served the public.

Retail—My dad was a man who could defend himself. He was strong. He knew how to box. And I know that he took care of himself. (When I was fifteen years old, I used to box with him and he could handle himself pretty well.) After the tent store business, Dad went into the jewelry business and became a very successful retail and wholesale diamond merchant. He had several retail stores in and around Chicago and a big diamond distributing house. I was a very spoiled, rich, young boy for seven years. Chauffeured around Chicago, I had an account at Morris Rothschild's and Co. and anything I wanted. At the end of World War I, the whole diamond market collapsed internationally with the European markets going sour. That eventually caught up with my father's business and the family never recovered from that. His wholesale and retail lines and buyers defaulted on their payments. We went downhill fast. But it was probably a providential result as far as I was concerned. I don't think I would have ever had the enthusiasm for making a go of it myself if I had continued to be a spoiled son of a wealthy diamond merchant in Chicago.

Salt Lake City—Dad went from Chicago to Los Angeles with some of his brothers to try and recoup his losses and they were doing pretty well for a few years. I think he was there about the time President Harding died, in 1924, and he stayed there until 1929 and found himself in the Intermountain West, just about the time the Great Depression broke. I came to Utah with him and decided to stay. I finished high school and then went to the University of Utah. He ended up in Los Angeles where he lived the rest of his life. So I don't really have any blood relatives in Salt Lake City except my family that I married.

Aspirations—I wanted to be a lawyer and this happened to be a nice place to settle down and get an education at a not very high cost. In the 1930s, you could go to law school, I think, for forty dollars a quarter, you could sign a note for it at 2-1/2 percent interest and pay it back after graduation. That was a good deal. I had the idea that once I got my degree, I'd go back to Chicago.

Fast Food—I lived at 322 University Street, right across from what is now Carlson Hall up on the campus, near the law school. I had a room in Mrs. Cooke's rented home in the basement for seven bucks a month, and spent an average of ninety cents a day for meals at various fast food houses: The Coffee Cup for breakfast and the Ute Hamburger Stand for lunch. You could eat pretty well for thirty to fifty cents a day. Even downtown at Scotties or Joe Vincent's Famous Cafe. I worked every afternoon after school at Roe's store downtown. I sold clothes for Ben and Harry Roe. In the summers, I worked at the Lagoon Amusement Park. Then I worked at the famous dog races when at the Coliseum at the Fairgrounds. Charlie McGillis, Dick McGillis's dad, promoted the races. He had a food concession and he gave me a job. He also had a promotion for not only boxers but wrestlers, and he was a boxer at one time, himself. A prize fighter.

I was a purveyor of foods, hamburgers, and hot dogs. You did everything in those days. You had to eat, so you had to make a living. And if you could earn twelve to fifteen dollars a week in the 1930s, you could live pretty well and pay all your costs for tuition and school. Yeah, fifteen to twenty dollars a week would be great. You know, the minimum wage law didn't come into effect until the second or third year under Franklin Roosevelt. The first U.S. minimum wage law was twenty-five cents an hour.

The AZA—The first contact I had with the Jewish community in those days was with the AZA (*Aleph Zadek Aleph*), a junior order of the B'nai B'rith organization. I met a number of fine young men in those days: Dick McGillis, Simon Ramo, Roxy Rothman.

I was the *aleph godel*, the president, of AZA for a year or two. I visited other communities and went to conventions. I also did some public speaking and debating. Simon Ramo, my debate partner, was the brightest guy I ever knew in my life. Si was a young Salt Lake military genius who got his degree in electrical engineering at the University of Utah in the early 1930s. He came from a very poor immigrant merchant background in Salt Lake, did his doctoral thesis on electrical energy at Hoover Dam, went to California State Polytechnic, and got a job with General Electric Company. Not because they needed a young Jewish scientist, but because they had an opening in their orchestra and he was a fine fiddle player. From there you couldn't stop Simon Ramo. He later became connected with Howard Hughes, eventually had a lot to do with intercontinental bombers and missiles.[2] So Si and I were partners in the AZA debate on the issue of having a Hebrew University in the United States. In those days the quota system against Jews being admitted into certain universities strengthened our argument. How'd we do? We won and we lost.

Silver Shirts—Roxy Rothman was another mensh. I'll tell you one of the things the two of us did something about. Roxy tried to put out a magazine called *Salt Lake Jewish News*. We were

To: Samuel J. Friedman,
Sec. B. F. Peixotto Lodge No. 421
Salt Lake City, Utah

From: Max Strasburg
Chairman of Past Presidents
Hollywood Jewelers
6730 Hollywood Blvd.

November 7, 1933

My Dear Brother Friedman:
The conditions under which we, as Jews, are laboring at the present time is one of such a serious nature that it is absolutely essential that each and every man make some sacrifice at this time.

Ten years ago, when Hitler first appeared upon the scene, no Jew had time to do his part, nor did they have time to do their part five years or three years ago, and yet today without a doubt if one percent or five percent of the Jews of Germany had realized their responsibility and were unselfish enough to do their part, they would not be facing the condition they are today.

Here in America, the Silver Shirts are gathering strength every hour. Their *Liberation Magazine* is going forth into thousands of new homes every week, and yet I find Past Presidents who understand the very traditions of B'nai B'rith haven't time to do their part. . . . Certainly there must be someone among the Past Presidents who is going to be big enough and strong enough to do his part in the organizations of its work, which are so necessary at this time. You as Secretary are the best man qualified to find that man for me. Our attitude today is more or less militant—it has to be—and yet it is with the great friendliness that I make this request to you.

Won't you kindly do your part in appointing a man who is unselfish, who is willing to do his share along this line.

Salt Lake's Jewish community found a willing volunteer in Simon Shapiro, chairman of the Past Presidents Association. On November 20, 1933, Max Strasburg wrote again:

My Dear Brother Friedman:
I assure you that we will appreciate at the present that it is a sacrifice to give any time to anything outside of your own business, and yet we are looking beyond today, looking to tomorrow. And as we gaze back into yesterday, realizing what Germany has gone through, we can't help but feel that it is not so much a sacrifice as it is self-defense, so that we, too, will not find ourselves tomorrow in the position that German-Jews find themselves today. And it is with this thought that I ask men to join me in this splendid work of educating Americans as to what the Jew really is and what he stands for. To tear down the libel and the lies and the falsehoods that are being broadcast about us. So that you and I may continue to live in this land of liberty, for which not only our forefathers but our children have given their life-blood that America might continue to be a land of freedom. As in the words of that immortal Lincoln, "The government of the people, by the people, for the people shall not perish from this earth."[3]

investigative reporters. In 1936 we knew that the developing American Silver Shirts, of the American Nazi Party, had a cell down here in the old Templeton Building on South Temple. What I mean by cells is a club. Roxy and I wandered into their place and listened to them. They wore swastikas and were as anti-Jewish, anti-Semitic, and pro-Aryan as Hitler. William Dudley Pelly was a nationwide organizer for this group; they were trying to mimic German nazism, and they used the Jews as their scapegoats for the economic problems that Americans were facing those days. They said unemployment was caused by the Jews who had all this money and that the Jews were in a big conspiracy to take over the world.

When you look into a little Jewish history, even Henry Ford, in the early 1920s, bought the notion that the "protocols of Zion" was some kind of world-wide Jewish conspiracy. Ford fell for it. I think the anti-defamation league of B'nai Brith put him on the right track. I remember as a young man listening to the radio or seeing a newsreel at the movies and hearing Ford's apology. Well, the Silver Shirts were little more than a fad here, but it worried us and we kept others informed of their doings.

Radio Days—In those days, it would have been difficult for me as an entering lawyer in Salt Lake since there weren't enough Jewish firms then. So after I got out of school, I went into business with two of my buddies rather than try to get into a downtown law firm. There was little business then. This was essentially an agricultural community around here with one major industry, Kennecott. And you have to remember this is 1939 and the depression was still on. But during the last year in law school, I had the opportunity to become a paid radio broadcaster for KSL radio. After that, I wasn't hurting for a living.

I was an imaginative and noisy and sometimes funny kid and I used to do imitations of great radio programs. In 1936, I was invited to do a show honoring the 25th Anniversary of the Rotary Clubs in Salt Lake City. If you are familiar with the program called "The March of Time," you'd know it was a news program that skipped around the country and brought you news of the week. We used it to depict the growth of the Salt Lake Rotary. Among the people who saluted the city were Franklin Roosevelt, Al Smith, Herbert Hoover. I got away with doing their impersonations and was offered a job by KSL's Earl J. Glade for three or four hundred dollars a month, good money in those days. I always wanted to be in business for myself and that's the way it worked out. I stayed in radio broadcasting until I married Helen Frank in 1940 and went into the Navy in early 1942. When I came back, though, I gave up broadcasting and stayed with the law.

High Holy Days—I've always been outward about my being Jewish. I've never tried to hide it or deny it. When I was in the United States Navy as an officer on an aircraft carrier, I let the skipper know I was Jewish. I conducted Friday night Sabbath services in the squadron ready room for the eight or ten Jewish kids who were on the ship; we celebrated the High Holy Days in the Pacific on an island in New Guinea. I was always happy and proud to let people know I am a Jew. Right from the beginning. In politics. My navy life. My law life. The thing that stirred me about being Jewish hasn't been the study of the Torah although I understand the notion of the law. Being Jewish to me is connected with social action. I've always been a liberal Democrat and a political activist, and I think being Jewish has directed me in that area. I see my religion as more of an opportunity to "do some good" rather than an opportunity for prayer and celebration.

Wally Sandack reporting. (Courtesy of the Sandack family)

Restoring the Faith—Franklin Delano Roosevelt was everybody's father, incredible and credible at the same time. You sat around the radio and you were broke or the banks had closed and this was a believable person who convinced us all that he knew the way out. And he did. It took a world war to end the depression. Nevertheless, he restored the faith we had all lost in America through the last days of Hoover's administration. The nearest thing that Herbert Hoover came to involving government with some of the problems was the Reconstruction Finance Corporation and that was only because a number of big businesses were in trouble and they were using it to bail them out. Nobody thought of using a reconstruction finance program for the average man on the street, until the reforms of the Roosevelt administration came along with the FHA [Federal Housing Authority] and the Homeowners Loan Corporation and the Farm Loan Administration.

The WPA Program—Roosevelt wasn't afraid to use government to solve some of the problems. It stopped the foreclosure on a lot of farmlands and homes. It closed banks and reopened them with guarantees for deposit. It provided a method by which people with few dollars could get into the home ownership field themselves. It commenced the social security program, which we've all relied on as being right for old age. It took kids from New York and elsewhere and put them into work camps and made menshen out of them. In those days the Work Progress Administration [WPA] gave writers, artists, dancers, playwrights, and poets the opportunity to be craftsmen in their fields. It made government work for the people. And the effect it had on me is that it fit in with my notion of what being Jewish meant. And that was being active in fields of social welfare and social reform. Get out in the market place and mix ideas with progress. Get moving. Get the country moving.

Utah went for Roosevelt and continued to from 1933 to 1945. The tide takes a little time to

SEN. MOSS "DISMAYED" BY RELIGIOUS ISSUE AT MEET

Sen. Frank E. Moss, D-Utah, said Sunday he was "shocked and dismayed" that the religion of the state Democratic committee chairman was brought up during the Utah Democratic convention.

Moss praised the newly elected chairman, A. Wally Sandack of Salt Lake City, as a "dynamic and respected leader" who would guide the Democratic party to victory next year.

Moss and Sandack, a member of the Jewish faith, called a Sunday morning news conference to repudiate the action of an Ogden real estate salesman, Bartley L. Lower, at the convention Saturday.

Lower, who was not a delegate to the convention, interrupted the nominations to urge the convention delegates to "recess for 20 minutes to consider that their nominee is a man who doesn't believe that Jesus is the Christ."

He was immediately hooted out of the coliseum and Sandack was elected by acclamation.

Moss told the news conference the Democratic Party "repudiates any attempt to discredit Sandack. There is no religious bigotry in the Democratic Party," Moss said, "nor, I believe, is there any religious bigotry in the state of Utah."

Sandack said he was "obviously upset" by Lower's actions, but considered it a "single, unfortunate incident."

"If it did anything," he said, "it unified the party."

Sandack was given a prolonged ovation Saturday night by the 1,200 Democrats who attended the annual Jefferson-Jackson Day dinner at the University of Utah Union.

The most vocal of the convention delegates who hooted Lower out of the coliseum Saturday was Charles Romney, a brother of Michigan's Republican governor, George Romney. Romney ran down the center aisle of the coliseum, shook his fist at Lower, and yelled, "This kind of thing doesn't belong here."[4]

get over these mountains, but it finally comes across, notwithstanding its conservatism.

Jewish Politicians—The Jewish mayor, Lou Marcus, was probably the brightest Salt Lake City mayor we ever had. He was elected in 1936. Hymie Guss was his campaign manager. Marcus was a top businessman; he operated theatres; and he gave this city a fine administration. Another notable person, this time in the 1950s, was a feisty Jewish character related to my wife's family by the name of Sol Selvin, a Russian immigrant. Lived in Tooele, Utah, became the mayor of Tooele, was elected to the Utah State House of Representatives in the 1930s, and stayed there for quite a number of years. Both in the House and the State Senate. Selvin was responsible for passing the first sales tax act in Utah. Primarily as a relief mechanism. It came in at a 2 percent sales tax with the understanding and commitment that [laughs] it would be used exclusively for State Relief, Welfare; and as soon as the economic woes were over, it would be abolished [chuckles].

A Jew, Selvin was probably the first real New Dealer that we had in the Democratic Party in this State. He fought for equal opportunities. He fought for job opportunities. He was thirty years ahead on the Civil Rights position. He was a great fighter. He reminded me a lot of Menachem Begin in his stature and in his looks, his dialect and his feistiness.

The Democratic Party and Running against J. Bracken Lee—In 1947 or 1948, I went back into my law practice and became very active in the Democratic Party. In 1952, I was elected Salt Lake County Democratic Chairman and I served a couple of terms in that spot. I remember I was part of the campaign for Earl J. Glade, who was the man who gave me a break in radio in the early days. He decided to run for governor in 1952 against J. Bracken Lee, who had been elected in 1948. Earl was a distinguished and high-class guy who knew nothing about politics and probably shouldn't have gotten into the race. He asked me to give him a few ideas, and I guess he ended up sounding more like Wally Sandack than Earl J. Glade.

J. Bracken Lee was a master politician and he got away with some things that you just couldn't believe in terms of his conservative attitude towards schools. He made a statement once if we haven't got enough money to afford the schools, let's close them up for a little while. Things like that. Earl couldn't contend with that kind of campaign. He was rather handily defeated.

Getting into Politics—During that time, I was elected the delegate of my voting district and I went to legislative meetings and to senatorial district meetings. Then I was on the County Central Committee, and from there to the Platform Committee, and Chairman of Fundraising. Gradually I got to be known as a worker in politics. I decided it was time to run for Salt Lake County Chairman and I was elected from 1952 to 1957. If you make up your mind to get into politics, there's no way you can really lose because organizational politics is hard work and most people shy away from it. A lot of work. I loved it. I worked practically every night. I had very little home life. I went out to meetings six nights a week. I was the epitome of "what makes Sammy run?" I guess I was doing it for a number of reasons. I was convinced it was necessary to make a contribution to the party. I was becoming known as a pretty fair politician. I got a few clients that way. And I proved that I was capable of being something other than a radio announcer.

And Winning—In 1956 I was elected to one of the delegate positions of the Democratic National Convention in Chicago. This Convention again chose Adlai Stevenson as Presidential Candidate and Estes Kefauver as the Vice President. It turned down the bid of that great young senator from Massachusetts, John Kennedy, who told me on the floor of that convention, "Wally, if I get the vice presidential nomination, I'll come to Salt Lake City early in the campaign and speak for you." (I wanted to raise some money at a county meeting.) He said, "If I don't get it—I'm exhausted, and I'm going to take my wife Jackie and spend about a month in Europe." Kefauver got the nomination, and Jack Kennedy took a vacation. I didn't really have much to do with him again until 1960.

Next Thing to Royalty—I ran a party campaign but the most involved I became in any individual campaign was in the 1960 Kennedy campaign where I was on the committee to elect Jack Kennedy president. He was a charmer. He was the nearest thing we had to royalty in politics in this nation. He was the guy that was coming, and I knew it, and everybody else knew it. He didn't know a lot about the problems in the Far West. He was a congressman and a senator from Massachusetts and he knew about fishermen's problems and things that were dear to commerce in that state. But he didn't know about the water problems in the West. But he was a sharp guy and he opened his mind to it and he got a pretty good amount of help on it.

Kennedy was traveling with another fine guy, Ted Sorenson, who helped him. The two of them both had bad backs. When I put them up to sleep in the old Hotel Newhouse, I came in there one morning to see how they were doing and they were both sleeping on the floor because the mattresses were too soft for them. Kennedy made several important appearances in Utah when I was County Chairman, and finally paved the way for his nomination in 1960.

Human Rights—I was a delegate to the 1960 Democratic Convention in Los Angeles. And I was a member on the National Platform Committee. The product of the Platform Committee was entitled, as I recall it, "The Rights of Man." It was a real declaration of Human Rights cast in the mold of liberal Democrats. With Kennedy's support, it just covered the A-to-Z of human rights. A lot of it was pre-done by people in Washington who saw the combination of this new declaration and the campaign of Kennedy as an opportunity to elect a president who stood on the campaign and to adopt a campaign that was advocated by the President. You know, platforms and political parties, *they say,* are things to run on and to take down after you've been elected. But this platform was a great platform and much work had been done on it in the prior months before the Platform Committee convened. But we had the duty and the ten days before the Convention to clean it up and to make the compromises that were necessary to go on. We were fortunate in having the strength in the Platform Committee to overrule the solid South and their opposition to those civil rights at the time.

 LETTER TO THE EDITOR: "CAN'T DO THAT" §

Somewhat unaware of what I was saying last Saturday, I found myself shouting at the top of my voice, "You cannot say that in a Democratic convention." I had lost my temper at the time. A speaker, I assume, proposed to nominate someone to run against Wally Sandack for State Chairman of the Democratic Party. Instead of telling the convention what his candidate could do for the party, he began by throwing mud at Sandack because of his Jewish religion.

Perhaps if I had my wits about me I would have said you cannot say that in the state of Utah. Time was in Utah when the Mormons nominated political candidates on the "People's Party" ticket; and the non-Mormons on the "Liberal Party" ticket; and much bitterness among the people resulted from political activities.

Those days, I hope, are gone forever in Utah. Many of us who are Republicans or Democrats fight each other with everything we have for a week or so before the election. But on Wednesday mornings after the political battles are over, we congratulate the winners and the losers start making plans to win the next round.

One of America's greatest and most unique contributions to political thought is the separation of the church and state. This is not toleration of another man's religious views. It is the complete freedom of conscience in religious matters. It is the right of every citizen of the United States to be a devoted member of any church he wishes and, every citizen should in no way be handicapped in his economic, social, or political activities because of the way he chooses to worship his creator. [Signed by] Charles W. Romney, 451 East 33rd South[5]

Bigotry Again—While I was in politics, I did have one event that disturbed me by reason of the fact that I was Jewish. It occurred on April 1, 1967 when I was running for the office of Chairman of the State Democratic Committee, and had no opposition. I was running with the support of all the candidates and the then-governor of Utah, Cal Rampton. I was drafted. I had been urged to take it. I didn't want it. I felt that I had served enough in organizational politics, but Governor Rampton insisted . . . and so I accepted it.

During the Convention, some character demanded the floor after I had been nominated. He was allowed the use of the floor. He walked up to the microphone in front of an audience of three to four thousand people and charged the delegates with the statement that "Sandack" should be disqualified because—and, he didn't say I was Jewish—but "Sandack does not believe that Jesus Christ was the savior." While it wasn't a very friendly experience for me to go through. But it passed. I was elected. By the way, it made the papers nationally. One of the Washington headlines read, "Utah Democrats Select Jewish Chief." I wasn't frightened [by the experience]; I felt like my head was being pushed. It felt like somebody had my head and was twisting it off of my neck.

So there you have it. I resigned the State Chairmanship in 1970. Rampton was re-elected as Governor, so I finished my responsibility. From time to time, I'm called on as an elder statesman to help raise money, figure out strategy, and help candidates win.

EIGHT

Shochets and Cattle Dealers

SCHMALTZ FOR THE HOLIDAYS

Harry J. Doctorman

Utah Native—I don't know what the "J" stands for in my name.[1] I've just had it all my life. I was born June 30, 1919 in Salt Lake City. I have two sisters, Irene Levine and Marjie Rosen. I grew up right here in 2nd West and 9th South. It was a big old six-room house. Dad got married and bought the house in 1918. He used to have a barn. He'd buy a couple of milk cows from a farmer, put an ad in the paper, and sell them off. He'd make a few dollars that way.

When I was a little kid, we'd always have two or three cows there. People would come on Sundays and buy these cows for milk. He'd sell others to the slaughterhouse for meat. I was right there. I used to go with him, help him in the barn, milk the cows. He had a little old Ford truck. He'd have some farmers slaughter the cows out in his barn, and then he'd deliver the meat to the butcher shops and charge them two dollars for slaughtering.

The Edge of Town—There were a lot of farms right close by. Sixty years ago, 21st South was at the edge of town. All vacant. Even 2900 South and Main. Even as close in to town as 13th and 17th South was all farms. All farms. A lot of people would buy a milk cow to feed their kids; they'd raise a calf or two. Then, they'd sell the calf and when the cow dried up, they'd sell the cow.

Working with Dad—I was awfully close to my dad. When I was six or seven years old, I went along with him. He always tried to teach me: this was a bull, this was a cow, and this was a young one. He'd pick me up after school in his little old Ford truck and we'd go out, get the beef, and deliver it to the butcher. I always wanted to be a meat packer. I'd tell him, "Some day, I'm going to have my own packing house." He'd say, "Oh, you're crazy." Later, we bought his business out.

Butchers Abound—Most of the butchers used to be around 1st South and West Temple. Alec Winters on 6th South and State Street was one of our best customers. He'd buy one or two beef a week. Block and Guss had a pretty good-sized slaughterhouse on North Beck Street.

There were nice old-fashioned meat markets with meat counters and little hanging scales. There were quite a lot of retail butchers in those days, I guess around fifty or sixty shops, but no chain stores, and very few stores that had groceries and meat. It used to be either a butcher shop or a grocery store. A butcher would buy a cow, or a butcher would have turkey, and geese and pork, veal and lamb. If people wanted meat, they'd go to a butcher like old man Kaplan. If they wanted groceries, they'd go somewhere else. A lot of the butchers didn't have refrigeration at that time. They used to bring in 50–100 pounds of ice and put it under the counter so they could put the meat on top of it to keep it cold. Auerbach's, on 3rd South, was a big department store. They had a big meat market down in the department store, and an elevator. They'd bring the meat down and I'd have to carry it about a block 'til we'd got to the back in the meat market. I'd take it down the elevator and [over] to the other end of the building.

The Shochet—We used to kosher slaughter for old man Kaplan, the butcher. We used to kill his cattle for him. When we got our own packinghouse, we used to kill kosher, but we had to give it up. It just took too much time [in the later years] when we had 10 or 12 butchers working for us. The *shochet* would come around for two or three hours to kill one beef and two calves and two sheep. He'd kill one and if he didn't like the lung on it, we'd have to go get another one to kill. That held up the whole crew. We were kosher for the Jewish community up 'til about 1955. It wasn't much then. Maybe two cattle a week. They'd only use the forefronts of the animal, the kosher part. They wouldn't use the hind quarters, so we'd sell the hind quarters out with the beef for *trayf.* Now, there's very few kosher slaughterers left; most of the kosher meat comes in from Denver.

Schmaltz for the Holidays—Years back, my parents always kept kosher. And for Passover, Dad would keep five or six geese in a little shed in the back of the house and feed them a lot of corn. Then, some of the Jewish ladies would come over and help my mother flick them and dress them. This was a big event. To get all the geese flicked so they'd have schmaltz for Passover. I was five or six years old at the time and the kitchen would be all full of feathers.

Losing Mother—My mother died in childbirth when I was eleven years old. It was really a shock. I was in school and they came and got me out of school. Told me my mother died. It hit my dad pretty bad. He had a hard time with us three kids. He had a hard time getting a woman to take care of us. He kept writing to my mother's sister and a year later, he went back to Poland and married Celia in 1930. She raised us.

Saturdays at Shul—When I was a kid we were always at the Shaarey Tzedek shul. It was just around the corner from us. Dad wouldn't work on Saturdays. He'd go to the shul on Saturdays and he observed all the holidays. My father was always involved in meetings, elections and politics. Nobody talked in English. It was all Yiddish and Hebrew. Temple B'nai Israel was Reform, the rabbi started in giving little English speeches and then some of the Hebrew was in English. A lot of these old-time Jews didn't like no Reform. They thought Congregation Montefiore wasn't Orthodox enough, either. Shaarey Tzedek was Orthodox.[2]

Tumult, or Kopdrayenish, at the Shul—But they were always fighting. One year, I remember they had such an argument so they went to Mr. Bernstein's house, about ten of them, for services. They wouldn't come to Shaarey Tzedek. Why, I don't know. So, they were davening right in Mr. Bernstein's living room. Right there on Edison Street. It was like this a lot, and there were a couple of cliques. Sam Hayden used to be president for about ten years, and if they didn't like what he'd done, they'd leave. I remember this. My dad would get mad for some reason or another, and we'd be back at the Bernstein house to have a minyan. Two weeks later, they'd all make up and go back together to the shul. But Shaarey Tzedek never did have anyone to teach Hebrew classes. There was no heder. And there weren't enough people to run it, so I think they closed that *shul* and everybody went back over to the Montefiore shul. My father paid his dues but he never got involved in politics again.

Traditions—I was bar mitzvahed in the Montefiore shul. I actually started going there when I was 8 or 9 years old because, I told you, we had no teacher at Shaarey Tzedek. It was a nice bar mitzvah. Rabbi Krikstein prepared a speech and I memorized it.[3] We were poor in those days. On Sunday, we had a few people over. That was around 1932, or '33, during the depth of the depression. My parents kept a kosher home until Mr. Kaplan died. I think Ben Davis took over for a year or two, but there wasn't enough business for him. So then we started *trayf.* To this day, though, we keep kosher over Rosh Hashanah, Yom Kippur, and Passover. We never eat pork, just beef, veal, and lamb.

Another Opinion—When I was about 20 years old, I went over to B'nai Israel. That was a *goyisheh shul.* That's what I thought. A lot of the men sat without yarmulkes. The service was mostly in English. I thought it was really like a Mormon church. [Laughs.]

Working through the Depression—During the depression, my father was always peddling three, four, five cattle. He did that for ten years or so. Then about 1931, he slaughtered at the Salt Lake Sausage Company on 3400 South 10th West. He used to kill maybe 10–12 cattle a week. They went into bankruptcy so he went down to the bank and bought the plant from them for $5500, with five years to pay it out, this whole meat plant. It did real well and every month, I'd go to the bank and give the vice president of Utah Savings and Trust $500. I had five years to

Young Harry Doctorman. (Courtesy of Gary Doctorman)

pay it and we paid it off in about eleven months. When I went with my last check and said I wanted the deed and the property, Mr. Nicholson, the vice president, sent a messenger over to the Continental Bank, across the street, to see if that check was good for $500. The messenger came back with the cashier check and they gave us the deed to the place. We had about ten years of building up a little business. We just killed cattle, some sheep and goats.

Extra Credit—Between '33 and '47, we were able to put aside a little money. At first, it was real hard to buy cattle. You know, we had to buy them for cash, and we didn't usually have any cash, and during the depression days, you couldn't borrow no money. So we floated our checks, never let a check go bad, and never had a check bounce. We worked like heck to get the money into the bank before the checks came in. It was hard work. We started at 10–12 a week, then right to the war, we were killing thirty cattle a day.

Licensing—We bought another plant and, during the war, we sold a lot of meat, 80 percent of our stock to the government. Before, we only had a Salt Lake inspected meat [license]. They came to us and said, "We'll give you a temporary federal inspection [license] if you give us 80 percent of the quota you're killing." So we did. With a federal inspection, we could sell all over the world. There's thousands of specifications for a federal inspection that you have to have, but we did it and soon bought the Jensen plant, in 1948, had some architects come in, tear down the killing floor, the offices, and some of the coolers, and rebuild it to USDA Inspection. We had enough money saved up to pay cash for that plant and 34 acres of land. We paid around $60,000. Then we started getting bigger, and we shipped all over. Before long, we were selling meat to New York and meat to San Francisco.

A Full Day's Work—Originally, my dad only had one butcher and one driver. When I got out of high school, I pretty well took over all the selling and we hired some more help. I had about 200 little stores around Salt Lake City, on the westside and on the eastside. Right after the war, from 1945 through 1946, I'd start my calls from 7:00 o'clock to 10:00. Then I'd pick out the beef I sold; the drivers would load the trucks up and deliver it. Then I'd get in the car and start selling for the next day. About 4:30 in the afternoon, I'd come back to the plant and call those I didn't call on that day. I had a morning list and a night list. I used to have two phones on my desk and every time I picked up one phone, the other would be there waiting. During those days, we didn't hire no managers, no supervisors, or salesmen. I did all the selling. When I first started selling meat, I bought me a new, really bright, yellow Studebaker, and it had "Doctorman and Son" written on it. Everybody in town seen that car; they knew us.

Me and My Dad—Later on, I took over the buying. I loved buying. I know cattle. I was brought up in the cattle business as a little kid. I'd seen thousands of cows and I know what's a good cow and what's a bad cow; I know which is a choice steer. You'd see if they were nice and plump and round with a nice layer of fat or you get an old, bony cow, a rack of bones. They're not very good but you can use them for different purposes. I'd get to go to some of the auctions. I'd go to Idaho quite a bit. Tuesday was Ogden. I'd go down to Delta. Thursday was Spanish Fork; Friday was Salina. Saturday, back to Spanish Fork. We needed a lot of cattle, two or three hundred cattle a day, and so we had buyers in Idaho, Montana, and Colorado. In the local auctions around here, me and my Dad: he'd take care of one and I'd take care of the other. As he got older, I'd go farther and he'd stay closer to home. It was easier than selling, believe me. And I loved it.

Sending Meat to the Coast—After we got into the bigger plant at Jensen's, I got some good out of town customers and instead of selling a guy one beef or a half a beef, I started selling them by the carload. We got into sausage factories, in some of the boning factories, and in some of the chain shores in California. Gradually, during the next twenty years, we worked up and started buying more trucks and hauling our own dressed meat to the Coast.

Journeymen—I never killed a cow. You couldn't get a young kid to go out and work on the killing floor. Never did have any other Jewish people working for us. We had a little apprentice program where the union would start them out as apprentices and then every three months, they'd raise them so that at the end of three years, you'd have to pay them journeyman wages. Most of the guys knew each other and took care of their own. Brothers-in-law, brothers, and sons worked under the same roof. And the relatives really brought them up so they became journeymen within three or six months' time. A good butcher was a guy who knew how to skin and saw and how to drop the guts out of the cattle without cutting them, and knew how to hang them up and shoot them, and cut off their legs and heads.

Between Telephone Calls—I used to be a champion veal skinner. I could skin a veal in seven minutes. In between telephone calls, I'd be skinning veal. I could cut meats very well, too. Break up the meat into pieces. But I never killed cattle. I never worked on beef or on the killing floor.

New Business from Old—We got into hides and shipped our own hides out of Utah. At first, we sold them to a hide dealer who would salt them and cure them and ship them off to the coast. Then I started thinking, I've got plenty of trucks and a beautiful high basement. We started salting and curing our hides. Then we got trucks and had a crew come in and roll them and tie them and stack them and ship them to San Francisco. Then I started selling direct to Japan. We got a reputation in Japan for having the best hides. Doctorman's Hides. Before I knew it, tanners from Japan were coming out here and calling on me.

Changing Times—Everything was working good, but then it changed. The unions came in 1936. At first they just organized one or two of the plants. Then they started with the butchers, and every year it got a little worse and a little worse. It got so unless we belonged to the union, the Meat Cutters Union, butchers couldn't buy beef off of us. It was all right until we couldn't produce enough and the cost of production per animal got up too high and big companies in the East put up automated killing floors and got twice the production for the same money. They started squeezing us down so we couldn't compete.

Labor Strikes—We had two strikes. One in 1967 and the other in 1973. One lasted 60 days. We had a lot of guys working for us at the time who went on strike and we had 800 head of cattle in the coolers and no hope. They thought they had us, but they didn't. We got our friends and relatives and our trucks—our truck drivers weren't on strike—and we loaded the trucks, worked like dogs, and got all the meat delivered. The strike was settled. The second strike, that time, we didn't want to fight. So we just quit.

We Did Okay—It's all right. We did all right. We made some real good real estate around the plant and started building some commercial buildings. We did all right and no aggravation.

Evelyn Doctorman on her honeymoon. (Courtesy of Gary Doctorman)

I used to go out with Gentile girls. Nice Gentile girls. But I didn't want to marry a Gentile. And pretty near all the boys of my age went out of town to find somebody and to get married. I met my wife at Manny Pepper's wedding in San Francisco. I tried to be nice to her but she kept running away from me. She was going to night school and wouldn't go out with me. So, it was near Yom Kippur, and I was in a flower shop and just for the heck of it, I said, I'm going to send that Eleanor Stein an orchid. I told her. She said, "Don't send me an orchid. I don't want an orchid from anyone but the man I'm going to marry." Just for spite, I sent her an orchid. She didn't know where I lived, and I was back in Salt Lake City, so she wrote me back a thank you note, and on the envelope, put, "To thank Harry Doctorman in Salt Lake City. Postmaster, please find." We were well known in the post office.

I was always brought up Jewish. And that's important. I am really a devoted Jewish person in my own way because certain things mean a lot to me in the Jewish religion. I don't know how to explain it. I kiss the mezuzah and I always put a tallis on when I go to shul. When I was young, right after my bar mitzvah, I used to put tefillin on every morning and daven. I had to give up a little bit over time. I pray at home. Before I go to bed, I usually give a little thanks. I've done this since before I was married and still continue. I feel if I don't say my prayers every night, my own way, then something's not right. So I do it every night before I go to bed and sometimes in the afternoon.

MY MOTHER-IN-LAW'S RECIPE FOR *Mondelbrodt*

Given by Karen Fjeldsted

This is what Eleanor Doctorman typed for me when I was a young bride, so I could make my husband, her son Gary, his favorite cookie for the holidays. Note how the spelling changed from *mandelbrot* to *mondelbrodt* over time.

3 cups flour
3 tsp. baking powder
1/2 tsp. salt
1/2 cup shortening
1 cup sugar
3 eggs
1 tsp. lemon juice
chopped almonds

Mix dry ingredients. Cream shortening and sugar. Add eggs, one at a time. Add flour mixture, chopped almonds, and lemon juice. Shape dough into four loaves and place on greased baking sheet. Bake at 350 degrees, 30 to 35 minutes. Cut into 3/4-inch thick slices. Turn them over to their cut side and brown in the oven. Sprinkle with cinnamon and sugar on top.

"THE BUMPER"

PAULA BLOCK DRAPER

Paul Weinstein Block

An Orphan in Military School—My father's younger years were like that of an orphan.[1] Paul Weinstein Block was born July 29, 1920, in Pennsylvania. His mother, Pearl, died in childbirth. Having been left with two other sons, his father was in no position to take care of an infant, and sent the child to his relatives. When my father was five or six years old, his father entered him at Greenbriar Military Academy in West Virginia. He stayed night and day, right through all the holidays and throughout the summers from the time he arrived until the day he left for Utah. I think he was around eleven years old. When the family was still intact, his father had been a salesman for Pendleton Mills out in the garment district of New York. When the depression hit hard, I think his dad could no longer afford to keep his son in military school. Heading west to try to make a living in California, I believe my grandfather sent my dad to Utah. Here he would stay with his mother's half sister and her husband, Gertrude and Louis Block, in Salt Lake City.

The Block Family—Gertrude and Pearl were born into the Guss family. I believe my great-grandfather, Isaac Guss, had eight living children from each of the two marriages. Gertrude and her husband, Louis, had no children so they took my father in. Dad's last name is Weinstein, actually. He took the name of Block much later out of respect for his aunt and uncle.

No English Spoken Here—When my dad met the Blocks, the childless couple spoke only Yiddish and he thought he had been dropped into a foreign country. They put him in the basement of their bungalow house on 320 East and Ninth South. You know how they have those rock-wall shelf basements that are not all dug out? Well, it was just two rooms like that. Mr. Block had been brewing beer in one of the rooms, storing it while it fermented. In the other, they put up a bed for my dad. So here he is a young boy from a military academy unable to speak Yiddish and here are the Blocks barely able to speak English. On that lonely night, his first night in Utah, the beer bottles exploded! My father thought it was the end of the world.

Almost an orphan: Paul Weinstein Block. (Courtesy of Paula Block Draper)

Gertrude Guss Block and her husband, Louis Block. (Courtesy of Paula Block Draper)

Afternoon Soup—But the Blocks were good to him and Dad said he was always wild for Gertrude. She was nice, she gave him a nickel every day he went to school, and made him soup every afternoon for lunch. Mr. Block was very much an Orthodox Jew of the old school. He was a small, dapper man, and very driven. Never having had any children of his own, I think he might have been a little distant. But he was trying to be a good person and take this child in and that's what he did. They did not adopt him. Louis Block would not adopt him, but my father honored him enough to take his name. He went into the military as Paul Weinstein and he came out as Paul Weinstein Block.

Fleeing Pogroms—I believe Louis Block came here in the early 1900s, probably before the Russian Revolution in 1917. The story is that he and his wife had a good business in Poland at a time when Jews were not allowed to own businesses. The ownership was in the name of an associate who wasn't Jewish, but that didn't protect them from risks. During a pogrom, the czar's solders came and raided the business. They raided their home. They could have killed them, too, had they not been able to escape. With the help of some non-Jewish friends, Gertrude and Louis went out the back window and were hidden under a manure wagon, right under the manure, and taken out through the gates of the city. The two of them made their way to America. I don't

The Guss children with grandparents in the Old Country, Russia. Sarah Guss is seated on right. (Courtesy of Paula Block Draper)

know how they did that but they were survivors, and in New York Louis became a junk dealer trading in bottles.

Setting Up Business—Louis's true "deal" was managing a slaughterhouse. That was his business in Poland and he knew what to do. Little by little, he made his way to Utah on the train and worked by selling hides. He did whatever he could to earn enough money and set up his own business. When he brought his wife's brother Sam Guss over from Russia, the two of them established the Block and Guss Meat Packing business.

Sam was Sarah Guss's father. Sarah's mother also died at childbirth, and when Sam decided to go to America, he left his children, including Sarah, in the care of his parents. When the revolution broke out, the grandparents worried about the fate of the children and put them on a boat to New York. They traveled alone. Sam's sister's husband, Rabbi Baskin, met them at the pier and sent them on to Salt Lake. By this time, Sam had remarried.

Jewish Rancher—Sarah eventually married Max Cowan who came out of Denver and had feedlots throughout the Intermountain West. Anybody who had herds to hold and feed would contact Max because he had feedlots up and down the railroad line. Mr. Cowan worked with Block and Guss since they could bring the cattle to the slaughterhouse only after they weighed a certain amount and were ready for slaughter. So they would fatten up at Max Cowan's feedlots.

Sarah Guss Cowan on her wedding day. (Courtesy of Paula Block Draper)

Getting Others Out of Russia—There were a number of Guss family members who came to Utah. People like Irvin Guss, old Abe Guss, and Esther Guss Shapiro. It was a big family, two marriages, a lot of children; and for some reason, Louis Block's goal was to get all of his wife's brothers and sisters out of Russia. I believe he did this because he was a moralist, and he knew what life was like for the Jew in Russia. Other Jewish gentlemen were trying to get family members out of Russia as well. Because of this desire, they established what was called the Hand-in-Hand Society. That meant, once the emigrants were established in Utah, the only requirement asked of them was to help bring other family members over, who in turn would bring others. Louis Block helped fulfill his mission up until after World War II when they found one relative left: a physician who had been in a concentration camp in Poland. Fortunately, he survived the Holocaust and they managed to get him out to Palestine. My father told me that in trying to help, Louis Block also sent medical supplies to Israel.

Kosher in a Slaughterhouse—My father worked at his uncle's slaughterhouse most of his life. Of course, the Block family was strictly kosher. My father had a joke at the meat-packing business. He used to say he never tasted steak until he was in the army. That's probably not true because one day a week, a *shochet* came to slaughter animals for sale to Jews. Maybe he meant he never had a *trayf* steak; that would be more like it.

Gathering the Herds—In the spring, Block and Guss made deals with surrounding ranchers in places like Heber and Park City to buy their herd in the fall. So many head of cattle would come in from one direction, so many head coming in from another, all of them had to be gathered and corralled until they could be pulled together and brought down as a herd into one of Max Cowan's feedlots.

"The Bumper"—Louis Block's expertise was what he called "the bumper." This means he could go to a cow, bump it with his knee, and see if the cow was with calf. He could tell just by bumping it. And that's the ones they wanted because they'd get two for the price of one.

"Pishing Out a Nickel"—In the old days, they marched cattle down the canyon, then they trucked them in, and where there happened to be a railhead, why, they could bring them in by train. They'd be weighed at the feedlot. My father would tell the story that he was riding with Sam Guss one time and he said, "Uncle, can't we hurry up a little bit?" Sam said, in Yiddish—and I imagine my father understood it by then—"There's no hurry. Don't you understand, that one is *pishing* out a nickel?" Because they're getting thinner as they come in, see? And you pay by the weight. When they're in the feedlot, that's when you try to fatten them up. "We don't want to hurry," he'd say, before pointing at the herd. "There's another one *pishing* out a nickel."

A Mensh—My dad always worked hard. I believe the adversity in his life made him feel tremendous empathy for the human condition. In his own way, he was a civil rights activist who understood the needs and wants of ethnic communities. In World War II, when he was a sergeant working with a black unit for the Army Air Force, the experience made his ties very close to the problems that they suffered. Years later, when he died, a friend of my dad, a black man, came to my house, specifically to tell me a story about my father when the two of them were young men working at the slaughterhouse.

"Your father said to me, 'Let's go to lunch,' one day. I said, 'There's no place around here that I could go to lunch with you.' He said, 'I'll take you to the restaurant down the street, where we all go.' I said, 'That's fine for you, but they're not going to let me in.' Well, your father disagreed. He said, 'They'll let you in if you're with me!' Your father was a good guy, but I figured he had to find out for himself how black people are often treated. So I agreed to go with him and we walked over to that place for lunch. They wanted to throw us out. Your father told the man that if he didn't let me have lunch there with him and the other men, he would see that the place was closed down. He probably thought that would have done it, taking a stand for me. But that didn't change the man's mind. He said no, and we left. We didn't have lunch that day and your father was true to his word. He never went back. Neither did any of the other men. And that place went out of business. That was the first time I knew I had power as a person."

The Meat Business—In one way or another, it seems like the Gusses were always involved in the meat business. Maybe it had to do with what they did in the Old Country; I don't know. But by the time my dad married my mother, Block and Guss Meats had become Jordan Meat Company, which is part of the Guss family business, owned by Irvin Guss's dad, and run by Irvin's daughter Nadine Guss and her husband, Clayton Johnson. Abe Guss, who had polio as a child, ran his father's company, Granite Meat, all his life. Although my dad never went far from his former trade, he eventually did leave meat marketing and opened up grocery stores. His store, Bargain Basket, was on Sixth West and North Temple; one Half Price store was on First South and Seventh East in Salt Lake City; and he had another store in Layton. He understood these businesses. He sold quantity goods of dented cans and boxes. Large quantities. I think he was one of the forerunners for the warehouse store concept that has taken over the country.

Blind Dates and Differences—My parents met on a blind date. Now, when my father married my mother, who was from a Mormon family, she visited Mr. Block. She explained that although she was never a practicing Mormon, she couldn't convert to Judaism while her parents were still alive. She did promise to raise the children in a Jewish home. And we were raised in a Jewish home. I don't know the reasons behind it, but Mr. Block disinherited my father. My father never talked about why, never said a word against him, and none of us seemed to be ever really affected by it. So I don't know what happened. I do remember as a kid when Mr. Block's nephew Norman Nathan and his wife moved into the Blocks' house. Why, we used to sit together on the porch to watch the Days of '47 Parade pass by. I think a lot of our friends used to come by to watch the parade, we had such a good view of the celebrations. There never seemed to be any problem.

True to Her Word—That we were raised in a Jewish home credits my mother's character. She grew up around Bear Lake, and was rodeo queen of the state of Utah during Governor Blood's administration. Her father was a cattle rancher outside of Lake Town. They ran the ranch in the spring, summer, and fall. In the winter, they'd come down to Salt Lake City where they had a home and grocery store on 131 J Street. My mother's mother was a well-educated woman. She was a teacher. Her father was a good man looking that his daughter be cared for. My father was embraced with open arms. It was a good marriage. If there were ever a conflict or question about religion, my mother would quote the Ten Commandments. That was her answer. There was never anything about organized religion that came into it. She would just sit us down and find the answer in the Ten Commandments. She had a good amount of common sense.

A Loving Father—The moon rose and set on my father's children. He was loving, warm and openhanded in every way. Maybe because of his early solitary years at military school. Maybe because he wanted something that for years he never had. It was the way he was and I could count on him, just like his friends could count on him.

A Visit—I don't remember Louis Block. My mother tells a story about him. I was just a baby and my mother and I were at home. Mother said she looked up suddenly and standing in the dining room, without a knock on a door, was Louis Block. She said, "He had just come in. Was just there. Unannounced. I asked him if he'd like to sit down, and he said, 'No.' He had just come to see the child. Whereupon he took a long look at you, Paula, and then turned around and walked out without a word." That was it. My father never speculated on it.

NINE

Knishes and Kashrut

DEVOTION TO TRADITION

Ed Eisen

Utah-Denver Connections—I was born November 11, 1916, in Denver, Colorado.[1] My parents immigrated from Russia and Poland to Colorado in 1911 or 1912, and then came to Utah when I was three months old. My mother's sister lived in Salt Lake and all my family was born here: Max, Joe and Freda.

In Europe, my father and mother both lived lives of comparative poverty. They were subject to the persecution prevalent at the time of the Jewish people under the czarist regime and in Poland under the various anti-Semitic groups. My father came here at a very young age as an orphan boy, and later was financially responsible for bringing most of the members of his family to this country.

A Peddler—Dad went to Denver because he had family and friends there. Denver, at that time, was one of the attraction cities in the United States for Jewish people mostly because of health reasons. It had high altitudes and people with asthma and things of that nature felt it was the ideal place to live. When my dad first got there, he was a baker. In Salt Lake, he became sort of a junk peddler. Many immigrants became junk peddlers because they were cast into that type of occupation nobody else wanted.

You can see by his status as a junk peddler, he wasn't accepted into society because that was about the most demeaning occupation you could have. But it was a way of making a living, and my father was a supporter of his family. He wanted to see to it that his family had bread on the table, so he was a hard worker. He worked day and night, I recall. My father was the type of peddler who knocked on doors and asked for junk. He would get a wagon full of junk, take it to a junkyard, and get paid for it. He used to rent a horse and wagon, but later graduated to a truck. Then he became ill with bad eyesight, so he had to have a man drive the truck. Later he went into the steel and wooden barrel business, which is where I am now. I inherited his business.

Salt Lake's Jewish Community—There were many Jews here before my family arrived in Salt Lake; however, I grew up among most of the Jewish people in the city and the city was so small, you pretty much knew every other Jewish person. My father was not a leader of the synagogue so much as he was an attendee. A traditional Jew, and by that I mean he was an observant Jew. He knew when the various holidays came, took time off to observe them, and educated his family in the same tradition. He was a member of the Orthodox synagogue; and we were reared in that environment. Of course, Orthodoxy has such stringent regulations in Judaism, I doubt if anybody could live up to the fullest extent in Salt Lake.

Kashrut—I might mention that one of the most important facets of Orthodox Judaism is a matter known as kashrut, which is eating foods that follow the Jewish dietary laws. Now, today that has practically disappeared from the entire Jewish community here in the city. But in those days, we had a kosher butcher shop, two of them in fact. One of them was the well-educated man Mr. Kaplan. He was also our *shochet* and my mother would send me by foot to his shop with a live chicken under my arm to prepare for the ritual slaughter. I think he also served as the synagogue's mohel. Trained in the field of ritual slaughter, this man knew how to kill an animal in a more humane way. We had a Jewish baker. Mr. Sussman baked only the breads and various other baked goods that were usually eaten by Jews. Every Sunday, he would make bagels in limited supply.

Distracting Women—In 1918, in addition to the two existing synagogues in Salt Lake, there was another one named Shaarey Tzedek. It was located on 2nd East between 8th and 9th South, and it was created—as are most synagogues—as a result of arguments between groups of congregants which cannot be resolved. The answer, form their own synagogue. The argument in question was the Orthodoxy of Congregation Montefiore. This new shul—it was always considered the new shul—separated the men from the women in a division known as the *mechitzah,* and, as I recall, the women sat in the balcony. The reason for this is many-fold. I'd say one of the most practical is the fact that women distract men from prayer. Therefore, they cannot pray with a full heart. So they put them where they can talk among their own and let the men do the praying.

Leaders—I believe Mr. Kaplan, a well-educated man, was the new shul's religious leader. He maintained the kosher butcher market and performed as the cantor during the High Holy

Ed Eisen with his new Wheelabrator. (Courtesy of Jean Eisen)

Days. Another strong leader who was at the dedication and at the laying of the cornerstone was Ben Garelick. They regarded themselves as strictly Orthodox Jews.

A Matter of Opinions—Now the old time Jewish synagogue attendee, congregant, or whatever name you want to tack onto him, was emotionally very active. They were dedicated to their religious endeavors. And as in this case, everyone had an opinion of his own. I recall certain people, like Mr. Sussman, who was the proprietor of our Jewish bakery, and Mr. Hayden, used to be the ring leaders of this little synagogue. We heard stories about them fighting among themselves and, in fact, the term "the Bolsheviks" was used by many. Why Bolsheviks? Because they were always engaged in some sort of an argument. The rumor going around the Jewish community was that rather than have real law-abiding meetings where the majority ruled, they even threw chairs at one another. The truth is, no such thing ever happened. Yes, there were outbursts of emotion and discussions were lively but there were no fist fights.

More Opinions—The same unbridled enthusiasm for debate existed at Montefiore, as well. Growing up, I do remember one religious leader, Mr. Harry Guss, standing up during services and yelling because he disagreed with something. And then my Uncle Motel Pepper, whose enthusiasm together with a Mr. Weber, created enough excitement in synagogue to warrant going to services just for the comedy. Once, when the new rabbi at Congregation Montefiore was chastising parents for not taking their children out of public school during religious holidays, he told them they would go to hell. Mr. Weber jumped up and shouted, "You can go to hell! I'm not going to go!"

Jewish Neighborhoods—We lived on the westside of the city. The area around 9th South, Main Street, State, and West Temple used to be the areas where many Jewish families lived because of its proximity to the synagogues. Many observant Jews walked to shul. The Weiss family, the Doctormans, the Spitzers, and Cohens, the Gusses, Friedmans and Garelicks all lived there in the early days.

Synagogues and Temples—Some Jews belonged to Shaarey Tzedek. My family belonged to Congregation Montefiore. And in my growing up years, I recall an unquestionable cleavage between the Jews of Congregation Montefiore and B'nai Israel. Why, I cannot say. Perhaps, and this is only my thinking, most of the people with any sort of wealth became members of the Reformed temples, such as B'nai Israel, whereas Congregation Montefiore had people from all ranks in life from the peddler to the shopkeeper. This is what I believe, while certainly there was a distinction. It is quite possible that the parents of either synagogue would not like a person from one synagogue marrying a person from the other synagogue. Of course, this happened and the parents accepted it because both people were Jewish, even though they didn't belong to the same synagogue.

No Crossing the Line—As a youngster growing up, we all associated with each other, going from one synagogue to the other to meet friends and socialize. But as children, we would never give a second thought to dating a non-Jewish person from the standpoint that we had obligations to our own faith. I cannot remember the prevalence of intermarriage as it exists today. But I think rebellion against organized religion is universal among every religious faith today. In my mind it is that way.

Jewish Life—The synagogue was central to our social activities. There was no little league baseball, no football, soccer, or skiing for us. I received a more thorough Jewish education than the average youngster because, from the time I was five years old until I was about fifteen, my parents made me go to religious school after my day at public school. My father provided transportation from school to synagogue and we spent two hours there every night except Friday. On Friday nights, we went to services; again on Saturday mornings; and then I went to Sunday school.

Mentoring—At my bar mitzvah age, I was taken under the wing of Mr. Louis Block, who insisted upon my attending morning religious services and made me subject to all of the religious obligations extended upon adults. From his teachings, I learned how to conduct services and be a Torah reader. Mr. Block was one of the synagogue's *machers.* Always excitable and sometimes irreconcilable to the problems of our congregation, he was a mentor and developed in me a strong love for traditional Judaism.

Reading by Rote—During my entire childhood, this religious schedule existed on an Orthodox basis. The teachers were not what you might call demagogues arousing an interest in studying. They were the types that taught you by the rote method. "Repeat this. Repeat this. Repeat this." It was a foreign language, Hebrew, that we were studying. Difficult to learn. They didn't explain the meaning of the words to us, as they do today, they wanted us to memorize the passages. As long as you learned how to speak Hebrew, in order to pray, you were satisfying the requirements. Today, we have teachers who are qualified to teach you the rudiments of the language just as you would in learning Latin, French or English. Back then, it was a bore; and if you didn't do it right, you received a smack from the teacher. Of course, you were afraid to tell your parents that the teacher used physical force because parents used physical force on you too. So that's how we learned in those days. The Reform Jews, on the other hand, while they had Sunday school, they had no such daily Hebrew School in Salt Lake City, and their use of Hebrew was limited.

Synagogue Support—Like with all religious organizations, donations and dues are crucial to their health. There are a lot of stories that are almost worth putting into a novel with regard to what some of the people did to pay their dues in those early days. Herman Finkelstein, a sprightly gentleman of ninety-five-plus years, was the secretary of Congregation Montefiore for years. He told me about one man who came in and plunked down five hundred dollars in gold bullion from a mine in Magna. He did this just so he could buy his own bench in the synagogue, so only he could sit there every time he came.

And Stories—Mr. Finkelstein also told a story about himself going to a dance, a ball to raise money for the synagogue. He found he was the only man there among twelve women. So, what could he do? He danced with all of them. At our home with us for High Holy Day dinner, Judge Herbert Schiller mentioned that Mrs. Rosenblatt, of blessed memory, who was the mother of the prominent Rosenblatt family here, ran a boarding house in the early years. You could see his eyes sparkle as though he was right in the boarding house. Mr. Bloom from Brigham City is another interesting man with a story that might not be told. He is more than one hundred years old, but so hard of hearing, you probably couldn't get through to him in order to hear his story. But this same man is so active and alert, even at a hundred and one years old, he would still get up, get dressed and go to the stock market every day. An extremely wealthy man, he was one of the early settlers here.[2]

Circuit Rabbis—Getting rabbis to come to these "hinterlands" is another story. Whether it was Montefiore or B'nai Israel, rabbis would come and go throughout the years. Some of their departures had to do with finances (in the 1890s, both synagogues had little money to keep up with the building maintenance, let alone pay a rabbi, a cantor, or a Hebrew teacher). Some of it had to do with personalities. Some of it had to do with our location and what it had to offer. You know, a rabbi is a paid professional. Trained graduates from theological seminaries and ordained, they seek out pulpits by determining what the closest areas of culture are, whether there are day schools similar to Jewish parochial schools to which their children can attend. They want facilities for kashrut, and a synagogue that's within walking distance. Riding to synagogue on the Sabbath or High Holy Days is regarded by observant Jews as a flagrant violation, tantamount to creating "energy" at a time one is commanded not to work. For one reason or another, many of our rabbis did not stay long. We had one rabbi stay with us for about thirteen years. Rabbi Cardon. He was a very fine gentleman.

A Gathering Place—The Jewish Community Center at 411 East So[uth] Temple was the saving factor for the Jews of the community for many, many years. As I look back on it in my mind's eye, it has a great deal of nostalgia for me because I attended many events there. It was a regular community center with some Jewish or traditional, not religious, content. We had at the time a strong AZA organization for boys, B'nai B'rith for girls, senior organizations, women's organizations. We had dramatic activities, plays, shows. During the war, the USO found that building a haven for hundreds of thousands of servicemen. We had a cross-section of American Jewry in the war. So, we offered religious services for those who sought religion, social services for those who sought friendship, and various other affairs to make the boys feel at home away from the army base. Orthodox and lonely, many of them were taken in the homes of the community. We also had several marriages take place among servicemen and local girls. My sister Freda married one of those boys, Dr. Victor Kassel who came from New York and was at the Salt Lake Air Base. They settled here.

Support for Israel—Our Jewish community, to my knowledge, has been pro-Zionist always. There has never been an objection to the establishment of the state of Israel. In fact, they were all behind the movement, and gave not only of their time but also their money to see to it that the State of Israel became a reality.

A Home for Holocaust Survivors—After World War II, there were also movements in this community to resettle a lot of refugees who had been in concentration camps or were displaced persons. In fact, some of the most successful people in our community today were formerly refugees. Names like Eric Tollich, Lou Dornbush, Gene Hertz, Mr. Helwing, and Isaac Rose come to mind. We also had several people who fought in World War II; and two that were killed in the line of duty: Sherman Pomarance and Harold Glasen.

Selling the Wonders of Utah—We have a very homogeneous community here. It's not often you can have any secrets among the Jewish community here. If a bit of news starts up here, it gets downtown in about half an hour. Over the past forty years, the years that I can remember, we have had very little increase in the Jewish population in our city. What increases we had were offset by attrition on the other side, death, and people moving away. We've always been approximately a 500-family community here in Salt Lake City. Lately, with the influx of scientists and academic people to the university in the fields of medicine and other professional fields, a lot of Jewish educators have arrived on the scene. How they identify themselves with the Jewish community remains to be seen. I've maintained over and over again that we need immigration. The only way you're going to get immigration is by offering people some type of reward at the end of the rainbow. And there is an achievement. Come to Utah and you can become a farmer, a scientist, a doctor. But all this is dependent on the existing Utah Jews and what we can offer others. This is a wonderful country. Now, we need to tell others.

The Blending of a Community—Recently the two congregations have merged into one, Congregation Kol Ami. I remember years earlier being party to a plan to do the same thing that was accomplished, but we always met with some type of a rebuff in connection with giving up one particular activity in favor of another. In other words, certain people from both synagogues could not let loose of customs, not so much tradition, but the customs they had been used to for years and years. I, too, have my own personal qualms about certain things that I have had to give up in favor of this merger. Yet, we have a new young rabbi in the community who seems to be able to impart this new type of religious meaningfulness to both the old and the young. And there is some hope that as a result of this, the consolidation will be successful. It has only been a year since the merger, and I am going to see if it works.

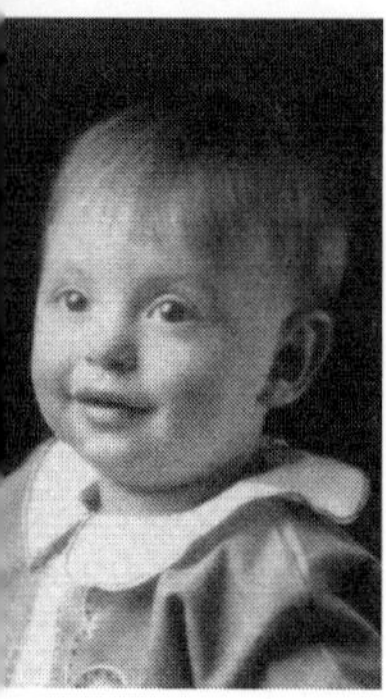

Cheverta Kaddisha, AN HONOR

Sade Tannenbaum

The Golden Medina—I was born in Poland and came to New York when I was five years old.[1] We came for the mere fact that this was the Golden Country, they called it the Golden Medina. Everybody was rich in America. Originally, my Dad went to New York first, then he came home, went to England, returned to Poland, and then back to New York where we joined him.

He sent for us, because at that time, you could be sent for. I remember, though, when we were leaving Europe, there was a little, well, we were smuggled across. I couldn't understand why it wasn't my father but a different man who carried my mother and another man who carried me across this water bridge, until we were taken across to the other side. Then we got on the boat and came to New York. I think this was in 1903. We came from Warsaw.

The Sea Voyage—I remember the trip. We went by steerage, because we were on the upper deck there and we had quite a rough time. I remember vividly coming to Ellis Island, and that they [the guards] pulled every one of us by the hair, and I had long hair, and showered us. Scared us half to death. And vaccinated us. And then we got off in New York, and lived in what they considered a tenement house. It wasn't bad. We had everything we needed. Dad had an apartment furnished when we got there.

Picking Up English—After a short time, we moved to St. Louis. They were demanding tailors. I even remember the man who sent for my father. Mr. Gilbert. Evidently they had some connection. We had to stay with another family because housing was impossible. The woman took me to the grocery store and said, "I'm buying a cake." That was the first word that I learned. Then of course we went to school and I gradually picked up English.

Learning New Meanings—We had landsmen in Kansas City, and so that's how we moved there to stay for many, many years. There were only two or three Jewish families that we knew. When I went to public school, I had quite a distance to go and there was a little boy who used to come out and call me, "*sheeny.*" That used to irritate me very much. Naturally, anyone would be sensitive to such remarks. I don't know how my mother got ahold of this, but she said, "You know, *sheeny* means smart." So I told the little boy, and from then on, I wasn't called *sheeny* anymore. Actually, Kansas City was, and I think still is, a very Catholic town and the Catholics and Jews get along pretty good. There was no proselytizing like there is here with the Mormons. So we lived there. I went to school and helped my Dad in business. I've actually been working since I was in the seventh grade. A tailor, my father made new clothes. He made the men's suits and then on the side, he would make ladies' clothes. He had a shop of his own for awhile. Then, when he got older, he worked for one of the big concerns until he retired. We lived in the back of the store. I can tell you we weren't rich, we struggled, but it was a good happy life. I graduated public school and went to high school. I went in the front door and came out the back and had to go to work. So that was my education. We stayed there until my father contracted asthma. The doctors suggested my father move from Kansas City to Denver for his asthma, and we stayed there until I was married.

Denver Shuls—We didn't live in West Colfax. We lived closer to town, on 26th Street, where there were many Jewish families. But I would visit West Colfax. It was really a Jewish community with many shuls. We always said, whoever got mad used to build their own shul. Most of the people were strictly Orthodox. We didn't know of Reform then. I think the Reform was more uptown. There's no hardship keeping kosher, keeping separate dishes and towels, observing the Sabbath, and all the Jewish holidays. But gradually, as you get older, things change; people move away.

We didn't have a Hebrew School at our synagogue on 24th and Curtis, so a *melamed* came to the house and taught the boys, just the boys. They didn't think—the girls, we were nothing. At the time, at synagogue, we sat upstairs, separated from the men.

A Need to Take Over—My father was the sick one for years; and it was my mother who died in August 1922 at forty-two years of age. I must have been around eighteen years old. It was very sad. It was the first death in the family and it was very hard on me. You know, the real Orthodox say, don't mourn, and when I got my black dress, my father thought it was terrible. So I had to get a black apron and I kept that for nine months. I had quit my job working part time at Western Union, when my mother was sick, towards the end. She was bedfast for almost a year, and I had never cooked, only cleaned. So I'd have to ask her how to do this and how to do that. We were strictly kosher then. We didn't have the convenience that you do today where you can buy kosher chickens. Of course, we had kosher butchers in Denver. I had it koshered. I had to cut up the chicken. And, fish, I had to get live fish. I'll never forget the first time my Dad helped. We'd take the hammer and hit the fish on the head, and the more we hit it, the more it jumped. I didn't know how to do it right. We had no canned foods. Everything had to be fresh, and made from scratch.

We had a coal stove and a gas stove. No washing machines, just a stationary tub and a wash board, and the laundry hung outside. We had a few throw rugs on the floor, but every week, we got down on our hands and knees and scrubbed the wooden floors with soap and water, and the stairs. It was hard work.

A Bride—After my mother died, I kept house for my father and two brothers. For three years. I went to work at the *Denver Post* on Saturdays, in advertising, which helped me a lot. It was very interesting work. I met my husband and became a bride in 1924. He came from the same town in Europe that I did. He lived in Salt Lake City. I was a friend of his sister. When his wife died, his sister said something about that and it just turned out he was a grand man. I raised two of his children; the boy that died in 1973, Lou, was three years old at the time and his sister was eight. And then we had three more. After I married, Papa remarried and they got along very nicely.

I came to Salt Lake City as a bride. My husband had been a milk deliveryman when he came here. Then he and his brother Jack, Ralph and Ira's father, became partners in the National Army and Navy. They had army surplus merchandise, some new stuff, and always workman's clothes. When I first came here, I kept kosher until Fred was born. Kaplan had a butcher shop and then after he died there was a man on 2nd South who used to have a butcher shop, and the *shul* ordered meats from Denver. When my father-in-law visited, I tried to make *milchedig* for him, and I'd order kosher chickens from a man named Davis that I could cook and take down to my sister-in-law's house, but at one point, I just quit. I said, no more.

A Matter of Persuasion—I remember when Mormons would try to convert us. They came in pairs, two men, to the house and in their own way. "Couldn't we come in and talk with you?" they asked. And my husband would say, "Let them come in." And they talked and talked and talked. My husband said, "You know, I've lived half my life as a Jew and I'm very happy with it." I had one neighbor, a Mormon, who was very nice. We minded our business and she minded hers. We were very close. It's the others that are so *farbrent.* I never had a fear about the children converting. I tried to keep the home as Jewish as possible. We knew Friday night. We light the candles, observed the holidays. Fortunately, they married into their own.

Congregation Montefiore was my first love. It was a pleasure to work at the shul, too. It's a small place but we had so many lovely dinners there. After my husband died, I still belonged to Montefiore but joined the B'nai Israel Sisterhood because we had quite a time having Sunday school for the youth. We didn't have bar mitzvahs then; we had confirmations. So my children were eventually confirmed. During the war, we had all our Jewish boys at the Jewish Community Center, in the old LDS building on South Temple. We fixed meals for them. I remember one year, we had our kitchen *kashered* so we could have a real Pesach for the soldiers.

Death Is Hard on Children—My husband passed away in 1939, and I've been a widow all these years. My oldest son was seventeen or eighteen years old. I had to sell my husband's share of the business because we had no partnership insurance, and I wasn't capable of becoming a partner. Since he was self employed, there was no social security like they have now with the children.

There was nothing at all. His death was very hard on the children. One of the boys had to go up and get Lou at the University, he was a student there, and then the other children had to be told. It was hard for the younger ones. Dan was nine and when he'd come with other children, and they spoke of a father, he didn't have one. But they all got along beautifully. All my children were just great. And we made it. We managed. I got the money from the business, sold my home, put us on a limited amount, and was able to stay home with the children until they were old enough for me to work.

A little mensh, Fred Tannenbaum, ten months old. (Courtesy of Fred and Irene Tannenbaum)

An Honor—For a long time, I have been involved with the preparation of the dead. I know you can't ask everybody to take part in the *Cheverta Kaddisha.* I know that some people can do it and others cannot. Claire Bernstein did it sometimes. Rose Nord did it for a time, as did Mrs. Eppeson. I deemed it an honor that I was asked to join the group of women that do that. I believe Clara Bernstein asked me at the time. As women, we only wash women's bodies. Actually, the body has already been washed before we begin the rituals. Rosie Pepper and I do this; and Janet Spitz too, and Nomi Loeb, I remember. Rose Pepper's and Claire Bernstein's mothers were probably among the first women to do this, because the ceremony has been done all the time. I think Rosie Pepper's son and Hertz and Sammy Sapitsky wash the men.

There was a time we used to have a man, a *shomer,* who would sit with the body until it was buried. And women who would sit and cry. I remember when my mother died, it was very hard. She died at home in her bed. They brought her down into the living room. They put something on the floor and put her body on top of it and covered it. They washed her there. They didn't do it in a funeral parlor. And you know, it was very, very, very difficult to have it done in the house. And then they brought in a very crude box, just plain wood, and placed her in that. The shroud was just a sheet. One woman was there. A friend, a neighbor. She was crying. I said to her, you're not going to bring her back. I told her to stop. Another neighbor, who was non-Jewish, wanted to see my mother, but was told if she comes in, she'll make my mother *trayf.* I

A YEAR OF MINYANS

by Fred Tannenbaum

Friends— I was born at the old St. Mark's Hospital on West Temple.[2] My earliest remembrance of living in Salt Lake was at 955 Fairview Avenue, off 9th South and 15th East. There were a few Jewish families in that area. The Grossmans and the Munzies. Art Munzie, Howard Grossman and Ira Tannenbaum went to the same elementary school as I did. I think we were the only four Jewish kids at Unitah Elementary School.

Life and times— My family belonged to Congregation Montefiore and I never graduated from Sunday school because it was interrupted at the time I would have been there to finish. There was no one there to teach. As far as Hebrew school, the cantor sometimes taught and I learned to read Hebrew. I studied for my bar mitzvah under the rabbi's father, Mr. Krikstein. My mother was far more religious than my father. A good number of the retail people were in the Reform congregation. While a number of people were observant, for example, the Eisens who were in the barrel business, in the downtown retail district, stores were all open on Saturdays. Maybe they had somebody else watching the store. I remember, a lot of young people worked in the stores. Milt Rosen's father had a store, Mike Arnovitz was a little retailer, and my Uncle Mike Sher had a small, inexpensive men's clothing shop. That was my first job, working for him during one summer in high school. I was fourteen years old. That's where I learned to sell. If a person was looking at your window and you didn't bring him in off the street to sell him something, you got a lecture. Mike didn't know how to sell, but his wife, my father's sister, was a very good saleslady and I learned a lot from her. They had a good way to teach selling: go out and do it! I earned ten cents an hour, a dollar a week at first; I saved it, and to earn more, I used to cut lawns and shovel snow.

We didn't have much money after my father died. My mother had four children to take care of. We certainly weren't destitute, but she was frugal. I'd say that 80 percent of what we spent socially was in charitable giving. My mother was always involved in the Jewish community. And our whole community life was the Jewish community.

Boy Scouts—We didn't go on many vacations. We rarely went out for dinner. But you didn't have television then, so you didn't see all these things you wanted. If you had a nickel, you could go to the movies, catch a serial. I had been a Boy Scout in a Mormon ward but was told in order to get promoted, I would have to go to

Seminary, so that's when I dropped out. My mother and some of the other parents got together and found Harold Chesler who volunteered to be a Scout Leader, so we did have a Jewish Boy Scout troop. We probably had about six to ten kids, not a lot, and since Mr. Chesler lived across the street from Liberty Park, we'd have our meetings there. Mr. Chesler owned theatres. He had one on 9th South and 9th East, the Tower Theatre, and another in Kennecott, up near the mines. He also had a distributor company, called Theatre Candy, and sold candy and popcorn to theatres.

So we didn't go to many places. To get to the synagogue, I used to ride the narrow gauge streetcar. That was my transportation. I'd buy a book of five-cent tickets, twenty tickets for a dollar, ride the streetcar from Unitah School, which was on 15th East, and come down to 1st South, and walk a few blocks over to synagogue. Then I'd usually get picked up by my mother or father.

Making a Minyan—I was thirteen years old when my father died, and every morning, we went to a minyan. We said kaddish for eleven months. We had an old car and my brother drove, he was old enough to drive, and we'd drive down 5:30 or 6:00 in the morning. We couldn't walk then because we lived too far away from the shul. But I remember the smog. My dad passed away in December and the smog was just terrible during that time, you couldn't see the side of the street.

Abe Guss, the greeter of the congregation, was always there. He was very good to the kids and he'd help us. How did I feel about going to minyan? It was the thing you had to do and you did it. It was a sign of respect.

After that, I didn't start in again going to minyans until my brother Louis died and I can't tell you exactly how long ago that was. But then I started going to the Thursday morning minyan. Ed Eisen was the organizer and we had a nice group of men. Sam Shapiro, Abe Guss, I don't remember everyone but it was very, very seldom that we didn't have a minyan of ten men. I liked going to minyans then. It became quite a social event. We'd have a table reserved at various places downtown, so that after a minyan, we'd take turns buying breakfast at a restaurant and kibitz, visit, and relax for a half an hour or forty-five minutes before going to work.

I remember going to the restaurant in Little America, the hotel. We used to have a waitress who would keep track of whose turn it was to buy and she'd give the check to the person she thought should pay. When they opened Dee's Restaurant on 4th South, why, we'd go there, too.

In those years, women didn't attend minyans. Not at Montefiore. Abe Guss was the one who said, absolutely not. He'd walk out of a minyan if a woman came in and

Mazel tov! Fred and Irene Tannenbaum's wedding. (Courtesy of the Tannenbaum Family)

they wanted to count her in to make a quorum of ten. At synagogue, men and women sat together, but women were never part of the minyan. Now, times have changed and women are counted in a minyan.

If I am impassioned about Jewish causes, most likely, it comes from my mother's belief that one Jew should help another Jew. It's part of our social life and our upbringing. My whole philosophy is if you're going to ask others to help, whether it's in life, in charity, or in business, you have to set an example. And my example has always been by doing.

A Merger in the Air—In my generation, Congregation Montefiore was too religious, and they weren't bringing in any of the young people, and the Reform synagogue, B'nai Israel, was too reform. I'd go once in awhile, the rabbis were always good friends of mine, but the service had almost no Hebrew in it. Financially, neither synagogue could afford to go out and build a new building. And actually, most members belonged to both synagogues, so they knew each other. To bring us together, the first move was to establish a community religious school. That was Max Siegel's doing.

From then on, it took a long time with a lot of meetings at various people's homes. And fortunately, there was a group of my generation that felt we were close enough together that we could join and build a new building, and fortunately, we had a rabbi, Rabbi Bergman, who could take care of two congregations and make it work.

I signed on the mortgage for the building and took care of all the monies during the process of building. I don't think there was any time that there wasn't a conflict. People like Abe Guss were far more religious than most of the others; my wife Irene, who is Reform, never did like the service; and I never experienced a choir during services, never had an organ, and didn't like it. But the conflict was livable, compromises were made, and a number of people changed from both. For me, I was very satisfied. The Reform movement has moved far closer to the Conservative movement and in turn the Conservative movement has moved closer to the Reform.

said she was a very good woman, probably someone my mother would have loved to see, so she came in to say goodbye. There were a lot of responsibilities then to burying the dead. They had to be buried quickly and with a small bag containing Israel soil; she couldn't be buried unless we had that in the coffin. It was hard for me, as a young girl, to see that with my mother. Now they take the deceased to funeral parlors and you don't see all of that. Now, why do I do this? You see, my mother would always take care of someone who was sick. In her short time, she did much good for people. It was natural for her. And so I will do anything to help as well.

When we prepare a body for burial, we wear gloves and we sponge the body a little at a time, while all the time we are saying a special prayer. Then we will put the shrouds on. They used to be very plain, drab, but now they have a little lace on them. And the little caps have a veil over the face. Then we will put the deceased into a casket. Of course, the casket is closed and ordinarily, there's no viewing. It doesn't take long to do this and I'm glad that I can help.

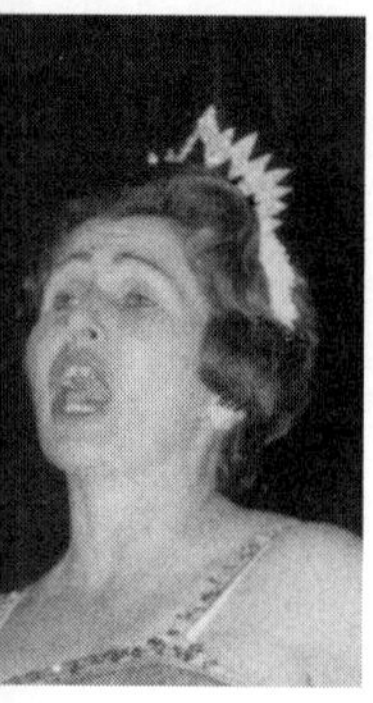

EVERYONE'S GOING MESHUGGE IN THE KITCHEN

Jean Eisen

Who Needs It?—Originally, I'm from Pittsburgh, Pennsylvania.[1] I moved to Los Angeles with my three-year-old daughter, Kelly, and my first husband, Manny Greenfield. He died from all the effects of diabetes at the age of 38. By then we had another child, Ed. My late husband's cousin actually introduced Ed Eisen to me. He was divorced and had one daughter, Sherry. We met each other, went out once or twice, but I thought, "Who needs it?" I have two children. I have a house. I'm busy at work. Life was busy enough as it was. Well, when Ed knew that our children went to the same Congregation Beth Am, he called and asked if it were all right if he picked up all the children and we did something together. I always say he married me because he fell in love with my kids. The kids liked him. My in-laws, who more or less looked after me, thought he was a very fine gentleman.

Ed and I dated off and on, then he decided to move back to Salt Lake City. Okay, so he's gone. And my life goes on. Well, a couple of months later, in fact, it was almost Rosh Hashanah, I was at my husband's sister's house across the street and a neighbor comes running in. "Mrs. Greenfield, Mrs. Greenfield. You know that man that drives a red and white car that used to come here? Well, he's back and he's knocking on your door."

We Do—I married Ed. I was 36 years old. I had two children, he had one, and after we married, we moved back to Salt Lake while I was pregnant with David.

Family Business—We moved back because Ed wanted to build up the business—the American Barrel—that had gone down to nothing. It was his Dad's business originally. American Barrel reconditioned steel drums for the oil companies. When Ed returned, they took out loans, bought new equipment, and built it back up. They even put in equipment to make new steel drums. A lot of people have misconceptions about the business. They think you can use steel drums once and then dump them. But you don't. Companies like American Oil or Phillips use drums over and over again, so they would bring in the drums to be washed and, what you call reconditioned, so they can be reused. Now, when the steel becomes worn, the companies can't use them, so they have to be refinished. If they can't be fixed, then you can sell them new ones. Ed bought new equipment to make new drums.

Modernization—We had two plants between North Temple and 1st South, with our office in the middle. On one side we had a new tumbler machine called a Wheelabrator that would clean open drums. These are barrels without lids. The barrel would be placed inside this huge machine and a rush of air would shoot bb's around and around the barrel inside and out as it turned. In our other plant, on the other side of our office, we cleaned closed drums. You've seen a drum with the little round opening in the lid? They had to be chain-cleaned. Chains would be dropped inside the barrel and the machine would shake the hell out of it. It was loud, so noisy, you couldn't go near it. The men working the equipment had to wear earplugs. We went into a lot of debt after he came back and took over the business, but he got it up and running again, so we were all right.

Jewish Public Relations—Ed was not religious, as far as he drove on *Shabbes*, but his life was the synagogue and the synagogue was his life. We did not keep kosher, but we never had *trayf* in our home, not then and not now. Ed worked very hard getting the business back on its feet, and seeing to the day-to-day running of the company. But he took time off during the day, which a lot of people in business think they can't do, just so he could go around to schools to talk about what a Jew is. He had a small book that answered a lot of questions that non-Jewish people would ask if they felt they could. He ordered a lot of these books from Montefiore's gift shop to give them to teachers. I was gift shop chairman and filled his many orders so people would better understand what a Jewish person was like. He'd get calls from schools, parents, and ward houses because people were curious as to what was that miner's light on top of a Jewish man's head or questioned whether Jews really did have horns on their heads—a widely held misconception. Whenever there was a call, he used to go and explain.

Combating Prejudice—He knew the importance of it. I felt the same way. Our kids were being made fun of, you know. This is a nice community here, but it's a Mormon community, and they didn't know about our traditions or cultures let alone our religion. I didn't have a Christmas tree up. Why didn't I have a tree up? And I'll tell you: it was "dirty Jew" that came from the mouths of some of them. It was frustrating. One year, I think it was David's first grade class, I called Bonneville Grade School, that's on that side of 19th East and close to the house. I asked if my son's class could come to our home during their recess and listen to Chanukah music and hear the story of Chanukah. On the mantle, we had several menorahs and candles. In the meantime, I baked Chanukah cookies and made twenty-one little gifts for each child. During their lunch period, they arrived at the house. Ed read them the story of the Chanukah. We ate cookies; in fact, they're the very same cookies my kids ask me to make today when they come back to visit. And we played dreidel games. Years, later, I met the first grade teacher at Emigration Market. She said, "Jean, I'll never forget how that day enlightened me. I never knew that you had that kind of holiday." She never even knew about it; many people don't know about Jews or others. And how many of our kids are going to schools where nobody knows anything about them? Even now, can you believe it?

Sisterhood, Song, and Food—We belonged to Congregation Montefiore. Now, I had left Congregation Beth Am in Los Angeles, which was so large it had three rabbis, to go to a tiny congregation, but it turned out to be the warmest place in the community. I remember, when I first got here and I was pregnant with my son David, and Ruth Eisen, Joe Eisen's wife, called me and asked if I was going to Sisterhood. "Oh, I'd love to," I said. When I got there, though, no one approached me. Finally Ethel Henteleff came over—she's Ruthie's cousin—and asked me to sit with them. That was very nice of them; and I think from that day on, pregnant and all, I went down to Montefiore and met with my friends, to kibitz, to cook, to be! I remember Rosie Pepper and Clara Pepper and we all, until 2 o'clock in the morning, would prepare for big fund raiser dinners, and then for one function and another. I'd get a call, I'd help, and I never stopped. I did all the baking for *Shabbes* just as a volunteer because that's my calling.

I found that companionship and friendship were created in Montefiore's kitchen. I wish Clara Pepper was here to tell you about Sisterhood. We'd cook together. And we had a lot of laughs doing it. We made latkes. We made our own rolls. Rosie Nord made the best little challahs. We made a potato roll with loads of sautéed onions and a pie crust that everyone drooled over. It was shaped like a jellyroll, sliced, and served with meat. Sometimes we made sweet potato and carrot *tzimmes.* Cheese blintzes with fruit. Knishes. At that time, there were so little packaged goods with kosher symbols on them, like "U" and "K" or parve on them, that we had to order our kosher meats through Denver and make everything from scratch. We got kosher chicken livers from Denver. With liver, boiled eggs, sautéed onions, and chicken fat, we made chopped liver. Now, you have to be careful that there's no gall on the liver or else your chopped liver will be so bitter, you can't do anything about it. Rose Arnovitz and Marion Sher cooked kosher filet mignon to perfection. We used to spend half the night making hamantaschen for Purim. We made latkes for Chanukah, matzo ball soup for Pesach. And delicious honey cakes! One of the best cooks was Mollie Shapiro, Marion Sher's and Sam Shapiro's mother. Her recipes could fill a book.

Oh, we had so much fun. Dinners at Montefiore were on Sundays. We often had plays. For Purim or other holidays, we'd sing songs with lyrics written by Frances Sapitsky. You could just give her a thought, a known tune, and she would come back with lyrics like gold and fast, fast, fast. Our sisterhood plays were corny, but based on real life. "Everyone's going meshugge in the kitchen. Everyone's telling you what to do." We were old-time cooks. Who needed a caterer!

More Food—We always had food. At the synagogue, people didn't just run in, pray, and run out. We went in, we prayed, we had kiddush afterwards where there was always a bit of wine, a little challah, maybe some herring, a cold drink, some pastry. It was a tradition and it came down as a tradition in our home.

Our Home—No one ever visits our home without a little something to eat. You know, you

Jean Eisen and the Montefiore Purim play, circa 1950s. (Courtesy of Jean Eisen)

break bread together. It's a part of our life. It brings warmth. It brings closeness. It brings comfort and it opens you up for conversation. And like Ed believed in, it helps enlighten people.

Exuberance in Life and Song—Ed Eisen sang louder than anyone else. Everyone at Montefiore and, later, at Kol Ami knew it. I used to sit next to Sam Shapiro. It used to be Sam, Mariam, and I and Ed. Sometimes they'd go like this, and tap, tap, tap him on his knee, so he wouldn't sing so loud. But he had a nice voice, and he davened louder than anyone else. I think he wanted God to hear him. The first *yontif,* Ed always had the honors, you know on the High Holy Days. Then Irwin Berry carried on. I remember Irwin said, "I'm following my dear friend Ed Eisen who did this for twenty years. But Ed didn't only say the High Holy Day prayers, he told the story with everything, and he wrote it himself." Oh, I cried to hear that.

Mergers and Minyans—Ed was against the merger. He used to tell everyone—of course, I knew he wasn't serious—that he was going to buy that old building, you know. He would get a couple of men to go in with him and buy the building. He wanted to go back to his shul. In the end, he said, "I have to go [to Kol Ami]. I'm the one that's in synagogue four days a week. So I have to live with it." He did. With his brother Max. They never missed a Saturday or an early morning minyan on Monday and Thursday. He never missed a date at shul until he had to go on oxygen and all.

B'nai Israel, *There Is Nothing Like a Dame*. Among the dancers: Jack Goodman, Jack Sweet, Verner Zinik, Howard Marcus, Wally Sandack, Milton Rosen. (Courtesy of Helen Sandack)

Among the B'nai Israel Sisterhood beauties *(l–r)*: Eva Siegel, Sari White, Bernice Roe, Janet Rosen, Sally Frank Weinstock, Hazel Provol, Sylvia Arnovitz, and a girl named Donna. (Courtesy of Helen Sandack)

After the new synagogue for Congregation Kol Ami was dedicated on December 12, 1976, the new *Sisterhood Follies*, led by Helen Sandack, Joanne McGillis, and Shirley Tannenbaum, brought to the stage real life issues regarding the merger between B'nai Israel and Montefiore, and got away with it! For "Mission Um-Possible," the curtain opened on an unusual star-studded cast including Iris Weinstein, Linda Bergman, Vivian Shapiro, Suzanne Goldsmith, Nomi Loeb, Irene Tannenbaum, Connie Weinstock, Marge Pepper, Diane Eisenberg, Rose Pepper, Shirley Tannenbaum, Mandy Harrison, Judy Wolfe, Alan Frank, Roger des Rogier, Hal Harrison, Ed Eisen, Louis Borgenicht, Milt Rosen, Wally Sandack, Lee Lovinger, Herm Bernstein, Sandy Pepper, and Marv Gallenson. Whatever the presentation, their scripts were flawless, they held back no punches; tongue in cheek, they brought the house down with songs strong, sensitive, and definitely real enough to help rekindle the spirit of community, as the two synagogues merged into one.

"There Are Good Times Just Around the Corner," by Helen Sandack

There's trouble at the Temple. They're crowded to the door.
So many hate to alternate from there to Montefiore.
Conservatives are cranky at the Congregation's growth.
They haven't got a parking lot—that's big enough for both!

Third East criticizes when Fourth East remains aloof
But now we have a Rabbi to put us under one roof.
Hooray! Hooray! Hooray! Abner is here to stay!

There are good times just around the Corner.
He will stop dissension and disrepair
Say goodbye to *[kvetching]* about a kosher kitchen
For we know that the liberal members don't much care.

No, they won't try to fool a fellow from the shul
Just by wearing a yarmulke on the head.
We're going to pack up our tsoriss in our old kit bag
And Kol Ami will move ahead.

The Tannenbaums are troubled. The Peppers are perplexed.
They don't know where to have their prayers.
And the Siegels are very vexed.

The Cohens are confused now. The Goodmans have never shown—
Perhaps they're at the Rosenblatts'
For services in their home.

Dealing with the problem, we overhead Mr. Guss,
"I'll go and pray in Denver—and that will stop the fuss!"
But now let's give a cheer. Abner is finally here!

There are good times just around the corner.
With the Rabbi balancing each page.

Now the left and the right will stop their silly fight
And diversion will unify us instead.
And then tomorrow the Sister will brag, brag, brag
'Cause Kol Ami will move ahead.

[All singing:] A likely story . . .
Don't be meshugge . . .
Kol Ami will move ahead!

A BOAT TO AMERICA

Abe Guss

A Promise of a Future—My father wasn't doing too well financially, so he left for America in 1912 to see what he could do for himself.[1] My mother, my two brothers and one sister and I were left behind until he could bring us over in 1920. When Dad left Russia, we moved to Antapolia, near the city of Brest-Litovsk, which was the demarcation point set up between the Germans and the Russians in the First World War. All my mother's family lived in Antapolia.

Left Behind and Waiting to Leave—I was eight years old when Dad left. Mother didn't work, and we didn't have any income. He had to send us some money to live on. It was a hard life. Difficult. Her brother in the city was a druggist; and their family was very interested in our welfare so they looked after us very much. Her father also helped out. I think we rented a very small, two or three-room house.

There was little entertainment. (I had never seen a show until I came to Salt Lake City.) My maternal grandfather had a large family and a big house. The youngsters used to get together Saturday afternoons to visit, talk, and study. I was too young to participate with them, but I remember going there. Our parents were extremely Orthodox. I didn't go to public school. I studied at the *heder,* and was there all day long from early morning until evening.

Liberalism—Zionism became very prominent and the younger men started to give it a lot of thought. There was some radicalism, not so much that, but liberalism. People would say, "You know so-and-so smokes on Saturday." Nobody ever heard him or seen him do it, but there was a rumor that he did and it was a terrible thing to smoke on a Saturday. Religion was a way of life: you went to shul in the morning and you went back before sunset. There was no exception. If you had a problem, you found the answer during services. I remember a certain individual deciding then that he would stop reading the Torah, not permit anyone to honor the service until the problem was solved. And most of the problems were dealt this way, within the religious community. There was no center. There was no secular meeting house. There were several synagogues and two rabbis.

Caution Taken—There were limitations on everyday life, of course. The church was very strong and you had to be very careful. Most of the non-Jewish people were uneducated and of the farming element who followed the advice and counsel of the priest. When Easter came, the Jewish community was advised not to show themselves on the street, not to do anything objectionable or conspicuous. There was great anti-Semitism.

When World War I began, the Russians drove out a lot of the Jews close to Brest-Litovsk. If not in Antapolia, rumors started that soldiers were assaulting Jewish women. My grandfather had several daughters and they decided they had to go further into Russia. They couldn't go by train, the trains were used by the army, so they got a horse and wagon and left in that. We were all ready to go with him—mother and the children, but the druggist, a very fine individual, went up to the wagon and asked my grandfather, "Where will Sarah go?" Sarah is my mother. "She'll be lost. Her husband won't know where to find her. Let her stay. I'll stay here. Whatever happens to us, will happen to her." And we remained.

War and Decisions—The Russians burned part of the town, burned part of the Jewish homes. Not because they were Jewish homes, but it was the war. Then the Germans occupied us for about two or three years. Their rules were very rigid, very difficult, and very strict. After the war, many of the stores and homes were destroyed. My mother decided to move into a village about ten miles from where her grandfather had lived earlier and had some non-Jewish friends. She opened up a little store in the house. The house itself wasn't any larger than two rooms. She would buy kerosene, head covers, and other things for the ladies and exchange them for corn and potatoes. We'd grind the corn for flour and that's how we would live.

Brutal Reality—When the Soviet Revolution took place in 1917, there wasn't a lot of discussion among the youngsters. In the small towns, we didn't feel it very much. We had lived, as I said, part of the time under the rule of the Germans. When peace was signed in Brest-Litovsk in 1918, the Germans left and the Poles occupied the country. They were vicious. It happened that one night, in the city of Antapolia, when the new Russian government, the Communists, came through the town, the Poles came in and chased them out. They were so unreasonable, so insensitive, and so murderous, they also went down to shoot any Jew. One man broke into a home, took a sword and put it through the covers of the bed to see if anyone was hiding in the bed. Under Polish hands, it was brutal.

A First Meal—There were so many soldiers around, we left by horse and buggy, and traveled part of the day to the county seat, a city called Kobryn. We then traveled to Brest-Litovsk. Before the war started, no Jews were permitted to stay. After the war, many of them came back. (Incidentally, the Prime Minister of Israel, Menachem Begin, came from Brest-Litovsk.) My mother's aunt lived in Brest-Litovsk with her family. She met us, when we arrived, and we had dinner at their home. I remember that. They served chicken. We hadn't had chicken for four or five years. I still remember it being the best I ever ate.

Making Arrangements to Leave—There were many soldiers there as well, making it difficult to travel. But there were Jewish agents in Brest-Litovsk who arranged to get tickets for families to travel by train from there to Warsaw. After three or four days in Warsaw, straightening out our visas, we went to the free port of Danzig.[2] We were all afraid in the city of Danzig. Again, having been under the Germans, any kind of rumor would excite us because we were fearful of the government and what might happen. When we finally left after several days and got into Liverpool, it was a different world. In Liverpool, we felt safe. Now we only had to wait for passage to America. My father, and an uncle, Nat Levine, had sent us a little money to travel to America, and we traveled a week or so by boat. Our only worry then was about food. We were afraid there might not be enough food for all of us, but we arrived safely in Philadelphia.

Reunion—My uncle's father met us in Philadelphia and, three days later, put us on a train to Salt Lake City. It was exciting seeing Dad. We hadn't seen each other for seven or eight years.

Down and Out—But my father had lost everything he had by the end of World War I. He was selling hides and pelts and, as I understand it, a load of goods when the Armistice was declared. The buyer refused to accept it because the prices tumbled. Dad took a loss of six or seven thousand dollars, which was all the capital he had. He borrowed on his life insurance and was able to get some money at the bank, just enough to get a horse and buggy to go out and peddle junk. In other words, when we came here, he was down and out. And now he had a wife and four children. Life was hard for about four or five years. Once he earned enough money to buy a truck, then he started doing a little bit better.

To Be a Child Again—I went to public school for the first time in my life. I was sixteen years of age. I think I was in the sixth or seventh grade. There was a teacher there who insisted I do everything that kids do. What a wonderful thing that was for me, because that was the only way I could learn, to start as a child again. The only problem was there were two young Jewish teachers in that school and they were beautiful girls. Of course, I had an interest in girls then, so sometimes I'd be embarrassed when my teacher would make me play with the sixth grade kids at recess. They were so much younger than I was! But I stayed a year there and then went on for another year at South Junior High on the northeast corner of 13th South and State Street.

Finding Employment—My father was having such a tough time making a living, I decided to go to business college and learn bookkeeping so I could get a job right away. I studied day and night and by luck found a job at an insurance agency. That's the agency I went to work for in 1923, the same one I bought out in 1941, and sold in 1969. It was first called Ashton-Jenkins Insurance, then Lauren Gibbs, and finally Guss Insurance Agency. I had a pretty successful business.

Teaching at Montefiore—My father worked hard, but he was also involved in the Jewish community and very active in the synagogue. It was his whole world. It was that way because he was a very learned man. Because of him, I got involved. I was a schoolteacher for two or three years in Congregation Montefiore. As I tell my story, I say I was fired more times by the synagogue than all the other teachers that have ever been hired by the congregation. The reason for this? Every time there was a meeting, my father would go and he had no inhibitions. If he didn't like what was being addressed, he'd speak up. Nothing bothered him. He didn't care who was opposing, even if the man were a prominent member of the synagogue.

And Subsequent Firings—Well, sometimes he would offend such a man. And they'd say, "Well, let's get rid of his kid here in Hebrew school!" They'd come down and fire me right on the spot! Of course, I'd be rehired almost immediately. Finally, I had to quit on my own, but I became even more active in synagogue life after I married Sophie. I was the president of Montefiore for two years. I was the president of the B'nai Israel Lodge. I was the secretary of one council or another for five or six years. I became the drive chairman one year. In the old days, there wasn't a meeting I missed. But then I got old and stopped going to meetings. Now, I just hate meetings.

Sophie and Abe Guss dancing. (Courtesy of Sophie Guss)

Life—Congregation Montefiore was an Orthodox synagogue in its early days. When I came in 1920, it had changed its seating system so that men and women could sit together.[3] Then they wanted to make more liberal changes. I was amazed because my mother and father sat apart for as long as she lived. My mother wasn't inclined to go to any meetings. Her world was her children, her family, and her religion. It wasn't a question of liking! "That" was the world to her! But it was difficult for her to be in America, let alone being in Utah where she was so isolated. The language was difficult for her to speak; moreover, her now Americanized children were becoming a problem.

Liberalism in America—They started to become more liberal. My brother occasionally would light up a cigar or a cigarette when they weren't in the home, and my mother didn't approve of it, was adamant against it. But she had to live with it.

When Is It Kosher Enough?—After I married Sophie, my mother never touched any food in our home. Dad was not as bad. But a glass of water, my mother wouldn't take. In Salt Lake City, she would never touch any ice cream either. She wasn't sure whether it was kosher or not, so she wouldn't touch it. Never. That's how extremely religious she was. There were others in the community like her. But with the passing of time, death, and people leaving, before long, she was one of the few, the very few Orthodox Jews left in Salt Lake.

GOYISHEH POTATOES AND KOSHER HOMES

Rose Guss Nord

Kosher Homes and Shabbes—My folks were ultra religious.[1] Dad left Russia in 1913 and went to New York, but couldn't make a living there. He would stop working Friday afternoon and wouldn't work on Saturdays. He left New York and went to visit some relatives in Denver. He stayed there awhile, but there were more Guss families here in Utah. He didn't ask permission to come. He just came. Claire Bernstein's mother-in-law had a kosher boarding house on 8th South. Dad was one of her boarders.

The minute my father got to Salt Lake, he bought a horse and buggy, used it to buy furs and hides; later he'd pick up iron scrap. He peddled his wares. But, like I said, he wouldn't work on *Shabbes,* and wouldn't work after twelve noon on Friday. I guess, he worked enough to make a living.

In a Small Shtetl—We came over from Russia in 1920.[2] From Antopole, or Antapolia, it's not even on the map, we looked. I was almost fourteen years old then. I don't remember Dad going to America. He was gone for about eight years, and my mother had the brunt of the burden, raising the children. We lived in a little house with a roof made of straw. That I can remember. It was one room. A narrow room with an old fashioned oven, like a baker's oven, heated with wood. My mother had needles and thread, crochet hooks; and some days, she would get a ride with one of the goyim that went to the nearby town to sell at the market. Instead of getting money, I think she got food for us. And milk. I don't know, maybe she bought them. But that's how she supported us. When the Germans were there, they pushed education. So when they moved out, and the Polish came in, some of us went to Polish schools. But it was hard. I remember my grandfather and fighting in the town when the Polish soldiers came. The day the Germans left, my grandfather left, he cried and cried.

Abe Taught the Children—My brother Abe taught us how to read a little bit of Hebrew. I couldn't write too good. Later, when I went to New York to live with my aunt and her husband, if I typed a letter to my mother, she *could* read it. But she didn't understand English too good, and Dad would try to explain it to her. Later in life, Mother talked better English than Dad. But she would tell me, "Write a few words, but write it in Jewish the best way you know how." I would have my aunt and uncle help me and I would copy it out. I mean, I knew how to speak *Yiddish,* but I didn't know how to write it. But I say, little by little I learned to write in *Jewish.* My father was a very educated man and so we belonged to Congregation Montefiore.

An American Sister—We had an American sister. When she was a baby, I would wheel her in the carriage, up and down the street. People would say, "You're so young to have a little girl." Mother was approaching forty years old, and to have her pregnant, oh, I didn't think people [that old] even got together!

Growing Up and Already Grown—I didn't date too much. Most of the fellows that would date me were buddies of my brother and no boy likes to take out his friend's sister. So when Mother's sister in New York said, "Wouldn't it be nice if I got to see Rose," I went there, to a small community in Long Island. That must have been around 1930. There were a lot of Jewish people in my aunt's neighborhood and I was the girl from out of town. I started going out with boys. I was like an animal escaping right out of a cage. My mother's youngest sister was not much older than I am, maybe eight or nine years. Her husband was the same way, not much older than I was, so I just stayed on. I got a job. In the height of the depression, I worked in the merchandise control office at the Paris Company for a year and a half. Within a short time, I became an assistant buyer at another department store. I worked and lived in New York until 1943. That's when I came back to Utah.

A Dated Affair—I married my husband in 1933. The first time I met him, it happened that one of my friends had a dance in one of the rooms of the synagogue. It was more or less a dated affair. A couple of days later, he called me and wanted to know if he could take me out. I remember we went out. But it took me three years to get him round to where we would [talk about marriage]. Then we were engaged for a year. My aunt and uncle were good to me and they idolized my husband-to-be.

First a Religious Marriage and Back to Work—We got married on a Saturday night and by Monday we had to go back to work. Since this was during the depression, people were selling apples out on the street. My husband worked as an insurance man. He would go from house to house, collecting policies for twenty-five or fifty cents apiece. He was scared he would lose his job because he was single; married men needed the work. On the other side of it, I was an assistant buyer and I was scared I'd lose my job if I got married. So, we were married first by a rabbi in his home. We didn't have a civil ceremony, the legal one, until six months later. All that miserable time, we didn't tell anybody that we were married.

My husband's parents had died and he moved in with a sister, so he just continued living with her. I continued living with my aunt and uncle, and had a curfew! If I went out at night, say, to a show with my "husband," and wasn't home at 11:30 P.M., my uncle would walk that street back and forth until I did get home.

A Legal Wedding and Births—Finally, after six months, we were married again and put an end to the separate living. We got our own place. We lived in Brooklyn first. It was noisy. My husband didn't like Brooklyn; he missed Long Island so badly that we moved back. My children were born in Long Island. I didn't have a hard time delivering them. My first one was a breech birth, feet first. But even then, by the time we got to the hospital, in Astoria, and my husband went home to change his clothes and return, I was already in the delivery room. When the time came for my daughter, I got to the hospital at 7:12 and she was born at 8:12, an hour later. So fast, they hadn't found the doctor yet! They said if I had another child, they'd put me on the hospital steps by the time I got into my ninth month! Oh, those were the days when you stayed in the hospital for ten days after giving birth. I was bored to death. You get up, you get dizzy, you get sick, you know, from just laying in that bed for a whole week and then some. Too long, and there was just so much to do at home that I wasn't getting to.

They brought the baby in a couple of times a day. I wanted to nurse the baby, and I was, but they were giving him a bottle anyway, and he'd drink that bottle dry. I thought I had enough milk. My mother said, "Rosie, you haven't got enough milk in there." I was waiting to see the doctor, and she said, "Forget it." She sent me one of those great big long linen dish towels to wrap around my breasts. Wrapped it around real tight, but once I stood up, I didn't have enough to hold the towel up. So my mother changed her mind, told me to go to the doctor and I found out I didn't have enough milk. My kids were bottle-fed. I was ninety-nine pounds when my son was born and with my daughter, I was one hundred and eight.

Buggy Brigade—I had my son in 1936. My daily routine was much like that of the other women in the neighborhood. You got up in the morning, and did your work. By ten o'clock, you were all dressed up with makeup on and everything else. You're living on the second or third floor of a walk-up apartment building. So you take the child downstairs, and put him in a buggy that you pulled out of the storage room downstairs. What you did was drag the buggy out with one hand while you're holding the baby close to you with your other hand, and then carefully bounce, bounce down the stairs to the outside. Once in the fresh air, he'd sleep and sleep in the buggy, and you'd wheel him to meet the buggy brigade. That's everybody who's out there doing the same thing. Twelve o'clock, you put the buggy in storage again, come upstairs, into your apartment, give the child a bath, give him his lunch, and put him down for his nap. Then you go ahead and do your housework. Three o'clock, you take the baby out again. And it's the buggy brigade again. In the spring, at about 4:30 P.M., you go back upstairs and start dinner. You get a big playpen and put that poor child in it. You call it the jailhouse, and throw everything in it to keep him occupied. Then he watches you make dinner for your husband. My husband gets home at seven and dinner is ready. This Paul, my son, was a lively one, and so I'd give him his bath earlier, except of course in the summer when it was light outside, and I'd put him down to sleep by six o'clock. That's the way it was every day.

She Visited, She Criticized, and She Left—Paul was born in March and my mother arrived in

June. After his nap, as usual, I got us ready to go outside. It was a hot day and my mother asked, "Where are you going with Paul?" I told her I was taking him for a walk to get some fresh air. She said, "Why put the baby in the terrible sun! Look at the shade, right here. Put the baby down. Open the window for fresh air, and forget about it." So? I did, but right after she left, I was taking my baby out in the buggy to meet the buggy brigade. That was the style then in New York.

And Then There Were Two—When we had two children, we couldn't afford a nursery. Few people could in those days. Babysitters were cheap, maybe thirty five or fifty cents, but if you didn't have that, you couldn't even get a babysitter. So you stayed at home and took care of your kids. It was just an old struggle, this time, doubled. You'd drag the buggy out again, bouncing up the stairs, and all the time you'd hold one baby to your chest with one arm and your toddler would hold on like this [at your side], and you'd pull the buggy with a free hand, and go out with the two of them. We used to take these children out every day. Hot weather or bitter cold.

Pinky—When Paul was born, my husband, whose father's name was Pinkus, started calling him Pinky, because there was one "Paul" relative already ahead of him. I remember, when I was expecting my second child, my son was already three and a half years old and we were outside taking a walk. Paul was active, like I said, and for a moment, I thought he was going to run right into the street. I hollered, "Pinky!" Out of nowhere, there was a little dog on the street and that damn dog came running up to me so fast, it must have thought his name was Pinky. But the other "Pinky," my Paul, if I didn't grab him right away, he would still be running.

Blues—My husband was the ninth child of ten children. I had nine sisters-in-law. Once you get married, you kind of go into that family. And I did; after all, there were a couple of sisters-in-law that lived nearby. I remember at first I was nervous about meeting them, but everything they did was just like in our home. Still, I missed my own family and in 1937, I took Paul by train back to Salt Lake City. When my daughter was born in 1939, I needed to go back home again to see my family, so in December of 1941, I took the train with both kids. No one could afford to fly then. I stayed in Salt Lake City for almost two months. It wasn't enough time, and I missed them terribly when we went back to Long Island. During the war, my son would come home after school wearing a nametag on his shirt. The schools were afraid that New York would get bombed, and they needed to know who the children belonged to. That frightened me. But, nonchalantly, I wrote a letter to my family, saying, wouldn't it be nice if I came back? Two days later, I got a special delivery letter, "Pack up and come!" That's what I did. We had a two-bedroom apartment at the time and what I didn't sell I gave away. Just took my dishes. We had gone back and forth from New York to Utah so many times, it got so even my husband couldn't take New York.

But, still, at first it was different moving back here. You know, your first years of married life are so informative. You develop your own sets of friends, and way of living, and when you come back, they knew you as a single girl. So they have to meet you again. After a few years, though, even my husband, when we would go back to New York, wouldn't want to stay there for more than two weeks.

Kosher in the City—In Salt Lake, my husband opened up a beer tavern, called Duffy's Tavern. It was on 2nd South, just past West Temple. The children didn't like their father having a tavern, I didn't like it, so he sold it and worked for my brother. My husband insisted on one thing, though, bless him. He said, "We're going to keep kosher here, too." I said, "I'll have to." But what a struggle it was. We had just one butcher shop on 2nd East and 8th South. So, of course, when Paul was in school, I used to take my little girl on the bus to get the meat and then take the bus home. It was inconvenient, but my husband would say, "You've got to keep the house kosher." It wasn't just for us, anymore, because by then we used to go out to eat and who could find a kosher restaurant here? But my parents were kosher and if anything ever happened to my mother and dad, and my sister was getting married, and my brother was still at home, "it would be up to us to keep a kosher home for them." That's what my husband believed. Kaplan, the butcher, was a doll. A very nice man. There was another butcher, on 4th South, and soon there was a third butcher shop on 7th South and 5th East. But it wasn't like Kaplan's.

Kosher Meat Orders—Much later, after Kaplan closed his shop, we got our kosher meat from the next nearest town, which happened to be Denver, Colorado. I became the middle man for the Jewish community. People would call me with an order, I'd write it down, and send it on to Denver. Every other week, the meat would come. It wasn't too hard because we lived at Mother's home for awhile and the meat would be dropped off by truck at Congregation Montefiore. Each of us could get it easily. This was in 1954. We had maybe twenty or twenty-five families who ordered kosher meat. After we moved to our own home, though, we had trouble. See, the trucks carrying the meat weren't refrigerated and so we had to have it flown and delivered somewhere, which turned out to be our house. During the holidays, there would be packages of meat from one side of the living room to the other. Not a place to sit for anybody. Everybody's meat was there. People would have to come to my house to pick it up, and some days, life got even busier. Then, this one would call me, saying, "Rose, I can't come tonight. Can I come the day after tomorrow?" Another one would call, "Rose, can I pick up my order tomorrow morning?" For one reason or another, the refrigerator, I had it filled with all the meat and little place for our own. So one day I almost cried when I knew the meat was coming. My brother, may his soul rest in peace, just felt so sorry for me, he went right out and bought me a freezer so I could keep my own meat and everybody else's. As it happened, I took care of the kosher meat orders for about twenty-five years. I still have meat come every couple of months, and some of my friends will get me a couple of kosher chickens. Now [in 1983], though, we order kosher meats through Julie Jacobson.

A Kitchen for Rabbis—Having a kosher home, I believe, I've fed more rabbis on Friday nights than any other kosher cook in town. Most of the rabbis who came wouldn't ride to Montefiore,

Making dinner for the soldiers at the old Covenant House (*l–r*): unknown, Gussie Bernstein, Bessie Friedman, Sally Zingol, Mrs. Joseph Sobel, Rose Arnovitz, Sonya Pepper, Elizabeth Grossman, Sade Tannenbaum, Claire Bernstein, Vickie Pullman, unknown, Freda Kassel, Abe Bernstein, Doris Guss, Frances Oliner, Hattie Feldman, Bettie Richtel, Mollie Shapiro, Sadie Appelman, Jennie Segal, Liona Poliner, and Ida Sobel. (Courtesy of Gail Bernstein Ciacci)

so I'd have to feed them at 3:30 in the afternoon so they'd have enough time to walk back to the synagogue and be there before it got dark.

Organizations for Women—I belonged to Hadassah. I belonged to Ort. I belonged to B'nai B'rith. I belonged to Sisterhood. And there used to be a Talmud Torah Club, named after the teaching of the Torah, whose members helped out in lots of ways. The members were usually older women who took care of the children who went to Hebrew School, and were active in the community. During wartime, all the different Jewish organizations took a turn helping at the old Covenant House. On Sundays, one organization would serve breakfast to soldiers, and then the Talmud Torah ladies would have their turn.

A Contradiction in Ethics Steeped in Humor—Sometimes the Talmud Torah ladies would serve lox. It wasn't expensive. But on this [particular] Sunday that I'm thinking about, they served pickled herring. One woman said, "We'll serve the herring on lettuce." Another one said, "Who serves pickled herring on lettuce?" The one who wanted it placed the herring on the lettuce, just like that; the other one took the lettuce off. Someone shouted, "Who's the boss today?" I was with Claire Bernstein and we were speechless. After all, this was her mother-in-law and somebody else's mother!

For a Piece of Rye Bread—Oh, those women were priceless. I loved the organization. We used to get our baked goods at Sussman's bakery. I think it was on 5th East and 2nd South. You could buy rye breads. Well, one time, we, the younger ones, said we'd serve the soldiers rolls. Well, the Talmud Torah women almost killed us. "Give them a piece of pumpernickel, or a piece of rye bread! White bread they get every day! Not white bread!" Oh, were we told! Half of them couldn't speak a word of English, and they wrote their minutes in Yiddish, but, boy, their books were always balanced, and they knew rye bread from white.

Goyisheh Potatoes—Once we had a seder for fifteen hundred soldiers—and I remember somebody served fifteen hundred little tiny potatoes, each one the same size, cooked in their jacket, then peeled, browned and sprinkled with parsley. One Talmud Torah woman saw the servings and remarked, "Goyisheh potatoes!"

Pinfeathers—That's how I learned how to cook, with the Talmud Torah women. My first job was peeling onions and carrots. I never knew you had to peel grapefruit! And then there's the kosher turkeys! You had to pluck the pinfeathers out with tweezers. Tweezers! Mrs. Pepper brought a dozen tweezers and gave one pair of tweezers to each girl. We sat there pulling the pinfeathers out, and I'll tell you, people were so dedicated then. See, dinners were made late Saturday night, after *Shabbes,* for Sunday's meal. And it took a lot of time. Sometimes these women would work until four o'clock in the morning. But, oh, how they liked to make fun of the younger ones who didn't "know from nothing!"

And Cooking Instructions—Once I asked my own mother how long to cook a certain piece of meat and what did she say? "Rose, you cook it 'til it's done."

A Soldier's Mother—One year, we had a soldier stationed in Tooele who came up to me. Put his arms around me, and I'll never forget what he said as long as I live. "You're too young to be my mother," he said. "But my mother always put her arms around me and kissed me just before we went to Kol Nidre services. I don't know if I'll be here next week." You see, he must have gotten his orders. "But I just want to put my arms around and kiss somebody's mother," he said. "Might it as well be you?" I cried, and he cried right along with me.

A Promise Kept—In 1957, my mother was ill and suddenly died. I had promised to look after my father and my bachelor brother. My dad had felt the whole word had gone under. We didn't want them to go and live alone or anything like that. And so this house needed to be where our family could gather. That's why, when the kids were teenagers, we moved back into my parents' home. As difficult as it was bringing teenagers into a quiet home, it was an asset, too, to have my children and a very wonderful husband. He was very good to my dad and the children saw the respect and honor that we gave to my father, and they learned from that.

Living with Grandpa—Still, it was very hard, living under one roof and being a wife, a mother, a daughter and a sister all at the same time. My first obligation was to my husband and it was hard to divide my attention. At the time my son was almost nineteen years old and my daughter was about fifteen. We never left Dad alone at night. If my husband and I went out, and my daughter had a date, my son took over and stayed home. Boys would come around, ask him to go out and have a coke with them and he'd say, "No, we're with Grandpa." And he stayed with him. I think that was really wonderful. When my son did go out, then my brother stayed home. My dad drove a car until he was eighty-three years old; he died at eighty-four.

Two Good Men—My husband was very helpful. When I complained, he'd say, "Now, look. You said you'd take care of your Daddy. This is how it is and this is how it's going to be and this is how you've got to do. My own father didn't live long enough for that, to see us all grown. So that's what children have to do." I guess he was right. It was hard at first, but God was good to me. We took care of my father, and then after he died, my brother, who never married, stayed with us. After my husband died, my brother helped me. He took up driving me to synagogue, and helping in the house. When he died, I felt like a widow again. I cancelled my Passover order this year, because I still have kosher meat from the last order.

A Kosher Home—I realized last November [1983] would have been fifty years we were married and I've always kept a kosher home. I used to kid my husband. That he told me he loved me, asked me to marry him, and keep a kosher home all in one breath. I thought I better say yes before he asks me for anything else.

IT'S IN THE BAG

I. J. Wagner

Serfs—You could call them serfs, my parents.[1] That's the way every Jewish person lived on farms in Russia. Farms were owned by barons, barons were under the rule of czar, and Jews, who couldn't own land, worked the land and paid taxes with their crops. My mother lived in Kraslava, Latvia, just a hundred miles southwest of the capitol of Riga. Her family grew potatoes. Their farm was right by a river, where they used to bathe. There were three brothers and four sisters. They also had a little bar on the farmhouse, and made a little bit of money. Soldiers would come in; my mother's parents would feed them. Some of the soldiers were German and they taught my mother German. She also spoke Russian, Latvian, Yiddish, Hebrew, and good broken English.

Tour of Duty—My mother's sister Mary was married to Abe Karras. For six years, Uncle Abe was in the army, where if you're Jewish you're always a private no matter what you do. After his tour of duty was over, instead of letting him leave the service, they made him enlist for another six years, so he took off to America with Mary. They went to Boston where Mary opened a little grocery store in an apartment building, you know, on the ground level. Then she opened another one in Newton, just outside of Boston, and another at the beach in Revere. In the long run, they made a good living.

A New Life—My mother Rose must have been maybe twenty-two years old when she decided she had had enough. Their mother had passed away, and my brother Abe remembers hearing a story that Rose may have been speaking out against the czar, got into a little trouble, and had to get away. So she came to America with her youngest sister Ethel in 1907. They went to Mary's house and slept on the floor for maybe a couple of weeks until they got their own place in a boarding house and a job at a shoe factory in Jamaica Plain. My mother marked the shoe buttons; my aunt sewed them on. Mother didn't like the work, but three dollars a week was a good wage, and she always said one thing. "I'd rather sleep on the floor in America than on a silk bed in Europe." That was her statement. Why? Because she was finally free to say what she wanted.

I. J. and Abe Wagner and their parents in horse and wagon. (Courtesy of I. J. Wagner)

And being Jewish didn't seem to make any difference to anybody, at the time. In the summer on Sundays, they'd make a sandwich and take the streetcar down to Boston Commons and listen to the band. That was my mother's big deal. She always loved music. And she was glad to be in America.

So that's how Rose got here. Then she met my father, who was from Vilna Goberna, near Kiev in Ukraine. Dad had six sisters and was the only boy. He was good looking and spoiled. After he arrived in America, he went to Lawrence, Massachusetts and opened up a fruit market. He didn't do well and moved into Boston; he found a room at the same boarding house where my mother and aunt were. It was there that he befriended Mr. Harris, who was in finance of some kind. I guess they kind of helped each other out, because when Mr. Harris went to Portland looking for work, he kept in touch with Dad.

My parents married, but Dad didn't have a job. I guess he did have few bucks, though, because after Mr. Harris sent word about job opportunities in Portland, my parents got on a train and went to Portland. Dad rented a horse and wagon and got into the express business, picking up people and their luggage. Soon after, Mr. Harris moved on to Salt Lake and into the house on 144 West Broadway. When my folks came, they moved to a house on 4th South and

5th East. Across the street, Isadore Coleman had a grocery store. He was a good man who gave my parents a dollar's worth of credit.

A Bowl of Soup—My mother was five feet tall, always smiling, and a meticulous housekeeper. She was good to people. People getting off the freight trains, many of them out of work, would stop by her house and knock on the door. She was always ready with some soup, a piece of bread, or fruit. She donated to the Orthodox Jewish men who were traveling west, soliciting funds for Israel. She was heart-broken to learn that her three brothers had been killed by the Nazis during the Second World War. They had stayed behind with their father; they never wanted to leave like she did. During that time, my mother also discovered she wasn't an American citizen. She was so determined to get her citizenship papers, she not only ran the business during the day, but she studied late into the night. This was going on during the time her husband died and she was left alone with teenage sons trying to make ends meet.

Finding Work—Times were hard for my parents, even in the early years, but my mother always had a lot of spirit. When I was six months, I was told she would carry me to the silent movies at Mahesy Theatre, half a block from the house. That's now the Clift Building and the Broadway Theatre. But I'm getting ahead of myself. Soon after my parents arrived here, Dad got the horse and wagon from Fisher Stables for about six dollars. Then he'd go down to the Denver and Rio Grande Depot. People didn't have cars, and if they were carrying heavy luggage, Dad would stop and pick them up. Dad had a little sign that said *Express* and he'd take the passengers and their trunks uptown, because the little hotels were all on 3rd South. There was the Rio Grande Hotel, the Boston Hotel, the Wasatch Hotel, and the Rex Hotel. I think the Rex Hotel was the site of the first synagogue. It had a lot of rooms and a big porch in front. I don't know what they called the synagogue.[2] When Dad needed extra help carrying luggage into the hotel, he'd pick up Jack Dempsey, a young kid, who would be playing pool, and the two of them would lug the suitcases and bundles into the building.

So that's the way my Dad started in business. Then one day, he went into the grocery store and moved potatoes; he helped the owner out by dumping 100-pound burlap potato bags into a bin so that customers could buy one or two pounds of potatoes at a time. After he did that, Dad asked the owner, "What are you going to do with these empty potato bags?"

The owner said, "You've done a good job, Harry. You take those down to the junk yard and they'll buy them from you." So Dad picked up about eighty bags, and he got four dollars. My God, he thought, that's more than he made all day long picking up passengers from the depot.

So, my mother said, "What happened?" He said, "I made all this money." She said, "It must be a mistake. See if they'll buy some more." He said, "I ain't got no more." She said, "See if you can get some more from other grocery stores." That's how my Dad started picking up empty bags.

Chutzpah—The next thing my mother does, she tells Dad to find out what the junkyard does with the bags. She said, "Buy a package of cigarettes for the man unloading the bags." A pack of

The Wagner family in Salt Lake with Abe (*left*) and Izzy. (Courtesy of I. J. Wagner)

cigarettes costs about eight or nine cents. "Ask him what they do with the empty bags," she told my Dad. So he found out they sold them to Bailey & Sons Seed Company, which is now about the middle of the block between Regent Street and State Street on 2nd South. She said, "What do they do with them?" When he found out they used some of them for seeds and took about five thousand others up to Globe Mills in Ogden, she told him, "Why don't you go up to the mill and see if they'll buy them from you."

That's how it started. Mr. Harris, who had gone into the finance business in the old adobe house, moved on to California; this time, we stayed in Salt Lake and moved into the adobe house. Owned by the Peery Estate, out of Ogden, we rented it from them. I think it must have been a polygamist home at one time. It was all on one level, no basement, no second floor, but lots of rooms with coal stoves and a front porch where we slept in the summer.

Pool-Hall Baths, Spigots, and Lilac Trees—If you walked in by the front door, the living room on one side of the hallway had a davenport that opened, and we had a bedroom. There were two or three other bedrooms on the left side of the house and a kitchen towards the back. We had no water in the house. We used a cast iron spigot out in the front. Nearby were lilac trees. In the winter, we wrapped the spigot in burlap so it wouldn't freeze and break. Mother would heat the water in a pot on the stove, pour it into a galvanized tub and bathe us little kids. When we got older, why, three or four years old, Mother would march us up to the Japanese pool hall on 1st South, behind the Salt Palace, what is now the Japanese Buddhist church. It was a public pool hall with a bathtub in another room. Two of us could go in at a time. We'd bring our own towels and soap, wash up, get dressed, and watch them shoot pool while Mother took her turn bathing. Mr. Fugio (Fudge) Iwasaki's father and uncle owned the business. Fudge now owns the Pagoda Restaurant on the Avenues. His family was always very good to us.

At home, we had a pull chain toilet up in the back and my mother bought a gas hot water tank for the house. Eventually, we put a bathtub in the house, and a shower. When the lilacs were blooming, my mother would put up a sign: "Lilacs for Sale." People could pick a bouquet for a nickel. You know, a nickel could bring you a loaf of bread. Ten cents could buy you a quart of milk and gas was—what—nine cents a gallon. In 1938 or 1939 we moved to Sugarhouse. I remember that. Mom wanted to get out into the country. So, that's the way it was.

Fishing—When my dad was alive, he'd go fishing for carp. He was a good fisherman and some of the Jewish fellows, Abe Mishkind, his dad was a peddler, and Abe Moskowitz, who had a fruit market, and other guys you wouldn't know today, would go along with him. In the 1920s and 1930s, 1st South and West Temple had a row of Japanese and Jewish stores. That's where we shopped. Well, I went many times with my Dad to fish Surplus Canal. The canal was just west of Jordan River, where we'd swim. Sometimes my pals and I would walk all the way down to the Canal or hop a freight train out to the Morton Salt Company, jump off when the cars stopped at Morton Salt, and go swimming in the saltwater ponds. We lost one fellow doing that. He fell off the train and got killed.

Friends—Our home playground was Pioneer Park at 3rd South and 3rd West. There were two swimming pools, one for the boys and one for the girls. Sometimes we'd have diving contests and the Pioneer Park Swimming Team would swim against the Liberty Park team. We had a place where we could play checkers, and two softball fields. At nearby Central Park, between 2nd South and 3rd East, on the north side of the street, we competed in teams. On my team there was the Downing boy, T. Diamond, three Eccles boys, not related to the Ogden Eccles, a kid named Cole, four brothers who were black, and an Italian, Henri Milano. I was the only Jew there. I've known Milano since I was twelve years old. His mother had the Elms Hotel, which is now the parking lot for the New Yorker Restaurant. She rented rooms for thirty-five or seventy-five cents a night. He played the accordion. Thirty years later, this childhood friend—he's still living—became vice president of Wagner Corporation.

Unfair Practices—Well, we had a hedge maybe three feet high all around the park, and a pavilion on Sundays where we would listen to a band or see silent movies. Charlie Chaplin was in some of them. When my mother learned we were going to the movies, she called us "candy cowboys." I don't remember those movies costing anything. But we used to go to the Victory Theatre. Cost a nickel or a dime. We'd play with kids at Pioneer Park and then we'd go to the matinee. The Black kids we played with would have to go upstairs. We never knew why. We didn't think about it. When we were kids, nobody thought about it, never questioned it. When it finally dawned on us what was happening to our friends, making them go to what they called "nigger heaven," we thought that was awful. Here we'd play together, go swimming together, go to the parks, and go into the movie theatre together. It made no sense that once there, the Black kids would have to go upstairs. Afterwards, we'd just meet up and go back to the park to play. None of us ever questioned it then. What a terrible shame.

Jewish Boxers—So that's what we did; and we boxed. I had three fights in McCullough's Arena on 9th South and Main. Mr. McCullough had a gym, a grocery store, and quite a few other things. In those days there were a lot of Jewish boxers. Max Baer was the World Boxing Association's heavyweight champion of the world in 1934. Barney Ross was a welterweight world champion boxer. I think he actually held two titles. I was in the Marine Corps with him. Boxed with him once, kind of a training session. It was a little bit rough; although he said he was supposed to take it easy with me. Locally, we had Imey Garfinkle and Abe Mishkind, my Dad's friend.

Floating on Salt—When my Dad was alive, he took Abe and me fishing. He'd take us for rides in his 1927 Lincoln. We'd go to Murray, which was like going out to the country. He'd take us to Saltair where the water used to come up almost to the road. You'd walk down the pavilion stairs and step right into the lake. You couldn't sink because it was almost 22 percent salt. You could go to sleep, if you wanted. You could stretch out on your back, float on the water, and go to sleep. Dances were held in the pavilion. We had Phil Harris and his orchestra coming through; all the big bands came through Salt Lake City to play. For a time, the pavilion had the largest dance floor in the United States, I think, and there were restaurants, giant racers, and all kinds of rides, like Lagoon. The Democrats had their day at Saltair, and we'd all go out there for picnics. I imagine the Republicans had their day too.

Big Bands—Bamberger's train would take you out to Saltair. From right on 2nd South, you'd pay maybe ten cents or fifteen cents and ride out there. Then you'd pay something to get in. Now, this is when I was older, see. There'd be a stag night when single girls would stand in front of the band and you'd walk up to a girl and ask, "May I have this dance?" On Monday nights, they did that at the Coconut Grove, on 4th South and Main. Now I'm talking about Prohibition, in the '20s and '30s, so there wasn't any legal liquor then. I remember later when I saw Bing Crosby for the first time. He and his trio had a show in the Ambassador on Wilshire Boulevard, singing with Paul Whiteman and his orchestra. A lot of people enjoyed the music. Liberty Park also had musicians playing; and every Sunday, Held's band, a group of local musicians, would play. Mother would love to go hear them. She'd sit and listen to the music.

In the Aisles—We used to go swimming at Warm Springs, around 3rd West and 8th North across from the old Holy Cross Hospital, where my Dad died. He was young; fifty-two years old. Warm Springs had a bathhouse with lockers, and a good size outdoor swimming pool. Beck's Hot Springs was another good place to go. A good many Jews were there, usually, those who belonged to Congregation Montefiore or Shaarey Tzedek. Speaking of the old *shul,* Shaarey Tzedek, there used to be a basement where they'd have programs and floor shows. My sister Leona and I played a duet on the violin. I still think about that. We had them in the aisles! They were leaving.

I went to the Fremont School, then junior high school, which became the Horace Mann School—it's gone now—and graduated from West High. I don't remember any other Jewish kids in my class except for Max Grobstein and Rachel Garelick, whose parents had a junk yard on Edison Street below 9th South. Rachel died when she was about sixteen years old.

I did get in a couple of fights, whenever anybody called me "Christ-killer," but the teachers treated us all good; and once in a while, I figured, if you had to fight, you did and nobody bothered you after that. In school, we didn't think in terms of being Jewish or Mormon. At Christmas, you'd stand in line for a little gift from the Elks Lodge. At home, we were kosher. I remember my brother Abe bought kosher bacon and then decided to buy the real thing. Dad ate it and when he found it was real bacon, he threw a glass full of water at my brother, he was so furious.

A Lesson—I think the first shul was on 202 First South West. It was an old house across from the Rex Rooms. I don't recall the name of it. It was a big wooden structure, with a porch. I remember that, but when we were young, Alfred Klein and I went to heder at Montefiore. The Rosen brothers, Milton and Ted, their family had a clothing store, went to heder with me. I got kicked out. No, I ran out. The Hebrew teacher hit me on the hand with a ruler. He should have been an orchestra leader. I took off and I never went back. My brother Abe stayed in and had a bar mitzvah, and always went to synagogue. My sister Leona had a bat mitzvah. Later, when I could drive, I'd take my mother and Mrs. Harry Guss to synagogue. But when I was seven, I wasn't having anything to do with getting hit. I was out of there.

I don't remember any other Jews living where we did, but a lot of Jewish families lived in Custer Court. In 1926, the Kleins, my friend Sidney Klein; Benjamin Ramo, Si Ramo's dad; and William Goldenberg lived there. Mrs. Millie Levy and Adolph Berkowitz lived in the Custer Apartments, and in Custer Annex there was Benjamin Arnovitz.

Buying Bags—My mother was a good cook. She made *tzimmes* and gefilte fish, and chicken. Mostly chicken. We raised chickens in the back yard. There was no zoning so there was nothing to worry about. Even when it came to manufacturing. See, what happened was my dad started bringing bags in from peddlers like Herschel Guss, Max and Hymie Guss's dad. That's because by the time Mr. Guss finished his work, he couldn't make it to the junkyard before closing time, so my Dad would buy up the bags. If anybody had bottles, Dad would buy bottles. Ketchup bottles we bought. In fact, we'd get a truckload of ketchup bottles and take them down to Springville Canning Company. They weren't plastic then. They'd wash them and refill them. We'd pick up empty whiskey and brown beer bottles from the bellhops at hotels and take them over to Becker Brewing Company in Ogden or to Fisher Brewing in Salt Lake, whoever would give us the best price. So we made a little on that. We'd buy anything the peddlers had to offer.

Recycling—Today, we would be called "recyclers." We'd take burlap bags and clean them ourselves. One worker would put the bag on two broomsticks, turn it inside out, and another person would take it off and the dust would fall out. Couldn't wash them; burlap would shrink, and then you couldn't use them. We bought and resold fruit jars and old batteries. Automobile batteries. Peddlers would come to us because we paid as much as the junkyard did. We had a fellow on South State Street, just below 9th South, who rebuilt batteries. We'd take them over to him. My brother Abe would go down every six months or so and buy old torn overalls from the prison, which was down on 21st South and 13th East, where Highland Park is today. Then we'd take the overalls to American Linen where they'd be cleaned and cut up for grease rags in service stations. We'd go to Pillsbury, which was Globe Mills at the time, and buy all the broken white flour bags. After we saved a ton of them, we'd take them down to American Linen. They'd take the one good side and make a dish towel out of it and tear up the other side for wiping rags.

Two-Cent Bags—Sweet Candy Company, one of the few Jewish-owned companies still in business today after a hundred years, used to give school kids a tour, and show us how they made candy. Before we left, they'd give us a little candy bar of chocolate. Later, we got their business, buying up their empty sugar bags and chocolate bags, and finding a market for them. The sugar bags we'd sell to seed stores; we'd sell potato bags to farmers, and then we'd buy the empty bags from potato chip manufacturers like Clover Club. Depending on the year, we'd pay two cents, three cents, and sell them back to farmers for four cents. The chocolate bags were big, heavy, and blue-striped. We sold them to a company in Vernal who used them to package batteries made out of Gilsonite.[3]

Nothing went to waste. If somebody in the neighborhood moved, my mother would buy all the furniture and resell it. She sold barrels, bottles, and oil drums, even though a lot of people were doing barrels then. The Peppers had Utah Barrel and Isadore Eisen had American Barrel. They were brothers-in-law and competitors.

Building Blocks—The first Wagner Bag Company was in the old adobe house. Maybe four or five women worked there with my mother, and for a long time, all our extra rooms were full of empty bags. If we weren't out looking for them, peddlers would drop them off at the house. My dad built a wooden hand baler that would press down two hundred fifty bags at a time. You'd put wire through them and make a bale. We bought a patching machine from Ben Redman of Redman Van and Storage. One of the women would cut up torn bags and use the material for mending holes in other bags. I think we paid her a dollar a day. Later, we built some galvanized iron sheds in the back. My Dad built up the business. He'd go out to Los Angeles and buy carloads of bags and sell them in Utah and Idaho.

Bread Lines—When I was thirteen or fourteen years old, I started working for Maurice Warshaw, whose real name was Moishe Warshawsky, at his Grand Central Market every summer. I worked there with Asher Moskowitz, Abe's son. I sold fruit and got fifteen dollars a week for fourteen hours a day, and that was all right with me. I was tickled to death to have a job. After all, how many people could get jobs during the depression? There were long bread lines, and here I had a job. I saved money and went on in school where I played football and basketball and was the sports writer for the school paper.

During the depression there wasn't enough money to pay teachers, so we graduated after two years in high school. I went to the University for two weeks in 1932. I was seventeen years old and was going to be a lawyer. In that year, 1932, my dad died of cancer and I had to quit school. We didn't take out bankruptcy, but we owed Utah Savings and Trust $6,000. Mom never missed a beat. She took over the business and got all of us working in the company. We made the living room into an office, put up used brick on the outside of the house, and painted a sign that said, The Wagner Bag Company. Some of our workers were miners like Houghey McCarten and Tobin O'Reilly who were good workers but had trouble finding jobs. One of our best men, Joe Moran, had been a cook in a mining camp. A streetcar ran over his toe, took it off, so he stayed with us. Mom gave out room and board for labor and an additional dollar a day. She kept the overhead low. She paid off the debts.

Push-Button Heat—Around 1939, we moved to Sugarhouse to 2121 South 10th East. We had a furnace that all you had to do was press a button and you'd have heat. At the other place, the adobe house, you had to put paper and kindling, and coal into a coal stove. Then you'd have to get up at three o'clock in the morning and add more coal to keep us warm.

More Building Blocks—I started buying property when I was around nineteen. I put a down payment on the adobe house, paid about fifty dollars a month on it, and soon my mother, brother, sister, and I owned Wagner Investment Company. When I came back from the service, we kept building on, building on, buying another piece of equipment, another piece of land. In later years, we bought the building next door, which used to be the Carver Sheet Metal Company. We bought the parking lot around the Peery Hotel. Then we bought property west of that. My wife Jeanné loaned us sixty-five hundred dollars to buy that piece of property, which is funny because that's where the Jeanné Wagner Theatre is built, on that same piece of property that she helped us buy. The building now belongs to Salt Lake County.

Jeanné—I met Jeanné Rasmussen when I worked at the Hotel Utah, on the roof. Jeanné Dore, that was her stage name. Mrs. Robins, one of the booking agents, called her at home. She was on vacation after working the circuit. She wanted to relax, but her agent insisted. When I saw her dance, I thought she was a beautiful woman and a good dancer. I asked her if she would mind a call from me. She gave me her name, her stage name, and of course, I couldn't find it in the Polk Directory.

A little while later, I was at the Brass Rail, a small club, waiting to meet a friend of mine when I saw someone dancing. I looked closer and it was Jeanné. I tapped her partner on the shoulder, and cut in. "Do you mind?" I asked. Well, she and I started talking and there wasn't anybody after that. Jeanné and I were married August of 1942. The morning I went overseas with the Marine Corps, I didn't see my perfect wife for almost two years. In the fifty-one years we were married, we never had an argument. She was born Mormon. I was born Jewish. That was never a problem with us. And I'll tell you, she would never let anyone say an anti-Semitic remark without speaking up against it. My mother loved her.

The Marines—I was twenty-six years old when I enlisted in the Marine Corps. I went down to the Post Office on 4th South and Main. There were three of us. Morris Epstein, Aaron Skolnick, and I. We knew about Hitler, about the camps. I thought I was going to fight the Germans. First I went to New Zealand. I was at the Second Marine Corps headquarters in Guadalcanal working in the general's office. When the bombs came from the air, we were all scared. I mean, you never really expect it. We had dugouts, and of course we never used electricity at night, no lights, just candles. But the bombs were something else. I had many attacks of malaria. It's ironic that a mosquito bite probably saved my life. I'd get malaria, have to go to the hospital, get discharged, go back to work, and get sick again. Just before leaving for duty, I was in the hospital again and my division went on without me. Most of them became casualties.

Changes—Over the years, Wagner Bag Company went through a lot of changes. We were making flour bags, potato bags, cement bags, new cotton bags, and new burlap bags. I was going to India to buy burlap, which is made from fibers of the jute plant. The workers would harvest it, soak it in water until they could get the fiber out of it and weave it into burlap. We'd buy millions of yards, and our machines would knock out twenty thousand bags a day.

We bought a hand-feeding machine out of Louisville, Kentucky that printed bags in two colors, and we bought a cut-and-fold machine. Sewers would stitch up the sides. Workers would count them, and put three hundred and sixty in a bale, because three hundred and sixty empty bags weighed one hundred pounds. When they were full of potatoes, they'd weigh thirty-six thousand pounds. Our territory covered Utah, Idaho, where we had an office in Twin Falls, a little bit of Wyoming, and Colorado. There was a time when we had a few hundred people working for us. Of course, by this time we were in another building. When the war came along, burlap was no longer available from India. Afterwards, someone figured how to eliminate bags completely and go directly from loaded trucks to receiving flour mill elevators. That's when Abe and I decided to sell the business to St. Regis Paper Company and go into a new direction. That's what I did; that's what I'm doing now.

WOLFES IN THE WEST

Michael Wolfe

In a Name—My great-grandfather, Elias Wolfe, was the first immigrant in my family to get here.[1] My grandfather Hubert was born here. My father Elliott was born here. I was born here as was my son, Mathew, the fourth generation Wolfe.

My great-grandfather's parents were Nathan and Sarah Reva Wolper. They were innkeepers and had a mill and a little farm in Vieksniai, Lithuania. Their primary business, however, was running a large ferry across the river where they lived. How they got from Wolper to Wolfe is an interesting story that my grandfather's sister, Ida [Levy], used to love to tell.

"It happened this way," she said. "In my grandparents' day, if a boy of a large family was bright, and his parents could not afford to give him a higher education, it was the custom for a wealthy family to adopt him and send him to a yeshiveh to become a rabbi or a scholar. The family that adopted Elias was named Wolfe. And that's how we got the name."

It seems not only did Elias get a good education, the name Wolfe served him well. It saved him from being conscripted into the army. Registering for the army under the family name of Wolper, when he came of age, his name was Wolfe, and the Russians could never find a boy named Elias Wolper.

Imported Jews—My great grandmother's family, the Katz family, was brought into Kurland, Latvia, by German barons to facilitate commerce. The Jews were always good peddlers and merchants and money handlers, and so they were bringing Jews out of the Pale to work for them. I know there was a lot of anti-Semitism then, but I think it wasn't as true for the Katz family since they were "imported Jews" who lived on the baron's estates, in what was like a village.

Elias was educated in the major cultural city of Vilnius. He married Etta Lena [Katz] in 1884; it was the result of an arranged marriage. There had been a surge of pogroms in that period of time, and I don't know how Elias left the country, but I did learn that Etta sneaked out by dressing in peasant clothes on the outside and wearing her good clothes underneath.

They had two children in the old country, and they did get to London. Since they didn't have enough money to get the entire family over to America at one time, they left for America separately: Elias in 1889 and Etta with the children Nathan and Abraham in 1891. Elias went first to Minneapolis to see one of his brothers. He didn't stay long because he had another brother, Morris Wolper, who didn't change his name, living in Salt Lake City. I would say Morris was one of the original Jewish mountain men. He was a fur trader, trading with the Indians.

Etta in America—When Etta arrived in America, she went to see her brother in Baltimore. She then went on to Salt Lake where she joined her husband. At first, Elias tried to be a *shochet,* but I don't think there was any money in being a *shochet,* so he became a peddler, going door to door selling. His brother, Morris, moved to Blackfoot, Idaho and I think Elias spent a lot of time with him, working there, too, because the family said he was gone a lot of the time.

I'm sure he had a horse and buggy, and he was around when Grandpa (Hubert) was born. There's a story that Hubert's sister actually delivered him. The family was living out on 9th West and 4th South. The story is that Elias hitched up the horse and wagon to go into town to get a doctor because Etta was in labor, and by the time they got back, Hubert was already born [1899] and his oldest sister, Rachel, was the midwife. She must have been seven years old at the time.

Etta was a kind, strong woman who did what needed to be done. She was generous. She had bread for the Indians when they'd come by her home. Even though the family had little money, she always had a little something for homeless or destitute people.

Elias was a better scholar than a businessman and the family moved around the country quite a number of times. They had six children in Salt Lake, and two in Cleveland. They spent some time in Portland, Oregon, where the family opened a men's haberdashery and clothing store, and then moved to Chicago to open up a dairy store. The eighth child, Reva, was born there in 1901.

Hot Goose Fat and Salt—There was a story told about how Etta had been sent to the hospital in Chicago because she had fainted on the street. Reva was just an infant and the family had to get a wet nurse to take care of her. While Etta was in the hospital, she was asked to nurse a baby whose mother had diphtheria. She did and apparently brought the germs home with her. Everyone in the family, except for Jack and Ida, got sick, quarantined for three months. Nat and Hubert were sent to the hospital. Nat was sent home. He was sick, but not as bad off as Hubert. The doctors said they couldn't do anything more for Hubert. Etta said her son was going to live, and she nursed him through it. What she did was heat some goose fat, put some salt in a woolen sock, dipped the sock in the fat and put it on Hubert's throat. He gave one loud gasp, which is what she wanted, and it opened his windpipe, and got air into his lungs. She saved his life. Hubert lived to be almost ninety-nine years old.

After Hubert got better, Etta went home and took care of Nat. Put him in a big tin bathtub, surrounded by chairs, filled it with just hot-enough water, spread sheets over the top to trap whatever steam was inside, and he got better, too. The house had to be fumigated. Everybody was put behind closed doors in the back rooms. In the front rooms, they hooked up some clothes lines, hung sheets and bed clothing over them, and sprayed them with disinfectant.

Finding Work—At the time, Elias hadn't been in town, and when he did come back, everything was over, everybody was well. Again they moved. This time to Minneapolis to run a bakery. They lived near the shop, upstairs over a feed store, and then they moved into a house. But it seemed that every time the Wolfes left Utah, they would come back. Elias liked it here, and I know Etta took in boarders to help pay the rent when Elias wasn't around. They bought a brick house on 7th South near 7th East and my great grandmother built a barn in the back for a cow and a horse. She built the structure herself. Then she built a summerhouse cold enough to hold the milk, and dug a cellar for storage and canned foods. In 1907, her last child, Jerry, was born.

I don't know if Etta kept a kosher home. I know she made gefilte fish, though, with my grandfather's fish. He'd slough religious school, heder, and go fishing out at Jordan River. He'd bring in a mess of fish and get scolded for missing school. Then, she'd make use of the fish. Fishing always played an interesting role in my grandpa's life.

A Divorce in the Family—Etta worked hard, keeping the household going, but Elias never could make a living. Everyone said his nose was always in a book. But I'm sure she had a better life in America than she would have had in the old country, and I'm pretty sure he was quite a charming man. But it was a hard life for Etta. After twenty-two years of marriage, in 1907, my great-grandparents divorced.

Almost everyone went to work then to help out. Those who were in school had to get out. Most of the children only went to the sixth grade. Grandpa went to the eighth grade. His older siblings were tailors, newspaper salesmen, or they did odd jobs, like chopping wood. The girls became seamstresses. So, in this environment, my grandpa grows up, and they live in about four or five different houses between 9th West and 4th South and 7th East, and up on G Street. They probably didn't get as far as 21st South, that was real country then, almost a hundred years ago. Once I asked him, point blank, "Grandpa, how come you moved so much?" He looked at me, smiled and said, "Every time the rent was due, we moved." It was a hard life, great-grandmother on her own with six children living at home by then.

Newsies!—My grandpa sold papers as a kid for the *Tribune.* He had a street corner, and he would fight over the corner with his brother Jack. Jack was older so he would pound him and tell him to get the hell out of there. "This is my corner." And my grandpa Hubert would start crying and when he cried, everybody would buy the papers from him. They felt so sorry for him. [Laughs.]

Wolfe Brothers Store—Nat and Abe, the oldest two, had moved out. They were following the miners, setting up little stores out in places like Eureka and in Bingham Canyon. In some towns, they put up tents and sold shovels and mining gear, things like that. Nathan was a good businessman, and when he and Abe stopped selling to miners, they came back to Salt Lake and

Wolfe's and Wolfe's, 1920. (Courtesy of Jeff Wolfe)

started the Wolfe Brothers store. The two of them did that. They put up a store on Regent Street and then moved it to 225 South State Street.

I don't know exactly when Etta left Salt Lake for Cleveland, but I'm sure her brothers were helping to support her. Grandpa went with her at first. But he wasn't a city boy. He got in a fight and punched in the nose. When his nose started bleeding, it wouldn't stop for a long time. He ended up in the hospital, and Ida said it took almost three months for him to recuperate. That must have been miserable for him. He just wanted out of there. He wanted to be with his father and his brothers. So as soon as he could, he and his older brother Jack got on a train and headed West. Well, they got lost or else they fell asleep, and wound up in the wrong part of the country. They didn't have a train ticket, so they were hopping trains. They slept in barns a lot, he told me, and they chopped wood for a month to get here. It must have been quite an adventure for those two boys, but Hubert was a tough guy. He took after his mother, and she was a very strong-minded woman.

Hubert was very disciplined. I think if you're growing up with a single woman who has a lot of kids, you have to pitch in and help with the family. So you become independent. Even when he ended up living with his father, although the father wasn't there very often, he still had to be able to get on by himself. His father out peddling, not making much of a living. So I think fishing became very important to my grandpa. He said they had to go fishing so they could eat.

Hubert in Business—Hubert lived with his father or with his older brothers. During World War I, Hubert and Jack signed up and went into the army together. Hubert was sixteen years old. He was sent to France. He told me when he was there he mailed half of his checks back to his mother in Cleveland. At this time, his father, Elias, was in Blackfoot, Idaho. By 1919 or 1920, Grandpa was back and had his own store in Pocatello, Idaho. He described it as a nine-foot by nine-foot hole-in-the-wall store.

Jack had a family by then. They were living in Pocatello, too, working with Hubert. Around 1924 or '25, Abe and Nat called and said they needed someone to manage their Ogden store. So Hubert gave the Idaho store to his brother, and moved down to Ogden to work in the store. It was called Wolfe's Brothers, and was one of several stores the older brothers had. A short time later, Jack's store failed. His wife had taken ill and he was always taking care of the three babies that he had. Eventually he moved to Ogden and worked for my grandfather. Abe then decided he wanted to go to California, so Grandpa bought him out. Nat got sick and moved to California, too, so Grandpa bought him out. They closed down a couple of stores and got to the building at 225 South State Street. I believe it was in 1927 when Grandpa decided he was tired of selling ladies dresses and straw hats, and turned the store into a sporting goods store.

A Wedding Match—First, though, I want to tell you about the time, years earlier, when Nat went to Winnipeg, Canada, met my Uncle Ed Mitchell, and did some jewelry business with him. He made about twenty-five thousand dollars, which was a lot of money back then, and married Ed's sister. So he comes back with the money and my Aunt Augusta. A few years later, they have my Cousin Bud Wolfe and then about ten years later, after World War I, Augusta's sister, Shirley Mitchell, comes out to Utah and marries my grandpa. That's how it worked: brothers from one family married sisters of another.

Well, Grandpa married Shirley in 1926, and I think that's about the same time he changed the store. He told me he was doing eighty thousand dollars a year, but when he switched to sporting goods—skis, fishing rods, wool shirts, swimwear—his first year sales went down to forty thousand dollars and he didn't think he was going to survive. Dad was born in 1927, so Grandpa had a very young family and it was a pretty bold move for him to make a switch in merchandise. But he did it, and the store prospered. When my Dad, Elliott, became the owner of Wolfe's Sportsman's Headquarters, he had the drive my grandpa had, and like his father, a love of sports.

Love of Sports—I never knew Nat Wolfe. He died when he was in his sixties, the only one of the ten children that died young. I think he had rheumatic fever when he was a child and it caused heart problems. But all the rest lived into their late eighties or early nineties. And they all liked sports.

The outdoorsman Hubert Wolfe. (Courtesy of Michael Wolfe)

Hubert was an outdoorsman: fishing, hunting, skiing, riding horses. They fished all over the Intermountain West, and in every river they fly-fished. All the family trips were spent fishing. I think he took up golf later in life. In 1921, Grandpa went to Yellowstone. He rented a Model T Ford and drove it up over the Teton Pass into Yellowstone, stayed at a camp way over on Jackson Lake. It was pretty primitive up there, but Grandpa just liked being outside. He and his friends would pack in on horseback to the Wind River Mountains in Wyoming. My earliest memory is they were getting ready for a big pack trip into the mountains, this would have been around 1960, and he had his dogs with him. He was fascinated with dogs and training dogs. That was his big love, besides fishing.

Potato Salad—Jewish fishermen are not uncommon. You either love it or you don't like it at all. Most fishermen around here became catch-and-release fishermen—they didn't need to eat the fish anymore. But all of them felt there's nothing more calming or relaxing than just being outside with your family and friends. Before leaving on a trip, they always made a big deal out of going over to Lou Dornbush's delicatessen to get the potato salad and the corned beef sandwiches.[2] Everything had to be just right. They might have complained about the price, but they went back every single time. They loved his potato salad better than anybody else's.

Hubert—My Grandpa walked every day. Never missed a day. He told me he weighed one hundred fifty-three pounds when he got out of the army in 1918. And most of his life, that's what he weighed. When he had his dogs, he was always walking with a dog. When he didn't have dogs, he'd walk the entire Salt Lake Country Club every single day at 6:00 A.M. He lived right next to the Club. I think Grandpa took care of everybody in his family. His father was not much of a businessman. He'd rather be reading, they'd say. But Hubert never said anything about him. He would never say a bad word about him. No, Hubert took care of his mother, his sisters, and his brothers. He took care of them all.

Etta and Elias—And my great grandmother Etta? Well, there was a time when Elias got sick with stomach cancer, and my great grandmother took him in. After all those years, she brought him into her home. She didn't know who else would take care of him, so she did. And after he died, she brought him back to Salt Lake City.

SWEET TOOTH

Tony Sweet

Suss to Sweet—That my grandfather happened to get into the candy business and our last name is Sweet is purely coincidental.[1] My grandfather was born in Visalia, California in 1871; and his parents immigrated to the United States from Germany in the late 1840s. My grandfather's father and his great uncle arrived in New York, went to Chicago, and went over the Isthmus of Panama into California. They were in the mining camps during the gold rush of 1848, selling merchandise to miners. After that, they settled in Visalia, and ran a mercantile store that they called Sweets Mercantile Store. The name "Sweets," as far as we know is from the German Suss and then it was changed to Sweet.

Sugar and Rice—My great-grandmother didn't like living in Visalia very much. She spent a lot of her time, nearby, in San Francisco, and that's where my grandfather went to high school. After he graduated, my grandfather met Alfred Saroni, who was in the commodity business in San Francisco: the sugar and rice business. Mr. Saroni was an entrepreneur and he went into business with my grandfather, sent him to Portland, Oregon, where the original Sweet Candy Company was founded in 1892. Mr. Saroni was the major financing arm of the business, and for one reason or another, they decided to close the Oregon company and relocate in Salt Lake City. They came here in the early part of 1900, bought two or three smaller companies for a very, very brief period of time—perhaps three months, and called their business the Salt Lake Candy Company. On May 7, 1900, they were incorporated as the Sweet Candy Company.

Mr. Saroni was Italian, and I think his wife might have been Jewish because they were both involved somewhat in the Jewish community and somehow related to the Zellerbachs. I think one of the reasons they came to Utah was because of the ready supply of sugar. This entire valley used to be planted in sugar beets. Of course, now it's all houses. Another motivator was the fact that the knowledge of the Mormon population and the economic climate indicated that this would be a good place to start a candy business.

Leon and Beatrice—My grandfather's name was Leon. Leon Sweet. My father's name was

Sweet Candy Company, 1917. (Courtesy of Utah State Historical Society)

Leon Jack Sweet. He always went by the name of Jack. He was not a junior. I know that my grandfather didn't like his own name and he wasn't particularly happy about giving it to his son, but his wife, Beatrice, decided that was a good name for him. Beatrice Weirthimer was from the south, Mississippi, but they met in Salt Lake City. She came out to visit a friend up in Ogden. She had a number of Jewish friends here. During that visit, my grandfather and she were introduced and they were married in 1905. They had two children, Emily and my father.

The Sweet Candy Company—Between 1900 and 1909, the Sweet Candy Company was just east near 79 South Main. In 1909, the year my father was born, the company moved to 1st West and Second South, which later became 2nd West and 2nd South. We occupied that building until 1998. When they originally bought the building, it was 40,000 square feet. In 1920, they doubled the size, adding on in 1950 and again in 1982.

The candy business is a good business. In the early days on 2nd West, we used to get corn syrup in rail cars. The cars would be positioned over a spout on a railroad track, a connection

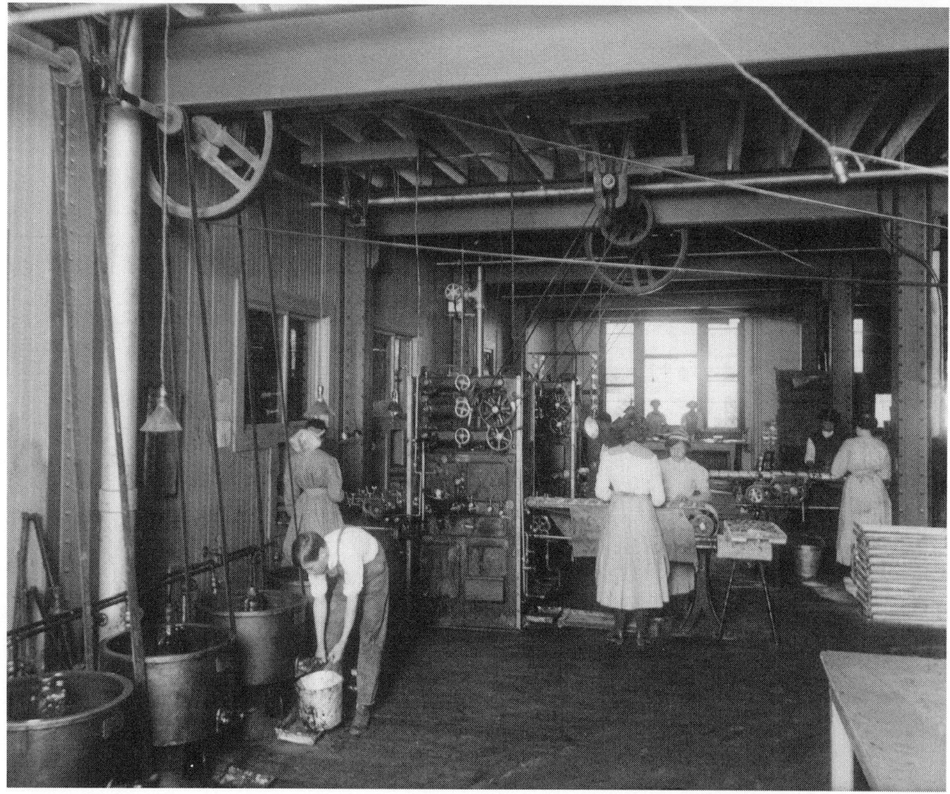

Boxing saltwater taffy. (Courtesy of Utah State Historical Society)

opposite top Making cordials. (Courtesy of Utah State Historical Society)

opposite bottom "Enrobers" and chocolate. (Courtesy of Utah State Historical Society)

fitted, and the syrup would flow by gravity from the railcar into a storage tank. Later, they took out the railroad tracks, and we received corn syrup in tanker trucks.

Making Chocolates—For many years, we made our own chocolate from raw materials. We bought chocolate liquor, which is like bittersweet chocolate, cocoa butter, milk powder, and sugar, blended them and mixed them together. Between 1911 and 1920, there could have been as many as 175 working in the factory. All the candies, all the chocolates, used to be hand dipped.

Cordials—To make cordial cherries, women started with a cherry dipped into a fondant cream. Letting it sit to set up, the cream covered cherry was then hand dipped into chocolate. This action would cause a chemical reaction because the acid in the cherry would break down the fondant cream almost entirely and turn it to a semi-liquid. Fondant is a basic building block of candy. That sweet, delicious, creamy sugar paste that's almost a liquid. Today they do it slightly different but in the old process, this is the way it's done. When women worked with nut meats, they hand dipped them into the fondant cream, put them on trays, stored them on racks to cool and, once dried, hand dipped them in the chocolate, too.

Chocolate-Covered Treasures—We had vats of melting chocolate and *enrobers,* area coaters, used to make chocolate-covered candies. This process involved a line drive with leather belts so that everything came up a common shaft and followed a continuous route. Chocolate coating would be put into a machine that would circulate the chocolate, something like taking a chocolate bath. Agitators stirred the mixture. Ladies would hand feed caramel and nut meats onto an in-feed belt. It would go through the machine where a curtain of chocolate would be released over it, showering both top and bottom with chocolate. The excess chocolate would circulate in the machine until the next drenching. After the candy was transferred through the machine, it would come out onto a tunnel where cold air would cool it.

Caramels—Caramel was poured onto a slab six feet long and three feet wide. It would be run through a caramel cutter, that would cut strips of caramel into square or oblong pieces of candy. A machine wrapped the caramels in waxed paper. Then people packed the wrapped pieces in a wicker tray, starting on the outside and working around and around and around until they got to the inside. It was a beautiful packaging process. My grandfather had a carpenter making wooden boxes, which were then embossed with our name. We also had a handsome array of labels.

Saltwater Taffy—We made a lot of different kinds of candies. My grandfather liked to do candy bars. We did a lot of candy bars. We made hard candies like all day suckers, Christmas candies, ribbon candies, jelly beans, Easter eggs, and saltwater taffy. We've been making saltwater taffy for more than eighty years, and we're probably the largest saltwater taffy producer in the United States.

Making taffy was a strategic business decision made in the late 1920s by my grandfather. In the early 20th century, people had no way to keep chocolate from melting during the summer months. No way to store it, transport it, or keep it in a house. Candy producers would virtually stop making anything that had to do with chocolate. As a result, to keep our workforce stable, my grandfather did a lot of chocolate in the fall and winter months; in the summertime, when the candy business was very soft, very flat in sales, he developed saltwater taffy.

I've always been led to believe saltwater taffy is a confection that was developed for the seashore, the eastern and western shores, because it was a product that didn't easily melt in the heat. Individually wrapped in waxed paper, it would keep out the sand, so you could take it down to the seashore. That's how we got into the saltwater taffy business: to even out our production schedule throughout the year. Many people think that because of Salt Lake City, there's salt from the Great Salt Lake in the saltwater taffy. That's not true. But business just continues to grow.

Another Sweet—After my father went to the University of Pennsylvania in 1927, he came back with a degree in finance and decided in 1931 to work in the family business. That was just at the beginning of the depression. My Dad used to tell me the story that the first year he worked there, the volume of the business fell in half, the next year, business fell in half again. So it was a very tough time. To counteract the depression and keep all his employees working, my father staggered the workers. We didn't want to have massive layoffs, so everyone was asked to co-operate and they did. People worked on part-time shifts so everyone was able to weather the depression. But it was a very tough time, and like the people of that era, my father was always very conscious of what a serious depression can cause. He was a very conservative businessman.

In 1986, we bought the warehouse that was adjacent to but not connected in the back. All told, we had about 115,000 square feet. In 1995, we moved our distribution, our warehousing out to the International Center and built a warehouse there. And then in 1999, we started construction on a brand new building, 185,000 square feet, all on one level.

Ethnicity—It's interesting. Over the years, when the labor movement was much stronger in the 1930s, we have had elections for labor unions, but they never have been successful. Our employees overwhelmingly vote to stay independent. I think our work force is stable. We have a lower turnover than most of the other businesses. In the early days, one would notice a homogeneous work force in Utah. No minorities of any kind. That was really true in our operation until recently. Today, we have five different major cultural groups working for us. We teach English and have English mentoring during the working hours. It's working out.

Where the Sweets Are—We are a wholesale manufacturer. This business has certainly changed. We had as many as 40 salesmen just selling our candy, and more than 4,000 accounts. Utah was our biggest territory. Stores like Keith O'Brien, the Paris, Montgomery Ward, J. C. Penney's, Kress, Woolworths, Sears, all of them had bulk candy, and we supplied them year round with assorted and seasonal candies. Now, with mergers, there's few candy departments in major department stores. We had to make a change. Today, we're a national marketer with business all over the country.

Yet, Some Things Remain the Same—One of our famous products is the chocolate orange stick. They've been around forever. Twenty times a month, I'll hear, "My grandmother always put one of those in my Christmas stocking." We used to individually cello-wrap them and put them in the dining cars on the D&RG Railroad and the Union Pacific when rail travel was more important than it is today.

Sweet Tooth—My grandfather and Mr. Saroni made a good decision to move to Utah. This has been a good candy community. Our company is still a family business, now into its fourth generation American born. In business for almost 110 years, we've become one of the oldest continually existing companies in Utah.

A Jewish Life—My mother, Corinne Heller, born in New York, married my father in 1937 and moved to Salt Lake knowing no one other than her husband, and became very involved in the Jewish community. All my family belonged to Congregation B'nai Israel, but my mother Corinne was the force behind any of our religious activity. When I was growing up, my father used to call her "Madam Chairman," because she was always working with Jewish organizations, the public library, and education. She and Esther Landa and Mrs. Dolowitz initiated the HEADSTART program here for children. I believe they did a lot of good for this community. So, I am from the Jewish tradition. I was born a Jew. I am a Jew. And I am an American, grateful that my great grandfather ventured out West. And I am a candy maker.

TEN

Standing Up to Bigotry

RAGTOWN

Sidney Matz

A Regular Little Jewish Store—My dad, Sam Matz, came down to Utah and opened a business in Magna, where he had a store on Main Street.[1] It was called the Fair Store. And he paid rent every month. In Russia, they couldn't own nothing. Whatever they had was always taken from them. So my Dad never bought nothing. His philosophy was not to buy, not to own. He paid for the store fifty times over what he could have bought the whole building, the hotel above it, and the two buildings beside it. But he had his principles.

Tzedakah—Dad ran the same store all the time he was there. He had stuff hanging from the ceiling down, like a regular little Jewish store. And he made a lot of friends. If he ever saw a kid with raggedy shoes or going barefoot, he'd bring him into the store, sit him down, and fit him up with a pair of shoes. If they said, "How can I repay you?" he'd say, "When you grow up and work at Kennecott, you'll know where to come and buy your shoes."[2] He gave away hundreds of pairs of shoes during the depression. He'd never let a kid walk by his store that didn't have a good pair of shoes on. And he built his whole reputation out there. People would come in, buy

Sam Matz with his family in Russia.
(Courtesy of Berenice Matz Engleberg)

something, take it up to the counter, write down the price, and leave. And all the while, he'd be sitting over there with a bunch of people, telling stories, this and that. That's the way he run that business for years. And he never lost a dime. To him, everybody was honest.

Faster Than a Speeding Machine—My dad could add faster than you could put numbers on a machine. He just had a system. Sometimes people would bring in numbers and an adding machine like it was a game: Sam Matz beating an adding machine. He'd do it in his head and beat the machine. He'd know if you were lying, too. I'd get in trouble and want to fix the story. So I'd walk in and he'd look at me, know what I was thinking, and I'd just tell the truth. He wasn't a big guy, about five feet five inches or five feet six, and this is no lie, these big railroad men, six feet, two hundred fifty pounds, would come in and want to arm wrestle with him, double or nothing. There wasn't a man in town who could put his arm down. He said it was a matter of "leverage," and he could hold his arm like a piece of iron. Then, when the guy would be tired, my dad would put him out.

Agnosticism—My Dad knew the bible, too. You could ask him about a passage in the bible, and he'd tell you the page and how many lines it was down. He went to *shul* and he spoke Hebrew. His father was a rabbi and he could have been one too. In fact, he officiated at a couple of our uncles' funerals. One was in Rexburg, Idaho, where they didn't have a rabbi. Yet, this man was an agnostic who took a scientific view of everything. He believed in a Supreme Being as something that's holding this universe together, but he didn't believe the way they got God pictured.

Ragtown—Magna used to be called Ragtown by the old-timers. Maybe because the town was built up from the tailings from the mines. They built on top of it. In fact, the mountain used to come all the way down right into the dike and there was a stream that run right down to the bottom of a beautiful little valley. When my Dad had the Fair Store, it came with two rooms, and a kitchen and a little bathroom in the back. That was our home. Sometimes Mother and Dad would have to go into town on a buying trip. They'd go into the Hotel Utah, and as the salesmen set up their goods, they'd pick out what they wanted. That's the way they run their business.

Little Sidney Matz with his dad, Sam, in the Fair Store. (Courtesy of Berenice Matz Engleberg)

Another Kind of Mishpoche—When our parents went into Salt Lake, us kids would be left in Magna. But when dinner time come, we'd run down to Andy Dallas's restaurant. He was a Greek. We'd sit down at the counter and he would bring us hot beef sandwiches smothered in gravy. It was a treat for us. Two doors up would be Shorty the Shoemaker, an Italian. He'd say, "Come on up, I'm fixing spaghetti." He'd sit us down in the back of the shoe shop where he lived and in his kitchen he'd give us the best spaghetti dinner I'd ever tasted in my entire life. Shorty had big thumbs and he could fix anything, fast. This man would put tacks in his mouth and spit them out into the shoe and hit 'em right in. It was fascinating to watch him; he was that good. One day, I guess he was in his forties, Shorty announced he was going back to Italy to get a wife. He came back with the most sweetest and most beautiful girl. They had two boys and then three girls. One of his kids is a professor at the University, Phil Notarianni.

And the barber. If my hair was messed, I'd run into the barbershop, and the barber, a Greek man, would cut my hair and off I'd go. If he remembered, the old man [my dad] would give him a quarter or whatever for the haircut. I was raised among Greeks and Italians and Japanese. That's the way we lived on Main Street and it was really a good way of life for us. Just everybody watched us.

Chicken Soup in the Mountains—When Dad closed the store, nobody could talk business with him. He left it right there. No matter what he owed or who owed him, he never brought it home. Sometimes in the summer, my mother would run the store and Dad would take us kids to the Lava Hot Springs. In them days, it took all day to get there. He'd pitch a tent and then go back and get mother. We practically spent the whole summer living there in a tent in the park. It was like living at home because Mom always had a good hot meal for us. She cooked like the old country people. You couldn't beat her chicken soup. She put in chicken feet and you can't believe the taste that soup had. It was good. Sometimes my Dad would go to this Coon Chicken Inn and they'd give him plastic bags full of gizzards and chicken livers. Free. They didn't want them and she'd make chopped liver out of that.

Bigotry—There was quite a bit of discrimination in those days. The KKK [Ku Klux Klan] used to burn crosses up on the hill by Kennecott and I heard stories that they wanted to run people out of town. We'd see them on their horses, riding through town, intimidating people. In fact, when the Klan would start, everybody would get to their homes. Once, me and my friend, Pete Karakas, snuck up in this canal and looked. We'd seen a couple of the people that were in the Klan. It was hot and they took their hoods off. And when they did, we saw a couple of people we knew. I can't mention any names because I don't want to start a big deal. But one of them was a Mormon bishop and the other was a businessman from Magna.

The Kidnapping—Well, one time the KKK kidnapped a Greek kid from Magna. A young kid. They took him up the mountain. They said they weren't going to do nothing to him. Just scare him. That was the biggest mistake they could make. The story is the Greeks got together and went up there with guns and trucks and that put an end to the Klan right then and there. That broke them up.

The Backbone of Kennecott—The Greeks were really the backbone of Magna. The backbone of Kennecott, they made Kennecott what it was. They started the first unions and they'd go on strike. The people that worked for Kennecott didn't want a strike. Some of them would get together with guns and shoot the [strikers] because they were stopping work. They didn't understand what a union does to protect your rights. But I talked to this guy later and he said, "We fought the Greeks because they wanted to unionize. If I only knew what good it would of done, we could have had this union in here twenty years before."

"Go See Sam Matz"—Dad got a lot of people jobs for Kennecott. He was a Mason. Most of the Kennecott officials were big Masons, so if people were looking for a job, they'd be told to "go into Sam Matz. He'll get you on." He did. He'd call the hiring boss and he'd put him on. Of course, they'd come and trade in the store, too.

Company Town—Most of the people who lived around here worked at Kennecott. In fact, Kennecott was like a family affair. Your dad worked at Kennecott, your mother did and your brothers. There were schools nearby and company houses in Garfield were cheap. Fifteen dollars a month got you a five-room home with two bedrooms. A wooden construction. You couldn't grow much grass because the smelter smoke would kill the grass and flowers. So [the houses] didn't look too good on the outside, but the inside was clean and comfortable. Gas cost next to nothing. Lights was for nothing. Kennecott furnished the power.

Through the Hard Times—During the depression, the town kind of stayed alive because Kennecott didn't shut down. They kept working. Maybe they'd only work three days, but everybody worked three days a week and got a paycheck. It was better than being on welfare. During those hard times, water was the most important thing. Kennecott would send a crew man up and down the street with a drill. They'd drill wells just so people could pipe water in to grow vegetable gardens and get them through the hard times.

Family Ties—Growing up, Pete Karakas was my first friend and the toughest kid in town. In fact, the first time we met, we got in a fight and he beat the hell out of me. But, the next day, we played. A couple of years older than me, we were inseparable. He could build anything or fix anything. He was that type of person. We'd build bikes by the parts we found. We built a shack. Then, as we got older, if my car ever went wrong, I'd take it to Pete and he'd fix it. We hung around in school, went to California together, and even joined the army together. The people in Magna always said that the Karakases had twin boys, and that they took Sid Matz, Pete's twin, and dropped him on Sam Matz's doorstep. Karakas got the good twin and Matz got stuck with the bad one.

Standing Up to Racism—Any time I ever heard any kind of anti-Semitism, I've always stood up to it. In 1938 or 1939, Pete and I were walking by a Mormon seminary. There was a little convertible car with swastikas on the windows and on the side. Swastikas. The guy was a guest speaker in that seminary. And I don't know if I should say this to you or not, it might cost me some money. But it had an impact on me and me and Pete got a whole bunch of bricks and knocked out every window in that little convertible. That was the only way we could fight back then. My dad claimed that a farmer came in and looked over the old man's store and told my Dad, "When Hitler comes here, I'll own this place."

And Then There Was War—I joined the army when I was twenty. They shipped us down to California for a year and then, two months before we were going to get out, we were shipped to the Philippines for six more months. We're on the high seas and all of a sudden, the ship turns around and heads back to California. December 7th, 1941. They bomb Pearl Harbor and we're taken straight over to the Hawaiian Islands. Then we're in the Philippines in the Second Marine Corps. And Okinawa. We were the first ones in there. We went in with the 7th Division. My outfit had seen a lot of combat. We were in for five years. Over four years overseas in the war; and in all kinds of battles. We're fighting the Japanese. I had good Japanese friends in Magna. One of our friends from back home was in the Japanese-American 442nd Battalion.[3] I wasn't mad at the Japanese. How could I be angry now? A lot of tragic things happen.

We were sweeping through this minefield and this Japanese soldier came right out and was sitting there like this, looking at me. I was trying to tell him that I wouldn't shoot him. Had the safety on my gun. All of a sudden, he just went flying all over the place. He had a hand grenade, something like that, and he blew himself up. Parts of it hit me in the chest. When I got out of the army, I had to go to the VA Hospital.

You Pass On It—What do I remember most? Ten or fifteen guys you're buddies with, you know, and all of a sudden, they're all just blown to hell. A guy was leaning up against some ammunition and we had a gun blow up near him. He's still standing, so we went over to him and asked if he was all right. He was just standing there, but all his bones were pulverized. So you pass on it. The real bad things, you just forget about it, so you can go on.

Sam Matz's Boy—Kennecott had a policy to rehire everybody that worked for them before the war. When I got back, I went up to Kennecott, hired out, and got a job. But I just couldn't sit still. I moved to Miami, came back, then went to California, came back again. I quit Kennecott nine times, and the hiring boss told me, "that's the last time you'll work for this company." I went down to San Francisco, into Mexico, Montana, Wyoming, Denver. Then I married, had two adopted children, and was ready to settle down. With help, and because I was Sam Matz's boy, I got rehired. I went out there determined to stick with it. When everybody else would go on a break, I'd keep working. I worked and worked. I did pretty good. They made me a lead man, even offered me a foreman's job. I didn't take it. I started at Kennecott when I was sixteen and I worked there for thirty-four years until I retired.

PEDDLER IN THE STORM

Ruth Matz McCrimmon

The Scribe—My father's brother, Aaron Matz, left Russia and went to Germany to study at the university.[1] He was very smart and wanted to be a doctor. A couple of years later, the Germans kicked out all Russian Jews attending school in Germany. Aaron didn't want to return to Russia. They wouldn't let him in the United States. The only place that was open to Jews like Aaron was South Africa. So he went there. Right after my father, Sam Matz, had his bar mitzvah, he left Russia too and joined Aaron in South Africa. My grandfather wanted him to go. He stayed behind in Russia. He was a very religious Orthodox Jew and a scribe. I always thought he was a rabbi, but he was a scribe. His handwriting was wonderful. He wrote many letters in Hebrew to his son in America, asking him to write more often. You know, my grandfather was a leader in his community and I was told he was a really good chess player. But I think their lives were quite drab. They were very poor people.

Curing a Sick Man—Dad stayed in South Africa for several years and told us of an experience he had during the Boer Wars in South Africa when soldiers from England and Canada fought the Dutch colonists.[2] Several natives told Dad, who at this time ran a little store, about a white man who was really sick with jungle fever, or malaria. Dad instructed them to bring him to his house, although he wasn't sure how he could help. This Canadian soldier was really ill, and my father didn't know whether his "patient" would survive. Nevertheless, he took care of him for almost six months. Six months, yes. When he was well, the man became a policeman in Johannesburg for several months and then went home to his family, and they lost track of each other.

A Peddler in Foreign Places—My Dad loved to travel and eventually he decided to leave South Africa and go to Canada. His brother had a shipping business; he sent bananas and oranges and all kinds of fruit to China, India, and other exotic parts of the world. So Dad got on the boat with the cargo and traveled to many unusual places. He went to the Forbidden City of China, to the Taj Mahal in India, and Sphinx in Egypt long before it was totally uncovered by scientists in 1926. When he arrived in Canada, I think he went to Montreal and worked in a large department store. But he wanted to travel and so he bought a small wagon and a horse, became a peddler, and headed West towards Vancouver.

No Room in the Barn—My Dad sold household goods out of the wagon and traveled around the country with his horse and wagon. One late afternoon, he got caught in a sudden snowstorm and went to a nearby farmhouse for shelter. When the woman of the house answered the door, he asked if he could rent a spot in the barn for himself, his wagon and his horse for the night. The woman said, "You're the Jewish peddler, aren't you?" When my father said yes, she told him they didn't take in Jews. Her husband came to the door and told him to leave. My father had no choice but to get back on the wagon and set out again. The snow was coming down hard. He could barely see in front of his horse; it was slow going, and he was getting cold.

Just as he was trying to figure out what to do next, a man walked by pulling his horse by its reins. He cautioned my father not to go any further as the storm showed no signs of letting up. "You'll never make it in this storm," the fellow said. "You better stop for the night, and begin again tomorrow."

The man's voice sounded strangely familiar and my father began explaining that he had tried to find shelter in a nearby house, but they wouldn't take him in because he was Jewish. Suddenly the man shouted, "Sam! Sam Matz! Is that you?"

Amazingly, this man was the same fellow Dad nursed back to health in South Africa. After asking which house had refused him lodging, and finding out it was his parents' home, the man turned the horse and buggy right around and headed back to the house. When they arrived, the man told his family, "This is the man who saved my life in Africa. I'd be dead if he hadn't taken me in. And you just refused to help him!"

Oh, I wish I could I remember his name. Well, of course, they cried, and took him in. They kept him all winter; for that matter, they wouldn't let him leave for three months, and still wasn't enough for them. They wanted him to live with them. They wanted to give him part of their farm. I still cry every time I tell that story. It was such an unbelievable happening, a snowstorm in some rural part of Vancouver, far away from anyone my Dad really knew. And there it is.

Heading South—In time, Dad left Canada and made his way down into Idaho, where he met my mother's brother, Uncle Ike. How did my dad learn about him? You know, there were not too many Jews around in the West, especially in places like Idaho, so word got around. Dad went to Uncle Ike's ranch and found out that the family was from a Russian village just a few miles from where Dad grew up. More than that, he found out there was a sister living there. Annie Simon. Or, Fogel. Now, I have to tell you, when our relatives, the Lewises, sent for Aunt Ida who sent for Uncle Ike, Ike got a little *farblondjet* when he landed in New York. When asked his name, he suddenly forgot, and looking around saw an advertisement on the wall that read something like "Simmon something" and that was it. Simon. But their name is really Fogel. Annie Fogel was my mother.

Berenice, Sidney, and Ruth Matz in Magna. (Courtesy of Berenice Matz Engleberg)

First Impressions—When my dad met her, I think he wanted to make an impression on her because he arrived at their house by motorcycle. He said he thought he was the first man in Idaho to have a motorcycle. This had to have been around 1914 or '15. Well, the story is he took my mother for a ride in the countryside and sometime during their little trip, unbeknownst to him, she fell off the motorcycle. He didn't know until he turned around to talk to her and she wasn't there! He went back on the same route and finally found her sitting by the side of the road. She must have had a good sense of humor even then, because they did end up marrying each other soon after. Then they moved to Wyoming.

"There Go the Christ Killers"—My sister Berenice and I were born in Wyoming, and later, we moved to Garland, Utah where my brother Sidney was born. Then we moved to Magna. At the time I think we were the only Jewish family that lived in Garland and Magna. I know that because we were called Christ killers. Little kids said that, "There goes the Christ killers."

What happened was one day when I was about six and Berenice was seven or eight, the

Mormon bishop came to talk to my Dad. He said, "Why don't you let the kids come to Church? They could come to Sunday School with their friends." So my Dad said, okay, he'd send us to church. Well, when we got to the class, the teacher started telling everyone that the Jews killed Christ. That Jesus was the Son of God and that we killed him. All the kids started shaking their finger at us, saying, "Shame on you."

I whispered to Berenice, "We didn't do it. Who did it?" And she said, "Well, Momma didn't do it. She's too nice. It must have been Dad." And I said, "Why would Dad do a thing like that?" Berenice said, "I don't know, but I think he did it." When we got home, we were so mad at our father, one of us finally said, "Why did you kill Christ, why did you do it?" He said, "Christ died more than two thousand years ago." That didn't mean anything to us. Two thousand years. We said, again, "Why did you do it?" He said, "I didn't do it." We didn't believe him because out of all of us, he was the *only* one who could have done it. We just kept asking him why.

Well, my poor dad was furious. He called the bishop and said, "You asked me to send my kids to Sunday School. I did so they could learn bible stories, and the teacher tells them that the Jews killed Christ and they come home and tell me that I killed Christ. My kids aren't going there anymore!"

Tzedakah—My family owned a store in Magna. Dad was really nice to people and there were a lot of immigrants working in that town. Dad knew Italian and Greek, so he could talk with them. If he met someone who was really poor and couldn't afford work clothes, he'd give them clothes.

Bias Restrictions—Nobody that I know ever refused to shop at the store because we were Jewish. So many stores were owned by Jews, like Auerbachs on Main Street in Salt Lake City, so nobody thought anything of it. I had more trouble when I got married and moved to the Avenues in Salt Lake. When they thought I was Italian, everything was fine, but when they found out I was Jewish, some people threw rocks and bricks at the house. One time they broke my front window.

I'll never forget that. I was pregnant, and had just got up from the couch to get a cup of tea. A rock came bursting through the window and there was glass everywhere. Oh, it was a mess to clean up. Then they started a petition to have us evicted from our home. Fortunately, my next-door neighbors refused to sign it. Of course, after many years there were three Jewish families that lived on the same block. That was in the late '40s.

No Room—Even my Dad had a hard time finding a place, though, when he and my mother were first married. I'll never forget when he was in Afton, Wyoming, he told us no one would rent to him. Momma was pregnant with Berenice, and he went to a woman who had a house. He asked if they could rent a place. She said, no, she couldn't rent to Jews. Dad said, "Well, now I know why Jesus was born in a manger."

A MINORITY CHILD

Berenice Matz Engleberg

One God and No More—My dad always believed in Judaism.[1] He told us when he was younger, around eleven or twelve years old, he helped teach other kids Hebrew and was immersed in Jewish religious life. But after immigrating to America, and maybe even before that, he was influenced by Thomas Paine and his book, *The Age of Reason.* That was his favorite book. Yet, at the same time, he was a devoted Jew. He knew passages of the bible and seemed to understand one side of religion and then the other side of it. During High Holy Days, he would close the shop, put a sign on the store, and take the family to Congregation Montefiore for services. I have to say, I was not always comfortable there because I think they thought we were "Magna hicks," unsophisticated people. Of course, Dad couldn't sit through the whole service anyway. Neither could Sidney. Maybe for different reasons, it was just too much for the two of them. But he took us to *shul,* and on every Jewish holiday, we would sit with him and he would quote from the Old Testament, and tell stories—he was a wonderful storyteller—until we understood about each holiday.

Kosher in the Country—Mama too tried to keep a kosher home, as far as living way out in Magna would accommodate her. She would cook all the right foods, and never mix *flayshig* with *milchik.* To this day, I can't put a piece of butter on a slice of bread that has meat on it. We never, ever ate bacon or ham. During Passover, we would bring out our two different sets of dishes, and Mama would place a separate block of wood in the sink and do the dishes on top of it.

Finding Landsmen—It was tough to live in a small town and be Jewish, but my parents had Jewish friends, in Salt Lake City, and even in Provo. I think the Perlmans had a junk store in Provo, and my cousin Leo Lewis had a store there too for many years. We would visit them in Provo and then go see Mr. and Mrs. Spitz who had a big house on 8th South and West Temple in Salt Lake. I remember the family going with them to Yellowstone and to Lava Hot Springs. So we did go places, but my Dad loved small towns. He said it was easier to be a big fish in a small pond than a little fish in a big one. And he got along with people; he told great stories, his store was open to everyone, and people respected him. But it was still difficult being a minority child.

A Stigma—I know my sister told you the story about going to the ward house and being accused of killing Christ. So I won't tell the story again. But what she didn't say was that it took me a long time to get over it. Maybe because I was young the teacher's remarks made an imprint on me. And it followed me for years. Why would someone say such a terrible thing to two little kids? What was the reason behind it? We had been invited there just to socialize with other kids, and the moment we went into the room and sat down, we were accused of killing Christ. That just stunned us. What could we say to that? We were kids; what did we know about two thousand years ago. Mama did that? Papa did that? Yes, it took me a long time, a long time to get over that. In Magna, when we were going to school, kids would walk by us, Mormon kids. "There goes those Jews," they'd say in a demeaning way. Or follow along us, saying, "Jews, Christ killers." Not the ethnic kids. They didn't do that. Magna was a fairly diverse town and we were raised around Italian and Greek people. They would never say anything like that. I used to go to Greek School with my friends and was proud to learn the Greek alphabet.

"The Sheik"—We had good times, too. What we did in the store, when we were kids, was so much fun. Sidney was such a funny boy, quick to joke, and easy with words, like his dad. Sid and Johnny Papanikolas went around together all the time. Whenever Sidney and Ruth would go to a show, they would put on the show right in the store and the Papanikolas family would come down and watch us do our act. Once, when Sidney did "The Sheik," his friend Dave Littlefield was the girl and Sidney was the hero. It was so funny, almost like vaudeville coming to town! Every time they saw a show, they would put it on the next day, and all our friends would come round to see it.

Wide-Open Spaces—I was born in Malad, Idaho in 1915, at home, delivered by a doctor who was drunk. He came to the house drunk. I was a breech baby, my feet came out first, which is why I have a bad leg. Maybe it should have been put in a brace, I don't know, but I'm lucky to be alive. Sidney was born in Garland, Utah. Ruthie was born in Afton, Wyoming. So within a radius of about 150 miles, the Matz kids managed to be born in three different states.

Small-Town Stores—In Garland, my dad worked for the Abramsons, who also had family in Malad, Idaho. We lived in that small town near Tremonton for several years. That's when we went to the ward house, but you know about that. After the Abramsons moved to Boston where they had relatives, Dad set up a store of his own and we went to Magna. Now, Magna was a bigger town than Garland. And it was a boom town then, with lots of activity and business because of Utah Copper Company business.

A Protest—When we got ready to leave Garland, though, Dad told us we couldn't take our dog Ted. He was a very sweet dog, had been with us for a long time, but Dad didn't think it would be smart to take him into a busy town. We rebelled. When the car was loaded up and

Berenice Matz's graduation picture, early 1930s, Magna. (Courtesy of Berenice Matz Engleberg)

ready to go, Ruth, Sid, and I locked hands together through the wooden porch rails of the house and refused to budge. If Ted wasn't going, we weren't going either. We stayed that way for quite a long time until Dad took the dog and put him in the car. Then we all made the move to Magna.

Bartering—During the depression, Dad bartered with customers at the store. They would bring in a chicken or they would bring in eggs, and he would sell them produce or merchandise. That's how everybody made it back then. We lived in the back of the store for a couple of years. We moved to a house up the street from the store. It was a small house, but then we moved further down Main Street and got a bigger house with a yard. Our house and the store was always open to people.

Dialects—Dad had a real good sense of humor. He was a dedicated Mason and was active in the Lion's Club. Whenever the Lion's Club made lunch with ham, they'd call Dad and ask what they could fix for him because he never ate ham. He could tell good stories. People just loved to listen to him. When he was in Arko, Idaho, one time, they thought it was so interesting that he came from South Africa and said words like "umpossible" instead of "impossible." When his friend, who was a bishop, left town for a few days, he turned his work over to Dad who gave a series of lectures and conducted services. Wherever he went, he usually got along with people, unless they didn't like Jews. Dad was prominent in Magna and very well liked. If he had had an education, he could have gone into public relations because he knew how to talk to people.

Known about Town—During the war, he was one of the only people who could go in to Kennecott without a pass because he knew everybody there. He had a lot of pull and got jobs for people at the mill. Joe Hadley was the personnel manager of the company. They used to come down to dinner with my family.

Interfaith Marriages—Ruthie and Sid both married non-Jewish people. Ruthie's husband was liberal and not a religious man, so Ruthie led a traditional rather than religious Jewish life. Sid's wife is an Italian. They get along very well. A nice woman, she had two children when he married her after our mother died and he was back from the service. He adopted them, and they took his last name, Matz. I never dated a non-Jewish boy. When we were growing up, my father would not allow it, and I couldn't do it to my mother. So I didn't date until I was at the University and even then there were few Jewish boys in Utah. When Ruth and her husband moved to California, I went to school at Berkeley. I got into social work.

A Denver Connection—When I was home on vacation, Estelle Appelman introduced me to Ben Engleberg. This was in 1942. He was from Denver. Denver has a very large Jewish community, far more extensive than Utah. A lot of Jewish people from all around the country went there because they had tuberculosis and Denver was the place to go for a cure. That's how Ben wound up in Denver. His mother went there first for the cure and was followed by her husband and their three kids. When Ben came to Salt Lake, he worked for Harry Miller at his print shop. He also did iron work. We married in 1944 and moved to Provo where Ben worked for my Uncle Leo Lewis at the store. Later they set up a kind of saloon in Provo.

Commitment to Judaism—I believe I married a Jewish man because even though we lived far away from most Jews, we always knew we were Jewish. Holidays, traditions, Jewish cooking. We grew up with Jewish food. The cheapest cuts of meat, usually. Jews were very poor people who learned how to make most delicious meals out of any kind of meat. And they still do.

And Food—Mother was from a line of bakers and she made the best rye bread you have ever tasted. She didn't use an electric or a gas stove. Would never do that. Dad had to get her a coal stove to make her bread. She could put her hand in the oven and tell what the temperature was exactly. She also made the most wonderful bagels by hand, and tongue. I feel so sorry that I didn't write down all her recipes, that I didn't ask her more about her family. You know, it seems to me that when our parents came to America, they left lives of poverty behind and they never wanted to talk about it. And then we got so busy, we didn't take the time to listen to their stories. I remember when my parents spoke Yiddish and how embarrassed I got listening to them. And now I would give anything to have learned Yiddish and be able to speak it today.

And Recipes—I do remember some recipes and make them to this day. Do you know *Pitcha*? Calf's feet jelly? Don't make such a face, it's a delicacy in Denver. Some people will have nothing to do with it. Blanch Tannenbaum won't touch it, nor will the Rothenbergs, while Mel Richtel loved it and my son David requests it. When my mother made it, she had to burn all the hair off the bone and scrape it clean. Now, you can buy it at Fred Meyer's, the supermarket, already cleaned. I still wash it off, then I put hot boiling water over it and let it steep for an hour or so. Finally, I cook it in water with lots of onions and garlic until the gristle and meat fall apart from the bones. My mother-in-law used to put hard-boiled eggs in it. It has a wonderful flavor. We had foods like that; and kishkeh, and kreplach, and knishes. People would say, "Oh, you eat the funniest things here." And then they'd taste it and like it.

A Change of Names—People changed their name when they arrived in America. You know my uncle's name went from Fogel to Simon. There was a joke at Ellis Island that when a newly arrived immigrant was asked his name, he was tired and said he was "*fargussend*," confused. Well, his name became Ferguson! I didn't know my real name until I applied for a passport and had to show my birth certificate.

A Matter of "e"—Ever since I could remember, my dad called me Bernice. I didn't like the name. One day I was reading a novel and saw the name Berenice. It's an affectation, I realize, but I liked it. So I added an "e" to my name. When I received the letter concerning my birth certificate, I expected "Bernice," Matz. Instead, written was Ziva Bertha Matz! That's who "I" was. That was my name. I couldn't believe it. I never knew it. I don't use it, of course, since I never heard about it before. It's Berenice for me. My granddaughter, Rachel, said to me, "If I have a daughter, I'm going to name her Ziva."

Pitcha (CALF'S FEET JELLY, ALSO CALLED *Sulze*)

2 calf's feet, cleaned and sawed to fit pot
cold water to cover
1 onion
1 clove garlic
3 bay leaves
1 tsp. peppercorn (optional)
salt to taste
2 Tbsp. lemon juice or 1/2 cup vinegar
3 hardboiled eggs, sliced
sliced lemon for garnish and parsley

Cook feet in water for ten minutes. Skim and add onion, garlic, bay leaves, and peppercorns (if desired). Cook over reduced heat for one hour. Skim again. Simmer for three hours or until the bones stand away from gristle and meat. Strain. Cut usable meat and gristle into fine cubes. Add to the strained liquid. Taste and add salt, if needed. Add lemon juice or vinegar. Bring to a quick boil and cook for five minutes. Turn into an oblong glass dish about two inches in depth. Let cool until partly jelled. Place some egg slices on top and stand remaining egg slices along the inside of the dish. Refrigerate. When completely chilled, jelled, and firm to the touch, unmold onto a serving plate. Garnish with parsley and lemon.

BAGELS (WATER DOUGHNUTS)

3 cups flour (plus 3 Tbsp. for kneading dough on board)
1-1/2 tsp. salt
2 Tbsp. sugar
1 package yeast
2/3 cup lukewarm water
3 Tbsp. salad oil
1 egg
4 quarts boiling water to which you add 2 Tbsp. sugar

Sift dry ingredients into a deep mixing bowl. Dissolve yeast in 1/3 cup lukewarm water. Add salad oil to the remaining water and stir into the dissolved yeast. Make a well in the center of the flour mixture and stir in the liquid, adding a slightly beaten egg when half the liquid has been used. Stir briskly to form a ball of dough and knead on a lightly floured board for two minutes. Return dough to mixing bowl, smooth side up, and punch down three times. Cover and let rise at room temperature for twenty minutes or longer, until the dough has come to the top of the bowl. Knead again until smooth and elastic. Divide dough into twelve equal portions. Form into lengths not more than 3/4-inch thick and pinch the ends together. Place on a floured cookie sheet and put under the broiler for three minutes. Then drop each bagel into a large kettle full of rapidly boiling water and cook for fifteen to twenty minutes. Skim out and place on a cookie sheet. Bake at 375 degrees for ten minutes; increase heat to 400 degrees for five or six minutes until bagels are browned and the crust is golden brown and crisp.

"THE JEWISH KID"

Eugene Levetan

Paying in Cash—When I was four, my parents bought a store in Bingham, a rough and tumble mining town.[1] We paid in cash. Besides, whoever heard of going to the bank and borrowing money?

At the time, Bingham City was home to thousands of immigrants and newcomers. We had Greeks, Irish, Italian, Spanish and Jews. Yes, Jews. We also had gangs then. Youth groups. Cliquish. If you were alone and went into somebody else's territory, you were pretty likely to get beat up before you got out.

Fighting My Way Home—These were kids of miners. Underground miners, mostly. And tough. They were very tough kids. When I was young, my mother dressed me like Little Lord Fauntleroy. No matter how much I protested, she insisted. And I did protest. Every day before school, I had a difficult time finding an outfit to wear that I wouldn't have to fight my way out of coming home.

"The Jewish Kid"—I was known as the "Jewish kid." It was a little unusual because my dad was a *yeshiva bucher* and very well educated, but since coming to Utah, he didn't practice his religion. Even my mother stopped lighting Friday night candles. So I didn't know much about Judaism. I did know about Jewish cooking, though, because that's what my mother did. And I knew I was Jewish because everybody told me I was. And sometimes, I'd have to fight my way out of conversations that had to be with my being Jewish.

Rocks—When I think about the past, the word "kike" comes to mind readily, because that's what I was called. One day, these guys were coming down the mountain and started throwing rocks at me. See, you've got houses and you've got a mountain, like a wall behind you. And these guys were throwing rocks at me and got me cornered. They were coming down the mountain at a run and there was no place for me to go. So I stood there, and thought, "Oh, boy, I don't know how I'm going to get out of this one."

Then along comes my dad, and he says, "We have to go now." That was it. The guys stopped. We went home.

My parents were cautioned by friends. "This is not a place to raise a young man," they said. And for me, they were right. I didn't have any friends. I felt like I had a monkey on my back all the time. But when I was twelve years old, we moved down to Salt Lake City. That's when I learned more about Judaism and my heritage. I found friends among the Jewish community and I studied to become a bar mitzvah.

As a kid, I remember Sam Shapiro and Moe, Sylvia Rosenthal and her cousin Bert, Gertrude Movitz and Mitzie Perlman. We were all synagogue friends, and everyday friends. It was fun. We had social clubs. Jewish clubs.

The Young Men's Hebrew Association was out of the old synagogue, Shaarey Tzedek. For awhile there was also the Herschel Club. It didn't last more than six months. We thought, maybe if we changed its name, the club would survive. But Mr. Herschel personally bawled me out for that idea!

ELEVEN

L'Chaim

MERCHANTS, MAVINS, MILITARY, AND MERGERS

Ralph Tannenbaum

A Story of Two Sons—My father Jack came from Polish Russia at the age of about five.[1] My grandfather's brother had been here prior to their arrival and was living in Denver, Colorado. He was actually a Zeidenfeld. The story is told that Zeidenfeld was actually the oldest Tannenbaum son who had been conscripted into the Russian cavalry. A Talmudic student, he went to live with a farmer by the name of Zeidenfeld as a way of hiding. Zeidenfeld had a son. The son died. They buried him, and Tannenbaum took on his name. To this day, that branch of the family is called Zeidenfeld. He has a little store on West Colfax, which my great aunt ran, while he sat in the back and studied throughout the day. This man lived in Denver until his death, he was a Zeidenfeld and a Talmudic student.

"Chicken Today . . ."—My father's family went to Denver from New York. His mother died in childbirth and his father remarried. My father didn't get along with his stepmother, so he left home at an early age and went out on his own. He worked as a bellboy at the Old Albany in Denver. Got board and room free with the job, and then joined a traveling sales crew working

for Fairbanks Morris which, I believe, was marketing borax soap, known as the Gold Dust Twins. In 1916, when he was sixteen or seventeen years old, he came to Salt Lake, liked it, and stayed on. My mother Edna was born in Evanston, Illinois. On her side, my grandfather had relatives in Salt Lake City, and so the family joined them in about 1916. Grandfather Samuel Levy was a "chicken today, feathers tomorrow" kind of guy. He'd have money today and, since he was a bit of a gambler, maybe not have it tomorrow. He and his brother Dave had a bar on State Street. I don't remember the name, but they were making a go of it. Then, the Volstead Act of 1919 struck hard and all of a sudden you had Prohibition![2] Federal authorities came into these bars, seized all the liquor, lined the bottles up on the sidewalk, took an inventory, paid for them, took axes and smashed them all. The liquor ran down the gutters, and that was the end of the business. Eventually, my mother's father worked with my father in his store.

A Patriotic Man—For the most part, my mother's family tended to be Reform Jews; my father's family was very Orthodox. I believe this is one of the points of dissention with my father and his parents. There was no question about his being a Jew, but he certainly wasn't an observant Jew. He was raised in a religious home that observed strict dietary laws, but I think he had no interest in it. He rebelled and then, of course, the military finished that rebellion. My father went into the Colorado National Guard; probably lied about his age to get in, and followed a quasi-military career throughout his life. He served in WWI, had been over to France, and stayed in the National Guard for quite a number of years. He was a Mason, a state officer in the American Legion, very active in the Reserve Army, and retired as a major. He was an honored officer in the military and an extremely patriotic man. He believed he had a tremendous debt to this country. After all, here he was a poor immigrant boy coming to America with his immigrant family and virtually little else, and he found he could make a good life.

Army Surplus—My father had been in business with Joe Arnovitz who sent my father to Filer, Idaho, to help liquidate a store. Filer, Idaho, is near the town of Burley and it's where I was almost born. At the last minute, my mother decided she wanted to come back to Salt Lake to be with her parents, so they moved back. At some point, my father worked for Ben Rosenblum on 2nd South between State and Main. Ben was one of these people who could look somebody in the eye and decide right then and there whether or not to give him credit. His losses were infinitesimal; he trusted people and they trusted him. My father worked for Nate Wolfe, Elliott Wolfe's oldest uncle who had an Army and Navy store on the corner of Regent Street and 2nd South. They sold surplus out of World War I. The government had a lot of surplus in their warehouse that they'd put out on auction, sealed auction. You'd write your bid and if you knew what you were doing, you bought what you could sell. My father decided he would like to go into his business, but it was a question of money. He wrote to his brother, Abe, who worked as a dairy-route man in Denver, and asked him to become a partner. Abe, my cousin Fred's father, apparently had enough money saved, because he sent it with the understanding that my father would open the store and when he got it running, Abe would come to Salt Lake with his family. Now, my father was a self-made man. He achieved a certain success and a degree of affluence, but I would say that is not uncommon for men similar to my father. In April of 1922, the National Army and Navy Store opened on 242 South State. Abe came to Salt Lake with his family. His first wife, Lottie, died not too many years after they arrived and Abe married Sade, a wonderful woman, who took care of Lottie's kids. Their son, Fred, was born in Salt Lake and had significant input in the growth of this community.

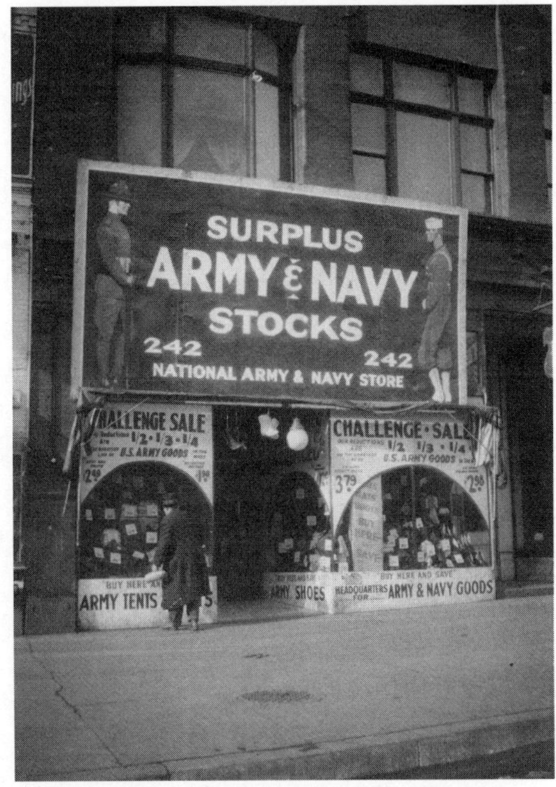

The early National Army and Navy Store, South Salt Lake Street. (Courtesy of Ralph Tannenbaum)

Glass Plates—Now, I have to explain that my grandfather was an extremely pious man. When he came to visit, my mother would always buy glass plates in order to cook and serve for him. As a child of six to ten years old, I used to watch him put on his tefillin when he would do his morning prayers. I have very fond memories of him. My father attended synagogues and was very interested in anything Jewish, but not from the standpoint of organized religion, not like my grandfather.

Officer Lessor—I was born in 1921. At the time, we lived in the old Avalon Apartments between 2nd and 3rd East on 3rd South. In those days, merchants put in very long hours, as late as ten o'clock on Saturday nights. When I was probably around four, at 6 o'clock in the evening, my mother would take me across 3rd South on my tricycle so I could meet my father at the store. Then she would take me across 2nd East and I would wheel down 3rd South, Broadway, to the corner where the Center Theatre now stands. I can remember a wonderful old Irish policeman by the name of Officer Lessor. In those days, on the corner, a policeman would sit up in a box mounted like a light pole. Officer Lessor would climb down a little ladder, take me by my hand, and walk my tricycle and me across State Street. Then I would wheel up to the middle of the block where the store stood.

Forty-nine-Cent Shirts—I remember the original store. It was roughly twenty-five feet front by one hundred feet depth. In the early 1920s, the store was stocked largely with military surplus out of World War I. We sold used shoes, chambray shirts for 49 cents, dress shoes for $1.98. Wages were very low. You didn't have withholding, you didn't have social security, and people were paid in cash right out of the till. As far as the payment of invoices, there was a spindle that had bills to be paid and there was a one-drawer filing system for paid bills. A bookkeeper used to come in once a week to do whatever he had to do, including making out checks. Later, I had a cousin who was exactly my age and the two of us would work on weekends. I'm talking about from the time that we were 14 years old until we went away to military school.

A Touring Car for Dad—The tricycle rides stand out most clearly for me, as does my father's first car, which I believe was a Dodge. It was an open touring car with plexiglas-like side curtains; just vaguely I remember a rainstorm in which my father had to pull the car to the side of the road, get out and buckle on the "windows." No one had a garage in those days. You parked in a public garage. My father used a garage on the southwest corner of 2nd South and 2nd East. I'm sure he paid a small amount, maybe less than five dollars a month.

Custer Court—We moved out of the Avalon in about 1924 or 1925 and into an apartment on 3rd Avenue and I Street. If my parents had been strong synagogue attendees, why, both Congregation Montefiore and Temple B'nai Israel were within walking distance of where we lived. There was a time more Jews lived down in the area of 9th South and 3rd East, over to Jefferson Street and a great number of Jews lived in what was known as Custer Court, on 5th South between 4th and 5th East. We stayed on 3rd Avenue there until 1926, when my brother Ira was born, and then we moved into a home on Gilmer Drive and 15th East where we lived for some twenty years.

No Kashrut—We attended Temple B'nai Israel.[3] It was my mother who insisted that my brother and I go to religious school at the old Jewish Community Center on East South Temple. Jewish education in those days was very elementary. In other words, we learned more about Jewish history in the United States and very little theology. We had fine teachers, people like Rabbi Sam Gordon and Dr. Louis Zucker. Very often I went to services with my mother on Friday nights and definitely on the High Holy Day. So in that sense I was raised in a very classical Reform background with a Reform rabbi. Services were said exclusively in English. We didn't observe *kashrut.*

Vaudeville—As for entertainment, I think the first movie I saw was "The Sheik," or "The Son of the Sheik," starring Rudolph Valentino. I went with my mother and grandmother. It was a silent movie and I was very bored because it was a romantic film. In 1929, my father took me to the Capitol Theatre to see Al Jolson and the "Jazz Singer." I remember the Capitol Theatre particularly because it had a very famous organ played by Mr. Farney, the organist. But for really vivid remembrances, I'd have to pick vaudeville. You see, on Saturdays, this one friend of mine—we were about six years old—and I would go to the kids' movies in the morning, about ten o'clock. Sometimes you could get in with a milk cap. Later, you could get into places with two empty milk cartons. Local dairies would sponsor that, and they would have special western movies, probably silent ones. But, then you got to see vaudeville shows after that with comedians, or tap dancers, maybe even an animal act. The Capitol Theatre had stages that could accommodate vaudeville. And they'd give away a million prizes to kids. Now, I remember that.

Boy Scouts and Mormons—In the early days, it's understandable that I was active in the Boy Scout program. I started in an LDS ward house. That's where most of the boy scout meetings were held in Utah. Surprisingly enough, we had a non-Mormon scout leader, Dr. Folsom. From 7:00 to 8:00 in the evening, everyone was supposed to go to what was called an Assembly where there was a certain amount of religious Mormon teachings going on. I had permission not to go to that, but rather come to the meeting at 8:00. Then it was strictly boy scouting, no LDS theology at all. Later we had a Jewish scout troop at the old JCC under the leadership of Howard Chesler. I can remember going to Camp Steiner, a Boy Scout Camp in the Uintah mountains. We had about twenty Jewish boys in that troop.

In 1935, when I was about fourteen years old, we were supposed to go to a Boy Scout International Jamboree in Washington, D.C., but there was an outbreak of polio and the event was cancelled. The Salt Lake Council had worked so hard on this project, and there were as many as a hundred boys from all over the area who were ready to leave, so it was decided that we would go on the trip to Washington, D.C. anyway. We slept in the Pullman cars. I shouldn't say Pullman cars, either, because those are sleeping cars and what we had were regular coach cars. To sleep, the back of one seat was removed and placed between the seats. Then they'd put two boards on top of that and a sleeping bag on top of the planks. That's the way you slept. The trip was very educational, we went all over Washington, D.C, and then up to New York City and to Cumorah, the hill near Palmyra, New York, where we saw Mormon enthusiasts still looking for the golden plates that Joseph Smith interpreted. I would say I was the only Jew on that trip, but I never felt any particular difference.

Too Few—In public school, my cousin Louis Tannenbaum and I were also about the only two Jews in that particular grade. The only time we ever faced a difference, kind of a setting aside, was in the early years when the Mormon kids would go from one activity to another, which had religious overtones, and we would become separate. Still, that didn't bother me. I didn't have one Jewish teacher in elementary school, but remember fondly a Bertha Rappaport who taught in junior high. Since I went to school during the depression, they did away with the 12th grade and after graduating in the 11th grade, I went right to military school in Roswell, New Mexico. Joel Shapiro attended that school as well as Jerry Hersh, whose father had a store on State Street, and Dick Schubach.

Jewish Row in the '20s—Back in those early days, though, when I was a kid, on State Street, between 2nd and 3rd East, there were so many Jewish stores, some people called it "Jewish row." It wasn't a ghetto and I can't give you numbers, but I can see them in my mind. The first store I remember is Ben Ramo's Golden Rule Store. It wasn't long after that Wolfe's moved over to State Street; we're talking about the 1920's. I can't tell you who was there next but eventually Sam Shapiro moved in with the Eagle Company. Sam Shapiro and Harry Sher were brothers-in-law and partners. Their business was commercial uniforms. They got into bowling shirts and had their own embroidery equipment. But that's much later. Sam had a store over on

Regent Street with Harry. They sold used suits, and had like a loan office. Before them, the store was owned by Sammy Movitz, Dick Movitz's father. Before that, there was Jack Shapiro who had a delicatessen in the United Grocery, a leased section on 3rd South between State and Main, on the north side. I can remember that store very well in the late 1920s.

Straw Hats, Warm Weather—Next was Charlie Porizky's store, Eastern Hatters. Sig Porizky had two stores. My maternal grandfather worked for him for a while. He had a store on Main Street, in the middle of the block, and then one further down on State Street. Eastern Hatters carried nothing but hats. You see, in those days, a well-dressed man certainly would never think of going out without a hat on. In the fall, I'm talking about a felt hat; in the summer, a straw hat. I believe Decoration Day, what we call Memorial Day, was always on a Sunday, near June 14th, and the following Monday was Straw Hat Day. The men would literally line up outside of these stores to buy a straw hat. They sold anywhere from ten to fifteen dollars. Of course, after Labor Day, the first Monday in September, you wouldn't be caught dead wearing a straw hat.

Our store was next and next to it was a place called Western Outfitters. There was a store owned by two brothers named Berkowitz; and across the street, you had Axelrad's Furniture; that's Irene Tannenbaum's uncle, A. Z. Axelrad. Finally, I think, there was Western Furniture, and that was Rachelle and Myron Finkelstein's business. Now, that's just in that area alone.

Credit Stores and Cash—There were a lot of Jewish stores throughout the city and actually many small stores that were scattered throughout Utah. In the early 1920s, a man by the name of Cohen had a men's clothier on Main Street between South Temple and 3rd South. Mr. Cohen was a charter member of B'nai Israel. The firm disappeared many years ago. Mose Lewis had a store on the west side of Main Street between South Temple and 1st South. A store by the name of the Paris Company on 3rd South between State and Main was originally started by two partners, Jules Dreyfus and Mr. Simon. I would call it a junior department store when contrasted to an Auerbach department store or a ZCMI. Paris was always considered a credit store, a good quality store. It was a friendly store, and in its heyday, did a big job. I think they went out of business in the late 1960's.

The Finest Store—The big store "was" Auerbach Brothers. Their store grew and grew and grew. At one time, and there was no question about this, Auerbachs was the finest department store in Salt Lake City, including ZCMI. Aaron Hersh had what was known as a continual going-out-of-business sale. This would have been when he was on 2nd South between State and Main on the north side of the street.

One Shoe Not Too Many—Now I'll tell you an interesting story that Ben Roe told me about the first store he ever opened in the town of Payson, south between Spanish Fork and Santaquin. He and his brother, Harry, opened a store and between the two of them had about two thousand dollars. Yet in the store there were boxes and boxes and boxes of shoes on display. It looked like a well-stocked store. The truth is maybe one box out of ten had a pair of shoes in them. They understood competition, and got away with looking good. Their business grew.

A Hole in the Wall—I could go on and on and on, there were so many Jewish businesses and their stories. First of all, there were many of these fellows, particularly these Jewish men who came from the old country. They had been *schneiders,* tailors. They had a little knowledge and they were hard workers. They would open a little hole in the wall as a tailor shop where you could take a pair of pants and have it altered. In many cases, these men were not content to stay altering someone else's pants. So they went out and they bought a few suits, and some cases. Maybe they bought them on consignment. And from this grew a store. This is what happened to the Mednick brothers. They bought one thing and then another until one of the brothers opened a sports store at a time when Mandarin shirts became the rage. In the 1950s, he did extremely well with dozens upon dozens of these shirts stacked up to the ceiling. I think we all have one still in our closet.

Traveling Salesmen—The Pullmans had a factory and actually made suits right here in town and sent men out on the road. Traveling salesmen. A cousin of mine got involved with this. What happens is a salesman is given largely samples and he'll go to a rural town, advertise in the local paper, and run a sale for two or four days. Five hundred suits at $50.00 a suit. Farmers will flock in and buy these suits. Then the salesman packs it up and moves on to the next town, where the same thing happens again. He'll go to Idaho, Montana, or Southern Utah, all the small farming and mining communities, put an ad in the paper and run a sale. That's what they did then.

Hired Help—Old man Finkelstein, who passed away not too long ago at the age of 101, was pretty sharp up until he died. He told me the story about coming to this country when he was about fifteen years old and on his own. He looked around and looked around for a job. One morning, he walks into this little old furniture store on 2nd South. He walks in, and it's a dimly lit store, with a man in the back sitting on a chair with his feet propped up on a desk, reading the newspaper. The kid, Finkelstein, walks in, doesn't say a word, but takes a broom and starts sweeping the floor. Pretty soon, the man looks up and says over his newspaper, "Hey, kid, who are you?" Finkelstein says, "I'm your new janitor. I just swept your floor." The man says, "How much am I paying you?" The kid says, "Twenty-five cents a day." The man says, "You're hired." That was his first job. Years later, this *mavin* in business, Herman Finkelstein, opened the Western Furniture Store that became a very well known credit and popular-priced furniture store.

Military Aspirations—I had always been interested in the military. As far back as I can remember, I always saw my father in uniform. My happiest moments were when my father would take me to Fort Douglas where the Reserves were camped. While my father was there, he allowed me to come up and sleep over in his tent. After awhile, I became friends with the sergeant in charge of the machine gun company and—now, I'm talking about when I was eight years old—I could field strip a 30-caliber machine gun! I became sort of a mascot of the machine gun company. This was the fulfillment of a little kid's fantasy!

Another thing I did was during Decoration Day, when the American Legion put flags on

Ralph Tannenbaum at the Civilian Military Training Corps at Fort Douglas. (Courtesy of Ralph Tannenbaum)
On board the USS *Honolulu*, Ralph on right. (Courtesy of Ralph Tannenbaum)

graves. I'd get up at 5:30 in the morning with my father and put these flags on veterans' graves in the Salt Lake City cemetery. It was like going on an annual outing and remains a very fond recollection in my memory.

In high school, I was very active in the ROTC. I also attended what was known as the Civilian Military Training Corps, the CMTC, during the summers at Fort Douglas. After I graduated from military school, I went on a one-month cruise and was selected to go to Midshipman School for three months. I was then commissioned as an ensign in the Naval Reserve and sent to Pearl Harbor March of 1941.

On the Chicago—Regardless of how much of a surprise the bombing of Pearl Harbor was, this country knew that the war was coming shortly. I had my orders to go to Pearl Harbor to join the cruiser *Chicago,* a heavy cruiser. The *Chicago* was escorting the carrier *Lexington,* which was delivering planes to Johnston Island at the northern end of the Gilberts, not too far from the equator. We were out to sea when the Japanese bombed Pearl Harbor and America entered the war.

I was in the gunnery department as a division officer responsible for a section of the ship and one of the turrets, a heavily armored structure that contained three of the larger guns. These cruisers were big ships. The *Chicago* was an eight-inch cruiser, which meant it had nine 8-inch

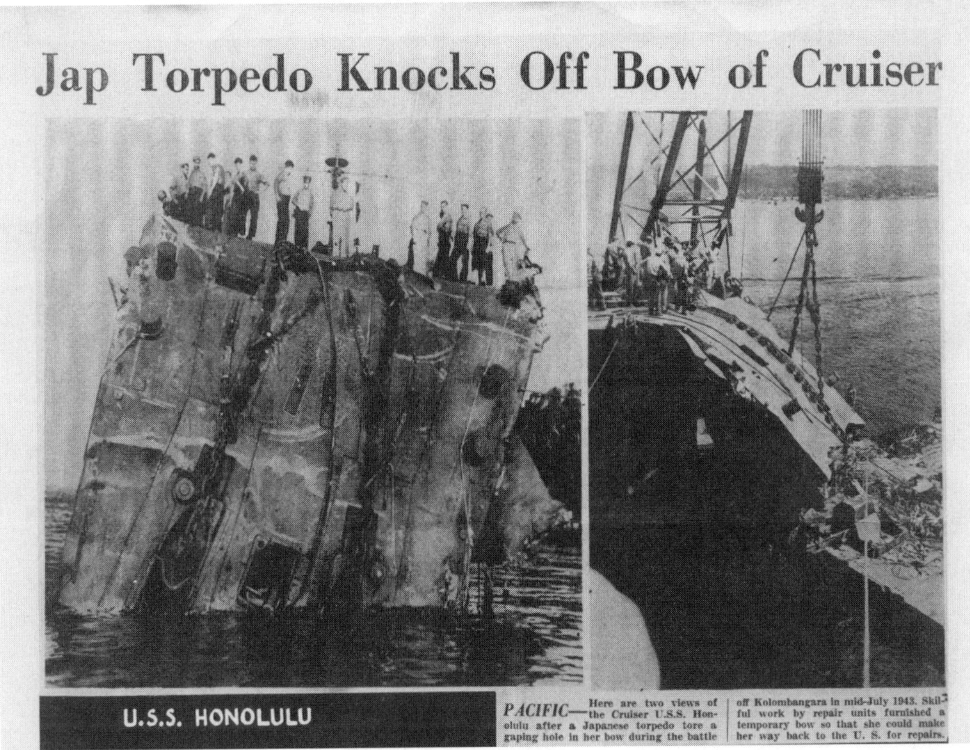

Jap Torpedo Knocks Off Bow of Cruiser

U.S.S. HONOLULU

PACIFIC—Here are two views of the Cruiser U.S.S. Honolulu after a Japanese torpedo tore a gaping hole in her bow during the battle off Kolombangara in mid-July 1943. Skillful work by repair units furnished a temporary bow so that she could make her way back to the U. S. for repairs.

USS *Honolulu* torpedoed. (Courtesy of Ralph Tannenbaum)

diameter guns with a projectile that weighed approximately two hundred sixty pounds. They were powerful weapons.

Hit by Destroyers—As the war progressed, I took part in several of the island landings from Guadalcanal, Solomon Islands, Guam, and Pelelui to the Philippines. The first time we were hit, the *Chicago* was torpedoed off Guadalcanal. Going back to San Francisco for repairs, we returned to the Pacific only to have the *Chicago* hit again by Japanese destroyers. This time, it sank the cruiser. I, of course, ended up in the water. Out of a thousand people, we probably lost about three hundred.

The reason we didn't lose any more than that was because large ships don't go down that fast. These ships have what they call damage control. In an emergency, the interior acts almost like a little beehive, all of the doors close shut so they can flood one compartment to counterbalance the area that's been ripped open and flooded. One compartment can be flooded, two compartments can be flooded, but if you flood too many, then the heavier section sinks. The ship dips and then little by little, it sinks. It took roughly thirty minutes for the *Chicago* to sink, so we did not lose too many people.

On the Honolulu—After we lost the *Chicago,* I was reassigned to a staff in Noumea, New Caledonia. There for a month, I had had enough and asked for sea duty again. That's when I was given the position of main battery assistant on the *Honolulu.* The *Honolulu* was a light cruiser, and had 15 6-inch guns. Well, I had been at gunnery control for pretty close to twenty-four hours without sleep when we landed in the Philippines and heard General MacArthur's "I have returned" speech on the ship's announcing system. Relieved from the battle station, I was on my way to my bunk in the stateroom. I went down into the bowels of the ship to the gunnery plotting [computer] room to see how things were going. As I was leaving, one of the ensigns I knew went off duty and came up the ladder with me. I passed through the ward room, where the junior doctor, the chaplain, and a couple of communication officers were sitting with a big bowl of ice cream. They asked me if I would like to have some. I said, no, I'm just absolutely dead on my feet.

Kamikaze—I got undressed and no sooner had I laid down in my bunk, the ship was hit with a torpedo. Now, this was one of the first Kamikaze attacks we experienced. Planes coming in low. The ship was hit in one of its ammunition magazines. Flames ripped through an elevator and blasted out where these friends of mine had been eating ice cream. Two of them were killed instantly. The junior doctor was very badly burned and the chaplain was badly wounded. There were thirty men in the plotting room. Each one of them was killed.

Call It What You Want—I was not scathed. Not hurt at all. That tends to make one think, when your time comes, it comes. I also understand the saying, "there's no such thing as an atheist in a fox hole." Nor on a ship. I think that's why I've got to believe in a Supreme Being. Call it what you want, but there's no question that any religiosity that I may have came about as a result of my experiences. I was in the service on active duty for five and a half years.

Something to Think About—Now, I bring up this young ensign, his last name was Kerr, for a reason. He survived the blast, stayed in the regular Navy, but started losing his hearing and got the Navy to send him to law school. Later, he became an attorney with General Electric, and then Chief Counsel for the Secretary of Defense, John B. Connally. Now, what I'm getting at is this. Lee Harvey Oswald had been ousted from the U.S. Marine Corps with a dishonorable discharge in 1959. He wrote a letter to the Secretary of Defense, asking for a reversal to his discharge. It was denied by Connally and passed through Kerr. On November 22, 1963, President Kennedy and his wife rode in an open limousine with the then Texas Governor John. B. Connally and his wife. They were on their way to the Dallas Trade Mart. On the last leg of the trip, three shots were heard. Kennedy was hit twice, in the head and neck; Connally got a bullet in his back. Kennedy died. Connally was seriously wounded. The theory is that Oswald was not trying to kill Kennedy but Connally. So there you have it. Something to think about.

Choices—Before the war, I had two ambitions. One was to go to West Point or Annapolis, which I could have gone to, or to become an attorney. But my father had already given me a partnership in the business. In the meantime, I married Shirley and we had one child, a daughter, Edna. So I came out of the service to Salt Lake in December of 1945 and immediately went to work.

The business had continued to grow throughout the depression. I credit my father and my uncle for all their hard work in those days. We were a value-low-priced store. That means we had clothes for the average man. When people didn't have the money to buy luxuries, they still had to have shoes, they had to have a pair of pants, or a shirt or a jacket. And they found values with my father.

Father Remarries—My mother passed away in 1940 and my father remarried in 1942, about two months before my wife and I were married. There is a very strong possibility that my attitude and my decision to get married were occasioned by my father's marriage. He had been in the service then, too, stationed in Ogden. He was also very much into the business when I came back after the war. I went to work there and little by little assumed more responsibility, even though I'd say he never did completely retire.

Into the Jewish Community—In 1946, a fellow by the name of Seymour Friedman asked me to join Congregation B'nai Israel. Shortly thereafter, I was asked to be on the board. Then I became the secretary, and held the position for quite some time. My wife Shirley was also very interested and became president of B'nai Israel's Sisterhood. We became very immersed in the Jewish community. When we decided to build a Jewish Community Center, in 1957, I got on the building committee. Alvin Smith was its first chairman, but when he was elected to the presidency of the United Jewish Council, Abe Bernstein took over as active chairman. I served with him, Al, Bernie Rose, Clara Pepper and Dal Siegel. In December 1957, about one hundred fifty Jewish members gathered at Foothill and 1700 South for the ground-breaking ceremony. In the spring of 1958, they began the construction of the James L. White Jewish Community Center.

The Merger—Earlier, in the mid-1960s, we attempted a merger with the two congregations, Temple B'nai Israel and Congregation Montefiore, but it failed. I would say there were many, many things that were bones of contention between the two groups. In my opinion, we did not have two congregations, we almost had six: 1) liberal and 2) more liberal and 3) classical Reform and 4) slightly Conservative members made up B'nai Israel; 5) Conservative and 6) more Orthodox members belonged to Montefiore. Maybe 90 percent of the mid-group were willing to merge, but the "traditionalists" in both synagogues could not iron out their problems.

During the merger, I was president of the Reform temple and Jerry Pepper was president of Montefiore. Why did later efforts succeed? I think it's because both congregations saw a need for new buildings. Things had gone financially worse, and both buildings were in serious need of repair. It would cost more and more money to attract rabbis to Utah. So, in 1969, the two congregations agreed to form the United Jewish Religious School to see how students from both congregations could learn together. This effort was greatly enhanced by funds from the United Jewish Council. Our leaders were Rabbi Nason Goldstein from Montefiore, and Rabbi Abner Bergman from B'nai Israel; Max Eisen was the first principal.

With a successful educational program and the graduation of its first combined confirmation class of 1971, talk of a merger took on new life. Each congregation appointed a committee and under the chairmanship of Samuel Bernstein, they met regularly and conscientiously for several months. After holding preliminary parlor meetings at many homes to discuss the pros and cons of the proposal, a vote was held by mail in the early summer of 1972 and an overwhelming percent of the Jewish community voted for the merger.

Reform and Traditional Coexisting—Rabbi Bergman was readily accepted as the rabbi of the newly merged congregation. His ordination as a Reform rabbi was tempered by a traditional background and the charisma needed to meld the divergence that was obviously apparent. All of us worked together. There was a fear people would disassociate themselves from one or the other synagogues. Some did, many of them returned. I remember an interview that another friend and I had with Joe Rosenblatt, the patriarch of the family. His attitude was "Fellows, you wait and see. Their ardor [and by that he meant the Conservative group] and their enthusiasm is going to make this new congregation Conservative." I won't say he's been proven correct. In fact, there have been many compromises made on both sides. It used to be that some Conservative members would walk out of the room if a woman went up on the bimah. Reform Jews who have not studied Hebrew have felt left out, and maybe they still do. But there's ways to work things out. Among the diversity of Jewish thought, Jewish ideas, and Jewish people, we are all one, which is probably why we were able to accomplish a merger of two distinct congregations. Of course, in the end for some of us, if you're a man 70 years old, it's pretty hard to change.

Chanukah Lights—I'll tell you another story that affected my attitude about Judaism. As a youngster, we never had a Christmas tree. We lit Chanukah lights. When Shirley and I married, we did have a small Christmas tree when we were in California and when our oldest daughter, Edna, and her younger sister Sandra grew up, we had a Christmas tree in the home for, oh, probably five years. Then Edna started religious school and I clearly remember hearing her say, "Dad, I don't think we should have a Christmas tree because we're Jews." That was the last Christmas tree we ever had.

Learning Hebrew—Then I remember going to a district Jewish welfare board convention in San Diego. On Saturday morning, I attended services at the synagogue. One of the district leaders was given an aliya and absolutely made a botch of it with his faulty Hebrew. I vowed to myself that if I were ever called upon in a similar situation, I would know what to do. I learned to read Hebrew and in the 1970s, went through a b'nai mitzvah with my wife, Shirley.

Zionism—I had always been a strong believer in Zionism. Possibly not as ardent a follower as Dr. Zucker or Joel Shapiro were, but there is one particular event I can remember. See, the Zionist Organization of America [ZOA] was largely a membership; it was a question of numbers on the role. And then there would be a strong cadre of people who would take an active part in sending telegrams to Congressmen, to President Truman, and other officials. I believe, during the time of Israel's Declaration of Independence, in 1948, Dr. Zucker had a group of twelve or fourteen of us send massive telegrams urging support for Israel. That's the sort of thing we did.

A Sanctuary for Holocaust Survivors—It wasn't until I visited Israel in 1967 that I understood the need for Israel. I think we envisioned a sanctuary for the Holocaust victims. I think that was our motivating factor. I was happy for myself. As a Jew, I'm an American first, last and always. Whether it's my military background or what, I don't think anyone can accuse me of dual loyalties, even though I have a great affinity for my fellow Jews in Israel.

Envisioning the Devastation of Humanity—Had I been in the European Theatre, I might have understood more. But my awareness grew by an education through pictures and writings on behalf of the United Jewish Appeal [UJA]. I was stunned by the numbers, six million people killed. Do I make myself clear? The whole concept was beyond the realm of possibility. And it was a long, long time before I think the average American was able to really envision the devastation of humanity. Little by little, you got talking with people who had been in concentration camps and immigrated to this country. People like Curt Brooks who lost a tremendous part of his family, Lou Dornbush, and many others whose paths I have crossed who came to this country having been in concentration camps. As I talked with them, I realized that a person's loss, a father, a sister, a mother, a cousin, a friend, could have been my loss. It brings it closer to home.

Freedom—When I got to Israel, I began to understand just how much we owed them for giving Jews a home. Here, we Jews in America were in an affluent and secure community while others of our identical backgrounds somehow did not have the ways or means or foresight to leave Poland, to leave Russia, to leave Germany, to get out to freedom; and there but for the grace of God go I.

"THE AMERICANS ARE HERE!"

Harry Miller

Getting Out Fast—My parents were from Grodno, in the Russian Pale of Settlement, in what used to be Poland.[1] My father's last name was Mueller. That means bricklayer, which is what he was. He never went to school. I never heard anybody talk about school other than heder. Yes, they all went to heder. When he was seven years old, he worked with his father laying bricks for chimneys or ovens. He was so small he could climb up the chimney, clean it out, and lay the bricks in there. When my dad was in his twenties, he left his wife and daughter and went to America. There was no money to bring them. He ran away because he didn't want to be in the Russian army. He'd never get out. No, he ran to New York and worked for his brother Phil who was a bricklayer, too. He worked, raised some money, and then sent for my mother and sister Sadie. The rest of us, Ethel, Rose, Annie, and I were born in America. I was born in 1905.

Moving All the Time—My father was a small man, maybe 5′3″, but he was a physically strong person and a hard worker. No such thing as strikes then, plenty of work, and there wasn't a moment when he wasn't laying bricks. His hands were moving all the time. All the time. And at the drop of a hat, he'd fight anybody! All they had to do was say "something" to him.

Running Away Fast—My mother was no weakling either. In Russia, she worked in a tobacco factory, rolling cigarettes by hand. I think the tobacco came from Turkey. She used to talk about pogroms. She said her friends would have meetings in the woods and when the Cossacks came, they'd run away, disperse, fast. She told us about how they would come in on their horses and destroy everything in sight, torching the houses and killing or beating up people.

Hard Times—And then, my mother talked mostly about once a year she would get a pair of shoes with buttons on them for Passover. But it was a struggle. My father's family lived in a one-room house with a big stove, at least seven or eight feet long that they would sleep on to keep warm. His father built it with a chimney. You put wood in there and you could adjust the fire. Everybody slept on it.

Never Forget the Injustice—In America, my mother looked out for us, worried about us. Once a year, she'd buy us a new suit of clothes for *Pesach.* Of course, I would only let her get my clothes at Klee Brothers because they'd give you a baseball bat when you bought a suit. Two dollars and ninety-five cents for a suit and a baseball bat to boot! My mother was a Socialist and an intellectual. All of the injustices that were done to her in Russia stayed with her. She became an actively liberal person, went to night school, learned how to speak English, and became aggressive in the affairs where she could better herself. When I was a kid, she and my Dad took me to hear Eugene V. Debs.[2] He was running for President on the Socialist ticket. They held me up by the arms over everyone's heads so I could see him face to face.

My Dad had a difficult time speaking English. He'd work eight or ten hours a day, and when dinner was all over, he'd meet with some of his friends to play pinochle for pennies and nickels. They'd pass the time away. But I remember when my Dad heard about a massive pogrom in Russia where thousands of Jews were being killed. He took me to a public meeting at the City Auditorium. It was dark, stormy, raining, and the place he took us was packed with four or five thousand Jews. A speaker was standing up in front asking the Lord to hear their plea. "Our people in Russia are being killed," he cried. "Stop them from being slaughtered. Let them come to America." Oh, that man's words had a big effect on me all my life.

Mean Streets—We moved from New York to Chicago, following my father's brother. Even though he couldn't speak English and couldn't write, my uncle became a successful contractor building homes. We never went hungry. We always had something to eat: barley soup, a piece of meat, black bread. We lived in Chicago on 2046 Division Street until I was about six or seven years old. That was a tough area with a lot of troubled kids.

I could have gone that way, too, but was fortunate to meet a man named J. P. Hardgroves. He took an interest in kids; got us off the streets and into the Association Club. It was known as the Lincoln AC or the Lincoln Athletic Club and it was a character-building organization with debating, chess, checkers, basketball, softball—all kinds of sports and competitions. It was my hangout and a big turning point for me.

Buy Bonds—When my grandmother had TB, we left our dad working in Chicago and moved to Denver to stay with our grandfather. After a few years, we returned to Chicago; a year or so later we made a final move to Denver where my Dad had made enough contacts by then to earn a living. World War One had just ended and I remember that day in 1917, Chicago, when everybody hooked up buckets and cans to streetcars and automobiles and the whole town was crazy with whistling and screeching. I was still in grade school making speeches to buy bonds. They called me a three-minute man because that was all the time we were allocated to talk—three minutes.

Orange Slices—My grandmother had to live at the Jewish Consumptive Relief Society. We would go there to visit her. She was a tall, thin, beautiful woman. She wore all white clothes and she had one of those little buckets she carried, to spit in. Her name was Hanna and I can see her now peeling an orange at the JCRS, part for my brother and part for me. We'd stay by her bed and she would tap us on the back. "Ari," she'd say, handing me a slice of orange. "Ari." That was on my birth certificate, but we never used it. So my name is Harry. The JCRS was an old hospital made by Jews, built by Jews, Jewish doctors. There were beds all over and sick people wearing white walking around with their buckets, but it was nice, clean, peaceful, and the air was dry.

Dolly—My grandfather had his own house and we lived three blocks away. When my father bought a house on Holden Place with three bedrooms and a yard where he kept his planks and bricks, my grandfather moved in with us. He didn't have much business. He was just a good man. He'd go out and buy junk, make a quarter a day selling paper, anything! He never knew what the word charity was. He was always at the synagogue. This man would get up in the morning, wash his hands, and the first thing he'd do was feed Dolly, his horse. Then he would go to the shul, which was right across the street, where he'd sit and study. Then come back for breakfast. I used to go with him, sit next to him in the wagon, when he went junk peddling, hollering through the alleys. People would come out with bottles and rags. I remember one day he came home from the alley with a baseball shirt from the Allison Candy Company. They had a team in 1920, and, oh, it was such a find. When I'd seen that baseball shirt, I wore it every day! That was my life!

Ganveh—In 1925, '26, Jewish immigrants came to Denver in droves. It wasn't a ghetto where we lived—those who became wealthy in the cattle business or merchandising moved up the hill—but Rudy Park, in back of West Colfax, was where many of us lived. Here, a lot of kids couldn't speak a word of English. When we played ball, our signals were always in Yiddish. Like, if we wanted to hit the ball, we'd say, *"derlang."* If we wanted to steal a base, it was *"ganveh"* which means to run. If you wanted to throw the ball, it was *"varf."* And that's the way it was. Sunday was the day of the ballgames! And when we played softball with those Jewish boys who moved up the hill, it was the "Ups" versus the "Downs." But on Saturdays, nobody played games; everybody went to synagogue. There was no such thing as not going!

Old Bread and Skimmed Milk—Now what I'm going to tell you is going to be quite a surprise. Our rent was $3.00 a month. It was a small house, a very small house but even then we had somebody that lived in the back of the house. I don't remember his name. All I know about him is that he lived on old bread and skimmed milk. Yes, this was an area for Jews, and there were many that moved here, to Salt Lake City. Big Ben Engleberg was one; he lived in Rudy Park; and Charlie McGillis was another. He was a West Colfax boy.

The Two-Fisted Fighter—Now, Charlie was well established in Denver and in Salt Lake City. He was the circulation manager of the *Salt Lake Tribune* and was one of the outstanding personalities when it comes to, shall I say, promoting street sales. See newspapers were "the king of the walk," and kids sold papers on the streets. That's where Charlie came into the picture. On the corners, he was a little on the rough side because he was, without question, a two-fisted fighter. He wasn't nasty or vicious, but when he went to do a job he would do it, and he would do an excellent job. He came right to the point. He didn't talk in circles or riddles. If he had something to say, he said it. He knew the town, the area, and the people. He was a one-of-a-kind guy, who would help anybody out. And he would stand up and fight for his rights. If anybody said anything anti-Semitic, he went to the person, because he could fight with both hands, and he would go, and no *ifs, ands, or buts* about it. No, Charlie wouldn't walk backwards. He was into amateur boxing shows.

The Jewish Boxer—You might not think Jews were involved in that kind of sport, but you're absolutely wrong. I would say that in the twenties, we had outstanding boxers who were Jewish. You take Charlie White, Benny Lambert, King Levitzski, Barney Ross, Hymie Garfinkle, and Jackie Fields. Two outstanding fighters were Hymie Garfinkle and Abie Mishkind. Of course, times were tough in those days and people had just come over from the old country. Louis "Kid" Kaplan, who was a feather-weight champion, couldn't even speak a word of English, and when he came to Denver and got into boxing, he was a by-product of the depression. So it was a good choice for him. I knew Jake Cobel, who was the circulation manager of the *Post,* and his brother Billy. They were close friends of Jack Dempsey. Billy had a haberdashery store in Denver; I had about five or six bouts for Billy. He was a great guy and a great sportsman from the old school; a two-fisted fighter, like Charlie McGillis.

SOFTBALL

Softball was a big thing then—in the late '30s. We had an all-Jewish team in Salt Lake. There were people like Harry Goldberg, Harry Guss, Max Guss, and Izzy Wagner in the MMCs. That was Congregation's Montefiore Men's Club. We played together a couple of years. At the time, we had a strong team and we played against the best of them: the Ziniks, the Knight Brothers, there were about forty, fifty teams playing out there at White Park on North Temple across the street from the State Fairgrounds, and we were among them, playing two or three times a week. We got good.

"Nanny Goat" Dupler—Joe Dupler, the owner of The Brass Rail and Dupler's Furrier—oh, and he had a mink ranch—was also in the business and was one who moved to Salt Lake City. He was a good-hearted man, always gave the newsboys money and presents on Christmas because he remembered when he was a kid on a street corner yelling out headlines. Of course, if you really wanted to get Joe Dupler mad, all you had to do was call him, "nanny goat." In Denver, he used a nanny goat to carry his ice cream he went selling in Broadway Park. So we got used to calling him "Nanny Goat" Dupler.

Into Utah—For a while, I boxed, too. I boxed in as a flyweight; had sixteen fights, won fifteen of them. So how's it happened I ended up in Utah? Well, I used to manage a Piggly Wiggly basketball team for the grocery chain that ended up being Safeway. In 1934, we had quite a number of kids from Utah play on our team, and passing through the state in 1935, I stopped in on one of the ball players I had just released. A nice guy on the highway patrol, he introduced me to the road commissioner, Pres Peterson, whose boy was also active in sports at Utah State University.

Street fighting in Cherbourg, June 1944. (Courtesy of Harry Miller)

Looking for the enemy in Cherbourg. (Courtesy of Harry Miller)

He asked me what I was doing and I told him I was managing the team and going to law school. One thing led to the other and I added that I was working on the school publication, selling ads for the newspaper, and that I used to sell on corners.

Fast Deals—He said, "I like the way you talk. You move fast." And he offered me a job publishing a Utah magazine, the Utah State Road Commission's official monthly magazine. He talked about what he wanted—to cultivate tourist activities—and I tell him, "I'm interested." He said, "What do you want, Miller?" I said, "Two hundred dollars a month, I'll keep all the money from the ads, pay the printing bill, and give you so many copies." He went out of the room, came back a few minutes later, and said, "That's good." I said, "You made a deal." I went back to the Hotel Utah, where I was staying, unpacked my clothes, and that was it. I published the magazine until the war started. Then, since gas was rationed and cars were rationed, and the road commission didn't have

Fighting in the streets. (Courtesy of Harry Miller)

Surviving in the ruins. (Courtesy of Harry Miller)

enough money to develop roads, you couldn't have a magazine telling people to come here, we stopped publishing until after the war.

Overseas—I enlisted in the army, was in the 79th Infantry Division, and went overseas. We were there a day or two after the initial invasion began until the end of the war. At one point, I was transferred from H Company to the Regimental Headquarters in the 314th division, and was close in combat. We were in five battles, and always under artillery fire. We lost a lot of soldiers going to Cherbourg for the main assault at Fort de Roule. Without the port of Cherbourg, we might not have stood a chance. I wrote about it in my book. Come over here, you can read it all there.

First American in Paris during the liberation, Harry Miller (*2nd from left, front row.*) (Courtesy of Harry Miller)

> Less than a mile away from Cherbourg, Fort du Roule was built into a cliff overlooking the port. The French had first fortified it, but the Germans had added murderous finishing touches. The approaches were covered by concrete emplacements and pillboxes from which interlocking bands of machine-gun fire sprayed the whole area. There were heavy and light artillery, ack-ack guns swung low to play point-blank into the attackers, an anti-tank ditch thirty feet deep, and a mess of barbed wire to slow the advance. To take it seemed an almost suicidal mission. But there was no taking Cherbourg without it.[3]

The Germans were dropping bombs around us, all right. They were fighting from here and they were fighting from there and evidently we were in the middle and had to dig foxholes. They seemed to be coming from all directions. Oh, I can tell you what it was. People killed. Friends. Faces you knew. We just lost a lot of people. It was hard and we were so tired. It was like all our feelings were gone.

The First American—But I remember one detail. We were in Paris just days before the liberation of Paris, we came to town, ahead of troops. Because we were the Cross of Lorraine, we were told our outfit, the division, was going to be there to liberate Paris. So we were there but something happened and they were going to have the Second French Armory Division enter the city. But I was already there and, of course, the French are fighting the Germans and, of course, I was hard and calloused by this time. But I believe I was the first American in Paris.

Disbelief—They thought at first I was German and I had a hard time convincing them that I was American. When they finally believed me, they threw their hands up in the air, shouting, "The Americans are here!"

Stark Reality—Fighting was still going on, like I said, but I met an English woman, Connie McGibbeny, I think that's how you spell her name. She became my interpreter. She convinced other people that I was American. But it was hard. Mind you, everything was dark. Everything was pitch black. There was no food. There was no heat. Zero. She took me across the street where there was a Nazi seal in red wax, not a Jewish star, but a seal on the door branding the occupants as Jews. I knocked on the door. They let me in. Again, I had to convince them I was an American. Living there was a brother and his father; the mother was already killed. They said they weren't Jewish, but I knew they were lying. I knew they were afraid to tell the truth, because they had been broken. I could see their wrists were red from where the skin had been ripped off from being tied with wire.

It happened, see, the Nazis would put Jews in prison, tie them up with wire, and beat them until they would admit to being Jews. Then they would put the Jew in a harness. What I mean by that is, they broke them and forced them to work for them. See, this other man I met had been in the jewelry business. He was taken into prison like the others, and beaten, but was allowed out of prison provided he would bring in so much gold every week. His sister had not been taken as a Jewess, because she was living with a Frenchman who protected her, denying she was Jewish. But their father was killed. I talked with them for long hours. This man, his name was Louis Bass. He enlightened me. I understood what was going on. Later, I met the Basses again, and others who had come out of hiding in Paris. Tragic stories. It hits hard. So I'll tell you. I brought a K-ration, what you call a No. 10, with spaghetti and meatballs and managed to get some potatoes from the field, if you know what I mean, and I remember we had our own kind of seder, and they ate and ate and talked for hours and hours. I will never forget it. Remember, the Germans had not succumbed yet, the fight is really just beginning, soldiers are dying on the streets, and the teardrops are huge.

They wanted to go to Israel, these Parisian Jews told me. Nobody had protected them in Paris and, as one man told me, their only hope was "to have a pillow under our heads in Israel."

Reunion—Outside of Paris, I met a Jewish fellow wandering in the woods, heading for the city. He gave me a little inkling of what was transpiring, but we were moving fast, so I didn't have much time to talk with him. I did give him some money and some K-rations. But our conversation was *F&F*, fast and furious. In Brussels, I met this one young girl, who must have been seventeen or eighteen years old. The Nazis had captured her, put her in a truck, and were taking her away when somehow she managed to jump off the truck. Broke her leg. She wound up in a Catholic convent. They kept here there. Safe. They'd done everything possible to convert her to Christianity, but she would not be converted. When I saw her, she walked with a real limp. In fact, I don't know how she walked without crutches. Outside of what became a Jewish community center building, they had a big billboard on the wall. Of those who returned, they would list their names and post it on the board. We'd go there, this girl and I, to look, and lo and behold, there was her brother, he must have been eleven or twelve years old, standing right in front of the billboard looking at the list of names! And when they saw each other, you couldn't believe the sight!

I'm a Jew definitely. When I got out of Brussels, I was looking for Jews all the time. Wherever I went. Wherever I went. You know, when you see your own people, you're one of them, and they're being slaughtered, and, you got to know, the resentment is strong. I was always an Orthodox Jew, even though I never practiced at it, at heart that is who I am. I could tell you stories, one after the other after the other that would bring you to your knees. Terrible stories. Life-affirming stories. It makes you wonder. I had some real experiences that taught me that I am a Zionist and will always be a Zionist. But the war is all water under the bridge now, I'll tell you.

Home Again—After the war, I went back to publishing. Yes, my contract with the state was renewed for a few years until my company, Lorraine Press, got too active, too busy. I published the weekly newspapers for Kearns, and then a weekly paper, the *Sunset News,* on the westside of town, and the *Daily Legal Record.* Let's see, what else did I create? That's enough for the time being.

Digging foxholes outside Paris. (Courtesy of Harry Miller)

TWELVE

Surviving

ESCAPE FROM KRISTALLNACHT

Minna Margaret Loser Praijs and John Price

Minna Margaret Loser Praijs—FULL JEWISH DESCENT. My husband, Selmann (Simon) Praijs (Price), was born on 30 May 1890 in Wislitza, Poland, the son of the merchant Isaak (Samuel) Praijs and his wife Florentine Praijs née Bloch. He was of full Jewish descent.[1]

To emigrate in April 1939, my husband had to have his birth certificate. This document, ordered in a hurry from Poland, indicated my husband's birth year as 1893 instead of the year 1890. In order not to risk our emigration, we decided not to correct the year of 1890.

GERMAN CITIZENSHIP. When Simon was five, in 1895, he and his parents moved to Berlin, Germany where he [eventually] attended the middle school. Upon completion Simon began a three-year apprenticeship in a men's clothing department store [owned by] Albert Goldberg in Spandau. He became a merchant in the same store. In the First World War, he volunteered to enlist in the German Army, which automatically gave him German citizenship.

After the war, he started his own business. Together, with a partner, they opened a cigar and cigarette shop. (It was during this time, in 1924, that I met my husband.) That business opportunity led to five or six stores, which were later sold, and eventually he had ownership of several men's clothing stores and investments in property.

Before Kristallnacht. A portion of the block of stores owned by Simon Price. (Courtesy of John Price)

KRISTALLNACHT. In 1928, we were married and the business became well known in the middle class public. By 1936, however, his income went down and was between 8,000 to 9,000 reichsmarks. In the year 1937, because of a boycott on Jewish businesses, our income went lower and lower, dropping to 4,000 reichsmarks per year.[2] In 1938, we hardly sold anything and because of this we did not purchase new items. In the period of Kristallnacht (November 9, 1938), the losses were staggering.[3]

DAMAGED GOODS. After Kristallnacht, we returned [to the store] and the business was a total disaster. Two show windows were broken and all the displays were destroyed by people walking on them. Merchandise such as sweaters, shirts, ties, and socks were pulled off the shelves and thrown about the floor. After we cleaned up, the damaged items were estimated to be 4,000 reichsmarks. The rest of the items were dirty, wrinkled, and not worth the original price. To this date, we do not know the correct amount of the damage or the amount of each item lost.

That same day after Kristallnacht, we packed the items in boxes and took them to a room in the store. From there, we still sold them secretly to old customers until Christmas. We could only sell the items dirt cheap because they were damaged. At this time, we still had half of the building and items that were worth 10,000 reichsmarks and sold for 2,000 reichsmarks. The rest of the building was 5,000 reichsmarks, which was estimated by the Industry Chamber. The items were

The Price family: Simon and Margaret with Wolfgang and Hans (John), 1938. (Courtesy of John Price)

3,700 reichsmarks at cost and retailed at 5,000 reichsmarks. The estimator estimated the tax amount of only 2,537 reichsmarks. Everything was sold for this amount. The buyers are not known to us.

In early 1938, an anti-Jewish economic campaign was in full throttle with laws and decrees that tumbled one onto the other to shatter the Jewish economic existence in Germany. On April 26, 1938, all Jews were ordered to register their property. Jewish assets, estimated five years earlier at ten to twelve billion reichsmarks, were reduced to half that amount. On July 6, a law was passed listing commercial services were forbidden to Jews, such as real estate brokerage and credit information. On September 30, licenses of Jewish physicians were withdrawn; within that same month, Jewish lawyers were forbidden to practice law. On November 12, 1938, after the Kristallnacht pogrom, a ban was placed on all Jewish business activities.[4]

ESCAPE. In April 1939, we emigrated with our eight- and five-year-old sons, Wolfgang and Hans (John).

John Price—A BEAUTIFUL AREA. My father's name was *Selmann.*[5] Over here, it became Simon, of course. Greta, my mother, became Margaret. I have one brother, Wolfgang, which is William over here. In Germany, my name was Hans Jochaim Praijs. I grew up in the city of Spandau, 16 kilometers from Berlin. Spandau was more like a town. Apartments could have been two to four stories high, the streets were paved, and you had squares with parks in them. A lot of the buildings had parks in the middle; my father's had grass, and there were public parks. It was a very beautiful area.

A NORMAL LIFE FOR JEWS. This district in Spandau was mainly Jewish. There were quite a few well-off professional people there, too. Jewish doctors, a lot of artists, you had a lot of performing arts, musicians and such. It was a very, very cultured area. Lawyers hung out their shingles and practiced law. Teachers taught at schools, in colleges. It was a normal life there for Jews.

THE EARLY SHOPPING MALL. My father had stores in Spandau. He had had a city block with a courtyard in the middle. On the first floor, there were stores; on the second, living areas. A city block would have been, my guess is, five-acre blocks. They were good-sized blocks with many stores; some he owned and many were rented out to other people. He owned, for example, the dry goods store where he sold towels, linens, and things like that. He had a lot of relatives running the stores. That's how he got his employees. After my parents married, Mother worked in the stores too. She was good with figures and helped on the books.

There was a cooking store where they had pots and pans, cups and saucers, those types of household goods, and a meat store where they cut and sold kosher meats. My father had a men's clothing store and a haberdashery. There was a pastry shop that he didn't own but rented out. And there was a movie theatre on the same block. It was a two-level theatre that showed movies with quite primitive sound. I remember going down the stairs right into the courtyard. The design of this area was like a predecessor of an early shopping mall. That's what you really had, all the way around the block were stores and shopping areas, and we were living above that.

THE 1936 OLYMPICS. I was born in 1933. I went to a Jewish school at the synagogue, maybe a few blocks away is all. We never really had a problem. I didn't personally see it. I was young at the time. I think all the horror stories my parents heard starting in the 1920s and 1930s took place in some of the larger areas, probably Berlin. The Brownshirts harassed everybody right from the beginning. But during the 1936 Olympics, they ended up taking down all of the signs against Jews. They stopped publishing newspaper articles that were derogatory towards Jews. They kind of whitewashed everything. Then when the Olympics were over, of course, they started up again.

SILENT VOICES. My father was a Teutonic type of man, very strong, and a doer. But he wasn't much of a speaker and he would never think to talk to us about what was happening. We were isolated from that. It wasn't happening in our own town. Or maybe my father actually isolated us from knowing. Even when he was in America the few years he lived before he died, I don't recall that he ever talked about it. It just isn't something you talk about.

WANTING A GOOD LIFE. My father was born in Poland and in World War I, he became a soldier in the Germany army, thus becoming a German citizen. He met my mother through mutual friends. He had already started the businesses and did a lot of activity. She was at least twenty years younger than he was when they married. In Europe, that's a very natural thing. People establish their business, establish their livelihood, and then they get married.

Other than basic schooling, neither my mother nor my father had a higher education. My father had tenacity. He had a couple of brothers to help him start out; both of them were champion prizefighters. One was a light-heavyweight fighter, the other a heavyweight fighter, and father was a middleweight prizefighter, so they made money doing fisticuffs in the ring. Strong, hard working, driven, they wanted to improve their lot. I remember seeing pictures of my parents, when he was courting my mother, in cars. I think everybody thought they would have a very good life.

BEGINNING TO HIDE. I know that my mother was not as kosher as my father was. But after awhile, it got too difficult to do that. Towards the latter part of our lives in Germany, before we left in 1939, it was too dangerous to go out. We were told to stay as close to home as we could, so I think they gave up on keeping kosher.

WARNINGS. There were early warnings that Jews were in danger and there was talk of people getting out of Germany. I had aunts and uncles and grandparents and cousins all living on the block or in adjacent blocks of our home. Some had started to go on trips and disappeared. No one ever talked about it. A lot of them decided to stay and then it became very difficult to get out. Everybody was trying to convince my father to go many years earlier, in the early 1930s, when he could have gotten out with some money by selling his business. But he believed he had no reason to go. He didn't want to leave. By the time it got to 1938, why, there was nothing to sell. And still, I'm not sure he wanted to go. They didn't believe, they couldn't believe, they couldn't fathom it, that it was going to last. Like everything else, it would be over with. They were going to oust Hitler. He was not going to continue to be the Chancellor forever. But it didn't work out that way.

THE SHATTERING OF GLASS. Kristallnacht happened to us, to our district. In apparent retaliation for the assassination of a German diplomat by a young Jewish boy, storm troopers or Brownshirts got together and went from block to block with bats and you name it, breaking all the glass in store fronts, breaking into shops, destroying property and pillaging everything in sight. What was left as a remnant, they marked with big stars. They painted the walls and glass with big yellow stars. We were all hiding upstairs above one of the stores. They didn't have ladders to get up and break those windows, but they broke all the shop windows and destroyed everything in their way to put the Jewish merchants out of business. It sent a very strong mes-

The Price Boys on the banana boat to freedom. (Courtesy of John Price)

sage. And you know my father couldn't do anything about it.

GOING INTO HIDING. It was frightening. I don't know exactly where we were in the apartment when it started. I mean, it just happened. We were upstairs, above the shop, and all of a sudden, you could hear the roar of big crowds coming. You closed your drapes, turned off the lights, hid where no one could find you, and made believe you didn't exist. And they just broke in and looted and you were literally left without a business. You're not going to start a new inventory. Just board-up the windows.

KILLING. They broke into all the synagogues, torched Torahs. I'm just glad they didn't torch the buildings. They beat up people. If you were a Jew out on the street, you got beaten up. You could be dead.[6] I can't say that I saw it, but at least one hundred people were killed in Spandau that night.

FINES. The next day, everybody had to muster up and start to wear yellow stars. My father had insurance and applied for compensation, but the insurance never paid. If anyone did get anything, it would have been confiscated as a collective fine on the Jews of Germany for the assassination of the German diplomat.

SILENCE. For the next month or so, we stayed close to home. We never left the house, as I recall. My parents never discussed leaving Germany. I guess they were fearful I would say something to one of my childhood friends. So nothing was ever said. And just one night we packed, and the next morning we were gone. After February 1939, nobody got out.

BRIBES. I remember one couple. I don't know what happened to them. But when we went into hiding, they helped us until we could really get out. They were very good friends of my father's and had one of the shops on the block. They helped. When it got down to late 1938, you had to amass a lot of money to try to get out. My father gave up everything. He got four visas. Did he bribe anyone? Absolutely. He bought them illegally, no question that he bought them. He didn't stand in line with thousands of others waiting to go to an Embassy. He bribed our way out.

DEPARTURE. We didn't take much. I remember a couple of paintings, surprisingly, two feet by three feet. I think my father brought three of them over. One was by a student of the Dutch painter Rembrandt, another was a scenic painting done in very heavy pointillism, and a third one was very dark and dim of a person praying.

And I don't remember how we left, but it had to have been in secrecy and I know these people helped. We ended up in Bremerhaven, which is an exit port to the North Sea, and we left on a small freighter that was returning to Panama. The boat came to Bremerhaven to deliver bananas and we hid down in the hold of the banana storage. There were four of us and then there were another four, a family. So there were eight on this boat. That boat could have taken a hundred people or more. But two families are all they took. That was the last boat that left Bremerhaven for a foreign country. When we arrived in Panama, it was more difficult for my parents than for us. They had difficulty speaking, while we were young and could pick up the language.

Minna Margaret Loser Praijs (Price)—In Panama, my husband worked as a painter in the canal zone. He painted apartments of American families but because he had not learned this trade, it was very hard for him. He was extremely underpaid.

STARTING OVER. In 1940, we were able to emigrate to the United States of America. We stayed in New York, where my husband found employment working nights in a machine factory. He worked with a lathe producing a variety of metal screws. Myself, I made a little money by working out of our home. Our income was always just enough to meet our needs. The end of 1943, we tried to establish our own business, which were ornamental pins made of leather and fur. This business did not meet our life needs, but because we did not belong to a union, and had to do it ourselves, our life standard was a little better than the previous years.

In 1946, my husband's sickness, which later resulted in his death from lung cancer, made him unable to work as much as he desired. Another problem was the industry development after World War Two was so fast, we couldn't keep up with it working out of the house. Because of this our income was barely enough in the year my husband died. When Wolfgang joined the American Army and our youngest son, Hans, age twelve, made enough for his allowance by delivering packages, we managed to get by and life got a little better.

John Price—DIFFICULT CHANGES. My parents were able to take as much as they could carry and no more. They left everything else behind. My mother was always sad. I don't think either one of them were ever really happy. They couldn't speak English. They had little money left. And very few relatives were left or could be found. It was a very sad existence, and we worked all the time.

TO MAKE A LIVING. In New York, my parents manufactured plastic tablecloths and shower curtains in the house. The house was full of material in every nook and cranny. My brother and I would haul them on the subway to the customers. They were very heavy to lug around. Later, we made fur and leather pins. My mother was tenacious and a hard worker. We worked all the time. Even though our first household was very religious, and my father was kosher, that was secondary to survival. Making a living and all that was crucial. When everyone's working these long hours with few breaks, eventually the traditions die away. We didn't stop celebrating Chanukah then; in fact, we celebrated the holidays. My father still went to synagogue, and I would go with him. After he died, I went for a year.

DISCRIMINATION IN AMERICA. In the 1940s and 1950s, there was a lot of anti-Semitism in corporations. You couldn't break into work. I remember in New York, there weren't many Jews in the upper management and professional businesses. I worked in the very early days with a producer, a company that produced television series and several soaps. Nobody in that company was Jewish. It didn't matter because they didn't know I was Jewish, but you knew by the things they said, that if you were Jewish—or if they found out you were Jewish—you wouldn't grow through that company. Then I had an experience with a worldwide company. I started out in their duplicating department as others did. But after a year, I was still in the duplicating department while the others had graduated to draftsmen, junior draftsmen, junior engineers, and so on, and I had just as much of a background as they did. But they knew I was Jewish. There was one Jewish person who worked in their drafting department. He was much older than all the others. He told me, "Don't stay. I stayed too long and look where I am. I got nowhere. Now it's tough to find a job elsewhere. I'm too old." He said the company would never promote Jews. I understood that.

YOU FORM YOUR OWN BUSINESS. Corporate America at one time had few Jews at the top. There are very few of those old-line companies before the war that had, at the upper business level, Jewish people. That's a very broad statement to make. We had a lot of friends that were engineers and ended up working for the subway system and public systems. I think it was the same with other nationalities, other minorities. So what you have to do is you don't bother with that. You just go out and make your own life. You ask about the compulsion to succeed? I think a lot of Jewish men went out and did extra duty work. They realized it doesn't matter if you run the race with a crutch [of anti-Semitism]. You run it. You form your own business and you do your job.

A TOSS OF A COIN. After that last job in New York, in 1954 I left the East Coast with a friend and knew right away I didn't want to go back to New York. We went to Grand Junction, Colorado, and worked on a survey crew for about two months, and made some money. Then we flipped a coin because I really had to go back to New York to finish up a semester of school. If I won, my friend would have to return with me because I had the car, a 1950 Ford Victoria. I paid for my car working summer and weekends, and what have you, in the Catskills. These resorts were all Jewish and all kosher. I started as a busboy, then as a waiter. I made enough to go to school and get a car. I think the idea of making money was always key in my life. I was making money when I was six or seven years old, doing odds and ends. I always had a way of making a buck. You see your father working and I think it's something you realize early that if you don't have something and you want something, you work for it. But, to get back, we were in Colorado ready to leave for New York and my friend talked me into coming to Utah. He said there were colleges here. I could get into geology. So we flipped a coin, headed West and never did get past Utah.

HELPING HANDS. I didn't know anybody when I first came. But when I was looking for a job, someone said, go and see Joe and Celia Doctorman. I went out and saw them and they hired me. They hired me to work in their meat packing plant. I worked for about a year while I was going to school. I lugged meat, cut meat, and helped deliver meat. The Doctorman family, Joe and Celia Doctorman, their son Harry Doctorman, and his brother-in-law Nat Levine and his wife Irene were great people who extended themselves to me. They invited me to dinners because I was a bachelor, in school, and they took a liking to me.

When I decided to go into the construction business, I got a little bit of help from Henry Pullman, from Pullman Clothing. He was remodeling his store. New walls and new ceilings. I built a couple of other little buildings for him and a warehouse in Salt Lake. He helped me but it was Maurice Warshaw who helped me open doors for business. I built stores for him. He was funny, he was hard hitting, he was a good businessman, and a very nice man. He was my main mentor.

SETTING MY OWN RULES. One thing just led to the other when I got into the construction business. Now, the company owns a lot of community centers and has eighteen malls around the West. There's no question I knew that I was going to be a businessman, though. From my earliest years, I knew that I had to work for myself, making my own business decisions. I like to set my own goals. In many cases, I want input, I want to hear what people have to say and how they can improve a process, but I want a place at the table, to sit at the table. And that, I found, comes from working hard and wanting to achieve success. We are building selectively now and finding projects that are workable with a good bottom line to it. I have a responsibility to make a profit for the shareholder, so there has to be a good bottom line. Having people around me who are challenged makes me challenged too.

GOING FORWARD. I believe now I'm trying to extend my productive life longer than others because the mind shuts down when you don't have a lot of activity. You can't retire, you have to move forward. The mind has to be exercised like muscles. If you've reached a point where you're satisfied with what you've done, then start to do other things. Whether it be charity or civic involvement, educational goals, traveling, or taking up sports. If there's nothing stimulating the mind to work harder, you don't move forward. Your thought patterns change, so that's why I will never stop. Maurice Warshaw never stopped. And so you just go forward.

"I HAD ON WORKING CLOTHES AND A COAT, THAT'S ALL"

Isaac Rose

Third-Generation Tavern Owner—I was born of course in the Jewish section of town in Krakow, Poland.[1] It wasn't strictly a Jewish section; in Krakow, people lived all over. But this was predominantly Jewish. My father's name was Zacharias; my mother had two names, Rachel-Ruchla, kind of a Polish-Yiddish expression. My father was a third-generation tavern owner. Until my father married my mother, he just spent his time studying. When he got married, there was a dowry, naturally. But he lost a part of it by getting into a venture with his brothers-in-law. So all he had left was enough to buy the tavern. We lived next door to the tavern, the same building. The business was in front, the living quarters were in back. After I was born, the third boy, we moved upstairs to a larger apartment.

The tavern existed until 1936 under my father's ownership. At that time, I was 25. The tavern was just a front room with a bar and taps of different sorts of beer coming out. Behind the bar were shelves with bottles of various liquors, whiskey that we sold by the drink. There were always some snacks. We sold sliced herring, pies, cookies, and we had a couple of other rooms where people who wanted some privacy could sit at their tables and order.

Taking Turns—My mother ran the household. She also worked with the customers at the counter, made sure they paid before leaving. My dad was an easygoing soul. We had a maid to do the heavy work. A Catholic maid. [Young girls] used to come from the surrounding villages where they had to work hard anyway and got nothing, to where they still had to work hard but got room and board and some money every month. The business was open from 6 or 7:00 o'clock in the morning until after 10:00 o'clock at night. My father would open, mother would come down about 8:00 o'clock, after we had gone to school, to relieve him so he could go to the synagogue for morning prayers. Then he would do some shopping for the business; besides selling beer and liquor, we sold tobacco which had to be bought from the distributor because the tobacco industry was government run. When he returned to the tavern, my mother would go shopping for the house, and then make lunch. In Europe, you eat at 1:00 o'clock because lunch is a big meal. In most places, stores were closed between 12:00 o'clock and 2:00. So whether we were at school or at work, we had to be home at 1:00 o'clock for lunch. For dinner, we had a light meal.

A Lesson in Study—My father was a religious man, very observant. He spoke some languages besides our Polish. He studied German classics, was familiar with philosophy, and very well educated in Hebrew, Hebrew Law, Talmud, and commentary. When we were young, we studied at home with him.

I attended school. After finishing my regular seven grades, I attended a kind of combination Hebrew seminary and high school where I got a very broad Hebrew and traditional education. By the age of thirteen, my older brothers finished school and went to learn a trade. One became a watchmaker, the other learned to become a jeweler. But my father, regardless of what they had been doing, spent every day with them, studying. In the long winters, when we were through with our Friday night traditional meal, by 6:00 o'clock, there were two or three hours of studying the bible. He would discuss with the older brothers what they had been studying to see how much they benefitted from it. I didn't get too much of this routine with him because at school, I was under the auspices of a religious organization with Zionist leanings. I graduated in 1929.

The Blue Coin Box—My father was a good Jew who in the spirit of a Jew supported Zionist ideas. He was supportive financially of all kinds of drives. We used to have a blue box at home from the Jewish National Fund and money was put in there very often and collected and sent to the Jewish Agency to buy land in Palestine.

Many Synagogues—Where I come from, first of all, the city's total population was approximately like Salt Lake City. Even the area was similar, surrounded by little hills. However, we had at least fifty different congregations, big and small, modern, ultra Orthodox and Conservative. Our Council, or the governing body, was responsible for maintaining four or five big synagogues. They maintained the grounds and paid the help. There were also quite a number of congregations who were grouped by trade or background. They were places where members assembled for prayers or social events, and paid dues to so they were able to meet all the expenses.

Rights for Jews—Under the Austrian monarchy, from 1848 until 1918, Jews did not experience too much anti-Semitism. We had rights. I tell you, 1848 came like a fresh wind over Europe and people could demand rights. By 1870, even Jews had all their rights. Jews were elected to parliament. We had a rabbi elected to parliament. They became judges. They attended universities. But in 1918, under Polish rule, it was a little different. When the Polish army came back, they didn't turn in their guns because there was no Austrian government. Instead, they organized bands, beat up Jews in the street, robbed people, and plundered stores. In our own hometown, we had to organize Jewish people who knew how to handle a gun, many of them like my Dad had been in the Austrian army and knew how to use a gun. These people patrolled the streets.

Taken Away—I remember we had a neighbor who lived next door. A tailor by profession, a very fine gentleman, nice family, two or three children, and a lovely wife. They were walking in the street and he was hit over the head by a club. He was paralyzed. He couldn't see. He couldn't talk. The poor fellow suffered for four years and in about 1922 or 1923, he died. This was not an isolated case, but it is one that was close to me and I remember it well. In other towns it was worse, but we took care of it by having a self-defense group patrolling the streets and keeping watch on the front of every house and holding a gun to scare away someone who intended to do harm. I was young then. Maybe eleven at the time, but my father kept watch in front of the house. He didn't carry a gun. He believed if something happened, he could alarm the people.

Anti-Semitism—I would not say that the Polish government encouraged this, but I wouldn't say they tried to protect us either. The Poles, by nature, didn't like the Jews. Few liked the Jews anyway, but under the Austrian rule, they had to keep their mouths shut. But when they got the Polish government, "Jews, go to Palestine" was the slogan. These slogans were on billboards, smeared on walls. "Jews, go to Palestine." Later on it leveled out, but for a while, it did a lot of damage.

Youthful Obsessions—As a kid, though, I remember going to soccer matches and sports events. My oldest brother was hooked on wrestling. In the early 1920s, there were regular movie houses. They showed a lot of western movies. I also remember seeing the Al Jolson.[2] He was born in Russia. But actually the Wild West was an obsession with me. I knew about America.

Stopped Short—After I finished my gymnasium, high school, and religious school, I went to a "university" in my hometown. I lived with my parents, but I wanted to be a little more independent and so I took office jobs. For awhile I even worked for my uncle who was a prominent lawyer in my hometown. I was a law clerk. I was intending to pursue my career in law and business. In 1939, I was only 28 years old at the time and to be an independent lawyer, independent, you must be thirty years old before you can practice. I never got a chance to do it. The war affected everyone.

Air Raids—In January 1939, we experienced the first air raid by the German *Luftwaffe* on a Friday morning. It lasted only a few minutes, and then periodically until noon you got about five or six raids over the town. On the third day of the war, on Sunday, there was a kind of panic in town. People started leaving town en masse. Jewish and non-Jewish people alike. I remember one bomb destroyed my grandfather's house. He lived in a different part of town in a two- or three-story house. There was a platoon of soldiers marching through the street near their barracks and a German plane saw them from the air and bombed them and their barracks. But the bomb didn't hit their barracks. It hit my grandfather's house. He happened to be in the living room downstairs. The impact knocked him off the chair. Fortunately, he wasn't injured. We ran to the house, went through the back alley and dragged him out through the window. My father took him home and he stayed with us for another two years.

POW—Several years earlier, my eldest brother moved to Vienna to broaden his skills as a jewelry maker. Then he moved to Paris. He was still a Polish citizen and went to the Polish army in France and fought alongside the French army against the Nazis. He was captured six months later in Belgium in 1940 when the front collapsed. He spent five years in a POW camp in Germany, then returned to Paris.

Invasion—My younger brother left town, but I didn't want to leave. I figured, why run when they can run faster. As it happened, two weeks later, Russia invaded from the East. They partitioned Poland between the German part and the Russian part. My brother wound up in the Russian part of Poland in the zone, which came under the Russian administration.

German Occupation—We had 90,000 Jewish people in my hometown of Krakow. Under the German administration, they decided to limit the Jewish population, cut it down to nothing practically. They created a ghetto. It was a very small area on the other side of the river that was populated by Jewish people before the war. Normally it housed maybe ten thousand people. They packed in about thirty thousand, and the rest had to get out. Conditions there were very bad. The apartment that used to be occupied by two or three people, now had eight or ten. There were not enough beds around. People went to work nights and when they came back in the morning, they took the bed of the people who slept at night and were now getting up and going to work. The bed was occupied twenty-four hours a day.

Businesses Seized—Some Jews who had been in business in other areas of town got permission to leave the ghetto and go to work in those places. They thought they still owned their business, but actually it came under a German trustee that was put in to oversee the operation. So, they'd let him go to the business, make him feel like he still owned it, but he didn't. He didn't own his business any longer. Other people went out to an army installation and worked like a handyman or a custodian. A lot of women worked there, too, sewing uniforms for the army. You had to get permission to stay in the ghetto. I didn't get it, but was not unhappy about it.

Terrible Things Happened—I seen sometimes people getting beaten up in the streets, being dragged to work, mistreated. Until the war started, there were all these big and little synagogues and places where people went in to pray. On the first Saturday that the Germans marched in, people went to the synagogue for *Shabbes.* Trucks came by one place after another and stopped while soldiers dragged out people from their synagogues and put them to work unloading coal in yards or doing other manual labor. We had to quit congregating in the synagogue because we would become a target. So we found some places to pray in private homes. Ten people here, twenty people there. We didn't want to give the German soldiers any place to go and pick up people.

Looking for Refuge—My wife and I had been married eight months before the war broke out in 1939. By 1940, we could not move around freely. So I did not live anymore in my hometown. We had to move to a neighboring city about 30 or 40 kilometers away. Town called Bochnia. My wife had some friends there, Jewish and non-Jewish. These Jewish friends arranged for us to get registered over there as local residents. The non-Jewish friend was a baker and had a truck. This was quite unusual because all the trucks had been requisitioned for the Army. But he had to bring flour to the bakery and he had to make deliveries, so they let him keep the truck. He took the truck and came to our home in Krakow, picked up our furniture, our belongings, and moved it all there to Bochnia.

No Plans—I stayed there for around two years. I still had to wear the yellow star of David on my sleeve, but I got permission to travel by railroad to my place of work, because I worked for some businesses that had been taken over by German administration. I worked in the offices as an accountant. One was a retail store with articles for shoemakers. Another was a wholesale business. Knowing the language and knowing the procedures, I not only kept my job, I was recommended from one administration to another to work. So I worked in different places. But in 1939, you couldn't make plans. You could get shot on the street, rounded up and sent away to some place. You didn't know what was going to happen tomorrow. You just went day by day. No, we tried not to make any special plans. Unless you had a lot of money, you couldn't escape.

Nowhere to Go—No, escape never crossed my mind. The civilian population would not give me any support. No, the Poles would not give any support because they didn't like the Jews. They didn't want to jeopardize their own lives. There were very isolated cases when Poles saved the Jews. For instance, when things started getting bad, some people thought they could hide in a village with some Polish families. And pay them. All right. Some Poles consented and kept them as long as they had the money. When the money was gone, they turned them over. No, there was no support from the Poles. And in Germany, you didn't know anybody, how could you expect to get some help for anybody else. No, you [believed] you were safer in the camp.

Picked Up—In 1943, my parents were deported; and the Germans were already rounding up people in Bochnia. I picked up a job with a German army unit, in order to be protected from further persecution. I did this because I protected my wife, too. I worked in the ordnance depot and she remained in Bochnia, worked in a store, sewing uniforms for the Germans. I was able to get a stamp on my passport and my wife's passport which kept us safe. But it didn't last long. A year later, on my birthday, we'd been surrounded by some guards and taken to a concentration camp. My wife was not there. She was still in a ghetto in Bochnia. Later, they liquidated this ghetto and sent what was left of the population over to a small concentration camp in southern Poland. She was there only for a few months and after they liquidated that camp, she was sent to Auschwitz. She was there a year before me.

The concentration camp they sent me to was built on a Jewish cemetery. I could see the markers. I was with a detail that went to Krakow to clean out the places where people had been rounded up and deported. We came to some apartment houses and you could still see the food on the table from where they had to get up and go fast.

Ostrowiec—In November 1943, I was coming back from the work with about twenty people and they didn't let us go in our barracks. They took us to the railroad station, packed 80 to 90 people in a railroad car. And I remember the commandant and someone else writing in chalk on the car where the destination of this particular railroad car is going. We went to a place called Ostrowiec, near central Poland. We went to several camps after that. We had what we had on our back. I had on working clothes and a coat. That's all I ever had. I had had a suitcase earlier, shirts, underwear, shoes. But they wouldn't give it to us.

Davening—We were housed in a barrack with a couple of hundred people. Slept in a bunk, upper berth and lower berth, like in a farmhouse. They gave us straw sacks that were infested. No bathing facilities. An outhouse. Some water, dirty from the faucet. You could wash your face and that's all. The food was very bad. I do remember in one of the barracks, there were some people from Hungary that were very religious and knowledgeable. After work, I managed to go to the barrack and one of the men was reading aloud so we could hear him and repeat after him some prayers. And I remember on a Saturday afternoon, they assembled us in the square and there was a rabbi and he talked to us, whether we would like to daven. So he started out, reciting the whole prayer. I remembered the prayers well because I was doing them since I was a kid. In another camp, I don't remember any kind of religious services.

Putting Up with Us—There was a factory and I worked in this factory with some civilians. Some of them were very friendly and some didn't like Jews anyway. But they put up with us. We transported and carried things for them, helped other Polish people push carts, did construction work. This was going on from about November 1943 until the next July of 1944.

Trying to Escape—In July, the Russian army advanced from the east and was very close to our area, divided only by a river. The minute that we found out that the Russians were close by, a lot of young people started running away, breaking off from the camp. Especially people who were familiar with the area; they figured they could hide among the Poles or some of their friends.

To Auschwitz—So one day, I remember the director of the factory, a German, assembled us in the square. He was doing some kind of head count. He said, "It's no use running away. The Poles hate you. Our German army is strong and will repel the barbarian Russians. But should a situation arise that we should have to evacuate the factory, you will be taken to a similar factory in Germany. We wouldn't move one hair on your head." He said, "Nothing will happen to you. Just sit down and don't run."

They surrounded the camp with some German army soldiers. Not SS, just army soldiers, mostly older people who were friendly with us. Figured we had some watches. Some tobacco. A little bartering, you know. Maybe. I didn't have anything to offer. A week later, they loaded us upon a train and we traveled one day and one night and wound up in Auschwitz.

We knew about the camp in Auschwitz. We knew Auschwitz with the gas chambers. We knew about everything. How? Polish people could still travel. They see the smoke coming out of the chimneys; they could smell the air. So they talked and we knew.

A Terrible Stench—I came over there in the morning. It looked like a strange place. Different from the other camps. Very nice, clean. Flower beds. Grass. Strange. And the barracks looked so strange, too, different than what we had been in before. And we see some strange characters running around. Persons. Wearing a dress. And no hair. They shaved the heads of the men and

Isaac Rose, survivor. (Photo by Eileen Hallet Stone)

women. When we came out of the train, we had to leave everything behind, and march to a bathhouse. And when we walked to the forest there was a terrible stench.

Gas or Water—In the bathhouse they gave us a cake of soap. We didn't know whether it would be gas coming out or water. Fortunately, it was water. After we went through the bathing, they handed out some articles of clothing. Some so big, they fell off. We had to laugh. Later we switched the clothes around. There's no reason to dwell on it.

A Bowl of Soup—They said they needed some skilled people to send away to a factory. Before the war, the factory manufactured mostly paints and chemicals. During the war, they do everything. The factory was very big and was constantly building, in the process of expansion. There were about thirty thousand civilians working there and about ten thousand prisoners, mostly German Jews and Polish Jews. I was working on all jobs as a group, construction and cleaning, from 7:00 o'clock in the morning until about 6:00 o'clock in the evening. When we got back, we had a bowl of soup.

Work—Every other Sunday was a free day. American fliers come out and bomb the factory. They seemed to know exactly when it's going to be free so they won't kill innocent people. But when we come back on Monday, we'd have to clean up and build it up again. Then I was assigned to a group of about twenty people to work in the office, outside the camp and close to the factory. What we had to do was check invoices. Another twenty people were preparing payrolls for the thirty thousand civilians. All of us were Jewish.

Two Days Together—In January 1945, we marched two or three days by foot to a big station in Germany. We came with nothing and we left with nothing. We stayed a day or two. And I'll tell you. Other groups from other camps were coming. One fellow comes up to me and says, "Listen, there's a lady with the name of Rose. She was asking about her husband." I ask, "Where is she?" I come over there and find my wife. She was in the women's division of Auschwitz. She was evacuated too. I knew she had been in Auschwitz, but I couldn't make contact. We hadn't seen each other for about two years. We were together for two days.

My wife had to work in the kitchen and she was able to bring me a whole loaf of bread. We went to the trains. I had the bread with me and some other food I was able to get. The women were put on a separate railroad car. A boxcar. Going elsewhere. And we traveled for eight days and eight nights until we came to central Germany.

Where Are They Taking Us?—In central Germany, we came to the master camp, called Drora. It was next to an installation, which produced guided missiles. I didn't work for three months because I developed an infection in my leg and I couldn't move around. They put me in a hospital, where a Polish doctor, a prisoner, took care of this by draining out the infection. I limped a little for about a week or two. After a month, they rounded us up from the barracks. We didn't know where we were going or if they were going to gas us. But they loaded us up on a truck, and brought us to a camp about ten kilometers away. There were already hundreds of people there. It looked like army barracks but there was not even a place to sit down or lay down. They put straw on the ground, there was one tap to wash with or drink from. We did nothing for about four or five weeks. Then I heard my name called out and I did paperwork for the Internal Revenue in Poland.

Allied Bombs—The 29th and 30th of March, our Passover came. On April 1st and April 2nd, it was the Christian Easter. The night before Easter, one of the SS sergeants walked into the barracks and said, "I want you to have a nice Easter." Something very unusual happened. Sunday and Monday was the Christian Easter and there were airplanes flying all over, bombs falling in the distance. By Tuesday afternoon, I was standing in one of the rooms talking with two Polish men and all of a sudden bombs were falling all over. The allies had in their plan that this was an army installation.

Saved!—Bricks were falling down. I lost my glasses at that time. I was up to my knees in bricks and rocks. I wasn't injured and neither were the two Polish men I had been talking with. My father used to tell me, if you are in a situation where your life is in danger, connect yourself with a person from a different faith or country. Because, he said, there's some place written somewhere that the angel of death does not have any power on two different nations or two different faiths. And that was it. By the 10th of April, I saw the first American soldier. We were saved.

Finding Mrs. Rose—I didn't have any doubt that I would survive. I figured if I just keep a low profile and don't get involved with any problems. And if I were lucky, I would survive. I was in an office, typing a list when a lady came over and started to ask questions. I handed her my list and she said, "Are you Mr. Rose?" I said, "Yes." She said, "Your wife is over in northern Germany. She's been liberated."

Finally Together—I remember April 15 hearing on the radio that Roosevelt had died. That's what I heard on the radio and this must have been a few days later, maybe even the beginning of May, when I met my wife again.

FORCED LABOR, LOST YOUTH

Michael Schafir

Many Concentration Camps—I was twelve years old when I saw my grandparents being herded into a railcar and taken away by the Nazis.[1] A year later, when I was thirteen and a half, I was picked up by the SS troops and sent into many different concentrations camps for five and a half years of forced labor. You could not find the names of these camps registered in any of the books that have lists of such concentration camps.

Obviously, there are a lot of camps that people know a lot about, and there were the small camps that were transitory. That is, they didn't [maintain them]. When no more jobs were needed to work, we were transferred elsewhere and this camp was demolished. This was in eastern Germany. And that's all I can tell you.

For instance, the first camp that I was taken to actually was not even a camp. The camp wasn't there. The supplies to build the camp were there. And we worked in a quarry, but when we came back at night, you had to build a camp to stay warm. This was in March in 1940, at the first camp: Bischmarchen.

Forced Labor—I was transferred from Bischmarchen to Reigezfeld to build a chemical plant. As I understood the system, and as I understand it now, the builders of this chemical plant were private people, or maybe it was the government. They would contract with the SS to supply labor for so many numbers of marks per hour. The SS was paid for our work. The SS was paid for our labor. But we didn't get anything. My job, I was doing manual labor, carrying pipes, digging.

Always Hungry—We were hungry. We were always hungry. And, I believe, my life was saved by a man, a German man who was working for the Nazis. He was a tall German. He was a professional. By that, I'm saying, he distinguished himself in his dress compared with the other Germans. First of all, he was a civilian. Second of all, he was not a guard. But he came over to my side and I survived because of him.

Michael Schafir survived five and a half years in concentration camps. (Photo by Eileen Hallet Stone)

He Saved My Life—He was a Nazi Party member, I know because he had a Nazi Party emblem on his lapel. We never talked. We were not allowed to talk to anybody unless we were addressed, ordered to do something. And he came over to my side and dropped a sandwich. I couldn't make any sense of it. And he did this day in and day out, whenever I worked. In fact, I became so used to it that I looked forward to go back to work on Monday to get a sandwich. We were starved. They were starving us.

I don't have any information to go on, to know whether he was an architect or an engineer. I surmise that he must have had an important position because he walked around very loosely, wherever he wanted to go. This is important because even Germans were restricted in some places. In other words, any German off the street couldn't just walk in there. Also they—German civilians—couldn't come to us. We were separated from the public. They would see us working, but they would not, could not, talk to us.

No Eye Contact—So he had to have been a kind of person who had a superior position. We never made eye contact. Never. If I tried to make eye contact with him, he looked away. What he did, though, was he looked around when he came to my side of the fence. He looked around to make sure he was not observed by a guard. The guards were scattered about and he made sure when he came over to my side, that he would not be caught doing what he was doing.

Taking a Risk—He took such a risk. If he had been caught giving me food, helping a Jew, helping a concentration camp inmate, giving me any attention that was kind, I'm sure the Nazis would have—I don't know what they would have done, but—he could have been killed. I learned from my experience with him that he had a purpose to what he was doing. He came in every day. That is something. For a Nazi party member to come to the site every day.

I was the youngest concentration camp prisoner. Barely a teenager. My high school years were taken from me in this place. I had no schooling. I don't know if he knew that. But he tried to help me. He did. And he did it for three years. Yes. Now, this is unusual also among the Germans to stay in one job for so long. I don't know anything about him. We never talked. We never exchanged any words. He obviously surprised me. And he just dropped a sandwich that saved my life. I don't know his name. I never found out what his name was. This man who saved me, I know nothing about him.

Alone—That was just one of the camps I was in. This was in the second camp. I was in six camps all told. This was the second camp. I know I could not have done what I did to survive had I not believed that God was watching me. I was convinced that God would not let me down. It gave me strength at first. Being a Jew, knowing what people can be, what people should be, yes, that gave me strength. You have to know I was a young boy. Alone. I lost everyone. Believing gave me strength but when I saw such atrocities in those camps that people committed against other people, I just couldn't reconcile it with my beliefs that I grew up with. It just didn't make sense. The God that I grew up with as a child, to revere, to cherish, to listen to, is guiding me, and watching over me. If there were such a God, how could he possibly, possibly tolerate what was done. How could he allow this to happen?

A Jewish Tenet—So, yes, I was religious when I went into the first camp, but gradually my beliefs went away. To me, life is common sense and Jewish ethics. I was brought up in Jewish ethics in which every human being is an equal. I treat others as I would want them to treat me. It is all common sense. I believe this. I am very fair in dealing with people. I am very concerned and, in fact, this is one of my basic tenets and this is a Jewish tenet. So, if you ask me am I spiritual by believing in God, no, I am not. Am I spiritual that I have understanding for fellow human beings, that each fellow human being to me is the same, that every human being deserves respect, that we need to be good to one another? If you want to call this spirituality, then, yes. I am a Jew. I was brought up with that history, that culture, and those ethics. And I am very proud of it. And if you want to call humane, kind, and ethical treatment religious, that's fine. Then I am that. I have no problem with it. But whether it is a Jewish God, Christian God, Muslim God, the fact remains that people have suffered in the name of God. I cannot reconcile myself to that.

> I believe with a perfect faith
> In the coming of the messiah
> In the coming of the messiah
> Do I believe
> And although he may tarry
> Yet do I believe.
>
> Thus sang survivors on their death-trek toward the crematorium. Was this a theological statement being made? That is, did they genuinely believe in the coming of the messiah—as articulated in their song based on Maimonides' twelfth Principle of Faith—or was it a chant of high courage, a refrain of defiance and an expression of Jewish solidarity in the moments of their mortality? Or was it perhaps a composite of all those elements?[2]

HIS WIFE, DIXIE SCHAFIR. I have to interrupt here to say something. Michael was born a Chasidic Jew, trained by his grandfather who was an intellectual. Grandfather Abraham ran a boy's school and was respected in his town because of his intellectual acuity. Michael was so religious that when he was a little boy he used to study with his foot in a bucket of water so he wouldn't fall asleep. And Michael loves God. He cries because he can't believe any more. But rather than think that God is a horrid being, he'd rather turn his back on God. Michael is deeply imbued with the ethics of the Jewish people. He is so totally Jewish and he is in such solidarity with the Jewish people, to hear him say he's an atheist is contrary to the way he lives.

No Explanation—I don't know that I am saying that. I have no explanation of how the Holocaust happened. Even years and years before, during the Spanish Inquisition which lasted into the nineteenth century, how could auto-da-fés have taken place.[3] This is a technical word for "execution," and I am totally speechless. I cannot understand at all when these Christians, who consider themselves holy, can simply make this a parade and they can watch people—heretics, Jews, and others—being burned. People being burned. Watching it like they were on a picnic. Can you imagine that? People being burned. And they did it over and over again. And how the Holocausts are happening right now, today, in other countries because of differences in beliefs and cultures! I have no explanation.

A Healer—I am a pediatrician. Why did I decide to become a physician? I have no physician in my past. None of my relatives were physicians. I had no role model that I wanted to emulate. What I was impressed by as a child was when I was about ten years old, my grandmother was sick and my grandfather called what was known as a healer. I was surprised by the impact he had on my grandmother and grandfather. And I realized, this is what I want to do. I want to grow up to do good for people. So this was a childhood dream. I had nothing else to go on. I want to help people. Even in the concentration camp, I kept this belief.

Liberation—After I was liberated, I was eighteen and a half years old. And alone. No home to go to. No family. No schooling. I never went to what you call high school. What was I to do? One of the dilemmas I faced was to get a place to live and I had to get an education. The first thing I did, I stood in line to register for a place to live. At that time in Germany, all housing was registered by the state and assigned to people. People had to take me in, whether they liked me or not. They had to take me in. This was a law, German law. There were millions of German refugees. But I stood in line and somehow expressed my interest in learning to a Quaker woman, who was there helping the British army. I can't remember her name, an Englishwoman. But she heard me, took an interest in me, and we became acquainted.

She spoke English, of course. I didn't speak English at all. We went on walks together. She was about thirty-five years old; I, of course, was eighteen and a half. She told me if I could learn to speak English, and since I was fluent in German—see, I was born and raised under Polish-German borders, so speaking German was easy—I could become an interpreter in the British military zone. She felt I had a knack for languages; and I did. Over time I've learned seven languages. When she talked to me, I thought, well, that would be great. So I looked around for individuals who could teach me. This woman, my friend, taught me, too. I owe her so much for what she's done for me.

A Lesson Learned—I will tell you one more example of what she did for me that has never left me. Never. I was accommodated in a hotel requisitioned by the British to house Holocaust survivors. I was assigned to a room. I had a room by myself. One day we were walking, she and I, this was in early 1945. I saw some Germans walking on the other side of the street. A couple and two children. I made a comment to her. I said, "Now, there go two murderers." To me, every German was a murderer. What I had been through, can you understand?

Now, obviously I was wrong with that concept. Who knew what this couple and their children had gone through and didn't I remember that this one German risked his life to help me? My friend was quiet. We kept walking and she stopped me. She said to me, "Mike, How do you know this, that they are murderers." I thought about it; I didn't know. She said, "You have to assume they are innocent until proven guilty." And that concept was so wonderful to me. She taught me this. I thought about it. I'm wrong. Somebody had come along to teach me something good; something that makes sense. Common sense I could believe in.

We became good friends, this woman and I. She arranged for some people to give me English lessons. And then I became conscious of the fact that to become a physician, I needed a high school education. I looked around and fortunately, at that time, there were many Germans who were unemployed, including some teachers. Somebody referred me to a Latvian who had been a teacher in his home country, between Russia and Poland. He was a wonderful teacher. Since

I already learned enough English to be a paid interpreter, I employed this man as a teacher to further my education. The Latvians were pro-Nazi, but I had no idea about this man, either. I really don't know what this man was. Or why he was teaching me, spending a lot of time with me. But I could feel he liked teaching me and he taught me everything I needed to know.

Ingenuity—And how did he do this? There were no textbooks. You couldn't get any textbooks. So this man wrote the textbooks for me. Physics for instance. How does a motor work? A diagram. Chemistry. He did it all for me; page by page, each page written by hand. He wrote every word down into a textbook for me to learn. He wrote all the textbooks for me. I still have them. Handwritten.

Then I learned about a German lady who was a professional teacher. Her husband was in prison at that time. I think he was an ex-Nazi in prison. I'm not sure. I turned to her to teach me Latin. In Germany, to go to medical school you had to have Latin. And I learned elementary Latin from her. She also taught me more English.

After about three years, in 1948, this man who taught me decided I had enough knowledge to pass the exam for high school. I took the exam with a class. I passed. I didn't have any grades. I just passed.

When I finally qualified to go to the University, I went to medical school in Germany before I came to America. For three years. I was admitted to medical school. The first day I walked into the class, there were nine hundred German students and I was the only Jew. I remember asking myself, "How can I spend time, so much time that I would have to interact with these other students?" Because in medical school, you have to interact in groups of eight students. And I asked myself, "Can I spend all this time in a class with people that I, at that time, still considered to be my enemies, because they are Germans?" And I said, "Well, I have to do it because I have to get an education. I want to become a physician. And this is the only opportunity."

It took time. Each survivor has a unique story to tell. So unique, you cannot identify me, myself, with any other survivor. The experience has been unique with each of us.

REVISIONING THE HOLOCAUST

Hilda Parker

University of Utah professor Hilda (Morganstern) Parker is a survivor of the Holocaust.[1] A native of Czechoslovakia, she was first sent to the concentration camp Theresienstadt when she was fifteen years old and, later, to Auschwitz. Her parents were exterminated. She escaped death three times and credits her age, self-identity, and luck for her survival.

The Best Ages for Survival—"I happened to be there between fifteen and nineteen, possibly the best ages for survival," Parker says. "At that age you are not young enough to need your parents' constant care and not old enough to be established and have your own children, but you *are* old enough to be separated from your family, to take the cold better, to sleep on bare floors, to go with less food, be independent, and live through the indignities."

Psychologically, Parker was strong. "I had a fairly good self-concept to begin with," she explains. "I came from a family with a strong identity and felt good about myself. As a result, I didn't collapse internally."

First Brush with Death—When interned in Theresienstadt, Parker became a shepherdess and had her first brush with death. Although she was "protected" by her work, quotas needed to be filled and her name was put on a transport list of those to be sent to the gas chambers. "The day before the transport was going to leave, Adolf Eichmann, who used to come by on his horse and talk to me while I was taking care of the sheep, saw me on the transport and took me off right away."

Life Spared a Second Time—Hilda Parker's life was spared a second time. "It was a strange incident and I could never figure it out," she says. "My mother and I had just arrived at Auschwitz. A friend of mine and her mother were in front of us. When they were separated to be loaded onto the trucks by the SS men, my friend asked one man if she could go with her mother. He said, yes. When it was our turn, I asked if I could go with my mother, too. He said, 'No, you go here and she goes there.' As my mother walked off to one side, I went behind his back and rushed to her. As if by accident, he turned around, saw me, grabbed my hand and pulled me back. 'You go there,' he shouted. I don't know why he did that but that saved my life." Parker's mother died in the gas chamber.

Escape—Four years later in a work camp, Parker says the SS promised them they wouldn't get out of Auschwitz alive. "The Russians were very close and the SS told us they were going to do away with us." Not willing to wait to be killed, Parker and two girlfriends escaped in the night. Undetected, they crossed the border, and three days later, they were liberated.

After the war, Parker returned home and she realized psychologically the enormity of the tragedy. "At first, it was very difficult to even get used to walking freely on the streets. But as a young person, I adjusted."

Choices—She didn't adjust to the injustice she witnessed, however, and she warns that unless people and governments make choices to condemn racism and discrimination, few will understand the horror of what happened then and what can happen now.

"Ignorance and fear stopped some people from helping," says Parker. "Anti-Semitism stopped others. But who knows what prevents the rest."

When war was imminent and people were trying to leave Germany, many countries refused refuge. They closed their borders and sealed the fate of millions. Says Parker, "Had countries responded to save Jewish lives like the individuals and governments in Denmark, Holland, and Italy did, many more innocent people could have survived."

LIBERATING DACHAU, A SOLDIER'S OBSERVATIONS

Joel Shapiro

I was assigned to the G2 unit as a "general outfielder," as they say.[1] Our job was the acquisition of battle information; find out what's happening on the other side. I ended up doing a little typing and interrogating. There were two German-Jewish boys [who] were superb interrogators. They never threatened a German prisoner and I never saw one who declined to answer.

Dachau—The unforgettable fact from my military career, though, was the experience of going into Dachau. A small detachment from our office had been sent in and I asked to go with them. So, "unofficially," I was in on the liberation of the Dachau concentration camp. And that's a Jewish memory that won't go away.

The countryside around Dachau was beautiful. White houses, neatly painted, well-kept flower beds. Peach trees. Grass. Neat streets. No dust or dirt. There was a railroad spur leaving the town and then there was this tremendous encampment. A trench, eighteen feet wide and cut deep into the earth, was built around the camp to prevent escape. Inside of that were high fences, a double row of fences. The camp covered acres. Tens of thousands of people [had] lived there.

American Troops—After the American troops arrived, they placed guards all around the camp to prevent a mass exodus. The first irony that struck me was that one guard had been replaced with another. However, the atmosphere of those being kept in was completely different. There was joy.

Railroad Spur—Along the periphery of the camp, we found SS guards lying dead with their fingers cut off. The prisoners did what had been done to them; they took the gold from their hands. The railroad spur coming into the camp had little cars. They were full of human corpses, and one could see that the side doors had been opened and a machine gun had sprayed down the sides. Each car had a pile of bodies. In the crematoria, there were two rooms with a pyramid of naked bodies, skeletons of inmates, who had not been burned. And now, under American guard, each [corpse] was waiting to be burned and cremated because there was nothing else do with [these decaying bodies].

In my youthful mind, the two or three days I was there observing and taking some photographs could be part of the total war experience that had its effect on me. I was twenty-two years old. As one matures and grows up, perhaps, you single out wartime experiences that you know, in retrospect, were the most important. The Dachau experience is an historical experience. It is related to the whole Hitler story and it did have an impact on me as a Jewish person, to this day.

The Holocaust Happened—To this day, when we see political forces that would deny the existence of these experiences and tell others there was no such thing as the extermination of ethnic groups in Germany, my witness to that, my personal experience to that, has some value.

I have shown these pictures and have related the experience more in the last eight to ten years, than I did in the first twenty years after the war. It seemed that [there were] young people who had no intimate, direct experience with the war. And that these stories were once again useful in interpreting what happened in this world. I have shown these pictures and have told my own personal story to people who work with me, and to others. So, yes, the impact of the event goes on and on.

We Need to Be Reminded Again and Again—I try to impress two points. Given the political climate, where there are those who deny that it ever occurred, I try to make clear that it did happen. It wasn't imagination. It's not a fabrication. It happened. And, more principally, I would think it again points out man's inhumanity to man. It appears that people need to be reminded, all of us need to be reminded, again and again and again.

Joel Shapiro, soldier. (Courtesy of Joel Shapiro)

After liberating Dachau: bodies awaiting cremation to avoid infection. (Courtesy of Joel Shapiro)

STALAG 19

Dr. Ernst Beier

Warnings—Maybe my father wanted to protect me.[1] He not only named me Ernst, but he called me Ernst Gunther. Gunther is a very German name. It means the head of an army. My father had been in the German army.

I had an uncle who was a colleague of my father. He was a Zionist and during the big holidays would go and drink some wine. I remember when I was six years old, I sipped wine with him. We went to synagogue maybe once a year because of this uncle. We went to a liberal rabbi. I resented this man because he, now this was in 1936, and I felt he should have warned people, Jews, particularly if you did have any money because money still could manage to get you out. People who didn't have money, eventually they got killed. So I felt the rabbi should have dealt with it, but I didn't hear much of it except from other people.

A Curse—In school there were problems. I wasn't beaten up. Occasionally someone would say "Judenicht" you know, "Jew boy." But it didn't hurt. So I didn't have that type of direct trouble that some of the kids had. But I know constantly there was discrimination. And I felt very early on in my life that being Jewish was a curse. Very early. I must have been six years old, in grade school. It was a private grade school. Very nice. And a guy asked about religion and I know that I got all red and mumbled that I was Jewish. I was very hesitant. I remember that even today, it shakes me up. So I must have sensed even at an early age, I was six in 1922, that there was a lot of hatred against Jews.

Partners—In my hometown, there wasn't really much of a Jewish ghetto at that time. We had a nice place near a park. We had a house, but I always compared it to my uncle's house. He was what we call a *macher.* He and my father were partners, but he was always taking advantage. When the factory made a lot of profit, it would be 60:40, the 40 percent for my father. And if he were losing business, it would be worse for my father. So my father did not establish himself too well with him. I heard them fighting each time they played cards in our home.

Days of Normalcy—In Germany, you have one room that is called *Herr zimmer,* the father's

Ernst on motorcycle just before fleeing Germany for Switzerland. (Courtesy of Ernst Beier)

room and it's a most elegant place in the house. The children were not allowed to get in, but, of course, we did get in when they were gone. The women could get in only when invited, I guess. It wasn't a huge home. We had three bedrooms, and a small fourth bedroom for two maids. A governess and a maid. That was common. They lived there.

In the summer, we always went to the Baltic Sea. It had become a habit. For a long time, we went to Helgoland, which is the North Sea almost to the beach. We rented a place, a *strandkorp.* It was like a beach hut, not a cottage—more like a cabana. Yes, a cabana. Shaded. Oh, we really enjoyed our summers. You could sit in the *strandkorp* and look at the ocean. Then you would make a sand wall around it. I remember we did it every year. It was a most beautiful beach at the Baltic Sea. *Schwimmenbunder,* floating in the waters. It was a summer resort area.

Political Identities—But back in, say, 1924, when I was eight, even then, Germany was very much divided then. People proclaimed their various political identities by hanging flags, you know, at the beach. They would have a black, white, and red flag, which was a nationalistic flag, and they would have it to show that they are nationalists, and later as Nazis. The flag Germany should have had was a black, red, and gold, *schwarz* gold, flag. That was the Democratic flag after the Weimar Republic, which was still a majority at that time.

Fleeing Germany—When I grew up, in my youth in Germany, I belonged to a group of Jewish boys, called *Greifen.* We met often and wrote anti-Nazi material. Of course, we did it foolishly. Germany was supporting Franco in Spain with weapons and planes. We printed messages about this on paper. Folding the paper into a small flyer, we then stuck them in matchboxes and distributed them. We were earnest but foolhardy. At school, one of the small flyers dropped to the floor, accidentally, and was picked up by a teacher. We got into a lot of trouble. We knew what was happening and so most of us left Germany as soon as we could. I got on my motorcycle, rode out of Germany and headed towards Switzerland without looking back. Once there, I waited for a visa. My brother who had gone to Israel earlier was now in the United States. He gave me the prerequisites for a visa.

Night of the Broken Glass—My mother described *Kristallnacht* as to what happened to people whom I knew were still living there. They didn't fare very well. My mother, herself, didn't fare badly. They "nazified" the factory, they took it over, you know, so it was totally lost to us. But she had enough money to survive and you wouldn't believe this but she was a very skillful woman. She actually arranged the German government to send me money in Switzerland every month. I don't know how she did it. I could have lived without it, because I was working for a laboratory there. But I was very lucky and she was very good.

Crisis at Sea—So I got here, with my brother's help, and I went on what might have been the last boat. I went on a German liner, the *Columbus,* because my mother couldn't get a ticket on any other boat, and I didn't really have enough money for passage. This is now in 1939. As we were in mid-ocean, the captain received a telegram to turn around immediately and go back to Germany because war was pending.

There was much excitement on the boat. Half of its passengers were Jewish. There were some nasty guards, who would have taken control of the boat and turned it around, but we were thinking there were enough engineers and very learned people and passengers to immobilize the boat. Still, it was absolutely frightening waiting to hear what he would do, or what we were going to do, or could do. After two days of waiting, the captain addressed all the passengers, including the ones who were in steerage. They were permitted to come up. He explained that because of the proximity to America and his lack of water and coal, or oil, he would go first to the United States before he turned around to go back. I know he didn't do it for that reason.

Refuge—When I arrived in the United States, I was exceedingly lucky because I got from the Jewish Joint Committee in New York an address to visit a chemical factory. The owner told me I could own this whole factory, which was huge in New Jersey. And I found out why he said that. He had a daughter. I didn't work there. I then went to Boston on a motorcycle and for some reason, the head of the English Department of Harvard, a guy by the name of Howard Mumford Jones, who had written twenty-seven books, wanted to have a Jewish refugee to live with his family. They contacted the Joint Jewish Committee and the Committee contacted me and Jones liked me and so I lived with them.

Back in School—Professor Jones thought I was bright enough to go to college, which I didn't have in mind to do. I hadn't gone all the way in college in Germany. But he called Amherst College, said he had a pretty bright refugee here, and could they send somebody over and see if there were a scholarship. The next day, two guys came to Cambridge and interviewed me. I started going to Amherst. Well, I was lucky. I graduated in 1940, and went to work in New York as a chemist, then became part of a research group to test gas.

I brought my mother over shortly thereafter. She had hidden thousands of dollars worth of stamps in what was at that time called a lift, a huge box where all her furniture was stored. In the furniture, she had it all hidden. But the Germans told her it was gone, so she never got anything. She came over with some stuff that she carried on her body, but no money. She was over seventy years old. She was an artist.

The Youth Group—Of the boys who were part of my group, one died recently. He came to America and was a musician, who learned to build organs. Another friend became a professor. Another friend escaped later and went to Africa first. He had a much harder time than I did. He came from a very well-to-do family and they wanted him to stay because his father was not Jewish and he, my friend, didn't look Jewish. But the Nazis went after him and he barely escaped by going to Africa. Now he's in Australia. We're still writing each other.

All of my friends got out but one. He wrote me a letter, I'll never forget, because I was his leader of the group and he felt I could just swing to get him out. I couldn't get him out. It was too late and I think he died. I don't know, but I assume.

Trying to Enlist—And then it was December 7, 1941, Pearl Harbor broke, and I went to join the army. I did not say I was Jewish because I believed they would have kicked me out right away. So I didn't say anything. But they kicked me out, anyway. They said I was an alien. Can you imagine? So they kicked me out, but they said, whenever you want to come back to work [as a civilian], you have a job with us. They wanted workers. My brother was working in a

Ernst brings his mother to New York. (Courtesy of Ernst Beier)

Ernst Beier, U.S. Ski Patrol. (Courtesy of Ernst Beier)

munitions factory, and I got a job there, too, from 1942–1943, so I could support my mother.

The Mountain Skiers—During this time, I still wanted to enlist in the army. I wanted to join the mountain troops because I was a skier. Howard Mumford Jones called President Roosevelt. That's all true. And Roosevelt got something going and I was accepted within a week. I went to Fort Dix and then to Camp Hill, in the 10th Mountain Division. I was there for about six to eight months. The base was about ten miles from Leadville, Colorado, and I got to know a lot of friends and skied a lot. I bought a car, actually, an old Ford. In the meantime, I had a lot of training, including glacier- and mountain-climbing training. Then they discovered that I spoke French better than I speak English, and of course, I speak German, so they yanked me out. They figured, well, we need some German-speaking soldiers in the army.

The Twenty-eighth Infantry—They sent me to Hagerstown, in preparation for going into military government. President Roosevelt decided he needed all the manpower he could get, so they yanked all of us out and put us into the 28th Infantry Division in the U.S. Army. That was called the "bloody buckets," and it was. First we went to Ireland and then to Southern England.

The First Battles Are the Worst—Yes, I killed. What you can't understand is when you see your first body, dead, and you're in uniform, the uniform plays a big role. If that's another American boy that's been killed, at that point, everybody who wears another kind of uniform than yours will be killed. You know that, you just do it. The first battles are worse because the military doesn't know everything about it. We got out of our landing camp in France and we went to the hedges, see, huge hedges, very large and tall, ideal for hiding. You never know who's going to come out and surprise you, shoot you. And so you have to walk very carefully. As soon as you see somebody, and you are sure nobody of your own is there, when you see the movement, you shoot. You have to, to survive. I had no feelings about it, no feelings at all. People can say, "How can you shoot people you grew up with?" Well, I did grow up with some Germans, but I had no feelings then. In the war, you shoot uniforms, you don't shoot people.

Five Major Battles—I was on "D" Day and, of all things, Utah Beach in France. We fought five major battles. I know because they gave me a Battle Silver Star for having been alive for five battles. It was pretty rough. We got into a rest area in Luxembourg. But then the Germans came on a big attack, in what is later called the Battle of the Bulge.

Captured—That's where I was captured by the Germans. It was stupid, how we got captured, because we didn't need to be captured. We were waiting to leave, actually escaping, when I overhead the officer say that the German army was surrounding us. A very stupid lieutenant, an American lieutenant, said, "Turn the jeep around. You have to defend the command post." The driver said, "Are you crazy? How can you defend a command post just with our carbines? They're coming with tanks." The lieutenant said, "I order you to turn around now." So the driver turned around and numbers of people on board got killed right when the Germans came in. The rest were captured.

Stalag 19—We were sent to a camp. To Stalag 19, which was near Frankfurt. It was very, very hard, a real hardship. First of all, we lost a third of our weight within a few months. We didn't get anything to eat but one light, thin soup and a piece of bread. It was a prisoner-of-war camp, a POW camp. I became a barracks leader. And people died of what a leader would call "moroseness." That meant the person mentally gave up on living. The reason for this is a lot of guys came directly from the U.S. They were not with the 28th Infantry Division but with the 106th Division. When they came over, they were captured the day after they arrived. They hadn't had time in battle, and they didn't understand what hardship was to come. They gave up drinking water most of all. They didn't drink any more. Most of the soldiers in my barracks died of this "moroseness." They weren't tough enough. Nobody from the 28th that I know died. We went through our battles and we survived.

Hunger—As barracks leader, I had to make decisions. There were 120 people per barracks. The Germans would give you a ladle of soup and a piece of bread and the prisoners could cheat if they wanted to have chow twice. If they did, the last prisoners wouldn't get anything to eat because there'd be nothing left. So the first thing I had to do was make rules of how to eliminate that. It was very difficult. We were all hungry.

Suspicion—At Stalag 19, I had a very intense interview with the head of the Gestapo of the camp. He didn't know I was Jewish, and was very suspicious of me, in spite of the name Ernst Gunther. He even asked a close buddy of mine, whom I met earlier, in Manila, in the Philippines, if I were German. My friend Hans Kasment looks German and speaks German fluently. But he is an American. His father was a Senator. Hans saved my life.

The Confidant—All the barracks leaders select a man to represent the GIs in camps and the POWs and we selected him. Hans was acceptable to the Germans because he spoke German and looked terribly, terribly, I mean, terribly German. He became the confidant. When they asked him about me, this remarkable man from an old Protestant family, an American brought up in Switzerland, risked his life and said no, Ernst Gunther wasn't Jewish.

Then they asked him to separate all the Jews. He said to them, "We don't do that in America." And he got a lot of trouble for it. Hans was sent to the Jewish camp *Bergen-Belsen,* where people were tortured and made to work without food. Many of them died. At Stalag 19, we hardly had anything to eat but we didn't have to work. Somehow, Hans escaped from that camp. (He is a fascinating story himself. About my age now, he's married to a fairly young Filipino woman and has twins eleven years of age.)

A Tragic List—Nobody identified the Jews in our camp, although some threatened to, but somehow the Nazis came up with a Jewish list and those on the list were all shipped out to Bergen. In compiling the Jewish list, they made an interesting but tragic error, which I thought was so typically stupid of them. They had one bathhouse. I never did go to the bathhouse, but a lot of the other GIs did. Many of them were circumcised. [These] Germans assumed that anybody who got circumcised was a Jew. So they gave the names of the guys who went down to the bathhouse and all of them went to Bergen. I mean, it was terrible. The whole thing was terrible.

Good-bye—The Gestapo man who interviewed me, he was a murderer. He was known to take Russian and Turkish prisoners, interview them, say to them, "You're free. You can walk out." Then when they would start to walk out of the camp, he would shoot them. When I was called, I said goodbye to everybody.

Saved—I was interviewed by that Gestapo man. He was a doctor not a physician, but a Ph.D. For some reason, I mentioned the philosopher and poet Goethe, whom I knew better than now, and that changed the entire interview. Suddenly, he was hungry for German culture and he found a prisoner with whom he could talk. We quoted Goethe to each other for about a half an hour. Abruptly, he said, "You better go now." I ran. My life was saved. Fortunately, he who killed so many was later killed himself. He deserved it.

Survival—How did we survive not knowing whether we would live to see the next day? Every day we survived, because you don't think about it. You think about the people you love. My mother, my girlfriend, my brother. I actually had a German Goethe piece of poetry from "Faust" that helped me a lot. I quoted it to myself every day. I was quite sick. I was sick with yellow jaundice. There was no medicine. Nothing. People thought I would die, but I didn't. I survived.

Close Calls—I was in camp for one hundred and three days, as a prisoner. When I got out, we were shipped to France and it was the first time I heard music again, which made me cry. Then I heard that Roosevelt had died. That really upset me because I believe Roosevelt really was the guy who saved our lives. I was in France for maybe ten days, and then shipped back to the U.S. where I got reassigned to the Air Force. I was supposed to be reassigned to go to Japan. I was always surprised in a way that I made it out alive. I mean, we had so many short, close calls. I never got wounded, no.

GI Bill—Eventually, they shipped me back to New York and I had a disability rating. You always had a disability rating of 40 percent, which was very useful along with the 20/20 that the USA gave us. Using that with the money and payment from the University, I was accepted at Columbia, where I got my Ph.D. You know, almost every friend of mine, except one, who escaped Germany and came to the United States got a Ph.D. Isn't that amazing? I lived like a king because I had $50 more than I expected. It was very nice.

Changing Directions—I decided after my POW experience with the Gestapo that I wanted to find out what changed this guy's mind from shooting me to letting me live. I wanted to find out what really saved my life, so I devoted myself to studies. I did all my research in this area and that's why I got into psychology. I wrote a book about it called *The Silent Language of Psychotherapy*, and I published one hundred papers on subtle cues.[2]

Frances—I met my wife at a party. Oh, Frances knew me before. We had been not living too far apart in New York. I was teaching in Syracuse, and she wanted to meet for a long time. Her mother warned her, "Ernst will never marry you." You know, in Germany, you have class structures, even among Jews. We came from a more money class and they came from a poorer group. The feeling was that this rich class would never marry this poor class. Even though I wasn't richer than she was. We lived together in Syracuse for a while and then I went to an American Psychological Conference and had to read two papers. One paper was at one o'clock; the other was at four. In between the two papers, we got married. We got married on September 6, 1949 and we've been married since.

Changing Course Again—When Frances applied to medical school in Syracuse, the head of the medical admissions committee said she was the best student ever to apply to medical school, straight A's. But she was a woman and, therefore, unacceptable, as they believed women don't give enough service to medicine. That's what she was told in 1954. Both of us got so mad and I'm still emotional thinking about that. Immediately, I started looking for another job, and since I'm a skier, I gave Utah a little preference. I came here because of the snow, and Frances, while she was pregnant with my son, was accepted to medical school here. She became a pediatrician and practiced here for thirty years. When I was at the University [of Utah], the Psychology Department had four people and when I left, as director of clinical training, we had thirty-eight. We really grew.

I never talked about being a Jew or being in a POW camp until 1997, when I started writing. You know, even in the POW camp, some GIs would come over and say, "I know you're a Jew and if you don't give me some bread, I'm going to tell the Germans." And I say to them, "You can go to hell."

THIRTEEN

Tzedakah

WORLDLY EXPERIENCES

Joanne Spitzer McGillis

Moving Out West—My Dad's parents came from Russia, although my grandfather, Morris Spitzer, liked to fancy that he came from Austria.[1] For years I heard wonderful stories about castles; I even believed for awhile that I was a princess. Not true. How my grandparents met and married, I'm not exactly sure. Morris was a tailor in New York, which was the only kind of work he could find. He and Minnie, my grandmother, probably married in New York. Then when my grandfather became a butcher, they moved to Chicopee, Massachusetts. That's where my father, Ed Spitzer, was born. My father's brother was in Connecticut. There was another move back to New York but when my grandfather developed a bad case of bursitis from lifting huge sides of beef and going in and out of cold icehouses, he took the family out West where he had a sister, Ethel Parver, living in Salt Lake City.

Fishing—I believe my grandfather opened a men's clothing store but it didn't do well, so in 1929 he bought a chicken farm right off 6200 South and Highland Drive. At the time, that was considered country. He sold chickens and eggs, and he had strawberry patches and a lovely orchard with peaches, plums, and apples. He also had a dog kennel. Although I was very young,

Young horsewoman, Joanne Spitzer. (Courtesy of Joanne Spitzer McGillis)

I have very pleasant associations and recollections of that farm. I have pictures of being on a little sled, all bundled up, with my grandfather and his dogs taking me around the farm. In the summers, we'd fish in a little creek. We'd use a safety pin for a hook and string for a line. Never caught anything, of course, but my grandfather and I would talk for hours on end about anything and everything. I told him my most private thoughts; later when he came to live with us, he would regale me with stories that were obviously not true. My father's father was really an honest man when he wasn't lying about royalty. Much later, we would talk about even more serious things and he would share with me the most unbelievable episodes familiar to living an immigrant life.

Back to the Land—My grandfather moved onto the farm as a matter of livelihood, of doing what you were best able and equipped to do. There are some things that we as Jews do instinctively, one of which is working the ground in an agricultural setting. I know that our entire family loves to be part of the soil, of nature and growing. Of course, maybe it has to do with association of my grandfather's farm. The peacefulness that comes with that kind of setting reinforces one's beliefs in life's many possibilities.

It was a small house, especially in terms of today's standards. Yet, before it was torn down in later years, I drove by it and thought how big it actually was. Except for the chickens, I remember it always smelled good. More than that, you felt like a free spirit just being there. Particularly for me because I was born and raised in an apartment.

My grandfather worked very hard on the farm as did my grandmother. I don't remember exactly when he left the farm for good. I was probably six or seven years old at the time, so it might have been around 1938 or '39. My grandmother died from a very painful form of bone cancer. There was no cure and it was so hopeless and frightening hearing her scream with pain. For a long time, it was difficult to drive by the farm. The memories are bittersweet.

Having to Do with Food—I was born in 1932 at the LDS Hospital in Salt Lake City. At the time, we lived in the Federal Heights Apartments right across the street from Reservoir Park. There were several Jewish families in the apartment building: one right across the hall, the Sobels; and one right down the hall, the Appelmans. Sadie Appelman's daughters and I were raised together until we moved from there. Interestingly enough, ex-governor Cal Rampton also lived there when he was a kid. My mother Navine was very kind to him so he has never forgotten her. What did she do? It probably had something to do with food. My mother was a great one for feeding others. She had a way of stretching a buck.

We used to go to, if you can pardon the expression, Coon Chicken Inn out on Highland Drive. I can hardly believe they ever called it that and I can barely say it without getting the chills. Can you imagine this—this label on a restaurant in a predominantly Mormon area? It was a long way out from downtown and it's very interesting to me especially since Mormons don't like to be labeled and know the meaning of prejudice. I don't know how it ever became named as such and perhaps there was some matter of pride because the food was very good. But the restaurant's façade was the face of a black man. You would walk through the mouth to get into the dining room. It was a chicken house and they used to give away chicken livers because few people wanted them. But my mother knew what to do with chicken livers. She made chopped liver, chicken liver omelettes, stewed chicken livers, and any kind of chicken liver concoction imaginable. You couldn't beat the price. They were free and we were poor. But what a horrible name. Anyway, that's the story of the chicken livers. When the owner realized that Jewish customers really loved chicken livers, he started charging for them.

Angel-Food Cake—Mother was a great soup maker and a baker. She won a contest put on by Granite Furniture, which offered a living room suite to the winner. I'll never forget it. She baked an angel-food cake and won a sofa, chair and table. Actually, since we already had furniture, she elected to take the money instead. We needed it then. Like I said, we didn't have much money, but we were never starving. My husband says I don't know the meaning of poverty because we always had food and clothes and shelter. That is true, and I'm grateful for it. Yet, I do know there were some very bad times, and my grandmother on my mother's side, Esther Findling, helped us through some difficult periods.

Crowd gathers to watch ticker tape on the *Salt Lake Tribune* building during the stock market crash, 1929. (Courtesy of the Shapiro family)

Good Times—The Findlings had lived in a beautiful home on Wolcott Avenue at the very top of South Temple by the University of Utah. It was a very big home with a ballroom in the basement; frescoes or murals on the walls; a rosewood bar; a huge kitchen with a walk-in refrigerator; and a big table in the middle of the kitchen that was always loaded with noodles being rolled out and sliced, coffee cake ingredients being measured, and pastry being put together with sweet fillings. My grandmother, who had a German maid, was constantly cooking, baking, and entertaining. Yes, they were well-to-do and quite charitable. My grandfather owned the Boston Store, a women's apparel shop, on 254 Main Street; and he was heavily into stocks and bonds. A Conservative Jew, he believed it was necessary for Jews to have a meeting place and a viable, active community life. Well respected in the Jewish community, he took it upon himself to help found our community center, the Wall Mansion on South Temple, by putting up the initial $2,000 and collecting the rest of the money from other community leaders for a down payment. He was loved. He was appreciated. He was looked up to and he was a leader.

The Bottom Falls Out—During the Stock Market Crash of the late 1920s, my grandfather lost a lot of money; and then with the deepening depression from 1930 to 1933, he found no way whatsoever to recoup his losses. He felt like an albatross around his family's neck. He ended up committing suicide. It was a terrible tragedy. He and Nana had a loving relationship. They were devoted to each other and she was devastated by his death. Never remarried. Never. She worked the store well into the late 1950's. But, of course, she had to sell the house on Wolcott right after his death. They auctioned off all the beautiful artifacts that were in this home. Fortunately, over the years a few small pieces have been returned to me. It was very tragic and sad; and it was also interesting because that left both sides of the family without any money. I was about sixteen months old at the time of his death, but I didn't know how he died until I was nine or ten years old.

Raising Funds—My mother was a religious woman, and would have been more observant had my father not been so irreligious. Oh, he was tolerant of my mother's views, supportive in all her efforts, and very much in love with her so there was never any conflict in my home, which may or may not have been a blessing. On High Holy Days, he would attend Temple B'nai Israel with my mother; but more often than not, I would go with her. She was a Reform Jew, president of Sisterhood at B'nai Israel, always did whatever was required. My earliest association is of mass cooking, pots and pots of food, to raise funds for the synagogue. After the Covenant House was sold and before we had a Jewish community center, Sisterhood members would rent the Blind Center on First South, and make really nice meals to feed to the merchants for lunch. That's how they made money: feeding the merchants. I remember standing on a stool stirring a large vat of turkey á la king; wondering if I was going to fall into it and drown. It was a lot of work, but wonderful to see what dedicated women did to raise funds.

Dancing—My mother carried herself like a queen; in fact, she resembled Queen Elizabeth in stature. She was kind, caring, loving. She and my father—their one great love in life and their one luxury was to go dancing at the Hotel Utah. Anyone who saw them dancing would always remember them. I suppose some of it had to do with rhythm, but you could sense how they adored being with one another.

Worldly Experiences—My mother wanted me to have the best education possible and to be open to all kinds of very worldly experiences because she had married young and always faced a struggle in life. The only luxury that my family could provide for me was a first rate private school education. I went to Rowland Hall School, an all-girls school; and actually my Nana Esther and Sammy Makoff paid for my tuition. (Sammy Makoff had married Ethel Parver's daughter.) Although there was a social distinction among the girls—the haves and the have-nots—I made it a point not to be stymied by it but rather focus on my studies. I was told that only good grades would get a scholarship to college, so there were many times I'd be up at four in the morning studying. We had very rigorous exams in this school and if you weren't prepared you could be in a lot of trouble.

One year, the school did something wonderful for me. They asked a donor to give some paints and because I was a budding artist and we had a wonderful art teacher by the name of Rose Salsbury, they allowed me to spend many hours painting murals for the school's entry. One was a picture of a group of women in long, long dresses, playing croquet in front of the school; the other was of Bishop Tuttle, the Episcopalian bishop, coming over the valley and designating where this little school would be built. I have never forgotten that they gave me that opportunity. It helped my self esteem, and it made me feel a part of the larger group.

One of Many—My father was one of the many Main and State Street Jewish merchants in the clothing business. He worked for my Uncle Sam Parver at the Golden Rule, and he might have had a little store of his own for a short time. But I believe that business went broke and he eventually worked quite a while at Makoff Department Store until there was a falling out—I'm not sure what happened—and he and a partner opened the Cameo Room at ZCMI.

Exploring Utah—Like his father, my Dad had a way with words and was a great storyteller. Dad thought that nature was an essential part of all our well being. He awakened in me a sense of adventure and an appetite for knowledge. He loved the beauty of the mountains, the turning of the leaves, the falling snow, and the profusion of wildflowers prevalent to this state. He wanted to explore it all and have us share the experience with him. So as soon as we could afford a car, we would be up in the canyons.

Friendships—My parents' friends were mostly Jewish. They had what they called a little Saturday night club in which the Siegels, Goldsteins, Karshes, Bernsteins, Peppers, and my mother's brother and sister-in-law, Harold and Bernice Findling, would have dinner at someone's house and then they'd all go out dancing. Sometimes, the Saturday Night Club would slip into a Sunday brunch in Millcreek Canyon with all the children. I can't remember who owned the big cast-iron grill, I think it was Bernstein's, and I'm not sure who brought the lanterns that light up the night, but everybody had their assignments for cookouts. We'd get firewood and stoke up the rock ovens, put on the grill. Everybody had a specialty. Mom's was potatoes with onions.

Almost Like Siblings—More often than not, we'd have breakfast in the canyon and then dinner in the canyon. I learned how to chill a watermelon in a running stream. We played baseball. We hiked, went on hayrides, or went on horseback rides. We fished and waded in the stream. The kids? Gail Bernstein Ciacci, Sandy Pepper, the Karsh kids, the Goldsteins, and Danny Siegel. We never dated each other. How could we? We were all like brothers and sisters. But we did learn about friendships. Our parents taught us to love and respect each other. And if there were ever a problem with one of the couples and/or their children, everybody would rally around that group. It was a very compact, loving, caring relationship that we had, similar to living with an extended family, and those lessons have been with me ever since.

Some of their friends, like the Peppers, Bernsteins and Goldsteins, belonged to Congregation Montefiore. Others were members of Congregation B'nai Israel. Montefiore had a cantor, which was unheard of in the Reform movement. The Reform temple had an organ, which was unheard

Young newlyweds, Dick and Joanne McGillis entertaining. (Courtesy of Joanne Spitzer McGillis)

of in the Orthodox movement. Yet, everyone worked very hard at being good Jews, and they didn't let their religious differences prevent friendships. Often we would go from the synagogue to the temple and back visiting with our friends. In fact, marriages occurred between members of the two congregations.

Bleeding-Heart Liberal—My grandfather Morris had a very strong personality and was religious until he became disenchanted with what he considered the abuse of power and pandering to the elite. Adamant in his views, he was socialistic in his thinking, partly due to his bad financial experiences, typical of what happened to so many immigrants beginning a new life in America. He was not uncomfortable talking about Karl Marx, Friedrich Nietzsche, or any other philosophical writer with whom he felt a connection. He was very suspicious of politics and very suspicious of any power play. I believe he influenced my way of thinking, and was responsible for turning me into a bleeding-heart liberal. He was also the one who told me about my Grandfather Jack's suicide. When I saw my grandfather's picture on the wall at the Jewish Community Center, and knew how much he had done for the community, I couldn't let it go. I believe my Grandfather Jack's legacy influenced my decision to become involved in charitable work in the Jewish community. I had to follow in his steps.

Never Too Young to Understand—Even though I was young, I knew the Jews were in trouble during World War II and that the war was being blamed on them. I remember hearing snatches of Hitler's speeches on the radio. My grandfather, who understood and spoke German, would talk about it in Yiddish so we wouldn't know to be afraid. But I was worried about the plight of Jews. (My mother died when she was forty-five years old; much too early, too young a woman. She was an inspiration to me. Among everything else she did, she worked at the USO and would bring Jewish soldiers home for dinner. She'd carry on a correspondence with them and if we didn't hear back from one, we would all worry.)

It was at this time I had pneumonia and was bedridden for almost four months. When I was well, I was told not to walk back and forth to school. My mother made arrangements with a woman who lived in upper Federal Heights to pick up her son and me at the same time. The second time I entered the car, the son called me a "dirty Jew" and said he didn't want to be in the same car with me. I was so embarrassed and afraid, I didn't know what to do. I stayed in the car but didn't say a word all the way home. I never took a ride with them after that.

We used to see a lot of newsreels at the movies and I remember the newsreels of Allies going into Hitler's death camps. It hit me how America's "wait-and-see stance" resulted in the tragic outcome. I was outraged. Somehow I realized that Americans could have prevented some of what happened. I became more than casually observant and I still am today. We need to educate our Jewish children, all children, to the importance of tolerance and understanding so that people of divergent faiths can live and work together in peace.

Tzedakah—My husband will say he did not grow up in a religious home, although his mother was a fairly traditional Jew. I say, he knows and practices *tzedakah;* and I am fortunate that he respects my views and honors my commitment to Judaism. Dick has difficulty in articulating about his Judaism. Being his wife for fifty years, I would say he has a huge sense of responsibility and *Yiddishkeit* in terms of living all the tenets of Judaism. He's righteous in a lot of ways; when he sees injustice, he knows it has to be corrected. When we came back from our honeymoon we went to a Welfare drive, it is now the United Jewish Federation of Utah [renamed United Jewish Communities]. Well, he gave an amount of money that nearly bowled me over. I didn't know that we'd be able to afford it. And why did he give? Because he knew it had to happen. What Dick doesn't tell you is that he was president of B'nai B'rith, chairman of the Bonds for Israel drive, yes, it was then called the Welfare drive, and he always assumed his role.

A Debt Paid—When Dick and I first traveled to Israel in 1980, we held candles as we walked along Wilson Bridge, through the Gate of Priests to the newly excavated subterranean hall of the Second Temple. The men recited the pledge to Jerusalem and with our arms encircling each other, we joined them singing *Hatikvah.* When Dick gave his gift, he said to the Prime Minister, "This is not a gift. This is a debt I owe you as a Jew living freely in America." This is his belief, and this is the action that he takes.

Later, I was led to the women's section of the illuminated Western Wall. I laid my cheek against the cool stone of this ancient wall, which symbolizes the long drama of Jewish survival, and I tucked in my prayers: Peace for mankind, health and happiness for my loved ones.

THE CCC CAMP

Anne Dolowitz

Fine Stitching—My grandfather Samuel Moskowitz and his wife Lena lived in a village that was situated at the bottom of hills or a mountain.[1] She was a fine seamstress, who did fine stitching for the more affluent citizens in that area. They weren't peasants, nor were they part of the aristocrats. I guess we would consider them as lower middle class. They had already moved away from the farm. They did not own their own land. One of my aunts was born in Turkey and, because the borders kept shifting, another sister was in Rumania. I suspect they were very close to the Russian border. My grandfather was a furrier.

Conscription—As a very young boy, my father, Simon, told us he remembered sitting at the family's square kitchen table listening to two Russian Army officers discussing the fact that his father was going to be conscripted into the army. I strongly suspect my family had witnessed the pogroms, and when the Russians ended up in my grandfather's house, my grandfather decided it was time to get out of the country. He and his brother left their families behind in 1911, and went to New York. I suspect there must have been a network among the workers, because within two years my grandfather had found his niche, and was working again as a furrier. When they saved enough money, the brothers then sent for their families.

A Picture of My Grandmother—My grandmother married at an early age and had already lost several children, two of them in Rumania. There's a picture of my grandmother, my aunt has it now, sitting on the side of the road with a bundle and a suitcase and babushka on her head. It was she who traveled by herself with the children when she left Rumania in 1913 with my father and his two older sisters. She took very few possessions. They went on the *Ryndam,* steerage class, I have the transit ticket, and they came through the Port of Amsterdam to Ellis Island. I know they came by steerage too because my father had memories of that. He must have been a character, with a mind of his own, because at four or five years old, he already got in trouble with the crew. He turned the handle on what would have been, I guess, a fire hydrant, and it was flooding the upper deck. He remembers being yelled at.

Two Rooms—My grandparents lived in a tenement building in New York, right in the middle of a Jewish neighborhood. By this time, though, my grandfather's brother had gone on to Canada, to Ontario, and eventually we lost contact with them. My grandfather was cutting and selling furs, but it was a hard existence. My grandmother worked as she had in Rumania, not in a sweatshop but in her home, taking in things, and she took care of the family. They lived in two rooms. My father and his sisters remember having their heads washed with kerosene to rid them of lice.

Everyone Worked—It was a tough life. Everybody had to work, including the children. By the time my father was eight or nine years old, he was out on the streets working as a messenger boy delivering mail in Manhattan. He had a bicycle with a bell, and was right down there in traffic in 1915, 1916. His sisters, too, were working. One of them was a seamstress and in time opened up a shop of her own in Long Island.

For a long time, my grandparents wanted to move out of the tenements and into a home. They wanted to become Americanized. I imagine it took a family effort, with everyone working, to be able to make such a move but they ended up with a house in the New York area with space enough for a vegetable garden, clusters of grapes, and a place to raise chickens in the back yard. As far as I know, my grandfather always stayed in the fur business and apparently made very good wine from his grapes. They were very observant and raised their children as Orthodox Jews. I have the *Shabbes* candlestick holders that my grandmother brought with her from Rumania. My father went to heder. If he misbehaved, which he could do, he was rapped on the knuckles. Somehow that didn't turn him away, and he learned how to read and speak Hebrew. For that matter, he picked up many other languages.

McCarthy Era—My mother came from a totally non-religious background. My mother, Etta Kalin, the last name was changed at Ellis Island from Kalinfsky, and my father lived in the same neighborhood, about a block apart. My mom was born in here in this country, as was her younger brother Robert. He was a fine musician who had his own music school. His daughter plays with the Philharmonic Orchestra. Her three older brothers were born in Russia. I don't believe my parents met at the same synagogue because Harry, my mother's father, was an agnostic and a communist. Yes, he was and so were his sons. And his sons had such a library, that during the McCarthy era, part of their library was put into storage. They really were fearful. I remember growing up in Brigham City as a child being told by my mother to never use the word "communist." That's the kind of fear that McCarthy had instilled.

Floating Fish—My mom's father had been a carpenter in Russia and had great difficulty adapting to American life. The acculturation process for him was never completed; while he knew very little English, he refused to learn his new country's language, and spoke only in Russian or Yiddish. My cousins who lived in New York said it was difficult to carry on a conversation with him. My grandmother Esther did learn English. My mother said she was a fine cook and remembers her making gefilte fish. Now, that's an inconsistency since there was no practice of the reli-

Simon Moskowitz studying, first year in medical school, 1929. (Courtesy of Anne Dolowitz)

gion! But my grandmother must have kept up with some traditions. She would go to the market, buy a fresh fish on Thursday, and float it in the bathtub until it was time to fix for Friday night, *Shabbes.*

Quit Working—Harry managed to make enough to live on, yes, but he retired at a young age, and read and read, he was a voracious reader in Russian and Yiddish, and sent his sons off to work. I don't know what the problem was. His sons remembered their father saying, "It's time for you to be making a living." And he just quit working. He would have been in his fifties. His children supported him. Elementary school they would have all graduated from. High school they would have all graduated from. But none of my uncles went on to college and yet they were exceedingly bright and read all the time. Two of my uncles were into textiles; Uncle Bob, like I said, was a musician. And my mother put herself through school, never graduated, but she made sure she got herself educated.

Sweethearts from Elementary School—My parents met in the neighborhood. I think my dad asked her to go for a ride on his bike. So they were sweethearts from elementary school. Dad must have been a real tease; and my mom had a sense of humor, it just didn't manifest itself a lot. When they married she was twenty-one years old, the same age as he since they were both born in 1908. They married in September 1929, just before the Stock Market Crash, and left for Omaha, Nebraska.

All of my Dad's family stayed in New York. While Dad was educated in New York, accelerated through high school, and was accepted to medical school at a time when it was very difficult for a Jewish fellow to be accepted in most colleges, he decided to leave the city, and was the only one to do so. Mom helped him get through medical school at Creighton University, in Omaha, Nebraska.

Wit's End—Now, in my dad's family, there is a wit in that family. "Wit's End" is very appropriate. That's what they called our house. He was a real punster and joke teller. He loved to play with words, had an outgoing personality, and really enjoyed interacting with people. As a kid, he was the favorite. The parents, you know, "my son the doctor!" They were thrilled about Dad. But my dad really didn't have a choice. It was going to be medicine. That was the epitome of what a son could grow up to be—a doctor. Fortunately, he did want to be a doctor, and ended up being a damned good doctor. He loved people.

The CCC—In Omaha, my mother picked up a job as a proofreader on the *Omaha Herald Tribune;* and my dad did research and went to medical school. He was young when he started medical school and finished his internship around 1933 or 1934. He said he wanted to specialize in Radiology, but he didn't have the money, so decided the best thing to do would be to sign on with a Civilian Conservation Corps [CCC], where they sent him to Council Bluffs, Iowa. He worked at the CCC camp and was allowed also to have private patients. He told us a story about a hillbilly, that's what he called them, who came down from the mountains on a mule and carried a shotgun. He told my dad, "My wife's having a baby and you're coming." Dad remembered the shotgun very distinctly. He followed the man into the backwoods and delivered the wife's baby on the kitchen table. For payment, he got a big bottle of whiskey.

The CCC was set up during the depression as part of the New Deal Program which gave unemployed people out-door jobs like building dams, doing conservation work, or fighting forest fires. From Council Bluffs, the CCC sent Dad into a camp between Kanosh and Kanab in Utah. Once again, as a camp doctor, he could take on private patients. They lived with a farm family and my mom, the New Yorker, learned to ride horses. She'd go out with the farmer and round up the sheep. She had a great time.

Dad was transferred to a CCC camp in a place called Perry, just outside Brigham City on Fruit Highway 89. This time, patients started coming to him from Perry, Willard, and Brigham City because by now my dad's reputation was well known; he was an incredible diagnostician. Willard was really nothing but a row of those wonderful old Welsh stone houses, farm country, and my parents said from then on they fell in love with the West and didn't want to leave Utah.

Brigham City—They found an apartment in nearby Brigham City in 1938 or '39, and very soon after that started building a house of their own. It became my mother's dream house. She followed the plan of a typical New England stone home with flagstone, brick, dormer windows, and a white picket fence. Most likely, this fence was the first of its kind in Brigham City.

Jewish Shopkeepers—There weren't many Jewish people living outside Salt Lake City, and nearby Ogden, but there was an older Jewish couple in Brigham City before my parents came to town. Harry [Lion] Bloom was his name. He ran a clothing manufacturing company; the building's still there. That man lived well into his nineties, and had a son and daughter-in-law in Ogden. There might have been another Jewish couple, maybe a tailor, but I can't remember.

At home with Anne, 1945. (Courtesy of Anne Dolowitz)

Jewish Humor—This would also have been the same time that the Rosenbaum family lived there. Hal Rosenbaum would have been painting in a studio in his family home on Main Street. It was a Mormon household, although by then I think they were "non-practicing Mormons." I found out just from my friend, their nephew Paul that their Grandpa had more than one wife. I was just astounded. Paul said, "Didn't you know?" And I said, "No." Well, the family doesn't practice Mormonism or Judaism, for that matter, but let me tell you: You can associate humor to any culture but there's a particular kind of humor that says those Jewish genes are there. Quick, funny, smart, I always thought Paul had such a connection. I think that's why I was attracted to him in high school. He was very different from the Mormon boys who were preparing to go on missions. For one thing, he could date me. For boys going on missions, dating a *Gentile* was a *no-no.*

Minority Child—As a cultural minority, and we were a minority, there were very few ways of fitting in. Now, my father was Jewish to the core; and his values were incorporated in his lifestyle, in the way he treated his patients, the way he treated his family, and the way he treated his friends that became a pattern for my brother and me. He married a Jewish woman, and it was very much a statement in our household that we were to seek it out as well; that we were going to marry Jewish spouses. Now, how that was to happen was a mystery for a long time. Eventually I was sent to the University of Colorado because there was a large Jewish Hillel, the university was close to home, and the daughter of Jewish friends in Ogden was going there as

According to Etta, Anne's mother: "Anne won't smile because she is wearing braces on her teeth. They are coming off in March, then you will see how attractive she is, especially when she smiles." (Courtesy of Anne Dolowitz)

well.[2] I did marry a Jewish man, Sandy [David] Dolowitz, whose family come from Utah.

Picture Perfect?—Yet, if you look at photographs of our early life in Brigham City, you'll see pictures of a Christmas tree. I believe my mom wanted to replicate the "American" experiences that she saw in other families. So we grew up, knowing that we were not Mormon, realizing we were Jewish, but never knowing what Jewish meant in the positive way. Yes, there was a Catholic Church and a Unitarian Church, but we lived in a primarily Mormon agrarian community in the '40s and '50s, and knew we were different.

Anyone Not a Mormon, Stand Up—Different, oh, absolutely, and not, like I said, in a positive way. There were many things that we were not invited to right at the very beginning. I would use a word like ostracized, because how could we feel otherwise. At school, being Jewish meant from kindergarten to sixth grade, the teacher would ask everyone who was "not" a Mormon to stand up. My brother and I at the time were the only kids in Lincoln Elementary School who were not Mormon. So, of course we stood up and were singled out from the very beginning. That was isolating. Embarrassing. Devastating actually, to be pointed out that way because it meant that *we* were negative.

Off-Limits—Being different became worse in junior high and senior high school because of the social events connected with the Mormon teenage groups. You didn't attend because you really weren't asked to go. If you wanted to date a "nice boy," like I said, I was off limits. I wasn't a Mormon and they wouldn't date a Jewish girl. Fortunately, I had a couple of really good friends who were boys and we went to the movies. Once they were in their senior year, though, that was it. They were "otherly" directed.

I couldn't have been a cheerleader. I wouldn't even have tried because I was Jewish and it was one of those unwritten rules, you know, you just don't do it. I was in the Pep Club, and there were girls in the class ahead of me who took me under their wing. I had close friends within my own graduating class who were "on the fringes," non-practicing Mormons. And I think that's the way it worked. Pep Club, and being a co-editor of the high school paper, I'd say those were the kinds of things that really got me through my high school years. But there was a line you couldn't cross. You always knew it was clearly defined and, no matter how disputed, was always there.

Funny, it was only in going back to my 30th class reunion, the only one I ever went to, that I witnessed such a turnaround among the middle aged, Box Elder class of 1960. All of them, former students, voiced a tremendous respect for Judaism. They consider us related; and, all of a sudden I was asked to give the Jewish prayer over the food. And did I know what a splendid tradition I came from?

Home—It's interesting because I think as we hit our middle years, many of us seek answers and spirituality. It happened in my family. When my brother was 12, my father realized Peter had no religious education except going to the Unitarian church religious school during the summers. So Dad decided that my brother had a year to prepare for a bar mitzvah. My brother and I didn't know what a bar mitzvah was, so for one concentrated year, a blessed woman in Ogden, Lillian Rubin, who had taught many, many children at Congregation Brith Sholem, prepared my brother for his bar mitzvah. At that time, I attended classes at Brith Sholem, too. That's where I started learning about my religion and practices. I was a little over fourteen years old, and it was the first time I met Jewish boys. The first time! And what did I think? I felt like I was home.

My Dad said he was sorry about the difficulties we encountered growing up in Brigham City. He considered sending us to Ogden High School, which was rated high nationally, but decided it would be too much of an effort to drive back and forth every day. Still, he felt he had made a mistake, he should have continued on with the residency, and not settled in Brigham. At the same time, he had a fine life there and a fine practice. He was a general practitioner. He loved delivering babies, and he loved raising babies. He just loved the practice of obstetrics and pediatrics. It gave him a lot of pleasure.

A Town Still Wonderful—There was a lot about Brigham that was wonderful, that still is wonderful. A small town to grow up in, we never had to lock our front door. We were known in the community. If there was some sort of crisis, there wasn't a business on Main Street who wouldn't let my brother or me in to make a phone call. It was also very easy to learn how to drive in Brigham City. We'd go out by the old golf course, no freeway traffic, and just drive on the country roads until we got it right.

And another thing about Brigham and small town living. We became thoroughly acquainted with orange iced tea served at the Idle Isle Restaurant, and its homemade rolls smothered with homemade jams and jellies. Right next door, they still have hand-dipped chocolates. Brigham's fruit is legendary! When my dad had his practice, there wasn't a day from the time the fruit ripened that there weren't packages wrapped and left by grateful patients. It was incredible and still perfect for a harvest sojourn.

Grateful Hearts—I am glad we didn't leave Brigham City. If it hadn't worked for my father to go West, I wouldn't be a Utahn. I wouldn't be the person I am today. Like my other relatives, I probably would never have left Brooklyn. As it happened, being Jewish in Brigham City gave me the impetus to appreciate cultural diversity. I learned at a young age that schools like the

Intermountain Indian School are wrong to take children away from families, put them into dormitories, and strip them of their language. The day they entered that campus they could not speak their native tongue. They lost their stories; they lost their lore. That really impacted me. How we don't appreciate our differences. Over the years, I've gotten involved in working with other multi-cultural groups, ethnic populations, and religious communities. We've had religious dialogues going on for five or six years, and it's important that we keep talking. Yes, living in Utah offers a quality of life that can recognize and celebrate differences in a positive way. I've learned that.

And I've learned a lot from my dad. My father said we're all shy at heart. If you go into a room full of strangers, you could find yourself in a totally quiet room, unless you break the ice. My father said to go over, say hello, and be a good listener. He was very much my mentor. (He also mentored my four-letter word vocabulary; I certainly didn't pick up that habit from my mother.) He taught me how to listen; that comes directly from my father, and I hope I've learned how to hear what people are really saying.

"BUSY AS A BIRD DOG"

Esther Rosenblatt Landa

My Beginnings—I was born on Christmas night, 1912, in the Nelson Apartments on 3rd East between 3rd and 4th South, two doors down from the synagogue which my grandfather helped to found.[1] My parents were Simon and Sylvia Rosenblatt. Later we moved to the Knickerbocker Apartments on South Temple and 13th East. My grandparents were living in a big house on the southeast corner of 6th East and 3rd South, but then they moved to the Knickerbocker too. I remember my family had lockers in storage rooms and I would help my grandmother [Tillie Sheinbaum Rosenblatt] change the dishes for Passover. We had to get the house all clean, and cart everything upstairs from the locker. All the Passover dishes, pots, and pans. My mother never learned to drive a car, but those were the days when Mr. Warshaw, who later turned out to be a millionaire, would come 'round driving a vegetable truck with a running board so you could step up on the running board and see what the produce was.

"Good Yontif"—For High Holy Days, my grandfather used to stay at the Newhouse Hotel [during *Shabbes*], so he could walk to services at Congregation Montefiore. When I was growing up, we would go to services at B'nai Israel. They would get out first, and then we'd walk over to 4th East, down 3rd South and over 3rd East to Montefiore to see our grandparents. My grandfather sat on the front row, on the left hand side where he had a lectern. The fellows down at the shop made him a lectern to hold his prayer book on. We'd go up and say "Good Yontif," good holiday, get a kiss and hug and then we'd go sit with my grandmother in the back row and stay there for a while. Sometimes it was hard to concentrate, kids would be running up and down the aisle and talking. But I could always be patient and sit still. Then we'd go back to B'nai Israel.

Even though my grandfather stayed at the Newhouse Hotel, when the sun went down, he would come home and we'd have a big feast. I remember herring and rye bread and schnapps. I used to help make the horseradish for gefilte fish for Passover. Preparing for Passover used to take a solid week of cooking. My grandmother would do the cooking, but she would always have a girl to help with the dishes. In the dining room, they had a big china closet with a glass front, and the guys would sit in their chairs and then, after dinner, they'd start to lean back. Way back. We'd yell, "Be careful!" Or else they'd crash into the china closet. Then I remember the big buffet where Grandma used to keep the candy, on the side of it.

Moving West—My grandfather Nathan Rosenblatt was very good humored. We called him Gramps. He used to give us five dollars on every birthday until we started to get too old, then it started to run into money. My grandfather came from Europe and went directly to Denver because there were people from his town there. He stayed briefly and then pushed his way further westward and came on to Salt Lake City. I think he was ill for awhile because I believe a Mrs. Bamberger took care of him. When he got better, he went back to Denver and the family shipped him over a bride, my grandmother. They were married in Denver. Simon was born there. When they moved to Salt Lake, around 1889 or 1890, they stayed here thereafter.

The Scrap-Metal Business and Leaving School—My father actually quit school when he was thirteen to help my grandfather out in his scrap metal business. He never went beyond an eighth grade education, but he had marvelous handwriting and was very good with figures. He could play the piano, but he was really work-oriented and not too much interested in anything else. When he was older, Sarah Lieberman, who was married to Lou Smith, came out from St. Joseph, Missouri, and became neighbors of the Rosenblatts. Knowing there were two unmarried Rosenblatt brothers, Sarah invited her sister, Sylvia, out to visit. She meet Simon, and they ended up getting married back in St. Joe, in 1911.

Tomboy School Days—The first couple of grades, I went to the Wasatch School, then we moved way out to the country. At the time, Yale Avenue and 13th East was considered the countryside. I went to the Uintah School, tramping through the fields between 13th East and 15th East, following the principal, Mr. A. B. Kesler, who was a tall Lincolnesque figure who lived on Yale Avenue. He would start out before me. There weren't any houses between 13th East and 15th East at that time. We had a path through those fields, it was mostly wooded area, and in the snowy days, he would break the path and we all followed behind. I also remember the big hill going from 13th East to 11th East where we used to sleigh ride. I think the roads were paved by then and my father had a car. He had to or else we couldn't have moved to Yale Avenue, because the street car went only to East High School on 13th East and 9th South.

In school, the good teachers I had were the ones who inspired you to do more work than you were assigned to do and made it easier for you to work and understand. I don't really recall there were any great discipline problems. The only thing that I remember at the Uintah School was that there was one boy who was evidently from a poor family and he used to come to school in bib overalls and his lunch was wrapped in newspaper. The kids kind of made fun of him and that didn't set too well with me. I don't know if that was a sensitizing experience for me, but I remember it well.

"For love of riding": Simon Rosenblatt. (Courtesy of Esther Landa)

Roosevelt Junior High was between 9th and 10th East on Lincoln Street and 9th South. From there, I went to East High and graduated in 1929. I was only sixteen years old because at the Uintah School, you could do half grades. When I got to Roosevelt, they said, "Write a book review on *Ivanhoe* and you can have the other half of the grade." I did and I graduated at sixteen.

I was a tomboy as a kid. I still am one, probably the only one who [in 1982] is almost seventy and still likes high school basketball games. When I was a kid, it didn't bother me very much that the Mormon kids were always going out to their own activities. When they went to Primary or Mutual after school, I was outside playing with whoever was left. So, I wasn't bothered by it, but my kids were when they went to school; some of them even went to the same school that I did, but that was a good deal later.

Because I was a tomboy, I couldn't sew. At the Uintah School, we had to take sewing and it took me forever and a day. First you had to make a little sampler, a little yellow sampler, with pins and needles stuck in and you had to make different kinds of stitches around the outside. Finally, before the end of the year, I managed to make one apron, and the other girls whooped and hollered and applauded because I finally got through. That was a little embarrassing. No, domestic science was not for me at all. Otherwise, I had a pretty happy time in the schools.

For Fun—We did everything. Played marbles. By our back door there was a place that was filled with dirt. I remember lagging and shooting. I could never skate, never learned to ski. Couldn't swim for the longest time. My Dad wasn't interested in doing that, so we didn't do that. Although my Dad, in his early youth, had a lot to do with the bicycle races at the original Salt Palace, and we used to go to a lot of baseball games, and travel. Once we went through the Fourth of July Canyon up by Coeur d'Alene, Idaho. Another time, we went to Seattle. And Portland. I remember at my cousin's house in Portland, my brother stuck his head through the banister and couldn't get it out. They had to get the fire department to get him out. In 1932, my dad took us on a car trip to the northwest and all the way down the coast and ended up at the 1932 Olympic Game in Los Angeles.

Steel Castings—When I was a teenager, I used to help my grandfather at work. I think I was tolerated. He always had his hat on and he smoked cigarettes. I remember learning how to weigh stuff on the scales. There were big sheets of paper, and on it was copper, wire, batteries, old tires, etc., and you'd have to write down the name of the peddler who brought the stuff in and how much it weighed. At that time, I think my father was already at the American Foundry and Machine, on the corner of 4th West and 9th South. They made steel castings. In other words, they would melt the junk, and pour the steel into wooden pattern molds that were made by the carpenters in the pattern shop, and sell the castings to the railroads for wheels, and that kind of business. It was a big place with a black, dirt floor and huge steel furnaces.

College Days—I started Mills College in Oakland, California during the depression, in 1929, but stayed my junior year in Salt Lake until I had enough money to go back for my senior year. My father was managing during the depression; I mean, we still had our house and he was a hard worker. He used to go to work very early in the morning, be out of the house by six o'clock. I remember there was a time when we lived on the fifth floor in the Mayflower Apartments and my brother Barney, when he was going through his wild days, would get off on the fourth floor and walk up because he was afraid he'd meet Dad going out to work. So life was all right. My sister, Barbara, there's five years difference between us, got into Stanford and was in the Class of '38. A year before that, I went to Europe with a couple of Mills friends. I remember being apprehensive when we took the train from Switzerland to Holland because I think we went through some parts of Germany. This was 1937, so I must have had some inkling something was wrong.

At Mills, I wrote a weekly column called the *Old Rocking Chair.* I can't remember what I wrote about; the issues were probably topical, but the fact that I went to a women's college had a big influence on me. I think my subsequent activities would have been different if I hadn't gone to a women's college. It developed a feeling of independence. And then, of course, you started having role models. I was an English major and got into PR and publicity work, which shaped my career from that time on.

A Woman's Place—After I graduated—which, by the way, I had to learn how to swim before I could graduate—my family was living in California and I lived with my grandparents in Salt Lake. I went to the Stevens-Henager College of Business right out of Mills because a woman couldn't get a job unless she could type and take shorthand. I think we've broken that stereotype now. I worked as a reporter for the women's basketball league on the old *Salt Lake Telegram.*

Life in Washington, D.C.
(Courtesy of Esther Landa)

In 1941, I spent the summer at Bennington School of Dance, doing publicity. It didn't start out that way. Martha Graham had done a dance called *Judith* and wanted to bring the Bennington School of Dance to the West Coast, so they came to Mills College in the summer of 1939. I liked it. Then, in 1940, my cousin Margie and I decided to go to New York to seek our fame and fortune. We started out driving. I was driving. Between Laramie and Cheyenne, Wyoming, the car turned over on the curve and we were hospitalized for quite a while. Our mothers had come up to take us home. I was brought back on a stretcher. The next year, we attempted our trip again. This time, we went by train and my Bennington friends got me a job doing the publicity for the summer theatre on Nantucket Island, in Massachusetts. But, since they really wanted me at Bennington, I spent the summer there doing PR. It was wonderful. Martha Graham was there, Doris Humphrey, Charles Weidman, you name them, they were all there.

World War II—After Pearl Harbor, everybody wanted to go to work in Washington, D.C. We all went to 90 Church Street, took a typing exam and waited to get a little postcard that said, "Come to Washington." I got mine in January or February, and ended up in Arlington. I had a room in a house and shared a bath with two sailors, who worked at the Navy Department. I reported to work in what was an old roller skating rink on one side or the other near the Capitol. I worked under the Office of Emergency Management. My part of the job got known as the Labor Management Drive. We got into incentive work for factories. That turned out to be PR when you got all through with it.

Jerry—I came back to Salt Lake City to get married. I met Jerry through the Mills College friends of mine, from Texas. He was transferred to Salt Lake by his company, and they told him to look me up. I didn't happen to be here at the time. He took Barbara out, but Barney said he was too old for Barbara. So eventually I came home and we got together. We were married in

September 1943, and then my husband went overseas. After the war, his company sent him to Tulsa, Oklahoma where we lived for three years. Then after my father died, I kind of wanted to come home.

A Commitment to Causes—After I had a baby, in August of 1944, I stayed home to take care of her and got active in Hadassah, raising money for Israel. I became the secretary of Hadassah, then joined the National Council of Jewish Women [NCJW]. Later I joined the League of Women Voters, and I got on the board of the League. Got involved in politics, community services, schools, women's rights and children's issues. I was as busy as a bird dog. Still am, as a kind of "behind-the-scenes activist." I'm not denigrating those people who are on the cutting edge. But in order to make change, you have to have a good back-up of people in the mainstream who think the same way about an issue but are willing to bring about social change through less spectacular, non-violent, non-confrontational ways such as education and reason. Women have to be more interested in politics. They have to be interested in so-called women's issues, which are actually family and human issues. Pay equity is not just a women's issue, it's a human issue. Sexual harassment is a human issue. As people, we all need to pay attention to these issues.[2]

Why have I gotten so involved? I figured I'd been the beneficiary of a good education, and I owed something back to the community. In my days, the women in the family weren't allowed or encouraged to go into the family business, so I had to go into community work. That was part of it. The other part is that we learned from the Old Testament prophets that we are supposed to do justice, to help others, and do what's right.

THE MOUNT SINAI POKER, CANASTA, AND S****** CLUB

Carol Landa

This is how I remember it.[1] My parents' poker club was organized in 1946 when the men came back from the war. My dad, Jerry Landa, served in England; Alvin Smith in the Aleutian Islands; Herman Bernstein in the Philippines; Wally Sandack and Jack Sweet in the South Pacific.

They came home to Utah. Back then, Jews felt the need to make their own social life in Salt Lake City, which lacked good restaurants, open bars, and, in many instances, country club memberships. They wanted a drink before dinner, a good meal, and an opportunity for conversation with each other. The older generation of Salt Lake Jews, consisting of their parents, older siblings, aunts and uncles had its own club: the Cadillac Club named for the obvious reason. The younger generation needed to create a club of its own.

Smith and Sandack cooked up the idea of and the name for the Poker Club: The Mount Sinai Poker, Canasta, and "S" Club. It was to provide a men's night out or as we say now an opportunity for male bonding. However, the wives would have none of it. They had been meeting with one another during the war and wanted to continue the association and to include their husbands. Having gained a measure of independence in the war years, the women laid down the house rules: The Club would be co-ed.

Originally, the "S" stood for a Yiddish word for sex. Refer to *The Joys of Yiddish* by Leo Rosten if you want more details.[2] Later, as they aged they said the "S" stood for schmoozing, which is Yiddish for good conversation. Now that they are really old they say the "S" stands for sitting.

This is how it worked. The Club met every other Saturday night in a member's home. The host and hostess furnished the drinks, appetizers, and main course. Others completed the menu. There were some GOOD cooks in The Club and I always asked my mom to assign the dessert to Bernice "Baby Doll" Smith. I can still taste her chocolate roll.

It was a full house on the night my parents hosted the Club. I loved those evenings. My mother [Esther Rosenblatt Landa] would order beautiful flowers: gladioli in peach and salmon that matched the colors in our living room. I would go shopping with her and she would buy different brands of cigarettes for her guests. One of my tasks was to undo the packages and arrange the cigarettes in elegant silver holders. After the party was over, I had to put out bowls of vinegar to take away the smell. Now that no one smokes any more, the silver holders are used for toothpicks or are in the back of the cupboard gathering dust.

My mom, famous for many things, is not an expert in the kitchen. But when the Poker Club came she made a special effort. Often she hired a caterer. We children were allowed to stick around for the appetizers, usually clam dip and chips. Years later a friend told me that was very "middle class" but I still love it and make it for my own parties.

After dinner, the women would stay upstairs in our living room and play poker, canasta, or bridge. They would tally up the expenses for the dinner and tell each couple how much it cost. Later on, as they became more affluent, they abandoned this practice and the host couple footed the whole bill.

The men would go downstairs to our family room for serious poker. My dad had a special round wooden table built that we would assemble before the party. Sometimes my brother Howard, my sister Terry, and I got to play with the poker chips which were colored blue, red, and gold. The chips fit neatly into niches in a worn round leather container. My mom taught us all how to play. Once in awhile, Dad let Howard sit in on a hand or two with the men. Now 87, my mother teaches her grandchildren how to play and keeps in practice herself at the 5-cent poker slots in Las Vegas.

Eavesdropping on the adult conversations, I got my first exposure to Yiddish phrases and Jewish humor. I learned to appreciate the Jewish comics who later on came into our living room via the television we acquired in 1951: George Burns, Jack Benny, and Milton Berle. I still think that Burnett, Cohen, and Sandack could have given them a run for their money.

The couples were winning pairs with not a divorce among them. With some few exceptions, they all stayed put in Salt Lake and they've stayed friends all these years. They epitomize Tom Brokaw's "Greatest Generation." I think of them as a sociological phenomenon.

Some were born and reared in Salt Lake and their friendships date from childhood and the friendships of their parents. Others, like my Texan dad, married in. The Club had members who were sisters and who were cousins. My dad, Jack Sweet, and Sid Cohen were fraternity brothers in Phi Sigma Delta. They all worshipped at Temple B'nai Israel and usually voted democratic. It was the "in group" and the envy of other young Jewish couples in town. I remember being surprised when a B'nai Israel friend told me her mother longed to be in The Club.

Every summer, the group had a Mt. Sinai family picnic at the Lagoon amusement park. Members had T-shirts made up one year that were misprinted to say "Mt. Sinia." This generated lots of laughs and even a funny song or two. We all had great times at Lagoon. I think our parents would have liked to see some matches made among the Club children. There were a lot of us, baby boomers all. It didn't happen. The offspring were rather divided between those of us who

The reunion. *Back row:* Louis, Doug G., Steve, Max, Howard (Whitney); Nancy, Ted, Jack, Larry, Suzanne, Janet Goldsmith, Debbie, Art, Terry, Esther, Jules Jane, Jane Ann, Herman, Libby, Jon Sweet, Marty (Michael); Hannah, Joey B., David B., Jeffery, Rachel (Sweet), Jeremy, David, Helen Susan (Elliott), Allie, Amy, Patrick (Lovingers), Bernice Smith, and Tom Burnett. *Behind:* Doug B., Dianne, Ginny, Bernice B. (Heather); Barbara B., Emily Sandack, Lisa Burnett, Elizabeth, David Bernstein, Andre B. Nora, and Harriet. (The Sandacks, the Goldsmiths, the Landas, the Sweets, the Lovingers, the Bernsteins, and others.) (Courtesy of Helen Sandack)

went to public schools (East, Highland, Olympus) and those who were sent to private schools (Rowland Hall and St. Marks). Those of us in public school thought the others were stuck up. I think the private schoolers thought we were unsophisticated. The only neutral ground was Lagoon or Temple B'Nai Israel.

While my generation fussed and feuded a bit as teenagers, I only remember two major fights in the Club. At some point, two of the mothers bought the same dress for their daughters' prom night and couldn't agree on who would take hers back. More serious was a debate about admitting new members. Both storms were weathered.

Those kings, queens, and jacks—those winning pairs were the Landas, Burnetts, Smiths, Rosens, Goodmans, Bernsteins, Kremens, Cohens, Friedmans, and Lovingers, Sandacks, and

Sweets. Later on Schwartzes who came from Pittsburgh, and much later Benowitzes from Ogden joined the ranks. Salt Lakers may recognize these names as active, successful, philanthropic members of the community.

The men were successful poker players too. The exception was the resident intellectual, Jack Goodman, who wasn't interested in poker. He would sit out the game and read. My Uncle, Ted Burnett, made a big killing one night ($175). The next day, he used it to pay cash to the obstetrician who delivered his daughter, my cousin Lisa.

Milt Rosen kept the accounts. All the winnings from the last game of the year went to a local charity selected by the members. The Club also chipped in to buy presents for any significant life event of a member or a member's family: births, bar/bat mitzvahs, confirmations, weddings.

One year, the Club members and their children and grandchildren gathered for a reunion picnic in Burnett's large back yard. Even though not everyone was there, some 50 plus showed up. My famous photojournalist cousin, David Burnett, took the picture to commemorate the occasion. In 1986, the Club celebrated its 40th anniversary at a party in Rancho Mirage, California. Wally Sandack was the emcee. Long known as a stand-up comic, he attributed the Club's zero divorce rate to wife swapping. He had a descriptive quip for everyone. For Jack Goodman: "If the shoe fits, it's ugly"; for Herman Bernstein: "A closed mouth gathers no feet"; for Corinne Sweet: "Virtue is its own punishment"; for himself: "Don't allow dignity to depress you."

They enjoyed life. They worked hard, raised their families, paid their dues and lived by the rules in poker and in life. Most have cashed in their chips. Gone are my beloved father, Jerry Landa, my Uncle Ted Burnett, my cousin Marj Goodman, the Schwartzes, the Cohens, the Kremens, the Sweets, Milt Rosen, Alvin Smith, and Seymour Friedman. They were special people and a special part of my life. I learned many important lessons from them, including, never to draw to an inside straight.

FOURTEEN

Landsmen

SOVIET IN SALT LAKE

Alla Branzburg

Starting Over—We came from Ukraine.[1] We took only seven bags and in these bags, we put our dishes and plates, glasses and clothes, pillows and blankets. Everything else, we gave away to our family and our friends. It was a difficult time, almost a tragic time because much of everything that I had known, had grown up around, and loved, was no longer with me. And I had to start life all over again.

What We Left—My parents lived three blocks away from my home in Donetak, a coal mining town. It was a five-minute walk to their home. Every day, my daughter Elena would run over to her Grandmother, and every day after work my mother would walk over and visit us. I miss my life in Ukraine because it was my life and I did not know of any other kind of life. When I was a child, I had a father and a mother and two grandmothers and a grandfather who loved me and took care of me, so my childhood was not difficult at all. I lived among Jewish and non-Jewish people and had my own community of friends. It was only after I was grown that I realized the difficulties of living in Ukraine as a woman, a mother, a worker, and a Jew.

Alla Branzburg makes a new life in a new land for her family. (Photo by Eileen Hallet Stone)

Worrying about Status—When we decided to leave Ukraine, we received help from HIAS [Hebrew International Aid Society]. We were sent to Austria for two weeks and then to the seaside town of Nettuno, Italy, where we stayed for six months. That is a long time when you are preparing to go to America, but after our interview with the American Embassy, we had to wait for too long a time for the American government to make a decision about our status. Throughout this time, we worried about whether we would receive refugee status and government support for our first year in America, or whether we would be unfunded and have to find a job immediately without knowing the language or the country. But whatever the decision, we knew we would be coming to America.

Ukrainian Homes—We lived in a state-owned, low-rental, cooperative-housing project, as most Soviet people do. We were lucky because there were just the three of us and we had a one-bedroom apartment with a living room. We slept in the living room so our daughter could have her own room. In some cases, even large families have to live in an apartment this same size. Petitioning for more space can take years before a larger apartment becomes available. Old parents who lived with their married children could die before a large enough apartment could be found. But we had a nice place and even a tiny washing machine in our small kitchen. It was such a small washing machine that, like many Russian women, I spent a lot of time washing many, many things by hand, wringing them out and hanging them over the balcony to dry.

Shortage of Food—When we were living in Ukraine, there were food shortages. After working eight hours a day, just like Americans do, instead of going to a supermarket such as "Albertsons," I would spend my evenings waiting in lines at government stores. Often it was impossible to find food. There was no food, no meat, no fruits, no vegetables. The waiting in line was for nothing. And what use were food stamps? Our food stamps had specific items on them, but what good is having an "egg" stamp if there are no eggs? Or a "meat" stamp if there is no meat? There were only a very few vegetables or fruit. To get our food, we had to buy it in the peasant market and pay prices two or three times higher than charged in state government stores. When we lived in Donetak, we had only tomatoes, potatoes, onions, cabbage and apples. For one month in the summer, we had strawberries.

Black Market—But it's the clothes that are so exciting for us. If a Russian woman just walked into an American clothing store, she would be shocked. To get such quality clothes in Russia, one would have to buy them on the black market and pay four times more than they were worth. For my own mother, who is a retired accountant, one pair of pants bought in a state store would cost her more than three quarters of her monthly pension. In the marketplace, it would be doubled!

Pride—Our colors are mostly grey, brown, dark blue, and sometimes red. But Russian women take care of themselves. Our women have so many jobs in the house and so many jobs in the office and still they will take the time to look good. Long after the dishes are done, and everyone has gone to sleep, instead of going to bed, these Russian women will color their hair and take care of their nails so they will look well groomed in the morning for their families and for work.

Passed Over—I had wanted to go to medical school but it was almost impossible to be accepted into any medical institution because I was Jewish. Soviet Jewish doctors are very few. Mostly they are the older ones who graduated from medical schools many years ago. Since I couldn't get in, I studied accounting and graduated with what you would call a master's degree and got a job in the mining industry. My husband, Alexander, who graduated in economics, also worked in the mining industry as a buyer. He is a very smart man who had no trouble being educated, but did have trouble rising to a higher position in his department because he was Jewish. You see, it was denied to him because for a Jew it becomes impossible to have an opportunity for growth no matter how much it is deserved. My brother had an easier time of it because he carried the last name of his non-Jewish wife instead of his own. Many Jewish people do this, take a non-Jewish name, just to survive the "normal" difficulties of Soviet life.

No Changes in Society—My grandfather was a rabbi in Poland, but I had cautious grandparents so I became apolitical. But I had my thoughts and imagination. I hated the politics of Stalinism. I don't believe in the Communist way of living. I knew we had *perestroika* but I didn't see any changes in the society itself. Food was still not available and housing was scarce, although high-positioned Communists had nice apartments, vacations, food, and clothes. It was not for us. Advancement at work was not possible for many Jewish people. Yes, we had a total of 24 vacation days, but without the funds, where could we go? Who can afford an apartment

JEWISH FAMILY SERVICES

In 1989, the Jewish community launched an extensive campaign called Operation Exodus. The iron gates of the Soviet Union are open. After decades of struggle, the Jewish people from the Soviet Union are coming home to America.

Fifty years ago, there was no safe haven, no place Soviet Jews could call home in which they had the freedom to explore their religion, their heritage, and their identity. Today, we keep the doors open.

at the seaside? Who can afford to tour the countryside? No, many of us just vacationed at home, most in crowded one-bedroom apartments.

In America—I studied English in grade school and my husband and I continued to study English. I am now studying at the community college and want to go to a university too. My daughter is happy here. She attends classes at Congregation Kol Ami and goes to summer camp at the Jewish Community Center. For all the time I had been cut off from my history and my religion, now I too can learn and reclaim my Judaism to live with and share with my family.

Land of Opportunity—I believe I came to America mostly because of my daughter. I want my Elena never to have the trouble that I had as a woman in the house, in the schools, and in the work. I want her to be spiritually free and without trouble with her religion. I want her to be mentally free to pursue whatever she wants to pursue because America is a country of opportunity and can offer her that. Elena is happier here, healthier here. She doesn't get sick like she did in Ukraine. But I want you to know that I love my Russia because it was my entire life. Now I am loving America, too. All I need is perfect English for my next job interview. What do you think?

FRONTIER JEWS

Harris Lenowitz

Traditions—My father was in the clothing business.[1] He had gone to school at a yeshiveh in New York where his parents had sent him when he was thirteen years old. Torah Vedas, as it is called and still exists. This yeshiva combined aspects of modern education with traditional Jewish education. When my dad married my mother, who was a third generation Texas girl, and moved to Texas, there was a lot of expectation on the part of his brothers, and his parents, that that would be the end of his Judaism. So a lot of my Jewishness derives from my father's desire to prove his family wrong, to assert his Jewishness against the surrounding climate in Texas, and, particularly, against the lack of any real Jewish education in my mother's family.

It has to be said the scarcity of Jewish education in my mother's family comes from two different places. One of them is the winding down of Eastern European Jewish traditions that began a generation earlier on my mother's maternal side of the family, while the other has to do with my mother's father who was a Socialist. He, along with his brothers, came to the United States and was sent to Texas to establish an agricultural activity, which, as you know, was a real draw in certain parts of the West, like the Clarion Colony in southern Utah.

My father had liberal, or socialist, inclinations, so he didn't want to get rid of that either. So that's what happened to me. I grew up a leftist and, at the same time, as someone who was to have a Jewish education. My father taught me Hebrew at home, from the time I was about six years old, and actually we were still studying together until after my second year or so in college.

The home we lived in, on the other hand, responded more to my mother's Jewishness. That is, we didn't have pork products at home, or non-kosher aquatic crustaceans, but neither did we observe separate milk and meat rules with separate dishes, and so forth. Whenever my father's grandfather or brothers and their wives and children came to town, we always had to bring up the appropriate dishes, pots, and pans that were stored down in the cellar for their use in the house.

My two sisters and I were sent to religious school at Congregation Agudas Achim, in San Antonio. My mother's family had been involved in the founding of the synagogue. For me, its education was largely social. That is, I was exposed to other Jews, and to their daughters and interacted with them to some degree. I don't believe there was any Hebrew education that I got there; that came from my father. At home, there weren't any other Jewish boys my age, and I hung around with the son of the preacher at the Methodist Church. In fact, I went to Catholic School, so I could get an earlier start on my education. That only lasted until the first grade, I think, and then they took me out because I asked them for a rosary.

Dry Goods and Talaysim—Congregation Agudas Achim was a high Conservative congregation; that is, empathetically clerical. It was attended by the old Texas families that had lost a good deal of their Jewish background and knowledge, but was supplemented by a regular flow of eastern Jews moving out to Texas through Galveston or Kansas and Oklahoma. Many of these people were in the same trade that my father was in: clothing, or, as it was called, the dry goods business. Since San Antonio was a big military town, several Jewish businessmen were uniform dealers. The dry goods business very often ends up in the hands of Jews in a number of different places, including, of course, Salt Lake City, and it is these people who are often considered frontier Jews.

When the people at schools or churches in San Antonio wanted to have someone to come and talk about what being a Jew is like, my father would give that lecture. In fact, my Dad used to schlep around a box that had a tallis in it, a tefillin, a prayer book, and a shofar. So that's what it was to be a frontier Jew, and it's true that I have carried a lot of that over by myself into Salt Lake. It's also true that I have met that same self here in Salt Lake among several people who were themselves frontier Jews. In particular, I remember Max Cowan, who epitomized the frontier Jew.

Chumash on the Range—My mother's father's family had been in the cattle business and although they had never done business with Max Cowan, they had done business with people like cattle dealer S. Garinksy, who did business with Max Cowan. And Max was truly a frontier Jew. I mean, when he was out there with his Daddy, he used to tell me about riding the range with a Chumash [the five books of Moses] in their saddlebags. I believe that probably was the case for a number of people out here in the high plains.

So I met people like myself here. Yet I didn't get along particularly well with the intellectual semi-religious community because even though my father taught me all these sources, he never believed in the religion. He taught me also not to believe while studying, although one would think that the two automatically go together in one package. I certainly wasn't interested in Reform Judaism, considering that to be text-free Judaism. I went in the opposite direction. I was interested in the traditions without the belief.

The people here in the Jewish intellectual community at that time did have a tendency towards Reform Judaism. I knew most of them: Louis Goodman, Dave Dolowitz, Hal Rosenberg,

Max Wintrobe, Maurice Abravanel, and of course the fellow who introduced me into the community, Louis Zucker and his wife Ethel. I got along relatively well with almost all of them. But it wasn't going to be a community that I was going to be part of, I thought. They were old fashioned.

Harris Lenowitz. (Photo by Eileen Hallet Stone)

A Transition—On the other hand, I considered the young people, who were more or less my age, lacked a desire for it and any background in Judaism, although I suppose the person I would have gotten along with is Joel Shapiro. Thus, for the first couple of years that I was here, I was disassociated from the Jewish people. And then I thought being uninvolved reasonable, since I was going to be a Jewish teacher at the University of Utah. My second year here, I saw that I needed to share what I have with the community here. So I began first as a teacher at the combined religious school of B'nai Israel and Congregation Montefiore. The classes were held at B'nai Israel, and I began by teaching modern Hebrew. Gradually, I changed towards teaching prayer book Hebrew to the kids. Within a couple of years, I decided that my activity was not enough and that I needed to join with the praying community as well. Since we lived in the Avenues [beneath the foothills], I liked the walk down the hill to Congregation Montefiore, where the Conservative to Orthodox old congregation men of Salt Lake met regularly. And I enjoyed meeting a lot of these men; they were like my uncles and of my father's generation, or the generation before that. They were comfortable with their Judaism. The one person I came to know best and knew for the next twenty-five years was Ike Rose. I suppose they were all believers, but that wasn't anything that anyone ever talked about really. I mean, can you picture yourself coming to shul and asking a Jew who is standing there praying with a yarmulke on, and ask him if he believes in God? I've never heard anybody do that. I never would do that myself. I don't even know what I would make of an answer.

Caring about Practice—I believe Judaism doesn't really care about belief. Judaism cares about practice, about what you do. If your mother was a Jew, then you're a Jew. That's the end of it. If you're an atheist of a Jewish mother, then you're an atheist but you're a Jew. On the other hand, if you're a Jew who has converted to Christianity, then you're not a Jew. But somehow the conversion procedure that is so typical of Christianity, for example, at the point one becomes a Christian is the point in which one converts to Christianity, one makes one's conversion, one achieves baptism, one achieves communion. This doesn't happen in Judaism. So really, it is not as unusual in Judaism to have people who are non-believers and are Jews.

Another Congregation—I was an active member of Congregation Kol Ami, and a teacher in the religious school there from 1972 until 1991. I didn't want to be part of a Judaism that has become "de-Hebrewized." I don't have any interest in it, where I can't get at the texts, where I can't get at the history. As a scholar of Hebrew, I like to see people praying in Hebrew. So when [Rabbi] Benny [Zippel] came to town eight or so years ago to start the Lubavitch shul, Bais Menachem, I found my kind of congregation. Now that there is a synagogue within walking distance of my house, I can get there on *Shabbat,* on the holidays, and whenever there is a need for a *minyan.* And I get there early, before Benny gets there, to make the morning prayers before anybody else gets there. By myself at first, and then actively with others in the service.

Literary Art and Judaism—But for me, participation is like what it would be for a normal person of Western civilization to wander through a museum of western art. Because literary art is the highest of the Jewish arts, the most highly developed, most intricate, most complicated, and most reflective of the contexts of Judaism and the times of the poets who wrote the poems and the prayers. It is like wandering through these people's minds and feeling them through the best expression. So I do that.

Reading Torah—I read Torah for Benny, when he's not there, but I refuse to read it with the sing-song notes. I don't like the way those notes are there; they mark phrases that I don't think are phrases. Besides, a lot of it is poetry, a lot of it is very interesting building plans, and that's what I want people to hear. That this is a communication that takes place and not a performance of some kind or other that is impenetrable, or on a different plane than in life. Over the last six years, I've read the Haftarah, fairly regularly. And so I like to do that. At next *Shabbes,* I'll read Torah at Congregation Kol Ami because they're short of Torah readers.

Reading Torah means preparing yourself to read Torah; even reading the Haftarah means preparing yourself to read the Haftarah. So even though I spend all week reading Hebrew texts for my classes, when it comes to preparing for the public reading of the Torah, that's a religious act, somehow. I have to learn it extremely well so as not to betray in any sense the art of the people that made the Torah.

Maftir Yonah—For thirty years [reflecting the highest synagogue honor], Max was the maftir yonah, and the person who regularly read the book of Jonah for the Haftarah reading for the Mincha service on Yom Kippur. Max was an integral part of the Congregation Montefiore. He was somebody who had a Jewish education. He was somebody who knew a fair amount of Hebrew. He was somebody who people respected. He was a generous man, both in terms of the way he felt about people and his charity to Jewish organizations. In the last two years, when Max was dying, I became the maftir yonah to read Jonah, and so that's the closest that I come to doing theology, and it's the closest that I come to anything that could be called an engagement with terms of Jewish belief.

Understanding Diversity—I work with the University of Utah vice president of diversity [currently, Karen L. Dace], people like Ron Smelser, a history professor who teaches about the Holocaust, and with the Jewish community to produce cultural programs that will coordinate with academic activities at the university. For the past sixteen years, we have held the actual celebration on the Jewish calendar of the Day of Remembrance at the Capitol Rotunda, with survivors, rabbis, Jewish community members, members of the predominant religious community, the governor, the mayor, and others.

My reasoning behind this? I guess I want to show that this is a part of the history of the Jews and the observance of this holiday, the celebration of the holiday, is needed to be part of the history of a Jew living wherever a Jew lives. And that may be in line with my theology. It was more important than anything else in the Jewish calendar, and part of every Jew's life. So it was the event, the doing of the event that was the most important thing to me.

My Father's Belief—God? No. I don't have any belief in God. My father didn't have any belief. His father didn't either. His mother may have. On my mother's side there was no one. So, no, I don't have any notion of the activity that I'm involved in as a Godly activity. I have a notion of God as a Jewish term of reference. And the literature in which that figure appears as Jewish literature, at best, Hebrew Jewish literature. And that's where my obligation is. I don't wear tefillin. I've only recently started lighting the Shabbat candles again, since my divorce. And making havdalah, which I haven't done since [my son] Bernie died. Sometimes I write *ketubahs* [marriage contracts]. And how much more than that I would want to do, I'm not really sure.

THE CHABAD LIFE IN UTAH

Sharonne Zippel

A Sheltered Life—My father is an Orthodox rabbi in Toronto.[1] I was raised observant, growing up in what you could consider a sheltered life. I went to a Jewish grade school, and never interacted with non-Jews. The kids on my street were Jewish, but they were not religious. Still, I had enough friends in my Jewish community that I didn't have to start, you know, going out to meet them; they were in my life.

A Kollel—I was teaching at a Jewish girls' day school in New York and my husband was studying for a year and a half, in what is called a *kollel,* a place for married people to learn. Basically, this is your last chance to just sit all day and learn before you go out into the world and do what you have to do, to be a rabbi. So he did that from morning until night. We lived in what was like a little ghetto about five blocks by nine blocks. It was a really sheltered life and I didn't enjoy it very much. I hated the crime. When you walked down the street, you always had to hold your purse close to you. So I was thrilled to leave New York.

Utah Opportunities—My husband was given lots of options to open a Chabad synagogue in Denmark, Puerto Rico, England, or Greece. At first, he went with Greece, but I put my foot down. My husband's brother was flying into New York from Italy and came off the plane with an airline magazine that had an insert about Utah, saying how beautiful Utah was. Low crime rate, great health. I said, that's it. We never heard of Utah. My husband's Italian. I'm Canadian. What do I know from Utah? We're moving there, where people are friendly and we don't have to be afraid to walk out on the streets, I said.

Home Schooling—Today in Utah, when I go to the supermarket with my children, and people ask if there's no school today, I tell them, "We're home-schooled." And they'll say it's wonderful. Many Mormons in Utah home-school their children, so they have an understanding of it. I don't do it because I believe in it. I would much rather have a Jewish day school here that provides for their needs. As it is now, until we can send them away to a yeshiveh, hopefully, until bar mitzvah, I can teach them here at home.

Sharonne Zippel preparing for Shabbes. (Photo by Eileen Hallet Stone)

Making Friends—I don't think my five children are isolated though. Except for the baby, I send them to the Talmud Torah, the religious school on Sundays at Bais Menachem. So they see other children there. They go to synagogue every *Shabbes*, so they see kids then, too. My oldest kid was playing basketball at the Jewish Community Center, where most of the kids on the teams aren't Jewish. He had a great time. They were fascinated with his *kipa* and his tzitzit. They ask him when he's running, doesn't his *kipa* fall off his head and stuff like that. Some of the kids tell him he plays good for a Rabbi's son. My oldest is a very outspoken person who doesn't know if someone's Jewish or not Jewish, he just talks and is friendly with everybody.

Keeping Kosher—There is a problem, of course, when they get invited to other people's homes, even to those who are Jewish but don't keep kosher. Keeping kosher isn't difficult; and when you've grown up with it all your life, it becomes second nature. Besides, there's many foods in the supermarket that you can buy that are kosher already and people don't even think about it. If my husband performs a wedding, we will attend the reception too, but if the food is not kosher, we can't stay. Some of our friends will go out of their way to get kosher food. They will bring in packaged foods and unopened paper plates, and we appreciate that thoughtfulness. We've invited people to our home. We had a dinner for the redemption of our friends' firstborn son. I cooked the dinner, and it was very exciting to socialize. I would also like just to go out with my husband to a kosher restaurant. In Utah? So you know, my husband can never take me out for dinner. Yes, I miss the delis and the kosher restaurants.

A Tichel—In the home, my hair is always covered. If I'm not wearing a wig, I have what's called a *tichel*, a head covering. This is something that a Jewish married woman is supposed to do that is special and intimate between her and her husband. I don't have to wear it to bed, but when a woman is *nidah*, those two weeks, she has to have her hair covered. I have very thick hair, so I just cut it short with a slightly longer front part that goes back. A man wears a *kipa* to remind him there is always a G-d above him. They say a woman doesn't need that constant reminder because she is instinctively and naturally more spiritual. In the beginning, it was difficult to wear a wig. But now it doesn't bother me. Mine are made from human hair, which look more natural, and come in styles that are long, short, and even one with a ponytail. I tried one on here, but they have synthetic ones only, so I purchase mine from Toronto or New York.

A Spiritual Leader—With Chabad, Chasidic Jews have a spiritual leader, a rabbi, besides the rabbi of their congregation. The Orthodox Jew will just have a rabbi for his congregation. So, while we do things the same as the regular Orthodox Jew, we also do things slightly different. For instance, we'll have celebrations for the days that a rabbi may have been let out of jail in Russia, or it was one of their birthdays. And where Orthodox Jews live within their own community, we will do outreach to Jews who are not as religious and try to bring them closer to Judaism. We teach about holidays, like the celebration of Lag B'Omer. The students of Rabbi Akiba (who supported the leaders of the rebellion against Rome in 135 C.E.) suffered the effects of a plague which left them dying. On the thirty-third day (Lag meaning thirty-three) during the forty-nine counting period between Pesach and Shavuot, the plague ended. So it is a day of celebration. It is also the day that a very great rabbi who revealed a lot of the Torah secrets passed away, and he asked that it be a day of rejoicing, and that people shouldn't be sad. We also try to teach others to get to one more mitzvah, one more good deed. To try to keep Shabbat if they can; to try to keep kosher if they can; to understand the holidays they are celebrating; and for a woman, to go to a *mikvah.*

Spiritual Cleansing—A mikvah is a spiritual bath in which you say special blessings when you immerse yourself three times in water. The first time you immerse yourself totally under the water and upon rising, you say a special blessing. The other two times you dip into the water, you have the power to ask from G-d whatever it is you want. The preparations for the mikvah take time but are equally spiritual in their ritual. You must be very clean, so you have to wait until seven days after your last menstruation has ended. You then cut your fingernails and your toenails so there is no dirt under your nails. You brush and floss your teeth; you bathe in your own regular bathtub. Preparing for the mikvah becomes an exciting time because you have been separate from your husband intimately for two weeks and you're looking forward to that night. At nightfall, you will go to the mikvah. And, if you have children, it is now your husband's duty to take care of them, which is wonderful.

When you immerse yourself in the waters of the mikvah, some people find it spiritual and contemplative. One woman I know likes to sit in the peaceful water and reflect on her thoughts. When I am under the water, I like to say my prayers, but I don't like getting my face wet, so I probably spend more time on the preparations. Whatever part you like, participating in a mikvah is spiritually cleansing, and afterwards you're ready to go on and take on something new with your life again.

A Wonderful Life—One of the laws from the Torah is for a male to not shave five corners of his face, which is why my husband wears a beard. We are lucky because his beard is tame and not too long. I can't complain. Before my husband and I met each other, my grandparents lived in England where my husband was studying to be in a yeshiveh. They kind of checked him out and my grandfather reported to my mother, "If those two ever get together, they'll never have a serious moment between them." We have a good time. We talk, joke, go out and have fun with the kids. It's not the kind of serious *rebbetzen* life that people think I lead. It's quite a wonderful life.

AFTERWORD

Judaism illuminates not in the shadows of any other religion but in the hearts, minds, lifestyles, services, and attitudes of its believers in its theology or in its history or both. For poet and professor Jacqueline Osherow, living a Jewish life in Utah is an ideal life.[1] "There aren't a thousand of you here, so if you want something done as a Jew, you have to do it," she said. "And you have to participate, because if you don't things won't happen."

Raised in a traditionally Conservative home in Philadelphia, as a child Osherow did not write on Saturdays. She did play the game of Scrabble and kept score by turning pages of a book: "If you had forty points and you got another twenty, you'd turn the book page to sixty," she explained. Today, her children lead a similar life in Utah. "The Jewish calendar defines our life. Judaism defines our week. It defines my year. It defines how our children are raised. It defines my plans. And it seems to fit within my writing."

And what has been the impact of Utah upon Judaism? "Living here near the mountains, the canyons, and the national parks, you can see how closely related nature and Judaism really are," Osherow remarked.

"Utah has made me understand the incredible thrill of living in such a beautiful world. I think it very likely because I live in Utah that I started going to synagogue every week and getting so involved in the Jewish community. I want my kids to know who they are, and I want them to appreciate and live that life. A Jewish life. Here in Utah."

Axelrad Furniture Company, 1915. (Courtesy of Irene Tannenbaum)

APPENDIX A: THE MEMORIES ARE MANY, THE STORES NOW FEW

A Partial List of Jewish-Owned Businesses in Utah, Pre– and Post–World War II

**currently active*

Adrien 'N Emilie: ladies apparel, Adrien and Emilie Segal
Allied: surplus, Mark McGillis
American Barrel: Ed Eisen
American Fur: Abe Cohne
Arent's Furs and Apparel: Marv Arent; Lynne Cohne
Arthur Frank Men's Apparel, Arthur, Boris, Harry, and Simon Frank
Associated Specialties: building materials, Abe and Herman Bernstein
Auerbach Bros.: department store, Samuel and Fred Auerbach
Axelrad Furniture: A. Z., Sam, and Robert Axelrad
Bank Jewelry: Neisen and Barry Bank
Baron Store: Harris Baron
Block and Guss: meat packing, the Block and Guss families
Boston Store: ladies apparel, Jack and Harold Findling and Esther Findling
Brumby's: bistro, Paul and Karen Gladstone*
Bryce Millinery: the Newman family
Cactus and Tropicals: Lorraine Miller*
Capitol: pawn and loan, Leo Siegel

Cinegrill: restaurant, Robert Cohne
Classic Jewelry: Morris Berkowitz
Community Market: food, Jack Shapiro
ComputerLand: Ray Pederson
Copper Rivet: Amy Wolfe*
Cuban Cigar: vending machines, the Safran family
Cuisine Unlimited: catering and deli, Maxine and Marvin Turner*
Demeris and Rice: advertising, William D. Rice
Diamond Mattress: "Bunk" Fox*
Doctorman Packing: meat packing, the Doctorman family
Domus: gift shop, Florence Hallet and Michael Hallet
Dornbush's: restaurant and deli, Lou Dornbush
Dupler Furs: Joe and Abe Dupler
Eagle Company: men's apparel, Sam Shapiro; Harry Sher
Eastern Hatters: men's hats, Sig Porizky
Eastern Outfitters: men's apparel, Ed Berkowitz
EIMCO: machinery manufacturing, the Rosenblatt family
English Tailors: men's apparel, Henry, Dave, and Jack Pullman
Evdasin Bakery: the Evdasin family
Fair Store: Sam Matz
Feiler Optical: Jerry Feiler
Firmbilt: men's apparel, Morris and Milton Rosen
Floors, Inc.: specialty floors, Dan Kotler*
Gallenson: pawn and loan, Nathan and Leon Gallenson
Golden Rule: general store, Morris Ramo
Grand Central Markets: food markets, Maurice Warshaw
Granite Meat: meat packing, Abe and Morris Guss
Guss Insurance: Abe Guss
Honest Jon's Hills House Antique Gallery: Jon Sweet*
Hub: men's apparel, Eugene Levetan
Hudson Bay: furs, Fred Provol
I. Michael's: ladies apparel, the Michael family
Intermountain Furniture: Louis Henteleff and Sam Henteleff and Alan Cohen*
Jack Wolfe's Outdoor Apparel: Jack and Dan Wolfe
Jordan Meat: meat packing, Sam and Irvin Guss
Kaplan Kosher Butcher: the Kaplan family
Ladies Shop: Louis French
L and L Texaco: Larry Vigor*
Liberty Heights Fresh: specialty food retailer, Stephen Rosenberg

The Paris Company, 1913. (Courtesy of Utah State Historical Society)

Paris Beauty Salon, 1941. (Courtesy of Utah State Historical Society)

Liberty Store: Jenny Segal
Lord's: apparel and coats, Ben Roe; Seymour Friedman
Lorraine Press: printing, Harry Miller
Lovinger Company: janitorial supply, Jules Lovinger
Lowenstein Mercantile: the Lowenstein family
Makoff: ladies apparel, Sam and Richard Makoff and Sam Makoff Jr.
Marvin's Gardens: Marvin and Sarah Goldberg*
Mednick's Tailors: men's apparel, Irving Mednick and family
Midwest Railroad: rail services, Bob Wolff*
Mode Millinery: Mrs. Segal
Morgan Jewelry: Nate, Ted Morgan and Sons*
Mose Lewis: men's apparel, Mose Lewis
National Army and Navy Store: outdoor apparel, Jack, Ralph, and Ira Tannenbaum
Off Main Café: Jean Glaser
Paris Company: department store, Jules Dreyfus and father
Paris Millinery: Jerry Landa
Pepper's Allied Metals: scrap, Jerome, Fred, and Manny Pepper
Pullman Wholesale Tailors: men's apparel, Henry and Dave Pullman
Quality Flowers: the Goldberg family*
Raymond's: ladies apparel, the Raymond family; the Goldberg family
Roe's Department Store: Harry and Ben Roe
Sapitsky Loan: pawn and loan, Sam Sapitsky
Schubach Jewelry: William Schubach
Shapiro Advertising: Jack Shapiro
Shapiro Luggage and Gifts: the Shapiro family*
Sher's Men's Shop: Mike Sher
Siegel Finance: Max and Danny Siegel
Siegel's: pawn and loan, Dal, Gordon, and Max Siegel
Skyline Floral: Gertrude Goldberg family*
Slater and Son: apparel, Sam Slater
Sol's: general merchandise, Sol Pomerance
Standard Optical: Henry, Bob, and Dick Schubach*
Steel Encounters: building materials, Fred Tannenbaum*
Sunset Sports: sporting goods, Richard McGillis
Sussman Bakery: Sussman family
Sweet Candy Company: Leon, Jack, and Tony Sweet*
Teitlebaum Flowers: Sam Teitlebaum
Union Clothing: Simon Frank
Used Furniture Store: Morris Aronovich

Utah Barrel: Ben and Morris Pepper; Sandy Pepper*
Utah Beverage Co.: Ben and Wilford Arnovitz
Utah By-Products: animal products, the Soble family
Wagner Bag, Wagner Investment: containers, I. J., Abe, Leona Wagner, and Rose Wagner
Warshaw's: food notions, Keith Warshaw
Weinstock Insurance: Jack Weinstock
Western Furniture: Herman and Myron Finkelstein
Willie's Tavern: Morris and Willie Goldberg
Wolfe's Sporting Goods: Hubert and Elliott Wolfe
Yard Stick: fabrics, Shekie Frankel
Zinik Sporting Goods: David and Verner Zinik

Ready for Shabbat blessings: candles, kiddush cup and challah. (Courtesy of Donna Barnow Balandrin)

APPENDIX B: TRADITIONAL JEWISH FOODS

Donna Barnow Balandrin

Shabbat—Beginning at sundown Friday night, Shabbat (Sabbath) lasts through sundown Saturday night. Literally like having a holiday every week, its observance is specifically mentioned in the Ten Commandments: "Remember the Sabbath day to keep it holy." Jewish homes prepare by setting a beautiful dinner table, making wonderful food, lighting Shabbat candles, and saying prayers. Blessings are said over the wine and the challah (traditional braided egg bread). Shabbat is the time to relax, attend synagogue, and spend time with friends and family.

CHALLAH

Doris Krensky

2 heaping Tbsp. yeast
1-3/4 cups warm water
1 scant Tbsp. salt
1/2 cup sugar
1/2 cup oil
7+ cups high-gluten bread flour (divided)

4 large eggs, beaten
sesame seed or poppy seed

Preheat oven to 350°. Dissolve the yeast in the water. Add salt and sugar. When it bubbles add oil and 3 cups of the flour. Mix well. Then add the eggs and beat thoroughly. Now add the rest of the flour and mix it until no longer sticky. Turn out onto a floured board, knead, cover, and let rise until doubled. Punch the dough down and turn it out again onto a floured breadboard. Divide it in thirds. Cut each third into 4 equal pieces. Roll 3 pieces into strips about 12 inches long. Braid these strips, pinching ends together, and place on a buttered cookie sheet. Divide remaining 1/4 piece of dough into 3 equal pieces and braid, or just twist the strip. Lay the braid or strip over the first braid. Now brush the loaf with water. Cover and let rise until doubled. Brush with egg and oil. Sprinkle heavily with sesame seed or poppy seed. Bake at 350° until well browned and hollow sounding (approximately 1/2 hour). Makes 3 loaves.

NOTE: *This recipe works much better if you use an excellent quality high-gluten bread flour.*

§

AUNT EILEEN'S MATZO BALL SOUP

Kitty Kaplan

2 large yellow onions, skins on, quartered
3 leeks, white parts only, cut into large pieces
3 stalks celery with tops, cut into large pieces
10 peppercorns
3–4 sprigs fresh dill
3–4 pounds chicken, skin removed
1 box matzo ball and soup mix

Place first 6 ingredients in a large stock pot, cover with water. Bring to a boil, reduce heat, simmer for 3 hours. When cool, strain the vegetables and chicken from the broth. Prepare the matzo balls and soup according to directions. Add the strained broth and serve.

§

STUFFED CABBAGE

Lotte Hertz

1 pound ground chuck
1/4 cup uncooked rice

1 egg
1 onion, grated
1 carrot, grated
1/4 tsp. salt
12–15 cabbage leaves
1/4 cup lemon juice or 1/8 tsp. citric salt or 1/4 cup vinegar
1/2 cup brown sugar
raisins (optional)
water to cover

Combine meat, rice, and egg. Add onion, carrot, and salt. Blanch cabbage leaves by covering with boiling water and letting them soak about 10 minutes or until pliable. Drain leaves. Place a ball of meat mixture in center of each leaf and roll up, tucking in ends securely. Place close together in heavy pan and add other ingredients and enough water to cover. Cover tightly and cook for 30 minutes. Reduce heat and simmer 20 minutes more. If desired, place in 350° oven uncovered for 20 minutes to brown on top. Turn rolls to brown on both sides.

LUKSHEN KUGEL (NOODLE PUDDING) (DAIRY)

Etta Rosenberg Balkin

12 ounces medium or wide egg noodles, cooked and drained
6 eggs
grated peel and juice of 1/2 lemon
1/2 cup sugar
1 tsp. salt
1-1/2 cups cream-style cottage cheese
1/2 cup dairy sour cream
1 tsp. vanilla extract
1/2 tsp. cinnamon
1 small can crushed pineapple, drained, or 2 unpeeled apples, cut into small pieces
1/2 to 1 cup raisins
1/2 stick butter or margarine, melted
3/4 cup chopped walnuts (optional)

Preheat oven to 350°. Prepare noodles according to instructions on package, then set aside to drain. In a large mixing bowl, combine eggs and lemon peel and juice and beat until foamy. Gradually beat in sugar and salt. Beat in cottage cheese, sour cream, vanilla, and cinnamon. Fold in noodles, crushed pineapple, raisins, and optional ingredients, if desired. Place melted butter or margarine in a 9″ × 13″ baking dish or pan. Coat pan and pour the remainder into the noodle mixture. Mix well, then turn noodle mixture into greased baking dish. Bake at 350° for 45–50 minutes, or until knife inserted just off center comes out clean, and top is just golden brown. Cut into squares. Serves 12. This dish may be used as a side dish, or by itself as a luncheon dish. Good hot or cold.

Rosh Hashanah—Rosh Hashanah, or the Jewish New Year, lasts for two days, and marks the beginning of a period of ten days of reflection and soul-searching that culminates in Yom Kippur, or the Day of Atonement. The shofar (ram's horn) is blown, awakening the conscience, and it is said that on Rosh Hashanah you will be inscribed in the Book of Life, and on Yom Kippur the book will be sealed. It is a time for forgiveness and new beginnings.

Many sweet dishes are traditional on the Rosh Hashanah table; for example, sliced apples are dipped in honey to symbolize the sweetness of the New Year. Honey cake is also a common treat, and the challah, or traditional bread, is likely to be round instead of braided, to represent a full and well-rounded year to come.

GEFILTE FISH

Rose Nord

3 pounds fish (filet of sole, red snapper, halibut, or black cod)
1 medium onion, finely chopped
3 eggs
1/4 cup matzo meal
1 Tbsp. sugar (optional)
1 Tbsp. salt
white pepper to taste

STOCK
6 cups water
2 carrots
3 stalks celery
1 sliced onion
peppercorns

Apple and honey sweeten the New Year. (Courtesy of Donna Barnow Balandrin)

Grind fish with chopped onion. Using an electric mixer, at low speed, add eggs, one at a time, with matzo meal. Add sugar (if desired), salt, and pepper. Mix well and set aside. Using a large, heavy pot, bring water to a boil. Add carrots, celery, onion, and peppercorns, and return to boil. Wet hands and form 14 balls. Add balls to water, and return to boil. Reduce heat and simmer slowly about 2-1/2 hours. Remove carrots. Cool and slice for garnish with balls. Makes 14 fish balls.

YOM TOV POT ROAST

Eileen Hallet Stone

4 pound brisket or pot roast
small amount of olive oil
1 tsp. salt
1/4 tsp. pepper
1/4 tsp. garlic powder, or 2 cloves fresh crushed garlic
1 cup sweet Concord-grape wine

1 medium carrot, chopped
1 large onion, chopped
2 cups water
1 cup dried prunes, chopped
1 cup dried apricots, chopped
1 large apple, peeled and chopped
1 tsp. cinnamon; a little less cinnamon if using cinnamon sticks
1 tsp. ginger, powdered or freshly chopped

In a large, heavy pot, brown meat in a small amount of olive oil. Add salt, pepper, garlic powder, wine, carrot, onion, and water. Bring to a boil. Reduce heat, cover, and simmer on low for 2 hours. (Add a little more water, if needed.) Add chopped fruits, cinnamon, and ginger and continue cooking for another 1/2 hour or until tender. Remove meat and fruit to a warmed platter. Skim fat from pot and use remaining sauce as gravy.

HONEY CAKE

Donna Balandrin (Grandma Etta's recipe)

3-1/2 cups flour
1 cup sugar
1 tsp. baking powder
1 tsp. baking soda
1 tsp. cinnamon
1/2 tsp. nutmeg
1/4 tsp. cardamom
1/2 tsp. salt
1/2 cup canola oil (or vegetable oil)
3 eggs
1-1/2 cups honey
1 cup strong black coffee, cooled
1 Tbsp. lemon juice
grated rind of a lemon
OPTIONAL: nuts or raisins or both

Preheat oven to 325°. Mix dry ingredients together in a large mixing bowl. Make a well in the center, then add the wet ingredients. Mix well. Add raisins or nuts or both, if desired. Line the bottom of an 11″ × 13″ pan with wax paper and grease the sides. Pour in batter and bake at 325° for 50 minutes, or until done. (At higher altitudes, it may work better to use a tube pan, and bake 50–60 minutes.)

Yom Kippur (Breaking the Fast)—Yom Kippur is the holiest day of the year, when Jews all over the world repent for any sins they may have committed during the past year. Yom Kippur is a day of fasting and penitence, so obviously it has no special foods for the day! One must *break* a fast with food, however, and it is customary to have a light supper at the close of this holy day, perhaps including egg salad, smoked fish, lox and herring, and cheeses.

CHOPPED HERRING (DAIRY)

Bea Albert (Linda Bergman's mother)

1 (6 ounce) jar herring snacks in wine sauce
1 slice day-old challah, crust trimmed
1/2 small apple, peeled, cored, and sliced
1 medium egg, hard-boiled
3 Tbsp. sour cream
3 drops lemon juice

Drain liquid from herring and set aside. Trim off soft bones and black skin from herring. Soak bread in cold water for 3 minutes. Put herring, onions from herring jar, bread (squeezed dry), apple, and egg into chopping bowl and chop until fine textured. Stir in sour cream and 1 Tbsp. of the liquid from the herring. Add more sour cream and lemon juice to taste. This recipe is best made a day ahead to allow the flavors to blend. Yields 1-1/2 cups. (Eileen Hallet Stone combines herring, sour cream, chopped sweet pickles, chopped apples, sliced red onion, and red wine for a sweet variation.)

Sukkoth—Sukkoth, the Festival of the Tabernacles, is a harvest holiday when people build a "Sukkah," a booth or hut made from wood and branches through which you can see the sky. The family eats meals and often sleeps in the Sukkah (weather permitting), and they decorate it with fruits, paper chains, or other decorations to make it festive. In ancient times, the Jews would build these temporary dwellings during harvest time, because their fields were often far from the villages, and sleeping in these huts would save valuable time. Sukkahs are also a reminder to Jews of

Strudel: a Sukkoth harvest of fruits. (Courtesy of Donna Barnow Balandrin)

the nomadic days living in the desert, after the Exodus from Egypt. This holiday reminds Jewish people of God's generosity in providing both food and shelter.

STRUDEL

Pauline Reingold Mednick (mother of Frances Sapitsky)

DOUGH

1 cup vegetable shortening
2 eggs
1 cup sugar
4-1/2 cups flour
2 tsp. baking powder
1/2 tsp. baking soda
1/2 tsp. salt
rind and juice of 1 orange
rind and juice of 1 lemon
(1/3 cup juice total from orange and lemon)

FILLING

2 large pie apples
1 small jar apricot and pineapple jam
rind of orange and lemon
1 cup ground nuts
1/4 cup corn flake crumbs
1/2 cup sugar
1/2 tsp. cinnamon
1 cup white raisins, ground (optional)

Preheat oven to 350°. Beat shortening, eggs, and sugar. Add rind and dry ingredients, which have been sifted together, alternately with juice. Divide dough into four pieces. Roll each on floured board. Spread 1/4 of filling on each and roll as for jelly roll. Bake on foil-lined cookie sheet for 45 minutes at 350°. Cool and slice.

MANDELBROT

Belle Katz

2/3 cup vegetable oil
1 cup minus 2 Tbsp. sugar
2 Tbsp. sifted powdered sugar
3 eggs
1 cup walnuts, cut into pieces
1 tsp. vanilla
2-1/2 cups flour, sifted
2 tsp. baking powder
cinnamon-sugar mixture

Preheat oven to 350°. Mix oil, sugars, and eggs (1 at a time). Add walnuts. Add vanilla, sifted flour, and baking powder. Mix thoroughly. Make 4–5 rolls on a greased cookie sheet. If dough is too sticky, dip hands in cold water and shape the dough. Bake 30 minutes at 350°. Slice and return to oven to toast on both sides. After toasting, dip in cinnamon-sugar mixture on both sides while still warm. Makes about 6 dozen.

Chanukah menorahs big and small, with "Happy Chanukah" dreidl-music box. (Courtesy of Donna Barnow Balandrin)

Hanukkah (also Chanukah)—Hanukkah is a holiday that symbolizes the fight for religious freedom. Hanukkah (which means dedication), or the Festival of Lights, celebrates the rededication of the Temple in 165 B.C. after the Jews recaptured it from the Syrian King Antiochus, under leadership of Judah Maccabee. There was only enough holy oil to light the Eternal Light for one day, though it would take eight days to prepare more oil. The miracle of Hanukkah is that the one day of oil burned for eight days, until more holy oil could be prepared. That is why Jews celebrate by lighting a menorah (a candelabra with eight branches and one extra—the *Shamus*—which is used to light the others) by exchanging gifts, playing dreidl (a game using a special top), and, of course, eating. It is not surprising that traditional Hanukkah foods use a lot of oil—that *was* the miracle, after all! Among the favorites are potato latkes and jelly doughnuts covered in sugar.

ROSIE'S LATKES

Rose Altschule

6 potatoes
2 eggs
2 Tbsp. flour
1 tsp. salt
1 small grated onion
1/2 tsp. baking powder
pinch of baking soda
salt and pepper to taste

Grate potatoes, cover with water so they don't turn brown, then drain. Add rest of ingredients and mix well. Drop mixture by tablespoon into at least 1/4-inch-deep hot fat. Fry until well browned on one side and then turn over. Turn over only once so pancakes don't get soggy. Drain on paper. To freeze, layer in pan, separated by foil. Reheat frozen on cookie sheet at 425° for 10 minutes. Serves 6–8.

NOTE: *The author's father, Hal Hallet, was born Harry Hallet without a middle name, so he gave himself one: H. This makes sense, since many Jewish men in those days had no middle name. His family always called him "Eddie." Don't ask! When Hal made latkes, he'd slice several large pieces of onion and drop them into the fry pan as the oil was heating. This imparts a delicious aroma and taste. Hal liked his latkes thin and flat; the kids used to call them birds' nests. They ate them smothered in applesauce or with a dab of sour cream. Most important, Hal never froze his latkes! You ate them, hot, "right on the spot."*

Purim—On Purim, the story of Queen Esther, a Persian Jew who saved her people from destruction, is read from a parchment scroll called the Megillah. As the story is read aloud, every time the name of the villain, Haman, is spoken, everyone drowns out his name with booing, noisemakers, and stamping feet. People dress up in costume as characters from the Purim story, and everyone celebrates yet another miracle of the Jewish people being liberated from oppression.

HAMANTASCHEN

Edna Schettler

1 cup sugar
1-1/3 cup butter or margarine

2 eggs, beaten
1/3 cup water
1 tsp. vanilla
4 cups flour
1 tsp. baking powder
1/2 tsp. salt

FILLING

1/2 cup apricot-pineapple preserves
1/4 cup honey
1-1/2 cups ground white raisins
1-1/2 cups ground nuts
1 Tbsp. cinnamon
2 large green apples, chopped into small pieces
1 Tbsp. lemon juice
1 Tbsp. orange juice

Cream sugar and butter or margarine until smooth. Add beaten eggs, water, and vanilla. Sift dry ingredients and add to mixture. Form into ball and refrigerate overnight in plastic bag. Next day, roll out 1/4 of dough at a time onto floured board. Cut circles approximately 2 inches in diameter with a glass. Spoon some filling in center of circle and pinch sides together to form a triangle. Bake at 350° for 10–15 minutes until light brown.

OTHER HAMANTASCHEN FILLINGS

Cheese
12 ounces cottage cheese, sieved
2 eggs, well beaten
1 Tbsp. matzo meal
1/2 tsp. cinnamon
1/3 cup sugar

Mix together thoroughly. It is best to drain cottage cheese before sieving.

Poppy Seed
1/2 pound poppy seeds
3/4 cup honey
1/2 cup sugar
juice and rind of 1 orange

juice and rind of 1 lemon
1 egg

Scald poppy seeds, drain well. Put through food chopper. Add remaining ingredients. Place in saucepan. Bring to a boil. Boil 2–3 minutes. Cool before using.

Prune
1 pound prunes
1 cup raisins
1/2 cup finely chopped nuts
grated rind of 1/2 orange
1/4 cup sugar (or to taste)

Cook prunes until soft. Pit and chop fine. Pour boiling water over raisins and chop. Add to prunes. Add nuts, orange rind, and sugar. Mix thoroughly.

Apple
1/2 cup raisins
3–4 tart apples, peeled, cored, and grated
1/2 cup crushed walnuts
sugar and cinnamon to taste

Pour boiling water over raisins. Let stand until soft. Drain and chop. Add apples and walnuts to raisins. Add sugar and cinnamon to taste.

Passover (Pesach)—One of the oldest festivals in the world, Passover has been continuously celebrated by Jewish families for more than three thousand years. This holiday is a wonderful time for gathering the whole family around the dining table to tell the story of the Jews' Exodus from Egypt, and the journey to the Promised Land. The Passover seder combines the telling of the tale with prayer, a wonderful feast, wine, and songs.

A beautiful decorative seder plate is placed prominently on the table, which also displays six smaller dishes containing symbolic foods: a shank bone and a burnt egg, which symbolize the Passover lamb sacrifice and burnt offerings brought to the Temple in ancient times; charoset, a chopped apple-nut mixture representing the mortar and hard labor; horseradish (maror) for the bitter life under Egyptian rule; saltwater for the tears shed by the Israelites; and greens (parsley or sometimes sliced cucumbers) representing springtime and renewal.

A plate of matzo, or unleavened bread, is also on the table. Matzo is unleavened, because in

Passover seder plate on display with kiddush cup and Passover wine. (Courtesy of Donna Barnow Balandrin)

their haste to leave Egypt, the Jews did not have enough time to let the bread rise. It is customary during the Passover holiday not to use any foods that have leavening (yeast, baking powder, or baking soda). Therefore, many Passover cake recipes will use a lot of eggs to make them light and fluffy. Only matzo meal (ground matzo) and potato starch are used in cooking instead of flour. In very traditional Jewish households, every speck of food that contains wheat flour or leavening must be removed from the home (and any unopened food may be donated to the poor).

MOCK CHOPPED LIVER (MUSHROOM AND WALNUT PATÉ)

Lois Spiegel (adapted from Laya Kesner's recipe)

Chopped liver is usually made with chicken or beef liver. Here's a recipe that tastes almost like the real thing, but won't offend the vegetarians among us!

1 cup sliced mushrooms
1 cup chopped onion
3 Tbsp. olive oil
1 cup shelled walnuts
5 hard-boiled eggs
1 tsp. salt
1/4 tsp. white pepper
OPTIONAL: add fresh or powdered garlic to taste

Sauté mushrooms and onion in oil until soft. Process walnuts first (grind fine), then add everything else to food processor. Serve with crackers or celery and zucchini sticks.

HOMEMADE HORSERADISH

Mylene Adler

Horseradish, or the bitter herb, reminds Jews of how the Egyptians embittered the lives of our ancestors in Egypt. A really good horseradish should bring tears to your eyes!

1 large horseradish root, trimmed and peeled
2 medium beets, peeled
1/2 to 1 cup vinegar
4–5 tsp. salt
1/2 to 3/4 cup sugar

Shred horseradish on food processor grater. Then shred beets (directly on top of horseradish). Process horseradish and beets, adding vinegar, salt, and sugar midway, to make a pasty sauce. Let it stand (it helps diffuse some of the "heat"). Chill before serving. Flavor will mellow as horseradish matures. Makes about 2 cups.

CHAROSET

This dish symbolizes the mortar that the Jews in Egypt were forced to make for building the pharaoh's great stone monuments, and represents their hard labor. The following is the more European (Ashkenazi) recipe, whereas the Mediterranean (Sephardic) recipe sometimes adds chopped figs, dates, almonds, a dash of lemon juice, and ginger.

6 large apples, peeled and finely chopped
1 cup chopped walnuts
1–2 tsp. cinnamon
sugar or honey to taste
1/2 cup sweet Passover wine (Manischewitz or Mogen David)

Mix all ingredients together well. Mixture should not be too watery. The amounts of each ingredient may be variable, depending on your own taste. If you like cinnamon, add more. The same goes for the sugar, walnuts, and wine. If mixture is too sweet, add a tablespoon or two of lemon juice. People usually love this dish, so make a lot. It is very tasty served on a piece of matzo.

APPLE PASSOVER KUGEL

Eileen Hallet Stone

8 eggs
1/2 pound melted butter or margarine
2/3 cup sugar
1 tsp. cinnamon
2/3 cup orange juice
1 cup matzo meal
8 apples, peeled and diced (medium size)
1/2 to 3/4 cup pineapple tidbits

Preheat oven to 350°. Using a big bowl, beat eggs, then add butter, sugar, cinnamon, and orange juice. Mix in matzo meal, apples, and pineapple. Pour into buttered 7″ × 11″ baking dish and bake at 350° for 1 hour (maybe a little more, depending on your oven). Half of this recipe will fill an 8″ square pan.

SAVORY CARROTS

Margaret Siegel

1 pound carrots, cut into thin diagonal slices
1/2 cup orange juice
2 Tbsp. olive oil
1/4 tsp. salt

1/4 tsp. sugar
dash of ginger
seeded grapes
chopped parsley

In saucepan, combine orange juice, oil, salt, sugar, and ginger; stir to dissolve. Add carrots and cover. Heat to boiling, then reduce to medium. Cook until soft (about 25–30 minutes) or tender-crisp. Add grapes. Cook 5 minutes more. Sprinkle with parsley and serve.

SPONGE CAKE

Sonya Cohne

1-1/2 cups of sugar, divided
9 eggs
juice of 1 lemon
1/2 tsp. cream of tartar
3/4 cup potato starch
1 Tbsp. matzo cake meal

Preheat oven to 350°. Separate eggs. Cream 1 cup of sugar with 7 yolks, then add 2 whole eggs. Add lemon juice. In separate bowl, beat egg whites with cream of tartar. Add rest of sugar (1/2 cup), and continue to beat until stiff. Fold half of egg whites into yolk mixture. Sprinkle starch and cake meal and fold in a little bit at a time, very slowly. Then fold in rest of egg whites. Bake in tube pan for 50 minutes at 350° F.

Shavuot—The word *Shavuot* means weeks, and the holiday comes exactly seven weeks after Passover. Shavuot celebrates the ripening of the first fruits and wheat harvest. But even more important, it celebrates the Israelites receiving the Ten Commandments at Mount Sinai. Homes are often decorated with fruits, flowers, and greenery. And it is customary to eat foods made with grain (flour) and dairy or cheese, such as blintzes or cheesecake.

BLINTZES

Belle Katz

3 eggs
1 egg white
1 Tbsp. oil
1 cup milk
1/2 tsp. salt
scant cup flour

FILLING

1-1/4 pound dry cottage cheese
4 ounces cream cheese
egg yolk
pinch of salt
1 Tbsp. sugar (optional)

Beat 3 eggs and 1 egg white, oil, milk, and salt together. Mix well and set aside. Make filling and let stand a little while. Grease a 7- or 8-inch skillet. Place over medium heat. Pour 1/4 cup of first mixture into pan and tilt so that the bottom is covered. Fry slowly until browned. (Teflon pan works best in frying blintzes.) Place fried side up onto towel. Fill with cheese filling or any other filling desired. Fold sides in and roll up. Fry again, turning once to brown. These blintzes freeze very well. Take out of freezer and fry slowly until browned on both sides. May be served with sour cream or jam on top. Serves 8.

APPENDIX C: YIDDISH GLOSSARY, HEBREW TERMS, AND SOME EXPRESSIONS

Glossary

Abi gezunt! As long as you're healthy!

Aiver butel (sounds like *ibber butel*): Mixed-up or absentminded

Aliya: Recitation of the Torah blessings. When a reader is given an honor to "ascend" to the *bimah* to give a reading, it is also called an *aliya.*

Balebatim: Leaders in the community and synagogue.

Balebosteh: A good wife or homemaker; or perhaps even a bossy woman.

Bal Korah (or *Baal Koray*): The Torah reader.

Bar Mitzvah: Hebrew for the "son of the commandments," a *bar mitzvah* recognizes a Jewish boy who has reached the age of thirteen and is fully responsible for performing the commandments *(mitzvot)* as an adult. Traditionally, the event is solemnized by calling the *bar mitzvah* to read the weekly portion of the Torah in the synagogue.

Bimah: A raised platform in a synagogue, usually in the center of the room, on which a desk stands for the reading from the Torah and from the Prophets. Often, the *bimah* is placed in the center forefront of the room and represents the altar that once stood in the middle compartment of the Temple.

Blintzes: Crepes filled with cream or cottage cheese, served with jelly or sour cream (or both).

B'nai B'rith: Hebrew for the "sons of the covenant," the Independent Order of B'nai Brith was founded in 1843 by German Jews to unite Jews who, though differing widely in their religious views, would come together for social, cultural, and philanthropic purposes.

Borsht: Beet soup, best served cold with a hot, boiled potato and a dollop of sour cream. The "Borsht Belt" refers to the resorts in the Catskill Mountains that cater to and were patronized only by Jews.

Bubbe (or *Bubeleh*): Grandma. Bubeleh is also a term of endearment, used for "darling," or "sweetheart."

Bubbe-meisses: Old wives' tales, grandmothers' tales.

Chabad Lubavitch: Brotherly love. *Chabad* is made from the words *wisdom (Chuchmah); understanding (Binah);* and *knowledge (da'at).*

Challah: A traditional loaf of twisted or braided bread. Originally, challah meant the "tithe" taken from the dough before baking and given to the priest. Today, the tithe is represented by a pinch of dough that is burnt in the oven while the bread is cooking. For the Sabbath, two loaves of bread are prepared representing the "double portion of manna" God gave Jews on Fridays and festivals during the time they were wandering in the desert.

Chuppa (or *Huppah*): The wedding canopy, under which the bride and groom take their vows.

Chutzpah: Gall, or nerve.

Daven: To pray. A traditional Jew davens three times a day, with other prayers on the Sabbath and during festivals.

Draikop: Scatterbrain.

Farblondjet: Confused, mixed-up, lost.

Farbrent: Overly zealous.

Flayshedig (or *Flayshig*): Meats, poultry, or foods that are prepared with animal fats; these foods should not be eaten with dairy foods.

Frum: Observant; Orthodox.

Gentile: Any person who is not a Jew.

Get: Divorce.

Ghetto: A walled portion of a city in which all Jews were compelled to live. The first ghetto was in Venice in 1516. Today, the term refers to any urban area with a particular ethnic concentration.

Gonif: Crook, thief, swindler; also, a clever person.

Goy: Gentiles; (plural, *Goyim*): Anyone who is not a Jew.

Goyisheh: Something that is not Jewish related.

Hadassah: Founded in 1912 by Henrietta Szold, the Women's Zionist Organization of America, *Hadassah,* provides medical and educational services to Israel.

Haftarah: A portion from the Prophets, read or chanted after the Torah reading in synagogue on the Sabbath holy days and festivals. Each portion of the Torah has a specific Haftarah.

Haggadah: A narrative that is read aloud at the Passover (Pesach) meal (seder). Drawing material from the Book of Exodus and the Talmud, and containing psalms, prayers, hymns, folk songs, riddles, and jingles, the Haggadah tells the story of Israel's bondage in Egypt and the flight to freedom.

Halahah: The substance of traditional Jewish law based on the rabbinic interpretation *(midrash)* of the Bible. Also a specific ruling within the law.

Havdalah: A separation of the holy from the mundane. It refers to the way we separate Shabbat from the rest of the week. During the Havdalah ceremony, a blessing is recited over wine, candles, and spices. The wine cup is filled to the brim as a symbol of hope and sits on a saucer, the candle is made up of a braided candle with two wicks, and a spice box is filled with aromatic herbs and spices.

Hazzan: A cantor leads prayers, on Shabbat and festivals, and may read from the sefer Torah [the scroll that contains the Five Books of Moses). Draped in a prayer shawl, the cantor, considered a master prayer, recites the liturgy as the *shaliach tzibbur,* "the advocate of the congregation."

Heder: Traditionally, a one-room European Jewish schoolhouse.

High Holy Days: English term for the Days of Awe, Rosh Hashanah (the New Year), and Yom Kippur (the Day of Atonement).

Kaddish: A ritual prayer said for the dead. It is also a prayer that glorifies God's name and is recited at the close of prayers. It is one of the most ancient of all Jewish prayers.

Kasher: To make kosher.

Kashrut: Kosher. In Hebrew-Yiddish, it means "foods fit to eat." In Yiddish, it can mean being pious, sympathetic, sweet, and dear. In America, it takes on more meanings, such as the real thing (or, can I trust him?), legitimate, and ethical.

Kayn aynhoreh (or *Kineahora*): A phrase said to ward off "the evil eye."

Ketubah: A legal document that attests to a marriage, and details the legal obligations of the husband to the wife if he should die or divorce her. It is signed and witnessed before the wedding ceremony takes place.

Kibitz: To converse, chatter, gossip, offer unsolicited advice.

Kiddush: Sanctification. The prayer and ceremony sanctifying the Sabbath and Jewish festivals and holy days.

Kipa. See Yarmulke.

Kopdraynenish: Confusing, makes one's head spin. Also a compliment, flattery. "Stop *draying* me a *kop*" could also mean stop driving me crazy.

Kosher: Food that conforms to or is prepared in accordance with Jewish dietary laws. Among many definitions of the word, *kosher* may also mean pious and devout. In American slang, *kosher* stands for genuine, right, proper, or perfect.

Landsman: A Jewish person who comes from the same town, area, or region as another Jew; a Jewish compatriot.

Macher: A *gontser macher,* a big shot in the community; a doer; someone with connections.

Mavin: A knowledgeable person, an expert.

Mazel tov! Good luck! Congratulations!

Mechaieh: Great joy and pleasure.

Mechitzah: A divider that separates men and women so they will not see each other during services. The women's gallery (section) is called *Ezart Nashim.*

Mechutanim: Family-by-marriage.

Megillah: Scroll or Book of Esther, but in slang it means the whole thing, the works (as in, the whole Megillah).

Melamed: A teacher, usually of Hebrew.

Mensh: A human being; a good, decent, honorable person.

Mezuzah: A small oblong case containing a parchment on which the Shema is inscribed. Traditionally, the mezuzah (doorpost) consecrates the home. A mezuzah is affixed, in a slanting position, beside the door of one's home and rooms in which one lives. The printed verse is from Deut. 6:4–9, 11:13–21. The first sentence is of Israel's watchword: "Hear, O Israel, the Lord our God is one." The mezuzah serves as a reminder of God's law and as a symbol of a Jew's loyalty to the Jewish people.

Midrash: A collection of rabbinical commentaries and explanatory notes on the Bible. The term *midrash* means to examine carefully. It is the name given to the classical rabbinic interpretation of the Bible. Rabbis believe the Bible contained the revelation of God to man. They also believe the Bible is full of information, and can serve as a legal and spiritual guide for all generations. In searching the Bible for understandings and truths, rabbis are guided by established rules of interpretation, called hermeneutics (the science of interpretation). When analysis is applied to the legal portions of the Bible, it is called the *midrash halakhah.* When narrative and historical material emerge, it is called *midrash aggadah.*

Mikvah: A ritual bath.

Milchedig (or *Milchik*): Dairy foods.

Mincha: The daily late-afternoon religious service. Observant Jews pray three times a day; *Sachris* (morning), *Mincha* (afternoon), and *Mairev* (evening).

Minyan: A quorom for public prayer, traditionally consisting of ten men of bar mitzvah age or older. In egalitarian communities, women are included as well.

Mishpoche: Family, including the entire clan.

Mitten derinnen: All at once, suddenly; in the middle of something.

Mitzvah: A commandment of the Torah; a kind act, an ethical deed.

Mitzvot: The Commandments.

Mohel: A person who circumcises a male infant eight days after birth in a ceremony called *Brith Milah.* Traditionally, at the ceremony, the boy is named. The *mohel* is not a rabbi, but one who is an expert in performing circumcisions.

Naches: Joy, or pride, especially from children.

Nidah: The complete period of menstrual flow.

Nosh: Snack. A *nosher* is a snacker or nibbler; person with a sweet tooth.

Parve (or *Pareveh*): Food that contains neither animal nor dairy products.

Pentateuch: The Five Books of Moses, known in Judaism as the Torah.

Pesach: Passover.

Rabbi: An ordained scholar and teacher of Jewish law and rituals. A teacher of the Torah, a rabbi may perform ceremonies, interpret the tenets of Judaism, preach sermons, supervise religious instruction, make hospital visits, and represent the community. Among other duties, a rabbi may also become a lecturer, therapist, social worker, and counselor.

Rebbetzin: The wife of a rabbi.

Reconstructionism: Developed in the United States during the early twentieth century by Rabbi Mordecai M. Kaplan, Reconstructionists promote living in both worlds: the Jewish environment and the mainstream environment.

Schmaltz: Often rendered chicken fat. *Schmaltzy:* Corny, overly sentimental.

Seder: Order of procedure, which involves the reading of the Haggadah; the seder is also the ceremonial dinner observed on the first and second nights of Passover.

Shabbes (Hebrew, *Shabbat*): The Sabbath. To rest. *Shabbes* begins just before sunset on Friday and ends sundown on Saturday.

Shabbes goy: A Gentile that does work for a Jew on the Sabbath.

Shaygets: A Gentile boy or young man; sometimes, an uneducated boy.

Shehitah: Kosher slaughtering.

Shivah: Mourning period of seven days, beginning at the time of the burial, observed by family and friends of the deceased.

Shochet: A Jewish person authorized and supervised by rabbis to slaughter animals. A *shochet* must be knowledgeable of all the requirements that govern kosher food.

YIDDISH HUMOR

by Donna Balandrin

Yiddish humor plays counterpoint to a cynicism borne of countless generations of suffering. Like Klezmer music, Yiddish expresses joyful wit upon an undercurrent of mournful sadness. After all, when you are done with crying, what else is there to do but laugh?

Yiddish expressions are also creative. Look at Jewish curses, for example, compared with the crass, simplistic curses of modern American culture.

Er zol vaksen vi a tsibeleh, mit dem kop in drerd!" or "May you grow like an onion, with your head in the ground!" In other words, not only will you live in the dirt, but you will never have enlightenment. I can think of no worse fate.

Yiddish is also important to guard against the "evil eye." Never say anything good about your life or your family without saying, "Kain ein hora!" or "May no evil come to pass!" And when someone sneezes—a simple "Bless you" is certainly not enough. It is much better to say, "Tzu gezunt, tsum leben, tsum vaksen und kvellen," or "To your health, to life, to growth and be proud and joyful." If you're in a rush . . . just say "Gezunt."

Shofar: A ram's horn that is blown in the synagogue during Rosh Hashanah and Yom Kippur.

Shtetl: A Jewish village.

Shul: A synagogue.

Tallit (or *Tallis;* plural, *Talaysim*): A prayer shawl worn during prayers at religious services. The *tallit* has fringes *(tzitziyot)* on the four corners, as decreed by the Torah.

Tefillin: Phylacteries are two black leather boxes that contain passages from the Torah on parchment. Fastened to the arm and head with long, thin leather straps, they symbolize one's duties to live, act, and think according to God's teachings.

Trayf: Not kosher.

Tsatskeh (or *Tsastke*): A little decoration; something cute. (If you have too many *tsatskehs,* your home will look *ongepatshkeyd.*)

Tsoriss (or *Tsuris*): Troubles and woes.

Tummel: Tumult.

Tzedakah: Righteous, upright, and compassionate; charitable, helping one another, which is a part of one's duty.

Tzimmes: To make a "tzimmes" over someone is to give him much attention whether or not he deserves it. In food, there are many *tzimmes,* such as potato and prune, carrot, or peach and apricot. (A simple recipe includes combining 3–4 lbs. of brisket; a handful of prunes, pears, and apricots; 3 large sliced carrots; 3 yams; 1 lemon, sliced thinly; the juice of 1 orange; 1 Tbsp. brown sugar; 1 Tbsp. flour; and 5 cups boiling water in an oven-proof pot. Cook 1 hour in oven at 400°, reduce heat to 325° and cook 4 hours, uncovering the *tzimmes* during the last 30 minutes.)

Tzitzit: Fringes at the corners of the tallit.

Yad: "Hand," the Torah pointer, often made out of silver.

Yarmulke: Skullcap worn by observing Jewish people. Also called a *kipa.*

Yeshiva bucher: A student at the *yeshiva* (or *yeshiveh*).

Yeshiveh: Jewish traditional school of higher study; a talmudic academy.

Yiddish: A Jewish language, *Yiddish* was developed in the beginning of the Middle Ages by Jews who were pushed eastward from Germany. They wove Hebrew and Slavic terms into a German base of language. *Yiddish* was spoken by Ashkenazic Jews in Eastern European and in places of emigration. Unlike the men, Jewish women were not taught Hebrew, "the sacred language"; Jewish mothers spoke *Yiddish* (*Mama-loshen,* the mother's tongue) to their children who spoke it back to them and later to their own children.

Yizkor: Prayer in memory or honor of the dead.

Yontif: Any Jewish holiday (from Hebrew "yom tov").

NOTES

Introduction: A Brief History of Utah Jews in the West

1. Like the inception of most Jewish communities, Utah's Jewish pioneers' first task was to create a cemetery and meet the requirements of the dead. The land selected for B'nai Israel's cemetery was donated by Brigham Young in 1866. It was an arid wasteland on a gradual hill that overlooked the city and supported little but clumps of sagebrush and greasewood and an occasional sego lily, the state's flower. Since there was no water available, as late as the mid-1880s, water was carried in hand buckets. In 1887, women from the Ladies Hebrew Benevolent Society called upon Brigham Young at his summer quarters in southern Utah and secured from him a legal deed of the original grant. In 1889, with the help of people such as Charles Popper, water was finally piped to the grounds. See notes from Congregation B'nai Israel, Jewish Archives, Mar. 30, 1880, box 1, folder 9, Special Collections, Marriott Library, University of Utah.

2. Robert E. Levison, "American Jews in the West."

3. Jack Goodman with Michael Walton, "Jewish Community," in *Missing Stories: An Oral History of Ethnic and Minority Groups in Utah,* by Leslie G. Kelen and Eileen Hallet Stone, 131.

4. Leon Watters, *The Pioneer Jews of Utah,* 2.

5. Ibid., 6.

6. Carvalho, *Incidents of Travel,* 185–86, 150–51.

7. Eveline Brooks Auerbach, diary. For an edited manuscript, see Annegret S. Ogden, ed., *Frontier Reminiscences of Eveline Brooks Auerbach.*

8. William Mulder and Russell Mortensen, "Carpet Bag Crisis: Drummond and His Trollop," in *Among the Mormons: Historic Accounts by Contemporary Observers,* 292–95.

9. Edward W. Tullidge, *The History of Salt Lake City and Its Founders,* app. p. 9.

10. Whitney, *History of Utah,* 2:163–64.

11. Ibid., 164–65.

12. Ibid., 165–66.

13. Ibid., 167.

14. Watters, *Pioneer Jews of Utah,* 163–69.

15. Goldberg, *Back to the Soil: The Jewish Farmers of Clarion, Utah, and Their World,* xxv.

16. Bernard Solomon, "A Historical Overview of the Salt Lake Jewish Community Center," 16.

17. Eileen Hallet Stone, ed., Dal Siegel interview by Leslie Kelen, Salt Lake City, June 2, 1982, Jewish Archives, Special Collections, Marriott Library, University of Utah.

18. Congregation B'nai Israel board minutes, Jewish Archives, 1881, box 1, folder 1, Special Collections, Marriott Library, University of Utah; ibid., folder 9.

19. "Congregation Kol Ami," brochure, 1976.

20. Zucker, "James L. White Jewish Community Center," brochure.

21. Rabbi Frederick Wenger, interview by author, Salt Lake City, Feb. 1, 2001.

22. Rabbi Benny Zippel, interview by author, Salt Lake City, Apr. 30, 1999.

23. Elizabeth Paige, interview by author, Salt Lake City, May 5, 1999.

Chapter One: A Wandering Jew on the Thirty-eighth Parallel

1. Carvalho, *Incidents of Travel,* 234.

2. Bertram W. Korn, ed., *Incidents of Travel and Adventure in the Far West,* by Solomon Nunes Carvalho, 21.

3. Elizabeth Kessin Berman, "Solomon Nunes Carvalho: Painter and Prophet," 5–6.

4. Joan Sturhan, *Carvalho: Portrait of a Forgotten American,* 9.

5. Korn, *Incidents of Travel,* 20.

6. In 1843, the Reverend Isaac Leeser founded the first Jewish journal in the United States, the *Occident.* The Reverend Mr. Leeser translated both the Sephardic and the Ashkenazic prayer books into English, as well as revised the King James translation of the Bible, eliminating references to Christian interpretation. See Solomon Grayzel, *A History of the Jews,* 624–25.

7. Korn, *Incidents of Travel,* 31.

8. Carvalho, letter Dr. J. Solis-Cohen, in possession of the National Museum of American Jewish History. See Berman, "Carvalho: Painter and Prophet," 19.

9. In 1895, Baltimore's Congregation B'nai Israel, following a strict Orthodox doctrine, banned photography, relying on the prohibition of the Second Commandment (Exod. 20:4): "Thou shalt not make to thyself any graven image, nor the likeness of anything that is in heaven above, or on the earth beneath." See Bernard P. Fishman, "Solomon Nunes Carvalho: Photographer," in *Solomon Nunes Carvalho: Painter, Photographer, and Prophet in Nineteenth-Century America,* by Elizabeth Kessin Berman, 25–26.

10. Ibid., 26.

11. Korn, *Incidents of Travel,* 36–37.

12. Carvalho, *Incidents of Travel,* 17–18. Future page references will be shown in brackets.

13. Nine years earlier, in 1845, the Reverend Isaac Leeser conducted the wedding ceremony of Carvalho to Sarah Miriam Solis, a young woman who shared not only her husband's love of art and ethics, but also his attraction to travel and discovery. While on the expedition, he wrote often to her.

14. Meat-biscuits were prepared by saturating flour with the juices of boiled beef before baking into biscuits.

15. One might surmise Carvalho tried to retain a form of Jewish dietary observance in which *trayf*, that is, nonkosher foods, were to be avoided.

Chapter Two: European Jewry

1. This chapter is from Peter Black, telephone interview by author, Nov. 2, 2000.

2. The original quote from Ba'al Makhshoves (Israel Elyashev, 1873–1924), a Yiddish literary critic, is cited in Irving Howe, *The Immigrant Jews of New York* (London: Bnai Brith Books, 1976), 14.

Chapter Three: Early Jewish Utah Pioneers

JULIUS AND FANNIE BROOKS

1. The following excerpt is from the unpublished manuscripts of Eveline Brooks Auerbach, the late Mrs. Samuel H. Auerbach, graciously loaned to the author by collector Stan Sanders, Salt Lake City. For a complete memoir published by the Friends of the Bancroft Library, see Ogden, *Frontier Reminiscences.*

2. Bacon and ham are considered *trayf*, foods that are not kosher.

3. Between 1856 and 1860, nearly three thousand Mormons traveled to Utah by handcart. These handcarts were crudely constructed of green lumber that shrank in the heat and had wooden axles in need of frequent repair. Although a first company of one hundred handcarts, comprising nine hundred individuals, reached Salt Lake Valley without mishap, others did not fare as well, succumbing to early storms, lack of food, sickness, and death. For an excerpt from *Recollections of a Handcart Pioneer of 1860* (Denver: L. R. Hafen, 1938), see William Mulder and Russell Mortensen, eds., "Handcarts to Zion," in *Among the Mormons,* 281–92.

4. Watters, *Pioneer Jews of Utah,* 23. The scarcity and high cost of matches prompted Alexander Neibaur to manufacture sulphur matches that, according to the *Deseret News* (July 26, 1865), sold for seventeen cents a box. In 1837, both Alexander Neibaur and his wife converted to Mormonism.

5. Watters, *Pioneer Jews of Utah,* 134. Ornstein and Popper opened the first non-Mormon butcher shop in Utah.

6. Tullidge, *History of Salt Lake City,* 79–80.

7. See William Mulder and Russell Mortensen, "The Mormons and the Mines," in *Among the Mormons,* 377–82.

8. Watters, *Pioneer Jews of Utah,* 136.

9. In her diary, Eveline Brooks wrote that the Brooks Arcade land was owned by Elizabeth Spencer, a wife of the polygamous Mr. Spencer. This first piece of property measured 66 feet on Third South and 166 feet west of the corner. "The corner had a two story adobe house, which Dad rented, a little one story adobe further up, which Dad tore down and built three frame one story buildings which were rented for Chinese wash houses and brought $25.00 per month." The Brooks Arcade, built on the narrow lot in 1891, was a Richardsonian-Romanesque building of elaborately carved gray stone. During its time, it became a busy residence to oculists, violin teachers, dentists, printers, and milliners. More than one hundred years later, the building struggled for survival as Salt Lake City planners deliberated its fate, ultimately saving only the facade.

SAMUEL H. AUERBACH

1. The following excerpt is from the unpublished manuscript pages and drafts of Samuel Auerbach's diary, graciously loaned to the author from the private collection of Stan Sanders, Salt Lake City. For a

more complete memoir, see Judith Robinson, ed., *Utah Pioneer Merchant: The Memoirs of Samuel H. Auerbach (1847–1920).*

2. A lunisolar calendar is used by Jews and follows the pattern set by festivals, holidays, and fasts. Days were added, a pattern established by the Calendar Council of the Sanhedrin, led by Patriach Hillel II, to accommodate the Jewish calendar of 354 days in a year with the Gregorian calendar of 365 days. The twelve months are Tishri, Heshvan, Kislev, Tevet, Shevat, Adar, Nissan, Iyar, Sivan, Tammuz, Av, and Elul, with the twenty-nine-day interposed month of Veadar added seven times in every nineteen-year cycle to readjust the calendar to the solar cycle. When Samuel Auerbach wrote of Av (or Ab), he probably meant July or August.

3. Stan Sanders and Eileen Hallet Stone, "Family Stories from the Auerbach Brothers," 9, 22.

4. The Independent Order of Odd Fellows was founded in England during the 1700s. The American order was organized in Baltimore in 1819. A secret society with its own system of rites and passwords, its chief purpose is to give aid, assistance, and comfort to its members and friends.

5. Joseph D. Farmer had several stores in Idaho, Salt Lake City, and Corinne. He almost lost his life in a snowstorm in 1864, having walked on foot from Boise City to the settlement at Call's Fort. In 1882, the year he was elected vice president on the Board of Directors of Congregation B'nai Israel, Farmer was bathing at Black Rock on the south side of the Great Salt Lake and drowned. An unusual drowning, since the Great Salt Lake has such salinity, no one was witness to the mishap, and his body was not discovered until four years later, in 1886, in Tooele County. Farmer was buried in B'nai Israel Cemetery (diary of Samuel Auerbach).

Gumpert Goldberg was born in Germany in 1832, came to New York when he was thirteen years old, and spent time in Colorado and Montana before settling in Salt Lake City. An unauthenticated story in Montana folklore is that the city of Helena, Montana, was named in honor of Goldberg's wife, Helena. Goldberg had businesses in Ogden and in Corinne with his business partner, Fred J. Kiesel. See Watters, *Pioneer Jews of Utah,* 155.

6. Jay Gould was an American financier and a leading railroad owner in the late 1800s. By 1882, he controlled more than fifteen thousand miles of track in the United States. See Betty M. Madsen and Brigham D. Madsen, "Threat of the Narrow Gauge," in *North to Montana,* 213–26.

7. The Pacific Railroad Act of 1862 gave the Union Pacific Railroad and the Central Pacific Railroad the responsibility of building a railroad that stretched across the United States, roughly following the forty-second parallel from Omaha, Nebraska, to Sacramento, California. In 1863, work began on the Central Pacific track; by 1865, Union Pacific started laying track westward. More than a thousand Chinese laborers were hired by Central Pacific, whereas Union Pacific hired thousands of European immigrants and Civil War veterans. The Central Pacific had to cross the towering mountain range of the Sierra Nevada; Union Pacific had to cross the rugged Rocky Mountains. By 1868, the two railroads competed in a race to see which railroad could lay the most track in the shortest amount of time. On May 10, 1869, the railroad tracks met at Promontory, Utah, making the United States the first country to have a transcontinental railroad.

8. The Cohn brothers' advertisement that follows was found quite by accident as part of the backing of an old print archived at the Daughters of Utah Pioneers Museum in the Old Rock Church in Parowan, Utah. As part of a Utah Humanities Council program, preservation librarian Randy Silverman, the author's husband, was carefully dissembling a poorly framed picture. As two sheets of backing paper loosened, he found two advertisements for Auerbach Brothers, pitching "One Price to All," and the annual sale at the Cohn Dry Goods Company. Needless to say, they are now well preserved at the Old Rock Church.

1. The story of Simon Bamberger was dictated to Leon Watters in 1924 (*Pioneer Jews of Utah,* 163–69). A draft of the interview is in the Ben Roe Collection, MS 138, and in the Simon Bamberger Family Collection, MS 225, Special Collections, Marriott Library, University of Utah.

The date of Bamberger's birth is given variously in several sources. The date he gave to Watters is the one given in the text. Bamberger's son Julian, in a letter to Watters dated Oct. 12, 1950, stated: "My father's opinion was that he was born February 27, 1846; but shortly after his death, one of the insurance companies insisted that he had given 1845 as the year of his birth and that is the date which was put on his tombstone."

2. These temporary camps were often the scenes of disorder and violence. Bryan, Wyoming, which at one time had a population of three thousand, was described as a "town where gamblers and desperadoes held a brief but lurid carnival of lawlessness" (*Along the Union Pacific Railroad,* pamphlet issued by the railroad [n.p., n.d.]).

3. Penrose was at that time the editor of the newspaper the *Ogden Junction* and later became the crusading editor of the *Deseret News* in Salt Lake City, the first newspaper published in the Rocky Mountains (Tullidge, *History of Salt Lake City,* 140–41). The Utah Central Railroad was built by Brigham Young to connect Salt Lake City with the transcontinental railroad in Ogden. Feramorz Little was the fourth mayor of the city. He had purchased the hotel in partnership with Brigham Young (Whitney, *History of Utah,* 2:45).

4. W. S. McCornick was the leading Gentile banker of Utah.

5. Bamberger Family Collection, MS 225, box 1, folder 17, Special Collections, Marriott Library, University of Utah.

6. Beck's Hot Springs was a hot sulfur spring just north of the city, which was owned by John Beck, a wealthy mining man and friend of Bamberger. Bamberger's train went from Salt Lake as far north as Farmington, where Bamberger built the amusement park, the Lagoon, a popular resort for dancing, swimming, and horse racing. It became and still is a recreation resort for Salt Lakers, and, in Bamberger's time, provided passenger traffic for the struggling railroad.

7. Bamberger was a member of the Board of Education from 1898 to 1903, was a state senator from 1903 to 1907, and was elected governor for a four-year term in 1916 on the Democratic ticket. While Bamberger was governor, the legislature, under his guidance, created the Public Utilities Commission to regulate electric and gas companies and passed the Workmen's Compensation Act.

8. The following excerpt can be found in ibid., folder 21. In 1881, Simon Bamberger married Ida Maas, daughter of J. J. Maas, former principal of the Guilford School, Cincinnati (ibid., box 2, folder 5).

9. Louis Marcus arrived in Utah in 1907 and worked in the motion picture business. In 1931, Marcus was elected mayor of Salt Lake City. A lifelong Republican in good standing, he lost his reelection bid. Most people had assumed he would win and therefore did not show up to vote.

10. Idaho and Utah each elected a Jewish man for governor: Moses Alexander and Simon Bamberger, respectively. No other state had a governor of the Jewish faith. Moses Alexander, who left Obrigheim, Bavaria, and came to America when he was fourteen years old, entered politics in 1886 while living in Chillicothe, Missouri. Running on the Democratic ticket, he was elected to the city council; in 1888, he ran on a nonpartisan ticket for the office of mayor and won. Having health problems, he was advised to move to a dry climate in the West. After an initial scouting expedition, Alexander, his wife, Helena, and their children moved to Boise, Idaho. In 1892, approximately one hundred Jews lived in Boise, and Alexander became involved in organizing the Jewish synagogue, becoming the vice president of the board of Congregation

Beth Israel. Asked to run for mayor in 1897, he accepted and won. In 1901, he ran again and was elected. In 1908, he ran for governor, but was defeated. In 1914, he ran again and this time was elected. See Juanita Brooks, *The History of the Jews in Utah and Idaho,* 127–34. According to the *Kansas City Star* (Aug. 19, 1917), both Bamberger and Alexander were in the clothing business and rose to riches and honor. "[Bamberger] went to Utah and became a millionaire railroad and mine owner. He was elected governor . . . by the Progressives and Democrats, who wanted an honest governor who would sign a prohibition bill and make the state dry."

SAMUEL NEWHOUSE

1. Martha Sontagg Bradley, "The World Outside Comes to Beaver, 1870–1900," in *History of Beaver County,* 125–26.

2. Margaret D. Lester, *Brigham Street,* 56–57.

3. Ibid., 60.

JOSEPH ROSENBLATT

1. The following excerpt was adapted from Eleanor Swent, *Joseph Rosenblatt: EIMCO, Pioneer in Underground Mining Machinery and Process Equipment, 1926–1963.*

2. See Peter Black's overview of European Jewry in Chapter 2.

3. Thomas Kearns and partner David Keith made their fortune in the silver mines in Park City. In 1892, they had organized the Silver King Mining Company. The Kearns family moved to Salt Lake City where Thomas built a mansion, now used as the governor's home. Kearns, an Irish Catholic, became a senator and eventually bought the *Salt Lake Tribune.*

4. In 1899, thirty-five members attended the first organization meeting for Congregation Montefiore, including the Appelmans, B. Cohn, H. Edstein, M. Glassberg, E. Kahn, D. Kerenz, I. N. Levitt, M. Levy (president), G. M. Lewis, M. Mayer, Isadore Morris, Moses Nathan, J. Pesioritsky (vice president), Nathan Rosenblatt, M. H. Sachs, B. Salmenson, Joshua Shapiro, H. Singer, J. Siler, E. Wolff, and J. W. Zerre (Brooks, *History in Utah and Idaho,* 120).

5. In 1894, the members of the American Railway Union, led by labor movement leader Eugene V. Debs, struck the Great Northern Railway in a "sympathy strike" in Chicago to help Pullman Company employees who were in a wage dispute. Violence erupted, leading to estimated damages worth $80 million. Debs and other union officers were ordered by the courts to quit their strike activities. Debs called upon all union members to strike. The American Federation of Labor refused to endorse the sympathy strikes, and Debs was held in contempt of court and jailed.

6. As part of the Land Grant Act of 1862, which authorized grants of public lands to schools that offered part-time military training to students, the first commission granted to students was in 1908. By the fall of 1916, more than forty thousand students were enrolled in the ROTC program.

Chapter Four: Turn-of-the-Century Arrivals

ABE B. CLINE

1. Eileen Hallet Stone, ed., Abe B. Cline interview by Leslie Kelen, Salt Lake City, June 2, 1982, Jewish Archives, Special Collections, Marriott Library, University of Utah.

2. Ben Roe arrived in Salt Lake City in 1913 to join his brother Harry who had a clothing store. Securing a

job at I. Cline and Brother, wholesalers of notions and furnishings, on 136 West Temple, Roe made thirty dollars a month. He roomed in Joseph Friedman's boardinghouse where very little Yiddish was spoken, so he learned to speak English. He worked at his brother's store in Payson, moved to Eureka to work in the Tintic Mercantile Company, returned to Payson to become the "sole proprietor of a fully paid business," and then opened Roe's in Salt Lake City. In time, he became president of Temple B'nai Israel, a board member of the Jewish Community Center, and involved in numerous Jewish and civic organizations. In 1966, he was given the Chai Award by the State of Israel. Throughout the years, Ben, his wife, Bernie, and Abe and Mildred Cline were very good friends. They vacationed together and they shared *Shabbat.* In James M. Rock's book, *A Blend of the Two: Ben M. Roe,* Roe said, "I believe that every man in his humble way, in accordance with his abilities, must help make this a better world to live in for everybody. . . . I, as an immigrant who knows the value of freedom, liberty, equality, and opportunity, know better than many people what it means to be deprived of those things. Therefore, I've always tried to pay society back in whatever my abilities and education permitted for all the kindness and goodness and opportunities I was privileged to enjoy. America is the greatest haven in the world for the oppressed."

3. Many Jewish families lived on West Colfax Street in Denver.

4. Roseanne Cline Gordon, interview by author, Aug. 14, 2000.

SIMON FRANK

1. Eileen Hallet Stone, ed., Simon Frank interview by Lorraine Ferra, Salt Lake City, June 29, 1982, Jewish Archives, Special Collections, Marriott Library, University of Utah.

2. Excerpts from article in the *Salt Lake Tribune,* Apr. 4, 1953.

EVA SIEGEL

1. Eileen Hallet Stone, ed., Eva Siegel interview by Leslie Kelen, Salt Lake City, July 13, 1984, Jewish Archives, Special Collections, Marriott Library, University of Utah.

2. Hyman Basow paid land fees and taxes on his property in Clarion, but moved the family to Gunnison where he supported his family with a plumbing and general repair business. See Goldberg, *Back to the Soil,* 125. Ben Brown was the backbone to Clarion Colony's back-to-the-soil experience. After he resigned as the association's president, Brown left the colony, remained in Utah for a while, and, in 1923, organized the Utah Poultry Association, later renamed the Intermountain Farmers Association (123).

3. The Maimonides Club is named for the Spanish scholar, rabbi, physician, and philosopher Moses Maimonides (1135–1204), who with his father was a secret Jew. Maimonides wrote the *Siraj,* a commentary on the *Mishnah,* the authoritative source of *halacha* (Jewish law), second only to the Bible. Maimonides's second greatest work was the *Mishneh-Torah,* fourteen books of biblical and rabbinical law (Abram Leon Sachar, *A History of the Jews,* 178–81). The Salt Lake City Maimonides Club, organized in 1925, offered Jewish boys and girls weekly gatherings for social events. Max Siegel was elected its first president with Bertha Pepper, Claire Steres, and William Goldberg as vice president, secretary, and treasurer, respectively. It has been said that at least eight couples met one another at a Maimonides event. See Brooks, *History in Utah and Idaho,* 181, 194.

SOL J. SELVIN

1. Sol Selvin, autobiography, MS 489, box 26, folder 24, Special Collections, Marriott Library, University of Utah.

2. The unedited, untitled biography of Sol Selvin by Min Selvin Crutcher, ninety-five years old, was given to the author by Nancy Selvin. Receiving this remarkable biography was a matter of *bashert* (fate). Ceramist Nancy Selvin from California was teaching a pottery class at the University of Utah. One of her students, Jan Faught, who works in preservation at the Marriott Library, heard Selvin speaking about the Jewish senator, knew about the author's research project, and put the two parties in contact with each other. "The timing of this coincidence amazes me," wrote Nancy Selvin (Jan. 10, 2001). "I had literally just begun to prepare Min's material when I was interrupted by my trip to the University of Utah, and then, Jan just happened to be participating in my workshop. What luck!" This jewel of a manuscript details not only Selvin's life in Utah, but also life in Tooele. To review the biography in full, contact the Special Collections, Marriott Library, University of Utah.

CLAIRE STERES BERNSTEIN

1. Eileen Hallet Stone, ed., Claire Steres Bernstein interview by Floyd O'Neil and Ralph De Rose, Aug. 1, 1972, Utah Minorities Number H-3, Center for the Studies of the American West, Collection on Utah Minorities, now housed in the Special Collections, Marriott Library, University of Utah.

ABE BERNSTEIN

1. Eileen Hallet Stone, ed., Abe Bernstein interview by Ralph de Rose, Sept. 14, 1972, Utah Minorities Number H-12, Center for the Studies of the American West, Collection on Utah Minorities, now housed in the Special Collections, Marriott Library, University of Utah.

2. Gail Bernstein Ciacci, interview by author, Salt Lake City, May 6, 1999.

3. Shaarey Tzedek has its own cemetery above Eleventh Avenue in Salt Lake City.

ESTHER KLEIN

1. Eileen Hallet Stone, ed., Esther Klein interview by Lorraine Ferra, Salt Lake City, Apr. 4, 1983, Jewish Archives, Special Collections, Marriott Library, University of Utah.

2. Ben Roe left I. Cline and Brother, where he was paid $30 a month to work for "Goulash" Klein, a Hungarian Jew, for $40 a month. Along with his regular duties, he tried to bring in customers who were coming from or going to the Bamberger Railroad station. With his first paycheck, Roe bought a second-hand bicycle for $7.50. While learning how to ride it, he put it down and within moments it was stolen. Although he was paid more by Klein, he did not like working at the store and went back to work at I. Cline and Brother at his old salary. See Rock, *A Blend of the Two,* 36.

SIMON SHAPIRO

1. Eileen Hallet Stone, "The Traveling Salesman," *Utah Holiday Magazine* (Sept. 1985).

2. Eileen Hallet Stone, ed., Joel Shapiro interview by Leslie Kelen, Salt Lake City, June 20, 1982, Jewish Archives, Special Collections, Marriott Library, University of Utah.

Chapter Five: Minyan in a Railroad Town

RALPH BENOWITZ

1. Ralph Benowitz, interview by author, Salt Lake City, Dec. 7, 2000.

2. After the completion of the railroad in Ogden, often Jewish immigrants would arrive and spend some time before eventually going to Salt Lake City or north into Idaho or Montana.

3. In 1890, Ogden's first Jewish congregation was organized under the name of Ohab Sholem. Meetings were held at Ben Oppman's clothing store at 352 Twenty-fifth Street. The first president was Sam Rosenbluth. In time, charter members included D. Kraines, Joseph Benowitz, William Benowitz, Ben Oppman, and J. Kraines.

4. "Mrs. Siner Donates Synagogue Stone," ibid.

5. "Vandals Burn, Ransack Brith Sholem in Ogden; No Leads," Eileen Hallet Stone, *Intermountain Jewish News,* Jan. 5, 1990.

6. The *Salt Lake Tribune,* Apr. 16, 1939, lists several resident rabbis, including Ben Alcoff (1917–1918), A. Leherer (1918–1920), Rabbi Finkelstein (1920–1928), Hyman Bariss (1928–1932), Rabbi Blumenthal (1932–1933), and Rabbi Friedman (1934–1935). For the last fourteen years, Rabbi Wenger of Congregation Kol Ami has traveled to Ogden to conduct a variety of services.

7. "Synagogue in Ogden," *Ogden Standard Examiner,* Aug. 22, 1921.

DORIS NEIDITCH GUSS

1. Eileen Hallet Stone, ed., Doris Neiditch Guss interview by Leslie Kelen, Salt Lake City, July 9, 1984, Jewish Archives, Special Collections, Marriott Library, University of Utah. In Sept. 2000, further information was given to the author by Mrs. Guss's daughter Shirley Hertz.

2. The *Jewish Daily Forward,* established by Socialists in 1897, was a major Yiddish newspaper of its time, and a "journalistic institution" in immigrant Jewish communities. A useful vehicle of acculturation because of its in-depth coverage of the U.S. political system, it also provided answers to everyday problems at work and in the home.

Chapter Six: Back to the Land

A BRIEF VIEW OF CLARION

1. Robert Alan Goldberg, author of *Back to the Soil: The Jewish Farmers of Clarion, Utah, and Their World,* spoke to Congregation Kol Ami's confirmation class taught by the author, May 6, 1995. Goldberg's talk combined selections from his publications. Also see his "Building Zion."

2. Robert Goldberg, "Zion in Utah," 69–70. Future citations appear parenthetically in the text.

THE AGRICULTURAL COLONY CLARION

1. This chapter was gathered from the Robert Alan Goldberg Papers (1980–1993). The Clarion Collection consists of diaries, monographs, news articles by or about the Clarion colonists, interviews, research questionnaires, and correspondence with descendants of the participants. Benjamin Brown's reflections on Clarion are in the Goldberg Papers, box 1, folder 1. Ben Brown was the Clarion project's leader.

2. The Bund ("Alliance") is a political organization formed by socialist Jews in Vilna, Lithuania, in 1897. In Louis C. Zucker's translation of Isaac Friedlander's monograph, he explains that "Bund" is Yiddish for "League," short for General League of Jewish Workingmen of Lithuania, Russia, and Poland. In a note with his translation, Zucker wrote, "It was anti-Zionist, but it stood for a vital internal Jewish, specifically Yiddish-language, cultural life; Yiddish, because it was the language of the toiling masses; Jewish cultural autonomy within the larger national life, in the lands and cities of Jewish concentration. It was a Jewish nationalism of the Diaspora, within a non-dogmatic, utopian socialism. In the 1920s, the Bund concerned itself actively with revolutionary politics, chiefly in Eastern Europe. In the United States, it was, early and

late, a cultural government, which it has been everywhere since after World War II. During Clarion years, it was a vital cultural force among the Jewish workers of New York, Philadelphia, Chicago, and the like."

According to Zucker, during the first quarter of the twentieth century, Dr. Chaim Zhitlovsky (1865–1953) was "probably the most outstanding torchbearer of Bundism as a lecturer in Yiddish on literature and philosophy, Jewish and general. I, Louis C. Zucker, remember the audible flushed-face enthusiasm which an announcement of his coming to Philadelphia to lecture in some large hall would arouse among his followers in the downtown Jewish section." Zucker added that the opposition party in Clarion were "internationalists, cosmopolitans, 'one-worldists.' Their Yiddishism was but a means to the workers' utopia: one world for their ideal. Neither party cared anything about Jewish religion." He concluded, "The Yehudim of Salt Lake City knew little or nothing about either of these then potent *Weltanschauungen* [world outlook] and cared less, except for their general opposition to Socialism or any other threat to laissez-faire capitalism."

3. Isaac Friedlander's excerpts are from *Virgin Soil,* a monograph, ca. 1930s, translated from the Yiddish by Zucker and edited by Michael T. Walton (Goldberg Papers, box 1, folders 13–16).

4. Morris Bassin's son's remarks are based on interviews and telephone conversations with Robert Goldberg.

5. Samuel Chatzky's comments on Clarion are from his journal translated from Yiddish by Adah Fogel, 1912, Goldberg Papers.

6. Having worked in the sweatshops of Philadelphia, Samuel Levitsky was no stranger to working long hours, "as a furrier twelve hours a day, six days a week," whenever he could find the work. See Goldberg, *Back to the Soil,* 33.

7. The animal was possibly a coyote.

8. Harry Bernstein's commentary on his father's experience in Clarion is derived from the unpublished Bernstein memoirs, 1984, Goldberg Papers.

9. Moshe Melamed's reflections on Clarion are from his unpublished diary, translated from Yiddish by Adah Fogel, June 8, 1912, Goldberg Papers.

10. Yetta Bassin Farber's remarks are based on letters to Robert Goldberg.

Chapter Seven: Networking

HOWARD MARCUS

1. Eileen Hallet Stone, ed., Howard Marcus interview by Leslie Kelen, Salt Lake City, June 7, 1982, Jewish Archives, Special Collections, Marriott Library, University of Utah.

2. James L. White was considered a "community leader" and was instrumental in helping the Jewish Community Center project reach its goals. Unfortunately, before the community center on 2416 East and 1700 South was completed, White died, on Apr. 17, 1957. At the building's completion and dedication in Mar. 1959, the membership decided unanimously to adopt the name the James L. White Jewish Community Center. Mrs. White contributed significantly as she took over the finishing, decorating, and furnishing of the senior lounge. The Whites' daughters and their families commissioned a New York artist to create two pieces of artwork, one for the interior of the building and the other for its façade.

SID FOX

1. This section is from Sid Fox's autobiography, MS 559, Special Collections, Marriott Library, University of Utah.

2. Materials concerning KDYL are in Sidney S. Fox Papers, boxes 10–12, MS 559, in ibid.

3. The station had once been owned by the *Salt Lake Telegram.* Even after its sale to Fox, the *Telegram* continued to sponsor the KDYL orchestra, led by the violin-playing maestro, Eugene Jelesnik, at seasonal performances and concerts. In 1945, Jelesnik became the musical and talent director for Fox's radio and television station (Gerald M. McDonough, *An Improbable Journey: The Life and Times of Eugene Jelesnik,* 199).

4. Eugene Jelesnik clipping file, undated article, *Rocky Mountain Magazine,* in ibid., 191.

5. The *Rocky Mountain Magazine* described KDYL's "bold experiment" in a "small market" that gave "promise that television in the smaller cities is going back to the people" (see ibid., 191–92). KDYL was the first privately owned television station in the United States. Others were owned by the motion picture industry, newspapers, manufacturers, and experimental laboratories.

6. Ralph Tannenbaum, interview by author, Sandy City, Utah, May 23, 2000.

7. Ibid.

CHARLIE MCGILLIS

1. Richard McGillis, interview by author, Salt Lake City, Oct. 24, 2000.

2. Primo Carnera was the 1933–1934 U.S. heavyweight boxing champion.

3. Excerpt from the *Salt Lake Tribune,* Nov. 1933, recorded in the self-published book *Some Experiences of Russel Lord Tracy* (Salt Lake City, 1941), 139. A signed copy, no. 157 out of 500, was presented to Mr. and Mrs. Charles McGillis.

4. Located at 411 East South Temple, the Enos Wall Mansion (named for the mining entrepreneur Col. Enos Wall) was put up for sale and recommended for purchase by the B'nai B'rith members. A three-story structure with an elevator and thick cement foundations and walls, a large entry hall on the main floor accommodated a front entrance of iron grillwork. A walnut-paneled library was on one side of the hallway, a French room and a gold room were on the other. The dining room was large enough to hold banquets, membership dinners, and New Year's parties for two hundred people. The second floor held bedrooms, which were quickly converted into small meeting rooms and classrooms.

5. This *Salt Lake Tribune and Telegram* article (no name, no date) was made available to the author by Cal McGillis.

6. Max Goldberg, "The Publisher's Desk," *Intermountain Jewish News,* July 3, 1970.

7. Russel Lord Tracy, "Four Hobbies," in *Some Experiences,* 131–49.

8. Written by Lin Crone, this newspaper clipping was made available to the author by Charlie McGillis's son Cal McGillis.

9. This letter is in the possession of Richard and Joanne McGillis.

A. WALLY SANDACK

1. Eileen Hallet Stone, ed., A. Wally Sandack interview by Leslie Kelen, Salt Lake City, June 22, 1982, Jewish Archives, Special Collections, Marriott Library, University of Utah; A. Wally Sandack, interview by author, Salt Lake City, Dec. 2000; A. Wally Sandack Papers, Acc. 1481, Special Collections, Marriott Library, University of Utah.

2. American industrialist Howard Hughes owned, among others, the Hughes Aircraft Company and had a controlling interest in Trans World Airlines.

3. Jewish Archives, MS 224, box 1, folder 20, Special Collections, Marriott Library, University of Utah.

4. "Sen. Moss 'Dismayed' by Religious Issue at Meet," *Salt Lake Tribune,* Apr. 3, 1967.

5. "Can't Do That," *Deseret News,* Apr. 5, 1967.

Chapter Eight: Shochets *and Cattle Dealers*

HARRY J. DOCTORMAN

1. Eileen Hallet Stone, ed., Harry J. Doctorman interview by Leslie Kelen, Salt Lake City, Mar. 13, 1986, Jewish Archives, Special Collections, Marriott Library, University of Utah.

2. In the few years of Shaarey Tzedek's existence, three rabbis or educated laypeople are mentioned: Rabbi Joseph Strinkomsky, J. P. Benson, and Rabbi Reuben Kaplan.

3. A list of rabbis and pastors at Congregation Montefiore include Jacob Brodie and M. Levy (1904), Jacob Brodie (1904–1905), Zorach Bielsky (1908–1909), Joseph Hevesh (1910–1912), Dr. Leon Album (1913), Samuel Beskin (1914–1918), Moses Klerman (1919–1920), David Aronson (1921–1922), M. Z. Levine (1923), E. M. Burstein (1924–1926), Joshua Bach (1927), Hyman Krash (1928), Joseph Krikstein (1938), Benjamin Groner (1938–1939), Oscher Goldman (1939), Abraham Rosenblum (1946), E. Louis Cardon (1954), and Maurice Schwartz (1962–1964). This list is derived from Board Minutes of Congregation Montefiore, MS 224, Jewish Archives, Special Collections, Marriott Library, University of Utah; and Brooks, *History in Utah and Idaho,* 232.

PAUL WEINSTEIN BLOCK

1. Paula Block Draper, interview by author, Holladay, Utah, Oct. 13, 2000.

Chapter Nine: Knishes and Kashrut

ED EISEN

1. Eileen Hallet Stone, ed., Ed Eisen interview by Leslie Kelen, Salt Lake City, July 18, 1983, Jewish Archives, Special Collections, Marriott Library, University of Utah.

2. A prominent retired Brigham City businessman, Lion Bloom, 106, of 622 East First North, died Sunday, April 20, 1975, at McKay-Dee Hospital, Ogden, after a short illness. He was born December 18, 1868, in Omsk, Russia. He married Ida Milkoff in Russia. She died in 1948. He immigrated to New York from Russia in 1905. Soon after he moved to Ogden and after a short period, came to Brigham City where he established a livery stable and cattle and salvage yard business, buying and selling hides and furs (obituary, *Box Elder News Journal,* 1975).

SADE TANNENBAUM

1. Eileen Hallet Stone, ed., Sade Tannenbaum interview by Joyce Kelen, Salt Lake City, June 6, 1983, Jewish Archives, Special Collections, Marriott Library, University of Utah.

2. Fred Tannenbaum, interview by author, Salt Lake City, Feb. 7, 2001.

JEAN EISEN

1. Jean Eisen, interview by author, Salt Lake City, Dec. 15, 2000.

ABE GUSS

1. Eileen Hallet Stone, ed., Abe Guss interview by Leslie Kelen, Salt Lake City, Dec. 3, 1987, Jewish Archives, Special Collections, Marriott Library, University of Utah.

2. Danzig was a former autonomous state that, from 1920 to 1939, was under the protection of the League of Nations, which was organized to promote international cooperation among nations. Although U.S. president Woodrow Wilson was the chief planner of the league in 1919, the United States did not join it. The league was succeeded in 1946 by the United Nations.

3. In most Orthodox synagogues, women are separated from men either by a raised gallery or a *mehitzah,* such as a partition or a curtain. The women's gallery is called *Ezart Nashim.* See Rachel Biale, "Women and the Mizvot," in *Women in Jewish Law: An Explanation of Women's Issues in Halakhic Sources,* 26–27.

ROSE GUSS NORD

1. Eileen Hallet Stone, ed., Rose Guss Nord interview by Joyce Kelen, Salt Lake City, Apr. 21 and 23, 1983, Jewish Archives, Special Collections, Marriott Library, University of Utah.

2. Rose Nord was Abe Guss's sister.

I. J. WAGNER

1. I. J. Wagner, interview by author, Salt Lake City, Apr. 7 and June 14, 2000.

2. Notes from Congregation B'nai Israel, Apr. 12, 1881, MS 224, folder 9, Jewish Archives, Special Collections, Marriott Library, University of Utah, address the purchase of a schoolhouse lot on the corner of Third South and First West Temple. On July 9, 1881, Charles Popper read, "Resolved that the Directors purchase the corner lot on Third South and First West Temple, known as Tanners Lot, now owned by John Sharp, fronting 1/2 rods on First West Temple and 10 rods on Third South Street, for the sum of $2600. The President [Henry Siegel] authorized to consummate the Purchase." On July 30, 1881, $700 was borrowed from M. C. Phillips "at the rate of 8 percent a year." In Aug. 1884, a resolution was passed. "In the future, this Congregation shall hold its services as *Minhag America,* and Dr. I. M. Wise's books are to be used." The dues of members were set at $12 a year. On Feb. 24, 1889, the notes suggest the old synagogue as well as the school property would be sold, and that there were plans to build at a new location.

3. Gilsonite is a trademark for Uintate, a black, brilliant variety of asphalt, mined in Utah and western Colorado. It was named after S. H. Gilson.

MICHAEL WOLFE

1. Michael Wolfe, interview by author, Salt Lake City, Mar. 6, 2000.

2. Lou Dornbush, a survivor of the Holocaust, owned Salt Lake City's only Jewish delicatessen; in time, he added nonkosher foods and other items.

TONY SWEET

1. Tony Sweet, interview by author, Salt Lake City, Dec. 3, 2000.

Chapter Ten: Standing Up to Bigotry

SIDNEY MATZ

1. Eileen Hallet Stone, ed., Sidney Matz interview by Leslie Kelen, Magna, Utah, Nov. 11, 19, and 25, 1985, Jewish Archives, Special Collections, Marriott Library, University of Utah.

2. In 1917, the corporation was called Utah Copper. Kennecott Utah Copper was incorporated as a holding company for all Guggenheim-affiliated copper properties on Apr. 29, 1915, although the company did

not gain controlling stock interest in Utah Copper until 1923 (Leonard Arrington and Gary B. Hansen, *The Richest Hole on Earth: A History of the Bingham Copper Mine,* 66–67).

3. The all-nisei 442nd Regional Combat Team, known as the "Go for Broke" outfit, was established on Jan. 1, 1943. Three thousand Hawaiian and fifteen hundred mainland nisei (most from the American internment camps) served as combat soldiers for the 442nd. More than eighteen thousand men served with the unit. One of the war's most decorated combat teams, the 442nd received seven Presidential Distinguished Unit Citations and 18,143 individual decorations. In seven major campaigns, the 442nd suffered 9,486 casualties and 600 deaths. President Truman declared the nisei fought "not only the enemy, but prejudice."

RUTH MATZ MCCRIMMON

1. Ruth Matz McCrimmon, interview by Alene McCrimmon and author, Salt Lake City, Sept. 1 and 24, 2000.

2. The Boers were farmers of Dutch ancestry, colonists sent by the Dutch East India Company in 1652 to live in South Africa. The British occupied the colony founded by the Boers in 1795, withdrew in 1802, and seized the land, permanently, in 1806. In 1836, some Boers sought freedom from British rule by moving northeast, to lands that became the Orange Free State and the Transvaal. The first Boer War took place in South Africa from 1880 to 1881. Later, the Boers fought the British in the Boer War of 1899–1902 and were defeated.

BERENICE MATZ ENGLEBERG

1. Berenice Matz Engleberg, interview by author, Salt Lake City, Dec. 10, 2000.

EUGENE LEVETAN

1. Eugene Levetan told the story of living as a minority in a mining town at a United Jewish Federation community dinner held at Little America, Salt Lake City, 1995.

Chapter Eleven: L'Chaim

RALPH TANNENBAUM

1. Eileen Hallet Stone, ed., Ralph Tannenbaum interview by Leslie Kelen, Salt Lake City, Jan. 24, 1983, Jewish Archives, Special Collections, Marriott Library, University of Utah; interview by author, Sandy City, Utah, Feb. 12 and July 7, 2000.

2. The Volstead Act, introduced by Andrew J. Volstead of Minnesota, was passed to prohibit the use of intoxicating liquors in 1919. It sought to punish violations of the Eighteenth Amendment, which prohibited the manufacture, sale, or transportation of liquor within the United States. The act was passed by Congress in 1919, and was repealed in 1933.

3. In 1889, the first rabbi to lead services at Temple B'nai Israel was Rabbi Heiman J. Elkin. He was followed by Rabbi Jacob Ludwig Stern, and Rabbi Moses P. Jacobson. From 1894 to 1900, services were read by Sig. Simon and I. Kaiser. Beginning in 1900, Rabbi Louis G. Reynolds led the congregation for three years. The following rabbis led the congregation thereafter: Charles J. Freund (1904–1913), Dr. William Rice (1914–1920), Adolph Stein (1921–1925), Samuel Gordon (1926–1943), Alvin Luchs (1943–1953), Adolph Fink (1953–1954), and Mordecai Podet (1954–1961) (Brooks, *History in Utah and Idaho,* 231). By the time of the merger, Rabbi Abner Bergman had been the congregation's rabbi for several years.

HARRY MILLER

1. Harry Miller, interview by author, Salt Lake City, Feb. 21, 1986, and Sept. 3, 2000.

2. Eugene Victor Debs, who formed the American Railway Union in 1893, was a spokesman for the American labor movement and a Socialist candidate for president five times. He ran his 1920 campaign from prison—a ten-year sentence under the Espionage Law in 1918—and received nearly 1 million votes.

3. Harry Miller, *Through Combat: The 314th Infantry Regiment* (n.p., n.d.).

Chapter Twelve: Surviving

MINNA MARGARET LOSER PRAIJS AND JOHN PRICE

1. John Price Papers, copy in possession of author.

2. In Apr. 1933, the Nazi boycott of Jewish businesses was initiated.

3. *Kristallnacht* means "Night of Broken Glass." Under the pretext of retaliating for the assassination of German diplomat Ernst von Rath in 1938, riots occurred in Germany and Austria during Nov. 1938. Nazi soldiers set fire to 191 synagogues, 91 Jews were killed, and more than 30,000 Jews were arrested and sent to concentration camps. Nazi soldiers and citizens broke into and looted thousands of Jewish homes and shops. A fine of 1 billion marks was imposed upon all German Jewry. That same month, Jewish children were prohibited from attending German public schools. "In all its major decisions, the [Nazi] regime depended on Hitler. Especially with regard to the Jews, Hitler was driven by ideological obsessions that were anything but the calculated devices of a demagogue; that is, he carried a very specific brand of racial anti-Semitism to its most extreme and radical limits" (Saul Friedlander, *Nazi Germany and the Jews,* 20).

4. Ibid., 257–58.

5. John Price, interview by author, Salt Lake City, Mar. 15, 2000.

6. On Nov. 9–10, 1938, SS commandos divided into three groups to attack the Jews "silently." Engineer Graubart was stabbed to death in front of his wife and daughter. In the same building, Karl Bauer was dragged into the hall, stabbed, and beaten with pistol butts, and he died en route to the hospital. Richard Berger, president of Innsbruck Jewish Community, was taken outside in pajamas and a winter coat. He was put into an SS car to go to Gestapo headquarters, but the soldiers took a different direction. At the bend of the Innsbruck River, Berger was dragged from the car and "silently" battered with pistols and stones, thrown into the river, and then shot. "The SS men were old-timers, fanatically devoted to Hitler, extreme anti-Semites, and exemplary members of the Order" (ibid., 235–37).

ISAAC ROSE

1. Eileen Hallet Stone, ed., Isaac Rose interview by Leslie Kelen, Salt Lake City, Apr. 28, 1987, Jewish Archives, Special Collections, Marriott Library, University of Utah; interview by author, Salt Lake City, Sept. 4, 1997.

2. Al Jolson (1886–1950), whose real name was Asa Yoelson, was born in Srednike, Lithuania, near Kaunas. His family emigrated to the United States when he was eight years old. He appeared in minstrel shows, burlesque, and vaudeville shows before making his debut on Broadway in the 1911 musical *La Belle Paree.* His first important sound motion picture role was in *The Jazz Singer* (1927).

MICHAEL SCHAFIR

1. Michael Schafir, interview by author, Salt Lake City, July 7, 2000.

2. Reeve Robert Brenner, *The Faith and Doubt of Holocaust Survivors,* 137.

3. The earliest auto-da-fé of the Spanish Inquisition, which began in 1440 and lasted more than three hundred years, took place in Seville. "Heretics" were turned over to the secular authorities who burned them at the stake. Thousands of Jews were forced to convert to Christianity, put on trial, or burned at the stake as "heretics."

HILDA PARKER

1. Excerpt from Eileen Hallet Stone, "Revisioning the Holocaust: Anne Frank in the World, 1929–1945."

JOEL SHAPIRO

1. Eileen Hallet Stone, ed., Joel Shapiro interview by Leslie Kelen, Salt Lake City, June 15 and 20, 1982, Jewish Archives, Special Collections, Marriott Library, University of Utah.

DR. ERNST BEIER

1. Ernst Beier, interview by author, Salt Lake City, Mar. 10, 1999.

2. Ernst G. Beier, *The Silent Language of Psychotherapy: Social Reinforcement of Unconscious Processes* (Chicago: Aldine Publishing, 1966).

Chapter Thirteen: Tzedakah

JOANNE SPITZER MCGILLIS

1. Joanne Spitzer McGillis, interview by author, Salt Lake City, Oct. 20, 2000.

ANNE DOLOWITZ

1. Anne Dolowitz, interview by author, Brigham City, Utah, Aug. 29, 2000.

2. Dedicated to the cultural and religious participation of Jewish students, the B'nai B'rith Hillel Foundations established Hillel entities in major universities in Canada, Britain, France, Holland, South Africa, Australia, Israel, and the United States. See Sachar, *A History of the Jews*, 401.

ESTHER ROSENBLATT LANDA

1. This chapter was adapted from Esther Landa interview by Fred Buchanan, tape U-1354, May 17, 1991, Everett L. Cooley Oral History Project, Marriott Library, University of Utah; Eileen Hallet Stone, ed., Esther Landa interview by Leslie Kelen, Salt Lake City, May 16, 1982, Jewish Archives, Special Collections, Marriott Library, University of Utah; and interview by author, Salt Lake City, Sept. 12, 2000.

2. Excerpt from Eileen Hallet Stone, "The Incomparable Esther Landa."

THE MOUNT SINAI POKER, CANASTA, AND S****** CLUB

1. Carol Landa recently retired from the University of California, and is a freelance writer living in San Francisco.

2. Leo Rosten, *The Joys of Yiddish* (New York: McGraw-Hill, 1968).

Chapter Fourteen: Landsmen

ALLA BRANZBURG

1. Alla Branzburg, interview by author, Holladay, Utah, Aug. 14, 1990.

HARRIS LENOWITZ

1. Harris Lenowitz, interview by Randy Silverman, Salt Lake City, Jan. 15, 2001.

SHARONNE ZIPPEL

1. Sharonne Zippel, interview by author, Salt Lake City, May 14, 1999.

Afterword

1. This excerpt was take from Eileen Hallet Stone, "Glimpses of Utah Jewish Life," 35.

BIBLIOGRAPHY

In the preparation of this work, information was obtained from current and archived oral histories, bibliographies, letters, diaries, family histories, biographies, catalogs of manuscripts, Jewish community religious and community records, newspapers, and periodicals. Herein are listed the primary and secondary sources considered most beneficial for this project.

Manuscript Collections and Unpublished Materials

Auerbach, Eveline Brooks. Diary. In possession of Stan Sanders, Salt Lake City.

Auerbach, Samuel H. Memoir. In possession of Stan Sanders, Salt Lake City.

Bamberger, Simon. Papers. Special Collections. Marriott Library, University of Utah.

Center for the Studies of the American West. Utah Minorities. Special Collections. Marriott Library, University of Utah.

Cooley, Everett L. Papers. Special Collections. Marriott Library, University of Utah.

Crutcher, Min Selvin. "An Untitled Biography of Sol Selvin." 1961. Special Collections. Marriott Library, University of Utah.

Fox, Sid. Papers. Special Collections. Marriott Library, University of Utah.

Friedland, Isaac. "Virgin Soil." Translated from Yiddish by Dr. Louis C. Zucker, edited by Michael T. Walton. Monograph. In the possession of Michael T. Walton.

Goldberg, Robert. Papers. Special Collections. Marriott Library, University of Utah.

Jewish Archives. Papers. Special Collections. Marriott Library, University of Utah.

Jewish Community Interviews. Special Collections. Marriott Library, University of Utah.

Roe, Ben. Papers. Special Collections. Marriott Library, University of Utah.

Sandack, Wally. Papers. Special Collections. Marriott Library, University of Utah.
Selvin, Sol. Papers. Special Collections. Marriott Library, University of Utah.
Solomon, Bernard. "A Historical Overview of the Salt Lake Jewish Community Center." Ph.D. diss., University of Utah, 1974.
Tracy, Russel L. Letter to Charlie McGillis, 1941. In the possession of Richard McGillis.

Interviews by Author
Beier, Ernst. Salt Lake City, September 1999.
Benowitz, Ralph. Salt Lake City, December 2000.
Black, Peter. Telephone interview, November 2000.
Branzburg, Alla. Holladay, Utah, August 1990.
Ciacci, Gail Bernstein. Salt Lake City, April 1999.
Dolowitz, Anne Moskowitz. Salt Lake City, August 2000.
Draper, Paula Block. Holladay, Utah, October 2000.
Eisen, Jean. Salt Lake City, December 2000.
Engleberg, Berenice Matz. Salt Lake City, December 2000.
Gordon, Roseanne Cline. Salt Lake City, August 2000.
Landa, Esther. Salt Lake City, September 2000.
Lenowitz, Harris. Interview by Randall Silverman. Salt Lake City, January 2001.
McCrimmon, Ruth Matz. Salt Lake City, September 2000.
McGillis, Joanne Spitzer. Holladay, Utah, October 2000.
McGillis, Richard. Salt Lake City, September 2000.
Miller, Harry. Salt Lake City, September 2000.
Paige, Elizabeth. Salt Lake City, October 1999.
Price, John. Salt Lake City, May and April 2000.
Rose, Isaac. Salt Lake City, September 1997.
Sandack, Wally. Salt Lake City, December 2000.
Schafir, Michael. Salt Lake City, July 2000.
Sweet, Tony. Salt Lake City, December 2000.
Tannenbaum, Fred. Salt Lake City, February 2000.
Tannenbaum, Ralph. Sandy, Utah, February and July 2000.
Wagner, I. J. Salt Lake City, April and June 2000.
Wenger, Frederick. Salt Lake City, February 2001.
Wolfe, Michael. Salt Lake City, March 2000.
Zippel, Sharonne. Salt Lake City, August 1999.

Newspapers and Brochures
Box Elder News Journal (Brigham City, Utah)
"Congregation Kol Ami" (brochure, Salt Lake City)
Deseret News (Salt Lake City)
Intermountain Jewish News (Denver)
"James L. White Jewish Community Center" (brochure, Salt Lake City, 1957).

Kansas City Star
Ogden (Utah) Standard Examiner
Salt Lake City Herald
Salt Lake City Telegram
Salt Lake City Telegraph
Salt Lake Tribune
Vernal Express (Utah)

Books and Articles

Arrington, Leonard, and Gary B. Hansen. *The Richest Hole on Earth: A History of the Bingham Copper Mine.* Logan: Utah State University Press, 1963.

Berman, Elizabeth Kessin. "Solomon Nunes Carvalho: Painter and Prophet." In *Solomon Nunes Carvalho: Painter, Photographer, and Prophet in Nineteenth-Century America.* Baltimore: Jewish Historical Society of Maryland, 1989.

Biale, Rachel. *Women in Jewish Law: An Exploration of Women's Issues in Halakhic Sources.* New York: Schocken Books, 1984.

Bradley, Martha Sontagg. *History of Beaver County.* Utah Centennial History Series. Salt Lake City: Utah Historical Society, 1999.

Brenner, Reeve Robert. *The Faith and Doubt of Holocaust Survivors.* New York: Free Press, 1980.

Brooks, Juanita. *The History of the Jews in Utah and Idaho.* Salt Lake City: Western Epics, 1973.

Carvalho, Solomon Nunes. *Incidents of Travel and Adventure in the Far West; with Col. Fremont's Last Expedition across the Rocky Mountains: Including Three Months' Residence in Utah, and a Perilous Trip across the Great American Desert, to the Pacific.* New York: Derby and Jackson, 1857.

Friedlander, Saul. *Nazi Germany and the Jews.* Vol. 1, *Years of Persecution.* New York: Harper Collins, 1997.

Goldberg, Robert Alan. *Back to the Soil: The Jewish Farmers of Clarion, Utah, and Their World.* Salt Lake City: University of Utah Press, 1986.

———. "Building Zion." In *A World We Thought We Knew: Readings in Utah History,* ed. John S. McCormick and John R. Sillito, 441–51. Salt Lake City: University of Utah Press, 1995.

———. "Zion in Utah." In *Jews of the American West,* ed. Moses Rischin and John Livingston, 69–91. Detroit: Wayne State University Press, 1991.

Grayzel, Solomon. *A History of the Jews.* Philadelphia: Jewish Publication Society of America, 1968.

Hallet Stone, Eileen. "Glimpses of Utah Jewish Life." *Beehive History* 25 (1999): 32–35.

———. "The Incomparable Esther Landa." *Network* (June 1990): 14–15.

———. "Revisioning the Holocaust: Anne Frank in the World, 1929–1945." *Network* (April 1990): 30.

———. "The Traveling Salesman." *Utah Holiday Magazine* 14 (Sept. 1985): 72.

Kelen, Leslie G., and Eileen Hallet Stone. *Missing Stories: An Oral History of Ethnic and Minority Groups in Utah.* Salt Lake City: University of Utah Press, 1996.

Korn, Bertram W., ed. *Incidents of Travel and Adventure in the Far West,* by Solomon Nunes Carvalho. Philadelphia: Jewish Publication Society, 1954.

Lester, Margaret D. *Brigham Street.* Salt Lake City: Utah State Historical Society, 1979.

Levison, Robert E. "American Jews in the West." *Western Historical Quarterly* 5 (July 1974): 285.

Madsen, Betty M., and Brigham D. Madsen. *North to Montana.* Salt Lake City: University of Utah Press, 1980.

McDonough, Gerald M. *An Improbable Journey: The Life and Times of Eugene Jelesnik.* Salt Lake City: Deseret Book, 1997.

Mulder, William, and Russell Mortenson. *Among the Mormons: Historic Accounts by Contemporary Observers.* New York: Alfred A. Knopf, 1958.

Ogden, Annegret S., ed. *Frontier Reminiscences of Eveline Brooks Auerbach.* Berkeley and Los Angeles: University of California Press, 1994.

Robinson, Judith, ed. *Utah Pioneer Merchant: The Memoirs of Samuel H. Auerbach (1847–1920).* Berkeley and Los Angeles: University of California Press, 1998.

Rock, James M., ed. *A Blend of the Two: Ben M. Roe.* Salt Lake City: Friends of the University of Utah Library, 1978.

Sachar, Abram Leon. *A History of the Jews.* New York: Alfred A. Knopf, 1970.

Sanders, Stan, and Eileen Hallet Stone. "Family Stories from the Auerbach Brothers." *Common Ground* 1:6 (April–May 1998): 9, 22.

Sturhan, Joan. *Carvalho: Portrait of a Forgotten American.* Merrick, N.Y.: Richwood Publishing, 1976.

Swent, Eleanor. *Joseph Rosenblatt: EIMCO, Pioneer in Underground Mining Machinery and Process Equipment, 1926–1963.* Western Mining in the Twentieth Century Oral History Series. Berkeley and Los Angeles: University of California Press, 1992.

Tracy, Russel Lord. *Some Experiences of Russel Lord Tracy.* Salt Lake City: N.p., 1941.

Tullidge, Edward W. *The History of Salt Lake City and Its Founders.* Salt Lake City, 1886.

Watters, Leon L. *The Pioneer Jews of Utah.* New York: American Jewish Historical Society, 1952.

Whitney, Orson F. *History of Utah.* 2 vols. Salt Lake City: George Q. Cannon and Sons, 1893.

INDEX

EILEEN HALLET STONE is a writer and public historian. She is coauthor of *Missing Stories: An Oral History of Ethnic and Minority Groups in Utah.* She lives with her husband, son, and Labrador retriever in Salt Lake City.